Central Banking and Monetary Policy in the Asia-Pacific

Akhand Akhtar Hossain

Associate Professor of Economics, The University of Newcastle, Australia

Edward Elgar
Cheltenham, UK • Northampton, MA, USA

Published by
Edward Elgar Publishing Limited
The Lypiatts
15 Lansdown Road
Cheltenham
Glos GL50 2JA
UK

Edward Elgar Publishing, Inc.
William Pratt House
9 Dewey Court
Northampton
Massachusetts 01060
USA

A catalogue record for this book
is available from the British Library

Library of Congress Control Number: 2009936217

ISBN 978 1 84720 372 4

Printed and bound by MPG Books Group, UK

Contents

For my wife: *Nilufar*
and
our children: *Andaleeb*, *Ayeeda*, *Afeeya* and *Azleena*

Preface

This book is about central banking and monetary policy in the Asia-Pacific. The purpose of this book is as a reference text. It surveys the major theories, models and approaches to inflation and monetary policy, with a focus on developing countries of the Asia-Pacific. The subject matter is topical, as it highlights contemporary issues in the design and conduct of monetary policy for price stability. High interest rates, inflation, exchange rate volatility and large-scale capital flows since the early 1970s have indeed raised the importance of monetary, fiscal and exchange rate policies in developing countries. Most Asian developing countries have maintained high economic growth since the 1980s without experiencing serious policy-induced macroeconomic problems, such as inflation and large current account deficits. The 1997–98 currency crises in East and Southeast Asia did, however, expose the vulnerability of these economies to both domestic and external shocks. Since then, most countries of this region have undertaken both stabilisation and structural reform measures. As part of improving economic policy, they have given more importance to monetary and exchange rate policies for price stability with the goal of maintaining sustained economic growth without creating unsustainable macroeconomic imbalances. Recognising these macroeconomic developments, this book provides an overview of key concepts and principles of central banking and monetary policy and reviews contemporary issues in monetary policy in the Asia-Pacific. The ongoing global financial crisis that has originated from the US subprime mortgage crisis has raised a wide range of issues about the role and effectiveness of monetary policy in economic stabilisation. Given space constraint and its analytical focus, the book does not review in detail this and other global or regional financial crises. The book highlights aspects of these financial crises only to develop or illustrate the key concepts and principles in central banking and monetary policy in developing countries.

This book took formal shape as part of my sabbatical research in 2005. I have, however, thought about writing this book much earlier while teaching some undergraduate courses in the areas of money, banking and finance at the University of Newcastle, Australia. My frustration stems from using various popular texts on money, banking and finance which are often detailed in their exposition of macroeconomic and monetary concepts and have excessive exposure to monetary histories and institutions of developed countries, yet avoid adapting the concepts and principles of money, banking and finance to conditions of developing countries. Although the developing countries of the Asia-Pacific were outside the intellectual radar throughout the 1950s and 1960s, it is foolhardy to ignore these countries at this junction of economic history of this region. Therefore, I have been looking for a survey text that covers the concepts and principles of monetary theory and policy, and reviews contemporary monetary policy issues in developing Asia, but without going into the detail of monetary histories of countries of this region.

I acknowledge my debt to my colleagues Professor John Burgess and Dr Andrew Nadolny; both read the manuscript and provided suggestions for its improvement. I also acknowledge the comments of an anonymous reviewer for his/her constructive comments on an earlier draft and suggestions for its improvement. I wrote preliminary drafts of this book at Bank Indonesia. I acknowledge the hospitability of Bank Indonesia and the friendliness of its staff. My special debt is to my colleague Gregory Bauer who has drawn the figures and charts for this book. The professional team of Edward Elgar Publishing has taken care of transforming the final draft into a reference text with care. I am grateful to the Faculty of Business and Law of the University of Newcastle for awarding me a research grant in the form of some teaching relief that helped me to finalise the manuscript. Finally, I take this opportunity to thank my wife, Nilufar, and our children, Andaleeb, Ayeeda, Afeeya and Azleena, for their support and understanding while I worked on this book. I dedicate this book to them.

Akhand Akhtar Hossain
The University of Newcastle
2009

Abbreviations

AD	aggregate demand
ADB	Asian Development Bank
ADO	Asian Development Outlook
AS	aggregate supply
ASEAN	Association of Southeast Asian Nations
BB	Bangladesh Bank
BI	Bank Indonesia
BM	broad money
BNM	Bank Negara Malaysia
BOCa	Bank of Canada
BOCh	Bank of China
BOE	Bank of England
BOJ	Bank of Japan
BOK	Bank of Korea
BOT	Bank of Thailand
BPNG	Bank of Papua New Guinea
BSP	Bangko Sentral ng Pilipinas
CBC	Central Bank of China
CBIG	central bank independence and governance
CBP	Central Bank of Philippines
CDs	Certificates of Deposits
CI	Certificate of Indebtedness
Cu	currency
CBSL	Central Bank of Sri Lanka
CMA	Central Monetary Authority
CPI	Consumer Price Index
CRR	cash reserve requirements
DC	domestic credit
ECB	European Central Bank
EEC	European Economic Community
EFAC	Exchange Fund Advisory Committee
FDI	foreign direct investment
FOMC	Federal Open Market Committee
FR	foreign reserves
GATT	General Agreement on Tariffs and Trade
GDP	gross domestic product
GDPD	GDP deflator
GNP	gross national product
GNI	gross national income

HKMA	Hong Kong Monetary Authority
IMF	International Monetary Fund
LAR	liquid asset ratio
LRAS	long-run aggregate supply
MABP	monetary approach to balance of payments
MAS	Monetary Authority of Singapore
MB	monetary base
MLA	Monetary Law Act
MNC	multinational corporation
MPC	Monetary Policy Committee
NDA	net domestic assets
NFA	net foreign assets
NIES	newly industrialising economies
NIR	net international reserves
NM	narrow money
NRB	Nepal Rastra Bank
OCA	Optimum Currency Area
OECD	Organisation for Economic Co-operation and Development
OPEC	Organisation of Petroleum Exporting Countries
PBC	People's Bank of China
PD	Presidential Decree
PNG	Papua New Guinea
PPP	purchasing power parity
PRC	People's Republic of China
RA	Republic Act
RBA	Reserve Bank of Australia
RBI	Reserve Bank of India
RBF	Reserve Bank of Fiji
RBNZ	Reserve Bank of New Zealand
Re	commercial bank reserves with central bank
RM	reserve money
SAR	Special Administrative Region
SBP	State Bank of Pakistan
SBV	State Bank of Vietnam
SDR	Special Drawing Rights
SE	seigniorage
SRAS	short-run aggregate supply
SRD	statutory reserve deposits
TBs	Treasury bills
UK	United Kingdom
USA	United States of America
WB	World Bank
WDO	World Development Outlook
WTO	World Trade Organization

1. Introduction

MONEY AND CENTRAL BANKING

Money is the lifeblood of a modern economy. A monetised economy is significantly more efficient than a barter economy with respect to transactions, saving and investment. The main reason is that transaction costs in a monetised economy are lower than those in a barter economy. A barter economy in fact relies on the 'double-coincidence of wants' that is rarely achieved. Higher efficiency in production, distribution and trade in a monetised economy therefore leads to society's welfare gains (Clower, 1969; Dillard, 1954; Lewis and Mizen, 2000).[1]

Yet the relationship between money and real economic variables is not precise. Any relationship between them depends on the time of adjustment of economic variables to changes in the money supply. The classical dichotomy, which is postulated in the writings of David Hume (1752 [1970]), suggests that money does not affect real variables in the long run.[2] The idea is that real output is determined by real factors of production such as labour, capital and technology. Money can, however, affect output and employment in the short run[3] (Blanchard, 1990; Fischer, 1979a; Friedman, 1994; Patinkin, 1972). The nominal variables such as inflation and nominal interest and exchange rates adjust fully to excess money supply growth over the long run. Therefore, the real interest and exchange rates remain unchanged to changes in the money supply (Fisher, 1923; Friedman, 1968a, 1977; Lucas, 1996).

The primary role of money is to facilitate the transactions of goods, services and assets. When the value of money remains stable, it is also used as a store of value (Friedman, 1969a; Lewis and Mizen, 2000).[4] Monetary economists emphasise that real balances[5] smooth the production process to such an extent that they can be considered a complementary factor of production.[6] Monetary management in a modern economy, however, is not a routine affair. One problem is that there is limited control over the money supply and therefore it can go 'out of order'.[7] Experiences of high inflationary countries suggest that when the monetary authorities lose control over the money supply, it adversely affects economic growth and the welfare of the society (Easterly and Fischer, 2001; Sachs, 1987).

Monetary economists hold the view that there exists an optimal level of the money stock that allows the economy to function smoothly without causing inflation or deflation or business cycles.[8] An important policy issue is therefore setting the rate at which the money supply should increase in a growing economy so that it does not cause inflation or deflation (Friedman, 1959a). Indeed, for the practitioners of monetary policy, a policy rule can be derived from the equilibrium condition in the real money market,[9] which states that $M/P = m^d(y)$ where M is the money stock, P is the price level and $m^d(. .,. .)$ is the demand for real money balances, dependent on real income (y).[10] If the goal of monetary policy is price stability,[11] then, according to classical monetary theory, the growth rate of the money supply should be equivalent to the growth rate of the economy times the income elasticity of demand for money (Burda and Wyplosz, 2005).

For a better understanding of the movements of nominal variables such as inflation and the nominal interest and exchange rates, monetary economists emphasise that the money demand relationship should be viewed independently of the way money is created. The demand for real balances is determined by economic agents, contingent on their wealth and the returns on alternative assets (real and financial) (Friedman, 1956). The nominal money stock is a supply variable, which is set by the monetary authorities (Brunner, 1992; Friedman, 1992). As Friedman (1992) emphasised, there are important factors affecting the money supply that do not affect the demand for money. The price level is adjusted to the money supply to bring equilibrium in the real money market.

Usually the central bank is the monopoly supplier of money; therefore, it bears the responsibility of determining and controlling the level of money in circulation. There is, however, no consensus on how a central bank should perform this responsibility. The increasing role of a central bank in monetary management arises from the classical view that money can get 'out of order' in the sense suggested by J.S. Mill (1848). Hence a central bank has the responsibility of maintaining monetary (or price) stability by supplying money to the level that is demanded.

Price stability – defined as low and steady inflation – has the characteristic of a public good.[12] Monetary management is important for another reason. As indicated above, although money does not affect real variables in the long run, most economists agree that money has short-run effects on the economy. These effects are unpredictable and arguably should not be exploited by the monetary authorities (Friedman, 1961). In fact, whether monetary policy should be used to promote economic growth or stabilisation or both remain an area of policy debate. Modern monetary theory and policy revolves around this theme, especially in developing countries.[13] Central banks, as the authorities to issue and control the money stock, have therefore become the main (if not the sole) agent of monetary management for price stability. However, until recently, central banks, instead of being stabilising institutions, operated as a branch of the Ministry of Finance (or Treasury) (Fry, 1992; 1998; Fry et al., 1996). Some observers (for example, De Long, 2000) have even accused some central banks of causing monetary mischief in many countries.[14]

THE BOOK

As indicated in the preface, this book is about central banking and monetary policy. It surveys the major theories, models and approaches to inflation and monetary policy, with a focus on developing countries. Some features of the book are highlighted here to develop its broad theme in the context of Asia-Pacific.

The Asia-Pacific is a large geographic region.[15] It comprises a relatively large number of developing countries and a small number of developed countries. The developing countries are at different stages of development. Their economic, social and political institutions have considerable differences because of varied sociocultural and political developments over the centuries. This book does not intend to survey the economic or monetary histories of these nations. The institutional and organisational developments of their monetary systems are reviewed only on a selective basis with the aim of making readers familiar with the structure and governance of major central banks of the region. Moreover, although most Asian countries recognise that the primary role of monetary policy is to achieve and maintain price stability, the strategy of monetary policy varies across countries. This is reflected in varied exchange rate arrangements in these countries. In order to highlight this phenomenon, the book provides an overview of the principles in the conduct of monetary policy under different exchange rate arrangements with varied restrictions on capital mobility. Country-specific examples are then drawn to highlight key issues in monetary policy. This is accomplished using information on macroeconomic developments in selected countries of the region since the 1950s. Such information remains useful for establishing linkages between monetary, fiscal and exchange rate policies.

The centrality of central banking is highlighted throughout the book. All countries in the Asia-Pacific have a central bank (or monetary authority) and also their national currencies. Depending on capital controls and exchange rate arrangements, most of them conduct independent monetary policy to achieve a single or multiple objectives.[16] As a precursor to the review of central banking and monetary policy issues, Chapter 3 surveys the evolution of central banking and introduces the structure, function and governance of central banks in selected countries of the Asia-Pacific. Chapter 4 provides an overview of the concepts and contemporary issues in monetary policy. Thereafter, there is a brief discussion of monetary policy frameworks in different countries of the Asia-Pacific. The later chapters elaborate on themes developed in Chapters 3 and 4. This book also has several analytical features of note.

Monetary theory and policy deals with analytical and policy issues. In the literature, monetary issues are examined within competing analytical frameworks that show interrelationships between monetary and non-monetary variables (Barro and Fischer, 1976; Sargent, 1986). Monetary theory and policy issues are also subjected to empirical testing and validation (Friedman and Hahn, 1990). In general, policy lessons are drawn from real-world events. The book maintains this analytical approach. It refers to empirical evidence on monetary relationships and highlights real-world events that have monetary or macroeconomic implications. No attempt is, however, made to survey the body of empirical literature on contemporary issues in monetary theory and policy. The monetary literature is voluminous and expanding rapidly (Friedman and Hahn, 1990; Lewis and Mizen, 2000; Lucas and Sargent, 1981; Walsh, 1998; Woodford, 2003). The empirical literature also involves advanced econometric issues that are beyond the scope of this book.

Given the survey nature of the book, there is a comprehensive treatment of models and approaches to inflation, and the design and conduct of monetary policy. This is because monetary economics deals with a range of issues that can be analysed from different perspectives. Although economists agree on core insights in monetary economics, there remain disagreements on the short-term policy issues such as the relative costs of inflation and unemployment, the approaches to inflation control and their associated costs, and the role of monetary and financial policies for growth and stabilisation (Lewis and Mizen, 2000; Mishkin, 1997; Orphanides and Solow, 1990). Although this book does not examine these issues in detail within an integrated framework, the core ideas and contrasting views are synthesised and presented in a simplified form. The strength of this book is to highlight disagreements among prominent economists on issues in monetary theory and policy. At the same time it articulates a theme that Friedman (1969b: v) captured beautifully in the preface to his book *The Optimum Quantity of Money and Other Essays*:

> Monetary theory is like a Japanese garden. It has esthetic unity born of variety; an apparent simplicity that conceals a sophisticated reality; a surface view that dissolves in ever-deeper perspectives. Both can be fully appreciated only if examined from many different angles, only if studied leisurely but in depth. Both have elements that can be enjoyed independently of the whole, yet attain their full realization only as part of the whole.

Since the early 1970s the literature on monetary theory and policy has expanded rapidly. The monetary literature has also become sophisticated in dealing with both analytical and policy issues (Friedman and Hahn, 1990; Taylor, 1999). The growing body of literature has been associated with recent inflationary trends and experiences of both developed and developing countries. Economists have learnt more about the sources, dynamics and control of inflation over the past few decades than at any time before (Corbo, 1974; IMF, 1996; 2001; 2006; Jongwanich and Park, 2008; Loungani and Swagel, 2001). As inflation came to the forefront of policy debate in the 1970s, the 'art' of monetary policy-making has been developed in tandem (Blinder, 1998; Mahadeva and Sinclair, 2002; 2005; Mahadeva and Sterne, 2000). Monetary policy practitioners now acknowledge that to make monetary policy credible and effective, the public need to comprehend monetary policy principles and issues (Cukierman, 1986; 1992; Walsh, 1998; Woodford, 2003). Understanding the working mechanisms of monetary policy has therefore become important for both professionals and the public alike (Dornbusch and Giovannini, 1990; Fischer, 1990; Mishkin, 1995).

However, satisfying the needs of diverse groups of readers is difficult, yet not impossible. In fact, the mysteries of monetary theory and policy can be removed to a large extent without compromising analytical rigour and sophistication that is part of monetary economics. In general, students and researchers benefit the most when economic principles, models and their implications are set out in a precise form so that they do not need to navigate through massive institutional and organisational distractions. Peripheral theoretical and empirical issues tend to clutter a text and can make core principles and issues confusing. Therefore, this book avoids a detailed discussion on institutional and organisational matters, except those needed for expositional purposes. Instead the basic monetary policy concepts and principles are defined and analysed in a relatively simple manner. Emphasis is also given to the applicability of basic principles of monetary theory and policy to developing countries in general.

Other than an expectation that readers have familiarity with macroeconomic principles and policy debates, advanced knowledge of monetary economics is not required. Except for some algebraic relationships and the use of calculus, no high-level mathematics is involved. The figures used for illustration are simple to follow, as they do not require advanced training in geometry. In addition, to make the book accessible to non-specialists, it is written in a matter-of-fact style. Those readers interested in an in-depth analysis of monetary issues are expected to consult journal articles and advanced texts, as listed in the bibliography. Statistical information is drawn from both international and country-specific publications. Most data are reported in a summary form. All other materials are presented in a clear, accessible style. Instead of standardising symbols for consistent use throughout the book, the symbols are model- and/or chapter-specific. Therefore, at the risk of repetition, the symbols are defined or redefined as the text demands so that readers can remain afresh with their meanings while they navigate through the text.

The book is self-contained and remains suitable for one-semester undergraduate courses on monetary theory and policy. It can also be used as a complementary text for courses on money, banking and finance. As a bridge between academic literature and popular writings, this book is written to appeal to researchers who need a reference text that does not get weighed down with technicalities but develops monetary policy concepts and analyses issues with real-world examples. The book would also suit policy-makers who have an interest in macroeconomics in general and monetary and financial policies in particular.[17]

PREVIEW

The remainder of this book is organised as follows. Chapter 2 provides an overview of the scope of macroeconomics, introduces key issues in monetary theory and policy, and highlights the roles of monetary and fiscal policies in macroeconomic stability.

Chapter 3 discusses the evolution of central banking and its functions in a historical context and then introduces the major central banks in the Asia-Pacific. Chapter 4 reviews the basic concepts and principles of monetary policy, discusses the extent of independence of monetary policy under different exchange rate arrangements and restrictions over capital mobility and, finally, assembles a set of guiding principles of central banking and monetary policy. These principles are returned to in later chapters.

The theories, models and approaches to inflation and monetary policy are the subject of Chapter 5. The discussion encompasses the relationship between money growth and inflation, the relationship between inflation and economic growth, the role of money and finance in economic growth, and the models and approaches to the conduct of monetary policy.

Chapter 6 analyses issues in the choice of strategy of monetary policy for price stability. It defines the concept of a nominal anchor and examines the rules-based strategies of monetary policy, namely, exchange rate targeting, monetary targeting and inflation targeting. The generalised framework for the conduct of monetary policy is outlined and the key features of monetary policy under specialised exchange rate arrangements are also reviewed.

Chapter 7 explains the money supply process. It also illustrates the applications of various instruments for monetary management.

Chapter 8 analyses the generalised transmission mechanisms of monetary policy. The discussion covers both the money and credit channels of the transmissions of monetary policy. The transmission mechanisms of monetary policy under inflation targeting are outlined. Given its importance in the design and conduct of monetary policy, a brief review is made of issues in the money demand behaviour in developing countries of the Asia-Pacific. Unresolved issues in the transmission mechanism of monetary policy are also critically discussed in the context of developing countries.

Chapter 9 discusses inflation and monetary policy developments in selected countries of the Asia-Pacific. Policy lessons are then drawn from monetary policy experiences of countries of the Asia-Pacific region. Given the space constraint, although this chapter does not make critical assessment of the conduct of monetary policy in selected countries, it provides a brief overview of the ongoing global financial crisis and its implications for monetary and fiscal policies in developing countries of the Asia-Pacific.

Chapter 10 provides a summary of concepts and principles of central banking and monetary policy covered in the book, and makes some concluding remarks.

NOTES

1. For a historical review of the evolution of money and its importance in a modern society, see Tobin (1992). He described money as a social institution that 'is similar to language, standard time, or the convention designing the side of the road for passing' (ibid.: 770).
2. This idea was postulated in the early statements on the *Quantity Theory of Money*, such as the classic one by David Hume in his essays 'Of Money', 'Of Interest' and 'Of the Balance of Trade' (Hume, 1752 [1970]). In the modern context, the quantity theory of money represents a body of thinking about the relationship between money, output and prices in the short and long runs. The main proposition is that an increase in the money supply raises only the price level and not output. This is expressed in terms of the neutrality of money in the long run but not in the short run. For detailed discussion on this and related propositions, see Fisher (1926), Friedman (1992), Johnson (1967; 1972), Patinkin (1956; 1972; 1992), Tobin (1992), and Thornton (1802).
3. Friedman (1994: 48) stated the short run and long run effects of changes in the money supply as follows:

   > In the short run, which may be as long as three to ten years, monetary changes affect primarily output. Over decades, on the other hand, the rate of monetary growth affects primarily prices. What happens to output depends on real factors: the enterprise, ingenuity, and industry of the people; the extent of thrift; the structure of industry and government; the relations among nations; and so on.

4. Tobin (1992) pointed out an analytical issue in money's role as a store of value. He suggested that the institution of money has value to the society as a public good does not automatically give it value to individuals in market exchanges. Therefore some value is assigned to money in an overlapping inter-generational model in which money has the function of being the sole or the principal store of value that links one generation to the next. This works well when the world is infinite and its end is not in sight. However, money may become worthless as a store of value vis-à-vis real resources if the end of the world is certain and is in sight.
5. The demand for money represents a demand for real balances. Real balances can be defined as the ratio of the nominal stock of money to the general price level. The demand for real balances depends primarily on a real variable such as a measure of real permanent (or expected) income, which is considered a proxy for wealth (Friedman, 1956). Whether or to what extent the nominal interest rate affects the demand for money remains an empirical issue (Mishkin, 2007a).
6. Traditionally, money is viewed as a lubricant that greases the wheels of the economy. In a modern economy, money is more than a lubricant. This is evident from the linkage between money growth and the returns on various assets, which are linked to inflation and the interest and exchange rates. The monetary growth literature treats the stock of real balances as a 'complementary' factor of production, especially in developing economies (Ghatak, 1983; Stein, 1970; 1971). The use of money as a factor of production gives rise to an inverse relationship between the real rate of interest and the rate of inflation. For example, a rapid rise in inflation induces firms to switch from money to real capital, which lowers financial capital and therefore the marginal product of capital. At equilibrium, the real interest rate equals the marginal product of capital. The resulting decline in the real interest rate could be substantial in developing economies having capital market imperfections. This creates a repressed financial system that retards economic growth (Fry, 1998; Gylfason, 1999; McKinnon, 1973).
7. John Stuart Mill developed the idea in the mid-nineteenth century that money hurts the economy when it goes 'out of order'; otherwise, it does not have any impact on the real economy:

   > There cannot, in short, be intrinsically a more significant thing, in the economy of society, than money; except in the character of a contrivance of sparing time and labour. It is a machine for doing quickly and commodiously, what would be done, though less quickly and commodiously, without it; and like many other types of machinery, it only exerts a distinct and independent influence of its own

> when it goes out of order. The introduction of money does not interfere with the operation of any Laws of Value . . . (Quoted in Goldfeld and Chandler, 1986: 16–17).

8. There is lack of consensus on this viewpoint. The optimal level of the money supply ultimately depends on its relationships with such variables as inflation (deflation) and business cycles. For discussion on the role of money in business cycles, see Friedman and Schwartz (1963a; 1963b), Barro (1976), and Lucas (1973; 1975; 1977; 1981). For general discussion on monetary models of business cycles and other topics on new classical macroeconomics, see Barro (2008), Hoover (1988) and Pesaran (1987). One controversial idea in monetary economics is Friedman's rule that states that the target inflation rate should be negative and numerically equal to the equilibrium real interest rate so that the nominal interest rate becomes zero (Friedman, 1969a). This indicates that the optimal monetary policy could be a steady contraction of the money supply at a rate that brings the nominal interest rate to zero (Woodford, 1990).
9. There is scope for confusion about the terminology 'money market'. The money market is defined here as the market where the demand for money and the supply of money interact to determine the general price level, which is the inverse of 'the price of money' – measured by the quantity of goods and services that is sacrificed to acquire a unit of money (Friedman, 1992). However, in J.M. Keynes's liquidity preference model, the money market (defined above) is used to determine the nominal interest rate, although economists such as Friedman (1992) argued that the interest rate (the 'price' of credit) is determined not in the money market but in the credit market. Money and credit are two different concepts. Friedman (1983a: 244) explained this issue as follows:

   > Interest rates are the price of credit, not the price of money. The price of money is the quantity of goods and services that will 'buy' a piece of money (the reciprocal of the price level). Fluctuations in interest rates reflect instability in the demand for credit rather than for money properly defined, although interest rate changes may indirectly affect the quantity of money demanded. The so-called money market is really a credit market.

10. This specification ignores the nominal interest rate as a determinant of the demand for money. At a fundamental level, the linkage between money and prices is explained by invoking the classical *Quantity Theory of Money*, which has been developed and popularised by Fisher (1911) in the *Equation of Exchange*: $MV = PT$ where M is the nominal quantity of money, V is the income velocity of money, P is the price level and T is the transactions of final goods and services. According to Friedman (1994: 39), Fisher's *Equation of Exchange* plays the same foundation-stone role for monetary theory that Einstein's $E = mc^2$ does for physics.
11. In a strict sense, price stability means zero inflation (Fischer, 1996a; 1996b; Poole, 1999). In a general context, price stability refers to a very low rate of inflation; for example, in the range of 1 to 3 per cent per annum (Akerlof et al., 1996; Mishkin, 2007a; Phelps, 1973) or somewhat higher for developing countries (Khan and Senhadji, 2001).
12. Price stability (like national defence or street lights) is non-rivalrous. It provides benefits to the nation, irrespective of an individual's demand for it. For a discussion on the properties of a public good, see Varian (2006).
13. For early reviews of the literature on money and monetary policy in developing countries, see Coates and Khatkhate (1980), Khatkhate (1972) and Page (1993).
14. De Long (2000: 90) has summarised this view:

   > After all, a central bank not constrained by the constant nominal money growth rate rule can get itself into all kinds of mischief. It could use the inflation tax to gain command over goods and services. It could try to stimulate aggregate demand and manipulate the business cycle in order to create a favorable economic climate at election time.

15. The Asia-Pacific region represents the eastern part of Asia, some countries in Latin America, North America and Australasia that are located around the Pacific Ocean rim. This book does not cover all countries in the Asia-Pacific. For example, West Asia, Iran, Afghanistan and the newly independent central Asian states of the former Soviet Union are excluded. The focus is the countries of South, Southeast Asia and East Asia, and some developed countries such as Australia, Canada, New Zealand and the United States of America (USA). Along with Japan, these developed countries are used as a reference for comparison of developing countries of the Asia-Pacific. The above developed countries have close economic relations with developing Asia. As a special case, central banking and monetary policy issues in the United Kingdom (UK) are briefly reviewed. Some central banks in Asia are structured following the line of the Bank of England. The Bank of England is also one of the trendsetters for central banks across the globe.

16. Monetary and exchange rate policies are intertwined. They may represent the same policy depending on exchange rate arrangements and capital flows (Aghevli et al., 1991; Crockett and Nsouli, 1977; Saxena, 2008). Chapter 4 explains the relevant analytical issues.
17. As indicated in the preface, this book does not give an adequate coverage of the latest global financial crisis, which originated from the US subprime mortgage crisis, and its implication on the design and conduct of monetary policy in the Asia-Pacific. Just like the East Asian financial crisis of the late 1990s, the US subprime mortgage crisis has become an important global policy issue. Although the global financial crisis issue remains relevant, it is outside the scope of the present book. Chapter 9 makes only a general overview of this crisis and draws some policy implications. The critical issue is whether the global financial crisis would bring fundamental changes in the way monetary policy is designed and conducted. Most monetary economists do not think so. Some economists, however, believe that fiscal policy would gain more importance given the present crisis while monetary policy's role in stabilisation would be diminished. Some time is needed before an objective assessment can be made on such views. I intend to publish a companion volume of case studies of monetary policy in selected countries of the Asia-Pacific. In this volume I examine the pros and cons of monetary policy in selected countries of the Asia-Pacific. The book examines in detail the US subprime financial crisis and its impact on monetary policy in the Asia-Pacific.

2. Monetary and fiscal policies for macroeconomic stability: an Asian perspective

This chapter provides an overview of the scope of macroeconomics, introduces key issues in monetary theory and policy, and highlights the roles of monetary and fiscal policies in macroeconomic stability (Friedman, 1948; 1968a; Lucas, 1986).[1] The discussion revolves around the theme that the phenomenal economic progress in East and Southeast Asian countries over the past four decades took place within the framework of what may be called the East Asian development paradigm (Ichimura, 1993; James et al., 1987; Ranis, 1987). One characteristic feature of this paradigm is the maintenance of macroeconomic stability within an open economy context. Disciplined monetary and fiscal policies are credited for the low inflationary economic environment in East and Southeast Asia that has kept the real exchange rates closer to equilibrium levels (Bhagwati, 1996; Montiel, 2003; Pfefferman, 1985). Consequently, unlike most countries in Latin America, the East and Southeast Asian countries have avoided the problem of policy-induced exchange rate misalignment[2] and associated external crises (Campos, 1969; Corbo, 1988; Dornbusch, 1993; Edwards, 1989a; 1989b; 1998). According to the World Bank (1993), competitive real exchange rates contributed to export-driven growth in high-performing Asian economies. Another characteristic of the East Asian development model is pro-growth institutions that some economists argue have been even more important in explaining macroeconomic performance in developing countries than their exchange rate arrangements (Calvo, 1996; Calvo and Mishkin, 2003).

MACROECONOMICS AND POLICY DEBATES

Economic growth theory focuses on the determination of the level and the rate of growth of natural (or potential) output that determines the standards of living of the people. The determination of output relative to natural output (that is, output gap or business cycle) is the concern of stabilisation theory. They together constitute the theme of modern macroeconomics.[3] Macroeconomists in general suggest that a well-managed economy has two main features. First, in such an economy the level of output does not fluctuate much from its natural level.[4] Second, the level of natural output grows at a steady pace given sustained capital accumulation, growing population and the introduction of new, or adaptation of existing, technology. In such an economy, both inflation and unemployment remain at a low level and the standards of living of the people rises at a steady pace (Friedman, 1973; Lucas, 1988). The reality may, however, be different for many countries, as macroeconomic problems do arise and remain at the forefront of policy debate (IMF's *World Economic Outlook*, various issues).

Contemporary macroeconomic issues such as inflation, unemployment and balance-of-payment crises have come to the forefront of the policy debate since the 'Great Depression' of the 1930s (Agenor and Montiel, 1996; Burda and Wyplosz, 2005). The Great Depression is significant in the history of economic thought, as it triggered the development of what is called Keynesian macroeconomics. Keynesian economics started with the premise that the Great Depression undermined the classical view of the efficacy of market mechanisms in correcting macroeconomic imbalances. Government interventions in economic affairs were sought for and justified on the ground of market failures. For example, it was argued that high unemployment during the Great Depression was the consequence of a sharp decline in aggregate demand.[5] This was the interpretation given by J.M. Keynes in *The General Theory of Employment, Interest and Money* (Keynes, 1936). In fact such a message was present even in the writings of Thomas Malthus (Ritter et al., 2004). The Keynesian prescription[6] was to raise aggregate demand by increasing public spending and lowering taxes (Meltzer, 1988). Although monetary expansion can raise aggregate demand, it was considered ineffective during a depression because under such conditions there could be a sharp rise in the speculative demand for money and hence no increase in spending via the interest rate channel.[7]

The Keynesian policy prescription of raising output through expansionary fiscal policy seemed logical during a depressed economic condition. It was arguably damaging for developing countries when many of them adopted expansionary fiscal and monetary policies to raise economic growth (Aghevli, 1977; Corbo, 1974; Nichols, 1973). Many developing countries suffered from high inflation and balance-of-payments crises at different times since the 1950s. These problems were due to excessive monetary expansion, which was linked to large budget deficits. Large budget deficits were one of the consequences of increased public sector spending as part of a state-led development strategy (Edwards and Tabellini, 1991). Ironically, instead of rectifying alleged market failures, government failures became rampant across developing countries (Kirkpatrick and Nixson, 1989; Lal, 1985; Little, 1982). Macroeconomic problems took a serious turn in these countries during the 1970s and early 1980s following several adverse supply shocks, such as oil price shocks and associated recession in industrialised countries (Cornwall, 1992). This precipitated the debate of whether economic problems in developing countries arise from market failures or government failures or a combination of both.[8]

In the early twenty-first century, the debate is far from over. There is, however, an emerging consensus on the optimal level of government intervention into economic affairs of an otherwise private sector dominated, market-based economic system (Hughes, 1994; Streeten, 1993; World Bank's *World Development Report*, various issues). The international financial institutions, such as the International Monetary Fund (IMF) and the World Bank (WB), have supported developing countries to undertake financial deregulation and reform measures and to open up their economies for global competition. The idea is to develop the money and capital markets so that both the product and input markets work better. In a well-developed market economy, there should be little need for frequent government interventions into economic affairs. There is also acceptance that markets work better under prudential regulations and when there are institutional checks and balances for market-driven economic activities (Goldsbrough and Associates, 1996; World Bank's *World Development Report*, various years). Microeconomic reforms are also considered necessary to raise economic efficiency. Despite such consensus on broad issues, most developing countries are yet to develop economic and regulatory institutions to enable the smooth functioning of markets. Some economists with a Keynesian-Marxist persuasion still call for government interventions into economic affairs on a regular basis. Instead of stabilising markets, such interventions often have unintended repercussions (Agenor and Montiel, 1996; Hossain and Chowdhury, 1996).

The next section provides a historical overview of the debate on the role of monetary policy in stabilisation. This provides the context for reviewing key issues in monetary theory and policy in developing countries in Chapter 3.

THE ROLE OF MONETARY POLICY: GROWTH AND STABILISATION

Historically, monetary policy has been associated with the taming of business cycles in developed countries. The debate remains as to whether monetary policy should be used to stabilise an economy (Modigliani, 1977).[9] As noted earlier, Keynesian economists suggest the use of fiscal policy (rather than monetary policy) to fight against recession. They argue, citing the Great Depression of the 1930s, that monetary policy is ineffective in raising aggregate demand during recession. Monetarists[10] do not share this view. Friedman and Schwartz (1963a), in their most famous book *A Monetary History of the United States, 1867–1960*, demonstrated that the movements in money were the major contributor to business cycles in the USA. According to them, the Great Depression in the USA was the outcome of a sharp decline in the money supply, precipitated by bank failures. They argued that this could have been avoided if the Federal Reserve System (the Fed) increased the monetary base. The Fed did not increase the monetary base because it did not understand the consequences of bank failures on the money stock. Internal political factors also undermined the workings of the Fed. This indicates that monetary policy was not necessarily impotent in stopping the Depression, which itself was caused by a monetary shock. Indeed, Friedman and Schwartz (1963a) viewed the conduct of monetary policy in the USA during the Depression as a debacle.

The idea that monetary policy was impotent during the Depression was discarded by most economists by the late 1950s (Laidler, 1982). The debate, however, continues as to whether monetary policy should be used for economic stabilisation or price stability or both (Samuelson, 1994). Until the late 1960s, there was no urgency in most developed countries to resolve this issue. Note that unemployment was the number one problem for most developed countries during the Great Depression and it was expected to remain high after the Second World War. Rapid economic growth, however, kept the unemployment rate low in these countries during the 1950s and 1960s. Inflation was also relatively low in these countries during these decades. Therefore monetary policy in these countries remained in the shadow of fiscal policy (Friedman, 1968a; Mishkin, 2007a).

The policy environment was different in developing countries. Most countries in Latin America experienced high inflation throughout the 1950s and 1960s (Wachter, 1983). Such inflation was caused by both monetary and non-monetary factors (Bottomley, 1965; Corbo, 1974; Sunkel, 1960). It was during the 1970s that inflation became a global phenomenon. The Organisation of Petroleum Exporting Countries (OPEC) oil-price shocks and food-crop harvest failures were considered the triggers (Cline and Weintraub, 1981). The oil cost-push inflation that resulted was further exacerbated by excessive wage push by militant labour unions, especially in Australia and the UK. Moreover, inflation remained at a high level due to accommodative monetary policy in most developed countries aimed at keeping unemployment low. Although inflation fell in most developed countries during the 1980s, inflation in most developing countries remained high throughout the 1980s. Since then inflation nosedived for both developed and developing countries and remained at a low level for over a decade until the recent inflationary surge across the globe (Brown, 1985; Bruno and Sachs, 1985; IMF, 1996; 2001; 2006).

During the 1950s and 1960s the traditional role of monetary policy in developing countries was considered to be the promotion of economic growth and development (Coates and Khatkhate, 1980; Ghatak, 1983). The dichotomy in the role of monetary policy in developing vis-à-vis developed countries reflects differences in economic issues and the priorities of policy-makers. In reality, the issue is not as simple as it may appear. Although the preoccupation of policy-makers in developing countries is to raise economic growth and bring structural change in the economy, these goals cannot be separated from concern about price instability and external imbalances. For example, the experiences of Latin American countries during the 1960s and 1970s suggest that if the inflationary pressure that emerges from a policy-induced economic boom is ignored for long, the resulting inefficient allocation of resources and underutilised productive capacity can retard economic growth. The Latin American experiences also suggest that high inflation in these countries vis-à-vis their trading partners was the major cause of their lack of competitiveness in trade and balance-of-payments difficulties. The exchange rate crises that emanated from the worsening of the balance-of-payments problem were compounded by massive capital flight (Canavese, 1982; Chu and Feltenstein, 1979; Dornbusch, 1993; Edwards and Edwards, 1987).

The full-blown debt crises of the 1980s stalled economic growth and social development in most countries of Latin America. In fact the 1980s were dubbed the lost decade for Latin America (Corbo, 1988; Edwards, 1994; 1998; Sachs and Larrain, 1993). In contrast, the overwhelming lesson from the experiences of both East Asian (Hong Kong SAR, South Korea, Singapore and Taiwan) and Southeast Asian countries (Indonesia, Malaysia and Thailand) has been that sustained macroeconomic stability is crucial for economic growth (James et al., 1997; World Bank, 1993). Inflation was relatively low in most Asian countries during the 1960s. This was primarily due to conservative fiscal and monetary policies (Saini, 1982). They experienced high inflation during the 1970s due to external shocks. Inflation fell in these countries during the 1980s. They also avoided external debt problems. The currency crises of the 1990s in different parts of the world (especially in East and Southeast Asia) further point to problems associated with mismatches between exchange rate regimes, capital flows and monetary policy, rather than policy-induced macroeconomic imbalances per se (Fischer, 2001; Hossain, 2000; 2006a; Kaminsky et al., 2003). This suggests that the objectives of price stability, balance-of-payments equilibrium and economic growth are intertwined. Therefore, attempts at demarcation between the roles of monetary, fiscal and financial policies in economic growth and stabilisation in developing countries could lead to misguided policy (Agenor and Montiel, 1996; Montiel, 2003).

MONETARY POLICY FOR PRICE STABILITY

Since the 1970s there has been a fundamental shift in the view on the role of monetary policy in economic stabilisation in developed countries. Given the inflationary experiences of the 1970s, there is growing agreement that monetary policy should be conducted over the medium term and the primary objective of monetary policy should be price stability, meaning low and steady inflation. This reflects the emerging consensus on four economic propositions (Blejer et al., 2000; Debelle, 1997; Mishkin, 2000a; 2000b):

1. Monetary expansion has a lasting effect only on the price level, not on output or employment.
2. Inflation is costly in terms of resource allocation (efficiency costs) or in terms of long-term output growth (breakdown of super-neutrality of money) or both.
3. Monetary policy has transitory effects on real variables, but there is imperfect understanding of the nature and the size of such effects.
4. Monetary policy affects inflation with lags of uncertain duration and with variable strength, which undermines the central bank's ability to control inflation on a periodic basis.

The message is that although monetary policy does not raise long-term economic growth, it can promote economic growth in developing countries by maintaining price and/or exchange rate stability. The classical idea that money does not affect output in the long run is epitomised by the view that money is a veil over the real economy. Output depends on real factors of production, such as labour, capital and technology. Monetary expansion raises output or lowers unemployment but only in the short run because of expectational errors or market imperfections. According to the rational expectations hypothesis, there cannot be systematic expectational errors and therefore monetary expansion cannot raise output even in the short run (Barro, 2008; Lucas and Sargent, 1981). Policy-makers do not generally subscribe to the 'policy ineffectiveness hypothesis'. Nevertheless, most central bankers appear to have moved away from the Keynesian prescription of expansionary monetary policy for raising output. They have also accepted that the key (if not the sole) objective of monetary policy should be price stability, which does not necessarily mean zero inflation (Akerlof et al., 1996; Allen, 2004).

Strategy of Monetary Policy for Price Stability

Historically, the governments and/or central banks in developed countries have used different approaches to maintain price stability. The debate revolved around the choice between discretion and rule in the conduct of monetary policy. The argument behind a monetary policy rule has been to overcome what is called the 'time-inconsistency problem'[11] of monetary policy. The gold standard was the classical monetary policy rule that existed during the nineteenth century and the early part of the twentieth century (Bordo, 1992; Bordo and Kydland, 1995; Bordo and Schwartz, 1984). The gold standard contributed to long-term price stability.[12] The gold standard, however, led to short-term volatility in prices and was abandoned during the First World War. Some countries attempted to return to the gold standard after the First World War but were unsuccessful.[13] The gold standard was abandoned again in 1931 when the British pound sterling was made inconvertible into gold.

One of the problems during the depression of the 1930s was economic 'warfare' by competitive devaluations of currencies (Moosa, 2004). This suggested the need for a stable exchange rate system. The Bretton Woods fixed-exchange rate system was introduced after the Second World War, bringing stability in exchange rates. This system linked the currency of a country with the US dollar, which was pegged to gold at the exchange rate of US$35 per ounce. The delegates of 44 countries endorsed the Bretton Woods exchange rate system and created two international financial institutions – the International Bank for Reconstruction and Development (World Bank) and the International Monetary Fund. The Bretton Woods system remained in operation until the early 1970s. The fixed exchange rate system acted as an anchor for monetary and price stability across countries. Each country maintained an agreed-upon exchange rate with the US dollar and was ready to exchange its currency for dollars at the fixed rate. Since not many countries wished to import US monetary policy under this arrangement, their pegged exchange rates were associated with stringent capital controls that provided them some independence in the conduct of monetary policy. However the Bretton Woods system came under pressure during the late 1960s when US inflation started to rise. In August 1971, the US government under President Nixon officially abandoned this arrangement when the US dollar was made inconvertible into gold (Cecchetti, 2008; Eiteman et al., 2001). Economists hold the view that expansionary fiscal and monetary policies[14] of the USA since the early 1960s led to the ultimate demise of the Bretton Woods system.

Post-Bretton Woods Exchange Rate Arrangements in Developed Countries

Since the early 1970s most developed countries have adopted a floating exchange rate system. This has allowed central banks to conduct an independent monetary policy for price stability. Under a floating exchange rate system there is, however, no anchor for inflation. Price stability therefore requires the adoption of an implicit or explicit monetary policy rule (Aghevli et al., 1991). For example, inflationary expectations under a floating exchange rate system can be tied to money growth (monetary targeting) or inflation itself (inflation targeting). Some developed countries – for example the USA and Japan – with developed money and capital markets have, thus far, avoided deploying an explicit monetary policy rule. They conduct monetary policy through discretion in which the short-term interest rate or a monetary aggregate is used as a policy instrument for demand management. This has worked well for the USA since the 1990s until the outbreak of the present global financial crisis (Mishkin, 2007a; Taylor, 2008a). Japan was not, however, successful using discretionary monetary policy to revive its economy from a decade-long deflation. The Bank of Japan, which gained autonomy under a newly enacted law in 1998, was slow to introduce an extraordinarily expansionary monetary policy to generate inflationary expectations to lower real interest rates (Blanchard, 2006; Ito, 2006).

Post-Bretton Woods Exchange Rate Arrangements in Developing Countries

The monetary policy strategy has taken different forms in developing countries. The floating exchange rate system was not appropriate for most developing countries because they do not have developed money and capital markets. For smaller open economies, a pegged exchange rate system was appropriate so that foreign prices can act as an anchor for domestic prices. For highly inflationary countries, the suggested exchange rate arrangements were currency union, dollarisation and monetary union. The aim of such exchange rate arrangements was to prevent central banks from performing their function as the lender of last resort that may lead to excessive monetary expansion (Aghevli et al., 1991; Mishkin and Savastano, 2000).

Since the late 1990s most developing countries have moved away from extreme forms of exchange rate arrangement and adopted a 'managed float' regime. Such a move arguably diluted their commitment to price stability. In order to remove this perception, they have opted for monetary policy rules such as monetary targeting, or inflation targeting, or a combination of alternative strategies of monetary policy. Central banks have been given a large degree of autonomy to conduct independent monetary policy to achieve one or more well-defined objective(s) of monetary policy (IMF's *World Economic Outlook*, various issues; Lowe, 1997).

Although greater autonomy for central banks can be considered a positive development, the design and conduct of monetary policy is yet to be institutionalised in most developing countries. Price stability, as the main objective of monetary policy, is acknowledged but has not been adopted in most developing countries. At the operational level, a fundamental question is how much control central banks should have on the money supply or interest rates or both. In a market economy, inflation remains outside the direct control of the central bank. What the central bank can do is to use indirect monetary policy instruments to change aggregate demand and probably aggregate supply. The way monetary policy instruments affect different components of expenditure in developing economies (that is, the transmission mechanisms of monetary policy) remains uncertain (Montiel, 1991). Further, there is considerable lag between any policy action and its impacts on aggregate demand and aggregate supply. Another aspect is the presence in many countries of many stringent controls over capital flows. The interaction between monetary policy, exchange rate arrangements and capital controls is yet another important issue (Cheng, 1988). These issues are discussed in subsequent chapters.

MACROECONOMIC STABILITY AND ECONOMIC GROWTH IN ASIA

During the 1950s and 1960s Latin America acted as the laboratory for testing different macroeconomic models and approaches to development. From about the 1970s the bulk of literature on development studies has an Asian focus. Macroeconomic stability in general, and price stability in particular, are the hallmarks of Asian development. Most successful Asian economies maintained budget surpluses or small budget deficits, experienced low inflation, and kept both internal and external debts under control. This represented a non-inflationary policy paradigm which was distinct from the Latin American structuralist growth model, where inflation was considered a part of economic growth (Corbo, 1988; Edwards, 1983; Harberger, 1984; World Bank, 1993).

Openness, Macroeconomic Stability and Economic Growth

East Asian development experiences have been the basis of a development paradigm that suggests a virtuous circle of openness, macroeconomic stability and economic growth. The idea is that there exists a linkage between economic openness and macroeconomic stability (Lane, 1997; Terra, 1999), which in turn promotes economic growth. In particular, economic openness and macroeconomic stability have a feedback relationship. For example, the basis of an export-oriented development strategy is the achievement and maintenance of export competitiveness. This requires low inflation that helps prevent real exchange rates from appreciating. Unlike most developing countries, East Asian countries, in particular, managed to maintain real exchange rates at their optimal levels by keeping inflation low (Petrie, 1993; World Bank, 1993).

Figure 2.1 is a flow chart of such a development paradigm. Two relationships are indicated. First, trade openness and macroeconomic stability are interlinked, that is, they feed each other.[15] The logic is that in an open economy policy mistakes become obvious much earlier than in a closed economy because its international competitiveness suffers. To regain its competitive position, it must act quickly. Thus, in an open economy, both recognition and reaction lags are short. Policy mistakes cannot extend too far, for too long. From this viewpoint, trade openness acts as an external constraint on macroeconomic mismanagement (Hossain and Chowdhury, 1998). Second, macroeconomic stability reduces policy uncertainty. This promotes economic growth by raising investment and its efficiency (Fischer, 1993; Little et al., 1993). When these relationships are linked together, one testable hypothesis emerges: openness to international trade and investment promotes, rather than retards, economic growth.[16] As Krugman and Obstfeld (2009: 260) point out, it is indisputable that some Asian economies achieved high rates of economic growth via processes that involve rapid growth of exports, rather than substitution of domestic production for imports. There is, however, debate whether such growth of exports was due to 'free' trade policies. A corollary of the above proposition is that the impact of trade openness on economic growth diminishes as the economy develops.[17]

The close association between openness, macroeconomic stability and economic growth suggests that any dichotomy between short-term macroeconomic management and long-term growth policies is artificial. Summers and Thomas (1993: 248) indeed suggest that 'sound macroeconomic policies with sustainable fiscal deficits and realistic exchange rates are a prerequisite to progress'. There is overwhelming evidence to support the view that high and variable inflation, as well as unsustainable external imbalance, adversely affects economic growth (Hossain and Chowdhury, 1996). Figure 2.1 shows the virtuous circle of openness, macroeconomic stability and economic growth.

The Asia-Pacific data support the openness-growth hypothesis. Clearly, North East and Southeast Asian economies are more open than the others in Latin America and Africa (Collier and Gunning, 1999) and they stand out for their superior macroeconomic performance. Although any evidence on the implied causal relationship between openness and economic growth should be treated with caution, some aspects of East Asian development experiences are consistent with the openness-growth hypothesis (James et al., 1987; World Bank, 1993). The benefits of trade reforms are ascribed to efficient resource allocation following comparative advantage, exploitation of scale economies and the possibility that a freer trading system encourages innovation and dissemination

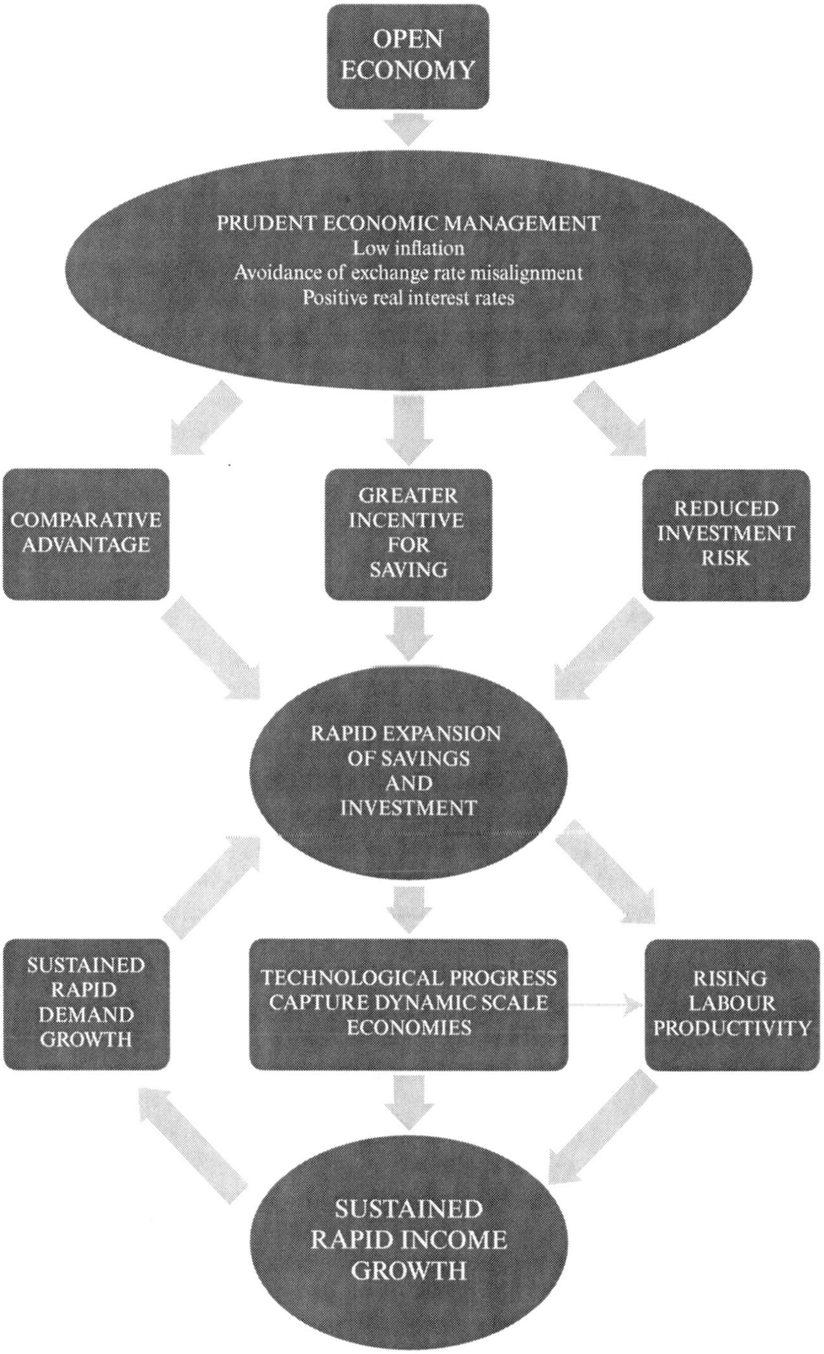

Source: Adapted from Hossain and Chowdhury (1998: 8).

Figure 2.1 Virtuous circle of openness, macroeconomic stability and economic growth of knowledge across national borders. To the extent that trade reforms remove structural distortions and maintain macroeconomic stability, they may raise the rates of investment and economic growth (Dornbusch, 1992a; Goldsbrough and Associates, 1996; Meier, 1985).

MAINTAINING MACROECONOMIC STABILITY IN ASIA

Globalisation remains the best option for rapid economic development in Asia. There is, however, risk from globalisation for developing economies, as they become heavily exposed to international shocks (Hossain, 2000; Reisen, 1996). The 1997–98 currency crises that created a gloom picture in Asia is largely past.[18] This is despite the present global financial crisis that has created a shadow on the growth prospects of some outward-oriented developing countries of Asia. Most affected countries have recovered and moved to their pre-crisis growth paths. They have undertaken reforms and improved their financial systems. Political reforms have also improved the institutional capacity of these countries to develop sound economic policies. The core idea of macroeconomic stability as a requirement of economic growth remains intact (Aziz et al., 2006). Despite the early fear that the currency crises may induce East Asian countries becoming protectionist, there has actually been an increase in economic openness. This has increased the importance of macroeconomic stability in a global context (Fischer, 2003).

Since the currency crises, monetary policy in particular has gained importance in most Asian countries. Conversely, the role of fiscal policy in stabilisation has lost its prominence. The future price stability in the region, therefore, would depend primarily on the stance of monetary policy. There is general agreement, for example, by central banks and the IMF, that price stability is important and every country should strive to achieve it.

Yet not all countries put equal emphasis on price stability. It appears that some countries put greater emphasis on economic growth. This influenced their policy-makers to downgrade the importance of price stability. For example, although Malaysia and Singapore maintained consistently low, single-digit inflation, South Korea and Indonesia experienced double-digit inflation throughout the 1960s and the 1970s. On the fiscal front, Singapore has consistently maintained budget surplus while Malaysia maintained relatively large budget deficits of around 7 per cent of gross domestic product (GDP) during the 1970s and 1980s. Hong Kong (China), Singapore and Taiwan (China) avoided borrowing abroad, while South Korea and Indonesia relied heavily on foreign borrowing during the 1980s and 1990s. These economies, however, financed their deficits in a prudent manner and avoided major macroeconomic problems. The situation has changed lately. Countries such as South Korea and Indonesia, which maintained high growth despite high inflation, may not be able to do so in the future. Financial markets have become sensitive to fiscal and monetary developments. In fact, Indonesia suffered during the financial crises of the late 1990s, even though it did not have unsustainable macroeconomic imbalances (Hossain, 2006a). Vietnam, which has made a tremendous economic breakthrough since the late 1990s, has apparently put more emphasis on economic growth, even at the risk of high inflation (Al-Mashat, 2004; Camin, 2008).

The challenge for Asian economies is to maintain low inflation and sustainable current account balances to maintain steady economic growth. In countries such as

Indonesia and Thailand, external debts of the private sector remain a matter of concern. Macroeconomic management has therefore become the focus of international financial institutions. The strategies that have been put in place by different countries suggest that macroeconomic stability has been taken seriously by most policy-makers in the region. Moreover, there are at least three recent positive developments that may help restrain fiscal excesses in developing Asia. The first is the rapid growth of domestic financial systems. Inflation is generally inversely related to the depth of domestic financial markets (Khan et al., 2006). A developed financial market lowers the cost of non-inflationary financing of budget deficits and reduces the need for seigniorage. Financial markets have distaste for inflation and they demand macroeconomic discipline which policy-makers can hardly ignore. The second development is the greater financial integration of Asian developing market economies within the world economy. In order to attract foreign capital, developing countries in the region must maintain fiscal prudence. International capital markets monitor country-specific fiscal developments, which determine the country-specific risk premium on sovereign or corporate debt instruments. The third is the diminishing public tolerance for inflation. This is a demonstration effect, which has originated from low-inflationary developed countries. This is also a reflection of the higher political weight of lower income groups in democratic regimes because these groups lose the most from high inflation (IMF, 1996; 2001).

NOTES

1. The later chapters review the contemporary issues in central banking and monetary policy in an expanded form.
2. Following Edwards (1989a: 8), the real exchange rate misalignment is defined 'as sustained deviations of the real exchange rate from its long-run equilibrium level'.
3. For a review of macroeconomic concepts, models, policies and issues, see Barro (2008), Blanchard (2006), Branson (1989), Burda and Wyplosz (2005), Dornbusch et al. (2008), and Gordon (1993).
4. There is debate over the factors which cause short-term economic fluctuations. New-classical economists suggest that such fluctuations reflect 'technological' shocks to the economy (Kydland and Prescott, 1982; 1990). In contrast, monetarists emphasise monetary shocks as the main source of business cycles. The Keynesians deemphasise monetary shocks but suggest autonomous shift in aggregate demand and/or wage and price rigidities as factors causing business cycles. For a detailed discussion on the different sources of business cycles, see Barro (2008).
5. Aggregate demand is known as effective demand in Keynesian economics.
6. This follows the works of Keynes (1936).
7. This is based on the Keynesian idea of the liquidity trap, which suggests that once the interest rate decreases to a very low level, the speculative demand for money becomes infinite such that any additional increase in the money supply is hoarded (rather than substituted for bonds) to avoid capital loss. Therefore, the interest rate does not decrease further and there is no increase in investment spending. Krugman (2000) has developed the idea of liquidity trap in the context of Japanese deflation of the 1990s.
8. For a review of the controversies in macroeconomics, see Dornbusch (2000) and Greenwald and Stiglitz (1988).
9. This is part of a debate on the efficacy of market vis-à-vis state among economists who belong to the two main schools of thought: Keynesians (and their neo-Keynesian heirs) and monetarists (and neo-monetarists). For a discussion on this debate, see Burda and Wyplosz (2005).
10. The term 'monetarist' is derived from the Latin 'moneta' (Burda and Wyplosz, 2005: 18). It refers to the view of Milton Friedman and others, who emphasise that the excess money supply is the key determinant of long-run inflation.
11. Time inconsistency refers to the temptations of policy-makers to deviate from any optimal policy stance that was announced previously and when private economic agents had acted or based their expectations on the original policy stance (Kydland and Prescott, 1977).

12. Under the gold standard, the money supply growth was limited to the rate at which additional gold was acquired by the authorities.
13. Cecchetti (2008) makes a strong point that the gold standard probably played a critical role in spreading the Great Depression of the 1930s throughout the world.
14. These policies were associated with the American War in Vietnam.
15. Although openness may lead to low inflation, there is lack of consensus on the direction of causality between them. For example, it is possible that openness and inflation are mechanically linked via budgetary effects. The higher the openness of the economy, then the higher would be the substitution of import tariffs for inflation tax in financing public spending. Lane (1997) provides some evidence which is not consistent with the endogenous openness hypothesis. An alternative budgetary channel predicts an inverse relation between openness and inflation, on the basis of a greater elasticity of money demand with respect to inflation in more open economies, which reduces the optimal seigniorage rate (Driscoll and Lahiri, 1983; Fair, 1987).
16. This hypothesis contrasts with the implication of Latin American dependency theory that economic openness is the root cause of underdevelopment of poor countries under the metropolis-satellite capitalist structure (Frank, 1967; 1996). Rodrik et al. (2002) argue that openness to international trade is not a major direct determinant of per capita income but it leads to better institutions that raise incomes.
17. Tariffs and seigniorage are both much more important sources of revenue for poor countries than for rich ones. The importance of openness is expected to decline with the wealth of the country if a budgetary explanation is important for the state of openness of an economy (Lane, 1997).
18. Although the present global financial crisis has created a shadow on the growth prospects of developing countries of the Asia-Pacific, Burton and Zanello (2007: 9) made the following assessment of Asia's post-crisis economic prospects:

> Ten years after a major financial crisis, Asia is looking at the future with renewed confidence and has good reason to do so. Ground has been regained where it had been lost, and Asia is well positioned to be an ever-greater force in the world economy. Encouragingly, policies are increasingly attuned to the quickening pace of globalization, and the foundations for a sustained expansion are being laid. Although the list of policy issues still to address might seem daunting at first, reforms must be a continuous process in today's fast paced and interconnected economy, and policies that address any one of these issues are likely to help on the other fronts as well.

3. Central banking in the Asia-Pacific: an overview

Central banks are entrenched as powerful national institutions with direct control of monetary policy for numerous countries. This is significant because until the late twentieth century, economists debated whether there was need for a central bank (Laidler, 2005). This debate has been linked to the issue of whether there is a role for discretionary monetary policy in economic stabilisation. Some prominent economists, such as Milton Friedman and Frederick Hayek, opposed discretionary monetary policy for economic stabilisation (Friedman, 1959a; Hayek, 1933; 1978). Following the tradition of the gold standard that put a natural limit to the growth of the money supply, they argued for a rule-based monetary policy in a fiat monetary system so that monetary policy can achieve price stability and create an environment for rapid economic growth (Friedman, 1991). They did not, however, maintain a common view on whether a central bank is needed once monetary policy is conducted by adopting a policy rule.

Friedman (1959a: 6–7) advocated a 'constant money supply growth rule' for price stability, that is, keeping the rate of inflation low and stable, by increasing money supply in line with the increase in money demand from increased output. Although such a rule may not be optimal, it was considered necessary for an effective check on the behaviour of policy-makers and to act as a yardstick to ensure accountability of a central bank. Friedman argued for the necessity of a central bank because it bears the responsibility of maintaining the sanctity of financial contracts, the prevention of frauds and the working of a monetary system in an uncertain world in which information is costly and scarce. The need for a central bank in the USA, in particular, originated from frequent bank failures (Mishkin and Eakins, 2006).

Hayek (1978), in contrast, argued for free competition in the provision of money by competitive commercial banks. He hypothesised that a system of competing private monies would be better at providing high-quality money, in the sense that the value of money remains stable over time. If citizens of a country are free to hold alternative monies, then private monies, as Hayek predicted, would outperform central bank monies in purchasing-power stability and dominate them in popularity. In such a monetary system, there is no need for a central bank (Selgin, 1988; Selgin and White, 1987).

The Hayekian view on the money supply and/or the competitive private banking led to an ongoing debate over this issue. Smith (1936), using the position of Bagehot (1873) that competitive commercial banking (with each bank holding its own reserves of gold) was a 'natural system', preferred in theory 'free banking' (that is, banking freed from the interference of a central bank). She opined that the mere existence of a central bank (even if it follows certain rules of conduct) represents a standing temptation for the monetary authorities to change the rules of the game and to debauch the currency. According to her, a free banking system would be inherently stable and perform satisfactorily, while a central bank in a free market economy would represent an undesirable intervention into the affairs of the banking industry.

In a broad sense, the idea of free banking is concomitant with the argument for free trade. Following the tradition in international economics that free trade and unhindered competition are beneficial to an economy, it is argued that the banking industry should not be seen as something special that justifies imposition upon private banks of outside controls, regulations or supervision. In a free-banking system, central banks therefore become superfluous.

Within a political economy framework, the idea of free banking, however, arises out of a distrust of the government's management of the fiat monetary system. Historically, central banks were established in the seventeenth and eighteenth centuries to provide credits to the government on subsidised terms. In turn, governments rewarded the central banks with monopoly rights to issue notes (Goodhart, 1988). The major concern was that under a fiat monetary system, central banks (without effective constraints) would have the temptation to engineer deflation (J.M. Keynes), or inflation (F.A. Hayek), or business cycles.

The major argument against free banking is that free banking could induce inflation because individual banks may have the incentives and opportunities to debase the liabilities at the expense of an ill-informed public. The proponents of the free banking system do not agree with this view. Instead, they argue that central banks, acting as an agent of the government, have the incentives and opportunities to debase the liabilities. Laidler (2005) argues that a fully developed free banking system would deliver price-level stability, not because any central agency decreed it, but because the self-interest of individual banks operating in a competitive environment would lead them towards such an outcome.

The idea of free banking, however, did not capture the imagination of policy-makers in developed or developing countries. Central banks were established in these countries with a sense of urgency. There were a number of reasons. First, the gold standard did not survive beyond the First World War, thus necessitating a reliance on fiat money. Second, the role of monetary policy was not merely to maintain price stability but was broadened to include output and employment (Laidler, 2005).

The broader role for monetary policy was a welcome relief for policy-makers. From the 1960s and 1970s, other functions were assigned to the central banks, referred to as 'central banking functions'. These include note issue and the supervision and regulation of the financial system. Over the years, central banks in most countries have gained the status of a national institution that instigates monetary and financial stability (Mizen, 2003). Financial stability is seen as a requirement for sustained economic growth. Hence central banks have been given the responsibility for financial stability, in conjunction with price stability (Siklos, 2002).

Having established the crucial role of central banks in modern economics, the rest of this chapter reviews the evolution of central banking and the functions of central banks in a historical context. The major central banks in the Asia-Pacific are then introduced, followed by a discussion on some institutional and organisational issues in Asian central banking.

EVOLUTION OF CENTRAL BANKING

Central banking originated in Europe in the second half of the seventeenth century (Collins, 1992a; 1992b; Fischer, 1994). The Swedish Riksbank was founded in 1664, the Bank of England was founded in 1694, the Banque de France was founded in 1800 and the Netherlands Bank was founded in 1814. Until such central banks were established, the 'Royal Treasury' or a large commercial bank performed central banking functions (Bordo, 2007). Central banking in its present form is a recent phenomenon. At the beginning of the twentieth century, there were only 18 central banks in the world (Capie, 1997). By 1950, there were 59 central banks and, by 2000, there were 174 central banks globally (Cecchetti, 2008).

Goodhart (1988) suggests that central banks evolved as a response to the private banks' inability to cope with recurrent banking panics, thereby representing a natural evolution. At the early stages of central banking evolution, some prominent private banks (in the course of their businesses) acted as the government bankers and/or for the ruling elite of the society. These banks later graduated into central banks. Smith (1936) argued that central banks evolved essentially as a tool for raising revenues for the government. She did not, however, say much about the role of central banks as the lender of last resort. Bordo and Redish (1987) argue that the origin of the Bank of Canada, for example, was political, as there was no economic rationale for its establishment. In the literature on central banking, economists have usually provided both economic and political interpretations for the origins of central banking.

The original impetus for the establishment in Europe of the first central banks came from two sources. First, under the pressure of financing war, the governments realised that, in exchange for their support for specific private banks, they could obtain favourable financial assistance and advantages from these banks. Such favouritism (supported by legislation) led to the transformation of a private bank into a central bank. The Bank of England and a specially established bank such as the Prussian State Bank are two prime examples (Goodhart, 1988; 1992; Santoni, 1984; Swinburne and Castello-Branco, 1991). Second, the purpose for establishing early central banks was to unify the note-issuing system, manage and protect the precious metal reserves of the country, and improve the payments system. This was the case for Germany, Italy and Switzerland.[1] Prior to this development, the regionalised note-issuing systems of these countries were costly and inefficient. A unified note-issuing system brought economic benefits such as economies of scale and increased confidence of the public in the note-issuing system. In addition, there were political attractions for the establishment of central banks, in the sense of having the sovereigns' access to seigniorage (Swinburne and Castello-Branco, 1991). In Japan, one urgent task facing the new government after the Meiji restoration in 1868 was to reform the chaotic currency system with inconvertible government money and coins, in conjunction with different kinds of private monies. After unsuccessful reform attempts, the note-issuing system was centralised in the hands of the Bank of Japan (central bank of Japan), which was founded in 1882 (Giannini, 1995).

Once the central banking institutions gained the privileged legal position as both the bankers to the government and having the authority to issue notes, they assumed the role of bankers' banks. Their privileged position gained the trust of other private banks, with respect to holding reserves for emergencies. Thereafter, individual banks sought, and gained, the liquidity support from the central banks to meet emergencies, especially during financial panics. At the early stages there were, however, some problems with the function of central banks as lenders of last resort. Early central banks had public charters, yet were still privately owned with policy independence. This was not compatible with the broader responsibility given to central banks. The problem that plagued the Bank of England in the early years was that it placed primary weight in its commercial activities. On several occasions, the Bank of England contributed to financial distress by neglecting its role of providing liquidity support to other banks. Bagehot (1873) formulated the public responsibility doctrine of the Bank of England in 1873: a provision of the lender of last resort support to other banks. This was the beginning of the central bank's core function as the lender of last resort (Bordo, 2007; Gorton and Huang, 2001; Lovell, 1957). Laidler (2004) emphasises that the function of the lender of last resort later became part of the British Monetary Orthodoxy.

As noted earlier, in countries where there were no central banks, quasi-central banking mechanisms were developed. Some financial institutions (because of their dominant position) became the source of emergency funds for the private banks that enabled them to economise on their reserve holdings. For example, in the USA, the clearing-house associations and some large commercial banks provided these services to smaller banks. The private Parisian bankers in their own initiatives established a separate institution in 1797 to undertake central banking functions. Three years later the Banque de France was created with official prompting and support (Timberlake, 1978; 1984; 1992).

This overview reveals that although there were political factors behind the establishment of central banks, the need for, and the emergence of, central banking was a natural phenomenon. Government interventions created specific central banks, or else endowed pre-existing banks with monopoly power to issue notes and any government banking privileges. Such interventions determined the particular form of central banking arrangements, or which institution should become a central bank, rather than whether there should be a central bank as a matter of principle. Activities of central banks expanded gradually as new issues emerged. Later, central banks developed more specialised activities, with which their position became institutionally stronger.

Central banks' position as the source of liquidity for the banking system meant that they gradually became increasingly tied both to the health of the banking system and the monetary condition of the economy. This created conflicts between the broader financial concern of central banks and their commercial banking operations. Central banks eventually moved out of their commercial activities and concentrated on central banking functions. For example, the Bank of England and the Banque de France undertook this transformation during the second half of the nineteenth century. Central banks established in the twentieth century were set up as entirely new and non-competitive institutions. They followed the traditions of their European forerunners. Where this was not the case initially, a separate central bank was subsequently split-off from its parent organisation. In Australia, for example, the Reserve Bank of Australia (central bank of Australia) was split-off from the government-owned Commonwealth Bank of Australia in 1959.

A monetary policy function was built into the traditional functions of central banks during the first half of the twentieth century. This followed the abandonment of guaranteed convertibility of national currencies into gold at the fixed exchange rate in the wake of the Great Depression. In the absence of a fixed external value of domestic currency, the growth rate of the money supply became the major determinant of the external value of money. Since then, central banks have assumed the responsibility of maintaining the value of money (external and internal) on the grounds that they have a monopoly over the supply of high-powered money (or central bank money) (Swinburne and Castello-Branco, 1991).

FUNCTIONS OF A MODERN CENTRAL BANK

The evolution of central banking suggests a number of functions of a modern central bank. The first and foremost is the issuing of currency notes, which is the major item on the liability side of the central bank's balance sheet (Cecchetti, 2008). Currency notes are the major component of the monetary base or high-powered money. They are a highly liquid asset and therefore used for transaction purposes. Currency notes and deposits also serve as a store of value, provided that the purchasing power of money remains stable in a non-inflationary economy. This was considered by Bagehot (1873) as the first order business for the Bank of England. As Laidler (2004: 4) writes, '. . . for him [Bagehot], a currency convertible on demand into one or other of the precious metals – preferably gold – was the *sine qua non* of the monetary system, and the preservation of that convertibility was the first order of business for the Bank of England'. This function of money may be undermined when a central bank performs its second function as the banker of the government. As the government's bank, the central bank accepts deposits of the government and manages its debt (domestic and external). The central bank also acts as the custodian and manager of the country's foreign exchange reserves.

The above functions and responsibilities of central banks are less controversial. Most central banks, however, remain prepared to finance most (if not all) budget deficits by accepting the government's treasury bills. The treasury bills enter into the asset side of the central bank's balance sheet. Therefore, this form of financing of budget deficits is equivalent to money creation (sometimes called *deficit financing*), which appears in the balance sheet as a liability. Financing of budget deficits through money creation is controversial, as the status of a central bank as an institution is lowered in the eyes of the public. Unless a central bank has the authority to say no to financing of budget deficits, the government's privileged access to the central bank for liquidity may lead to excessive money creation at least in the short run, irrespective of whether the country operates under a fixed or a flexible exchange rate system. Excessive money creation leads to high inflation or hyperinflation, which undermines the role of money as a store of value. This remains the most controversial aspect of central banking in developing countries. In fact, Fry (1992: 325–6) described the process how, until recently, many developing countries used central banks as a source of revenue:

> In many developing countries, the central bank has served as an important source of government revenue. Indeed, the central bank in these countries is the goose that lays the golden eggs. The free-range goose, conducting conservative monetary policy with a fair degree of independence, produces golden eggs worth less than one percent of GNP [gross national product] (Malaysia, Morocco and Thailand). The battery-farm goose, bred specially for intensive egg-laying, can produce golden eggs in the form of an inflation tax yielding five to ten percent of GNP (Mexico, Peru and Yugoslavia). The force-fed goose can produce revenue up to 25 percent of GNP for a

limited period before the inevitable demise of the goose and collapse of the economy (Chile in the early 1970s).

The third function of a modern central bank is to serve as the bankers' bank, which takes the form of a lender of last resort (Bordo, 1989). The central bank provides liquidity to commercial banks to maintain financial stability and/or smooth operation of the settlement system. Since opening-up economies in recent years and increasing banking competition, commercial banks have become vulnerable to both domestic and external shocks (Claassen, 1985). Central banks remain ready to meet the emergency needs of commercial banks and other financial institutions that arise from shocks and/or sharp changes in market sentiments. By ensuring that sound banks and financial institutions can continue to operate, central banks provide stability to financial systems. Currently this has emerged as an important function of a central bank (Cecchetti, 2008; Goodhart, 1999a; 1999b). This issue is elaborated below.

Monetary policy was added to the list of central banking functions in the 1950s. By the 1990s this had become the central bank's most glamorous function. Until recently monetary policy was usually used to achieve multiple objectives in developing countries, including economic growth, poverty alleviation and amelioration of business cycles (Ahmed, 1987; Chandavarkar, 1992; Coates and Khatkhate, 1980). The present debate is whether monetary policy should be used to achieve a single objective such as price stability. Chapter 4 reviews this issue in detail.

Central banks are the guardians of modern financial systems. The supervision and development of the financial system has therefore emerged as an important function of a modern central bank. The central bank and/or other regulatory authorities watch the operations of commercial banks and non-bank financial institutions to ensure that savers and investors have confidence in the financial system. To maintain financial stability, the central bank remains responsible for the operation and development of the settlement system. In fact the recent financial crises (for example, the late 1990s Asian crises and the 2008 US subprime mortgage crises) have exposed the problems of payment risks in a deregulated financial system. Traditionally, central banks helped commercial banks to operate under a net settlement system. One major weakness of this system is that the interbank settlement risk exposures may go unmanaged and even unrecognised. As a result, difficulties facing a financial institution may spread quickly to other institutions through payment defaults. The central bank's role in the payment system has therefore become critical in maintaining financial stability. Besides such settlement risks, the financial system in most countries has become vulnerable to both real and monetary shocks. One common lesson from recent financial crises is that financial instability leads to monetary instability. This is because central banks are required to rescue the troubled banks and other financial institutions to avoid any economy-wide meltdown. Central banks have therefore become heavily involved in preventing and managing financial risks and crises that seem inherent and inevitable in a deregulated financial system, especially in developing countries (Crockett, 2001; Mishkin, 2007a).

Finally, the research department of a central bank analyses macroeconomic developments in an economy and examines that economy's vulnerability to both domestic and external shocks. In the currently deregulated economic environment, the research function of the central bank is critical for the conduct of monetary and financial policies. Central banks publish both current and historical data. Furthermore, researchers working in central banks publish papers on contemporary macroeconomic and monetary issues. Since the effectiveness of monetary policy is enhanced when the public is informed of economic issues and reasons behind monetary policy actions, economic research performs the role of communication with the public in general, and financial markets in particular (Blinder, 1998; Bodart, 1990). Some central banks, such as the Reserve Bank of Australia and the Monetary Authority of Singapore, publish educational materials for both students and the general public.

The above list of functions of a central bank is not exhaustive; nor are all functions equally important. Their importance differs from country to country, depending on the stages of development. The tasks of supervising and developing the financial system and the payments system are critical for developing countries. The lender of last resort function is equally important, as it is linked to financial stability and settlement risks.[2] Further, developing countries have difficulties in establishing a balance between the traditional central banking and developmental functions of a central bank (Ahmed, 1987; Dorrance, 1969). Some developmental functions that central banks perform have historical roots. This can be traced to the way the central banks' roles and responsibilities were defined when they were established. For example, even under the gold standard during the early twentieth century, the functions of central banks were thought to be wide-ranging. This was authoritatively described by Montagu Norman while giving evidence before the Royal Commission on Indian Currency and Finance (Sayers, 1957).

In summing up: central banks remain unique in many respects. They carry well-defined, primary and secondary, functions. Historically, it is the primary function that differentiates central banks from others, although there is no consensus on the precise primary function of a central bank. According to Hawtrey (1932), the lender of last resort was the essential characteristic of a central bank, while Smith (1936) regarded the monopoly in note issue as the peculiarity of a central bank. Kisch and Elkin (1928: 72) considered that '[a]n essential function of a Central Bank is the maintenance of the stability of the monetary standard. This involves the control of the monetary circulation and the Bank therefore should be given the right of note issue, and preferably the sole right'. In the Statute of the Bank for International Settlements (BIS, 2003), on the other hand, a central bank is defined as 'the bank in any country to which has been entrusted the duty of regulating the volume of currency and credit in that country' (Article 56a).

CENTRAL BANKS IN THE ASIA-PACIFIC[3]

This section introduces the major central banks in the Asia-Pacific and reviews their key functions and governance. The relationships of central banks with the governments are also reviewed in a broad context. Chapter 9 reviews monetary policy developments in selected countries of the Asia-Pacific.

Central banks in the former British colonies of Asia were established after their national independence. These banks have organisational structures and functions similar to those of the Bank of England. Both economic and political factors played a role in the establishment of central banks in newly independent nations of the region (Davies, 1960). Central banks and other financial institutions were also linked to development initiatives that most Asian developing countries undertook after their independence. Since the 1990s most Asian central banks have curtailed their developmental activities. Some of them have gained autonomy and reputation, and have been assigned the responsibility of maintaining monetary stability for rapid economic growth.

In the context of this overview, the major central banks of the Asia-Pacific are introduced in an alphabetical order. Central banks of some developed countries are also covered for comparison of central banking activities and governance. They act as trendsetters for monetary policy, given their varied experiences.

The Reserve Bank of Australia[4]

Australia's central bank is called the Reserve Bank of Australia (RBA). The RBA assumed the functions of central banking in 1959. Until then, the Commonwealth Bank of Australia – which was established in 1911 under the Commonwealth Bank Act as a government-owned commercial bank to 'curb the money power' of the handful of private banks – discharged responsibilities of a central bank. By the time the Commonwealth Bank opened for business in mid-1912, it did not have the authority to note issue, which was administered by the Australian Department of Treasury. In 1920, the responsibility for note issue was transferred from the Treasury to a Notes Board. In 1924 the Commonwealth Bank Act was amended and the Bank was given control over note issue. From this time until 1945 (when there were changes to the legislation), the Bank gradually evolved its central banking activities under a stringent controlled regime. The Bank gained the powers for exchange control and a wide range of controls over the banking system such as the authority to determine advance policy and interest rates and to require private banks to lodge funds in its special accounts. The new Commonwealth Bank Act and the Banking Act, both of 1945, formalised the Bank's powers in relation to the administration of monetary and banking policy.

The Reserve Bank Act 1959 preserved the original corporate body, under the new name the Reserve Bank of Australia, to carry on central banking functions of the Commonwealth Bank, which had evolved over time. In order to carry out the commercial banking and savings banking activities, separate legislation created the Commonwealth Banking Corporation. The Reserve Bank Act 1959 took effect from 14 January 1960.

There were no major changes in the functions of the RBA until the abolition of exchange controls following the float of the Australian dollar in December 1983. The present deregulated system was the outcome of two major inquiries into the Australian financial system: the Cambell Committee 1979 and the Wallis Committee 1996. The banking supervisory function was subsequently transferred to a newly created authority: the Australian Prudential Regulation Authority. The Reserve Bank Act was also amended to create a new Payments System Board, with a mandate to promote the safety and efficiency of the Australian Payments System (RBA, *History of the RBA*).

Currently, two boards manage the RBA: the Reserve Bank Board and the Payments System Board. The role, responsibilities and composition of the Reserve Bank Board are legislated in the Reserve Bank Act 1959, in addition to recent amendments in 2003 (Act No. 42). Accordingly, the Reserve Bank Board is responsible for the Bank's monetary and banking policy, while the Payments System Board is responsible for the Bank's payments system policy.

The Reserve Bank Board comprises nine members: three ex officio members, comprising the Governor, the Deputy Governor and the Secretary to the Department of the Treasury; and six external members, who are appointed by the Treasurer but cannot be RBA staff and/or Commonwealth public servants. The Governor is the Chairman of the Board. The Treasurer appoints both the Governor and the Deputy Governor for seven years. They remain eligible for reappointment and hold office subject to good behaviour. The Treasurer appoints the external members for five years.

The relationship of the Reserve Bank Board and the government is set out in the Reserve Bank Act 1959, which directs that 'the Governor and the Secretary to the Department of the Treasury shall establish a close liaison with each other and shall keep each other fully informed on all matters which jointly concern the Bank and the Department of the Treasury'. Accordingly, the Governor of the RBA and the Secretary to the Department of the Treasury keep each other informed on all matters that jointly concern the Bank and the Department of the Treasury. In practice, this is done regularly in monthly meetings with the Governor, Deputy Governor and the Treasurer. Institutionally, the relationship of the RBA with the government is in the form of what the RBA calls 'one of independence with consultation'. This is outlined in documents such as 'Consultation with Government' and 'Accountability to Parliament' (Reserve Bank of Australia, 2009b).

In recent years the most important task of the RBA is the conduct of monetary policy. The RBA can be considered a trendsetter, together with the Reserve Bank of New Zealand (RBNZ), for the design and conduct of monetary policy in the Asia-Pacific region. According to the Reserve Bank Act 1959, Section 10(2), the Board's obligations with respect to monetary policy are stated as follows:

> It is the duty of the Reserve Bank Board, within the limits of its powers, to ensure that the monetary and banking policy of the Bank is directed to the greatest advantage of the people of Australia and that the powers of the Bank . . . are exercised in such a manner as, in the opinion of the Reserve Bank Board, will best contribute to:
>
> (a) the stability of the currency of Australia;
> (b) the maintenance of full employment in Australia; and
> (c) the economic prosperity and welfare of the people of Australia.

The objectives of monetary policy in Australia remain broad and there is scope for different interpretations of these objectives. However since 1993, the monetary policy objectives have been expressed in the form of Consumer Price Index (CPI)-inflation target of 2–3 per cent per annum over the business cycle. The aim of monetary policy is to achieve the inflation target over the medium term and, subject to that, to encourage a strong and sustainable growth in the economy. The logic is that controlling inflation preserves the value of money. This is the principal way monetary policy promotes long-term growth in the economy.

Within the present inflation-targeting framework, the Reserve Bank Board makes decisions on the conduct of monetary policy, such as setting the short-term interest rates (the cash rate) independently of the political process. The RBA Board normally meets 11 times a year (on the first Tuesday of each month, except January) and makes decisions on monetary policy. Five members form a quorum for a meeting of the Board, which is chaired by the Governor, or in his/her absence, the Deputy Governor. The Act provides for decisions to be reached by a majority of the votes of the members present with the Chairman having a casting vote. In practice, the Board achieves a consensus without the need for formal voting.

As part of the RBA's accountability, the Governor appears twice each year before the House of Representatives Standing Committee on Economics to answer questions about the Bank's conduct of monetary and banking policy. The Statement on the Conduct of Monetary Policy in December 2007 (issued by the Treasurer and the RBA Governor) has incorporated amendments relating to independence of the RBA and covering practices regarding transparency and communication (RBA, *Governance and Accountability of the RBA*).

The RBA remains responsible for its own budget, which has given the Bank financial independence from the government. In the conduct of monetary policy, the RBA in recent years has shown considerable de facto independence. This is important in a historical context because even in the early 1990s, the RBA was alleged to be under control of the then Treasurer). However, in the final analysis, monetary policy remains the joint responsibility of the RBA and the elected government. The RBA Act stipulates that in the unlikely event of a dispute over whether monetary policy of the Bank is 'directed to the greatest advantage of the people of Australia', the government can override the Reserve Bank's decision and direct the Bank to adopt its policy. The government must, however, table such policy and its rationale before the Houses of Parliament and remain responsible for it. In practice, such a conflict has never arisen.

The Bangladesh Bank[5]

The Bangladesh Bank is the central bank of Bangladesh. The Bank was established under the Bangladesh Bank Order 1972 (President's Order No. 127). The Bank Order 1972 was amended in 2003. As per the amended Order, the functions of the Bangladesh Bank are as follows:

1. to formulate and implement monetary policy;
2. to formulate and implement intervention policies in foreign exchange markets;
3. to give advice to the government on the interaction of monetary policy with fiscal and exchange rate policy, on the impact of various policy measures on the economy and to propose legislative measures it considers necessary or appropriate to attain its objectives and perform its functions;
4. to hold and manage the official reserves of Bangladesh;
5. to promote, regulate and ensure a secure and efficient payment system, including the issue of banknotes; and
6. to regulate and supervise banking companies and financial institutions.

The general superintendence and direction of the affairs of the Bank are entrusted to a Board of Directors. The Board consists of nine members:

1. the Governor;
2. a Deputy Governor, nominated by the government;

3. four directors (who are not government officials), nominated by the government, from amongst persons who, in the opinion of the government, have had experience and shown capacity in the field of banking, trade, commerce, industry or agriculture; and
4. three government officials, nominated by the government.

The Governor is appointed for four years and is eligible for reappointment until he/she attains the age of 65 years. The directors are nominated for three years. They remain eligible for re-nomination and hold office at the discretion of the government.

Monetary policy objectives in Bangladesh remain broad. Since late 2005, the Bank has formalised the framework for the conduct of monetary policy through monetary targeting with the aim of '[m]aintaining price stability while supporting the highest sustainable output growth' (Bangladesh Bank, 2006b: 1). As part of ongoing financial reforms, central banking functions have undergone changes. The Bank has gained some autonomy in performing its functions, which include the regulation and prudential supervision of the financial system.

The relationship of the Bangladesh Bank with the government is not transparent and the Ministry of Finance continues to exercise its influence on both monetary and banking affairs. The objectives of monetary policy, in contrast to the Australian example, remain vague and the Bank is yet to establish credibility by demonstrating its autonomy in the conduct of monetary policy. The Bank's communication with the public is minimal and is not considered effective. The Bank does not have control over its budget; it requires permission from the Ministry of Finance for most senior appointments and for policy measures that the Bank undertakes.

The Bank of Canada

The Bank of Canada (BOCa) is the central bank of Canada. It was established in 1935 as per the Bank of Canada Act passed in July 1934. Its preamble (Bank of Canada Act, 1934, c.B-2, Preamble), which has remained unchanged since the Bank was established, calls on the Bank to (Freedman, 1992: 161; Thiessen, 2000: 62):

> regulate credit and currency in the best interest of the economic life of the nation, to control and protect the external value of the national monetary unit and to mitigate by its influence fluctuations in the general level of production, trade, prices and employment, so far as may be possible within the scope of monetary action, and generally to promote the economic and financial welfare of Canada.

To ensure that the BOCa should not be subject to undue influence from either the government or the financial sector, the architects of the Bank made it a privately owned corporation with widely distributed shares. The government had traditionally minimal representation in the Bank, other than the Deputy Minister of Finance, who was expected to serve as a non-voting member of the Board of Directors. Subsequent legislations reversed the separation of the Bank from the government by eliminating private equity holdings and making the government exclusive owner of BOCa's shares (Thiessen, 2000).

The BOCa is governed by a Board of Directors, appointed by the government for a three-year renewable term. The Directors appoint the Governor (with approval of the government) for a term of seven years. Although the Board has the legal power to take initiatives on matters of monetary policy, as a practical matter, the senior management of the Bank formulates and implements monetary policy. The policy-making body of the Bank is called the Governing Council, which consists of the Governor and four Deputy Governors. The Governing Council makes decisions on monetary policy.

The BOCa Act was amended in 1967. According to the amended Act, the Governor and the Minister of Finance need to 'consult regularly on monetary policy and on its relation to general economic policy'. Although the Bank controls monetary policy, the government bears the ultimate responsibility of monetary policy. In the event of any disagreement between the BOCa and the government, the Minister of Finance has the authority to issue a directive that the BOCa must follow. Thiessen (2000: 71) makes the following remark: 'It was generally agreed, I believe, that such a "nuclear weapon" would only be used when there was a fundamental disagreement between the Governor and the Minister, and that following its use, the Governor would resign.' In reality, since the directive must be in writing and specific and applicable for a specified period and published forthwith, such directives are not likely to be issued. The directive power of the Minister of Finance, however, indicates that there is a dual responsibility for monetary policy. The government takes the ultimate responsibility for monetary policy and the BOCa accepts the immediate responsibility of its day-to-day operations without political pressure as long as no directives are in effect.

Canada was the first country to adopt a flexible exchange rate system, from 1950 until 1962. It returned to the Bretton Woods system on 2 May 1962, pegging the Canadian dollar to the US dollar. However, because of large inflows of foreign capital that put upward pressure on the Canadian dollar, it was floated in 1971. This allowed the BOCa to pursue independent monetary policy. By the early 1970s, inflation had become a major problem for Canada, causing the authorities to adopt monetary targeting in 1975. This strategy was successful initially but inflation began to rise during the late 1970s. Canada abandoned monetary targeting in 1982 and looked for a new nominal anchor for price stability. Although senior officials of the BOCa had previously extolled the virtues of price stability, they had not developed the concept or made commitment to achieving price stability through monetary policy. In 1988 John Crow, the then new Governor, was the first to articulate the idea of price stability as the main objective of Canadian monetary policy (Crow, 1988; Thiessen, 2000).

In February 1991, the BOCa, in a joint statement with the Minister of Finance, announced the introduction of inflation targeting. The lower and upper bounds of the annual inflation-target were set between 2 and 4 per cent, with a mid-point of 3 per cent. These bounds were gradually lowered to 1 and 3 per cent by the end of 1995. Since the introduction of inflation targeting, the transparency of monetary policy in all respects has considerably improved. Thiessen (2000) considers the present state of monetary policy in Canada a successful evolution.

The People's Bank of China[6]

The People's Bank of China (PBC) is the central bank of the People's Republic of China (PRC). It was established on 1 December 1948, based on the consolidation of the Huabei Bank, the Beihai Bank and the Xibei Farmer Bank. In September 1983, the State Council of the PRC decided to have the PBC as the central bank. The Law of the PRC on the PBC was passed by the People's Congress on 18 March 1995. Since then the PBC has gained the legal status of a central bank.

The top management of the PBC is composed of the Governor and a number of Deputy Governors. The President appoints the Governor of the PBC and the Premier of the State Council appoints the Deputy Governors.

The Law of the PRC on the PBC provides the following functions:

1. issuing and enforcing the relevant orders and regulations;
2. formulating policy on renminbi (Chinese currency) and administering its circulation;
3. regulating inter-bank lending and foreign exchange and gold reserves; and managing the State treasury;
4. guiding and organising the anti-money laundering work of the financial sector;
5. generating financial statistics and conducting surveys, analysis and forecasts; and,
6. participating in international activities of the central bank and performing other functions specified by the State Council.

Under the guidance of the State Council, the PBC formulates and implements monetary policy and safeguards financial stability. The PBC reports to the State Council its decisions concerning the (annual) monetary and other important matters for approval. The objectives of monetary policy are maintaining stability of the currency value and the promotion of economic growth. The main instruments of monetary policy are reserve requirements, rediscounting, central bank lending and open market operations.

The Reserve Bank of Fiji

The central bank of Fiji is called the Reserve Bank of Fiji (RBF). Although Fiji gained independence in 1970, the RBF was not established until 1 January 1984. Its predecessor was called the Central Monetary Authority (CMA), established in early 1973. A currency board preceded the CMA. The CMA (like the currency board) had the responsibility for printing, minting and issuing currency. It was also given the responsibility for promoting a healthy financial system and a strong economy, acting as a banker for commercial banks and a banker and financial agent for the government and other government agencies.

A Board of Directors, appointed by the Minister of Finance, guides the RBF's affairs. The Governor is the chairman of the Board of Directors and the RBF's chief executive.

The functions, powers, and responsibilities of the RBF are specified in the RBF Act 1983:

> The principal purposes of the Bank as stated in Part II, Section 4 of the Reserve Bank Act are as follows:
>
> (a) to regulate the issue of currency, and the supply, availability and international exchange of money;
> (b) to promote monetary stability;
> (c) to promote a sound financial structure; and

(d) to foster credit and exchange conditions conducive to the orderly and balanced economic development of the country.

The Monetary Authority of Hong Kong

Hong Kong is the Special Administrative Region (SAR) of China. It does not have an officially designated central bank. The Hong Kong Monetary Authority (HKMA) performs central banking functions. The HKMA was established on 1 April 1993 by merging the office of the Exchange Fund with the Office of the Commission of Banking. The Exchange Fund Ordinance and the Banking Ordinance govern the functions and responsibilities of the HKMA, which reports to the Financial Secretary of the Government.

The Exchange Fund Ordinance has established the Exchange Fund under the control of the Financial Secretary. The Exchange Fund is used primarily for influencing the exchange value of the Hong Kong dollar (HK$). It is also used to maintain the stability and integrity of the monetary and financial system of Hong Kong, with a view to maintaining Hong Kong as an international financial centre. In controlling the Exchange Fund, the Exchange Fund Advisory Committee (EFAC) advises the Financial Secretary. The Financial Secretary is the ex officio Chairman of the EFAC and appoints other members in a personal capacity under the delegated authority of the Chief Executive of the Hong Kong SAR.

The Financial Secretary appoints the Monetary Authority under the Exchange Fund Ordinance. The Office of the Monetary Authority is part of the HKMA, with the role of Monetary Authority also acting as Chief Executive of the HKMA. The Chief Executive's Committee is chaired by the Chief Executive of the HKMA, comprising the Deputy Chief Executives and the Executive Directors of the HKMA. The Committee meets weekly to report to the Chief Executive on the progress of major tasks being undertaken by various departments of the HKMA and to advise him/her on policy matters relating to operations of the HKMA.

The HKMA is responsible for maintaining monetary and banking stability in Hong Kong. Its main functions are:

1. keeping the Hong Kong dollar stable;
2. managing the Exchange Fund (Hong Kong's official foreign reserves) in a sound and effective way;
3. promoting the safety of Hong Kong's banking system; and
4. developing Hong Kong's financial structure to enable money to flow smoothly, freely and without obstruction.

The monetary policy objective in Hong Kong is to maintain exchange rate stability within the framework of the Linked Exchange Rate System, which is a currency board established in 1983. The underpinnings of the Linked Exchange Rate System include maintaining large official foreign reserves of Hong Kong, ensuring a sound and robust banking system, fiscal prudence, and promoting a flexible economic structure. The currency board system in Hong Kong requires both the stock and the flow of the monetary base to be fully backed by foreign reserves. Any change in the monetary base is therefore matched by a corresponding change in foreign reserves.

The Reserve Bank of India

The Reserve Bank of India (RBI) is India's Central Bank. It was established on 1 April 1935 in accordance with the provisions of the RBI Act 1934. The RBI was originally privately owned but nationalised in 1949. The preamble of the RBI describes its functions as: 'to regulate the issue of Bank Notes and keeping of reserves with a view to securing monetary stability in India and generally to operate the currency and credit system of the country to its advantage'.

A central Board of Directors governs the affairs of the RBI. The government, in keeping with the RBI Act, appoints the Board. The directors are appointed for a period of four years. The Governor and up to four of the Deputy Governors fall into the category of official directors. There are 10 non-official directors, nominated by the government from various fields, and one government official. There are four other directors appointed from local branches.

The RBI performs all traditional central banking functions: issuing of currency notes, acting as banker for both commercial banks and the government, regulating and supervising banks and other financial institutions, managing foreign reserves and conducting monetary policy. The main objectives of monetary policy in India remain the maintenance of price stability and ensuring adequate flow of credit to productive sectors for rapid economic growth.

Bank Indonesia[7]

Bank Indonesia (BI) is the central bank of the Republic of Indonesia. In implementing its tasks, BI is presided over by the Board of Governors. The Board of Governors consists of a Governor, a Senior Deputy Governor, and at least four (or at the maximum seven) Deputy Governors. The Governor presides over the Board of Governors, while the Senior Deputy Governor acts as the Vice Governor. The Governor, Senior Deputy Governor and Deputy Governors are proposed and appointed by the President upon approval of the House of Representatives. The President pursuant to the recommendation of the Governor proposes the Deputy Governor. The members of the Board of Governors are appointed for a five-year term of office, being eligible for reappointment.

Bank Indonesia is required to provide both an annual report and a quarterly report to the House of Representatives and the Government. To ensure accountability, independence, transparency and credibility of Bank Indonesia, the House of Representatives have an established Supervisory Body of five members, who are selected by the House of Representatives and appointed by the President for a term of office of three years, with allowance for a single consecutive term.

Bank Indonesia performs all traditional central banking functions, including issuing of currency notes, acting as cashier for the government and banker of banks, regulating and supervising banks and other financial institutions and safeguarding the payments system, managing foreign reserves and prescribing and implementing monetary policy. The main objectives of monetary policy in Indonesia are to achieve and maintain the stable value of the rupiah against both goods and services and foreign currencies. The formulation of monetary policy is coordinated with appropriate policies for fiscal management and promotion of economic activity.

The Bank of Japan[8]

The Bank of Japan (BOJ) is Japan's central bank. It was founded in 1882 during the Meiji restoration under the BOJ Act which was promulgated in June 1882. The Bank was reorganised on 1 May 1942 in conformity with the BOJ Law (Law of 1942). The Law of 1942 reflected the wartime situation. For example, Article 1 of the Law stated the objectives of the Bank as: 'the regulation of the currency, control and facilitation of credit and finance, and the maintenance and fostering of the credit system, pursuant to national policy, in order that the general economic activities of the nation might adequately be enhanced'.

The Law of 1942 was amended several times after the Second World War. Such amendments included the establishment of the Policy Board as the Bank's highest decision-making body in June 1949. The Policy Board consists of the Governor, two Vice Governors and six outside members, who are appointed by the Cabinet and approved by the Parliament. All of them serve for five-year terms of office. The Policy Board determines monetary policy.

The Law of 1942 was revised completely in June 1997 under two principles: namely, 'independence' and 'transparency'. The revised Law came into effect on 1 April 1998. While the ultimate power of the BOJ resided earlier with the Ministry of Finance, the new Law has given independence to the BOJ. According to this new Law, the objective of monetary policy is to achieve price stability, meaning maintaining an economic environment in which there is neither inflation nor deflation. The Law has granted greater instrument and goal independence to the BOJ. Before this, the government had two voting members on the Policy Board, one from the Ministry of Finance and the other from the Economic Planning Agency. According to the new Law, the Government may send two representatives from these agencies to Policy Board meetings, but they do not have voting rights. These representatives, however, have the ability to request delays in monetary policy decisions. In addition, the Ministry of Finance under the new Law has lost its authority to oversee operations of the BOJ, particularly the right to dismiss any senior officials. The Ministry of Finance still continues to have some control over the Bank's budget that is unrelated to monetary policy. The Ministry of Finance's veto power over the Bank's budget actually may act as a check on the BOJ's de facto independence in monetary policy and other matters.

The BOJ's Policy Board meets twice a month, announces its decisions at a press conference following each meeting, and publishes minutes about a month later. These actions, together with frequent public speeches by nine board members and numerous publications posted on the BOJ website, ensure that financial markets and the public remain well-informed about the stance of monetary policy in Japan. Cecchetti (2008) suggests that the BOJ's system of independence, accountability, transparent communication, and monetary policy framework meet the requirements of a modern, independent central bank.

The Bank of Korea

A central banking system was first introduced in Korea when the former Bank of Korea was established in November 1909. The issue of banknotes and coins, and the management of the National Treasury, which were handled until then by Daiichi Bank, were transferred to the Bank of Korea. The Bank of Korea was reorganised as the Bank of Chosun on 1 August 1911. The Bank of Chosun performed some central banking functions such as issuing banknotes and coins and managing the National Treasury. The Bank of Chosun continued to act as the central bank when Korea gained independence after the Second World War. These functions included issuing banknotes and coins, managing national treasury, holding foreign reserves, and offering rediscounts to commercial banks.

After considerable preparation for the establishment of a formal central bank in the midst of economic and political uncertainties in the late 1940s, the present Bank of Korea Act was promulgated on 5 June 1950 and the Bank of Korea (BOK) began operations on 12 June 1950. It acts as the bank of note issue, the bankers' bank and the government's bank, and remains responsible for formulating and implementing monetary and credit policies. There is also responsibility for managing foreign reserves (Bank of Korea, 2000).

The Monetary Policy Committee (MPC) is the policy-making body of the BOK. It decides on matters concerning the operations of the Bank, as well as monetary and credit policies. The MPC is composed of the following members:

1. the Governor of the BOK;
2. one member recommended by the Minister of Finance and Economy;
3. one member recommended by the Chairman of the Financial Supervisory Commission;
4. one member recommended by the President of the Korea Chamber of Commerce and Industry;
5. one member recommended by the Chairman of the Korea Federation of Banks; and
6. one member recommended by the Chairman of the Korea Securities Dealers Association.

The Governor is an ex officio member of the MPC and is appointed by the President, following deliberation of the State Council (the supreme policy deliberation body of the government). On the recommendation of each pertinent organisation, the President appoints other members. The appointed members have terms of four years and may be reappointed for a single consecutive term. The Governor serves as Chairman of the MPC.

The term of the Governor is four years; this may be extended for a single consecutive term. The Governor is given guarantee that he/she would not be discharged from office against his/her will, except as provided for in the relevant laws. The Governor appoints the Deputy Governor and Assistant Governors as his/her assistants. The BOK has an auditor, independent of its executive organs, who is appointed by the President on the recommendation of the Minister of Finance and Economy.

The BOK Act was revised by the Supreme Committee for National Reconstruction and enacted in May 1962. The revised Act changed the role of the MPC from devising policies on monetary, credit and foreign exchange to a new role of development of policies on monetary and credit operation and management. Responsibilities for foreign exchange policy development and foreign exchange management were transferred from the BOK to the government. Decisions arrived at by the MPC were made subject to reconsideration request from the Minister of Finance, and if a request was rejected, the final decision determined by the Cabinet. This gives the government the final say on monetary and financial policies.

The BOK's monetary policy has been exercised through both indirect policy tools and the direct control of bank credits. Until the early 1980s the Bank set maximum interest rates on some deposits and loans of banking institutions. Since 1982, the monetary authorities replaced direct credit controls (which imposed ceilings on credit expansion of individual banks) with indirect instruments such as the BOK rediscounts, open market operations and a reserve requirements policy. Because the effectiveness of these instruments was limited, the authorities frequently relied on direct credit controls in periods of accelerating inflation or pronounced monetary expansion.

Pursuant to the revision of the BOK Act in April 1998 following the currency crisis, the BOK has adopted inflation targeting as the framework of monetary policy. The BOK sets the target rate of inflation in consultation with the government (Bank of Korea, 2000; Nam, 1995).

Bank Negara Malaysia

Bank Negara Malaysia (BNM) is the central bank of Malaysia. It was established on 26 January 1959 under the Central Bank of Malaysia Ordinance 1958 with the following objectives:

1. to issue currency and keep reserves, safeguarding the value of the currency;
2. to act as a banker and financial adviser to the government;
3. to promote monetary stability and a sound financial structure; and
4. to influence the credit situation to the advantage of the country.

The policy of the BNM is entrusted with a Board of Directors, which comprises the Governor, the Deputy Governors and the Secretary General to the Treasury (ex officios) and other directors, who are persons of standing and experience in banking and economic affairs. All members of the Board of Directors (except the Deputy Governors) are appointed by His Majesty the Yang Di Pertuan Agong, holding office for a maximum of three years. They remain eligible for reappointment. The Minister of Finance appoints the Deputy Governors. The Governor is the Chief Executive of the Bank and is assisted by three Deputy Governors and six Assistant Governors.

The BNM plays a key role in managing the country's economy. It is charged with achieving monetary stability and promoting a stable financial system. As part of its work, the BNM issues currency notes, sets interest and exchange rates, regulates financial institutions (including supervision of Malaysia's Islamic banking system), manages the country's payment and settlement systems, overseas programmes for combating money laundering and terrorism financing, and establishes and implements monetary policies and programmes, including any initiatives for developing small and medium enterprises throughout Malaysia.

Nepal Rastra Bank[9]

Nepal Rastra Bank (NRB) is Nepal's central bank. It was established in 1956 and is entrusted with the central banking responsibilities, including the development of the domestic financial sector. The functions and objectives of the NRB have been recast by the new NRB Act of 2002. The preamble of the new Act lays down the primary functions of the NRB as:

1. to formulate necessary monetary and foreign exchange policies to maintain the stability in price and consolidate the balance of payments for sustainable growth of the economy of Nepal;
2. to develop a secure, healthy and efficient system of payments;
3. to make appropriate supervision of the banking and financial system to maintain its stability and foster its healthy development; and
4. to further enhance public confidence in Nepal's entire banking and financial system.

As per section 14 of the NRB Act 2002, the Board of NRB comprises seven members: four ex officio members – the Governor (who is the Chairman), the Secretary to the Ministry of Finance and two Deputy Governors, and three other Directors who are appointed from among persons renowned in the fields of economics, monetary, banking, finance and commercial laws. The Governor, Deputy Governors and other directors are appointed by the government of Nepal for term of five years. The government may reappoint the retiring Governor for another one term and, if deemed necessary, the retiring other directors for any term.

The Reserve Bank of New Zealand

The Reserve Bank of New Zealand (RBNZ) acts as New Zealand's central bank. It was established in 1934 and is government owned. The RBNZ is similar to other central banks in terms of its functions and responsibilities. Its three main functions are:

1. operating monetary policy to maintain price stability;
2. promoting the maintenance of a sound and efficient financial system; and
3. meeting the currency needs of the public.

The RBNZ also performs other central banking functions. For example, it:

1. acts as banker to the banks, providing inter-bank settlement facilities and related payment services;
2. manages foreign exchange reserves and, if required, enabling interventions into foreign exchange markets;
3. provides cash and debt management services to the government;
4. advises the government on the operation of the financial system; and
5. provides secretariat services to New Zealand's Overseas Investment Commission.

During the 1970s and 1980s New Zealand experienced high inflation and economic crises. By mid-1984 New Zealand introduced economic deregulation and reforms. The New Zealand dollar (NZ$) was floated in March 1985. A consensus had emerged among policy-makers that New Zealand required price stability in an environment of deregulation for sustained economic growth. This was formalised with the passing of the RBNZ Act 1989. This Act established the monetary policy framework in New Zealand for price stability, with considerable autonomy of the central bank for the conduct of monetary policy.

Prior to the 1989 legislation, the RBNZ acted as an adviser to the government and was subject to ministerial directions for monetary policy and other responsibilities. The RBNZ's decision-making was practically at the discretion of the Minister of Finance. In the case of monetary policy, the ministerial directions to the RBNZ were confidential and priorities shifted frequently. The complication was that monetary policy aimed at a number of sometimes conflicting objectives.

The 1989 Act has made the price stability goal of monetary policy explicit and non-negotiable. Ultimately, monetary policy is directed at 'achieving stability in the general level of prices'. The Act also requires that the operational details of the Bank's inflation target be made public in a separate agreement between the Governor and the Minister of Finance. This is known as the *Policy Targets Agreement*.

The Governor, as the chief executive officer, exercises powers of the RBNZ. The 1989 Act stipulates that it is the duty of the Governor to ensure that the Bank carries out its central banking functions. The Minister of Finance, on the recommendation of the Board of Directors, appoints the Governor for a five-year term. The Board has no executive authority over the Bank, with the Governor remaining solely responsible for the conduct of monetary policy.

The Bank of Papua New Guinea[10]

The central bank of Papua New Guinea (PNG) is called the Bank of PNG (BPNG). It was established by the Central Banking Act of 1973. The Central Bank Act of 2000 amended and consolidated all laws that established the BPNG as the central bank.

The objectives of the BPNG are:

1. to formulate and implement monetary policy with a view to achieving and maintaining price stability;
2. to formulate financial regulation and prudential standards to ensure stability of the financial system in PNG;
3. to promote an efficient national and international payments system; and
4. subject to the above, to promote macroeconomic stability and economic growth in PNG.

The BPNG performs the following central banking functions:

1. issuer of currency;
2. acts as banker and financial agent to the government;
3. regulates banking, credit and other financial services; and
4. manages gold and foreign exchange reserves.

Of these functions, the status of BPNG as official banker to the government has been well defined. When the government's financial resources are insufficient to meet public outlays, the government can draw on temporary advances from the BPNG, which are then converted into treasury bills at six monthly intervals. There are, however, limits on such borrowing, defined in the Central Banking Act on both flows and stocks of the BPNG's net claims on the government.

A Board of Directors acts as the chief policy-making body of the Bank. The Board consists of between 9 and 11 members. The membership of the Board includes the Governor, two Deputy Governors, and up to three persons appointed by the Head of State. The functions of the Bank of PNG Board are set out in section 26 of the Act: 'The Board of the Bank of PNG is responsible for determining the policies of the Bank, other than the formulation and implementation of monetary policy and the regulation of the financial system, which shall be the responsibility of the Governor.' It is the duty of the BPNG Board, within the limits of its powers, to ensure that the monetary and banking policy of the Bank is directed to benefit the people of PNG. Furthermore, the powers of the Bank under this Act and any related Acts, are to be exercised in such a manner as, in the opinion of the Board, best contributes to price stability, financial stability, development of efficient national and international payments systems, and macroeconomic stability.

The Governor is responsible for the formulation and implementation of monetary policy. The Money Market Operation Committee and the Monetary Policy Committee provide necessary information. The Monetary Policy Committee comprises the Governor, two Deputy Governors, the Managers of the Economics and Financial Markets Departments and the Manager of the Monetary Policy Unit. The monetary policy stance is issued on a six-monthly basis in the Governor's monetary policy statement. The BPNG Board and Treasury Minister are informed of the monetary policy stance.

The monetary policy framework in PNG is not well-developed. The BPNG does not have set specific targets for monetary aggregates, interest rates, exchange rates or output. It uses monetary policy to bring changes in these variables on an uncoordinated and ad hoc basis.

The State Bank of Pakistan

The central bank of Pakistan is called the State Bank of Pakistan (SBP). It was established in 1948 following the country's independence in August 1947. The SBP's functions are classified under two headings: the primary functions, which include the issuing of notes, the regulation of the financial system, the lender of last resort function, and the conduct of monetary policy; the secondary functions include the management of public debt, the management of foreign exchange reserves, advising the government on matters of economic policy, maintaining the payments system, and building and maintaining close relationships with international financial institutions.

The superintendence and direction of the affairs and business of the SBP have been entrusted with the Central Board of Directors, which consists of the Governor (chairman), Secretary to the Finance Division and seven directors (including one director from each province) who are nominated by the Federal Government to ensure representatives from the agricultural, banking and industrial sectors.

The top management of the SBP consists of a Governor, one or more Deputy Governors, executive directors, economic adviser and directors of various departments. The Governor is the chief executive officer, who directs and controls the affairs of the Bank on behalf of the Central Board. The President appoints the Governor for a term of three years. The Governor remains eligible for reappointment for another term of three years. The Federal Government appoints the Deputy Governors for a period not exceeding five years.

The legal documents governing the financial system of Pakistan include the State Bank of Pakistan Act 1956, the Banking Companies Ordinance 1962, and the Banks Nationalisation Act 1974. These Acts have changed several times to provide authority to the SBP for regulating the banking sector, conducting monetary policy and setting limits on the government's borrowing from the SBP. The SBP Act 1956 was amended in February 1994 to make monetary policy the sole responsibility of the SBP. The Board has also been entrusted with greater responsibility to regulate and supervise the monetary and credit system, in line with the national policy objectives of the government.

The Bangko Sentral ng Pilipinas

The central bank of the Philippines is called the Bangko Sentral ng Pilipinas (BSP). Previously known as the Central Bank of Philippines (CBP), it was established on 3 January 1949. The policy objectives of the CBP were contained in Republic Act (RA) No. 265. This Act guided the CBP in implementation of responsibilities such as promotion of economic development and the maintenance of internal and external monetary stability.

The RA No. 265 was amended by the Presidential Decree (PD) No. 72 to make the CBP more responsive to changing internal economic conditions. The PD No. 72 emphasised the maintenance of domestic and international monetary stability as the primary objective of the CBP. The (renamed) BSP remains committed to promoting and maintaining price stability and developing a sound financial system for sustainable growth of the economy. The BSP also aims to promote and preserve monetary stability and convertibility of the Philippine currency, Peso.

A Monetary Board exercises the powers and functions of the BSP. The Governor is the chairman of the Monetary Board, with five full-time members from the private sector and one member from the Cabinet. The Governor is the chief executive of the BSP and remains responsible for the direction and supervision of Bank's operations and administration. A Deputy Governor heads each of the three operating sectors of the BSP. These sectors are:

1. the *monetary stability sector* takes charge of the formulation and implementation of the BSP's monetary policy, including serving banking needs of all banks through accepting deposits, servicing withdrawals and extending credits through rediscounting facilities;
2. the *supervision and examination sector* enforces and monitors compliance to the banking laws to promote a sound and healthy banking system; and
3. the *resource management sector* serves human, financial and physical resource needs of the BSP.

The primary objective of monetary policy in the Philippines is 'to promote price stability conducive to a balanced and sustainable growth of the economy' (RA 7653). In January 2002 the BSP adopted inflation targeting as the strategy of monetary policy.

The Monetary Authority of Singapore

The Monetary Authority of Singapore (MAS) is the de facto central bank of Singapore. The MAS was established under the MAS Act of 1970. It started operations on 1 January 1971. Before this, several government departments and agencies performed monetary functions of the central bank. In April 1977, the government brought the regulation of the insurance industry under the wing of MAS. The regulatory functions under the Securities Industry Act 1973 were also transferred to the MAS in September 1984. Following its merger with the Board of Commissioners of Currency on 1 October 2002, the MAS is responsible for the issuance of currency notes.

The MAS is governed by a Board of Directors, which consists of the chairman, deputy chairman, managing director and five other members. The managing director is the chief executive, who is entrusted with the MAS's operations and administration. A deputy managing director and a team of assistant managing directors, executive directors and directors assist the managing director.

The main functions of the MAS are to issue currency notes, conduct monetary and exchange rate policies, manage official foreign exchange reserves and issue government securities. In addition, the MAS regulates and supervises the financial sector and plays a key role in the development and promotion of Singapore as an international financial centre.

The main objective of monetary policy in Singapore is price stability. Given that the Singapore economy is highly open and there is free capital mobility, it has adopted an exchange rate based monetary policy framework. This is where the exchange rate acts as anchor of the price level. Singapore maintains a conservative stance on fiscal policy. The commitment of the government to maintain a strong dollar and the holding of large foreign exchange reserves have ensured the MAS's credibility in maintaining price stability (Monetary Authority of Singapore, 1999; 2001).

The Central Bank of Sri Lanka

The central bank of Sri Lanka (CBSL) was established in 1950 under the Monetary Law Act No. 58 of 1949 (MLA). The main functions of the CBSL are to:

1. conduct monetary policy;
2. conduct exchange rate policy;
3. manage foreign exchange reserves of Sri Lanka;
4. issue and distribute currency notes;
5. license, regulate and supervise commercial banks, finance companies and primary dealers in government securities;
6. provide clearing and settlement facilities to the financial institutions (commercial banks and primary dealers); and
7. act as the economic adviser, banker and fiscal agent of the government.

The monetary policy objectives of the CBSL have been streamlined by amending the Monetary Law Act in 2002. The CBSL has two objectives of monetary policy:

1. maintaining economic and price stability; and
2. maintaining financial system stability.

Prior to the amendment of the 2002 Law, the CBSL had multiple objectives of monetary policy, such as maintaining stability of the currency value, maintaining stability of the exchange rate, promoting production and employment, and developing productive resources. These objectives were often in conflict.

Under the amended Law, the CBSL has been given autonomy to achieve its policy objectives. In doing so, the CBSL maintains liaison with the Ministry of Finance. The secretary to the Ministry of Finance is a member of the Monetary Board, which is the governing body of the CBSL. The Monetary Board consists of five members:

1. the Governor;
2. the Secretary to the Ministry of Finance (ex officio); and
3. three non-executive members.

The Governor is the chairman of the Monetary Board and acts as the chief executive of the Bank. The President, on the recommendation of the Minister of Finance, appoints the Governor and the non-executive board members. The approval of the Constitutional Council is required for the appointment of non-executive board members.

The term of office of the Governor and the non-executive board members is six years. The quorum for Monetary Board meetings is three members. The concurrence of three members is required for any decision of the Monetary Board to remain valid. However, in cases where a unanimous decision is required, the concurrence of the five members is necessary.

The CBSL has a unique legal structure, as it is not an incorporated body. In terms of the Monetary Law Act, the corporate status is conferred on the Monetary Board, which is vested with all powers, functions and duties. As the governing body, the Monetary Board is responsible for making policy decisions and for the management, operation and administration of the Bank. When there is a difference of opinion on monetary policy between the Minister of Finance and the Monetary Board, the Minister of Finance may inform the Monetary Board that the government accepts responsibility for the Monetary Board, thereby directing the Monetary Board to adopt the government's policy.

The Bank of China

The Bank of China (BOCh) is the central bank of Taiwan, China. It was established in 1923 and relocated from mainland China to Taipei in December 1949. The BOCh is the sole monetary policy-making and policy-executing entity in Taiwan. The decision-making body is composed of three parties: the Board of Directors, the Board of Supervisors, and the Governor and Deputy Governors.

The Board of Directors is the highest decision making body of the Bank. It consists of 15 directors, nominated by the Executive *Yuan* (cabinet) and appointed by the President. Five to seven directors of the Board are designated as Executive Directors. According to the BOCh Act, the Governor, the Minister of Finance and the Minister of Economic Affairs are ex officio directors. The directors (except for ex officio directors) are appointed for five years, remaining eligible for reappointment upon the expiration of their terms.

The Governor is the chairman of the Board of Directors. He/she is responsible for executing the decisions of the Board, as well as operations of the Bank. The Governor is appointed for a term of five years and remains eligible for reappointment. The Deputy Governors assist the Governor in handling affairs of the Bank. They are also appointed for a term of five years, again remaining eligible for reappointment.

The BOCh's main functions include conducting monetary and foreign exchange policy, issuing currency, and serving as the bank of banks and the government's bank. The four operational objectives of the BOCh are: (1) promoting financial stability, (2) guiding sound banking operations, (3) maintaining stable internal and external value of the currency, and (4) within the scope of the above three objectives, fostering economic development.

The Bank of Thailand

The Thai National Banking Bureau, set up in 1939 with the status of a department to the Ministry of Finance, was the first organisation to assume the central banking activities in Thailand. The Bureau started operations on 24 June 1940. Its initial operations were, however, limited to such central banking functions as managing the issue of government bonds, taking deposits from and lending to the government, government agencies and commercial banks, and transferring funds between the central region and other parts of the country.

In 1941 the Bureau started executing exchange controls. Once the Second World War spread to Asia, the government decided to change the status of the Bureau to that of a central bank. The Bank of Thailand (BOT) Act was promulgated in 1942, decreeing the BOT a juristic person responsible for central banking activities. The BOT started operations on 10 December 1942.

According to the BOT Act 1942, the Minister of Finance is empowered to oversee overall affairs of the BOT – the general control and direction is entrusted with a court of Directors, comprising the Governor and Deputy Governors – appointed by His Majesty the King as Chairman and Vice Chairman respectively – and at least five other members appointed by the Cabinet.

The BOT's roles and responsibilities are to:

1. promote monetary stability and formulate monetary policy;
2. promote and supervise financial institutions;
3. provide banking facilities and recommend economic policies to the government;
4. provide banking facilities to financial institutions;
5. manage foreign exchange reserves; and
6. print and issue banknotes.

The main objective of monetary policy in Thailand is the achievement of monetary and financial stability, including exchange rate stability. Economic growth does not seem to be an explicit objective of monetary policy, although monetary and financial stability is considered necessary for sustained economic growth. Thailand maintained exchange rate pegging as a strategy of monetary policy from 1947 until 1997. After it floated baht in July 1997 following a speculative attack, the BOT adopted inflation targeting as a strategy of monetary policy with the objective of price stability.

The Bank of England

The Bank of England (BOE) is the central bank of the UK. It was founded in 1694, making it one of the oldest central banks and a model for other central banks in different parts of the world. The Bank Act of 1946 gave the government statutory authority over the BOE. The Court (equivalent to the Board of Directors) of the BOE is made up of the Governor and two Deputy Governors, who are appointed for five-year terms, and 16 non-executive directors, who are appointed for three-year terms.

Inflation was a major problem in Britain during the 1970s. It introduced monetary targeting in 1973 but it was not pursued aggressively. In 1983 the BOE changed its strategy of monetary policy from monetary targeting to monetary base targeting. By 1992 it adopted inflation targeting. Success of this strategy is evident by inflation falling from 10 per cent in the early 1980s to 4 per cent a decade later. Since adoption of inflation targeting, the UK economy has grown steadily with inflation remaining at a relatively low level of about 2.5 per cent per year.

With inflation targeting there have been institutional changes in the BOE. Until 1997, the BOE was one of the least independent central banks because any decision to raise or lower interest rates resided solely with the Chancellor of the Exchequer, separate from the BOE. In 1997 the BOE was given power to set the cash rate. The Bank was not, however, given total instrument independence. The government can overrule the Bank and set rates 'in extreme economic circumstances' and 'for a limited period'.

The decision to set the interest rates resides with the Monetary Policy Committee, which consists of the Governor, four other central bank officials (two Deputy Governors and two other central bank officials chosen by the Governor), plus four outside economic experts appointed by the Chancellor of the Exchequer. Since the Chancellor sets the inflation target, the BOE does not have full independence. This indicates that the government and the BOE jointly remain responsible for the design and conduct of monetary policy.

The Federal Reserve System of the USA

The Federal Reserve System (the Fed) of the USA comprises 12 Federal Reserve Banks. These banks are located across the country. Therefore the Fed has an unusual decentralised structure, which was intended by its founders under the Federal Reserve Act to diffuse power along regional lines, between the private sector and the government, and among bankers, business people and the public.

The Federal Reserve Banks

Each of the 12 Federal Reserve districts has one main Federal Reserve Bank, which may have branches in other cities within the district. Each of the Federal Reserve Banks is a quasi-public (part private, part government) institution owned by the private commercial banks in the district which are members of the Federal Reserve System. The member banks elect six directors for each district bank: three more are appointed by the Board of Governors of the Federal Reserve System. Together, these nine directors appoint the President of the Bank, subject to approval of the Board of Governors.

The functions of the 12 Federal Reserve Banks include the following:

1. clearing cheques;
2. issuing new currency notes;
3. withdrawing damaged currency notes from circulation;
4. evaluating proposed mergers and applications for banks to expand their activities;
5. administering and making discount loans to banks in their districts;
6. acting as liaisons between the business community and the Federal Reserve System;
7. examining the bank holding companies and state-chartered member banks;
8. collecting data on local business conditions, and
9. undertaking research on issues in monetary policy.

Structure of the Federal Reserve System

At the head of the Federal Reserve System, headquartered in Washington, DC, is the seven-member Board of Governors. Each governor is appointed by the President of the USA and confirmed by the Senate. To limit the President's control over the Fed and insulate the Fed from political pressure, the governors serve one non-renewable 14-year term, with one governor's term expiring every other January. The governors (many of them economists) are required to come from different Federal Reserve districts to prevent the over-representation interests of one region of the country. The chairman of the Board of Governors is chosen from among seven governors and serves a four-year term. Once a new chairman is chosen, the old chairman resigns from the Board of Governors, even if there are many years remaining for his or her term as a governor.

The Board of Governors is involved in decisions concerning the conduct of monetary policy. All seven governors are members of the Federal Open Market Committee (FOMC) and vote on the conduct of open market operations.

The FOMC itself meets eight times a year and makes decisions regarding the conduct of open market operations, which influence the monetary base. The FOMC is referred to as the 'Fed' in the press. The Committee comprises seven members of the Board of Governors, the President of the Federal Reserve Bank of New York and Presidents of four other Federal Reserve Banks. The chairman of the Board of Governors presides as the chairman of the FOMC. Even though only the presidents of five of the Federal Reserve Banks are voting members of the FOMC, the other seven Presidents of the district banks attend the FOMC meetings and participate in discussion.

The objectives of monetary policy in the USA are price stability and maximum employment. For example, the mandate of the Federal Reserve System has been defined in the Humphrey-Hawkins Act, passed by the Congress in 1978. According to this Act, the Fed is required to: 'maintain long-run growth of the monetary and credit aggregates commensurate with the economy's long-run potential to increase production, so as to promote effectively the goals of maximum employment, stable prices, and moderate long-term interest rates'. According to Blanchard (2006: 546), in simple terms, the above quote suggests that the mandate of the Fed is to achieve not only low inflation in the medium and long run but also to stabilise economic activity in the short run.

The USA adopted monetary targeting in the 1970s but it was not pursued aggressively. Since 1982, the Fed decreased emphasis on monetary targets and by 1993 it no longer used monetary aggregates as a guide for conducting monetary policy. Since then the Fed has conducted discretionary monetary policy without an explicit nominal anchor such as a monetary aggregate or inflation target. However, as Mishkin (2007a) suggests, the Fed has a coherent strategy of monetary policy. This strategy, which he calls 'just do it' policy, involves an implicit anchor in the form of an overriding concern by the Fed to control inflation in the long run. In addition, the Fed involves forward-looking behaviour in which there is careful monitoring for signs of future inflation using a wide range of information, coupled with periodic 'pre-emptive strikes' by monetary policy against the threat of inflation. Although the conduct of monetary policy over the past decade or so has been successful in keeping inflation low while maintaining rapid economic growth, there is concern that such a strategy of monetary policy lacks transparency. The criticism is that success depends on personalities in the Fed rather than any institutional set up that may ensure accountability and policy effectiveness. Under Mr Greenspan's chairmanship, the Fed's success in maintaining low inflation was widely appreciated and there was not much criticism for the discretionary nature of monetary policy the Fed pursued. The latest subprime mortgage turbulence in the US financial system has, however, raised question whether the Fed under Mr Bernanke's chairmanship will be equally successful in maintaining low inflation, steady economic growth and financial stability.

THE RELATIONSHIP OF CENTRAL BANKS WITH THE GOVERNMENTS

The evolution of central banking reveals that there is a close but complex relationship between central banks and governments. Central banks are often the creation of Parliament and therefore, politicians have a stake in the way central banks function. In the early years central banks were treated as just another government agency with a status much lower than that accorded to the Ministry of Finance. In the literature, the relationship between a central bank and the government becomes apparent from the close linkage that exists between fiscal and monetary policy (Masciandaro and Tabellini, 1988). Chapter 4 discusses this linkage in detail.

Currently, central banks are expected to conduct an independent monetary policy and to achieve price stability, irrespective of the stance of fiscal policy. Yet the ability of a central bank to conduct independent monetary policy depends on the institutional arrangements of that central bank with its government. From an analytical viewpoint, the issue is whether fiscal or monetary policy dominates economic management of the national economy. Historically, fiscal policy dominated monetary policy. This was the legacy of Keynesian economics of the 1950s and 1960s when monetary policy was subordinate to fiscal policy. The goal of monetary (or credit) policy was to keep the interest rate low through direct controls and/or monetary expansion. A close linkage existed between fiscal and monetary policy because budget deficits were routinely financed by money creation. In effect, the central bank became an extension of the Ministry of Finance, with politicians having great influence over the way monetary policy should be conducted and how the central bank should function (Bhatt, 1974; Coates and Khatkhate, 1980).

In the present context, the interrelationship between fiscal and monetary policy is crucial for understanding the conduct of monetary policy (Siklos, 2002). There are two aspects of a monetary regime that determine the institutional position of a central bank:

1. The 'political' aspect, which is determined by the legislative and administrative rules concerning the appointment and the composition of the Board of Directors (or governors) and the relationship of the governing bodies with the legislature and the government.
2. The 'economic' aspect, which is determined by the requirement of the central bank to finance budget deficits, the use of monetary policy instruments, and the fiscal consequences of regulatory controls over the financial system.

These two aspects jointly determine the extent of fiscal dominance over monetary policy. Fiscal dominance is likely to be low when a central bank remains insulated from any political pressure that originates from the finance ministry or other government department. This may happen if, first, the self-representatives of the central bank, subject to approval of the legislature, appoint the governor and the board of directors; second, the governor remains responsible to the legislature, rather than to the government, for monetary policy decisions and performance; and third, the governor and the board of directors can be reappointed, subject to approval of the legislature. Conversely, political pressure from the finance ministry or the rest of government is likely to be high when there is over-representation of government in the central bank's decision-making bodies; and/or in the event of conflict, the central bank is required to obey the legal directives of the finance ministry or other government departments (Bank of Korea, 2000; Swinburne and Castello-Branco, 1991).

Financial Relationships

The main question in the central bank's relationship with the government is whether the relevant finance ministry has limited or unconstrained access to the central bank as a source of financing budget deficits. When the finance ministry has full discretion in determining the extent of monetary financing of budget deficits, the central bank loses control over the monetary base. Any excessive money creation generates inflation, which in turn raises the interest rate. The central bank may still come under political pressure to keep the interest rate low or to impose regulatory controls over the interest rate, since the interest rate is perceived to be determined by the central bank rather than affected by budget deficits or their mode of financing. Therefore, it is axiomatic that a high degree of fiscal dominance exists in a monetary regime in which the finance ministry has easy access to monetary financing of budget deficits.

Modern theories of monetary policy demonstrate the importance of the central bank's autonomy in the conduct of monetary policy for price stability (Fischer, 1994; Forder, 2000). Although complete independence of central banks from the governments is neither desirable nor practicable, the theory of central banking points to a number of principles that can guide modern central banks. It is revealing that Ricardo (1824: 283) provided a model of central banking which is remarkably similar in spirit to the way modern central banks are expected to operate:

> It is said that Government could not be safely entrusted with the power of issuing paper money; that it would most certainly abuse it . . . There would, I confess, be great danger of this if Government – that is to say, the Ministers – were themselves to be entrusted with the power of issuing paper money. But I propose to place this trust in the hands of Commissioners, not removable from their official situation but by a vote of one or both Houses of Parliament. I propose also to prevent all intercourse between these Commissioners and Ministers, by forbidding any species of money transactions between them. The Commissioners should never, on any pretense, lend money to Government, nor in the slightest degree be under its control or influence . . . If Government wanted money, it should be obliged to raise it in the legitimate way; by taxing the people; by the issue and sale of exchequer bills; by funded loans; or by borrowing from any of the numerous banks which might exist in the country; but in no case should it be allowed to borrow from those who have the power to create money.

In this statement, Ricardo has provided three key building blocks of what can be called the Principle of Autonomy. They are: (1) the institutional separation between those empowered to create money and those empowered to spend it, (2) the prohibition of monetary financing of budget deficits, and (3) the political accountability of central banks. Such criteria can be used to judge whether a central bank has autonomy in the conduct of monetary policy. While most central banks in developed countries have gained autonomy in the conduct of monetary policy, central banks in most developing countries have not yet gained genuine autonomy irrespective of their theoretical legal position. The main difficulty in these countries is to separate fiscal policy from monetary policy. For both economic and political reasons, central banks in developing countries carry out quasi-fiscal operations that lower their commitment to monetary and financial stability. Central banks' monetary operations are hence inextricably connected to the government's fiscal operations and with the management of public debt (Bank of Korea, 2000; Fair, 1979; Fischer, 1995a; 1995b; 1995c).

The quasi-fiscal activities that have monetary implications fall under five categories: (1) collecting seigniorage, (2) imposing financial restrictions, (3) implementing selective credit policies, (4) undertaking foreign exchange operations at non-market clearing prices, and (5) providing implicit or explicit deposit insurance at subsidised rates and recapitalising insolvent financial institutions. Not all central banks engage in such activities. Still the degree of fiscal dominance of a monetary regime is determined by the central bank's relationship with the financial system and by the use of direct instruments of monetary policy. Under repressed financial systems that existed in most developing countries until the 1980s, financial regulations were commonly imposed to facilitate financing of budget deficits. In general, regulatory restrictions such as credit controls, portfolio constraints and interest rate ceilings increased the private sector's demand for government securities. This in turn lowered the costs of government borrowings. Having such financial restrictions, the challenge that central banks faced was to insulate monetary policy from fiscal operations. In fact, the solvency of a central bank was dependent on explicit or implicit costs of such activities (Fry, 1998; Goodhart, 1992).

CENTRAL BANK INDEPENDENCE AND ITS IMPACT ON INFLATION IN THE ASIA-PACIFIC REGION

The main argument for central bank independence is that it raises central bank credibility and makes monetary policy more effective. Central bank credibility is, however, more complex. It is intricately linked not only to actual or perceived objectives of monetary policy and mechanisms through which monetary policy achieves those objectives, but also to policy-makers' actual or perceived objective functions. The issue becomes more complex when policy-makers have incentives to conceal their true stance on the role of monetary policy and are perceived to be motivated by personal, political and other factors.[11]

A central bank's credibility can be increased by providing it institutional independence for achieving a well-defined policy objective. This can make monetary policy more effective by a number of ways. First, an autonomous central bank is able to assign monetary policy a sole objective (for example, price stability), after consultation with the government. This can avoid a conflict that arises when monetary policy is given the role of achieving multiple objectives. When monetary policy has a sole objective, it becomes more credible. In contrast, when monetary policy is given the role of achieving multiple objectives, such as inflation control and the reduction in unemployment, it creates dynamic inconsistency that lowers monetary policy effectiveness. For example, when monetary policy has inflation and employment objectives, any anti-inflationary monetary policy may not be credible because at some stage in the future, the government will have a temptation to create inflation surprises to raise employment. When the private sector is aware of such dynamic inconsistency in monetary policy, then inflation risk premium is incorporated into interest rates and both price and wage decisions, and therefore monetary policy loses its effectiveness. Second, an independent central bank with an inflation target is able to lower inflationary expectations. This can lower inflation quickly with small or no reduction in output. Third, an independent central bank can provide disciplinary check on economic policies, particularly fiscal policy. Fourth, a transparent role of monetary policy and a well-defined relationship between the government and the central bank can strengthen accountability of both the central bank and the political leadership. The accountability of those responsible for monetary policy is weakened when there are multiple objectives of monetary policy because policy failure with respect to one objective can easily be excused by citing other objectives (Fraser, 1989; 1992; 1993).

Critics argue that central bank independence does not necessarily raise monetary policy effectiveness. The major difficulty of having an independent central bank is that it may cause a coordination problem between monetary policy and other areas of economic policy, especially fiscal policy. If the aim of central bank independence is to raise monetary policy credibility, it cannot do so unless the government's economic policy as a whole becomes credible. For example, if the government runs persistent large budget deficits and the central bank pursues a tight monetary policy, macroeconomic policy as a whole loses its credibility. This is because the private sector realises that at some stage in the future, the monetary authority must give way to fiscal policy. Sargent and Wallace (1981) have indeed shown the implication of the government budget constraint: that sustained debt-financing of budget deficits can be more inflationary in the long run than even money financing of those deficits. In other words, when a government runs persistent budget deficits, a tight monetary policy can cause high inflation in the future, and under certain conditions a tight monetary policy now can even cause a high inflation now. It indicates that monetary policy credibility requires coordination between monetary and fiscal policies. Such coordination is difficult unless the government is directly or indirectly responsible for monetary policy-making. In practice, no central bank can be fully independent to make its monetary policy by disregarding other policies. Therefore, dispersal of responsibility has the potential to lower efficiency of monetary policy.

In addition to the coordination problem, the question is often raised whether it is democratic to allow unelected central bankers to determine the major component of economic policy (Friedman, 1985). When politicians misuse monetary policy, they can be removed from office through the ballot box. When central bankers misuse monetary policy, there is no effective approach to their removal. For example, the performance of monetary policy in New Zealand is supposed to determine the fate of a single person (the Governor of the Reserve Bank of New Zealand). However, there are difficulties in enforcing any threat of removal of the Governor and/or other high officials in the central bank establishment. Central bankers are a part of public bureaucracy, which is able to play politics to survive and flourish.[12]

The key issue is whether independence of a central bank leads to independent monetary policy. Consider the cases of the Federal Reserve System and the Bundesbank, for example. They were (are) considered highly independent but their revealed actions were interpreted as if they had followed monetary policies for their governments (Auerbach, 1985; Frey and Schneider, 1981) so that they could exercise policy discretion and avoid accountability. Friedman (1962) argued for a constant money growth rule to stop central bankers from conducting discretionary monetary policy that allows them to follow prevailing political winds and thereby avoid accountability. They may do so by adopting clumsy monetary management procedures and resorting to secrecy.[13] Therefore, for pragmatic reasons, Friedman (1962: 219) made a statement that 'money is too important to be left to the central bankers'. When central bankers have their own objective functions and are motivated by factors that are different from those in any altruistic social welfare function, there can be inflationary bias in monetary policy even if central banks are made independent.[14]

Central Bank Independence and Inflation Performance

The issue of central bank independence and inflation performance has generated vast empirical literature, involving both cross-country and country-specific experiences. The most comprehensive early work on this issue is that of Cukierman et al. (1992). This study involved 72 countries – 21 industrial and 51 developing countries – and the period of study extended to the 1950s. The authors used a much wider range of information on central bank independence, including aspects of legislation (central bank law/charter) such as the terms of office, who appoints the governor and under what circumstances the governor is dismissed, who formulates the monetary policy, who has the final say, the role in the budgetary process, price stability and other objectives, how stringent is the lending criteria for the public sector, and so on. An index of legal independence is then constructed by first aggregating 16 variables into four principal components: the appointment and dismissal of the chief executive officer (the governor), the policy formulation cluster, the objectives of central bank, and limitations on the ability to lend to the public sector and then further aggregating these four into one.

Cukierman et al. (1992) and Cukierman et al. (1993) have found a significant negative relation between central bank independence and inflation for industrial countries but not for developing countries. Walsh (1998) and Franzese (1999) have found that central bank independence has the strongest impact on inflation when the government is not open, inflation abroad is high, the domestic financial sector is small and the wage bargaining coordination is low.

Since the late 1990s most central banks of developed countries have introduced measures to reduce time inconsistency in monetary policy. Provision of central bank independence has been the most prominent measure. Central bank governors have also been given a relatively long tenure to avoid political pressure. In addition, conservatives who dislike inflation are often appointed as central bank governors. In a deregulated economic environment, these measures have been adequate to keep inflation low. The general dislike of inflation by citizens also helped central banks to pursue directly a steady conservative monetary policy and indirectly put pressure on the government to run disciplined fiscal policy.

Unlike developed countries, central banks in developing countries have relatively less autonomy in pursuing a single objective of monetary policy. This is despite the general agreement that central bank independence may help to keep inflation low. Most developing countries still consider rapid economic growth more important than price stability. Central bank independence is therefore not seen as paramount, rather it can slow economic growth. It implies that there can be a reverse relation between central bank independence and inflation. For example, countries that dislike inflation tend to give more independence to their central banks and have lower inflation (Blanchard, 2006).

Ahsan et al. (2007) have constructed a composite index for central bank independence and governance for 36 countries of the Asia-Pacific. They have used data for the period 1991–2005 to construct an index for central bank independence and governance (CBIG). The index values for the sample countries suggest that Australia has the highest CBIG, while Vietnam has the lowest. New Zealand, Taiwan, the Philippines, Nepal, South Korea and Malaysia have relatively more independent central banks, while Indonesia, Japan and Pakistan have relatively less independent central banks. The authors have examined the bidirectional relationship between central bank independence and inflation for the sample countries. They have shown that central bank independence and governance has improved in the sample countries since the Asian financial crisis and that it has contributed to reduce inflation. Figure 3.1 confirms an inverse relation between central bank independence and inflation for 20 selected countries of the Asia-Pacific over the period 1990–2007.

SUMMARY AND CONCLUSION

This chapter has reviewed the evolution and functions of a modern central bank. The origins of central banking can be traced to the latter half of the seventeenth century in Europe when the government-sponsored Swedish Riksbank and the Bank of England were founded. From a historical perspective, central banks were founded for the financial advantage that the governments obtained from these institutions, unification of 'chaotic' currency issue systems, centralised management and protection of silver and gold reserves, and the improvement of inter-bank payments systems.

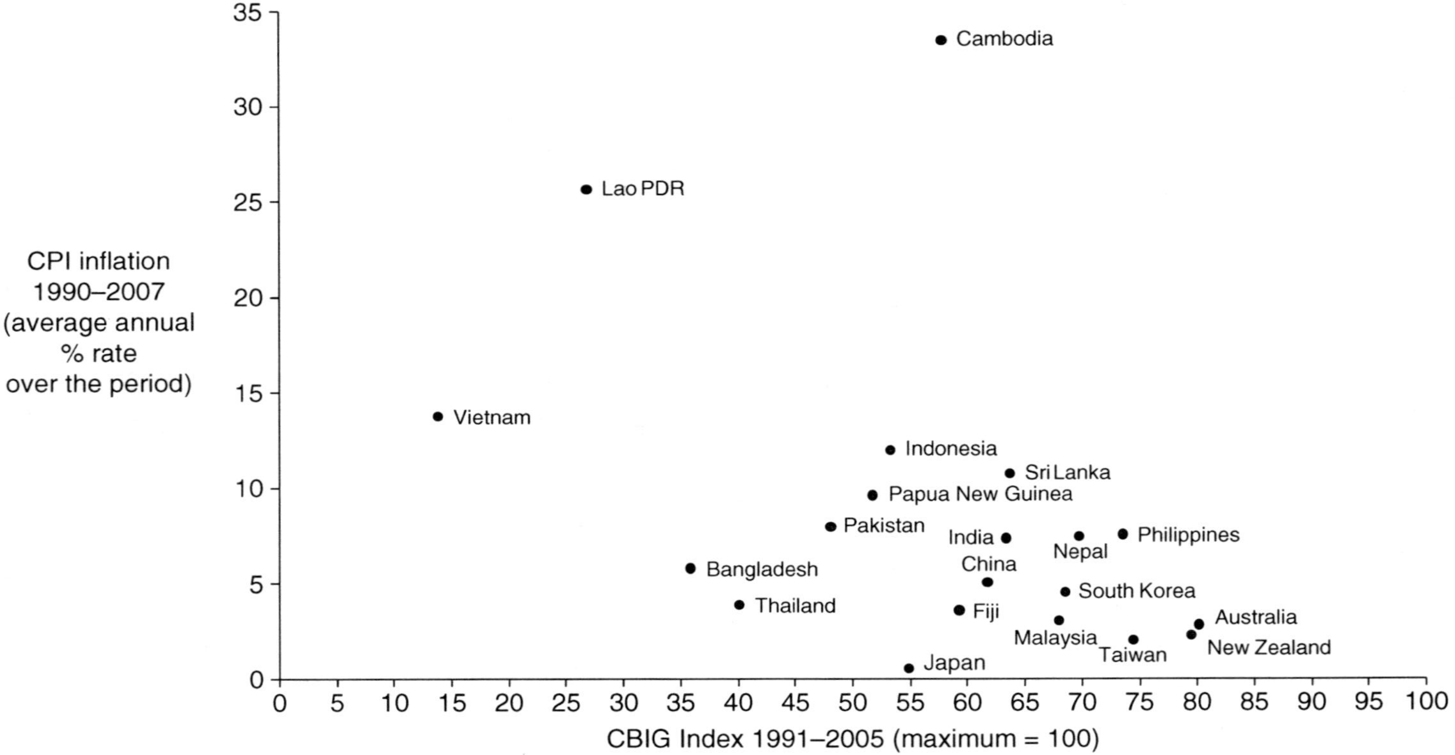

Note: Correlation coefficient: $\rho = -0.42$.

Source: Ahsan et al. (2007).

Figure 3.1 Central Bank independence and governance (CBIG) and inflation in selected countries of the Asia-Pacific

Contemporary central banks have evolved as an outcome of institutional adaptation of countries to reduce confidence costs in the fiat monetary system, as well as acting as a conduit for resource transfer from the people to the government for developmental activities. Central banks have transformed in recent decades, emerging as national institutions with the explicit role as guardians of financial stability. Because of this transformation of functions, there has been a corresponding change in the expectations of citizens in the ability of central banks to achieve and maintain macroeconomic stability in general, and price stability in particular (Capie et al., 1994; Siklos, 2002). This has happened at a time when there is also debate by some 'neoliberal' economists over whether central banks are even necessary (Collyns, 1983; Friedman, 1999; Goodhart, 1999a; 1999b).

The review of the organisational and administrative structures of central banks of the Asia-Pacific suggest that all the central banks in this region are governed by a board of directors/governors, who are appointed by the government for three or five years with the possibility of a renewal. Most central banks aim to maintain price stability through monetary policy for sustained economic growth. Central banks are also assigned the responsibility of supervising and regulating the financial system. Without resolving conflicts between them, the twin objectives of price stability and economic stability remain in the statute books of central banks as a reminder that economic stability cannot be ignored, although price stability is often the overriding objective of monetary policy.

Monetary policy is conducted under different frameworks, but is coordinated with fiscal policy. This is manifested in the close liaison between the Governor of the central bank and the Minister of Finance. Although most central banks appear autonomous under new central bank laws enacted in many developing countries, the government has retained control over appointments, nominations and reappointments of governors, and most members of the board of directors. Arguably, the provision of renewability provides an incentive to board members to appease politicians who are currently in power or expected to be in power in future. Most central banks also do not control their own budgets.

Since the 1990s, most central banks are not required to finance budget deficits or are even not allowed to participate in the auctions of Treasury bills. Open market operations can, however, be a back door for financing budget deficits. When government finances budget deficits by selling bonds, it may raise interest rates. Central banks can undertake open market purchase of government bonds with the aim of lowering interest rates (Burda and Wyplosz, 2005). Nevertheless, fiscal dominance appears to be diminishing in both developed and developing countries. Because of financial reforms there are fewer restrictions on the interest rates and credit allocation. The rules regarding the reserve requirements and the holding of government securities have been relaxed. Controls over capital flows and external borrowings still remain in force (IMF's *Exchange Rate Arrangements and Exchange Restrictions*, various years). Provided that there are no major financial crises, most central banks in developing Asia would move towards a more liberalised financial system, allowing them to use indirect monetary policy instruments for liquidity management (Downes and Vaez-Zadeh, 1991; Mahadeva and Sinclair, 2005).

The review reveals that there has also been a move towards increasing autonomy of central banks across the Asia-Pacific region. However, the issue of central bank autonomy or independence needs to be looked at from a historical viewpoint (Hetzel, 1990). Until the 1970s, the premier independent central banks were the Federal Reserve System and the central banks of Germany and the Switzerland. By the late 1990s the European Central Bank had become independent. Since 1997 the Bank of England has become even more independent than previously. This has implications for the central banks in Asia because, due to colonial heritage, most of them were cast in the mould of the Bank of England. The Reserve Bank of New Zealand and the Bank of Japan have emerged as the two highly independent central banks in the region. The Reserve Bank of Australia has also gained considerable autonomy and policy independence since the mid-1990s. In the wake of the East Asian currency crisis, the central banks of South Korea, Indonesia and Thailand have gained considerable autonomy in conducting monetary policy via inflation targeting. Central banks of some transitional economies have also taken greater responsibility in achieving price stability (Lowe, 1997; Wagner, 1997).

While these changes in the region are considered a positive development, the de facto independence of Asian-Pacific central banks remains limited because of the governments' control over appointments of directors and the budgeting of central banks (Banaian et al., 1983; Berger et al., 2000; Cukierman, 1986). Fortunately, central banks have shown enthusiasm for developing and protecting their autonomy and building policy credibility through institutional reforms and research activities.[15] Most central banks in Asia are also in the process of standardising their activities by following traditions established by the central banks of developed countries. International financial institutions (such as the Bank for International Settlements, the IMF and the World Bank) are helping these banks to streamline their activities and governance. Central bank officials are receiving advanced training in central banking, especially the modern approaches to liquidity management. Most governments in Asia have lately become reluctant to engage in expansionary fiscal and monetary policies for immediate economic or political gains. This is partly a reflection of an emerging consensus against simplistic macroeconomic populism for solving entrenched structural economic problems such as unemployment, poverty and income inequality. Under these circumstances, central bank governors have a better chance of working conservatively and maintaining integrity of central banks.

Provided that central banks work conscientiously and with tenacity, their status should be enhanced over time. This will bring policy credibility and make monetary policy effective. This is, however, not an easy task and it may not happen overnight. In fact the status of a central bank as an autonomous institution with the responsibility of conducting independent monetary policy remains complex, as it depends on much more than simply words in central banking legislations (Cukierman et al., 1992; 2002; McCallum, 1995a; 1997).

NOTES

1. Centralisation of note issue, however, did not happen easily. Countries with a long tradition of political fragmentation succumbed to monopolistic tendency. The legislation passed in the USA in the1860s, which created the 'national banking system', is a case in point (Smith, 1936). There are other examples. In 1881, Switzerland had 36 cantonal banks of note issue. A reform involving establishment of a federal bank was contemplated in the 1880s in the wake of a major banking crisis. This was rejected by a popular referendum. A further crisis revived the debate after a few years. The idea of establishing a central bank was rejected again in a new referendum in 1896. It was only in 1905, after a third referendum, that a federal central bank was established. Similarly in Italy, there was strong resistance to centralisation after the country's political unification – the process of unification started roughly in 1815 and ended in 1871. The early

attempts in 1863 and 1865 to create a central bank 'Banca d'Italia' were unsuccessful because of a deeply rooted tradition of local autonomy rather than doctrinal preferences. The Banca d'Italia became the sole bank of issue only in 1926 (Giannini, 1995).

2. In fact this issue has become significant since the 1970s when the Southern cone countries of Latin America experienced financial crises after financial deregulation. In the early 1980s the Latin American debt crises again posed a threat to the international financial system. On that occasion, the intervention of the IMF and other international organisations rescued the international banks and the financial system. Since then there have been a number of banking and financial crises across the world, including some in developed countries. For example, in the early 1980s the savings and loan crises posed a threat to the US financial system, which required a large injection of public funds. Major banking crises later developed in both Latin America and Scandinavian countries. The recent banking and financial crises were in East Asia and Japan. The present global financial crisis originated from the US subprime mortgage crisis that started in 2007. The central banks have acted as both the provider of emergency liquidity and the manager of those crises. In a global context, the central banks and the IMF remain the major institutions who share the task of lender of last resort (Hossain and Chowdhury, 1996; Mishkin, 2007a; Taylor, 2008a).
3. Unless specific references are provided, country-specific information on central banking is drawn from publications on country-specific central bank websites. The website publications of the Bank for International Settlements and the IMF are also consulted and references are cited in the text.
4. The information on the Reserve Bank of Australia (RBA) is drawn from various documents, including the Reserve Bank Act 1959, available at http://www.rba.gov.au.
5. The information on the Bangladesh Bank (BB) is drawn from various documents, including the Bangladesh Bank Order 1972, available at http://www.bangladeshbank.org.bd.
6. The information on the People's Bank of China (PBC) is drawn from documents available at http://www.pbc.gov.cn.
7. The information on Bank Indonesia (BI) is drawn from various documents, including Bank Indonesia Act 1999 (amended in 2004), available at http://www.bi.gov.in.
8. The information on the Bank of Japan (BOJ) is drawn from various documents (http://www.boj.jp; Ito, 2006; Mishkin and Eakins, 2006; Suzuki, 1992).
9. The information on Nepal Rastra Bank (NRB) is drawn from various documents available at http://www.nrb.org.np.
10. The information on the Bank PNG (BPNG) is drawn from various documents available at http://www.bankpng.gov.pg.
11. In the literature, policy-makers are classified as Type I and Type II. Type I policy-makers are strongly anti-inflationary in their preferences, and they do not seek to create inflation surprises. Type II policy-makers expose as anti-inflationary but are tempted to create inflation surprises. The problem for the private sector is to distinguish between a Type I policy-maker and a Type II policy-maker (Blackburn and Christensen, 1989).
12. Friedman (1985: 4) remarks that 'The person ostensibly in charge is like the rooster crowing at dawn. The course of events is decided by deeper and less visible forces that determine both the character of those nominally in charge and the pressures on them'.
13. Auerbach (1985) argues that when formal central bank independence permits substantial back-door political influence on monetary policy, it assists the political leadership to escape responsibility and accountability of monetary policy because of a non-transparent relationship between the central bank and the political leadership. In such a situation, the central bank has a tendency to adopt clumsy instruments and monetary management techniques to conduct monetary policy and resort to hiding under secrecy.
14. Milton Friedman, quoted in Fischer (1990: 1181), wrote: 'From revealed preference, I suspect that by far the two most important variables in their [policy-makers'] loss function are avoiding accountability on the one hand and achieving public prestige on the other. A loss function that contains those two elements as its main argument will I believe come far closer to rationalizing the behavior of the Federal Reserve over the 73 years.'
15. See, for example, Alesina and Tabellini (1987); Banaian et al. (1983); Cargill and Hutchison (1990); Cukierman (1992); Fazio (1991); Grilli et al. (1991); Lohmann (1992); Mittra (1977); Swinburne and Castello-Branco (1991); and Willett (1988).

4. Monetary policy: overview of concepts, debates and issues

MONETARY POLICY

Monetary policy is a key component of economic policy. It refers to policy actions taken by a central bank to change the monetary and financial conditions in an economy. The aim of monetary policy is to achieve either a single objective, for example, low and steady inflation, or multiple objectives such as low inflation, steady economic growth, equilibrium in the balance of payments, and interest and exchange rate stability. The policy instruments that central banks deploy to bring a required change in the monetary and financial condition in the economy include short-term interest rates, bank credits and bank reserves. These instruments are interrelated; their deployment and effectiveness depend on exchange rate arrangements, monetary policy frameworks, and controls and regulations over capital flows (Cheng, 1988; Mishkin, 2007a; Walsh, 1998).

Monetary policy and central banking are intertwined. Monetary policy as a concept, however, is not as old as central banking. As reviewed in Chapter 3, central banks were first established in Europe more than three centuries ago. Monetary policy as a distinct component of economic policy was not identified until around the time of the First World War. Since then the scope of monetary policy has become wider. It encompasses established activities of central banks, including nineteenth-century functions connected with implementing rules and regulations, rather than direct intervention of economic activity. In this historical context, it can be difficult to distinguish monetary policy from economic policy in general. Nevertheless, as a general principle, it is possible to define modern monetary policy as that part of economic policy that is designed and implemented by central banks to achieve one or more well-defined economic goals. The difficulty is that this criterion needs simplification. For example, although most controls over interest rates, exchange rates and credit ceilings are within the jurisdiction of central banks, these can be imposed and administered by the finance ministry (or treasury). Likewise, most central banks perform some quasi-fiscal operations that, in a strict definitional sense, should lie outside the ambit of monetary policy. The distinction between monetary and fiscal policy also becomes blurred in the long run because the key variables that are in the domain of these separate policies have feedback relationships. For example, budget deficits, public debt, interest rates, exchange rates, money growth and inflation all interact. Their long-term behaviour cannot be analysed satisfactorily in isolation without taking into account the feedback relations within a macroeconomic context (Agenor and Montiel, 1996; Fry, 1992; Fry et al., 1996; Goodhart, 1988).

In an operational sense, monetary policy is conceptually seen as a policy instrument separate from fiscal policy. Fiscal policy itself deals with government outlays, taxes/revenues, and the financing of budget deficits through monetary and non-monetary means.

Moreover, the transmission mechanisms of monetary policy are different from those of fiscal policy. The effect of fiscal policy on aggregate demand is direct because it operates through government spending and private disposable income (via taxes) that affects private consumption spending (Haliassos and Tobin, 1990). The impact of monetary policy on aggregate demand is, however, indirect because it depends on the responses of consumers and investors to changes in the monetary and financial condition that is brought about by a central bank's policy actions (Friedman, 1991; Modigliani, 1971). This does not preclude the possibility that when a central bank uses direct monetary instruments such as credit controls, they affect both aggregate demand and aggregate supply directly (Agenor and Montiel, 1996). This is the case of monetary policy in a repressed financial system, which has been discarded by most developing countries in favour of financial deregulation and economic openness (Hossain and Chowdhury, 1996).

Therefore, from a practical viewpoint, monetary policy remains within the domain of central banking. Its design and implementation are the responsibility of a central bank. This role of a central bank has been institutionalised in most countries in the present deregulatory financial environment. However, as noted earlier, whether a central bank performs this responsibility alone or in consultation with the finance ministry (or treasury) depends on the institutional arrangements in the particular country. There is variation in the degree of autonomy that a central bank enjoys in terms of its design and implementation of monetary policy. Also, the issue of whether monetary policy should aim at achieving a single (or multiple) objective(s) is yet to be resolved. As a general rule, most central banks coordinate monetary policy operations in conjunction with fiscal policy and maintain policy consistency. This is necessary for maintaining monetary policy transparency and credibility, which determines the effectiveness of monetary policy in achieving its objective(s) (Cukierman, 1992; Walsh, 1998). Hence the logical beginning of any discussion on monetary policy in developing countries is therefore the interaction between monetary and fiscal policies (Fischer and Easterly, 1990; Fischer et al., 2002). This is explained below by invoking the concept of the government budget constraint and demonstrating policy implications.

THE GOVERNMENT BUDGET CONSTRAINT[1]

The effects of budget deficits on macroeconomic variables are analysed within an analytical framework that is centred on the government budget constraint. This concept is developed below.

When revenues fall short of recurrent and capital outlays, the government incurs a deficit, which requires financing from monetary and/or non-monetary sources. The government budget constraint is one way of showing the linkage between budget deficits and the alternative sources of deficit financing. This is an essential tool for understanding both the linkage between monetary and fiscal policies, and the macroeconomic consequences of budget deficits (Dornbusch and Fischer, 1981; Sargent and Wallace, 1981).

The government budget deficit can be defined and linked with changes in government net debt as follows:

$$D_g - D_{g-1} = (G + I_g - T) + i \cdot D_{g-1} \qquad (4.1)$$

where $(D_g - D_{g-1})$ is the change in government net debt between the current and previous period; G is government consumption spending; I_g is government investment; T is taxes net of transfers; and i is the nominal interest rate. The right-hand side of equation (4.1) measures the budget deficit, showing that the change in government net debt is equal to the budget deficit.

When the government's budget is in deficit, the Treasury needs to finance this deficit by raising funds through issuing government bonds. The buyers of bonds can be classified into four categories: foreigners (public or private), domestic households and firms, the domestic banking system, and the country's central bank. In developing countries, the central bank often buys the bulk of Treasury bonds issued to finance deficits because there is limited demand for Treasury bonds from other buyers such as the private sector. The government may also be unwilling to sell large Treasury bonds to the public because that would require paying interest in the future (Fry, 1998). Because the central bank is often a key organ of the government, its only option is often to buy Treasury bonds or monetise the deficit.[2]

In most situations, however, both the public and the central bank hold Treasury bonds. Thus a change in debt held by the central bank $(D_{gc} - D_{gc-1})$ equals the overall change in debt $(D_g - D_{g-1})$ less the change in debt held by the public $(D_{gp} - D_{gp-1})$:

$$D_{gc} - D_{gc-1} = (D_g - D_{g-1}) - (D_{gp} - D_{gp-1}) \tag{4.2}$$

The effect of a budget deficit on the money supply can be shown from the following equation for changes in the monetary base (MB):

$$MB - MB_{-1} = (D_{gc} - D_{gc-1}) + NER \bullet (R_c^{\$} - R_{c-1}^{\$}) + (L_{cb} - L_{cb-1}) \tag{4.3}$$

where $R_c^{\$}$ is foreign reserves in foreign currency at the central bank, NER is the nominal exchange rate measured in terms of domestic currency per unit of foreign currency, and L_{cb} is the stock of loans made to commercial banks through the discount window. If the discount window component of changes in the monetary base is ignored, equation (4.3) can be written as:

$$MB - MB_{-1} = (D_{gc} - D_{gc-1}) + NER \bullet (R_c^{\$} - R_{c-1}^{\$}) \tag{4.3a}$$

Substituting the expression for $(D_{gc} - D_{gc-1})$ from equation (4.2) into equation (4.3a) and rearranging the resulting expression yields:

$$(D_g - D_{g-1}) = (MB - MB_{-1}) + (D_{gp} - D_{gp-1}) - NER \bullet (R_c^{\$} - R_{c-1}^{\$}) \tag{4.4}$$

This equation, which is another form of equation (4.3), can be called the *fundamental equation* for financing the budget deficit. It shows that there are three ways to finance the deficit, which is equal to the change in the government net debt $(D_g - D_{g-1})$:

1. by an increase in the monetary base, $MB - MB_{-1}$;
2. by an increase in the public's holdings of Treasury bonds, $D_{gp} - D_{gp-1}$; or
3. by a loss of foreign reserves at the central bank, $NER \bullet (R_c^{\$} - R_{c-1}^{\$})$.

In short, to finance the budget deficit the government will have to print money, borrow from the public, or run down foreign exchange reserves. Whether the government in a developing country has the luxury of alternative financing options is a matter of contention (Haliassos and Tobin, 1990). During the 1950s and 1960s many newly independent countries resorted to money financing of deficits (Coates and Khatkhate, 1980; Fry et al., 1996). The situation changed in the 1970s, when many developing countries resorted to external borrowing, leading to the debt crises of the early 1980s. Since then most developing countries have undertaken the IMF–World Bank-supported stabilisation and structural adjustment policies that have helped them to create a wider tax base and other options for non-monetary financing of deficits. Nevertheless, as Easterly et al. (1994) articulate, the point is that each of the three sources of deficit financing identified above can cause a particular kind of macroeconomic problem, namely, high inflation or high interest rate or large external debt or all of them.

The linkage between monetary and fiscal policies suggests that it is possible to trace most monetary problems in developing countries to expansionary fiscal policy. Because fiscal policy remains in the domain of the executive branch of the government, the government bears the responsibility of monetary problems. This indicates that when monetary policy is dictated by fiscal policy, there is not much that a central bank can do to avoid creating monetary problems such as inflation and balance-of-payments crises. This has been the case in most developing countries, where central banks have operated under the guidance of the Ministry of Finance; therefore, monetary policy remained subordinate to fiscal policy (Aghevli and Khan, 1978; 1980; Easterly and Schmidt-Hebbel, 1993; Fischer et al., 2002; Khatkhate, 1972).

Since the debt crises of the 1980s, the central banks in developing countries have had some autonomy in the conduct of monetary policy. Yet the issue remains what precise role the central bank and/or the government should assign to monetary policy. There is controversy as to whether monetary policy should be used as a tool of economic stabilisation or to bring long-term price and exchange rate stability. The main argument for price stability as the sole objective of monetary policy is that monetary policy cannot bring long-term economic gains. If monetary policy is conducted within a medium-term horizon and the fiscal authorities accept monetary policy independence, this may improve the conduct of fiscal policy or at least lower the temptation of the government for fiscal excesses (Masciandaro and Tabellini, 1988).

An emerging consensus is that monetary policy can bring long-term price stability but that it is not effective for economic stabilisation. In a deregulated system, the economy remains vulnerable to both monetary and real shocks (domestic and foreign) and therefore there is temptation of the government for the deployment of monetary measures to bring economic stability (Hossain and Chowdhury, 1998). Indeed, it is important to review the historical debate on the scope of stabilisation in a capitalist economy.

The next section illustrates the concept of independent monetary policy by invoking the *impossibility theorem* for open economies. This states that of the three desired economic policy goals – the stability in the exchange rate (exchange rate stability), free movement of capital (financial integration) and independence in monetary policy (monetary policy independence) – it is possible to achieve only two at a time (Krugman and Obstfeld, 2009; Shambaugh, 2004). The 'impossibility theorem' is a simplified form of the 'inconsistent quartet' which suggests that it is impossible for a country or a group of countries to simultaneously aim at free trade, free capital mobility, independent monetary policy and exchange rate stability: at least one of them must be abandoned (Padoa-Schioppa, 2004).

EXCHANGE RATES, CAPITAL FLOWS AND MONETARY POLICY

As indicated above, the impossibility theorem states that the three desirable goals of an open economy, namely, capital mobility (financial integration), independent monetary policy (ability to set the interest rate or control over the money stock) and exchange rate stability (fixed or pegged exchange rate) cannot be maintained simultaneously: at least one of them must be sacrificed (Figure 4.1).

For example, if the exchange rate stability is desired under a fixed or pegged exchange rate system for maintaining price stability, then this may be compatible with free capital mobility or monetary policy independence, but not with both simultaneously. Under a fixed or pegged exchange rate system with perfect capital mobility, the country loses monetary policy independence because its interest rate would shadow the interest rate

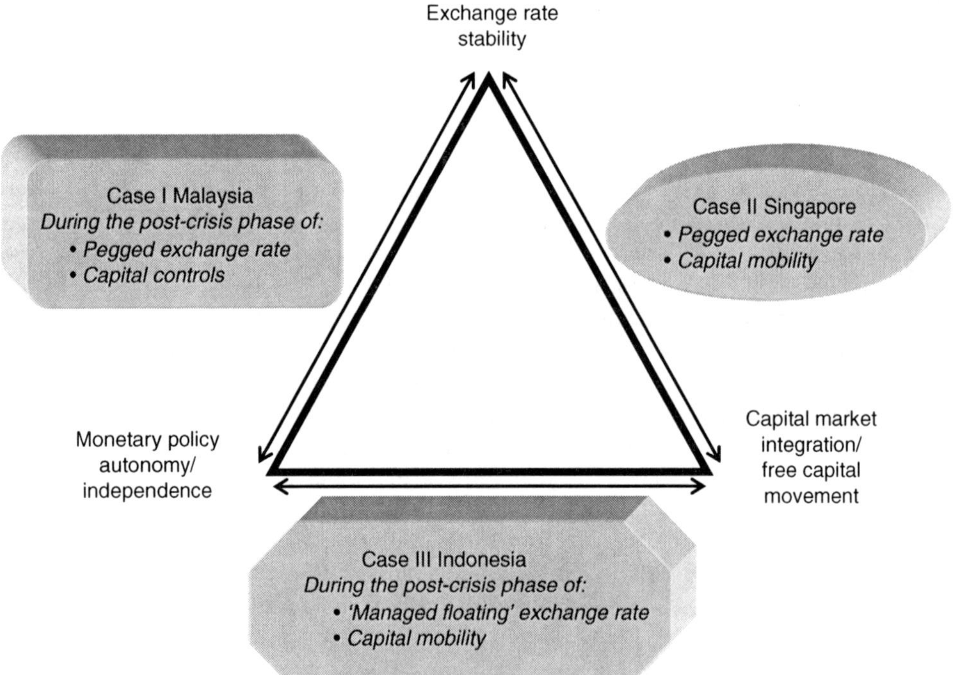

Source: Adapted from Krugman and Obstfeld (2009: 650).

Figure 4.1 Impossibility theorem for open economies and monetary policy in Indonesia, Malaysia and Singapore

of the pegged currency country. Any attempt to keep the domestic interest rate higher or lower than the foreign interest rate would trigger massive capital flows which would likely undermine the goal of exchange rate stability. If a country intends to gain monetary policy independence under a fixed or pegged exchange rate system, it may be able to achieve this partly by introducing capital controls (Aghevli et al., 1991; IMF's *Exchange Rate Arrangements and Exchange Restrictions*, various issues). China, India and Malaysia continue to maintain some monetary policy independence under capital controls. When a country adopts a floating exchange rate system, it can achieve monetary policy independence with or without capital controls. Therefore a corollary of the impossibility theorem is that when a country allows free capital mobility, it can have monetary policy independence under a flexible exchange rate system. However, the country will have no monetary policy independence under a fixed or pegged exchange rate system. The East Asian financial crises have led many economists such as Athukorala (2001), Bhagwati (1998), Rodrik (1998) and Stiglitz (2003) to argue in favour of capital controls in developing countries that may provide them monetary policy independence while maintaining exchange rate stability (Krugman and Obstfeld, 2009).

The key points illustrated in Figure 4.1 are further discussed. Some analytical results are also derived to highlight policy implications that remain useful to analyse contemporary issues in monetary policy in the Asia-Pacific.

Fixed Exchange Rate System: Interest Rate, Money Stock and the Price Level

Under a fixed exchange rate system, a country loses its monetary policy independence unless there are controls over capital flows. Under a fixed exchange rate system the stock of the money supply is endogenous and the domestic interest rate shadows the foreign interest rate.

Endogenous money supply

Under a fixed exchange rate system, the domestic money supply is determined by the money demand factors. This is explained as follows.

Consider the money multiplier model of the money supply:

$$M^s = mm \cdot MB = mm \cdot (DC + FR) \tag{4.5}$$

where mm is the money multiplier with an assumed value one and DC is domestic credit and FR is foreign exchange reserves in domestic currency, that is, $FR = R^{\$} \cdot NER$, where NER is the fixed exchange rate of domestic currency per unit of foreign currency (\$). Equation (4.5) defines the monetary base (MB) from the asset side of the central bank's balance sheet (Table 4.1). By definition, the central bank's assets equal liabilities, which include currency in circulation (C) (that is, currency held by commercial banks in vaults and currency held by the non-bank public) plus bank and non-bank deposits (bank reserves) with the central bank.

Under a fixed exchange rate system, the monetary authorities stand ready to buy or sell foreign currency for domestic currency at a predetermined exchange rate. Whenever there is a pressure on the exchange rate, the monetary authorities buy or sell foreign currency for domestic currency to ensure that the exchange rate remains at the fixed level.

Table 4.1 A simplified consolidated balance sheet of a central bank

Assets	Liabilities
Domestic credit (DC)	Currency in circulation (C)
Foreign reserves (FR)	Commercial bank deposits (reserves) (R)
Other assets (O^a)	Other liabilities (O^l)
Assets = $DC + FR + O_a$	Liabilities = $C + R + O_l$

In terms of the central bank's balance sheet, *ceteris paribus*, foreign assets (reserves) adjust in line with foreign exchange interventions and the monetary base adjusts in line with foreign assets. In other words, if there is any change on any component on the asset side of the central bank's balance sheet, this leads to changes on items in the liabilities side so that assets are balanced with liabilities. Adopting a fixed exchange rate regime therefore implies that the monetary authorities ensure that the officially fixed exchange rate becomes equal to the equilibrium level. The central bank then remains committed to adjusting the money base to the level that is needed to ensure that the exchange market clears at the predetermined exchange rate. This implies that the monetary authorities lose control over the money supply. In a policy sense, fixing the exchange rate means that the country has an exchange rate policy but no independent monetary policy, unless it imposes controls over capital flows. Algebraically, this is shown as follows.

The domestic interest rate shadows the foreign interest rate Consider the following interest rate parity condition:

$$i^d = i^f + \rho + \sigma \qquad (4.6)$$

where i^d is the domestic interest rate, i^f is the foreign interest rate, ρ is risk premium, and σ is the expected depreciation (or appreciation) of domestic currency against the foreign currency. Under a fixed exchange rate system, $\sigma = 0$, so that $i^d = i^f$ (assuming that $\rho = 0$). This means that when a country maintains a credible fixed or pegged exchange rate system, the domestic interest rate equals the interest rate of the pegged currency country plus risk premium. Any deviation of the domestic interest rate from the foreign interest rate represents a risk premium. When the deviation between the two becomes significant, it triggers massive capital flows under perfect capital mobility. This makes the exchange rate peg untenable.

The domestic price level determined by the purchasing power parity condition When an economy is small and all of its goods are tradable, the domestic price level is determined by the purchasing power parity condition:

$$P^d = NER \cdot P^f \qquad (4.7)$$

where P^d is the domestic price level, *NER*, as previously defined, is the exchange rate of domestic currency per unit of foreign currency, and P^f is the foreign price level.

Adjustment of the money market

To ensure that the foreign exchange market remains in equilibrium, the central bank must keep the domestic interest rate i^d equal to i^f. Given that the domestic interest rate is determined by the interaction of real money demand and the real money supply, the central bank's foreign exchange intervention must be such that the domestic interest rate equals the foreign interest rate and brings equality between real money demand and real money supply.

Consider the equilibrium condition in the real money market:

$$(M^s/P^d) = m^d(y, i^d) \tag{4.8}$$

where m^d is real money demand, which is an increasing function of real income (y) and a decreasing function of the domestic interest rate (i^d). In this specification the nominal money demand (M^d) increases proportionately to an increase in the domestic price level (P^d), leaving the demand for real money $m^d(y, i^d)$ unchanged. Imposing the restriction that i^d equals i^f, then equation (4.8) can be written as:

$$(M^s/P^d) = m^d(y, i^f) \tag{4.9}$$

Given P^d and y, equation (4.9) shows what the money supply should be to keep the fixed exchange rate consistent with equilibrium in the money market at the foreign interest rate i^f. The working process is explained below.

Given the equilibrium condition in the money market, any change in demand for money should be accommodated by a change in the money supply. An example makes this point clear. Recall that $M^s = DC + FR$. Assuming that DC (domestic credit) is constant, a rise in income (y_1 to y_2) will increase the quantity of money demand and this will raise the domestic interest rate (i_1^d to i_2^d). Assuming that there are no restrictions on capital flows (and no sterilisation), a rise in the domestic interest rate will increase the inflows of foreign capital (given a foreign interest rate). This will increase FR on the asset side of the central bank's balance sheet and the money supply M^s on the liability side (M_1^s to M_2^s). Similarly, the money supply will decrease when there is a decrease in demand for money (say due to a decrease in income), which will lower the domestic interest rate and induce an outflow of capital given the foreign interest rate.

This indicates that the domestic interest rate can vary from the foreign interest rate only temporarily, and only when there are restrictions on capital mobility. Under perfect capital mobility, the slightest difference between the interest rates prevailing in domestic and foreign capital markets can provoke large capital flows. Under a fixed exchange rate system with perfect capital mobility, a central bank cannot therefore keep the domestic interest rate at a significantly higher or lower level than the foreign interest rate. This means that attempts by the central bank to tighten monetary policy induce huge capital inflows into the country, forcing the central bank to intervene in the foreign exchange market to keep the domestic currency from appreciating. An increase in foreign assets offsets the initial contraction of money (that increased the interest rate), forcing the domestic interest rate down to the level of the foreign interest rate.

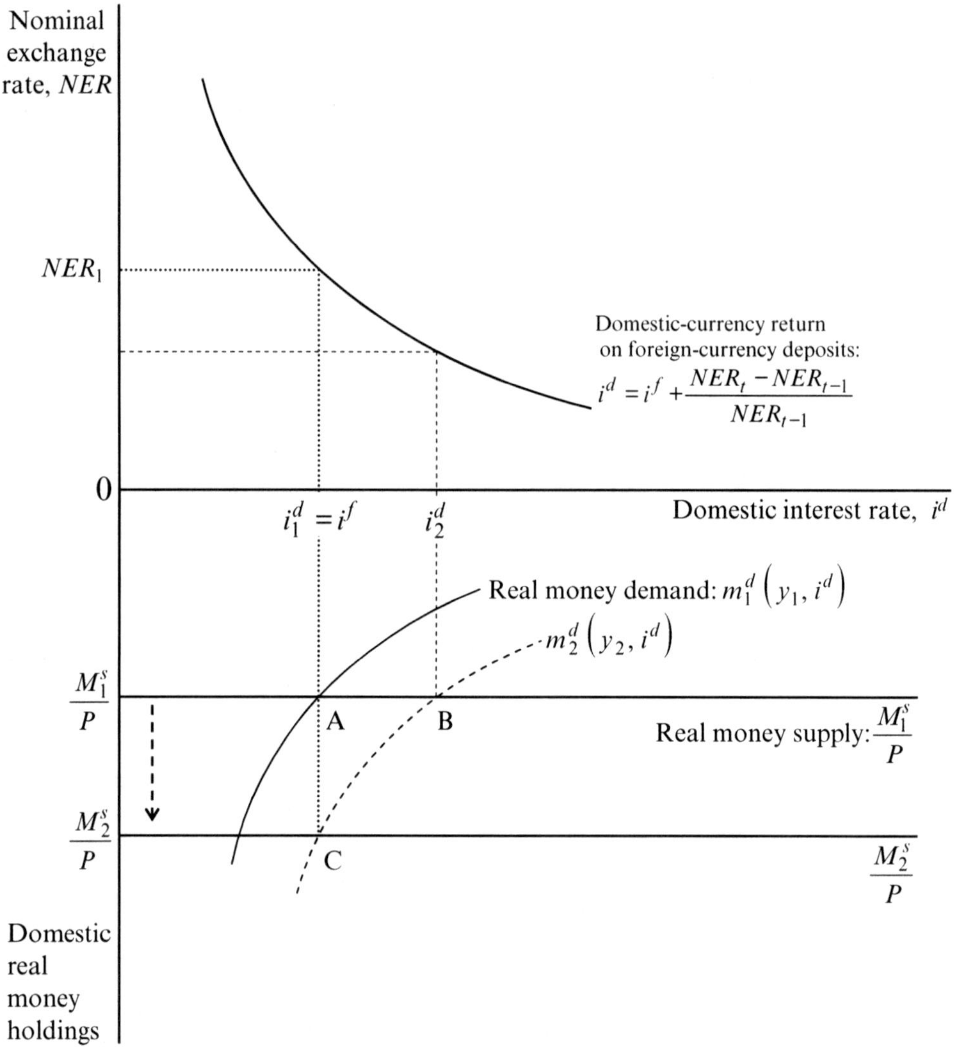

Source: Adapted from Krugman and Obstfeld (2009: 469).

Figure 4.2 Foreign exchange and domestic money markets under a fixed exchange rate system

Floating Exchange Rate System: The Money Stock, Price Level and the Interest Rate

Under the floating exchange rate system a country gains monetary policy independence with or without capital controls. This is reflected in the fact that the stock of money supply is exogenous and the domestic inflation rate (or the domestic interest rate) can deviate for a long period from the foreign inflation rate (or the foreign interest rate).

The exogeneity of the money supply

Under a floating exchange rate system the monetary authorities can exogenously determine the money supply. Recall that $MB = DC + FR$. Assuming free capital mobility, the balance of payments are theoretically in equilibrium and there are no changes in foreign reserves, such that $\Delta MB = \Delta DC$ (that is, $\Delta FR \cong 0$). The absence of intervention by the monetary authorities to stabilise the exchange rate implies no change in net foreign assets. The current account deficits are financed by, or become equal to, private and official capital inflows. The linkage between the money supply and the balance of payments is broken and the central bank regains its control over the money supply. That is, by controlling domestic credit the monetary authorities impose control over the money supply. When the monetary authorities create excess credit, this leads to depreciation of the exchange rate and through it a rise in the domestic price level. The exchange rate thus acts as a conduit through which any excess credit expansion by the central bank increases money supply and the price level. This idea is explained below.

Inflation: A Policy Variable

Consider the money market equilibrium condition, as specified above:

$$M^s/P^d = m^d(y, i^d) \tag{4.10}$$

Using this condition the following equilibrium relationship can be derived:

$$\pi = \lambda - \eta_y \bullet g_y \tag{4.11}$$

where π is inflation, λ is money supply growth, η_y is the income elasticity of demand for money and g_y is the growth rate of the economy. It is assumed that the domestic interest rate does not have a long-term trend (despite short-term fluctuations) and hence it does not affect long-run real balances. The nominal interest rate can therefore be excluded from the inflation equation (Burda and Wyplosz, 2005). If the trend growth rate of the economy is ignored ($g_y \cong 0$), the long-run inflation rate would approximate the money growth rate:

$$\pi = \lambda \tag{4.12}$$

Equation (4.11) represents the classical monetary model of inflation. The domestic inflation rate corresponds to the domestic money supply growth rate less the growth rate of money demand, which equals the income elasticity of demand for money times the growth rate of the economy. Assume that in the long run the condition of neutrality of money holds, such that real income is determined in the real sector by the factors of production: labour, capital and technology. This means that inflation is a policy variable, as it is determined by the money supply growth rate. The money supply growth rate is a policy variable under a flexible exchange rate system. The money growth–inflation relationship holds, provided that the money demand function remains a stable function of real income and the interest rate. Given that money supply does not affect output growth, an increase in money growth by 1 per cent is expected to increase inflation by 1 per cent (given the

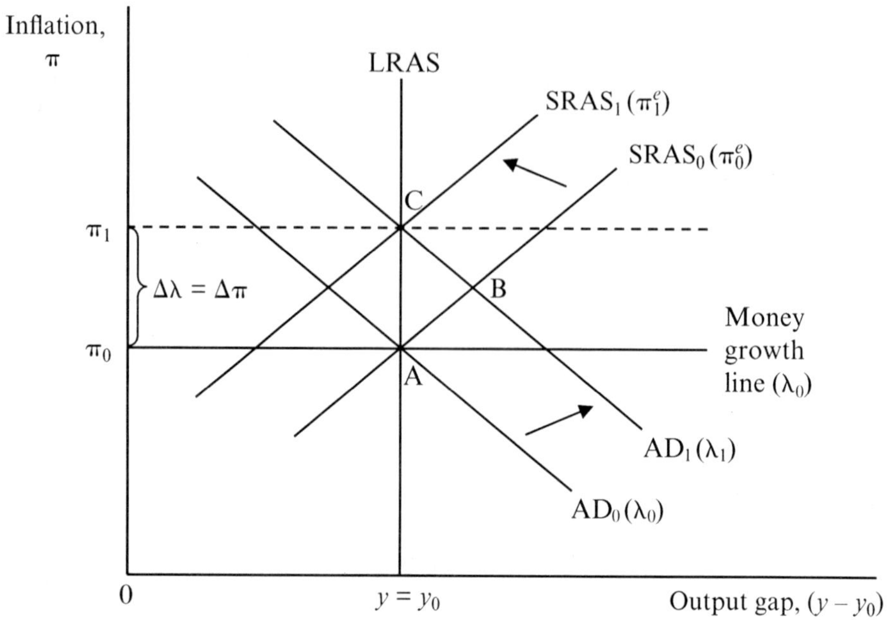

Notes:
1. $\Delta\lambda$ = increase in the money growth rate.
2. $\Delta\pi$ = increase in the rate of inflation.

Source: Adapted from Burda and Wyplosz (2005: 316–17).

Figure 4.3 Adjustment of inflation to money supply growth

zero growth rate of money demand). If the growth rate of money demand is positive, inflation would be less than the money supply growth rate.

Figure 4.3 shows that in the long run real output (y) is at its trend level, implying a zero output gap (LRAS line) and the money growth rate determines the inflation rate. Starting at point A, where the inflation rate ($\pi_0 = \pi^e = \lambda_0$), a monetary expansion from the growth rate λ_0 to λ_1 shifts the AD_0 line rightwards to AD_1. This moves the economy to its short-run equilibrium position at point B. However in the long run the economy settles at point C, with y equal to its trend level. By then, the inflation rate increases at the money growth rate. Thus in the long run the superneutrality of money proposition holds; that is, a rise in the money growth rate causes a proportionate increase in the inflation rate.

Inflation and the domestic interest rate

Consider the following simplified Fisher equation for the domestic nominal interest rate:

$$i^d = r^d + \pi^e \tag{4.13}$$

where, as defined earlier, i^d is the domestic nominal interest rate, r^d is the domestic real interest rate, which is determined in the real sector of the economy (that is, through the interaction of saving and investment functions), and π^e is expected inflation. According to the classical model of inflation, expected inflation (π^e) is equal to expected money supply growth (λ^e) minus the income elasticity of demand for money (η_y) times the expected growth of real economy (g_y^e). This shows that the nominal interest rate is determined by factors such as the money supply growth rate, which is within the control of the monetary authority, and the growth rate of the economy, which is exogenous insofar as the monetary authorities are concerned. Through control over the money growth rate (and inflation), the monetary authorities gain control over the domestic interest rate. Given that a change in the money supply growth rate does not change the real interest rate, it changes the nominal interest rate, such that:

$$\Delta i_t = \Delta \pi_t^e = \Delta \lambda_t \tag{4.14}$$

where t is a time subscript.

The nominal and real exchange rates

The real exchange rate, '*rer*', is defined as the ratio of foreign to domestic prices, expressed in the same currency: $rer = NER \cdot P^f/P^d$. Its rate of change is the sum of the rate of nominal depreciation of domestic currency plus the differential between the foreign and domestic inflation rates:

$$\Delta rer/rer = \Delta NER/NER + (\Delta P^f/P^f - \Delta P^d/P^d) \tag{4.15}$$

Note that in the long run, the real exchange rate is determined by real factors, such as the relative factor productivity, the terms of trade, technological progress and external asset position. If these factors remain unchanged, the equilibrium real exchange rate would remain constant, even though the actual real exchange rate may depart temporarily from its equilibrium level.

Equation (4.15) shows that the real exchange rate would not change if the nominal exchange rate depreciates at the rate σ ($=\Delta NER/NER$), which equals the difference between the domestic ($\pi^d=\Delta P^d/P^d$) and foreign ($\pi^f=\Delta P^f/P^f$) inflation rates:

$$\sigma = \pi^d - \pi^f \tag{4.16}$$

This shows that the real exchange rate may remain unchanged when a country, which has a higher rate of inflation than that of the foreign country, has a depreciating currency. Similarly, a real exchange rate may remain unchanged when a relatively low-inflationary country has an appreciating currency. Equation (4.16) represents the principle of the relative purchasing power parity (PPP) proposition.

The PPP and the long-run money growth–inflation relations suggest that the rate of exchange rate depreciation in the long run equals the gaps in money supply growth and money demand growth at home and abroad:

$$\sigma = (\lambda^d - \lambda^f) - (\eta_y^d g_y^d - \eta_y^f g_y^f) \tag{4.17}$$

A faster growth rate of the money supply at home (λ^d) than abroad (λ^f) leads in the long run to a depreciation of domestic currency *ceteris paribus*. In contrast, *ceteris paribus* a faster growth rate of output at home (g_y^d) than abroad (g_y^f) leads to an appreciation of domestic currency.

To conclude, this section has established some basic propositions in monetary policy. Under a fixed exchange rate system, the exchange rate acts as a nominal anchor and the domestic price level is linked to the foreign price level via the purchasing power parity condition. When the monetary authorities have a credible fixed or pegged exchange rate system, domestic inflation converges to foreign inflation. This happens when the economy is small and does not have a large non-tradable goods sector. Under a flexible exchange rate system, the monetary authorities gain control over the money supply and can determine the rate of domestic inflation. Whether the exchange rate will appreciate or depreciate depends on the inflation rate at home vis-à-vis the rest of the world. When domestic inflation is higher than foreign inflation, the domestic currency would depreciate and the opposite would happen when the domestic inflation is lower than foreign inflation.

Thus, under a floating exchange rate system, there is no exchange rate policy, as it loses its identity and becomes synonymous with monetary policy. In the long run the real interest rate parity condition holds and the inflation differential becomes equivalent to the nominal interest rate differential. In fact, the purchasing power parity condition underwrites the basic principles of monetary policy. This is the logical foundation of the view that monetary policy has a comparative advantage in achieving and maintaining price stability under a floating exchange rate system. Once the money supply determines the price level, other nominal prices adjust to the price level equi-proportionately and the relative prices remain unchanged. This is the essence of the dichotomy between the monetary and real economy. This explains why there is controversy over the use of monetary policy to tame business cycles, or to promote economic growth (Barro, 2008; Friedman, 1991). This issue is discussed next in a historical context.

MONETARY POLICY FOR STABILISATION AND GROWTH

Since the publication of Keynes's (1936) *General Theory of Employment, Interest and Money*, macroeconomists have become divided into two broad groups: those who favour active policy intervention (dubbed as Keynesians or post-Keynesians) to stabilise the economy, and those who oppose such intervention, except perhaps during exceptional circumstances (known as monetarists and new-classical economists). The idea of economic stabilisation[3] is indeed the heart of Keynesian economics. As indicated earlier, the Keynesian theory of aggregate demand provided an explanation for the Great Depression of the 1930s and suggested policy measures that could be used to prevent future depression. The basic Keynesian argument is that the Great Depression was the result of drying up of investment opportunities and an autonomous downward shift in investment and consumption spending. An implication is that the government could have undertaken an expansionary fiscal policy to avoid the onslaught of Depression. The Keynesian explanation of the Depression was widely accepted throughout the 1950s and 1960s. To many, it has become an orthodoxy that countercyclical fiscal policy can smooth out economic fluctuations in an inherently unstable capitalist economy, which is prone to recession spontaneously as a result of self-fulfilling prophecy (Dornbusch et al., 2008).

Fiscal activism has thus become an integral part of Keynesian economics. Although Keynes discounted the impact of monetary expansion on aggregate demand during a recession, its potential was nevertheless recognised. If there were no liquidity trap and/or investment pessimism,[4] an expansionary monetary policy can achieve full employment much quicker than waiting for the market forces to lower unemployment. The reason is that market forces rely on the adjustment of wages and prices, which could be rigid downwards and painfully slow. The slow adjustment of the economy because of wage and price rigidities provides a rationale for fiscal and/or monetary activism.

Much has changed since the heyday of the Keynesian economics of the 1950s and 1960s. Since the early 1960s, Friedman and Schwartz (1963a), Friedman (1968a) and others[5] have rehabilitated the classical/monetarist income determination model in which the money supply determines the level of nominal income.[6] As indicated earlier, Friedman and Schwartz (1963a) argued that in the USA, the Depression of the 1930s was the result of contractionary monetary policy, rather than caused by an autonomous downward shift in private spending. In Friedman and Schwartz's view, the 1930s Depression, far from proving that money did not matter, was 'in fact a tragic testimonial to the importance of monetary forces' (Friedman and Schwartz, 1963a: 300). The failure of the US Federal Reserve System to prevent bank failures, and the subsequent decline of the money stock from the end of 1930 to 1933, was responsible for deep recession. Such a monetary reinterpretation of the Great Depression rehabilitated the importance of monetary forces in economic activity.

The debate on the appropriate role of monetary policy still continues, almost a century later. The Keynesians assign it a demand management role in the same way they assign a stabilising role for fiscal policy (Modigliani, 1977). Monetarists are not impressed with such a role for monetary policy because they do not see the need for activist policies to achieve stabilisation (Cagan, 1992b). Even if a case for activist policies for stabilisation can be made, monetarists argue that monetary policy is not capable of playing such a role. The main role of monetary policy, according to Friedman (1968a), is to create a stable macroeconomic environment where real forces can operate rather than monetary policy itself becoming a source of economic disturbance.[7] Friedman elaborated his view in a later publication on the conduct of monetary policy in a historical context (Friedman, 1991).

The question of stabilisation traditionally has not received much attention in developing countries. It is argued that in developed countries, instability in output or employment originates primarily from the demand side, whereas such instability in developing countries originates mostly from the supply side (Cline and Weintraub, 1981; Hossain, 1989). Neither fiscal nor monetary policy is effective in smoothing out fluctuations in output arising from the supply shocks (Barro, 1981; Lucas and Sargent, 1981). The need for and the scope of stabilisation in both the demand and supply sides in developing countries are reviewed next.

Demand Shocks and Stabilisation

There are two pertinent questions about economic stabilisation in developing countries. First, how prevalent are demand shocks to developing economies? Second, how sensitive are developing economies to demand shocks? The Keynesians believe that demand shocks are rampant and tend to persist, while the monetarists suggest that demand shocks are infrequent and not persistent (Gordon, 1993).

Demand disturbances in a market economy can originate from a number of sources, including private expenditure demand shocks (such as a shift in private consumption or investment spending) and sharp changes in both budget deficits and net exports. In the early literature, the debate on private sector instability centred on the question of how unstable is consumption in developing countries? The Keynesian consumption function states that the level of consumption expenditure depends on current disposable income and on an autonomous component independent of this income. This implies that any shift in autonomous consumption component, due to changes in consumer confidence or optimism, may create instability in consumption expenditure. The Keynesian consumption function was later found theoretically inadequate and inconsistent with actual observations. It was superseded by Friedman's (1957) permanent income hypothesis and by Modigliani's life cycle hypothesis (Ando and Modigliani, 1963; Modigliani and Brumberg, 1954). Friedman's permanent income hypothesis suggests that consumption expenditure depends on permanent income. Modigliani's life cycle hypothesis goes one step further and suggests that consumers tend to stabilise consumption expenditures over their lifetimes. These forward-looking consumption theories imply that consumption expenditure is stable. In fact a consensus has emerged that consumption expenditure on non-durable goods and services is stable, although spending on durable goods could be pro-cyclical. Therefore, any outburst of spending on durable goods can be a source of instability in the private economy (Abel, 1990).

How unstable is consumption expenditure in developing countries? It depends on two main factors: first, whether current or permanent income is the determinant of consumption expenditure and, second, the share of durable goods in total consumption expenditure. Gersovitz (1988: 389) has reviewed the literature on consumption behaviour in developing countries. He concludes: 'the general sense of the literature on developing countries is that a permanent, or lifetime, notion of income . . . is an appropriate determinant of consumption, rather than current income'.

Nevertheless, current income has a role in consumption expenditure in developing countries. The high incidence of poverty is one reason why current income is linked with consumption expenditure. Such a link becomes stronger when underdeveloped credit markets create liquidity constraints for different categories of consumers. Liquidity constraints raise the short-run marginal propensity to consume from what is implied by the permanent income life cycle hypothesis. Consumption expenditure on durable goods is pro-cyclical in developing countries. However, the share of consumption expenditure on durable goods (monetised component) appears low in these countries. Most poor people simply cannot afford to buy many durable consumer goods. In addition, rural households produce various durable goods for their use, rather than purchase them from markets (Campbell and Mankiw, 1987; 1991; Flavin, 1981; Gersovitz, 1988; Hall and Mishkin, 1982; Morduch, 1995; Townsend, 1995).

Investment is the second component of private expenditure. Unlike consumption expenditure, investment expenditure is relatively unstable. Keynesians suggest that investment spending is autonomous, although it depends on business confidence or optimism. In contrast, monetarists suggest that private investment expenditure is stable as consumption expenditure. It can be expressed as a function of the costs of borrowing, measured by the real loan rate of interest, output and any factors relating to investment financing, especially credit rationing, which is reflected in monetary and fiscal policy (Dornbusch et al., 2008).

There is lack of consensus on factors that determine private investment in developing countries. The debate is whether the real loan rate of interest has any impact on private investment in developing countries, as the neoclassical theory suggests. Some empirical studies, such as Blejer and Khan (1984), Greene and Villanueva (1991), Khan and Reinhart (1990), Sundararajan and Thakur (1980) and Tun Wai and Wong (1982), suggest that the real interest rate, the inflation rate and economic growth are the primary determinants of private investment in developing countries. Therefore, the argument that private investment is autonomous or dependent on non-economic factors does not appear valid for developing economies. This does not necessarily imply that the investment function is highly stable. The question is whether any variation in the private investment rate can generate instability in the private economy. As the share of investment in private expenditure is small in most developing economies, a small change in the private investment rate is unlikely to create instability in the private economy. Moreover, even if private investment is relatively unstable, when consumption expenditure and investment expenditure are aggregated the resulting private expenditure function may remain stable (Hossain, 1995).

Although the early literature on demand shocks emphasised fluctuations of private consumption and investment spending arising from domestic sources, the focus has shifted towards the international sources of instability. In an open economy with a large external sector, autonomous changes in net exports can become a source of demand instability. As most developing economies are linked with industrialised economies, demand shocks to industrialised economies can affect the incomes and expenditures of developing economies. For example, the sharp rise in interest rates in industrialised countries was one of the factors that caused a debt crisis in many developing countries during the early 1980s. The resultant payment difficulties were responsible for recessions in debt-ridden countries (Sachs and Larrain, 1993). Sharp changes in the terms of trade are also considered another external source of demand disturbance for developing economies. Most of the developing countries, being net importers of oil, faced serious terms of trade shocks in the 1970s following two sharp oil price rises (Hossain and Chowdhury, 1998; Krugman and Obstfeld, 2009).

In sum, the possibility of demand shocks arising from domestic sources is not high for developing countries. This is because consumption is relatively stable and has larger weight in aggregate expenditure than relatively unstable private investment. Developing countries are relatively more prone to demand shocks from external sources. How frequent and severe are demand shocks, be they internal or external, remains an empirical issue.

Sensitivity of the Economy to Demand Shocks

How sensitive an economy is to demand shocks depends on the parameter values of key macroeconomic relations, such as the marginal propensity to consume, the interest elasticity of demand for money, and the interest sensitivity of investment spending. The higher the value of the marginal propensity to consume, the larger is economic instability after a demand shock due to the multiplier process. The lower the interest sensitivity of investment spending, the lower is the offsetting change in investment from changes in the interest rate arising from the initial shock, and therefore the greater is instability. The higher the interest elasticity of demand for money, the higher is the change in excess money supply from changes in the interest rate, and therefore the greater is instability (Aghevli et al., 1979). Therefore, the sensitivity of a developing economy to demand shocks can be determined by estimating the parameter values of the consumption, investment and money demand functions.

There are a growing number of studies on consumption, investment and money demand functions for developing countries. The findings can be used to determine the sensitivity of developing economies to demand shocks.

The main parameter of interest in economic stabilisation is the marginal propensity to consume. As suggested earlier, for reasons of absolute poverty and liquidity constraints, the marginal propensity to consume is believed to be close to unity in developing countries (Gersovitz, 1988). Empirical studies, however, do not confirm this view, although the marginal propensity to consume in developing countries is found to be somewhat higher than that in developed countries. Kandil (1991), for example, has found that the mean value of the marginal propensities to consume for 21 developing countries is 0.60 with a minimum value of 0.32, a maximum value of 0.79 and a standard deviation of 0.11. On the other hand, the mean value of the marginal propensities to consume for 18 developed countries has been found to be 0.56 with a minimum value of 0.43, a maximum value of 0.67 and a standard deviation of 0.06.

Another parameter of importance for the conduct of monetary policy is the interest elasticity of demand for money. Empirical studies suggest that the interest elasticity of the demand for money is low in most developing countries. In a survey study, Sriram (2000) reports estimates of the interest elasticities of demand for money for eight Asian developing countries (China, India, Indonesia, South Korea, Malaysia, Pakistan, Singapore and Thailand), which, except in one study for Indonesia, are significantly lower than 1. In an earlier study, Kandil (1991) found that the mean value of the interest elasticity of demand for money for selected developing countries is −0.58, compared with −0.66 for selected developed countries. She has also estimated the slopes of the LM curve for selected developed and developing countries and the slope of the LM curve for developing countries has been found steeper. Kandil's (1991) study also shows that investment spending in developing countries is sensitive to the interest rate. In fact, she illustrates 'a higher sensitivity of investment demand to changes in the interest rate in developing countries, compared to most developed countries' (Kandil, 1991: 271).

In sum, although a larger marginal propensity to consume indicates that developing countries are sensitive to demand shocks, the parameter values of the investment and money demand functions suggest otherwise. Overall, developing economies do not seem to be highly sensitive to demand shocks. The impact of demand shocks on economic fluctuations is therefore unlikely to be large. Meanwhile, whether or not the impact of demand shocks would persist, requiring policy interventions depends on the flexibility of key relative prices such as the real wage rates, real interest rates and real exchange rates. This issue is reviewed next.

Flexibility in Wage, Interest and Exchange Rates

The Latin American structuralist literature suggests that there are structural rigidities in the product and factor markets, which make wages and prices unresponsive to market conditions (Corbo, 1974; Taylor, 1979; 1983; 1988). As in the Keynesian model, the structural rigidities of wages and prices prevent the product and factor markets from clearing after demand and supply shocks. Yet most empirical studies do not support the assertion that the wages and prices in developing economies are rigid. They find that agricultural wages, and prices in particular, are flexible in these countries. The idea that agricultural real wages in developing countries are flexible contrasts with the implication of the traditional subsistence and nutrition-based efficiency wage theories which suggest that agricultural real wages are stable at subsistence or at an efficiency level. A number of empirical studies from developing countries, such as Bangladesh, Egypt and India, provide evidence that agricultural real wages show substantial variations and fluctuate during the peak and slack seasons. Market forces play a role in agricultural real wage determination in developing countries (Ahmed, 1981; Bardhan, K., 1977; Bardhan, P., 1979a; 1979b; Hansen, 1969; Hossain, 1990; 2008; Lal, 1984; Rosenzweig, 1988; Squire, 1981). However, unlike agricultural wages, there are downward nominal wage rigidities in the manufacturing and public service sectors in developing countries. Organised unions, minimum wage laws, and the difficulties in hiring and firing of public sector workers create wage rigidities (Amin, 1981). There are no wage rigidities, however, in the informal private manufacturing and services sectors, as wages are determined by the market forces (Hossain, 1989).

Tables 4.2 and 4.3 show that more than 50 per cent of the labour force in some low-income developing countries is employed in agriculture, with the share of agricultural output at more than 30 per cent of GDP. Thus the agricultural sector bears the burden of adjustment in these economies to both demand and supply shocks. The relatively more flexible real wages help to better adjust these economies to both demand and supply shocks (Hossain and Chowdhury, 1996).

In addition to flexibility of wages, the flexibilities of real interest and exchange rates are important in the adjustment of an economy towards equilibrium after demand shocks. The nominal interest rates in some developing countries are still institutionally determined and are not adjusted fully in response to money market conditions. Nevertheless, real interest rates are flexible because of the flexibility of prices.

Data for real interest rates (not reported) in selected countries in the Asia-Pacific are found to be highly flexible and volatile. Over the past few decades, the real interest rates have changed in most countries from largely negative to positive. This reflects inflation volatility in these countries, which was very high throughout the 1970s and 1980s.

In an open economy aggregate demand depends on the real effective exchange rate. A depreciation of the real exchange rate improves the competitiveness of exportable goods and induces a switch in domestic spending towards domestically produced goods. Although most developing countries follow a pegged or managed floating exchange rate system, the real exchange rates of their currencies fluctuate, sometimes sharply. This follows the principle that in the long run the real exchange rate is independent of the exchange rate regime (Sorensen and Whitta-Jacobsen, 2005).

Data for real effective exchange rates (not reported) in some Asian developing countries

Table 4.2 Distribution of employment (%) by economic activity in selected countries of the Asia-Pacific, 1960–2006

Country/region	1960			1980			1990			Latest year			Year
	Agriculture	Industry	Services	Agriculture	Industry	Services	Agriculture	Industry	Services	Agriculture	Industry	Services	
Australia	11	40	49	6	34	60	6	32	62	4.1	na	na	2004
Bangladesh	87	3	10	73	9	18	64	15	21	52	10	38	2003
Bhutan	95	2	3	93	2	5	na	na	na	na	na	na	na
Cambodia	na	na	na	na	na	na	81	2	17	60	10	30	2006
China	75	15	10	74	14	12	60	13	27	49	12	39	2003
Fiji	na	na	na	na	na	na	3	33	64	1	34	65	1999
Hong Kong, China	8	40	52	1	50	49	1	27	72	0	6	94	2006
India	74	11	15	70	13	17	62	15	23	56	19	25	2005
Indonesia	75	8	17	58	12	30	56	11	33	44	13	42	2006
Japan	33	30	37	6	39	55	7	34	59	na	na	na	na
Korea, South	66	9	25	37	27	36	18	27	55	8	18	74	2006
Lao PDR	83	4	13	80	6	14	na	na	na	82	9	9	2003
Malaysia	63	12	25	41	19	40	26	20	54	15	21	64	2006
Maldives	na	na	na	na	na	na	5	16	79	4	17	79	2006
Mongolia	70	13	17	40	21	39	33	17	50	39	12	49	2006
Myanmar	68	11	21	76	8	16	66	8	26	63	9	28	1997
Nepal	95	2	3	93	2	5	na	na	na	76	6	18	1999
Pakistan	61	18	21	60	15	25	51	13	36	43	14	43	2006
Papua New Guinea	89	4	7	82	6	12	na	na	na	72	5	23	2000
Philippines	61	15	24	52	15	33	45	11	44	36	10	54	2006
Singapore	8	23	69	2	42	56	0	26	74	0	17	83	2006
Sri Lanka	56	14	30	52	18	30	47	15	38	32	19	49	2006
Taiwan, China	56	11	33	37	26	37	13	32	55	5	28	67	2006
Thailand	84	4	12	71	10	19	63	10	27	40	15	45	2006
Vietnam	81	5	14	73	13	14	72	9	19	52	13	35	2006

Note: na = not available.

Sources: Author's compilation based on World Bank, *World Development Report* (various years), and ADB, *Key Indicators of Developing Asian and Pacific Countries* (various years).

Table 4.3 Sectoral distribution of output (%) in selected countries of the Asia-Pacific, 1970–2006

Country/region	Agriculture					Industry (all)					Manufacturing only			Services				
	1970	1980	1990	2000	2006	1970	1980	1990	2000	2006	1990	2000	2006	1970	1980	1990	2000	2006
Bangladesh	na	42	29.4	24.6	18.7	na	15.3	20.9	24.4	27	12.7	14.7	16.5	na	42.4	49.7	51	54.3
Bhutan	na	na	42	27.7	22.4	na	na	24.6	34.3	35.9	8	8.3	7.3	na	na	31.8	36.3	37.2
Cambodia	na	na	55.6	35.9	30.1	na	na	11.2	21.8	26.2	5.2	16.9	19.6	na	na	33.2	37.1	38.6
China	41.2	32	26.9	14.8	11.8	35.9	48	41.3	45.9	48.7	36.7	40.4	43.1	22.9	20	31.8	39.3	39.5
Fiji	26.8	22.5	22.2	17	14.3	19.8	21.7	24.1	22.3	21.9	11.3	12.2	11.1	53.4	55.8	60.4	64	68.1
Hong Kong, China	2.2	0.9	0.2	0.1	0.1	36.5	32	23.4	12.7	9.2	16.1	5.1	3.3	61.4	67.2	72.4	82.7	90.7
India	44.5	38	29.3	23.4	17.5	24	25.9	26.9	26.2	27.9	16.7	15.6	16.3	31.5	36.1	43.8	50.5	54.6
Indonesia	46	23.3	19.4	15.6	12.9	20.9	41.6	39.1	45.9	47	20.7	27.7	28	33.1	35.1	41.5	38.5	40.1
South Korea	28	14.2	8	4.3	2.9	22.4	37.8	37.3	36.2	35.2	24.5	26.1	24.7	49.6	48.1	54.6	59.5	61.9
Lao PDR	na	na	61.2	52.6	44.8	na	na	14.5	22.9	29.5	10	17	20.7	na	na	24.3	24.6	25.7
Malaysia	32	22.9	15.2	8.6	8.7	24.7	35.8	42.2	48.3	49.9	24.2	30.9	29.8	43.3	41.3	44.2	46.3	43.5
Maldives	na	na	14.9	8.8	8.4	na	na	12.8	15	16.7	9.2	8	6.8	na	na	72.3	80.1	78.8
Mongolia	na	na	15.2	29.1	18.8	na	na	40.6	21.9	40.4	35.2	6.1	5.8	na	na	44.2	49	40.8
Myanmar	38.3	37.2	57.3	57.2	48.4	14.7	15.2	10.5	9.7	16.2	7.8	7.2	11.6	47	47.6	32.2	33.1	35.4
Nepal	67.5	61.8	50.6	39.6	38.2	11.4	11.9	15.9	21.5	20.3	6	9.2	7.5	21	26.3	33.5	38.9	41.5
Pakistan	38.9	30.6	26	25.9	19.4	22.7	25.6	25.2	23.3	27.2	17.4	14.7	19.5	38.4	43.8	48.8	50.7	53.4
Philippines	28.8	25.6	21.9	15.8	14.2	29.4	36.1	34.5	32.3	31.6	24.8	22.2	22.9	41.8	38.3	43.6	52	54.2
Papua New Guinea	na	na	29	31.7	34.6	na	na	30.4	39.1	45.6	9	9.9	5.9	na	na	40.6	29.1	19.9
Singapore	2.3	1.1	0.4	0.1	0.1	29.8	38.8	32.5	33.5	33	25.7	26.2	27.7	67.9	60	67.2	66.4	66.9
Sri Lanka	31.8	26.5	22.9	19.9	16.5	16	27.4	27.3	27.3	27.1	17.3	15.1	12.2	52.2	46.1	49.8	52.8	56.5
Taiwan, China	16.9	7.9	4	2	1.6	35.5	46	38.4	29.1	25	31.2	23.8	21.4	47.7	46.1	57.6	68.9	73.4
Thailand	30.2	20.6	12.5	9	10.7	25.7	30.8	37.2	42	44.6	27.2	33.6	35.1	44.1	48.6	50.3	49	44.7
Vietnam	na	na	38.7	24.5	20.4	na	na	22.7	36.7	41.6	12.3	18.6	21.3	na	na	38.6	38.7	38.1

Note: na = not available.

Sources: Author's compilation based on ADB, *Key Indicators of Developing Asian and Pacific Countries* (various years), and ADB, *Asian Development Outlook* (various years).

are highly flexible; a smooth trend of depreciation has been exhibited for some countries since the 1970s. It is not possible to determine whether such movements of real exchange rates reflected changes in fundamental determinants of real exchange rates. However, the fact that most developing countries of the Asia-Pacific region have avoided major current account problems over the past two decades indicates that policy-makers in these countries have managed real exchange rates in such a way that there were no sustained exchange rate misalignments.

In sum, the developing countries appear less prone to demand shocks and these shocks are unlikely to be large. Furthermore, given the flexibility of real wages, real interests and real exchange rates, demand shocks to these economies adjust through price mechanisms so that there is not much need for stabilisation through government interventions. In the recent past, some developed countries of Asia such as Singapore, South Korea and Japan have used labour market intervention measures to cope with external shocks (Bercuson, 1995; Bhattacharya and Pangestu, 1993).

Supply Shocks and Inflation: The Role of Monetary Policy

Although demand shocks are not so prevalent in developing countries, they frequently experience supply shocks originating primarily from the agriculture sector which features droughts, floods and cyclones. Because agriculture is the dominant sector, supply shocks in this sector have macroeconomic consequences. Supply shocks are not, however, restricted to the agricultural sector. They also originate from the external sector. As noted earlier, the OPEC oil shocks to non-oil developing economies in the 1970s were regarded as a supply shock because higher import prices reduced the marginal product (in terms of external output) of domestic resources. To the extent oil was used as a raw material, the rise in oil price shifted the production function inward (Hossain and Chowdhury, 1998).

Given the nature of agricultural production, supply shocks are frequent but random. When agricultural supply shocks are negative, they lower output and employment and raise agricultural prices, especially for food. In developing countries, food prices are politically sensitive because of their dominance in the cost of living index, particularly for urban people. Hence the question of whether the monetary authority should adopt a hands-on or a hands-off policy after a supply shock has wide-ranging economic and political significance.

In the early studies, crop failures were considered a major cause of inflation in developing countries. The idea is that food crop failure can raise the general price level when non-food prices are rigid downward (Edel, 1969; Wachter, 1983). Yet in the absence of accommodative monetary expansion, such price increases are unlikely to be sustained. Why should the monetary authority increase the money supply in such a situation when there is danger of sustained inflation? This question was addressed in an early paper by Porter (1961). He argued for monetary expansion after an agricultural supply shock, in order to lessen the danger of inflation. In a developing country, any increased price level after a crop failure would remain at a high level, regardless of whether the monetary authority increases the money supply. Porter (1961) advocates an expansion of the money supply; otherwise, farmers may hoard foodgrains to balance the desired and actual levels of wealth-holding because disequilibrium in their wealth position is created after the price increase. Such an action by farmers may increase the price level further because of the decline in food supply in open markets.

Porter's arguments are weakened if the normal level of food supply in the market can be maintained from both domestic official stocks and imports. In that case, there may not be any significant increase in food prices after a food crop failure. Even if there is an increase in the price level after the crop failure, it is unlikely to generate a self-sustaining inflationary process without the support of expansionary economic policies. The adoption of such policies remains at the discretion of monetary and fiscal authorities. The question of whether farmers would hoard foodgrain after the food crop failure depends on the expected price of food. It is likely that any expansionary monetary and fiscal policies may increase expected inflation, which, contrary to Porter's view, may induce farmers to hoard more foodgrains rather than less.

The contemporary literature on monetary policy suggests that in the event of supply shocks, the monetary authorities should consider reducing rather than expanding the money supply, so that the inflationary expectations are not built into the system. Such a policy may not appear sound but could be effective in stabilising prices quickly once the supply shocks are over (Sorensen and Whitta-Jacobsen, 2005). Chapter 5 examines this issue in detail.

FINANCIAL DEREGULATION AND MONETARY POLICY FOR PRICE STABILITY

Whatever consensus might have existed in the 1950s and 1960s on the role of 'financial repression'[8] in economic growth, this has broken down since the early 1970s with the publication of two seminal works by McKinnon (1973) and Shaw (1973). The consequence of both financial repression and import substitution was economic stagnation, even in countries such as India which were thought to have a greater potential for rapid economic growth (Bhagwati, 1992; 1993). The then widely held view that an inward-oriented development strategy would both better protect developing economies from external shocks and reduce their balance-of-payment problems was not validated, even for semi-closed economies. Ironically, those developing economies which were relatively open coped better in managing the external shocks of the 1970s through both increased export earnings and relatively easy external financing (Hossain and Chowdhury, 1998; Krueger, 1993; World Bank, 1993).

The policy implications of different development strategies were apparent. By the early 1980s most developing countries started redesigning their development strategies by shifting emphasis from import substitution to export orientation. The enviable macroeconomic performance of export-oriented North East and Southeast Asian economies since the 1960s, and even throughout the turbulent years of the 1970s, softened the attitude of most developing countries towards export-oriented industrialisation (Bhagwati, 1984; World Bank, 1993). Further impetus to such an industrialisation strategy came from the World Bank and the IMF. Over the years these financial institutions have become too powerful and influential for most non-oil developing countries to ignore. At the intellectual level, the pendulum of ideas started to shift from state activism towards market mechanism as a means for efficient allocation of resources. By the early 1980s the stage was therefore set for resurgence of the neoclassical economics in development studies – a discipline which previously had been shaped and dominated by the Keynesian and structuralist ideas of the 1940s and 1950s (Hirschman, 1981; Lal, 1985; Little, 1982).

The next two decades witnessed the gradual ascendancy of neoclassical economics as the dominant paradigm of development studies. The collapse of the socialist economies of the former Soviet Union and East Europe, coupled with the market-oriented economic reforms in both China and Vietnam, removed whatever obstacles remained on ideological grounds on the way towards market-oriented reforms in developing countries. Even though the currency crises of the 1990s in Indonesia, South Korea, Malaysia, Mexico and Thailand are considered a setback to globalisation of developing economies, they demonstrate that open economies with sound fundamentals have some immunity to both domestic and external shocks (IMF's *World Economic Outlook*, various issues). For example, Hong Kong, Singapore and Taiwan arguably remained relatively unscathed from the contagion of the Asian currency crisis because of their fundamentally sound economic policies, open trade and exchange regimes, continual investment in human capital, and sound legal and institutional framework (Lane and Associates, 1999). This has led to the emerging view that sustained economic growth requires a macroeconomic management framework that operates through market forces, not against them. Working through market forces again requires both policy credibility and consistency; otherwise, market forces would impose 'stiff-low quality' or harsh penalty to economies which suffer from sustained macroeconomic imbalances (Guitián, 1998).

Price Stability as the Sole Objective of Monetary Policy

As indicated earlier, within the presently dominant market-based economic system, there is an emerging consensus that price stability should be the sole or overriding objective of monetary policy. At an analytical level, this reflects the emerging consensus on four basic propositions (Fischer, 1992; Friedman, 1963; 1968a; 1968b; 1969a; Masson, Savastano and Sharma, 1997):

1. monetary expansion has a lasting effect only on the price level, not on output or employment;
2. inflation is costly, both in terms of resource allocation (efficiency costs) and long-term output growth (breakdown of super-neutrality of money);
3. monetary policy has transitory effects on a number of real variables, but there is imperfect understanding of the nature and/or the size of such effects, and
4. monetary policy affects the inflation rate with lags of uncertain duration and with variable strength, which undermines the central bank's ability to control inflation on a period-by-period basis.

Chapter 5 will review each of these propositions in detail. For now, this section defines the concepts and provides an overview of these propositions.

Concept of price stability

In the monetary policy literature, price stability is defined in a loose form. Strictly speaking, price stability implies that the price level remains stable over time. That is, inflation at least over the medium term (if not annually) should be zero. However, as zero inflation is considered non-optimal in the formulation of monetary policy, price stability implies a condition of low and stable inflation. Although low inflation may include zero inflation, in practice it means a positive annual inflation rate within the range of one to three per cent for developed countries. Sorensen and Whitta-Jacobsen (2005: 606–607) provide a rationale for such a low rate of inflation for inflation targeting countries such as Australia, Canada, New Zealand and the UK: 'If policy makers want interest rate policy to be an effective tool of stabilization policy, they may therefore have to accept a positive average rate of inflation to preserve room for substantial interest rate cuts in times of recession.'

It is debatable whether the range should be higher for developing countries, given that the growth-maximising rate of inflation is as high as 7 to 11 per cent for developing countries (Khan and Senhadji, 2001). This shows that there is considerable ambiguity in defining price stability. This issue is elaborated further to highlight statistical problems in defining low inflation as price stability.

Statistically, the definition of price stability implies that the price level is a stationary process or at most, trend-stationary. That is, the price level has a mean and a constant variance, such that the price level is mean-reverting. When the price level is trend-stationary, this implies a base drift in the price level. Although this leads to non-zero inflation, the price level is predictable because it has a mean and a variance. However, when the price level has a stochastic trend or is characterised by a unit root, its variance increases without bound with the forecast horizon. This creates forecasting uncertainty of the price level as the forecast horizon increases. Such series can, however, produce inflation that may be a stationary process with a mean and a constant variance.

Hence, to refer low inflation as price stability is a misnomer. This creates complexity in the implementation of monetary policy under inflation targeting. For example, if the monetary authorities annually target a certain positive rate of inflation, the central bank is not required to compensate for any failure to achieve its target in the previous year. On the other hand, if the target is the price level or a path for the price level, the central bank may have to compensate for any missing of the target in the previous year. Fischer (1996a; 1996b) has illustrated this point neatly in Figure 4.4.

Assume that the monetary authority's target rate of inflation is 2 per cent, but inflation last year was 4 per cent. If the objective of the monetary authority is to maintain price stability, the target of monetary policy this year should be an inflation rate less than 2 per cent – say, for example, 1 per cent – since the central bank has an obligation to return to its target path for prices.

Therefore, the choice between the price level targeting and inflation targeting involves a trade-off between low-frequency price level variability, and high frequency inflation and output variability. Price level targeting has the advantage of reduced long-term variability of the price level. This is beneficial for long-term nominal contracts and inter-temporal decisions. However, this may come at the cost of increased short-term variability of both inflation and output. The intuition is straightforward: in order to stabilise the price level under price-level targeting, higher-than-average inflation must be succeeded by lower-than-average inflation. This results in higher inflation variability than would be the case under inflation targeting, since base drift is accepted in the latter case and higher-than-average inflation needs only be succeeded by average inflation. Given nominal rigidities, higher inflation variability can cause higher output variability (Fischer, 1994). One of

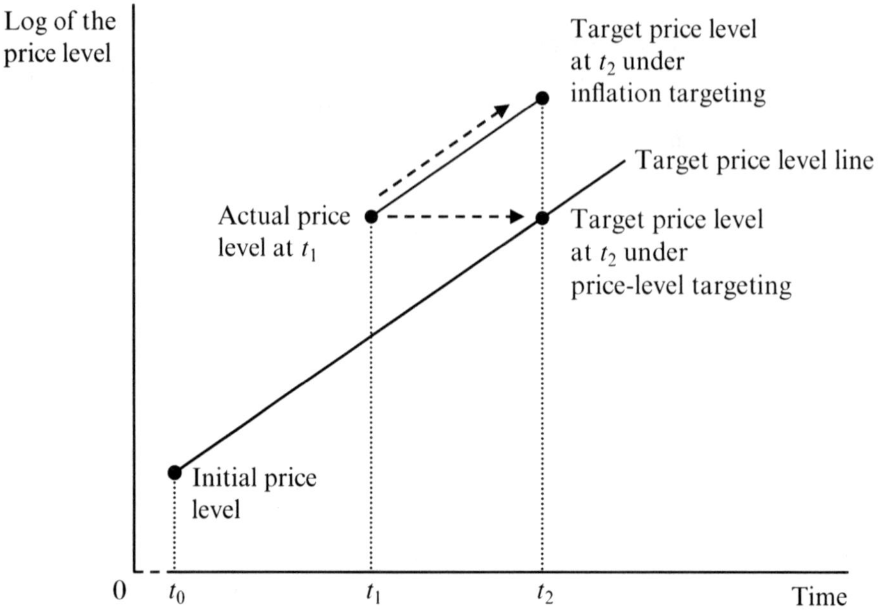

Source: Adapted from Fischer (1996a: 36).

Figure 4.4 Inflation and price-level targeting

the reasons many economists argue for a gold standard is that such a monetary system produces long-term price stability, meaning zero inflation.

Arguments for 'Price Stability' as the Single Objective of Monetary Policy

In the literature, there are both conventional and special arguments for price stability as the single objective of monetary policy. They are overviewed here; Chapter 5 will elaborate on them. In a general context, there are four arguments in favour of price stability as the sole objective of monetary policy. They are based on Tinbergen's principle, Mundell's assignment rule, the Phillips curve relationship, and the rational expectations hypothesis on the effectiveness of monetary policy.

Tinbergen's principle

Tinbergen (1952) developed an approach that shows the crucial steps of optimal policy-making. First, the goals of economic policy need to be specified in the form of a social welfare function that the policy-maker attempts to maximise. On the basis of the social welfare function, the policy-maker identifies economic targets. Second, the policy-maker identifies policy instruments that can be used to achieve policy targets. Third, the policy-maker must have a model of the economy linking instruments to targets so as to choose the optimal value of policy instruments. Tinbergen argues that if the policy-makers have '*n*' targets, they can be achieved provided that they have at least '*n*' linearly independent policy instruments.

Mundell's assignment rule

Mundell (1962) extended Tinbergen's contribution. His main insight is that where the detailed structure of an economy is not known and/or where policy-making is decentralised, the government may be able to proceed, on the strength of only limited information, by assigning a policy instrument to that target for which it has a relative advantage. Given that monetary policy has a relatively stronger effect on inflation than does fiscal policy, monetary policy should be used to target inflation, while fiscal policy is useful for adjusting output fluctuations (Argy, 1992).

Inflation–unemployment trade-off

The famous Phillips curve shows the inverse relationship between inflation and unemployment. This relationship has been used by the Keynesians as an argument for deploying monetary policy to lower unemployment by generating inflation. As this curve suggests a policy trade-off between inflation and unemployment, Keynesians rule out the possibility of a simultaneous rise in inflation and unemployment (stagflation). However, this was found to be an erroneous assumption. The monetarists, led by Friedman (1968a), predicted the end of the Phillips curve as early as 1967. Phelps (1968; 1970), a Keynesian, also predicted instability in the Phillips curve relationship. The stagflation experiences of industrialised countries during the 1970s confirmed that there is no long-run trade-off between inflation and unemployment.[9] In the long run the Phillips curve is vertical. Hence, any attempt to exploit the short-run trade-off between inflation and unemployment may ultimately result in higher inflation without any reduction in unemployment.

Discretionary monetary policy and business cycles

Although the mainstream monetarists acknowledge the presence of a short-run trade-off between inflation and unemployment, the new classical economists have established the view that under rational expectations there may not exist even a short-run trade-off between inflation and unemployment. In their macroeconomic models, they assume that expectations are rational and the wages and prices are flexible with respect to the expected price level. This leads to the policy-ineffectiveness proposition that anticipated monetary policy has no effect on output or employment: only unanticipated monetary policy matters (Barro, 1976; 1977; Lucas, 1972; Lucas and Sargent, 1981). Therefore, unlike the Keynesians, the neoclassical economists do not consider that monetary policy is effective to smooth business cycles. Moreover, to achieve price stability, credibility in monetary policy is crucial and this requires a rule-based monetary policy that avoids policy 'surprises' and uncertainties. The real business cycle theorists go one step further and explain business cycles as the equilibrium outcomes in response to a variety of real shocks, such as the technology shocks, that hit the economy perhaps every decade or so, while markets adjust rapidly and remain in equilibrium (Kydland and Prescott, 1982; 1990).

Besides the above general arguments that had their origins in the context of developed economies, there are a number of other reasons specific to developing countries that led to the view that price stability should be the sole objective of monetary policy.

Macroeconomic populism and economic crises

The concept of macroeconomic populism was developed by Dornbusch and Edwards (1990; 1991) in the context of Latin America. It is defined as 'a policy perspective on economic management that emphasizes economic growth and income redistribution and deemphasizes the risks of inflation and deficit finance, external constraints and the reaction of economic agents to aggressive non-market policies' (Dornbusch and Edwards, 1990: 247). Lately, the term is used in a broad sense to emphasise the economic and political costs of expansionary macroeconomic policies. The Latin American experience shows that populist macroeconomic policies ultimately fail, and when they do fail, it is at the cost to the groups of people who are supposed to be favoured in the first place. Therefore, it is suggested that when monetary policy is used to achieve price stability (and the central bank is given the responsibility to achieve price stability), there is less pressure from the government to undertake an expansionary monetary policy. This may improve macroeconomic policy-making in general, and the credibility and effectiveness of monetary policy in particular.

High inflation and poverty

Price stability is important for sustained economic growth and thereby the reduction of poverty. Most empirical studies suggest that inflation increases both poverty and income inequality. The poor do not have easy access to financial instruments that can be used as inflation hedges. Moreover, the poor are more likely to rely on fixed incomes, such as pensions, subsidies and transfers that are at best, only partially indexed to inflation (Easterly and Fischer, 2001; Fischer, 1984; Lucas, 2000). In a labour surplus economy, the nominal wages do not always adjust quickly to inflation. Real wages therefore decline sharply with inflation. The consensus view is that inflation hurts the poor more than it hurts the rich. In the long run, if inflation remains high and affects investment, it would cause economic stagnation and thereby hurt the poor most (Ball, 1992; Romer and Romer, 1998). One of the famous propositions of Friedman (1991) is that high inflation, if sustained for a long time, may lead to high unemployment, implying that in a high inflationary country the short-run Phillips curve could be positively sloped. High unemployment is certainly bad for the poor. High inflation could also be politically costly (Friedman, 1991). Therefore, from a social, economic and political point of view, a low and stable inflation is desirable (Easterly and Fischer, 2001; Ghosh and Phillips, 1998; IMF, 2001).

Implementation of monetary policy

There are a number of advantages from implementation of a monetary policy strategy that is designed to achieve price stability rather than multiple (often conflicting) objectives. The arguments are that a single objective monetary policy strengthens the implementation of monetary policy, makes monetary policy transparent and credible, allows the central bank to be independent, yet still accountable, and minimises policy inconsistencies. Since low inflation usually leads to stable inflation, there is significant gain in social welfare when price stability dominates the central bank's objective function (Sorensen and Whitta-Jacobsen, 2005).

PRINCIPLES FOR CENTRAL BANKING AND MONETARY POLICY

Having reviewed the key features of central banking and some aspects of monetary policy, this section synthesises the basic principles and guidelines for central banking and monetary policy in developing countries. Subsequent chapters build on these general ideas to provide a detailed blueprint for monetary policy in developing countries. The key message is that central banks that operate under the following principles and guidelines are likely to achieve and maintain low and steady inflation, which would create an environment for sustained economic growth and avoid creating macroeconomic or financial crises.

Central Bank Autonomy and Accountability of Policy-Makers

There is growing evidence that central bank independence (preferably autonomy) is necessary for achieving and maintaining price stability (Alesina and Summers, 1993). Independence does not mean goal independence; it implies instrument independence (Fischer, 1994). A country can have monetary policy independence (meaning choosing its own inflation or the interest rate) when it operates under a floating exchange rate system. While the conduct of independent monetary policy for price stability requires institutional autonomy of the central bank, monetary policy-makers should remain accountable to the public for their policy actions. In a democratic system, policy-makers should be accountable to the people's representatives at the Parliament and, therefore, they can be removed from their positions of trust if found incompetent or grossly negligent in discharging their duties. Accountability of policy-makers is vital because this results in efficiency in policy-making. When policy-makers are subject to 'punishment', competent policy-makers would replace those who are incompetent, this creates incentives for policy-makers to do their jobs well.

Price Stability as the Sole or Overriding Objective of Monetary Policy

As noted above, a developing country can reap a number of benefits by maintaining price stability. High inflation is costly in economic, social and political terms and should be avoided assiduously. Although it can be argued that low inflation facilitates economic growth, it is unwise to make efforts to exploit such linkage because overt inflationary measures by stimulating aggregate demand may ignite inflation, create inflation inertia and ultimately damage the economy. Therefore, on the basis of both economic theory and empirical evidence, the main objective of monetary policy should be price stability rather than promoting economic growth or reducing unemployment. In practice, price stability does not mean consistently zero inflation, it could mean on average, a rate of inflation within the range of say 3 to 5 per cent (or less) per annum over the medium term. This may not be the optimal rate of inflation but it could be compatible in the long run for steady economic growth. Of course, this rate may vary for different countries, depending on particularly inflation histories and the stage of social and economic development.

Monetary Policy for Taming Business Cycles

Although the overwhelming view is that price stability should be the dominant objective of monetary policy, price stability should be considered a means to an end (a healthy economy) and should not be treated as an end in itself. Therefore, policy-makers should not be obsessed with inflation control – the so-called 'inflation nutters' as characterised by King (1997). In general, policy-makers should remain concerned about both inflation and output fluctuations and attempt to minimise both, without neglecting the priority accorded to price stability. Modern thinkers on the conduct of monetary policy defines the policy-makers' objective function to embrace these considerations (Sorensen and Whitta-Jacobsen, 2005). However, in reality, central banks have multiple objectives of monetary policy. This lowers policy credibility and effectiveness and makes monetary policy less transparent. This issue – referred to as the time-inconsistency problem – is discussed below.

Rules-Based Monetary Policy to Avoid Time Inconsistency

Time inconsistency in monetary policy is a major problem that policy-makers generally face, especially in developing countries. The time-inconsistency problem of a discretionary monetary policy has been described by Calvo (1978a), Kydland and Prescott (1977) and Barro and Gordon (1983a; 1983b). It arises when the monetary authorities have in-built incentives to change any optimal policy in the future. For example, when policy-makers have both inflation and full-employment goals, a time-inconsistency problem arises for monetary policy because although policy-makers may declare that they would adopt, say, a zero-inflation policy which appears optimal in period one, they have incentives to reverse this policy in the future in order to engineer inflation surprises for short-term output gains (Barro, 2008; Swinburne and Castello-Branco, 1991). When the private sector recognises the time-inconsistency problem, a game-theoretic model can be developed to explain the inflationary bias in a discretionary monetary policy. The time-inconsistency problem also highlights the myopic nature of some policy-makers who try to exploit the short-run trade-off between inflation and employment. In the long run, the result could be high inflation without employment gains because economic agents adjust their wage and price expectations upward to reflect the expansionary monetary policy being adopted. To avoid the inflationary bias in discretionary monetary policy, policy-makers should follow a rule-based monetary policy and stick with it to gain policy credibility. This would lower inflation and prevent policy-makers from falling into the time-inconsistency trap (Barro, 2008; Romer, 1996; Sorensen and Whitta-Jacobsen, 2005).

Choice of Monetary Policy Rules

As pointed out earlier, monetary policy independence requires the adoption of a floating exchange rate system. Under a fixed or pegged exchange rate system, some monetary policy independence is feasible provided that there are effective capital controls in force. There is a body of literature that identifies factors that developing countries need to consider before making a choice of the exchange rate regime (Aghevli et al., 1991). Historically, the classical gold standard system was used to maintain long-term price stability. Under the present fiat-monetary system, there are three rules-based monetary frameworks: exchange rate targeting, monetary targeting and inflation targeting. Countries, experiencing high inflation, may adopt the exchange rate targeting for price stabilisation while undertaking other measures to bring fiscal and monetary discipline. In fact, exchange rate targeting becomes credible only when there is fiscal and monetary discipline. For high-inflationary countries, currency board, dollarisation and monetary union are also proposed to maintain price stability. All these frameworks use the exchange rate as a nominal anchor to keep inflationary expectations low, which gradually bring price stability (Dornbusch and Fischer, 1986; Flood and Mussa, 1994; IMF's *World Economic Outlook*, various issues).

Monetary targeting brings price stability by imposing control over a monetary aggregate and its growth rate. Assuming that there exists a stable money demand function, a central bank can control the money stock and thereby the price level in the long run. The monetary aggregate acts as an intermediate target. The desired rate of inflation is a choice for the central bank or the government, or both. Assuming that the central bank has no goal independence, the government determines the desired rate of inflation by considering the tolerance of the public, or the welfare of the nation. The task of the central bank is to use the monetary aggregate to bring inflation to the desired level. In doing so, the central bank may not attempt to stabilise the exchange and interest rates. The reason is that if the inflation rate is controlled and the monetary policy gains credibility, then the interest and exchange rates would naturally remain stable. This may not happen if the money and capital markets are underdeveloped, foreign exchange markets are thin and capital flows are unpredictable. In such cases volatilities in money and capital markets are created which induces central banks to intervene. Such interventions create problems for monetary control and therefore, inflation targets cannot be achieved and maintained.

Inflation targeting has the same philosophy. The only difference is that in this case, the central bank does not use an intermediate target to bring the inflation rate close to the desired level. Rather, the central bank uses a short-term interest rate to adjust aggregate demand to keep inflation close to its target level. The monetary aggregate may not be used to control inflation because the money demand function is considered unstable and/or the monetary authorities find it difficult to control the money supply. When there are large and unpredictable capital movements that create volatility in interest and exchange rates to such an extent that most developing countries cannot absorb, then central banks may intervene in foreign exchange markets to stabilise the economy. Such interventions affect the money supply and undermine the stance of monetary policy. In principle, however, monetary aggregates can be used as an instrument (rather than the interest rate) under an inflation targeting regime. This is contingent on the linkage between money and aggregate demand being well developed, especially in developing economies (Taylor, 2000).

Forward-Looking Monetary Policy

The effects of monetary policy actions are not immediate and their lag effects vary. Monetary policy should thus be forward looking. The monetary authorities should not wait until inflation is imminent because by then their policy actions could be counterproductive. For example, by waiting until inflation appears before tightening monetary policy, the monetary authorities could be too late and their policy actions may have unintended consequences. When inflationary expectations become embedded into the wage- and price-setting processes, they create an inflation momentum that is difficult to contain. Bringing inflation rate down is time-consuming when there is lack of policy credibility. Economic stabilisation therefore becomes costly in terms of output loss.

To avoid this problem, the monetary authorities should behave in a forward-looking, determined fashion and act pre-emptively and decisively (MAS, 1999; Sorensen and Whitta-Jacobsen, 2005; Walsh, 1998).

Financial Development and Stability

One major responsibility of a modern central bank is to develop the financial system and maintain financial stability. For sustained economic growth, financial development is important. Moreover, economic growth and financial development have a feedback relationship (World Bank, various years). The globalisation of developing economies has made financial stability an important goal of a central bank. Historical evidence shows that financial instability creates economic downturns and affects social and political development. In the past when most economies were almost closed with respect to international capital movements, good monetary policy could in theory work to prevent harmful effects on the economy and financial system arising from external shocks, especially trade shocks. In a relatively closed economy, if monetary policy is conducted efficiently in the sense that itself does not become an independent source of shocks to the economy, then monetary policy maintains both price and financial stability. Obviously this requires sound prudential regulation and supervision of the financial sector and prudent fiscal policy. In open economies, the relation between financial stability and monetary policy is much looser. Open economies are exposed to various external shocks, such as sharp changes in the terms of trade and large-scale capital flows. Monetary policy is not always effective in bringing financial stability. Other measures should also be in place. There is a body of literature on the linkage between financial deregulation and financial crises in developing countries (Hossain and Chowdhury, 1996). Some prominent economists such as Bhagwati (1998) and Stiglitz (2003) have indeed argued for cautious deregulation of financial markets, especially with respect to opening capital markets. As mentioned above, the choice of an exchange rate regime is also important, especially when the country allows free capital mobility. In short, while conducting monetary policy and performing regulatory supervision of the financial system, central banks should make every effort to prevent financial instability. A healthy financial system would promote a healthy economy and reduce output fluctuations. It is equally true that a healthy economy would create a healthy financial system. As a national institution, central banks bear this broad responsibility. The 1990s experiences of East Asian countries suggest that it is difficult to conduct independent monetary policy in the midst of financial instability and in a globalised system. In this environment, it has become difficult for domestic monetary policy to successfully support financial stability. Sutton and Tosovsky (2005) suggest that financial stability in an open-economy environment requires cooperation between the internationally operating financial institutions and domestic supervisory authorities, at both the regional and international levels.

Coordination Between Fiscal and Monetary Policies

Although monetary policy can be used to keep inflation under control, it cannot work for long in isolation if fiscal policy is ignored. Sargent and Wallace (1981) have emphasised this point in their model: 'Unpleasant Monetarist Arithmetic'. The 1990s literature emphasises that high inflation or hyperinflation in developing countries is essentially a fiscal phenomenon. The key point is that unsustainable budget deficits are not compatible with price stability. Sustained large budget deficits put pressure on the monetary authorities to monetise budget deficits, which generate inflation. In fact, expected inflation in the future may lower money demand and raise inflation, even in the absence of monetisation of budget deficits. Therefore, the responsibility of long-term price stability falls equally on both the fiscal and monetary authorities. The task of fiscal authorities is to maintain fiscal discipline and raise enough funds through the taxation system, while the task of monetary authorities is to keep the money growth rate at a level that is consistent with low and steady inflation. While institutional independence of the central bank may be useful to avoid the link between budget deficits and money growth, it may not be enough when there is no coordination between fiscal and monetary policies. When fiscal policy dominates, monetary policy loses its credibility and effectiveness (Romer, 1996; Sorensen and Whitta-Jacobsen, 2005).

CONCLUSION

This chapter has reviewed the fundamental concepts and principles of monetary policy and has explained how monetary policy is different from fiscal policy. It has emphasised that there is a close relationship between monetary and fiscal policy, especially in developing countries. Monetary policy cannot be conducted independently of fiscal policy unless there is close coordination between both. When budget deficits become unsustainable, monetary policy loses its credibility. The public become concerned about budget deficits and thereby monetary policy loses its effectiveness. This chapter has also highlighted the policy trilemma in an open economy that needs resolving before monetary policy can be conducted independently. Under a fixed exchange rate system, monetary policy loses its independence unless there are controls over capital flows. In a floating exchange rate system with free capital mobility, the central bank loses control over the exchange rate but gains control over monetary policy.

The chapter has examined whether monetary policy should be, and can be, used for stabilisation of developing economies. Although the literature suggests that there are possibilities of demand disturbances in developing economies originating from both domestic and foreign sources, they are unlikely to be rampant and persistent. The parameter values of the consumption, investment and money demand functions suggest that developing economies are not highly sensitive to demand shocks. Moreover, as real wages and real interest and exchange rates in developing countries are flexible, the demand shocks to developing economies are adjusted through price mechanisms. Hence there is less need for stabilisation of the economy in the form of policy interventions. Although demand shocks are not prevalent in developing countries, these countries frequently experience supply shocks originating from the agricultural sector. Agricultural supply shocks are however random and do not persist. Monetary policy is usually not effective in stabilising an economy following a supply shock.

Finally, this chapter has defined the concept price stability and reviewed arguments behind price stability as the major (if not the sole) objective of monetary policy. It has also put together a set of guiding principles of central banking and monetary policy in developing countries. The issues raised and reviewed in this chapter are examined in detail in later chapters.

APPENDIX: CENTRAL BANKING AND MONETARY POLICY IN AN ISLAMIC FINANCIAL SYSTEM[10]

Since the late 1970s an Islamic financial system has evolved in most Muslim countries. There are also a growing number of Islamic financial institutions in non-Muslim countries. The basic tenet of the Islamic financial system is the prohibition of interest in all transactions – financial or real. This follows the religious injunction in Islam, which prohibits its followers from paying or receiving interests of any form.

In Arabic the word *riba* is the term used for interest. *Riba* is defined as the additional amount to the principal of any loan, which in conventional accounting is calculated on the basis of duration of a loan, its amount and the predetermined interest rate. This method of interest calculation is applicable to loans in the form of both cash and commodity. In a monetary loan the nominal interest rate is used to estimate the amount of interest payment, while in a commodity-to-commodity credit system, the extra amount of goods and services that is added to the principal represents real interest. Islamic scholars confer that the term *riba* represents all forms of interest, whether it is usury, real or nominal, explicit or implicit (Khan and Mirakhor, 1992).

The Holy Qur'ān and the Sunnah (the teachings and traditions of the Prophet Muhammad) constitute the Islamic Law – the Shariah. In Islam, charging interest is an act of injustice and forbidden. In earlier days of Islam, the moneyed people took advantage of the poor's desperation and helplessness and charged very high interests that made the lives of the poor miserable and destroyed the economic and social well-being of the community. The motto that the poor and the weak need to be helped, rather than taken advantage of for the accumulation of wealth, provided the ethical basis for the prohibition of interest in the Islamic economic system.

In the absence of a well-developed analytical basis, Islamic scholars have needed to develop various reasons in a modern context for the prohibition of interest in financial transactions. It is suggested that even in a modern society, the interest rates charged for loans are exploitative. Furthermore, the theoretical basis of the modern theory of interest (a reward for saving) is considered at best partial and inconsistent with the Islamic notion of justice and the concept of property rights (Ahmad, 1984; Chapra, 1982; Khan and Mirakhor, 1990; 1992; 1993; 1994; Siddiqi, 1983).

The Islamic banks and financial institutions have grown rapidly since the late 1970s. In most Muslim countries, Islamic banks and financial institutions operate side by side with conventional banks. In non-Muslim countries, Islamic investment and holding companies operate and are expanding rapidly (Khan and Mirakhor, 1993; 1994). Only a small number of Muslim countries have, however, developed a full-fledged Islamic financial system. Pakistan, Iran and Sudan remain the three countries that have developed a complete or partial Islamic financial system (Iqbal and Mirakhor, 1987). Malaysia too has lately become a hub of Islamic financial products, while also hosting Western financial institutions.

Sources of Funds and the Financing of Projects

Besides their own capital and equity, Islamic banks rely on two sources of funds: transaction deposits and investment deposits. Transaction deposits are equivalent to demand deposits of the conventional banking system. The Islamic banks guarantee the nominal value of transaction deposits but pay no return on such liabilities. Banks cannot use transaction deposits for any profitable investment. Instead, they charge fees from the deposit holders to cover their costs of administering transaction deposit accounts. In contrast, the Islamic banks use funds in investment deposits, sometimes called the profit-and-loss accounts. These funds resemble the shareholders' funds in a firm, rather than the time and saving deposits of conventional banks. Banks do not provide any guarantee to the nominal value of investment deposits and do not pay fixed rates of return. Instead, they treat investment depositors as shareholders, as in mutual funds or investment trusts. Investment deposit holders are entitled to shares of the profits or losses of banks. The banks agree on a profit-sharing arrangement (especially the profit-sharing ratio) in advance of transactions between banks and depositors. Such a contract can be changed with the consent of both the bank and depositors.

The Islamic banks apply the same principles of profit-and-loss sharing with borrowers. Loans are made principally under two methods: the *Mudarabah* and *Musarakha* arrangements. Under these arrangements the banks share the profits and losses of enterprises with the borrowers. The main difference between the two arrangements is that in the case of Mudarabah, the financier is not allowed a role in the management of the enterprise. In contrast, in the case of Musharakha transactions all parties have the right to participate in managerial decision making. In cases where the profit-loss sharing arrangements cannot be made, there are a number of alternative instruments for investment and financing of projects. They include *Qard al-Hasanah* (beneficence loans), *Bai-Muajjal* (deferred-payment sale), *Bai-Salam* or *Bai'-Salaf* (purchase with deferred delivery), *Ijara* (leasing), *Joalah* (service charge) and cost-plus sale. This list is not exhaustive; there are numerous other variations. Since under the Shariah there is freedom of contracts with considerable flexibility, a wide range of contracts can be made between borrowers and lenders. The overriding restrictions are that any contracts between them do not involve interest payments and that both the parties are fully informed of contract details. Islamic Law permits profit-sharing as alternative methods of financing investment projects (Khan and Mirakhor, 1990; 1993).

Central Banking and Monetary Policy

The main task of central banking in the Islamic financial system is the provision of an institutional framework for smooth operation of financial markets in compliance with the Shariah. The central bank takes the lead in promoting financial institutions, deposit and loan instruments, and a yield structure conducive to efficient mobilisation of savings and the allocation of resources. The central bank in particular has the task of fostering development of primary, secondary and money markets. This is considered crucial because a mere adoption of the Islamic rules of finance does not in itself create significant impetus for financial and economic development. The shallow financial markets and the absence of attractive financial instruments can limit financial intermediation and retard economic growth.

The principal goal of monetary policy in the Islamic system is to ensure macroeconomic stability. This is characterised by price-level stability (zero inflation) and a sustainable balance of payments position. As in modern central banking, in the Islamic financial system macroeconomic stability is considered important for increased saving, investment and foreign capital flows. It is emphasised that macroeconomic instability can retard economic growth and cause economic distress. Since the well-being of the Islamic society depends on the equitable distribution of income and wealth through taxation (zakat) as an instrument of poverty alleviation, sustained economic growth is considered fundamental.

Monetary policy in an Islamic system takes place within a policy framework in which most modern monetary policy tools are available. The only exception is the discount rate and other policy instruments that involve the interest rate. All other tools, such as open-market operations (where equity shares rather than bonds are traded) and credit policies (selective credit controls) are used. Furthermore, in an Islamic system the authorities can use the reserve requirements and profit sharing ratios for monetary management (Khan and Mirakhor, 1993).

In conclusion, the role of money and monetary management in an Islamic economy must fit into the framework of the overall economic system as defined by Islam. In an Islamic system, the State is empowered to design specific economic policy to achieve specific economic and social objectives. Monetary management and policy in an Islamic economy is thus required to be designed with the overall aims of the Islamic society (Khan and Mirakhor, 1993).

NOTES

1. This section follows with Sachs and Larrain (1993).
2. The debt that the Treasury owes to the central bank does not necessarily have to be repaid in a genuine sense; it represents a claim by one organ of the government on another.
3. Sorensen and Whitta-Jacobsen (2005: 620) have defined stabilisation policy in a present context as the active use of monetary and fiscal policy to influence aggregate demand for goods and services with the aim of minimising the social welfare loss from the volatility of output and inflation.
4. Investment pessimism refers to a situation where investment is not sensitive to changes in the interest rate. This may happen when the economic environment and profit expectations are weak.
5. Along with the works of Milton Friedman and his collaborators, the works of Brunner and Meltzer (1963; 1968) have also been influential.
6. Bomhoff (1983) has reported early empirical evidence on the monetarist contention that the growth rate of money matters for short-term fluctuations in economic growth and for longer-term trends in inflation.
7. Monetarists consider economic policy as the design of institutions and rules, which they believe would lower uncertainty and variability for society as a whole. They also believe that activist monetary-fiscal policy can destabilise an otherwise stable economy. If minimising fluctuations is the goal of fiscal activism, then monetarists claim that in this respect they are close to Keynes (Meltzer, 1981).
8. Financial repression represents an economic condition where the government's discretionary monetary and financial policies indiscriminately distort financial prices, discourage saving, lower investment, and misallocate financial resources (Fry, 1998).
9. Coyne (1961), intuitively, came to a similar view in the early 1960s (cited in Thiessen, 2000: 68):

   > There are those who sometimes set out the false alternatives of either full employment with inflation, or stable prices with a high level of unemployment. They say the nation must choose between unemployment and inflation. No person in any position of responsibility could possibly subscribe to that doctrine. It is false. Full employment and stable prices are not only compatible, they are in the long run inseparable.

10. This appendix draws heavily from Iqbal and Mirakhor (1987), Khan (1986), Khan and Mirakhor (1990; 1992; 1993; 1994) and Mirakhor and Zaidi (1991).

5. Inflation and monetary policy: theories, models and approaches

Inflation and unemployment are the twin 'evils' in a capitalist economy. Their importance in the 'matrix of national welfare indicators' is expressed in the form of a 'misery index', which in a simplified form is defined as the sum of the inflation and unemployment rates. An interpretation of this index is that the society benefits from a reduction in inflation but loses from a rise in unemployment and therefore a reduction in inflation by say one percentage point may exactly offset the social cost of a rise in unemployment by one percentage point. An implication is that the society is indifferent in the trade-off between inflation and unemployment because this keeps the level of societal misery unchanged. When both inflation and unemployment rise (fall) simultaneously, the society's welfare deteriorates (improves) (Blanchard and Fischer, 1989; Blanchard and Sheen, 2007; Gordon, 1993).

There is, however, a lack of consensus on the above interpretation of the misery index. Not all economists agree with the view that both inflation and unemployment are equally bad. The Keynesian economists put greater emphasis on the costs of unemployment, while the monetarists put greater emphasis on the costs of inflation (Driffill et al., 1990; Evans, 1991). The late Noble Laureate James Tobin, for example, maintained the view that 'inflation is greatly exaggerated as a social evil' (Gordon, 1993: 284). This is apparently because the costs of lowering inflation in terms of lost output could be significantly greater than the societal benefits from a reduction in inflation. Costs of inflation also vary depending on whether inflation is anticipated or unanticipated and whether it is high or low. In a free market economy, anticipated inflation swiftly reflects in wages and other contracts and therefore it affects economic activity only temporarily. Conversely, unanticipated inflation can adversely affect economic activity, income distribution and other real variables in both the short and medium runs. This happens particularly in economies where there are market imperfections, which results in a slow and partial adjustment of wages and other contracts to actual or perceived inflation (Ball and Romer, 1990; Blinder, 1998; Fischer, 1977, 1981; Sorensen and Whitta-Jacobsen, 2005).

Although both Keynesian and Latin American structuralist economists suggest that low inflation could be good for economic growth in countries where there are wage and price rigidities (Canavese, 1982; Cardoso, 1981; Mikesell, 1969), economists in general remain averse to very high inflation and in its extreme form – hyperinflation. Both very high inflation and in particular hyperinflation destroy an economy and causes economic and political crises (Dornbusch, 1993). In general, monetarists remain averse to inflation, whether low or high. Although they are not indifferent to unemployment, they believe that there is a 'natural rate of unemployment' which is determined by real factors. In this view, unemployment cannot be lowered below the natural rate without removing market imperfections, making real wages more flexible, and keeping the rate of inflation low and steady (Friedman, 1968a).[1]

This follows the monetarists' belief that high unemployment is the consequence of policy distortions in labour markets, wage regulations and other policy-induced uncertainties. Monetarists suggest that high inflation could also be a source of unemployment. For example, high inflation is generally volatile, which creates uncertainties and lowers investment (Friedman, 1968a; 1991). Therefore, price stability is considered important for maintaining macroeconomic stability, which creates an environment for productive investment and technological innovations. Experiences of rapidly growing economies of East Asia have shown that sustained economic growth can keep the rate of unemployment low and steady (Treadgold, 1990; World Bank, 1993). Therefore, unlike Keynesians and Latin American structuralists, monetarists do not see any positive role of inflation in relation to economic growth. Indeed, any stimulus that inflation gives to economic activity is likely to be transitory and uncertain (Friedman, 1973).

Research has yielded conclusive evidence on the costs of high inflation (Easterly and Fischer, 2001; Fischer et al., 2002). Yet there remains no consensus on the 'optimal rate of inflation' (Cogley, 1997). Economists apply both positive and normative criteria to define the optimal rate of inflation. In an early contribution, Friedman (1969a) used a microeconomic principle to show that the optimal rate of inflation is in fact minus the real rate of interest. His reasoning was that since the cost of production of money is almost zero, the opportunity cost of holding money, which can be approximated by the nominal rate of interest, should be zero so that the public can maximise their holding of real balances. The Fisher relationship shows that the nominal interest rate equals the real interest rate plus the rate of expected inflation. A zero nominal interest rate therefore implies a rate of expected inflation that equals the negative of the real interest rate (Sachs and Larrain, 1993).

An optimal rate of inflation defined this way has become controversial. Most economists are against deflation and therefore suggest that the optimal rate of inflation should be positive but very low. They cite the experiences of the 1930s to illustrate the deflationary costs in the economy (Croushore, 1992). Japanese deflation of the 1990s can be considered a recent example. Ambiguity continues about the meaning of low inflation. Although Poole (1999) does not share Friedman's view that the optimal rate of inflation should be negative, he is against any positive rate of inflation. He favours zero inflation, arguing that it is good in all respects. The issue is whether zero inflation can be achieved and maintained on a sustained basis without adversely affecting the economy (Sorensen and Whitta-Jacobsen, 2005).

When inflation is brought to zero, there is a danger that it may lead to deflation. It indicates why some economists, who view inflation as pernicious and insist on zero inflation, are pejoratively dubbed 'inflation-nutters'. These economists supposedly believe that monetary policy should be such that it permanently eradicates inflation from the system, irrespective of any costs of unemployment. Furthermore, these zero inflation advocates do not mind if their policies lead to deflation; after all, Friedman's optimal inflation rate equals the negative of the real interest rate. It remains doubtful that such an extreme view is shared by many policy economists (Romer, 1996).

An alternative, but widely supported view, is that inflation is part of the economic growth process: a low but positive rate of inflation is fine, in so far as it does not distort economic decisions. A low rate of inflation may even be beneficial for economic growth (Summers, 1991; Tobin, 1965; 1972). Accordingly, the optimal rate of inflation could be in the range of for example, one to three per cent per annum. Phelps (1973) has provided a rationale for such a positive rate of inflation. He suggests that although inflation is distortionary, so too are all taxes. Therefore, it makes sense for a government to rely on some inflation tax to lower its reliance on other taxes.[2] Edwards and Tabellini (1991) have explained fiscal policy and inflation in developing countries from such a viewpoint.

With regard to monetary policy, the key issue is how to keep inflation low and stable. To begin with, it requires a better understanding of the sources and consequences of high inflation. It is equally important to understand the approaches to control inflation and the resulting costs on the economy. In current economic thinking, the design and conduct of monetary policy is considered both a science and an art. The scientific part of monetary policy encompasses a body of macroeconomic and monetary theories, models and approaches to inflation and unemployment. Chapter 4 provided an overview of the major concepts and propositions on monetary policy. This chapter reviews some of the theories, models and approaches to inflation and monetary policy. No attempt is, however, made to synthesise diverse theories of inflation and monetary policy. The theories and models that have monetary policy implications are presented topic by topic, albeit at the risk of repetition and digression.

PART I

MONEY GROWTH, INFLATION AND STABILISATION

As emphasised in earlier chapters, monetary policy deals with inflation over the medium term or a business cycle. To begin with, the analytical issue is the source of inflation (Parkin, 1992). Once the source of inflation is identified, it becomes easier to design the monetary policy framework to control inflation over the medium term or a business cycle. This section provides an overview of the sources of inflation.

The inflation literature begins with the classical view on inflation. It states that inflation in the long run is determined by the growth rate of the money supply (Baer and Kertenetzky, 1964; Harberger, 1978; Johnson, 1972). Non-monetary factors affect inflation, but only in the short run. Non-monetary factors, originating from both the demand side and the supply side, cannot lead to a self-sustaining inflation without monetary accommodation. Therefore, control of long-term inflation is equivalent to a control of the growth rate of the money supply.[3]

Money Growth and Inflation

In the monetary literature, inflation has a precise meaning. Inflation represents the condition of a continual rise in the general price level.[4] Inflation defined this way is different from short-term 'random' fluctuations of the general price level. For example, a change in the price level say of about 1 or a 0.5 per cent (plus or minus) over a year does not represent inflation or deflation. This does not suggest that such a change in the price level is not important to some policy-makers. Such a change in the price level reflects random demand and supply shocks that hit an economy. Yet random shocks do not represent a long-run source of inflation. In the absence of monetary accommodation, the net effect of such shocks on the general price level on average should not be significantly different from zero.

The situation could be different for some developing countries. Sometimes major supply shocks play a role in the inflationary process in developing countries. For example, consider the situation when a harvest failure of staple food crops raises the food prices sharply, which may take considerable time to fall to their pre-shock levels. Since food prices dominate the consumer price index in developing countries, this may cause a short-term spike in an otherwise low and stable inflation path (Cardoso, 1981; Swagel and Loungani, 1995; Vogel, 1974). Even in such a situation, there may not exist a stable long-run relationship between supply shocks and inflation, as defined above.[5]

Inflation: a monetary phenomenon

Following the classical tradition, monetarists suggest that money growth is the ultimate source of inflation. This is reflected in Friedman's famous statement that 'inflation is always and everywhere a monetary phenomenon' (1968a: 29). He has elaborated this view on inflation and its control as follows (Friedman, 1983a: 193, 200):

> Controlling the growth of money is important because, ultimately, inflation is a monetary phenomenon – nothing else. If you control growth of the money supply, you control inflation; if you do not, inflation cannot be limited. Secondly, this control is important because money is pervasive and affects the entire economy.

Some critics consider Friedman's statement on inflation tautological, in the sense that inflation by definition represents a fall in the value of money. That is, a unit of money buys fewer goods and services when the price level rises. Monetarists do not see merits in such criticism because Friedman's statement represents an approach to inflation rather than a statement that is rhetorical and hence vacuous. For example, Barro (1993) has provided a broad interpretation of Friedman's view on inflation. First, Friedman's view does not rule out the impacts of real disturbances such as supply shocks on the price level. These impacts are more important for isolated episodes of price changes than for chronic inflation. Second, the expression of monetary phenomenon incorporates variables that affect the demand for money as well as the nominal supply of money. Third, money growth behaves differently in different countries and at different times. Fourth, the monetary interpretation of inflation incorporates incentives structure that leads to printing money, as for example the financing of budget deficits on a sustained basis.[6]

Classical model of inflation

In the monetary literature the linkage between the money stock and the price level is well-established. This follows the tradition of the *Quantity Theory of Money*, which can be expressed in the form of the well-known *Equation of Exchange*:

$$MV = Py \tag{5.1}$$

where M is the quantity of money (\$), V is the velocity of circulation of money defined as the average number of times per annum a dollar is spent on final output, P is the price level and y is real output on which spending is made. This *Equation of Exchange* states that the money value of expenditure (MV) equals the money value of output bought (Py). Equation (5.1) can be expressed in the form of proportionate changes in variables, such that

$$g_M + g_V = g_P + g_y \tag{5.2}$$

This shows the sum of the proportionate changes in money (g_M) and velocity (g_V) equals the sum of the proportionate changes in the price level (g_P) and output (g_y). Assuming that the velocity of circulation of money is constant[7] ($g_V = 0$) and output is determined by the factors of production ($g_y = g_{y0}$) (and is not affected by the money supply), the *Quantity Theory* suggests that there exists a one-for-one proportional relationship between money supply growth (g_M) and inflation (g_P). When the money supply growth rate is determined exogenously by the monetary authorities, it leads to a causal linkage running from money supply growth to inflation.

One criticism of the *Equation of Exchange* is that the velocity of money is not constant but unstable or adaptable, which implies that there may not be any linkage between money and prices. Moreover, any linkage between money and prices does not imply a causality running from money supply growth to inflation. There can be a reverse causation running from inflation to money supply growth. Furthermore, both money supply growth and inflation may be caused by a third factor, such as a supply shock in the form of a trade-union militancy that leads to an excessive wages growth, or rapid rise in oil prices (Mishkin, 2007a). In response to such a criticism, monetarists refer to the historical evidence under the commodity (gold) monetary system that established a causal link between the expansion of commodity money (gold) and inflation. The Californian and Australian gold discoveries in the middle of the nineteenth century are examples when these gold discoveries led to rising price levels as suggested by the *Quantity Theory*. There were similar increases in prices in sixteenth-century Europe after the new world gold entered. In addition, there were episodes in the twentieth century when episodes of hyperinflation originated from exogenous increases in the money supply. Examples are the hyperinflation experiences of South America, Europe and Asia, following the First and Second World Wars. They provide evidence on the growth of the money supply (for exogenous reasons) as the major contributing factor to high or hyperinflation. The fact that there was no hyperinflation under the gold standard suggests that it was the slow expansion of the gold supply that put a check on inflation. Under the present fiat money system there is no major constraint on the growth of the money stock. Technologically it is feasible to expand the money supply at a very high rate. This is what happens in a country that experiences hyperinflation, as its money printing machine remains in operations 'full steam' (Sachs and Larrain, 1993). Zimbabwe is the latest example of a fiat monetary system that has allowed the government to expand the money supply at an extraordinarily rapid pace.

The aggregate demand and aggregate supply model of inflation

The aggregate demand and aggregate supply model can be used to explain the generation of inflation and its control. When inflation is defined as a continually rising price level, both monetarists and the Keynesians agree with Friedman's interpretation of inflation as

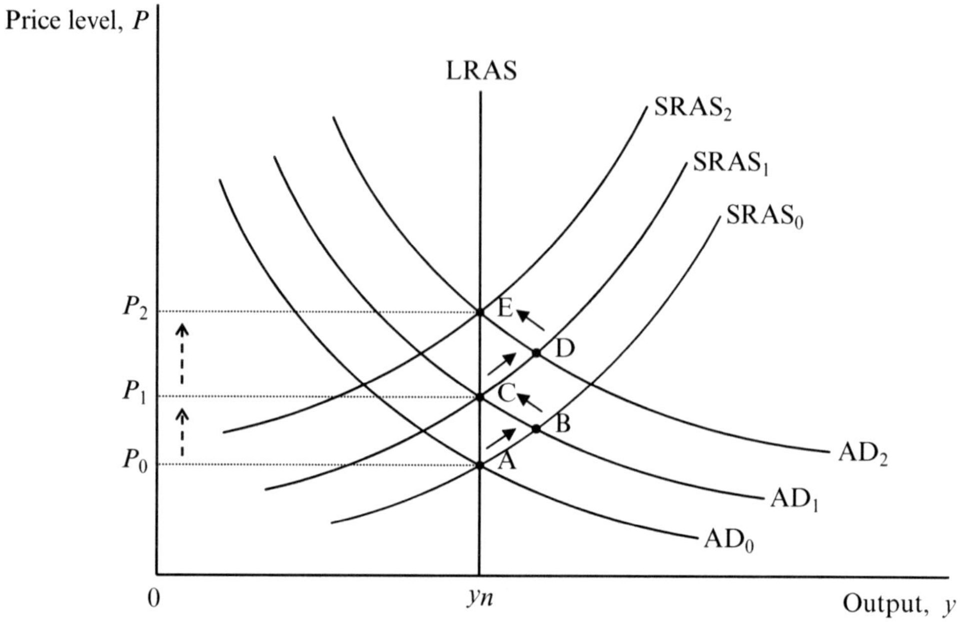

Note: Money supply with a high employment target shifts aggregate demand from $AD_0 \rightarrow AD_1 \rightarrow AD_2$, while $SRAS_0 \rightarrow SRAS_1 \rightarrow SRAS_2$ and so on. The outcome is a continual rise in the price level from $P_0 \rightarrow P_1 \rightarrow P_2$ and so on.

Figure 5.1 Money supply as the source of inflation

a monetary phenomenon. This follows the reasoning that a high rate of inflation, irrespective of its originating source, cannot be sustained without monetary accommodation. The original source of inflation could be both monetary and non-monetary. Monetarists suggest that even when the original source of inflation is non-monetary, it works through the monetary channels. For example, suppose that there is a non-monetary supply shock to the economy that raises the general price level. A one-off price increase does not lead to self-sustaining inflation unless there is an expansion of the money supply. Such an expansion of the money supply is not automatic but could be a reaction of the monetary authorities to lower the rate of unemployment that might have increased due to the supply shock. Even when the money supply is not increased, a supply shock can generate inflation through the money demand relationship. For example, an adverse supply shock by lowering output (and generating inflationary expectations) lowers the demand for money. This can create excess money supply and raise the general price level. When there is monetary accommodation after a supply shock, economic agents revise inflationary expectations upward which may lower money demand and sustain high inflation for a few years (Hossain, 2000). This broad idea of the generation of inflation is illustrated using a simple model.

In Figure 5.1 a continually rising money supply shifts the aggregate demand curve to the right from AD_0 to AD_1 to AD_2 and so on. The rising price level generates inflationary expectations and the aggregate supply curve shifts to the left from $SRAS_0$ to $SRAS_1$ to

$SRAS_2$ and so on. The result is that the price level rises continually from P_0 to P_1 to P_2 and beyond. This inflation generating process does not refer to any source of the money supply but it can be linked to money-financed budget deficits.[8] As Friedman (1983a) pointed out, budget deficits are one reason for money creation. There could be other reasons for rapid monetary expansion.

Keynesians suggest that an increase in the money supply may raise the price level depending on whether the economy is at full employment. If the economy operates below the full employment level, an increase in the money supply (which raises aggregate demand) would increase output but not the price level. Increased money demand, in response to increased output resulting from monetary expansion, may balance increased money supply and therefore leave the price level unchanged. Only when an economy reaches the full-employment level, then an increase in the price level may result from monetary expansion. Further, although Keynesians do not suggest that high inflation can be generated without rapid monetary expansion, other factors such as government spending, tax cuts and supply shocks can affect aggregate demand and aggregate supply. Therefore inflation cannot always be considered strictly a monetary phenomenon (Ball and Mankiw, 1995).

Monetarists do not deny that non-monetary factors can affect the price level but they suggest that they do so only temporarily. For example, a one-shot fiscal expansion or a supply shock cannot generate self-sustaining inflation. By definition, demand and supply shocks are a random phenomenon. They do not repeat systematically and therefore cannot be a primary source of inflation. There are also institutional checks and balances that prevent continual increase in government spending or a reduction in taxes. Indeed, continually increasing government spending is not a feasible policy. There is a limit on the total amount of government expenditure: the government cannot spend more than 100 per cent of GDP. In fact, well before this limit is reached, the political process stops such an increase in government spending. Similarly, any policy of continued tax cuts is not sustainable. Taxes cannot be reduced below a zero rate (Sachs and Larrain, 1993). In most developing countries, income taxes constitute only a small portion of total revenues. There is also usually no strong political pressure or lobby in these countries for tax cuts.

For these reasons, in the Keynesian analysis, high inflation is explained by rapid monetary expansion caused by large budget deficits. Keynesians also emphasise the cost-push nature of inflation. In cost-push inflation, there is continual leftward shift of the aggregate supply curve (from $SRAS_0$ to $SRAS_1$ to $SRAS_2$ as Figure 5.2 depicts). This induces the government to shift the aggregate demand curve to the right continually (from AD_0 to AD_1 to AD_2 and so on) in an attempt to keep the unemployment rate at close or below its natural rate. A continuing rise in the price level can result (Figure 5.2). What role does monetary policy play in cost-push inflation? As indicated above, cost-push inflation occurs only if the aggregate demand curve is shifted continually to the right because of the continual increase of the money supply. Therefore, according to the monetarists, cost-push inflation is exacerbated by aggregate demand policies and ultimately is a monetary phenomenon. It cannot occur without monetary accommodation, which is not automatic but could be in response to a policy that aims at keeping the unemployment rate close to or below its natural rate (Mishkin, 2007a).

In sum, aggregate demand and aggregate supply analysis shows that the Keynesian and

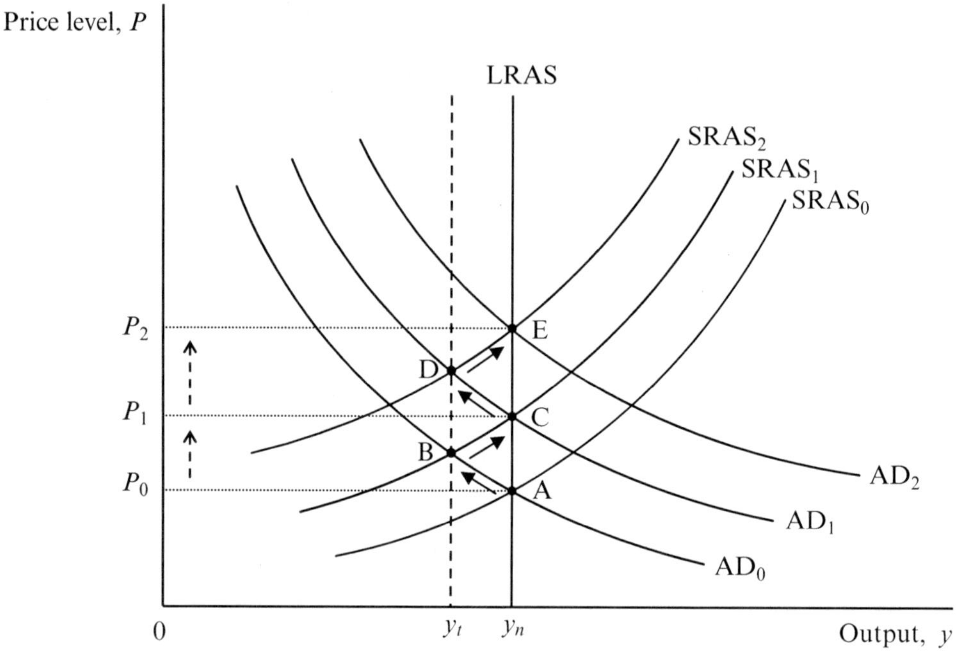

Note: A wage push shifts SRAS$_0$ → SRAS$_1$ → SRAS$_2$ and so on, while an accommodative money supply with a high employment target shifts AD$_0$ → AD$_1$ → AD$_2$ and so on. The outcome is a continual rise in the price level from P_0 → P_1 → P_2 and so on.

Figure 5.2 Cost-push and inflation

the monetarist views on high inflation are not that different. High inflation can occur only with a high rate of money growth. However, there are differences in the interpretation and focus on factors that cause inflation in the short and long runs. While the Keynesians emphasise the non-monetary sources of inflation and link them to structural factors, monetarists consider money growth a policy variable. The government bears the ultimate responsibility of monetary expansion, although the central bank bears the immediate responsibility of monetary policy and controls instruments that undertake monetary operations. The focus of the Keynesian analysis is the short run. Inflation is therefore seen to be affected by both real and monetary shocks. In the long run, such shocks dissipate and inflation is determined by the growth rate of the money supply. From a longer-term viewpoint, most economists agree with Friedman's view that 'inflation is always and everywhere a monetary phenomenon' (Mishkin, 2007a; Romer, 1996). Understanding sustained inflation is therefore equivalent to understanding factors behind the rapid growth of the money supply (Gordon, 1993). This explains why it is sometimes necessary to investigate the inflationary process in a developing country within a macroeconomic framework (Hossain, 1995). Economic openness also appears to have changed the dynamics of inflation, as most developing economies have been exposed to external shocks while their economic policies have been more disciplined in recent years due to external constraints (Ball, 2006; Iyoha, 1973; Lane, 1997; Romer, 1993).

Money Growth, Output Growth and Inflation in Developing Asia

In order to validify the proposition that there is a stable long-run relation between money supply growth and inflation, this section provides empirical evidence with data for developing Asia over the period 1950–2007. The model used is derived from the following equilibrium condition in the money market:

$$M^s = P \cdot m^d(y) \tag{5.3}$$

where M^s is the exogenously determined money supply, P is the price level and the demand for money $m^d(\ldots)$ is an increasing function of real output (y). For simplicity, in the money demand function, the nominal interest rate is ignored. Assume that the monetary authority sets the money supply to M_0, equation (5.3) can be written as:

$$M_0 = P \cdot m^d(y) \tag{5.4}$$

Divide both sides by the price level P to express the equation in real terms:

$$M_0/P = m^d(y) \tag{5.5}$$

This relationship can be used to explain why a real shock to output may not lead to self-sustaining inflation. Instead it can be demonstrated that the primary source of inflation remains money supply growth.

Assume an adverse supply shock decreases output (y) and thereby lowers money demand. Since money demand has decreased, the equilibrium condition in the money market requires M_0/P to decrease. Since M_0 is given, a fall in M_0/P requires P to increase. This shows that an adverse supply shock leads to a rise in the price level. However, such an increase in the price level is a one-off event in response to a decrease in output caused by an adverse supply shock. *Ceteris paribus*, P may continue to rise if there are similar shocks on a regular basis. Usually this does not happen and therefore supply shocks cannot be a regular source of inflation.

Rather than a sustained decrease in output, most countries experience steady output growth due to changes in the factors of production. This raises money demand and therefore real balances (M/P) show an upward trend. As equation (5.5) suggests, this can happen if M increases at a higher rate than P. If M is kept constant at M_0, M_0/P can increase steadily only if P continues to decrease (Barro, 2008). Since this does not happen, it is plausible that an increase in the money supply leads to an increase in the price level. Equation (5.5) can therefore be transformed into a simple monetary model of inflation:

$$\pi = \lambda - \eta_y \cdot g_y \tag{5.6}$$

where π is inflation, λ is money supply growth, g_y is output growth and η_y is the income elasticity of demand for money. This relationship is assessed by examining the long-term data for the Asia-Pacific region over the period 1950–2007.

Table 5.1 reports five-yearly data for broad money growth, output growth and

Table 5.1 *Broad money growth, CPI-inflation and output growth in selected countries of the Asia-Pacific, 1950–2007 (annual average over period; percentage)*

Country/region	Broad money growth rate 1950–69	CPI-inflation 1950–69	Real GDP growth rate 1950–69	Broad money growth rate 1970–89	CPI-inflation 1970–89	Real GDP growth rate 1970–89	Broad money growth rate 1990–2007	CPI-inflation 1990–2007	Real GDP growth rate 1990–2007
Australia	7.0	4.7	5.4	13.8	9.0	3.4	10.2	2.8	3.4
Bangladesh	na	na	3.5	20.3	17.6	0.9	14.0	5.8	5.2
Cambodia	na	na	na	na	na	11.5	51.5	33.4	7.7
China	10.1	1.1	6.2	20.1	4.0	8.7	16.1	5.1	9.9
Fiji	na	na	5.7	14.5	9.0	3.5	8.6	3.6	2.5
India	7.7	4.1	3.8	17.1	8.3	4.4	16.7	7.3	6.3
Indonesia	179.8	80.8	na	32.3	13.3	6.7	21.0	11.9	4.6
Japan	17.2	4.2	10.1	12.2	5.8	4.5	5.7	0.5	1.6
Korea, South	55.2	47.9	7.1	25.0	11.9	8.3	14.0	4.5	5.8
Lao PDR	na	na	na	na	na	5.6	37.8	25.6	6.4
Malaysia	7.4	1.7	5.8	16.0	4.6	6.9	14.9	3.0	6.4
Myanmar	7.8	0.9	4.9	14.4	10.5	3.5	32.5	24.5	8.7
Nepal	19.6	5.1	2.2	18.8	9.3	2.5	16.3	7.4	4.3
New Zealand	4.0	4.1	4.1	22.8	11.8	2.2	7.6	2.3	2.9
Pakistan	10.1	3.1	3.7	15.1	9.5	5.1	16.2	7.9	4.6
Papua New Guinea	na	na	na	12.7	7.5	2.7	10.8	9.6	3.4
Philippines	10.2	2.6	5.5	19.8	14.4	3.9	15.6	7.5	3.8
Singapore	na	na	8.9	14.9	4.4	8.2	10.0	1.5	6.7
Sri Lanka	8.0	1.7	3.7	18.3	9.9	6.8	17.8	10.7	5.1
Taiwan, China	na	na	na	na	na	8.3	na	na	5.3
Thailand	12.7	1.7	6.6	19.2	6.9	7.1	11.5	3.9	5.2
United States	7.7	2.1	4.0	9.5	6.3	3.2	6.8	2.9	2.8
Vietnam	na	na	na	na	na	6.0	na	na	7.5

Note: na = not available.

Sources: Author's computation based on IMF, *International Financial Statistics Yearbook* (various years) and IMF, *World Economic Outlook* (various years).

CPI-inflation for selected countries of the Asia-Pacific. The relationship between money growth and inflation is strong (Figures 5.3 to 5.5). The countries which experienced high inflation had high money growth rates over the sample period. The countries which experienced high economic growth had low inflation given the money supply growth. Without implying a causal relationship in a statistical sense, these findings are consistent with the proposition that inflation is an increasing function of money growth and a decreasing function of economic growth. This relationship holds for both low and high inflationary economies. Subject to econometric confirmation, these data can be deployed to validate the proposition that there exists a long run relationship between money growth and inflation in developing Asia.

BUDGET DEFICITS AND INFLATION

As indicated earlier, one strand of the money growth-inflation literature suggests that budget deficits and money growth are closely related in developing countries. Therefore inflation can be considered a fiscal phenomenon. The argument is that the linkage between money growth and inflation is superficial. The model is not complete without establishing a relationship between money growth and budget deficits. Furthermore, budget deficits are not always under the control of the government. Budget deficits could be the result of both structural and policy-induced constraints that governments face (Edwards and Tabellini, 1991; Roubini, 1991; Tanzi, 1982). Therefore, beneath the money–inflation relationship, there exists an inflation model that has structural elements. Latin American 'structuralists' suggest such a model of inflation for developing countries (Canavese, 1982; Corbo, 1974; Olivera, 1967; Pazos, 1972; Sunkel, 1960).

Although it is plausible that budget deficits are a source of inflation, the fiscal-monetary part of an inflation model is not stable. Any linkage between budget deficits and money growth depends on institutional arrangements which change over time. Friedman (1983a) himself acknowledged a linkage between budget deficits and inflation, but in his view any relationship between them is likely to be weak or episodic.

An understanding of the feedback relationship between budget deficits and inflation is essential to comprehend the impact of monetary policy. The following analysis suggests that high inflation is invariably linked to the fiat monetary system. Whether a government monetises budget deficits remains a policy decision. Disinflationary experiences in different countries suggest that high or hyperinflation stops suddenly when the monetary authorities make a strong commitment to stop printing money. Therefore the decision about monetising budget deficits should not be considered a routine or rigid affair. Any linkage between budget deficits and money growth is therefore likely to be unstable across countries and over time (Fischer et al., 2002; Hossain and Chowdhury, 1998).

Budget Deficits and the Balance-of-Payments Crisis

This section develops relationships between budget deficits and inflation under both the fixed and flexible exchange rate regimes.[9]

Consider an economy with an ongoing budget deficit. Assume that it is operating under a fixed exchange rate system. Also assume that the government does not have

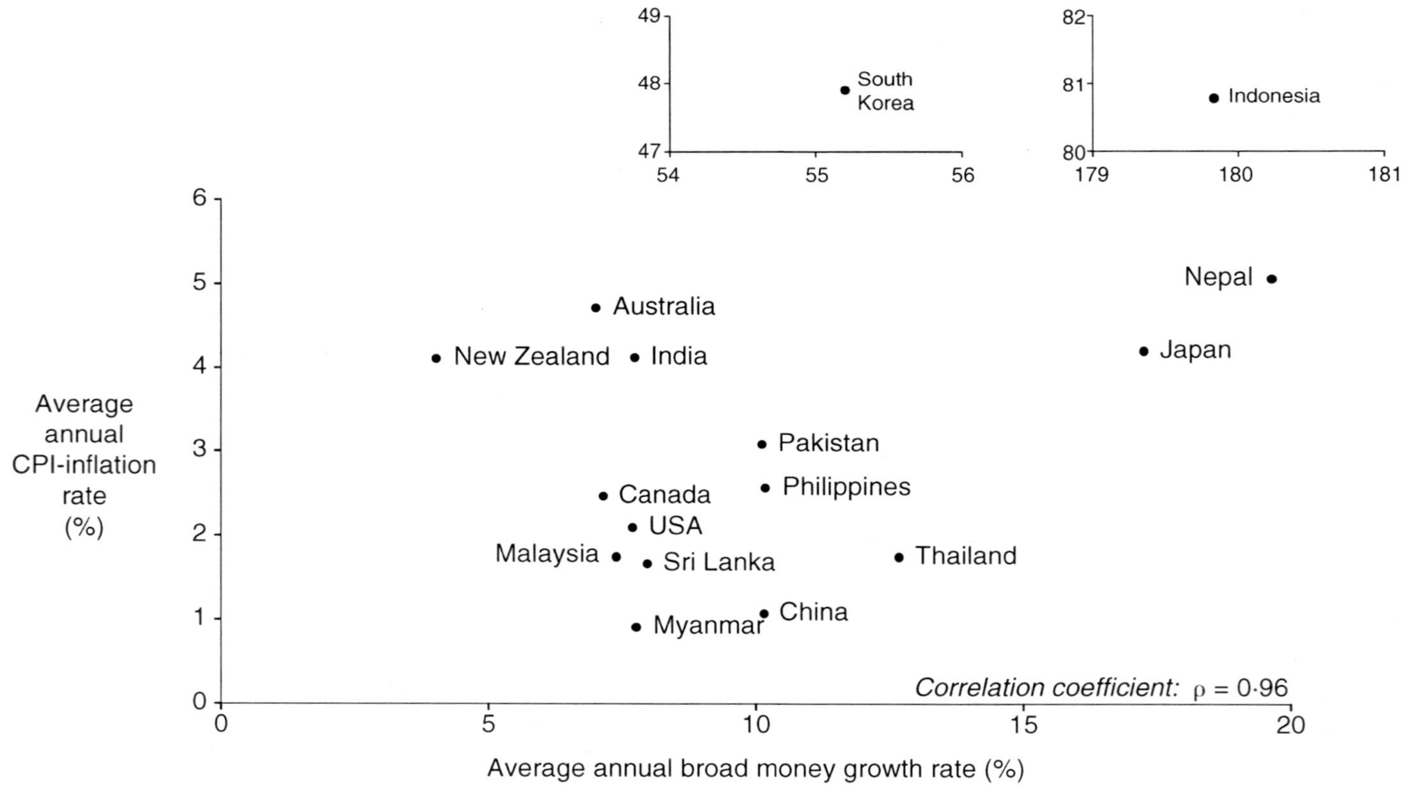

Note: Average annual data for some countries are for a shorter sample period than 1950–69.

Source: IMF, *International Financial Statistics.*

Figure 5.3 Broad money growth and CPI-inflation in selected countries of Asia-Pacific, 1950–69

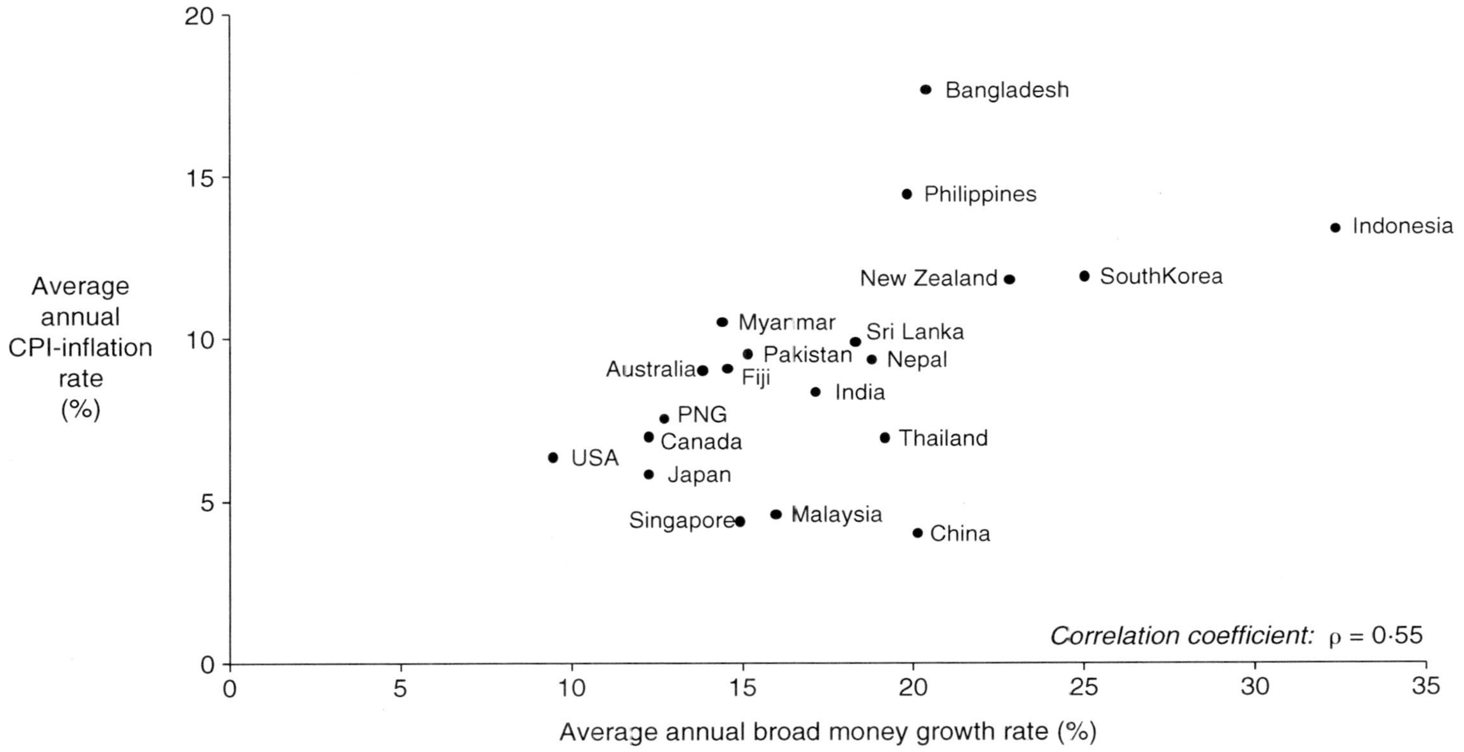

Source: IMF, *International Financial Statistics*.

Figure 5.4 Broad money growth and CPI-inflation in selected countries of the Asia-Pacific, 1970–89

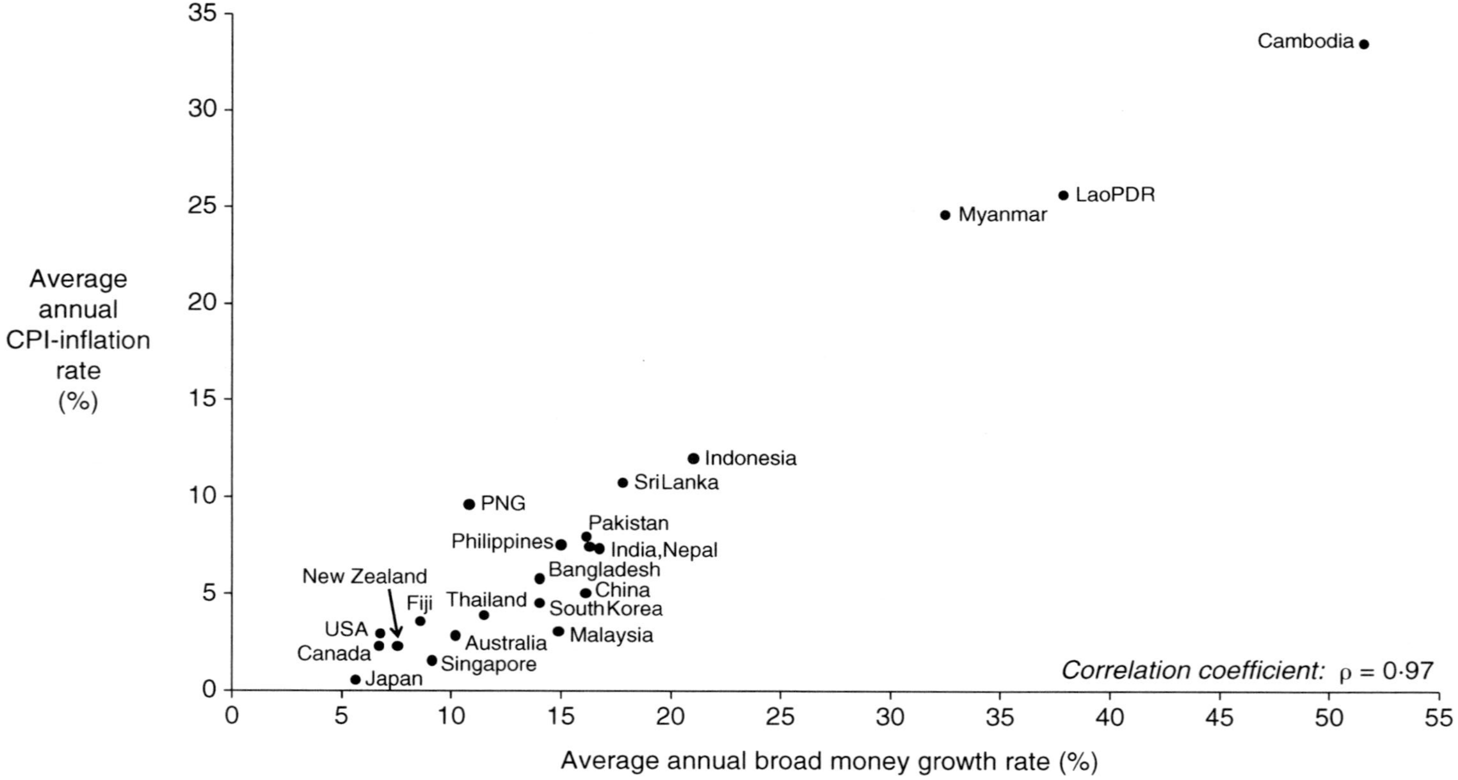

Source: IMF, *International Financial Statistics.*

Figure 5.5 Broad money growth and CPI-inflation in selected countries of the Asia-Pacific, 1990–2007 access to direct borrowing from the public (at home or abroad). The policy option for the government is to borrow from the central bank, which holds foreign exchange reserves.

Start with the consolidated government budget deficit, as defined in Chapter 4:

$$(D_p^g - D_{p-1}^g) + (M_h - M_{h-1}) - NER \cdot (R_c^\$ - R_{c-1}^\$)$$
$$= P[(G + I^g - T) + i^d \cdot D_{p-1}^g - NER \cdot (i^f - R_{c-1}^\$) \quad (5.7)$$

where D_p^g is government debt to the public, M_h is high-powered money, $R_c^\$$ is the stock of net foreign assets held by the central bank, NER is the exchange rate, measured in units of domestic currency per unit of foreign currency, P is the price level, G is the government consumption spending, I^g is government investment, T is taxes and i^d (i^f) is the domestic (foreign) interest rate.

The right side of equation (5.7) is the budget deficit: the excess of government spending over government income. The left side of the equation shows the sources of deficit finance. Since the government cannot borrow from the public, $(D_p^g - D_{p-1}^g) = 0$. Also, for simplicity, assume that high-powered money (M_h) equals the money supply (M). Finally, define DEF in real term such that it equals the nominal budget deficit deflated by the price level. Equation (5.7) then can be written as:

$$(M - M_{-1}) - NER \cdot (R_c^\$ - R_{c-1}^\$) = P \cdot DEF \quad (5.8)$$

Budget deficits and inflation under a fixed exchange rate system

Under a fixed exchange rate system, the money stock is endogenously determined by the determinants of money demand such as real income and the nominal interest rate. Assume that $M = M_{-1}$ when the economy is at full employment and there is no growth. Equation (5.8) can thus be written as:

$$- NER \cdot (R_c^\$ - R_{c-1}^\$) = P \cdot DEF \quad (5.9)$$

This shows that when an economy is at full employment and income is unchanged, the demand for money remains constant. Therefore when the government borrows from the central bank, then, in effect, all borrowing would be from abroad. Any attempt to borrow from the central bank leads to an increase in high-powered money that, in turn, lowers foreign exchange reserves and a subsequent reversal of the money supply increase through the external sector. Financing deficits by borrowing from the central bank is then equivalent to financing deficits out of international reserves.

What is the relationship between budget deficits and inflation under a fixed exchange rate system? Recall that the domestic price level $P^d = NER \cdot P^f$, where P^d is the domestic price level, NER is the exchange rate of the domestic currency per unit of foreign currency, and P^f is the foreign price level. Assuming that all goods are tradable, then the domestic price level remains unchanged as long as the nominal exchange rate remains fixed and there is no change in the foreign price level. To the extent that the purchasing power parity proposition holds, the domestic price level would therefore shadow the price level of the anchor country.

Table 5.2 Overall budget deficit/surplus and foreign reserves in selected countries of the Asia-Pacific, 1980–2007

Country/region	1990–94	1995–99	2000	2001	2002	2003	2004	2005	2006	2007
Australia										
Overall budget deficit/surplus (% of GDP)	1.8	1.8	1.8	1.8	1.8	1.8	1.8	1.8	1.8	1.8
Foreign reserves/GDP at current prices (%)	5.2	4.5	5.0	5.2	5.4	6.6	6.0	6.3	7.6	3.1
Bangladesh										
Overall budget deficit/surplus (% of GDP)	−3.4	−2.5	−4.5	−4.1	−3.7	−3.4	−3.4	−3.7	−3.3	−3.3
Foreign reserves/GDP at current prices (%)	5.9	4.6	3.3	2.9	3.6	5.1	5.8	4.9	6.4	8.1
Cambodia										
Overall budget deficit/surplus (% of GDP)	−4.4	−3.6	−2.1	−3.1	−3.4	−4.0	−2.0	−0.5	−0.8	−1.2
Foreign reserves/GDP at current prices (%)	2.4	11.5	17.5	19.4	22.9	23.3	24.2	22.1	22.5	29.1
China										
Overall budget deficit/surplus (% of GDP)	−2.9	−2.3	−2.8	−2.5	−2.6	−2.2	−1.3	−1.2	−0.8	0.7
Foreign reserves/GDP at current prices (%)	7.2	13.5	14.1	16.5	20.3	25.1	32.0	36.8	40.4	46.8
Fiji										
Overall budget deficit/surplus (% of GDP)	−3.2	−3.2	−4.8	−7.6	−6.9	−6.5	−4.4	−5.2	−4.0	. . .
Foreign reserves/GDP at current prices (%)	21.0	23.4	27.9	25.3	22.5	21.7	20.8	12.6	na	na
Hong Kong, China										
Overall budget deficit/surplus (% of GDP)	2.0	1.4	−0.6	−4.9	−4.8	−3.2	1.7	1.0	4.0	7.2
Foreign reserves/GDP at current prices (%)	34.1	48.8	63.6	66.7	68.3	74.7	74.5	69.9	70.1	73.7
India										
Overall budget deficit/surplus (% of GDP)	−5.4	−4.7	−5.7	−6.2	−5.9	−4.5	−4.0	−4.1	−3.4	−3.1
Foreign reserves/GDP at current prices (%)	4.1	7.3	9.4	10.8	15.1	18.8	20.5	18.3	21.1	na
Indonesia										
Overall budget deficit/surplus (% of GDP)	−0.4	−0.1	−1.1	−2.4	−1.5	−1.7	−1.0	−0.5	−0.9	−1.2
Foreign reserves/GDP at current prices (%)	7.8	13.6	17.7	17.1	16.4	15.4	14.1	12.1	11.7	13.2
Japan										
Overall budget deficit/surplus (% of GDP)	−2.2	−6.0	−6.4	−6.0	−6.8	−6.6	−5.2	−6.1	−1.1	. . .
Foreign reserves/GDP at current prices (%)	2.3	5.1	7.6	9.7	11.8	15.7	18.1	18.4	20.1	21.8
Korea, South										
Overall budget deficit/surplus (% of GDP)	−0.4	−1.4	1.1	1.2	3.3	1.1	0.7	0.4	0.4	3.8

Table 5.2 (continued)

Country/region	1990–94	1995–99	2000	2001	2002	2003	2004	2005	2006	2007
Foreign reserves/GDP at current prices (%)	5.4	9.6	18.8	21.3	22.2	25.5	29.3	26.6	26.9	27.0
Lao PDR										
Overall budget deficit/surplus (% of GDP)	−7.0	−6.6	−4.3	−4.2	−3.2	−5.4	−2.4	−4.3	−3.2	−2.7
Foreign reserves/GDP at current prices (%)	3.1	7.4	8.1	7.6	10.6	10.0	9.1	8.3	9.6	na
Malaysia										
Overall budget deficit/surplus (% of GDP)	−0.6	−0.2	−5.5	−5.2	−5.3	−5.0	−4.1	−3.6	−3.3	−3.2
Foreign reserves/GDP at current prices (%)	29.9	29.8	30.3	31.9	33.1	39.8	52.9	50.7	52.6	54.1
Myanmar										
Overall budget deficit/surplus (% of GDP)	−2.5	−1.0	0.7	. . .	. . .	. . .	. . .	. . .	. . .	. . .
Foreign reserves/GDP at current prices (%)	0.8	0.2	0.1	0.1	0.1	0.0	0.0	na	na	0.0
Nepal										
Overall budget deficit/surplus (% of GDP)	−6.9	−5.0	−4.3	−5.5	−5.0	−1.4	−0.9	−0.8	−1.6	−2.0
Foreign reserves/GDP at current prices (%)	13.1	13.8	16.6	17.7	17.4	19.0	20.2	18.2	na	na
New Zealand										
Overall budget deficit/surplus (% of GDP)	−1.5	1.6	2.1	2.0	3.8	4.2	4.3	5.3	5.9	. . .
Foreign reserves/GDP at current prices (%)	7.7	7.6	7.5	6.8	8.2	7.5	7.0	8.0	13.0	na
Pakistan										
Overall budget deficit/surplus (% of GDP)	−7.3	−6.5	−5.4	−3.3	−2.4	−1.2	−1.8	−4.2	−3.7	−4.0
Foreign reserves/GDP at current prices (%)	4.4	3.4	3.1	6.7	12.6	14.9	11.8	10.6	10.8	11.6
Papua New Guinea										
Overall budget deficit/surplus (% of GDP)	−3.7	−0.8	−1.8	−3.0	−3.3	−1.0	1.6	0.0	3.1	0.0
Foreign reserves/GDP at current prices (%)	6.5	7.2	7.7	12.4	10.0	14.7	16.8	15.2	25.6	na
Philippines										
Overall budget deficit/surplus (% of GDP)	−1.5	−0.9	−4.0	−4.0	−5.3	−4.6	−3.8	−2.7	−1.1	−0.2
Foreign reserves/GDP at current prices (%)	9.3	14.4	19.8	22.0	21.3	21.4	18.7	18.7	19.5	na
Singapore										
Overall budget deficit/surplus (% of GDP)	8.9	6.6	2.5	−1.8	0.1	7.4	6.9	9.0	6.9	12.2
Foreign reserves/GDP at current prices (%)	90.0	na	na	na	na	na	na	na	na	na

Table 5.2 (continued)

Country/region	1990–94	1995–99	2000	2001	2002	2003	2004	2005	2006	2007
Sri Lanka										
Overall budget deficit/surplus (% of GDP)	−8.0	−7.8	−9.3	−10.2	−8.2	−7.3	−7.5	−7.0	−7.0	−6.9
Foreign reserves/GDP at current prices (%)	11.3	13.2	6.9	8.5	10.0	12.4	10.7	11.2	10.4	11.3
Taiwan, China										
Overall budget deficit/surplus (% of GDP)	−2.2	−1.0	−4.6	−6.4	−2.9	−2.3	−2.5	−0.3	−0.2	. . .
Foreign reserves/GDP at current prices (%)	42.7	33.7	34.7	43.4	55.8	69.1	74.5	72.4	74.1	na
Thailand										
Overall budget deficit/surplus (% of GDP)	3.3	−0.7	−2.2	−2.4	−1.4	0.4	0.1	−0.6	1.1	0.0
Foreign reserves/GDP at current prices (%)	19.2	23.2	26.6	28.6	30.7	29.5	30.9	29.5	32.4	na
Vietnam										
Overall budget deficit/surplus (% of GDP)	−2.9	−2.2	−4.3	−3.5	−2.3	−2.2	0.2	−1.1	−1.8	−5.4
Foreign reserves/GDP at current prices (%)	2.8	8.3	11.3	11.5	12.1	16.1	na	17.4	22.3	33.8

Note: na = not available.

Sources: ADB, *Asian Development Outlook* (various years) and ADB, *Key Indicators of Developing Member Countries of Asian and Pacific Countries* (various years).

If budget deficits persist, the government eventually runs out of foreign reserves. At that point, residents may attempt to convert their domestic money for foreign money. For lack of foreign exchange reserves, the government cannot supply foreign currency to the residents and therefore the fixed exchange rate system becomes untenable. At that point, the central bank finds no other option than to float the exchange rate. The collapse of the fixed exchange rate system due to a speculative attack (well before the central bank runs out of reserves) is called the balance-of-payments crisis (Calvo and Guidotti, 1992). The breakdown of the fixed exchange rate regime is accompanied by a sharp depreciation of the currency, which may lead to both economic and political crises. This is reflected in a sharp rise in inflation, which is associated with a sharp depreciation of the exchange rate of the currency. The late 1990s East Asian currency crisis illustrates the mechanics of a currency crisis and the resultant surge of inflation (Hossain, 2000; 2006a).

Inflation under a floating exchange rate system

When the currency is floated, the domestic money supply becomes exogenous and linked to the central bank's holding of domestic assets (credits). When the government cannot borrow from the public but borrows only from the central bank, this increases the holdings of central bank's domestic assets. Equivalently, this increases the liabilities of the central bank, that is, high-powered money. With $R^{\$}_{c} - R^{\$}_{c-1} = 0$, equation (5.8) then becomes:

$$(M - M_{-1}/P) = DEF \qquad (5.10)$$

It can be written as:

$$DEF = (M - M_{-1}/M)\,(M/P) \qquad (5.11)$$

Recall the *Equation of Exchange*, which shows that $M = Py/V$. If DEF remains constant period-to-period and y (output) does not change, V would be constant. This gives the relationship: $M_{-1} = P_{-1}y/V$. Equation (5.11) then can be written as:

$$DEF = (P - P_{-1}/P)\,(M/P) \qquad (5.12a)$$

By multiplying the right-hand side by P_{-1}/P_{-1}, equation (5.12a) can be expressed as:

$$DEF = (P - P_{-1}/P_{-1})\,(P_{-1}/P)\,(M/P) \qquad (5.12b)$$

Define $\pi = (P - P_{-1}/P_{-1})$ and the fact that $P/P_{-1} = 1 + \pi$, equation (5.12b) becomes

$$DEF = (\pi/1 + \pi)\,(M/P) \qquad (5.13)$$

Equation (5.13) shows that under a floating exchange rate system, there is a linkage between budget deficits and inflation. One interpretation of equation (5.13) is that budget deficits are financed through the inflation tax on real balances. The tax rate is $(\pi/1 + \pi)$ where π is the rate of inflation. The tax base is real balances. The product of the tax rate and the tax base is total revenue, which finances budget deficits (Kimbrough, 1992).

The chain of causation running from budget deficits to inflation is as follows. Deficits lead to an increase in the money supply when the central bank buys Treasury bonds issued by the deficit-ridden government, which cannot borrow from the public or from abroad. This creates an excess money supply (given the prices and interest rates), which causes a depreciation of the exchange rate when households convert part of their excess money into foreign assets. When foreign exchange reserves are in short supply, the central bank cannot intervene into foreign exchange markets to prevent any depreciation of the currency. In so far the purchasing power parity proposition holds, the depreciation of the exchange rate would lead to inflation at the same rate.

HIGH INFLATION OR HYPERINFLATION: POLICIES AND ISSUES[10]

Monetary economists emphasise that most monetary relationships can be studied better during high inflations and hyperinflations (Hall, 1982; Siklos, 1995). High inflation is defined as the rate of inflation exceeding 100 per cent per annum, while hyperinflation is defined as the rate of inflation of more than 50 per cent per month (Cagan, 1956). An inflation rate of 50 per cent per month (when compounded for 12 months) results in annual inflation of about 13 000 per cent.

Cases of hyperinflation are not a common phenomenon. Until the 1990s there were only 15 cases of hyperinflation. Most of them happened within the decades following the First and Second World Wars (Bomberger and Makinen, 1983; Bresciani-Turroni, 1937; Cagan, 1956). Table 5.3 reports some information on seven episodes of European hyperinflation of the 1920s and 1940s. There was no hyperinflation during 1949 and 1983. Seven cases of hyperinflation, however, happened during the second half of the 1980s. Several countries also experienced high inflations during the 1980s and early 1990s.[11] Zimbabwe is the latest case of hyperinflation.

Cases of hyperinflation provide information on factors that cause extreme inflationary conditions and the damaging effects of such inflation on both the economy and society (Cagan, 1992a; Capie, 1986). In fact, some recent ideas about central banking and monetary policy originated from the bitter memories of hyperinflations during the 1920s and 1940s. The painful memories of the 1923 German hyperinflation had a lingering effect on the German people. These bitter experiences acted as a catalyst for the establishment of an independent German central bank (the Bundesbank), which jealously guarded against inflation. The present European Central Bank (ECB) is a 'replica of the Bundesbank' in its spirit. The ECB remains committed to low and steady inflation in Euroland. Central banks of other countries have followed the spirit of the Bundesbank, although most do not have the same fighting zest against inflation as an inflation fighter (Cecchetti, 2008; Mishkin, 2007a).

Conditions that May Trigger Hyperinflation

It is interesting to overview the conditions that may trigger high inflation or hyperinflation. As mentioned above, hyperinflation is a twentieth-century phenomenon. Such cases have common elements despite unique characteristics. Still, it is difficult to postulate a general theory of hyperinflation. Following Sachs and Larrain (1993), some of the common elements and characteristics of hyperinflation are described below.

Fiat money

There is consensus that hyperinflation is a monetary phenomenon. All cases of hyperinflation were preceded by a rapid expansion of the money supply. Monetary expansion at a rapid pace has been technologically feasible only under a fiat money system. Under a metallic money (or the gold standard system), there was limit on the supply of precious metals. Fiat money has removed this constraint and is therefore considered the basic condition of hyperinflation. However the need for rapid expansion of the money supply remains the root cause of hyperinflation. Such an environment is created when the taxation system breaks down and/or the opportunities for foreign borrowing dry up. This happened in Bolivia during the early 1980s (Blanchard, 2006). Facing both domestic and external constraints on borrowings, money creation becomes the only source of government revenues. High inflation or hyperinflation then becomes the outcome of rapid monetary expansion over a number of few years. Keynes (1923: 41) made the following observation on the predicament of a beleaguered government that runs out of options for deficit financing: 'A Government can live for a long time, even the German Government or the Russian Government, by printing paper money. That is to say, it can by this means secure the command over real resources – resources just as real as those obtained by taxation.' Barro (2008) reports that during hyperinflations in some countries, the revenues from money creation can approach about 10 per cent of GDP. This was

Table 5.3 *Seven European hyperinflations of the 1920s and 1940s*

Country	Beginning of hyperinflation	End of hyperinflation	P_T/P_0	Average monthly inflation (%)	Average monthly money growth (%)
Austria	October 1921	August 1922	70	47	31
Germany	August 1922	November 1923	1.0×10^{10}	322	314
Greece	November 1943	November 1944	4.7×10^{6}	365	220
Hungary-I	March 1923	February 1924	44	46	33
Hungary-II	August 1945	July 1946	3.8×10^{27}	19800	12200
Poland	January 1923	January 1924	699	82	72
Russia	December 1921	January 1924	1.2×10^{5}	57	49

Note: P_T/P_0 = price level in the last month of hyperinflation divided by the price level in the first month.

Source: Blanchard (2006: 494).

apparently the maximum amount that the governments were able to raise from printing money. Note that the revenue–GDP ratio in many developing countries is about 10 per cent. This indicates that money creation may entirely replace other sources of revenues in poor countries during hyperinflation.

War, civil war and revolution

Hyperinflation is sometimes preceded by war. Large budget deficits during a war are monetised. Some studies suggest that hyperinflation is actually linked to civil wars, revolutions and deep social and political unrest rather than a conventional war. Sometimes war creates patriotism and makes it easier for the government to finance war-spending through conventional taxes and/or borrowings from the public. In contrast, during civil war, hostility occurs between different groups or communities. Consequently, it becomes difficult for a government to collect taxes because some sections of the people avoid paying taxes. Increased war spending is then financed through money creation.

Weak governments

Not all revolutions and civil wars provoke periods of hyperinflation. Not all hyperinflation also emerges under these conditions. Weak governments are another condition that may trigger hyperinflations. There are, however, problems in establishing that weak governments produce hyperinflations. First, it is difficult to separate the government's weakness from any social unrest or civil war. A weak government leads to internal unrest, this in turn may feed back and weakens the government. Second, weakness is hard to verify. Third, the argument may become tautological: whenever hyperinflation happens, people may label the government weak. Nevertheless, in general, weak or inexperienced governments may not have the ability to raise taxes and to implement tough budgetary reforms. In addition, they may placate different groups with transfer payments and subsidies to build up political bases. Under these circumstances, governments may turn to inflationary finance of budget deficits and thus set the stage for high inflation. Historically, some developing countries after independence used inflationary finance for developmental activities. To remain in power, nationalist leaders also placated different groups in the society and thereby created an environment for high inflation or hyperinflation. As argued in Chapter 4, macroeconomic populism was a common phenomenon in many Latin American countries during the 1970s and 1980s, leading to high inflation and balance-of-payments crises (Dornbusch, 1993; Dornbusch and Edwards, 1990).

External shocks

Economists have found a parallel between hyperinflationary experiences of the 1920s and the 1980s. External shocks caused adverse effects on the budget on both occasions. In the 1920s the problem stemmed from war reparations of Austria, Hungary and Germany to the Allies. After the Second World War, Hungary made reparations and occupation payments that contributed to its fiscal crisis. External shocks raised budget deficits and caused debt crises in Latin America during the 1980s. The countries affected had high levels of public debt as a proportion of GDP. They serviced such debts until their macroeconomic consequences become unbearable. Several countries, namely Argentina, Bolivia, Brazil and Poland, made interest payments until the onset of hyperinflations (Dornbusch et al., 2008).

Economic Dynamics of Hyperinflation

In order to develop a general model of hyperinflation, economists look at both the demand and supply sides of the money market. The main feature of hyperinflation is the rapid expansion of the money supply, which originates from the need to finance large budget deficits. Typically, a major external or internal shock pushes the government to run large budget deficits. Once deficits continue for a few years, the government scrambles to find non-monetary sources of finance. Once the stock of debt builds up, creditors become reluctant to finance new deficits. They sense default risk in the event of foreign debt or inflation risk in the event of domestic debt. The government then turns to money financing of budget deficits as the last option. When deficits are large and sustained over a few years, monetary financing accelerates inflation. By the time inflation reaches a triple-digit figure, the people sharply revise their inflationary expectations upward. In the process they lose confidence in the government's ability to control budget deficits and/or the money supply. Available evidence suggests that a money-financed deficit of within the range of 10 to 12 per cent of GDP for a few years, is a recipe for high inflation or hyperinflation (Barro, 2008; Buchanan et al., 1987; Sachs and Larrain, 1993; Vogel, 1974).

The demand for money

It is possible to formalise discussion on the impact of inflationary expectations on money demand following monetary financing of budget deficits on a continual basis. Cagan's (1956) classic model of hyperinflation is built on this line. He was the first to observe that at times of hyperinflation, the demand for real balances depends entirely on expected inflation. Note that the demand for money depends on the nominal interest rate (i), which can be approximated as the sum of the real interest rate (r) and expected inflation (π^e). The money market equilibrium condition then can be written as:

$$M/P = m^d(i) = m^d(r + \pi^e) \tag{5.14}$$

where M is the money stock, P is the price level, and $m^d(\ldots)$ is a decreasing function of the nominal interest rate (i) which equals the real interest rate (r) and expected inflation (π^e). At times of high inflation, the shift in the nominal interest rate is due to the shift in expected inflation rather than any major change in the real interest rate. Cagan therefore simplified the money market equilibrium condition as follows:

$$M/P = m^d(\pi^e) \tag{5.15}$$

This simplification allowed him to focus on dynamics of expected inflation as an integral part of hyperinflation. When expected inflation is high, households hold very low real balances because the opportunity cost of holding money is extremely high. Conversely, when expected inflation is low, they hold larger real balances. When the inflation rate is very high, most debt instruments have only short maturity. Even short-maturity debt instruments may not exist during hyperinflations, implying a complete breakdown of the credit system. An alternative to money holding is durable goods, especially consumer goods which are necessities for living in difficult times.

At the early phase of inflation, expected inflation may lag actual inflation and this creates an opportunity for the government to raise seigniorage. As inflation accelerates, expected inflation catches up actual inflation. When the economy reaches the steady state, expected inflation equals actual inflation. Equation (5.15) then can be rewritten such that real balances become a function of actual inflation:

$$M/P = m^d(\pi) \qquad (5.16)$$

Equation (5.16) represents a money market equilibrium condition in which the demand for money remains stably related to an extremely high rate of inflation. This is the foundation block of the monetary model of hyperinflation.

Table 5.4 reports data for the money growth rate, inflation and real balances in Germany from 1920 to 1925. Importantly, they reveal a negative relationship between inflation and real balances.

The supply of money

The story of the money supply side is straightforward. The money supply increases continually because the government continues to borrow from the central bank to pay its bills. The government faces the constraint of financing a given level of real spending for running state machineries. Let *SE* be the amount of real spending that the government must cover by printing money. This can be expressed as:

$$SE = \Delta M_t/P_{t+1} \qquad (5.17)$$

where ΔM_t is the increase in the money stock between t and $t+1$, P is the price level for $t + 1$, and *SE* (seigniorage) is the real value of goods and services purchased by the newly issued money, $\Delta M_t/P_{t+1}$. The real revenue generated this way can be expressed using the growth rate of the money supply, $\lambda_t = \Delta M_t/M_t$. Equation (5.17) is rewritten as follows:

$$SE = (\Delta M_t/M_t)(M_t/P_{t+1}) \qquad (5.18)$$

This shows that seigniorage equals the growth rate of the money supply λ_t times real balances, such that

$$SE = \lambda_t \bullet M_t/P_{t+1} \qquad (5.19)$$

Seigniorage and inflation tax

In the hyperinflation literature, the concept seigniorage is used synonymously with inflation tax revenue (R^π). The inflation tax measures the decline in the value of real balances due to rising inflation:

$$R^\pi = \pi_t \bullet M_t/P_{t+1} \qquad (5.20)$$

It was demonstrated earlier that there exists a stable inverse relation between inflation and real balances. As inflation rises, money loses its real value. Therefore, households need to increase their nominal money holdings merely to keep real balances constant.

Table 5.4 Money growth, inflation and real balances during the German hyperinflation and thereafter, 1920–25

Period	Growth rate of total currency in circulation (M) (per cent per month)	Cost of living index (CLI)-inflation (per cent per month)	Real balances, M_t/CLI, (end of period, 1913 = 1)
February 1920 to June 1920	5.7	6	1.01
June 1920 to December 1920	3	1.1	1.13
December 1920 to June 1921	0.8	0.1	1.18
June 1921 to December 1921	5.5	8.4	0.99
December 1921 to June 1922	6.5	12.8	0.68
June 1922 to December 1922	29.4	46.7	0.24
December 1922 to June 1923	40	40	0.24
June 1923 to October 1923	233	286	0.03
Reform period			
December 1923 to June 1924	5.9	−0.6	0.44
June 1924 to December 1924	5.3	1.4	0.56
December 1924 to June 1925	2	1.6	0.57
June 1925 to December 1925	1.2	0.4	0.6

Source: Barro (2008: 286).

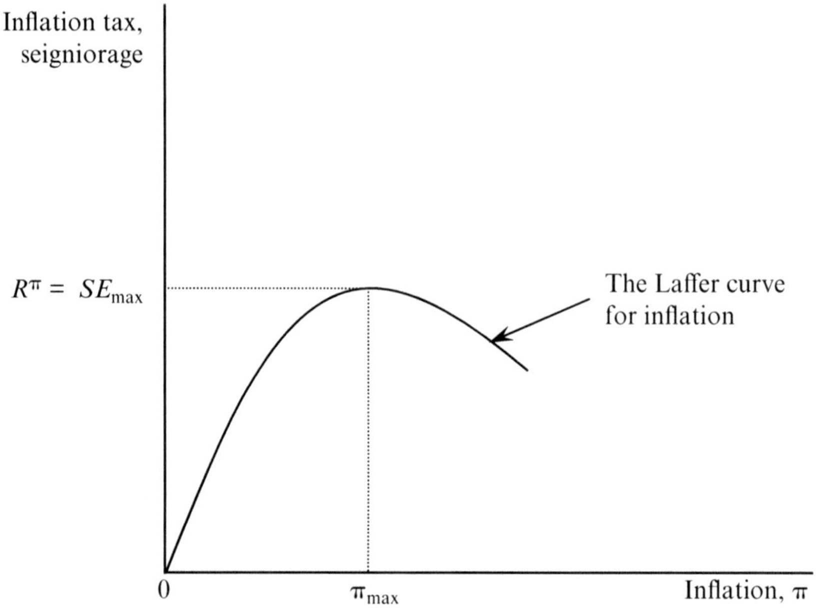

Figure 5.6 Relationship between seigniorage (≡ inflation tax) and inflation

When inflation remains constant (and real balances are constant), households increase their nominal money holdings at exactly the same rate that the government collects seigniorage revenue. That is, since $\lambda_t = \pi_t$, $SE = \pi_t \bullet M_t/P_{t+1}$. Therefore in the steady-state:

$$SE = R^{\pi} \tag{5.21}$$

The revenue maximising rate of inflation

Equation (5.19) represents an inverted U-shaped relationship between seigniorage and the inflation rate:

$$SE = f(\pi),\ \delta SE/\delta\pi > 0 \text{ for } \pi < \pi_{max} \tag{5.22a}$$

$$SE = f(\pi),\ \delta SE/\delta\pi < 0 \text{ for } \pi > \pi_{max} \tag{5.22b}$$

This relationship is based on two results. An increase in the money growth rate increases the rate of inflation and the nominal interest rate. The higher interest rate (or expected inflation) lowers the demand for real balances. Thus an increase in the money supply growth has two opposing effects: the rise in the money growth rate raises real revenue but a decrease in real balances reduces real revenue. The net effect of the money supply growth therefore depends on how the demand for real balances falls in response to an increase in the nominal interest rate or expected inflation. Figure 5.6 shows that there is an optimal rate of inflation (π_{max}) at which SE is maximum.

This relationship can be illustrated with a simple money demand specification. Assume that during hyperinflation the money demand function takes the form: $m^d = e^{-\beta\pi}$, where

m^d is the demand for real balances, π is the rate of inflation, e is the exponentiation parameter and β is the sensitivity of money demand with respect to inflation. Recall that $R^\pi = \pi \cdot m^d = \pi \cdot e^{-\beta\pi}$. The first-order derivative of R^π with respect to π (when set to zero) yields an expression for the rate of inflation at which the inflation tax revenue is maximum.[12] In the present case this is given by $1/\beta$. This suggests that the higher the sensitivity of money demand with respect to inflation, then the lower is the rate of inflation at which inflation tax revenue would be maximum.

In a highly inflationary economy, the sensitivity of money demand with respect to inflation is very high and therefore the inflation rate at which the inflation tax revenue becomes maximum could be relatively low. For example, Khan (1980) estimated the semi-elasticity of demand for money with respect to inflation for several countries – estimates were found to be between 3 and 5. Substitution of these estimates yields the revenue-maximising rates of inflation ranging from 20 to 33 per cent per annum.

Stabilisation Policies for Ending Hyperinflation

All cases of hyperinflation come to a sudden crashing end. The public cannot bear dislocation of the economy and the government becomes desperate to find a way to bring fiscal and monetary discipline. The central bank may introduce a new currency, while the government introduces tax reform measures that include new taxes for replacing inflation tax. The official exchange rate is devalued sharply and then pegged to a stable foreign currency, say the US dollar. This is expected to bring exchange rate stability and provide an anchor for inflationary expectations. These stabilisation measures constitute a package, although they may not always be successful. Success usually comes after several attempts.

Economists have examined different approaches to price stabilisation and their relative chances of success (Veiga, 1999; Vines, 1992). The key issue is whether stabilisation can be brought without affecting the real economy. Note that hyperinflation causes dislocation of productive resources. Many destabilising factors remain present in the system by the time stabilisation measures are put in place. The real economy remains at a standstill, implying that coordinated attacks have a chance of stopping hyperinflations without imposing significant costs in terms of unemployment. This issue is debated around two alternative approaches. The orthodox approach to stabilisation involves a policy package (as defined above) combining monetary, fiscal and exchange rate policies (Bruno, 1979; 1993b). An alternative is the heterodox approach which combines monetary, fiscal and exchange rate policies with income policies (Agenor and Montiel, 1996). Which approach to stabilisation is more effective in the end depends on credibility of the programme and the seriousness of the authorities in bringing the rate of inflation down. The populace respond positively when the authorities develop a programme that includes structural measures to achieve and maintain both fiscal and monetary discipline on a sustained basis. Such a programme can lower inflationary expectations quickly and restore confidence of the people in the ability of the government to preside over a smooth transition from high to low inflation. The programme becomes more credible when the government brings major institutional changes that deny the government access to money financing of budget deficits (Dornbusch, 1993; Dornbusch and Fischer, 1986; Dornbusch et al., 1990; Kapur, 1976).

Table 5.5 Seigniorage, inflation tax and inflation in selected countries of the Asia-Pacific, 1950–2007

Country	1950–69			1970–89			1990–2007		
	Seigniorage (% of GDP)	Inflation tax (% of GDP)	Inflation (%)	Seigniorage (% of GDP)	Inflation tax (% of GDP)	Inflation (%)	Seigniorage (% of GDP)	Inflation tax (% of GDP)	Inflation (%)
Australia	0.51	1.35	4.71	0.57	0.98	8.99	0.33	0.52	2.80
Bangladesh	na	na	3.49	0.80	0.75	17.62	0.92	0.44	5.77
Canada	0.36	0.44	2.46	0.48	0.91	6.94	0.14	0.46	2.25
China	na	na	na	4.78	25.89	7.45	5.72	15.47	5.05
Fiji	na	na	na	19.82	0.67	5.85	1.02	0.54	3.57
India	0.72	0.66	4.12	1.75	1.20	8.32	1.71	1.11	7.31
Indonesia	3.23	12.58	171.33	1.37	1.32	13.30	1.57	1.24	11.95
Japan	1.05	0.96	3.94	0.98	1.70	5.81	0.59	0.11	0.53
Korea, South	1.68	1.04	19.93	1.53	0.94	11.85	0.48	0.47	4.50
Malaysia	0.32	0.07	0.40	1.47	0.75	4.58	1.29	0.68	3.02
Myanmar	0.84	0.43	0.91	3.25	1.81	10.48	8.99	7.06	25.13
Nepal	0.90	0.35	5.06	1.33	0.92	9.33	1.88	1.06	7.33
New Zealand	0.07	1.07	4.11	0.41	1.29	11.75	0.42	0.31	2.29
Pakistan	1.12	0.70	3.08	1.78	2.18	9.49	1.76	2.05	7.93
Papua New Guinea	na	na	na	0.50	0.71	6.51	0.79	0.97	8.13
Philippines	0.57	0.29	2.56	1.18	1.08	14.40	1.64	0.68	7.51
Singapore	2.35	0.35	1.27	2.05	0.97	4.35	0.77	0.31	1.51
Sri Lanka	0.64	0.29	1.66	1.41	1.12	9.86	1.12	0.98	10.77
Thailand	0.91	0.39	1.61	1.05	0.68	9.86	0.93	0.34	10.77
USA	0.26	0.55	2.09	0.41	1.07	6.32	0.33	0.41	2.90

Notes: Seigniorage is measured in terms of the increase in reserve money stock as a percentage of GDP. Inflation is measured as the percentage change in the CPI. Inflation tax is measured as inflation times one period lagged narrow money stock as a per cent of GDP.

Source: Author's calculations based on IMF, *International Financial Statistics Yearbook* (various years).

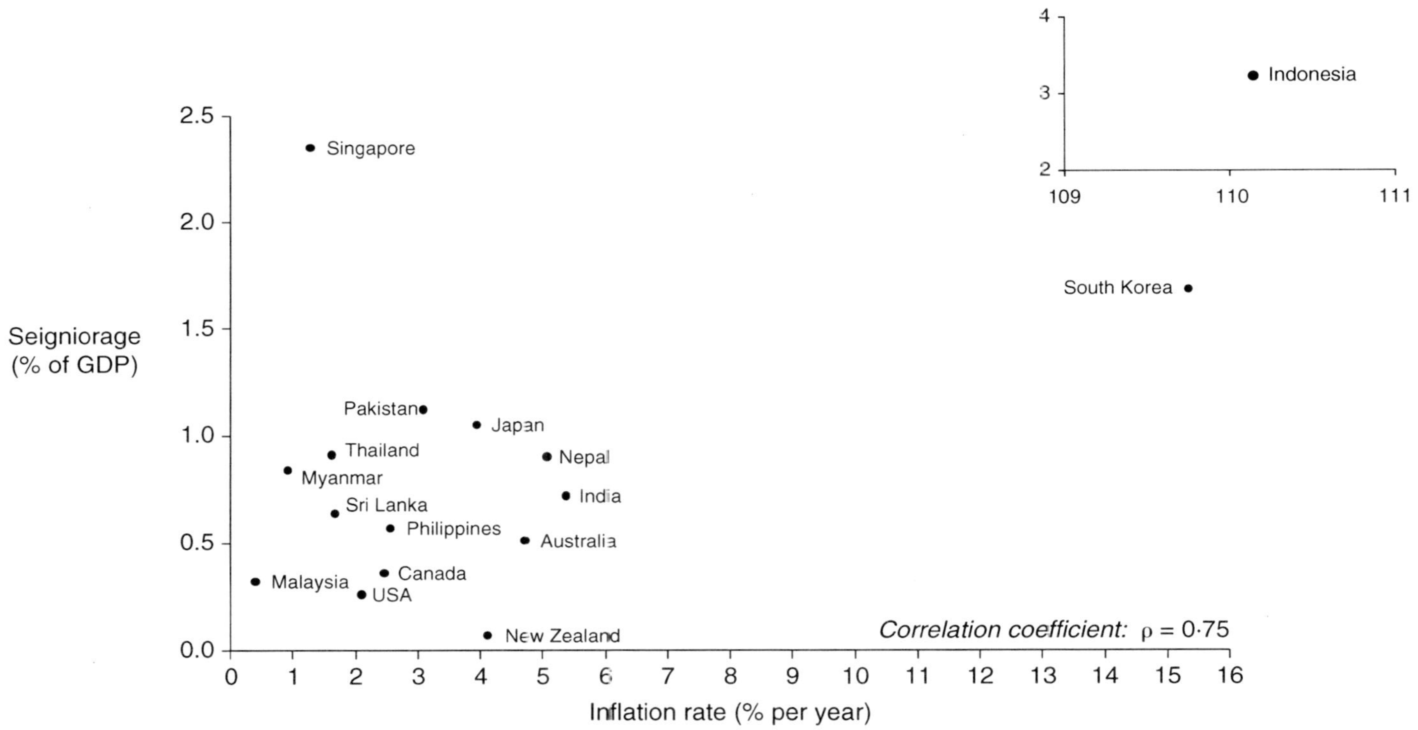

Notes:

1. Excluded for lack of data: Bangladesh, China, Fiji and FNG (Papua New Guinea).
2. Seigniorage is measured as an increase in the money base as a percentage of GDP.
3. Inflation is measured as the annual rate of change of the Consumer Price Index (CPI).

Source: IMF, *International Financial Statistics*.

Figure 5.7(a) *Seigniorage and inflation in selected countries of the Asia-Pacific, 1950–69*

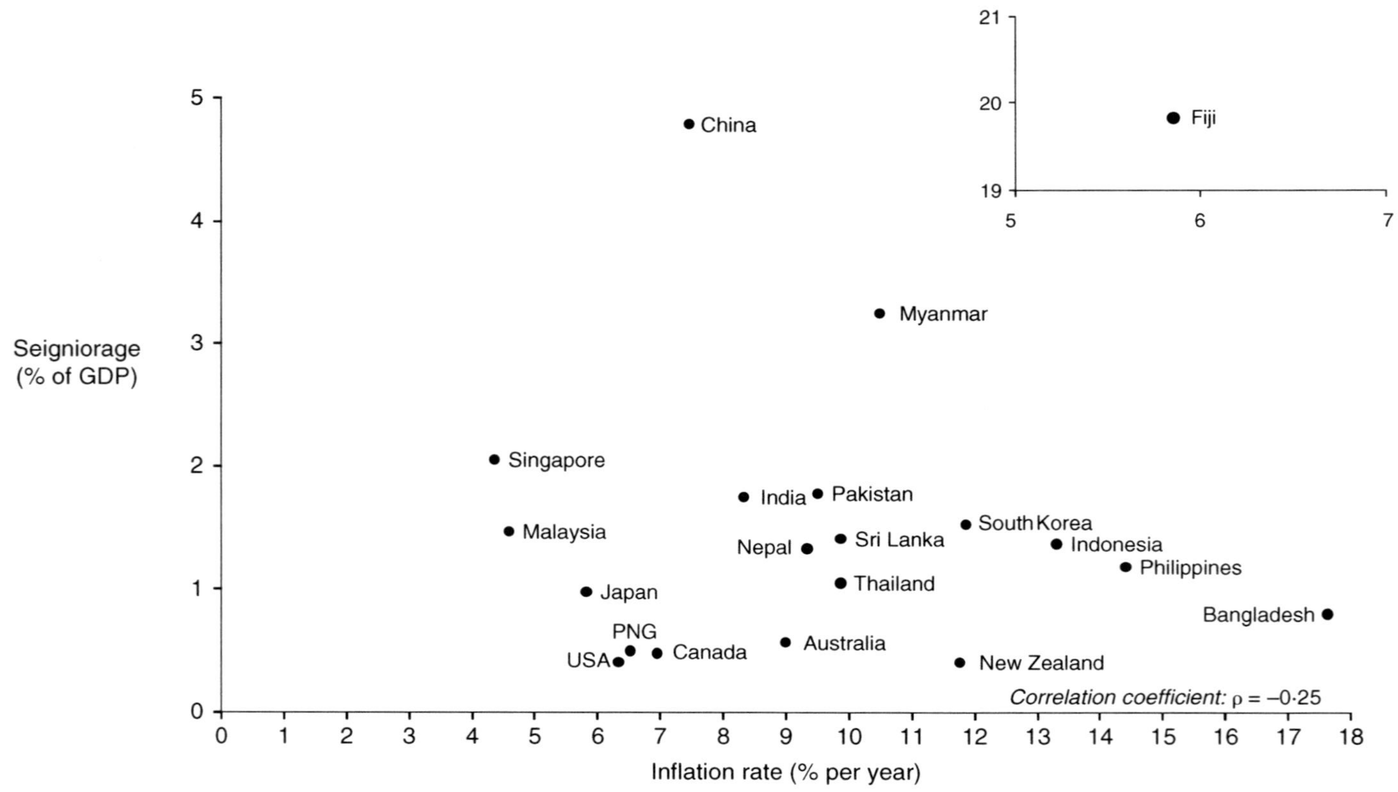

Notes: As Figure 5.7a, notes 2 and 3.

Source: As Figure 5.7a.

Figure 5.7(b) Seigniorage and inflation in selected countries of the Asia-Pacific, 1970–89

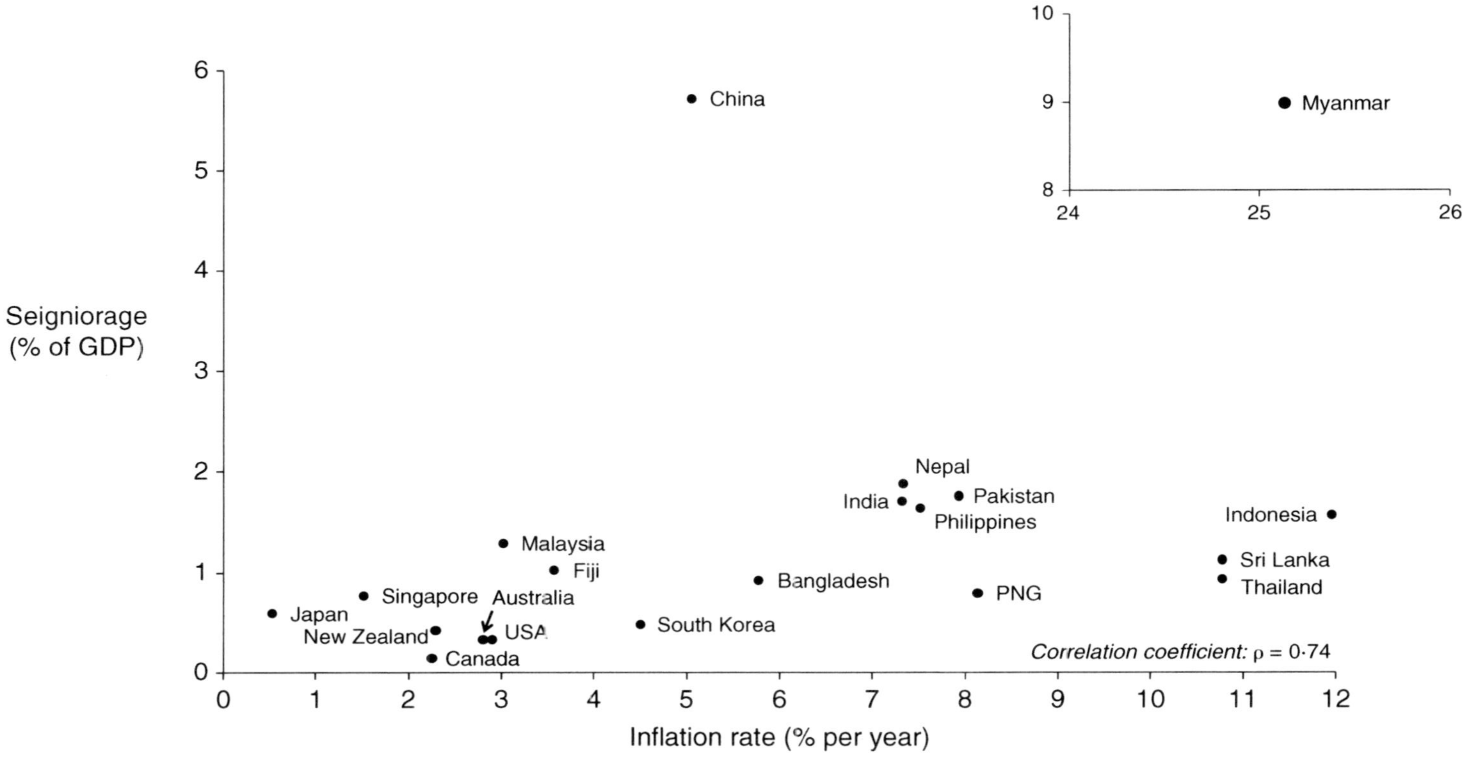

Notes: As Figure 5.7a, notes 2 and 3.

Source: As Figure 5.7a.

Figure 5.7(c) *Seigniorage and inflation in selected countries of the Asia-Pacific, 1990–2007*

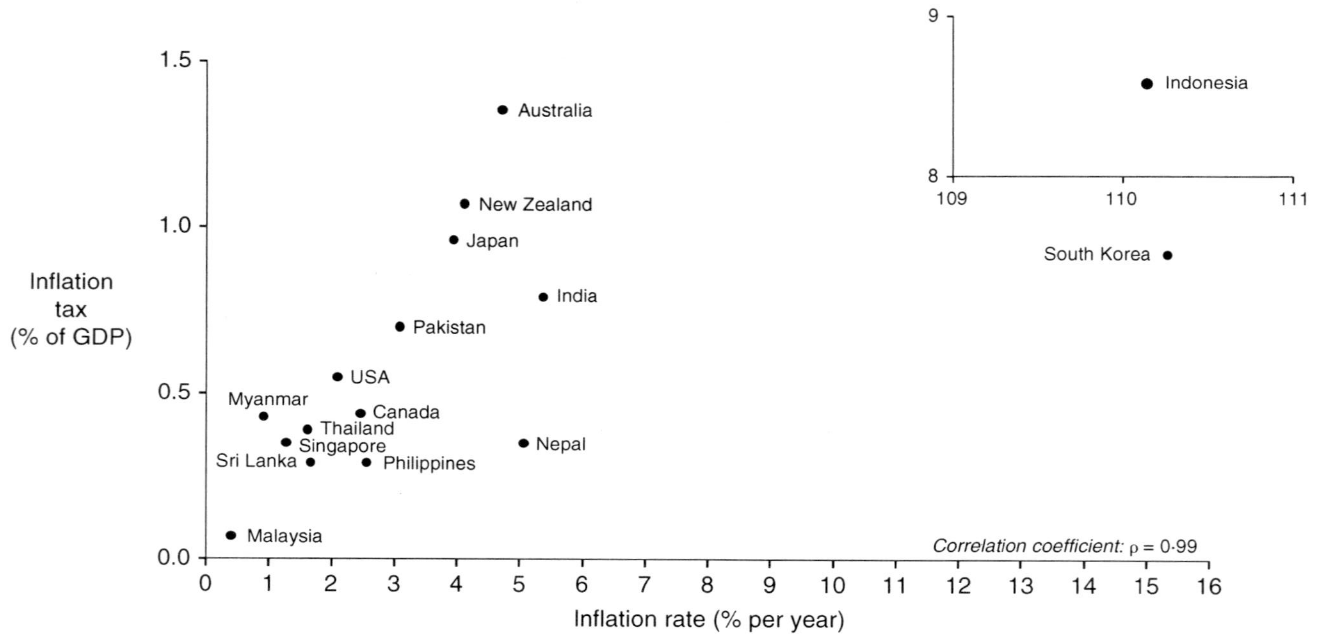

Notes:
1. Excluded for lack of data: Bangladesh, China, Fiji and PNG (Papua New Guinea).
2. The inflation tax is measured as:

$$\frac{(\pi_t \cdot NM_{t-1})}{GDP_t},$$

where π is the rate of CPI-inflation. NM is the narrow money stock, and GDP is gross domestic product.

Source: IMF, *International Financial Statistics.*

Figure 5.7(d) Inflation tax and inflation in selected countries of the Asia-Pacific, 1950–1969

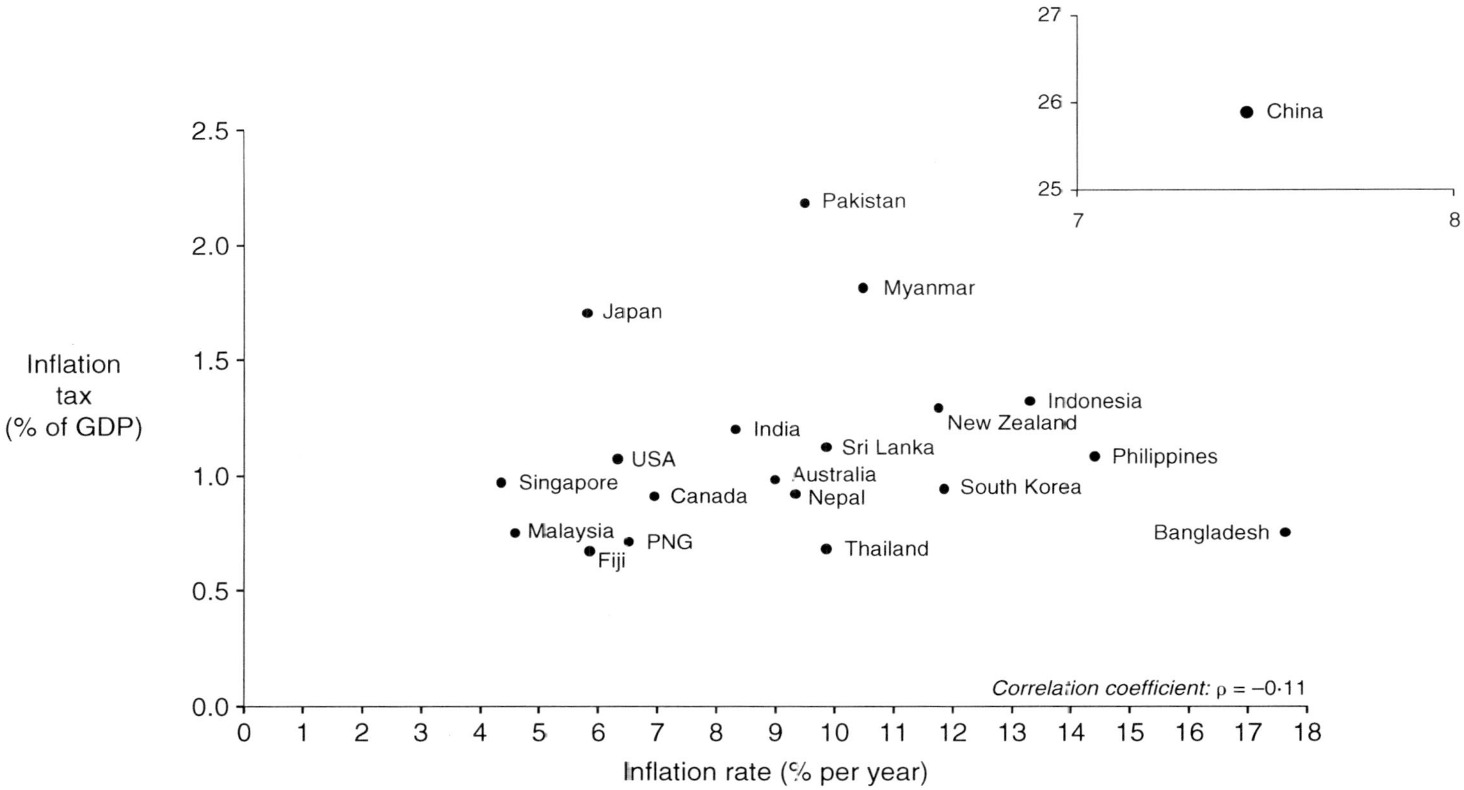

Note: As Figure 5.7d, note 2.

Source: IMF, *International Financial Statistics.*

Figure 5.7(e) Inflation tax and inflation in selected countries of the Asia-Pacific, 1970–89

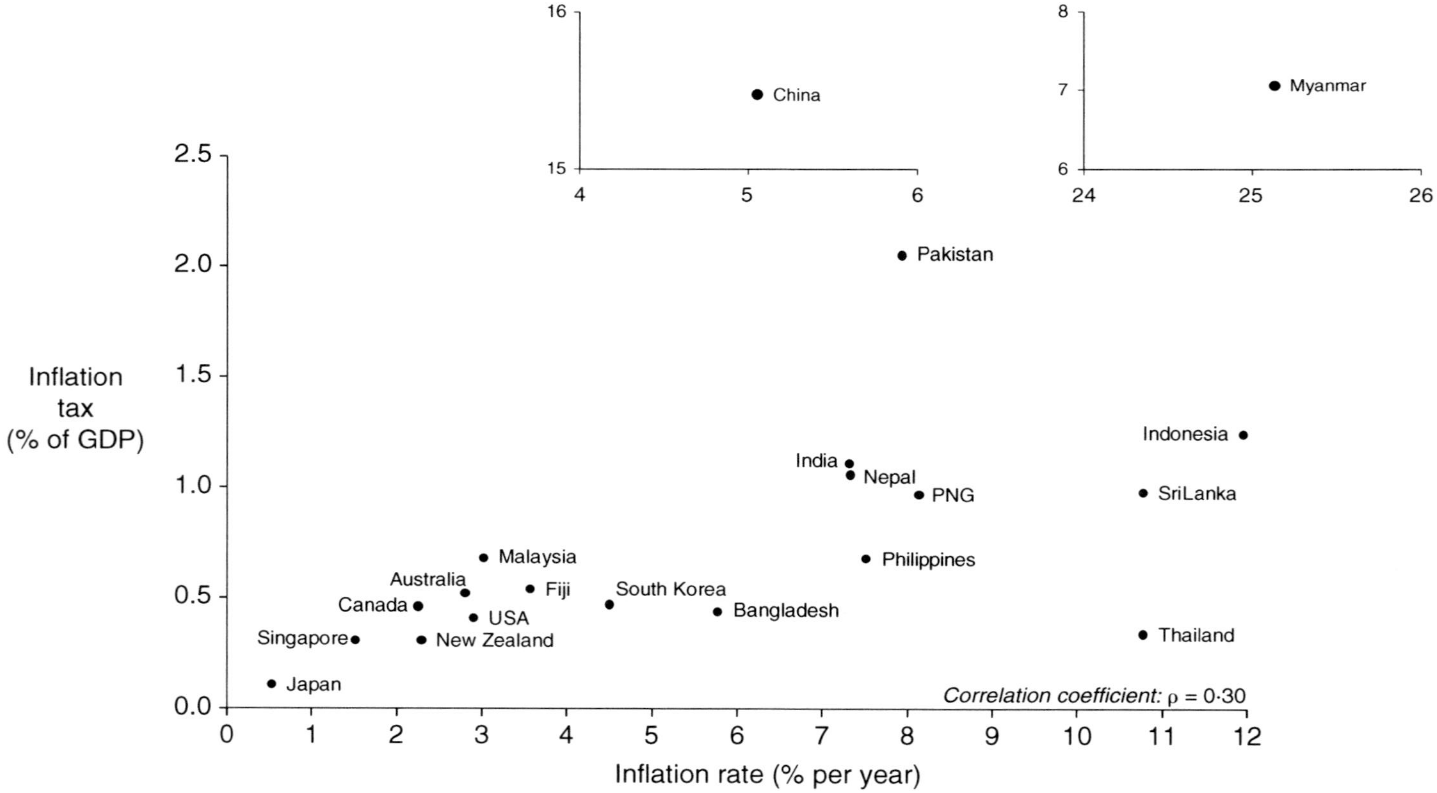

Note: As Figure 5.7d, note 2.

Source: IMF, *International Financial Statistics.*

Figure 5.7(f) Inflation tax and inflation in selected countries of the Asia-Pacific, 1990–2007

Exchange rate stabilisation

One of the characteristics of hyperinflation is that domestic residents substitute foreign (hard) currency for domestic currency. This is called currency substitution (or dollarisation). In a dollarised economy, the purchasing power parity (PPP) condition of the following form holds:

$$P^d = NER \cdot P^{f\$} \tag{5.23}$$

As defined earlier, P^d is the domestic price of tradables, NER is the nominal exchange rate of domestic currency per unit of foreign currency, and P^f is the price of tradables in foreign currency (\$).

In a hyperinflationary economy, most prices are quoted in foreign hard currency ($P^{f\$}$) and are converted into domestic currency prices by multiplying the dollar prices by the prevailing (market) exchange rate. The exchange rate therefore plays the crucial link between the dollar prices and the local currency prices for most goods and services. In a high-inflation or hyperinflationary condition, the exchange rate also depreciates at approximately the same rate as the rise in domestic prices. This provides a clue that the domestic prices can be stabilised through the stabilisation of the exchange rate of domestic currency (Dornbusch, 1988b; 1992b).

Yet bringing stability in the exchange rate is not easy. In a high-inflation or hyperinflationary economy, at least two exchange rates prevail: an official exchange rate and a free (or curb) market exchange rate. The free market exchange rate, defined as the number of domestic currency per unit of foreign currency, remains substantially above the official rate. The purchasing power parity applies to the free market rate and/or to a weighted average of the official rate and the free (or curb) market rate. As a strategy to stabilise the exchange rate, the authorities may require first a major devaluation of the official exchange rate to such an extent that it aligns with the free market rate. The next task is to stabilise the newly unified exchange rate at a sustainable level. The sustainable exchange rate may represent the value of the currency at a level that the central bank can defend without creating an environment for a speculative attack on domestic currency.

To defend the newly established exchange rate, the central bank, however, needs a large quantity of foreign exchange reserves that help to build the people's confidence in the exchange rate system. Once the exchange rate structure is in place, the medium- or long-term exchange rate stability requires both fiscal and monetary discipline. This can begin with a commitment of the government that it will neither run budget deficits nor finance them through money creation. This promise must be credible with the public, otherwise budget deficits and money creation would deplete foreign reserves and eventually there could be speculative attacks against the domestic currency. The country could again descend into turmoil (Blejer and Liviatan, 1987).

This indicates that a sharp devaluation of the domestic currency is not enough to stabilise the exchange rate. Exchange rate stability (and thereby price stability) requires tight fiscal policy that relieves the government of the need for financing budget deficits through money creation. In this context, Barro (2008: 285) cites the example of the 1924 stabilisation programme in Germany:

> A monetary reform occurred in November 1923. The reform included a new type of currency, a promise not to print new money beyond a specified limit to finance government expenditures,

reductions in real government spending, reform of the tax system, and a commitment to back the value of the new currency by gold.

Financing budget deficits

Hence the exchange rate cannot remain stable unless the underlying budget deficit is brought under control. During episodes of hyperinflation it is difficult to raise tax revenues, since taxpayers postpone paying taxes and reduce their real tax burden. In the final stage of hyperinflation, the entire deficits (and sometimes the entire spending budget) are financed by money creation. The new credit to the government acts like fuel to the fire. Therefore the fundamental step in ending hyperinflations is the elimination of budgetary problems that caused hyperinflation in the first place (Fischer et al., 2002).[13]

Central bank independence and fiscal reforms

Since mere announcements to reduce budget deficits are not enough, one effective strategy to reduce the budget deficit is giving autonomy to the central bank so that it can resist pressure from the government to finance the budget deficit through money creation. Side-by-side fiscal austerity measures should be undertaken. First, the prices of goods and services, which are provided by the public enterprises, are raised so that the prices reflect production costs. Second, tax revenues must be raised through stringent compliance measures. Other measures to improve the fiscal condition may include elimination of subsidies and tax exemptions. Many fiscal measures that reduce budget deficits – such as elimination of food subsidies, currency devaluation, raising prices of goods and services provided by the public enterprises and higher consumption taxes – may themselves raise corrective inflation (Blejer and Liviatan, 1987).

Heterodox stabilisation programmes

Heterodox stabilisation programmes include interventions into wage and price settings, in addition to monetary and fiscal measures. Heterodox programmes are based on the idea that inflation has a large component of inertia, which leads inflation to perpetuate. Inflation inertia originates from long-term labour contracts, backward-looking wage indexation and other mechanisms that introduce an automatic wage and price adjustment based on past inflation.

The rationale behind the heterodox approach to disinflation is that tight fiscal and monetary measures alone may not be sufficient to stop inflation. When inflation inertia is present, orthodox deflationary measures may cause deep recession and become unpopular. Therefore the proponents of the heterodox programmes argue that incomes policies (that is, wage and price controls) are necessary in stabilisation programmes. Some advocates of heterodoxy even suggest that wage and price controls alone are sufficient to stop inflation and that the orthodox fiscal and monetary restraints have no role to play in stabilisation programmes (Sachs and Larrain, 1993).

Heterodox programmes do have a number of shortcomings. First, the wage and price controls are often superfluous. If inflation inertia is low, inflation would soon stop on its own accord. Second, price controls are difficult to enforce beyond a small group of commodities. Administering price controls is difficult. Third, price controls are often anticipated. Therefore, private enterprises push up prices when they anticipate price controls. Fourth, price controls could be addictive, in the sense that policy-makers may have a mistaken view that inflation can be stopped without the pain of monetary and fiscal austerity measures. Fifth, price controls introduce a great deal of rigidity in the relative price structures, which may create shortages and breed corruption. Finally, most controls are difficult to phase out when they are no longer regarded necessary (Blejer and Liviatan, 1987; Sachs and Larrain, 1993).

Issues in Stabilisation

Costs of hyperinflation

High inflation or hyperinflation is obviously costly to the economy. A rise in inflation from a low level may initially bring some economic benefits but they do not last long. Once inflation reaches an extremely high level, the transactions system breaks down. Hyperinflations are an extreme condition when all prices rise so rapidly that it is difficult for consumers and producers to receive price signals from changes in the relative prices of goods and services. Informed decisions on consumption and production, however, require economic agents to make predictions about relative prices. The higher the rate of inflation, then the higher is its volatility. High inflation also makes relative prices volatile and therefore unpredictable. Real returns on, and costs of, investment are then difficult to predict. This means that credit markets work poorly or even cease to exist when lending and borrowing in a volatile inflationary environment turn out to be a gamble (Blanchard, 2006; Makinen, 1992). Likewise, productive economic activity stalls because everyone remains busy to protect themselves from the onslaught of inflation (Dornbusch et al., 2008).

Costs of disinflation

High costs of hyperinflations suggest the urgency of price stabilisation. The issue is whether deflationary measures that are commonly used to stop hyperinflations would lead to recession and/or cause other problems. Monetarists acknowledge the possibility of recession as a short-term cost of disinflationary measures.[14] In contrast, new classical economists do not believe that such a recession is unavoidable. In the theoretical literature, discussion on the costs of disinflation makes use of the expectations approach, which puts emphasis on the credibility of policy-makers (Vegh, 1995). Sargent (1982) has argued that the major European hyperinflation periods ended as a result of credible reforms of monetary and fiscal policies, without significant losses of output. When there is policy credibility and consensus among policy-makers about the urgency of stability, the people respond positively and hyperinflations come to an end quickly (Blinder, 1999; Croushore, 1992; Dornbusch, 1989; Fender, 1990). This argument can be made using the standard expectations-augmented aggregate supply curve relationship:

$$\pi = \beta\pi^e + \gamma\,(y_a - y_f) \tag{5.24}$$

where π is inflation, π^e expected inflation, y_a is actual output, y_f is full-employment output, and β and γ are adjustment coefficients. Equation (5.24) suggests that when there is policy credibility, then citizens would adjust downward their inflationary expectations (π^e). This may lower inflation sharply without raising the output gap ($y_a - y_f$). The adjustment path then can be traced along the long-run vertical Phillips curve schedule. This implies that the adjustment coefficients in equation (5.24) would take the following approximate values: $\beta \cong 1$ and $\gamma \cong 0$. As credibility is difficult to earn in a highly inflationary economy, the costs of disinflation could be high. In fact, in Bolivia, the costs of disinflation were substantial (Dornbusch et al., 2008; Morales, 1988; Sachs, 1987).

High interest rates

One major problem that a hyperinflationary country encounters following price stabilisation is the persistence of high real interest rates for a considerable period of time (Blanchard, 2006). This real interest rate problem can be understood in terms of the standard model of interest rate determination.[15] Consider the following money market equilibrium condition:

$$M/P = m^d(i, \ldots.) \tag{5.25a}$$

where real money supply (M/P) equals the real money demanded (m^d). In this specification, money demand is a decreasing function of the nominal interest rate (i). Output is assumed constant and is normalised to one. From this condition, the following interest rate model can be derived:

$$i = h(M/P, \ldots.),\ h_{(M/P)} < 0 \tag{5.26a}$$

As reviewed earlier, the standard stabilisation programme involves policies that stabilise the price level via fixing the nominal exchange rate to a level that is realistic and defendable. Such an exchange rate is defended by stopping money being printed for financing budget deficits. Assuming that the purchasing power parity holds, that is $P^d = NER \cdot P^{f\$}$, then the combined fiscal and monetary policies (with a zero money printing provision) may freeze real money stock (M/P) at the very low level that existed during a hyperinflation. Since the inflation rate (π) is reduced to zero once price stability is gained (that is, P is constant), the high nominal interest rate that existed during hyperinflation would equal the real interest rate, $i \cong r$.

The high interest rate problem may be aggravated if it is assumed that the demand for money depends not only on the nominal interest rate but also on the expected rate of inflation, π^e:

$$M/P = m^d(i, \pi^e, \ldots.) \tag{5.25b}$$

This expression yields an interest rate specification that includes the expected rate of inflation as a separate determinant of the interest rate, such that:

$$i = h(M/P, \pi^e, \ldots),\ h_{(M/P)} < 0,\ h_{(\pi e)} > 0 \tag{5.26b}$$

In this expanded model the equilibrium real interest rate would actually rise because of a shift of the money demand schedule to the right in response to the downward adjustment of inflationary expectations.

Therefore, one major reason why stabilisation programmes fail is that such high real interest rates undermine most stabilisation programmes. This can happen at least in three ways. First, high interest rates can create pressure for monetary expansion. If the

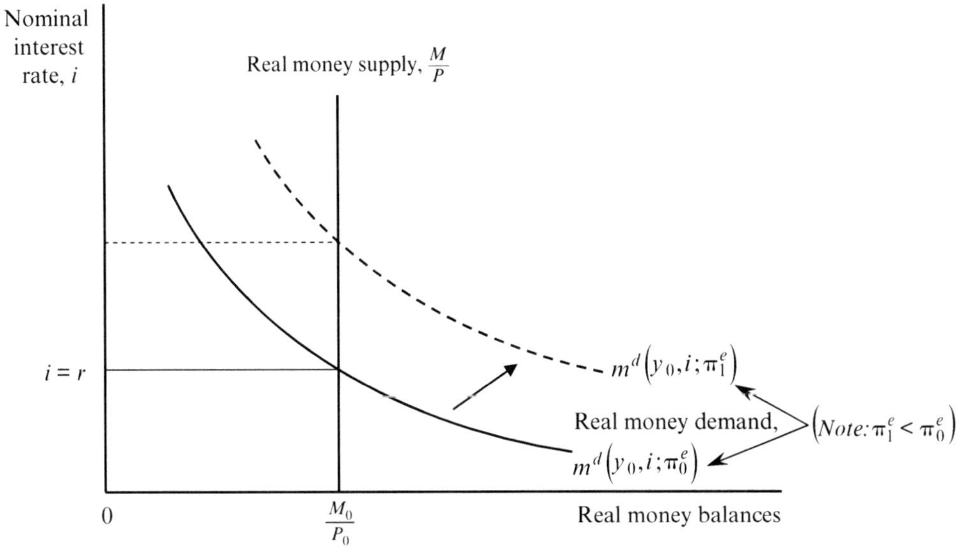

Notes:
Fisher's equation: $i = r + \pi^e$.
Money market equilibrium:

$$\frac{M}{P} = m^d(y_0, i) \rightarrow i = h\left(\frac{M}{P}, y_0\right)$$

when $M = M_0$ and $P = P_0$, $M_0/P_0 \approx$ constant after stabilisation and therefore $i = r$, given that $\pi \approx \pi^e \approx 0$.

Figure 5.8 High real interest rate after price stabilisation

money supply is increased, the exchange rate stability may be lost and consequently the stabilisation programme may collapse. Second, high interest rates may make the budgetary situation worse if the government needs to service debt at high interest rates. Third, high interest rates may lead to financial distress for enterprises, which may lead to bankruptcies, unemployment and political tensions.

Lessons from Hyperinflation and Stabilisation Programmes

Since the 1970s a large number of studies have examined different aspects of stabilisation programmes in high-inflation and hyperinflationary countries. As indicated earlier, Latin America remains the laboratory for investigation of issues in high inflation and hyperinflation situations. It is found that high inflation or hyperinflation does not happen overnight. It takes considerable time to develop an environment for either. The conditions that lead to hyperinflation are well documented (Dornbusch, 1993; Makinen and Woodward, 1989; Sachs and Larrain, 1993).

Stabilisation measures that ended episodes of hyperinflation vary across countries. The major lesson is that countries that experience hyperinflation make several disinflationary attempts before they finally succeed. There are well-documented cases of failed stabilisation attempts in Latin America to deal with hyperinflation. They include the

Southern Cone *Tablita* experiments of the early 1970s and early 1980s. The authorities in this region pre-announced the rates of depreciation of currencies in an effort to guide inflationary expectations. In heterodox programmes of the mid-1980s, stabilisation measures were accompanied by price and wage controls. Some Latin American countries, such as Bolivia in the mid-1980s and Nicaragua and Peru in the early 1990s, succeeded in stabilisations after a few attempts. In Bolivia, stabilisation programmes were launched in November 1982, November 1983, April 1984, August 1984 and February 1985. The last attempt was made after the election of a new President in September 1985, which proved successful (Blanchard, 2006; Morales, 1991; Sachs, 1987).

Hamann and Prati (2003) have investigated 51 stabilisation episodes and found that there are at least three factors, namely, 'luck, initial conditions and political institutions', determine the success or failure of disinflation plans. Both policy and non-policy macro variables also play some roles, although these are not decisive. Macro variables that have been found important include the real exchange rates, output growth, international reserves, and any other indicators of monetary and fiscal policies.

Good luck

Both domestic and external shocks make a difference to success or failure of disinflationary programmes. Disinflationary programmes have a high chance of failure if the country is exposed to external shocks, for instance, a decline in export demand and a sharp rise in foreign interest rates. Such external shocks make macroeconomic management difficult. Therefore 'luck' is considered an important factor in the eventual success or failure of a stabilisation programme.

Past failures of stabilisation attempts

Past failures lower the chance of success of a new stabilisation programme. Countries with a long history of high inflation at the start of a stabilisation programme often have less of a chance that a new programme would be successful. This follows the proposition that long-lived inflation creates institutions and practices that create inflation inertia and make stabilisation programmes untenable.

Crisis hypothesis

The 'crisis hypothesis' suggests that the worse the situation is the higher could be political consensus in favour of stabilisation through stringent measures. Therefore the higher the rate of inflation the greater could be the chance of success of a stabilisation programme.

International reserves

Stabilisation programmes that are backed by a relatively high level of foreign reserves create credibility and have a higher chance of success. Large foreign reserves act as an insurance against adverse developments and therefore lower the chance of failure.

Money-based versus exchange rate based stabilisations

Exchange rate based stabilisation programmes have a higher chance of success provided that stringent monetary and fiscal measures are undertaken to keep the exchange rate stable. Exchange rates play the role of anchoring inflationary expectations. Therefore the stability of exchange rates is crucial for price stability, as opposed to only fiscal and monetary policy changes to lower budget deficits and money growth.

Capital controls

There is debate whether capital controls are important for stabilisation. Although open capital accounts are perceived to accentuate external capital market shocks, open capital accounts may also improve the chance of success of stabilisation programmes. This may happen if such openness is seen by investors as a signalling device that policy-makers are serious about stabilising the economy through economic reforms and policy measures. Most developing countries still remain ambivalent about capital mobility. They do not have adequate financial infrastructure in place to manage large scale capital flows. Therefore, capital controls may make it easier for policy-makers to stabilise an economy in the event of shocks that might have been caused by factors other than weaknesses in economic fundamentals (Hossain, 2000; 2006a).

Political institutions

Political regimes and institutions play a role in the success of stabilisation programmes. In general, countries with established political institutions have a higher chance of success in stabilisation programmes. Such countries are also less likely to create hyperinflation in the first place. Political instability is generally high in countries which do not have developed political institutions. Such countries suffer from macroeconomic crises, which are reflected in high inflation and large current account deficits. As discussed, macroeconomic problems may originate from large budget deficits when they are financed by money creation. At a deeper level, they may represent structural and policy-induced distortions that generate large budget deficits which, when financed by money creation, make these countries vulnerable to macroeconomic crises.

Democracy versus authoritarianism

In a competitive democratic system, the constant political pressure from opposition generally induces the government to maintain economic stability. This may not necessarily be the case when an authoritarian government remains in power. Such a government does not face political opposition and can get away with economic mismanagement.[16] A government with a strong executive branch has a better chance of success of stabilisation programmes. Stabilisation requires tough monetary and fiscal policy measures. In addition, a presidential regime has been suggested to have a greater ability to limit government spending or to introduce large budget cuts.

Longevity of a government

A new government is more likely to succeed with stabilisation programmes. This follows the proposition in reputation models that a new government prefers low inflation, independently irrespective of its other preferences. The populace are more responsive to policies of a new government vis-à-vis an incumbent government that has been in power for a long time.

Social cohesion

Social cohesion brings success in stabilisation programmes. On the other hand, social tension lowers the chance of their success. Blanchard (2006: 504) elaborates this proposition:

> Sometimes failure comes from political opposition. If social conflict was one of the causes of the initial budget deficit and thus was at the root of the hyperinflation, it may still be present and just as hard to resolve at the time of stabilization. Those who lose from the fiscal reform needed to reduce the deficit will oppose the stabilization program. Often, workers who perceive an increase in the price of public services or an increase in taxation, but who do not fully perceive the decrease in the inflation tax, will go on strike or even riot, and the stabilization plan will fail.

Real exchange rate

Stability of the real exchange rate is critical for the success of a stabilisation programme. If the exchange rate remains misaligned for long or there is a sharp appreciation of the real exchange rate, this may encourage capital outflows and therefore derail stabilisation programmes.

Economic growth

High economic growth helps stabilisation directly by improving the fiscal position of the government and indirectly, by creating a consensus among the people for continuation of stabilisation policies and measures.

Foreign reserves

As indicated above, foreign reserves play an important role in stabilisation programmes. A faster accumulation of foreign reserves may strengthen stabilisation programmes and help to absorb external shocks. Having adequate foreign reserves also creates confidence among policy-makers in their ability to manage the economy and maintain exchange rate stability.

Monetary and fiscal adjustment

Monetary and fiscal adjustments are critical in stabilisation programmes. They create a stable macroeconomic policy environment that creates a sense of optimism and encourages productive investment. Stabilisation takes a long time to achieve if monetary and fiscal policies are not adjusted appropriately. Even when fiscal adjustment is implemented, it may take time to achieve low inflation if money, rather than the exchange rate, is used as a nominal anchor to prices (Park, 1973; Reinhart and Savastano, 2003).

To summarise the findings/discussion from part I, macroeconomic discipline alone may not be adequate for price stability. Other policy and reform measures may be necessary to restore confidence among the public and policy-makers alike. Hyperinflation is generally accompanied by a sharp reduction in financial intermediation. This creates economic inefficiency, especially if the credit system breaks down. Stopping hyperinflation does not restore the demand for domestic money or other financial assets to levels that prevailed before hyperinflations. Although a portion of capital that left the country during high inflation or hyperinflation may return once inflation is stabilised, dollarisation and other forms of indexation may dominate financial intermediation for many years. Therefore, policy-makers need to create confidence among the people about future prospects of the economy. Until the monetary disintermediation process is halted and the people's confidence is restored, there remains the danger that even minor problems on the policy front and shocks to the economy may ignite inflation. As Blanchard (2006) points out, the successes and failures of stabilisation plans have an element of self-fulfilling prophecy. In short, even well-conceived plans work only if they are expected to work. Good luck, good public relations and good policies interact to ensure stabilisation programmes become successful.

PART II

INFLATION AND ECONOMIC GROWTH

Approaches to Investment Finance

One common economic goal of developing countries is raising per capita real income on a sustained basis.[17] There is, however, no consensus on mechanisms through which per capita real income can be raised steadily over time, except that all the major approaches to development give emphasis on both capital formation and the effective utilisation of capital.[18]

Although investment has been identified as the major determinant of economic growth, there is controversy over the relative efficacy of different approaches to investment finance. In the literature two analytical approaches to investment finance can be identified:[19] the 'prior savings approach' and the 'forced savings approach'. According to classical economists, prior savings are the determinant of investment and all savings find their investment outlets. The proponents of the prior savings approach are averse to inflation and do not see any need for inflation to raise economic growth. As investment is an alternative to consumption, they argue that investment, if it is not financed by prior savings, may generate inflation but no real income.[20]

Economists who follow the Keynesian school of thought do not consider prior savings as a requirement of investment for growth. According to this view, the government without prior savings can increase investment autonomously through money creation. Such investment would generate its own savings in at least four ways. First, if resources are underemployed, monetary expansion would increase aggregate demand and hence output and savings. Second, if resources are fully employed or if there are supply rigidities (as expected in developing countries), monetary expansion would generate inflation. Inflation in turn would lower real return on financial investment, which would induce wealth-holders to change their portfolio by investing in physical capital. The resultant rise in capital intensity would increase output and hence savings. Third, inflation can also increase savings by changing income distribution in favour of profit earners with a higher propensity to save compared with that of wage earners. Finally, inflation imposes tax on real balances and transfers resources to the government for financing productive investment.

Therefore, the precise role of monetary policy in economic growth is dependent on whether 'prior savings' or 'forced saving' is appropriate for developing countries. According to the forced savings school, since investment (not saving) is the constraint on economic growth, a low or negative real interest rate is necessary for encouragement of private investment. To the extent that a high rate of inflation keeps real interest rates low, inflation can be considered a necessary price to pay for economic growth. Therefore the policy implication that follows from the forced saving approach is financial repression characterised by interest rate ceilings.[21] In contrast, the prior savings school believe that the role of monetary policy in developing countries should be mobilisation of savings and channelling them into productive investment. This can be done by keeping the inflation rate low so that the real interest rate remains positive over time. This forms the basis of financial liberalisation reform.

This section reviews the theoretical debate on the role of money growth or inflation in economic growth. The review is selective, in the sense that the pure monetary growth theories are analysed along with the linkage between inflation and economic growth. In fact, the ideas from these complementary branches of monetary economics have common threads and continue to be useful to deal with monetary policy issues in developing countries.

Neutrality and Super-Neutrality of Money

Economic growth is a dynamic phenomenon. It deals with changes in real economic variables over time. The core issue in the monetary growth theory (common to both the forced and prior savings schools) is whether money has any effect on real variables in a growing economy in the steady state or in the transition towards the steady state. Answers to these questions can be found in the literature on neutrality and super-neutrality of money. These concepts are defined first and then elaborated by introducing the monetary growth models.

One fundamental proposition in monetary economics is that money is neutral to the economy – that is, to the determination of relative prices, employment and output. It is a building block of the classical quantity theory, which states that a change in the quantity of nominal money causes a proportionate change in the price level, while real variables such as employment, output and the real interest rate remain unaffected.[22]

Fisher (1930) invoked the concept of money illusion[23] to account for short-run non-neutrality of money arising from fluctuations in real interest rates. He wrote that 'The erratic behaviour of real interest is evidently a trick played on the money market by the "money illusion" when contracts are made in unstable money' (Fisher, 1930: 415). The presence of money illusion violates the 'homogeneity postulate' (Haberler, 1941; Leontief, 1936; Modigliani, 1944), which in its refined form states that the demand and supply functions of goods and services are homogeneous of degree zero in money prices and in the initial quantity of financial assets, including money.[24]

The short-run non-neutrality of money is a prominent feature of the Keynesian monetary theory (Meltzer, 1988). It follows the contention that under the conditions of underemployment, the price level does not rise proportionately to an increase in the quantity of money.[25] Therefore the resulting increase in the real quantity of money lowers the real interest rate and, through the interest rate channel, raises investment and output.[26] Keynes (1936) accepted the classical view that the demand for labour depends on real wages and therefore employment can be increased only by lowering real wages. According to him, as nominal wages are more rigid than prices, monetary expansion that raises the price level increases output because the increased prices, given fixed nominal wages, lower real wages. Keynes's assumption of rigid nominal wages is interpreted as being based on the existence of money illusion on the part of workers. It follows from his suggestion that the supply of labour depends on the nominal wage rate, so that workers do not see an increase in the price level at a given level of the nominal wage rate as a fall in the real wage rate. They supply more labour as the nominal wage rate increases with the rise in labour demand, implying that workers suffer from money illusion (Leontief, 1936). Leijonhufvud (1968), however, provides an alternative interpretation to the Keynesian labour supply behaviour. He argues that workers may continue to supply the same amount of labour in the event of an increase in the price level, not because they identify nominal with real wages irrationally, but because in a world of less than perfect information, they may take time to learn about the changed value of money (Howitt, 1992).

The monetarists accept that in the short run money has effects on the economy. As Friedman (1992: 260) writes: 'In the short run, which may be as long as three to ten years, monetary changes affect primarily output. Over decades, on the other hand, the rate of monetary growth affects primarily prices.' His acceptance of short run non-neutrality of money is based not on money illusion; rather it arises from expectational errors or imperfect information.

Lucas (1972) developed a macroeconomic model with optimising agents, decentralised markets and imperfect information. The use of imperfect information leads to the effect of unanticipated money shock on output, but anticipated money does not affect output. Fischer (1979a) also developed a model in which nominal wages are preset on the basis of lagged information on money and demand disturbances. His model, like the Lucas model, shows that demand and money shocks affect output to the extent that they are unanticipated. The Fischer model works as in Keynes. Because prices are flexible but nominal wages are fixed within a period, monetary shocks increase prices, decrease real wages and increase output.

Therefore it is evident that the short-run non-neutrality of money is explained by the argument of imperfect information (Blanchard, 1990). Such an interpretation is more convincing than any argument which invokes the assumption of money illusion, because money illusion contradicts the rational behaviour of economic agents. Gordon (1993) argues that Friedman's explanation of the short-run effect of inflation on output is not convincing. According to him, it does not seem valid to suggest that workers hold incorrect expectations over such a period of time as to cause a major effect on output. It is also doubtful that employers have information advantage over workers to such an extent over a considerable period of time that can generate business cycles.

Super-Neutrality of Money

Closely related to the neutrality of money is the concept of super-neutrality of money. One question regarding the super-neutrality of money is whether a change in the growth rate of nominal money affects the growth paths of real economic variables in the steady state, with the exception of real balances, the steady-state value of which may decrease with the rise in inflation following an increase in the growth rate of nominal money (Danthine, 1992). Super-neutrality of money requires that the real interest rate, capital intensity and per capita output (or consumption) are independent of inflation and the rate of money growth.

Money growth may affect economic growth through its impact on the real interest rate and thereby on capital accumulation (Orphanides and Solow, 1990). The presence of such effect is postulated by Metzler (1951). He argues that the real interest rate is a monetary phenomenon and that an increase in the growth rate of nominal money can affect capital accumulation. According to him, the central bank can affect the real interest rate through money market operations (Metzler, 1951: 112): '[B]y purchasing securities, the central bank can reduce the real value of private wealth, thereby increasing the propensity to save and causing the system to attain a new equilibrium at a permanently lower interest rate and a permanently higher rate of capital accumulation.'

One criticism of the Metzler model is that he did not examine the effect of inflation on the interest rate and distinguish between a real and a nominal interest rate. He also did not link capital accumulation with economic growth (Orphanides and Solow, 1990).

By applying the Metzler model, Mundell (1963; 1971) shows that anticipated inflation raises the nominal interest rate by less than the inflation rate and therefore lowers the real interest rate and gives an impetus 'to an investment and an acceleration of growth'. One shortcoming of the Mundell model is that it does not consider the effects of anticipated inflation on real variables in the steady state, although he claims that any change in the real interest rate is a permanent change.

Tobin (1965) has formally developed the supposed link between monetary expansion, inflation and economic growth through the 'capital-intensity effect'. Indeed, the modern literature on money and growth has begun with Tobin's model, which establishes a case against monetary super-neutrality.

The Tobin model

The Tobin model is based on the one-sector neoclassical growth model of Solow (1956) and Swan (1956), and it rationalises the forced savings approach to development finance.

Assume that per capita real output (y) depends on the capital–labour ratio (k)

$$y = y(k) \tag{5.27}$$

where $\delta y/\delta k > 0$ and $\delta^2 y/\delta k^2 < 0$.

In the non-monetary model, individuals save by acquiring physical capital and therefore k is the only form of wealth. However in the basic monetary growth model, per capita real balances are considered an alternative form of wealth, so that per capita real wealth (w) equals per capita capital (k) plus per capita real balances (m)

$$w = k + m \tag{5.28}$$

Per capita real balances may be assumed to depend on per capita real output and the opportunity cost of holding money instead of capital. The opportunity cost of holding money equals the real rate of return on capital (r_k) plus inflation (π), so that the demand for real balances can be expressed as

$$m = m(y, r_k + \pi) \tag{5.29}$$

where $\delta m/\delta y > 0$ and $\delta m/\delta(r_k + \pi) < 0$.

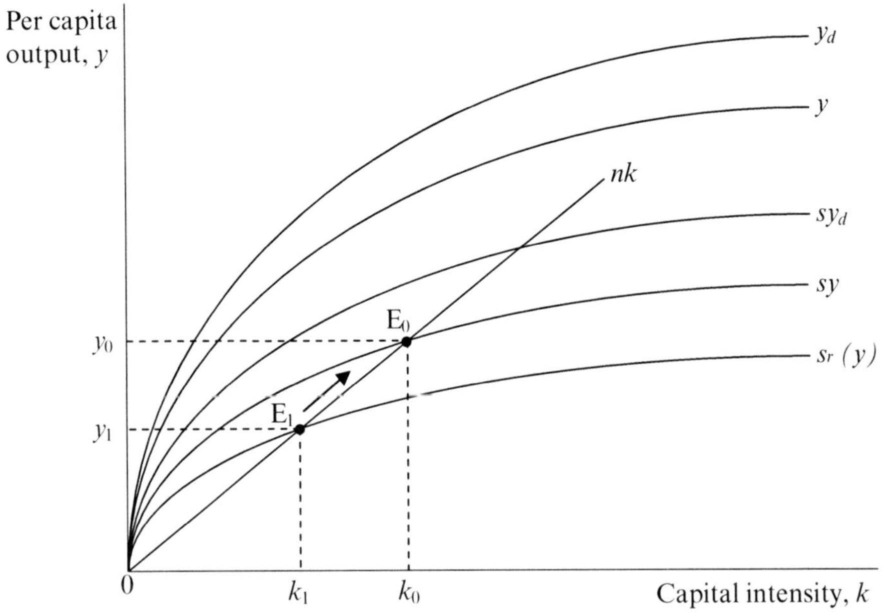

Figure 5.9 A neoclassical monetary growth model

Assume that the stock of nominal money is exogenously determined and that it grows at a rate of λ. When the demand for per capita real balances is constant, the equilibrium condition for the money market ensures that the rate of inflation equals the growth rate of nominal money less the growth rate of population (n), such that:

$$\pi = \lambda - n \tag{5.30}$$

Assuming that the nominal interest rate (or return) on money is zero, Tobin (1965) suggests that a rise in inflation would lower the real return on money and make real balances less attractive to hold, given that assetholders compare the return on money with the return on capital. Therefore a higher rate of inflation encourages a portfolio shift away from money and into capital and consequently raises real output because of the rise in capital intensity. This is known as 'the Tobin effect'. The presence of it suggests that money is not super-neutral.

Figure 5.9 presents the standard one-sector neoclassical growth model. It explains how a rise in the growth rate of nominal money raises per capita real output. The initial equilibrium is at point E_0, where the savings curve (sy) crosses the capital requirement line (nk). At equilibrium the capital–labour ratio is k_0 and per capita real output is y_0.

To modify the real growth model into the neoclassical monetary growth model, per capita 'disposable income' (y_d) needs to be redefined as per capita output (y) plus changes in per capita real balances $(\lambda-\pi)m$. That is, $y_d = y + (\lambda - \pi)m$. Per capita disposable income is so defined because changes in real balances in the 'outside money' economy are regarded as a change in wealth and therefore a change in income. Using the quantity theory relationship in growth form, $\lambda = \pi + g_y$ (velocity is assumed constant; g_y represents the growth rate of output), the above definition of disposable income can be rewritten as $y_d = y(1 + xg_y)$, where x is the money–income ratio (m/y). Assuming that per capita saving (s) is a constant proportion of disposable income, the savings curve sy_d is drawn. It shows that when the economy grows, due to an increase in k, y_d, from which savings is made – then the value of the ratio of savings to output rises. Note that not all, but a portion of total savings is devoted to increasing real savings and then to increasing physical capital. Precisely, from savings sy_d, savings devoted to increasing real balances are given by $xg_y y$, leaving real savings $s_r(y)$ which is defined as: $sy_d - xg_y y$. Real savings are plotted as $s_r(y)$. Given the capital requirement line nk, the equilibrium point is now at E_1 with the capital–labour ratio k_1 and per capita output y_1.

The effect of any monetary expansion that leads to inflation can be seen on the equilibrium capital–labour ratio and per capita output. From the definition of real savings $s_r(y)$ and its inverse relationship with the money–income ratio (x), it follows that any decline in the value of the money–income ratio (x) will shift the $s_r(y)$ curve upwards and therefore raise the capital–labour ratio and per capita output (Johnson, 1978: 165).

Since the rate of return on capital is fixed by either the capital–labour ratio or per capita output, the money–income ratio would vary inversely with inflation. Inflation is a policy variable which can be raised by raising the growth rate of the nominal money supply at a given rate of growth of population ($\pi = \lambda - n$). It suggests that the higher the rate of inflation, the lower the money–income ratio, and the intersection point E_1 is further to the right as the real savings curve $s_r(y)$ shifts upwards. The upper limit is the point E_0 where the rate of inflation is high enough to lower the money–income ratio to negligibility (Johnson, 1978: 165).

Critique of the Tobin effect

The conclusion drawn above is based on the implicit assumption that the stock of wealth remains constant with the rise in inflation. As Orphanides and Solow (1990) point out, the stock of wealth is endogenous, is dependent on the saving behaviour of individuals and is likely to change with inflation. When wealth is reduced because of the decline in real balances owing to inflation, inflation may not raise the capital–labour ratio and therefore the super-neutrality condition of money may prevail. It indicates that the net effect of inflation on capital intensity depends on the interaction of the portfolio composition effect and the saving behaviour of individuals during inflation.

Levhari and Patinkin (1968) specified the savings rate as a function of the rates of return on capital and real balances. They demonstrated that the steady-state impact of inflation on capital intensity could be positive or negative. They also noted that the role of money in the Tobin model is not adequately explained and showed that the Tobin effect cannot be obtained unambiguously when money is treated as consumption or a production good. Dornbusch and Frenkel (1973) showed that when inflation has a positive effect on consumption, the Tobin effect disappears.

The classic defence of super-neutrality of money came from Sidrauski (1967a; 1967b). He formulated a monetary growth model within a representative individual's utility optimising framework, where individual's utility is a function of real consumption and of the flow of services of real balances. Sidrauski's important finding was that the sizes of the steady-state capital stock and real consumption are independent of inflation and the rate of money growth, implying that money is super-neutral. However, as the opportunity cost of holding money rises with inflation, super-neutrality does not extend to real balances and therefore monetary expansion that generates inflation leads to welfare losses (Haliassos and Tobin, 1990).

Orphanides and Solow (1990) find that the difference with the results of Sidrauski and Tobin lies in the specification of savings behaviour.[27] As in the case of Dornbusch and Frenkel (1973), when inflation has a positive effect on consumption the Tobin effect is neutralised in the Sidrauski model in which the portfolio decision and the savings behaviour are derived simultaneously. Orphanides and Solow also show that Sidrauski's neutrality results can be obtained in a model in which the transactions role of money is explicitly modelled.

In Sidrauski's model the marginal product of capital depends on the level of capital stock. As his model shows, in the steady-state real balances are inversely related with the rate of money creation and the super-neutrality results cannot be sustained if real balances enter in the production function. Therefore, an important variation of the Sidrauski model has been the inclusion of money as a factor of production. It is assumed that firms hold real balances to facilitate production, so that money acts as a complementary factor to capital:

$$y = y(k,m) \tag{5.31}$$

Inflation lowers the productivity of and the return to the complementary input capital by lowering real balances in the steady state. The negative effect of inflation (or money growth) on productivity is opposite to the positive effect suggested by the portfolio view of Tobin (1965) in which money and capital are substitutable assets. Marty (1968) finds that, given the production function (5.31), the effect of a rise in inflation on capital accumulation is ambiguous and depends on the form of the production function. If the production function is concave, and the effect of real balances on the marginal product of capital is positive, inflation would lower capital holdings. Orphanides and Solow (1990) make the pertinent remark that whatever model is used for analysis, any complementarity between money balances and capital does create a negative effect of inflation on capital. Because inflation damages the efficiency of the transactions technology, the net productivity of capital, and hence the demand for capital, may be lower – particularly during high inflation.

Figure 5.10 shows that an increase in the growth rate of nominal money has an ambiguous effect on capital intensity and per capita output (or income). In the figure, an increase in the growth rate of nominal money from λ_1 to λ_2 is shown to have two effects. First, it would shift the consumption curve from c_1 to c_2 as the consequent higher rate of inflation reduces the real balances and hence the disposable income, $yd = y + (\lambda - \pi)m$. Second, a rise in inflation lowers the demand for real balances, and since real balances (m) are a complementary factor to per capita capital stock (k) in the production: $y = y(k,m)$, the decrease in the holding of real balances would lower per capita output. As a result, the net production curve would shift from $(y - nk)_1$ to either $(y - nk)_2$ or $(y - nk)^*_2$, representing two alternative positions. As both the consumption and production functions shift to the right, the net effect of an increase in the growth rate of the nominal money supply on capital intensity (or per capita output) would depend on the relative strength

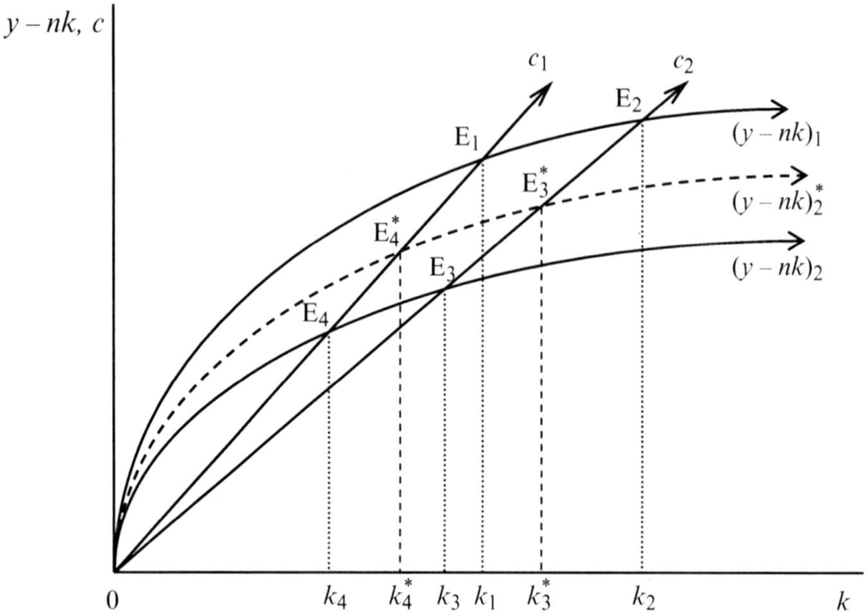

Figure 5.10 Effect of money supply growth (or inflation) on capital intensity (or per capita output)

of two opposite effects of monetary expansion.[28] For example, in the figure, the capital–labour ratio is shown to increase from k_1 to k_3^* when the production curve shifts from $(y - nk)_1$ to $(y - nk)_2^*$ and the consumption curve from c_1 to c_2. However, if the production curve shifts to $(y - nk)_2$ instead, the capital–labour ratio is k_3, which is lower than the initial equilibrium capital–labour ratio k_1.

In the literature on super-neutrality of money, the question has received attention of whether changes in the growth rate of nominal money are super-neutral when the economy is outside its steady state, but moving towards it. Fischer (1979b) develops a model similar to Sidrauski's with perfect foresight and shows that although in such a model the steady-state capital stock is invariant to changes in the growth rate of nominal money, such super-neutrality does not prevail during the transition path to the steady state. Cohen (1985) provides an explanation of Fischer's results. He shows that the nominal rate of interest varies along the transition path because of two conflicting factors. On the one hand, a rise in inflation raises the nominal interest rate, and on the other, a decline in the real interest rate due to inflation pushes down the nominal interest rate. When these two effects cancel each other out, monetary policy cannot affect the nominal interest rate; otherwise, the nominal interest rate during the transition path may remain above or below its steady-state value. In such a situation, monetary policy may affect capital accumulation by influencing the nominal interest rate towards its steady state value (Haliassos and Tobin, 1990).

In conclusion, this section has reviewed the basic theories of money in economic growth. The core question in monetary growth theory is whether money has any effect on real variables in a growing economy, either in the steady state or in the transition towards the steady state. In the literature such questions have been examined within the context of neutrality and super-neutrality of money. The review of the literature on the neutrality of money reveals that both the Keynesians and the monetarists accept that money is non-neutral in the short run. The short-run non-neutrality of money originates from workers' expectational errors or imperfect information. Closely related to the neutrality of money is the concept of super-neutrality of money. The core question with respect to the super-neutrality of money is whether any change in the growth rate of nominal money has any effect on the growth paths of real economic variables with the exception of real balances. The review of the literature on the super-neutrality of money reveals that the super-neutrality condition does not hold in a strict sense but it can be considered as a reasonable approximation.

Can Inflation be a Source of Economic Growth in Developing Countries?

The policy of inflationary finance has been criticised by a number of prominent economists, including Bailey (1956), Barro (1972), Dornbusch and Reynoso (1989), Mundell (1965; 1971), Marty (1967; 1973) and Friedman (1971a). The standard argument against inflationary finance is that it imposes welfare costs on money-holders. However, the most convincing argument against inflationary finance within a political economy context is that once a licence to print money is given to the government, then there is no guarantee that it would not end up creating high inflation or hyperinflation. Economists working on Latin America show that hyperinflations in this region were 'triggered by large budgetary deficits and sustained by subsequent ongoing deficits, virtual economic collapse, and steadily rising inflationary experiences' (Dornbusch, 1993; Gillis et al., 1992). Aghevli and Khan (1978) have developed an inflation model for developing countries, which shows that budget deficits perform a dual role of the original source of, and the propagating mechanism for, the inflationary process. They have used the idea of inflation induced budget deficits, which arise when government revenues rise more slowly than the government outlays with inflation because of structural constraints in the fiscal system. Inflation induced budget deficits may then become the dynamic force to sustain inflation.

Montiel (2003) has investigated the possibility of a positive relation between inflation and economic growth within a production function approach. He asks the question why there should be any relationship between inflation and the rate of growth of economic capacity. Assume that there is a production relation in the following form:

$$y_p = AF(L_p, K) \tag{5.32}$$

where y_p is the full-employment level of GDP, L_p is the full-employment level of labour, K is the capital stock and A is an index of the productivity of resources employed. The rate of growth of capacity output ($\Delta y_p/y_p$) can then be expressed as:

$$\Delta y_p/y_p = \Delta A/A + \theta\, \Delta L_p/L_p + (1 - \theta)\, \Delta K/K \tag{5.33}$$

where θ is the share of labour.

Within this growing accounting model, if inflation is to affect economic growth, it must do so by altering the rate of growth of the productivity or the rate of accumulation of productive factors. Economists have identified several potential channels through which inflation can affect economic growth. They include both the capital accumulation and productivity growth channels. They are discussed below with an emphasis on how inflation may affect economic growth.

The Mundell–Tobin effect

The Mundell–Tobin effect remains the major explanation for the positive relationship between inflation and economic growth. The story has been elaborated earlier as follows: if money and capital are substitute assets for domestic savers to hold, an increase in the steady-state inflation rate would lower the real rate of return on money, which pays no interest while leaving the real return on capital (in the form of the marginal product of capital) unchanged. This would increase the share of saving devoted to capital accumulation, rather than hoarding real balances, and therefore raise the rate of long-run economic growth.

Capital taxation

Because the tax laws are written in nominal terms, high inflation may raise the effective rate of taxation on the return to physical capital. For example, in an inflationary environment, depreciation allowances written in nominal terms (that is, in terms of the original nominal cost of capital) understate the cost in current inflated prices for replacement of capital when it wears out. This overstates profits and consequently, raises tax obligations compared with any proper accounting of the costs of depreciation. Other effects may also be important – for example, there could be an exaggeration of capital gains on real assets.

Unstable inflation and uncertainty

High inflation tends to be unstable. When inflation is unstable, prediction of future prices is difficult. Since prediction of future prices is important for investment decisions, inflation instability creates investment uncertainty. When investment is irreversible, capital accumulation and growth are unlikely to be high in a high inflationary environment.

High real interest rates

Under officially determined exchange rates, high inflation results in a real exchange rate appreciation. In a financially open economy, the resulting expectation of future real exchange rate depreciation tends to raise the domestic real interest rate through the open-economy financial arbitrage condition. This can be illustrated as follows.

Consider the uncovered interest parity condition:

$$i^d = i^f + \Delta NER/NER \tag{5.34}$$

where i^d is the domestic nominal interest rate, i^f is the foreign nominal interest rate and $\Delta NER/NER$ is the expected rate of depreciation of domestic currency.

Let π^d and π^f denote the expected domestic and foreign inflation rates. Since the domestic real interest rate is defined as $r^d = i^d - \pi^d$, it follows that:

$$r^d = i^d - \pi^d = (i^f - \pi^f) + (\Delta NER/NER + \pi^d - \pi^f) \tag{5.35}$$

It can be written in real terms as follows:

$$r^d = r^f + \Delta rer/rer \tag{5.36}$$

where r^f is the foreign real interest rate and $\Delta rer/rer = (\Delta NER/NER + \pi^d - \pi^f)$ is the expected real depreciation rate of the domestic currency. When the real domestic currency is overvalued and is expected to depreciate in real terms, the domestic real interest rate would tend to be high (given the foreign real interest rate). This would discourage domestic investment and lower output growth.

Capital flight

The basic portfolio problem in terms of a choice between domestic and foreign currency (by denomination and location) involves the comparison of rates of return on capital.

Let i^d be the expected after-tax return on a domestic asset, i^f the after-tax return abroad and $\Delta NER/NER$ is the expected rate of depreciation of the home (that is, developing country) currency. Foreign assets will be more attractive than home assets if the expected return from tax evasion and expected depreciation exceeds the home rate of after-tax return:

$$(1 + i^f)(1 + \Delta NER/NER) > (1 + i^d) \tag{5.37}$$

Alternatively, looking at real rates of return:

$$(1 + r^f)(1 + \Delta rer/rer) > (1 + r^d) \tag{5.38}$$

where $\Delta rer/rer$ is the expected rate of change of the real exchange rate. The above criterion shows that with an anticipated real depreciation, capital would move abroad unless home real interest rates exceed those abroad. There is an emerging consensus that one principal cause of capital flight from developing countries is the likelihood of a sharp devaluation of currency. This happened in both Argentina and Mexico (Cardoso and Dornbusch, 1989; Sachs and Larrain, 1993).

An expected devaluation of currency is not the only factor that may cause capital flight. An underdeveloped financial system or financial repression could be another related cause. In general, controls over interest rates and the lack of financial assets with high yields encourage wealth-holders to transfer funds abroad. Until recently, most developing countries had extensive controls over interest rates, which created negative real interest rates because of high rates of inflation. The reduced flow of resources into the domestic banking system during high inflation reduces the flow of credit that these institutions can make available for domestic investment, with consequent negative effects on economic growth.

Working capital

As reviewed earlier, real balances and physical capital complement in production. Real balances may be considered as working capital. High inflation raises the nominal interest rate and induces firms to economise real balances. This lowers the productivity of physical capital, which may lower investment and economic growth.

Inflation as indicator of government competence

Fischer (1993) argued that there are no good arguments for high inflation. The fiscal argument does not support high inflation because of the seigniorage 'Laffer curve', which, as explained earlier, suggests that inflation tax revenue initially increases with the rate of inflation but declines as the inflation rate exceeds the revenue-maximising optimal rate. Therefore when a government allows high inflation, it signals that the government has lost control. The public may then treat the government as incompetent in financial management. This lowers investment and economic growth.

Variability of relative prices

As reviewed earlier, high inflation tends to be volatile and therefore raises variability of relative prices. This lowers the information content of relative prices and interferes with the efficient allocation of resources.

Shoe-leather costs

As discussed earlier, high inflation raises the nominal interest rate. This induces economic agents to economise their holding of real balances. In doing so, they waste resources which they could have deployed for producing goods and services. This is the 'shoe-leather costs' of inflation, which lowers productive efficiency in the economy.

While the neutrality and super-neutrality of money has been the focus of growth analysis in developed countries in the context of a fully employed economy, an important branch of the money-growth literature has been concerned with the role of inflationary finance in economic growth in developing countries. The review of the literature on inflationary finance and growth reveals that any money creation to finance public investment may have some influence on economic growth but it is unlikely to be a major source of growth. Experience of Latin American countries suggests that inflationary finance is actually a hazardous means of economic growth. Rao (1952) delivered such a message to planners in developing countries about fifty years ago.

PART III

FINANCE AND ECONOMIC GROWTH

Recent theoretical and empirical research suggests that financial markets play an important role in economic growth. An efficient financial system transfers loanable funds from savers to borrowers and directs resources to productive and profitable investment projects. The more productive is investment the higher is growth of the economy (King and Levine, 1993; Zahler, 1993). An efficient financial market also enhances economic growth by pooling risks and facilitating transactions. Stiglitz (1994) considers the financial system as the 'brain' of the entire economic system.

During the heyday of the Keynesian revolution in the 1950s and 1960s, the importance of financial factors was ignored (Chandavarkar, 1992). Under the influence of the predominantly Keynesian forced saving approach, most developing countries favoured a development strategy that included low nominal interest rates, which resulted in negative or very low real interest rates given high inflation in some of those countries. The resultant financial repression was the major reason for low savings and underdevelopment of the financial sector (Honohan, 1992).

Since the early 1970s, the view that repressive financial policies raise investment and economic growth has come under criticism from the 'prior saving' school. The classic works of McKinnon (1973) and Shaw (1973) have changed the intellectual pendulum in favour of financial deregulation. Although there are differences between the McKinnon and the Shaw models, they essentially suggest that financial repression has a number of growth inhibiting effects. First, low or negative real interest rates encourage current consumption and induce the people to hold savings in real (rather than financial) assets. In developing countries, real assets are a better hedge against inflation. As a result, the financial sector remains shallow, which adversely affects the monetisation of economy and the efficiency of transactions. Second, low or negative real interest rates create excess demand for investible funds, which may lead to credit rationing and rent-seeking activities. Finally, low real or negative interest rates create inefficiency in investment and induce investors to make such capital-intensive investment, which may be incompatible with the country's factor endowments (Chowdhury and Islam, 1993; Fry, 1998). The McKinnon model of finance in its basic form is considered next.

The McKinnon model of finance in economic development

The McKinnon model of finance in economic development is applicable to a fragmented economy with rudimentary money and capital markets. Entrepreneurs in such an economy are constrained to self-finance, as they do not have access to bank credits. Before making investment in high-yielding physical capital, investors are therefore required to accumulate funds in monetary forms. Money thus serves as a 'conduit' for capital accumulation.

The McKinnon model of finance takes the following simplified form:

$$m^d = m^d\,(y, iyr, d - \pi) \tag{5.39}$$

$$iyr = iyr\,(r_k, d - \pi) \tag{5.40}$$

$$iyr = syr = s \tag{5.41}$$

$$s = s(g_y, d - \pi) \tag{5.42}$$

$$\pi = \pi(\lambda, g_y) \tag{5.43}$$

$$g_y = \rho\, s \tag{5.44}$$

where m^d is the demand for real money, y is real income (or output), iyr is the investment–income ratio, $d-\pi$ is the real deposit rate of interest, r_k is the real return on physical capital, syr is the savings–income ratio (or the propensity to save, s), g_y is the growth rate

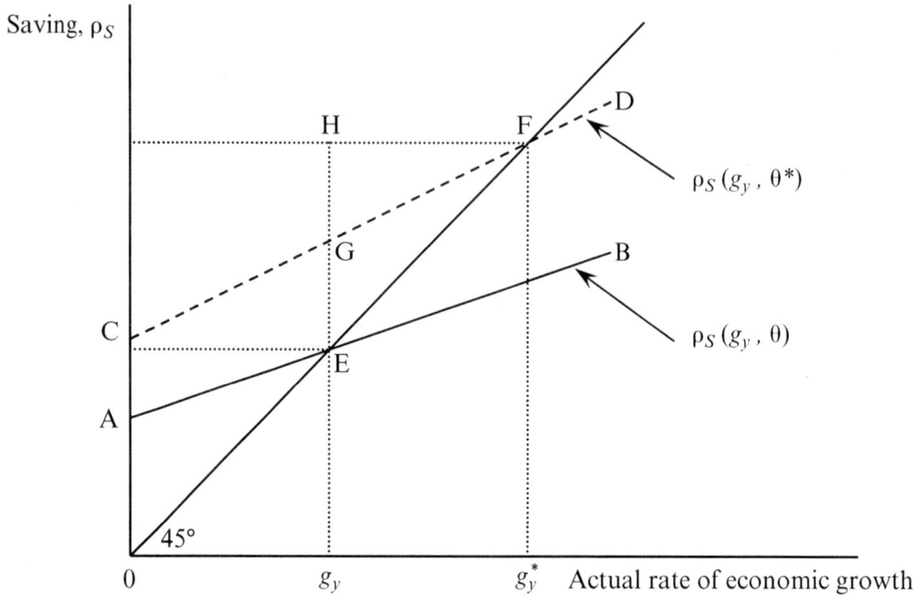

Figure 5.11 The propensity to save and the rate of economic growth

of income (or output), λ is the growth rate of exogenously determined nominal money stock, and ρ is the fixed output–capital ratio.

Equation (5.39) shows that there is a complementary relationship between money and capital. All the partial derivatives of real money demand in equation (5.39) are positive. The complementarity between money and capital is also shown in the investment function (5.40). All the partial derivatives of investment are positive. The investment function suggests that any exogenous change that raises the return on capital, such as opening the economy to foreign trade and the introduction of, for example, seed-fertilizer-irrigation technology in agriculture, would raise the level of desired investment. This increased demand for investment may lead to an increase in the demand for money. A rise in the real deposit rate of interest would also raise savings and therefore investment.

Equations (5.42) to (5.43) show the dynamic relationship between savings and economic growth. At equilibrium, the growth rate of income generates the desired level of saving which is sufficient to support the level of investment needed to maintain that growth rate of income.

Figure 5.11 shows the effect of financial reform on the propensity to save. E represents the initial equilibrium growth rate of output where the variable propensity to save line crosses the 45-degree line. The variable propensity to save line (AB) is drawn as a function of the growth rate of output.[29] Assume that the initial financial structure of the economy is repressed with a low or negative real return on holding money and a small money–income ratio. Such an economy is denoted by the parameter θ. The variable propensity to save line CD is drawn as a function of the growth rate of output after financial reform. Assume that this reform has raised sharply both the real return on holding money and the money–income ratio. Such a financial reform is denoted by the parameter θ^*. The consequence of such a financial reform is the shift in the saving line from AB to CD in which the slope of the line CD with respect to g_y is steeper than that of AB. The new equilibrium growth rate of output is g_y^*. It also represents a higher propensity to save.

The increment to the rate of saving has two parts. EG is the buoyant effect on savings of financial reform. McKinnon (1974) calls it 'the pure intermediation effect' – the increase in the propensity to save at a given growth rate of income. Since income is expected to grow faster when realised savings and investment rise, GH captures the growth dividend to savings – the portfolio effect when individuals maintain their portfolio balance in the face of economic progress. The steeper slope of the savings line (CD) indicates that the effect of growth on the rate of savings (reverse causation) is higher in a financially reformed economy compared with that of a financially repressed economy. Therefore the essence of the McKinnon model is that financial reform promotes saving and economic growth.

A developed financial sector performs two growth-promoting functions. First, by sharing risks, it facilitates trade and specialisation. Second, it promotes capital accumulation. Although the role of a developed financial sector in facilitating trade and specialisation is well understood, the capital-accumulation-augmenting role of financial reform remains a controversial issue.

There are three aspects in the financial development-capital accumulation-growth link: the relation between the real deposit rate of interest and the rate of savings (or the volume effect of the real deposit interest rate); the relation between the real deposit interest rate and financial savings (or the composition/efficiency effect of the real deposit interest rate); and the relation between the real loan interest rate and the efficiency of investment. Although economic theory does not offer a clear-cut prediction as to the overall influence of interest rates on saving, the proponents of financial liberalisation hold the view that a rise in real interest rates would encourage households to save more.

A rise in the real deposit rate of interest is believed to promote financial deepening because savings may be held in financial, rather than non-financial, asset forms. This improves the efficiency of intermediation between savers and investors. This can be compared with the condition when the nominal interest rate is set below the inflation rate, which creates a negative real interest rate that lowers the demand for financial assets, as savers are encouraged to invest in real rather than in financial assets. As a consequence of the decline in financial savings, the supply of loanable funds declines and the financial sector becomes shallow.

Effective utilisation of capital is one important determinant of growth. In many developing countries it is not always the lack of capital but the lack of effective utilisation of capital that might have retarded economic growth. It is argued that when real interest rates are negative or very low, there is little incentive to use capital more efficiently since excess capacity is costless. Hence a rise in the real interest rate is expected to raise the effective utilisation of capital (Fry, 1991).

The above contention can be explained with a simple diagram (Figure 5.12). MPK represents the marginal productivity of capital under a repressed financial system. If the ceiling interest rate is r_c, which is below the market (equilibrium) rate r_e, then the measured capital stock (K_m) would be higher than the equilibrium capital stock (K_e). When the interest rate ceiling is removed and the interest rate moves towards the equilibrium rate r_e at point E, the marginal productivity of capital would rise along the MPK schedule and the capital stock would approach to K_e so that the measured capital stock equals

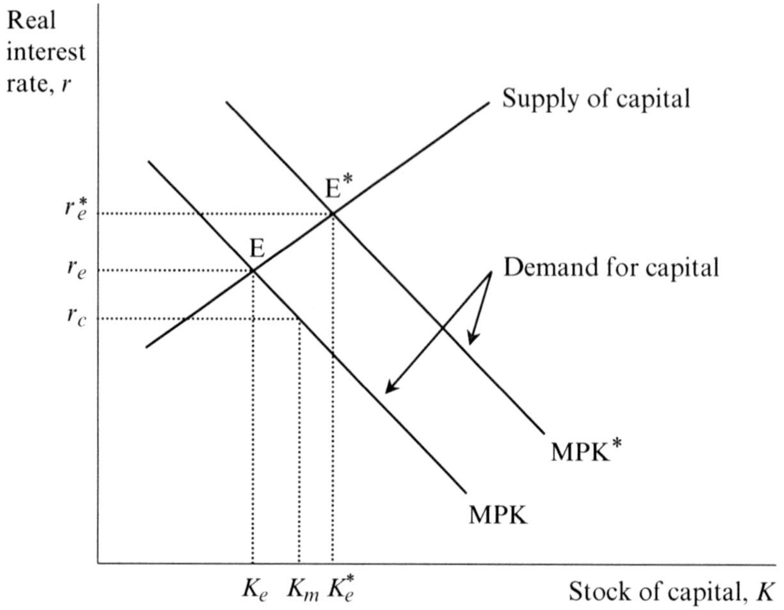

Notes:
1. MPK represents the marginal productivity of capital under a repressed financial system.
2. MPK* represents the marginal productivity of capital after financial reform raising the efficiency of capital.

Source: Adapted from Hossain and Chowdhury (1996: 36).

Figure 5.12 Relationship between the real interest rate and capital stock

the equilibrium stock. However, it can be argued that with financial reforms and the improved utilisation of capital, there could be an increase in the efficiency of capital that may cause a shift in the marginal productivity of curve to the right. This would result in an increase in both effective and measured capital stock. MPK* represents the marginal productivity of capital under financial reforms that raise the efficiency of capital. The new equilibrium is established at point E*, where the stock of capital and the real interest rate are higher compared with the corresponding figures before financial reform. Financial reform is therefore expected to raise both quantity and efficiency of investment.

Critique of the financial liberalisation hypothesis[30]

The empirical foundation of the financial liberalisation paradigm has not been robust. The doctrine of financial liberalisation has been challenged, both on theoretical and empirical grounds. One variant of the critique, known as the 'new structuralist' critique, uses empirical findings – for example, Wijnbergen's (1982; 1985) – that the major effect of financial reforms in South Korea was a huge portfolio shift of savings away from the unregulated (informal) to the regulated (formal) market without concomitant increase in the volume of savings. Thus whether financial reforms would enhance growth depends on the relative efficiency of the formal financial sector in allocating investable funds.

According to Cho (1990), informal credit markets are less efficient because they have a narrow information base and a limited capacity for risk pooling. On the other hand, informal credit markets can economise on overhead costs, which may outweigh their limitations pertaining to risk pooling. An implication is that it is not possible to make an a priori statement about the efficacy of the formal vis-à-vis informal credit market.

The new structuralist critique of the financial liberalisation hypothesis also draws on what is known in the literature as the Cavallo effect (Cavallo, 1977). The argument is that in developing countries firms depend on borrowing for their working capital. Thus the diversion of funds from the informal market as a result of financial liberalisation would reduce the supply of loanable funds because bank deposits require reserves. This may therefore create credit squeeze and raise working capital costs with a predictable outcome of stagflation (Bruno, 1979; Taylor, 1979; 1983). The validity of this argument hinges upon the substitutability between the formal and informal sector deposit instruments. Kapur (1992) argues that the informal and formal sector deposits are not close substitutes. The informal sector primarily provides high-yielding but illiquid deposit instruments, arising from zero reserves. In contrast, representing the formal sector, bank deposits are more liquid. Both these have their own roles in the utility function of wealth-holders. Even if there is some portfolio shift towards the formal sector, Kapur maintains that the total supply of productive credit may not necessarily decline. Kapur derives his results by considering the motive of the government which receives a 'windfall' seigniorage gain as the monetary base increases with the rise in reserves due to higher deposit takings. The government can channel this newly created monetary base to development banks or to commercial banks.

A stronger critique of the financial liberalisation hypothesis, often characterised as the new view of the role of finance, maintains that a repressed financial system would facilitate rapid economic growth (Amsden, 1989; Lee, 1992; Stiglitz, 1994; Wade, 1988). In developing this argument, Zysman (1983) makes a distinction between a capital-market based and a credit-based financial system. In a capital-market based financial system, securities are the main sources of long-term business finance. Lenders (and borrowers) can choose from (and use) a broad spectrum of capital and money market instruments.

On the other hand, the capital market, in a credit-based system, is weak and firms rely heavily on credit to finance investment. Banks are the main suppliers of credit, which makes firms dependent on banks. If banks are themselves dependent on government, then firms essentially become dependent on government as well. In such an institutional environment, financial repression (in the form of government-directed credit) is alleged to have certain advantages. First, 'a credit-based system permits faster investment in developing country conditions than would be possible if investment depended on the growth of firms' own profits or on the inevitably slow development of securities market' (Wade, 1988: 134). More importantly, productive investment is less affected by speculative stock market booms and busts. Second, a credit-based system tends to avoid the bias towards short-term profitability that often appears to be associated with a stock market system. It stems from the argument that lenders of long-term finance are interested in the ability of borrowers to repay the loans over the long term. Hence, long-term performance becomes the dominant consideration, entailing a focus on such issues as the ability of organisations to develop new products, cost competitiveness, and so on. These therefore become the criteria that managers are concerned with, rather than the short-run performance in the stock market. Finally, a state-dominated financial system provides the government with the necessary political clout to implement its industrial strategy. As Wade (1988: 134) comments, 'firms are dissuaded from opposing the government by knowledge that opponents may find credit difficult to obtain'.

Stiglitz (1994) argues that most of the arguments against financial repression are based on a number of errors in previous empirical studies. Foremost, earlier studies failed to distinguish between small and large repression, and let large repression influence the results. Second, high negative rates of returns are primarily a symptom of a wider range of government failures, and it would be incorrect to infer that the low level of economic growth is caused by financial repression. Third, the claim that financial repression leads to inefficient allocation of resources is based on the failure to recognise the distinction between credit and other markets.

Stiglitz maintains that market failures related to informational asymmetry is endemic in financial markets.[31] Moreover, economies with imperfect information or incomplete markets are not constrained Pareto-efficient.[32] In such situations, feasible government interventions can make all individuals better off. Stiglitz has outlined a number of ways in which financial repression (low interest rate) policy can enhance growth.

First, the low interest rate policy can be viewed as a mechanism of resource transfer from the household to the corporate sector where such transfers are costly. If the marginal propensity to save of the corporate sector is higher than that of the household sector, then the aggregate savings would rise. This argument is similar to the Kalecki-Kaldor-Robinson model.

Stiglitz's second argument is that lower interest rates could increase the expected quality of borrowers by minimising the adverse selection and incentive problems. This effect would be even greater if the government possessed some positive selection capabilities. Furthermore, by reducing the cost of capital, financial repression (low interest rate policy) increases the firm's equity which, in turn, reduces the prospect of bankruptcy. In addition, when more of their own capital is at stake, firms are more likely to select good projects.

Finally, because lower interest rates create excess demand, directed credit policy can be used as an incentive scheme. The government can set up a competitive situation where better performer in terms of some measurable target (for example, foreign exchange earnings) would get more access to capital.

A very similar argument in favour of financial repression can also be found in C.H. Lee's internal capital market hypothesis. Using the East Asian example, Lee (1992) suggests that a state-dominated, credit-based system operates as a de facto internal capital market. The State cultivates a long-term and close relationship with borrowing firms. The atmosphere of trust and cooperation created as a result of this close relationship allows lender monitoring to be carried out effectively and efficiently; in the case of East Asia, export targets were traditionally used to monitor performance. The outcome is that transaction costs are minimised. Hence, what is apparently considered a phenomenon of financial repression is, in effect, a de facto internal capital market that is more efficient than private capital markets.[33]

While the above arguments are persuasive, it is possible to construct cogent counter-arguments. For example, a credit-based system should not be confused with a state-controlled credit-based system. Financial repression is a necessary feature of the latter, but not the former. Importantly, the major advantages of a credit-based system as identified by Wade do not require the existence of state controls (and hence financial repression). The only way in which financial repression can contribute to economic growth in this framework is to presuppose that a strong-willed government has the capacity to overcome the inadequacies of private capital markets without the corresponding risk of government failure. Stiglitz (1994: 32) himself pointed out that governments may resolve market failure imperfectly as some interventions could be motivated by special interest group pressures. Moreover, the government is at a marked disadvantage in assessing risks and premiums due to the large element of subjectivities involved.[34]

There are also inadequacies of the internal capital market hypothesis. It is sufficient to emphasise that the notion of transaction cost minimisation is not unique to a state-controlled financial system. It is worth noting that the efficacy of the internal capital market has been exhaustively studied in the case of Japan, yet the state does not play a major role in the Japanese internal capital market (Frenkel, 1991).

The hypothesis of the superiority of lender monitoring in a state-controlled financial system is also questionable when one takes account of the interactions between formal and informal credit markets. Cole and Patrick (1986) report that in South Korea there is a widespread practice of re-lending by privileged borrowers in regulated markets to users in unregulated markets (and hence profit from arbitrage). This fact invalidates the notion that the State can effectively monitor the behaviour of borrowers. In addition to fallibility, state regulators are likely to be influenced by corruption. In such circumstances, a legitimate question is 'who monitors the monitors?' The experience of Bangladesh's Grameen Bank shows that a system of peer monitoring can perhaps overcome some of the associated problems (Calomiris and Himmelberg, 1994; Stiglitz, 1989; 1990).

Finally, the widespread scepticism about the financial liberalisation hypothesis can be seen as a reaction to the popular perception that financial reform is synonymous with a laissez-faire approach. Current developments in the literature, as well as the experience of a wide range of countries with financial reforms, have brought to the fore the issue of prudential regulation of the financial system (Diaz-Alejandro, 1985; Long and Vittas, 1991; Park, 1991). In order to avoid the recurrence of financial scandals, prudential regulations are necessary, which entail, *inter alia*, enforceable measures such as audits and disclosures. Thus the choice is not between a laissez-faire approach and a dirigiste system, but for a competitive financial sector within the institutional context of prudential regulation.

To conclude, the earlier discussions of financial factors in developing countries were primarily concerned with their role in mobilising savings. The predominantly Keynesian school believes that investment is the constraining factor for growth, and prescribes financial repression characterised by low nominal interest rate and high inflation. While a low interest rate is expected to encourage investment, inflation is used to create forced savings.

On the other hand, the followers of the Classical School argue that prior savings and financial development are key elements in economic development. According to this view, financial reform enhances the aggregate saving rate, induces financial deepening and improves investment efficiency. These salutary effects in turn contribute to rapid economic growth.

The empirical foundation of the financial liberalisation paradigm has, however, not been so robust, compounded by burgeoning arguments that directly challenge its doctrine. A stronger critique of the financial liberalisation hypothesis maintains that a repressed financial system would facilitate rapid economic growth. It is also argued that earlier studies of the adverse effects of financial repression were influenced by large repressions. The large repressions themselves may be symptoms of government failures, making it difficult to conclude whether the adverse growth effect is due to repression per se or to government mismanagement.

It is now increasingly realised that financial markets do much more than mobilising savings – whether 'forced' or 'voluntary'. Financial markets not only deal with intertemporal decisions but also with risk and information. As Stiglitz (1994: 23) comments, 'how well they perform these functions may affect not only the extent to which they can mobilise savings but, more broadly, the overall efficiency and rate of growth of the economy'. Because of endemic nature of market failures in the financial sector due to information asymmetry, moral hazard, and the high transaction costs of monitoring and information transfer, a consensus now seems to be emerging that small repression is perhaps growth promoting. Even the World Bank, which vigorously preached the financial liberalisation programme, appears to have accepted the emerging view (Cho and Khatkhate, 1989; World Bank, 1993).

PART IV

STRATEGY OF MONETARY POLICY

Rules versus Discretion in Monetary Policy

Whether monetary policy should be conducted through discretion or rules remains a perennial debate. Simons (1948) addressed this issue in the 1940s. Fischer (1990: 1157) points out that although Simons posed the issue as one of rules versus authority, such dichotomy should be seen as a continuum.

The debate has continued over the extent of discretion of the monetary authority in the conduct of monetary policy. In general, monetarists suggest that the design of monetary policy implies the design of institutions and rules, leaving limited scope for discretionary monetary policy. The problem with discretionary monetary policy is that it allows policy-makers to engage in policy actions with the view of influencing economic activity. Yet such policy actions can create uncertainties and economic instability, so monetarists argue that they should be avoided. The emerging view is that central banks should not conduct monetary policy in a discretionary manner. They should instead follow well-defined guidelines and rules so that the conduct of monetary policy becomes transparent and more effective.

Although the rules-based monetary policy is preferable to discretionary monetary policy, there is disagreement whether rules and discretion are mutually exclusive. One interpretation of a rule is that it is a preset policy that remains independent of contemporaneous circumstances; that is, it neither permits nor requires judgement (or discretion) on policy matters. Friedman's (1959a) proposal for a 'constant money growth rule' is interpreted as a policy rule. Under a policy rule, any deviation from the rule is interpreted as a discretionary act. Bryant et al. (2003) have, however, provided a broadest interpretation of the policy rule. They suggest that all monetary regimes can be described as a system of rules – even those with discretionary elements.

Economists focus on two kinds of (instrument) rules: the money growth rule and the interest rate rule. Since the 1950s, Friedman (1959a) argued for a money growth rule, reasoning that central banks do not possess detailed knowledge and information on the economy, which is essential for the conduct of discretionary monetary policy. In particular, it is difficult to forecast the future path of the economy. To predict the response of the economy to any change in monetary policy is difficult because of 'long and variable time lags'. A discretionary monetary policy may therefore carry the risk of destabilising the economy. Friedman instead recommended for a constant money supply growth, within the vicinity of 2 or 4 or 5 per cent per annum, to keep inflation low and stable. Through such a policy, monetary authorities arguably can make a contribution to economic stability (Friedman, 1968a: 17). Importantly, Friedman's approach was pragmatic, not intended to be a panacea for economic growth and stability (Friedman, 1983a).

Friedman's constant money growth rate is often interpreted as passive, even though such a rule requires setting the money growth rate and responding to correct or ignore past misses in attaining the set money growth rate. The main criticism against a money growth rate is that the velocity of money may not be stable (Fischer, 1990). McCallum (2000) has extended Friedman's rule to include a feedback element to correct for past mistakes or to adjust to permanent shifts in velocity. He notes that 'even the most enthusiastic promoters of rule-based policy making do not contemplate that central banks would turn the selection of instrument settings over to a clerk/calculator' (McCallum, 2000: 275).

Taylor (1993) has devised the most popular interest rate rule, which includes feedback elements. In its simplest form, the central bank raises the nominal interest rate when expected inflation rises and lowers the interest rate when the unemployment rate rises above an undesirable level. This idea is formalised under the famous Taylor's rule:

$$i_t = r^* + \pi_t + \alpha(\pi_t - \pi^*) + \beta(y_t - y_t^f/y_t^f) \qquad (5.45)$$

where i is the nominal interest rate, r^* is the real 'natural' interest rate, y (y^f) is the actual (natural) level of output, π^* is the central bank's target inflation rate, and α and β are policy parameters. If α and β are large, the monetary policy rule would dictate aggressive response to excess inflation and to economic booms. If α is large relative to β, the monetary authority responds more aggressively to expected inflation than to the level of economic activity. The case of $\beta = 0$ corresponds to pure inflation targeting.

Recall that the nominal interest rate equals the real interest rate plus expected inflation. By increasing the nominal interest rate more than the rise in expected inflation, Taylor's rule raises the real interest rate to cool off the economy. Given that the measure of economic activity is the output gap, this rule allows the central bank to manipulate the nominal interest rate to stabilise output around its potential level, not simply to increase output (Dornbusch et al., 2008).

In the context of a fixed price IS-LM model, Poole (1970) has examined the question of whether output would be more stable if monetary policy is conducted by keeping the money stock or the interest rate constant in the event of shocks to the IS curve and the LM curve. The standard answer is that money stock fixing is preferable if the shocks originate from the IS curve, and that interest rate fixing is preferable if the shocks originate from money demand. When prices are flexible and with rational expectations, monetary policy cannot change output unless the monetary authority has informational advantage, or if some prices were fixed before monetary policy decisions are made (Barro, 2008; Fischer, 1990).

Dynamic inconsistency and the rules versus discretion debate in monetary policy

Both theoretical and empirical studies demonstrate that there is no long-run relationship between inflation and unemployment (Appendix 5A3). Yet under certain circumstances, a short-run trade-off between these variables may exist. For example, a short-run Phillips curve may exist due to sticky wages and prices. Given wage and price rigidities in the short run, expansionary monetary policy can raise output or lower unemployment. This can create a game-theoretic scenario, in which the central bank has an option to generate an inflation 'surprise' to lower unemployment. This leads to the problem of 'dynamic inconsistency in optimal monetary policy'. As indicated earlier, Kydland and Prescott (1977) and Calvo (1978a) have independently developed this concept and demonstrated an inflationary bias under discretionary monetary policy.

Dynamic inconsistency has made a fundamental change in macroeconomic policy-making, especially in the context of the discretion versus rule in monetary policy. Although a policy rule is considered superior to discretion, dynamic inconsistency creates an inflationary bias, even when monetary policy is conducted by a rule that is not binding. This follows the idea that unanticipated monetary shocks affect the economy; therefore, the monetary authorities retain the temptations to exercise their power to generate money shocks that will affect output or employment. Under a binding rule, the monetary authorities would commit to follow the designated model of conducting policy. Under discretion, the authorities leave open the option of a surprise. Under rational expectations, expected monetary shocks do not affect real variables.

Various measures have been suggested in the literature to remove an inflationary bias in monetary policy, even if under a rule. The idea is to raise the central bank's credibility in monetary policy, making it costly for a central bank to break a preset rule. Authors like McCallum (2000) and Taylor (1993) maintain the view that, to be rules based, a monetary regime must satisfy certain minimum criteria. It is not sufficient for policy to be non-random. Even under a discretionary regime, the central banks should have policy goals and conduct policy predictably, not randomly. Monetary policy can only be effective if the policy rule is credible and binding.

The next section develops a model to illustrate the concept of dynamic inconsistency and then reviews how different strategies of monetary policy can remove inflationary bias. The discussion draws on Dornbusch et al. (2008).

A model of dynamic inconsistency

As indicated above, dynamic inconsistency refers to the difference between the optimal policy that a central bank announces that it would carry out and the policy that it actually carries out, once the public have made decisions on the basis of its expectations. If the central bank announces that it would target a particular rate of inflation (say zero) and the public enter into contracts based on that announcement, the central bank has an incentive to renege on its promise by exploiting the possibility of achieving a higher level of output by producing an inflation 'surprise'. This means that policy-makers, unconstrained by rules, have an incentive to 'cheat' the private sector to spur output gains. The public would, however, know this sooner or later and adjust upward their inflationary expectations, which would limit desired output gains. There may not even be an output gain; it depends on whether underlying wage and price rigidities prevent full wage and price adjustments. As rational agents account for incentives of policy-makers to produce an inflation surprise, they adjust their behaviour accordingly. The result is no rise in output but a rise in inflation. This theme is developed next.

Assume that the policy-maker chooses a monetary policy which results in a particular rate of inflation. The choice of the inflation rate leads to an unemployment rate, as suggested by the following expectations-augmented short-run Phillips curve:

$$\pi = \pi^e - \varepsilon\,(u - u_n) \tag{5.46}$$

where π (π^e) is actual (expected) inflation and $u(u_n)$ is the actual (natural) rate of unemployment. The coefficient ε captures the effect of inflation on unemployment, given expected inflation, π^e. When the rate of unemployment is above the natural rate, inflation is lower than expected; when the rate of unemployment is below the natural rate, inflation is higher than expected (Blanchard, 2006).

Both the policy-maker and the public prefer a low rate of unemployment and zero inflation. Also, both inflation and deflation are costly. When the price level is constant (that is, $\pi = 0$), the costs of inflation are the minimum.

Assume that the policy-maker's loss function L can be expressed as follows:

$$L = \alpha(u - u_n) + \pi^2 \tag{5.47}$$

This loss function suggests a decrease in the policy-maker's utility when actual unemployment is higher than the natural rate of unemployment and when inflation deviates from zero. The higher the value of the coefficient α, the greater is the relative weight to lowering unemployment for the policy-maker.

Figure 5.13 illustrates the three steps of a monetary policy game that the policy-maker plays to derive a policy outcome. First, the policy-maker chooses and announces a policy; for example, 0 per cent inflation (point A). This is the optimal policy when it is announced by the policy-maker. At this point, $\pi = \pi^e = 0$ and therefore, actual unemployment equals the natural rate of unemployment, $u = u_n$.

Second, economic agents choose the level of expected inflation ($\pi^e = 0$), which is consistent with the authority's announced policy. In the short-run Phillips curve the economy is positioned at the full-employment level (point A). This is the point where $u = u_n$. Given the short-run Phillips curve with $\pi^e = 0$, the policy-maker finds it attractive to move the

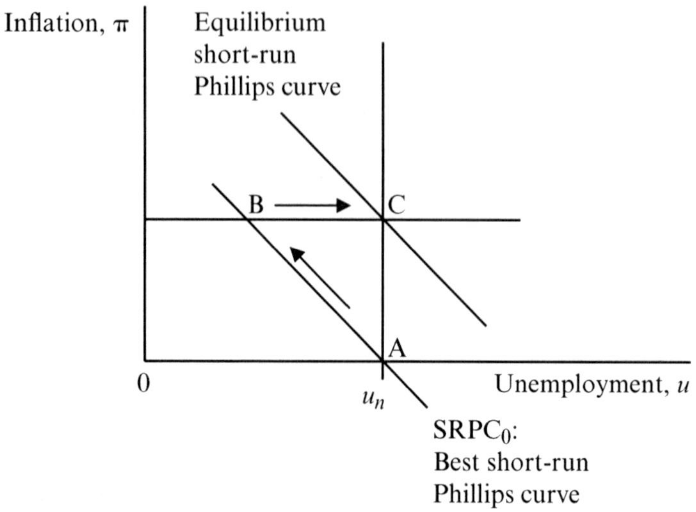

Notes: At point A, $\pi^e = 0$. At point B, $\pi > \pi^e = 0$. At point C, $\pi = \pi^e > 0$. This represents the equilibrium inflation rate, which is the greater than zero, although everyone prefers zero inflation at point A ($\pi = \pi^e = 0$).

Figure 5.13 Dynamic inconsistency and inflationary bias in monetary policy

economy to the point B by generating an inflation surprise, $\pi > 0$. This follows the minimisation of the following 'loss function':

$$L(\pi) = \alpha\,[-\,1/\varepsilon\,(\pi - \pi^e)] + \pi^2 \tag{5.48}$$

where, using equation (5.46), $u - u_n$ is replaced by: $-\,1/\varepsilon\,(\pi - \pi^e)$.

Take the first-order derivative of $L(\pi)$ with respect to π (given $\pi^e = 0$) and set the marginal loss function $ML(\pi)$ equal to zero, such that

$$ML(\pi) = -\,\alpha/\varepsilon + 2\pi = 0 \tag{5.49}$$

This gives the optimal inflation rate:

$$\pi = \alpha/2\varepsilon. \tag{5.50}$$

This shows that the optimal inflation rate is positive. It holds for any level of π^e.

At point B, actual inflation is greater than expected inflation. Economic agents would subsequently revise expectations and the short-run Phillips curve would move up and the equilibrium would be established at point C. At this equilibrium, the economy ends up with high inflation. The policy-maker would promise to lower inflation to zero (and bring the economy back to point A) but the promise may not be credible. Economic agents believe that if the economy returns to A, the central bank would cheat them again. Breaking the policy rule has thus created a credibility problem.

The result in equation (5.50) holds, irrespective of the value of π^e. Although everyone desires zero inflation, in the last stage of the game it pays the policy-maker to choose a positive rate of inflation. In fact, since anticipated inflation equals $\alpha/2\varepsilon$, if the policy-maker chooses in the last step to set an inflation rate below $\alpha/2\varepsilon$, recession would follow. The problem is that society has no way to commit to zero inflation.

Equation (5.50) shows that the optimal rate of inflation rises with the coefficient value α. That is, in the loss function, if the policy-maker's loss is weighted heavily against unemployment, the result would be more inflation. This perverse result occurs because a high value of α increases the incentive in the last step to raise inflation to lower unemployment. However, if the society can cede power to a policy-maker who cares less about unemployment (one with a lower value α), a lower rate of inflation may result.

Establishing credibility in monetary policy

Before the dynamic-inconsistency idea was developed, the rules versus discretion debate were articulated by non-activists. They argued that counter-cyclical policies were ineffective and could be destabilising. Kydland and Prescott moved the debate forward in a profound way. They showed that those rules which are not binding are time-inconsistent. Establishing a credible commitment to the rule is more important than the exact form of the rule. To be precise, the problem is how to tie the policy-makers' hands and to ensure that the rules are not broken (Blanchard, 2006; Persson and Tabellini, 1990; 2000).

The time-inconsistency problem reveals difficulties in bringing down inflation under disinflation programmes. If policy-makers had broken earlier promises by creating inflation surprises, the policy announcement of low inflation under deflationary programmes would not be credible. Facing high inflation, the government commonly announces a sharp reduction in inflation and expects that the public would believe its announcement. Often such announcements are not credible. The public may believe that the government would trick again once they enter into contracts. In doing so, the government would disinflate less than it promises to maintain output gains. The problem is that the public know that once they set their expectations and enter into contracts, then the government has an incentive to renege its promises.

Central bankers and policy-makers recognise the natural rate hypothesis and the idea of rational expectations. The actual or perceived loss function of the monetary authority that generates inflation has led economists to suggest measures that may lower an inflationary bias in monetary policy. A number of such measures are discussed next.

Central bank autonomy

An important solution to the inflationary bias is to give the central bank autonomy in monetary policy. The government and central bank can set the target of a particular rate of inflation and the central bank can then use its policy instruments to achieve that target. Central bank independence generally leads to lower inflation (Grilli et al., 1991). Empirical evidence on this issue is, however, tenuous because there can be a reverse causation. Countries that dislike inflation tend to give more independence to central banks and therefore have lower inflation (Blanchard, 2006).

Central bank independence by itself may not be enough. In the USA, the Fed, for example, has more independence than most central banks. However its anti-inflationary credibility is low because of the fact that, while the European Central Bank has the overriding statutory duty to stabilise prices, the Federal Reserve Bank Act of 1978 requires the Fed to pursue full employment as well as low inflation. This makes the Fed's monetary policy inconsistent over time. This is equally true for other countries in the Asia-Pacific. As reviewed earlier, the monetary policy in most countries has the responsibility to keep inflation low without raising unemployment.

Longer-term appointment

Assume that inflation and unemployment are the objectives of monetary policy. Given such an objective function, even if the central bank is not subject to political pressure, it may attempt to lower unemployment below the natural rate. When a central bank pursues such policy, it creates a long-run inflation problem. Central bankers, who are appointed by the government, may go soft with inflation and hence remain in favour with politicians. Therefore, it is suggested that central bankers need a longer-term appointment so that they can take into account long-term costs from higher inflation and have incentives to build policy credibility and/or reputation as an inflation fighter. Central bank governor and other high officials with a longer tenure can better resist political pressure to generate inflation surprises.

Appointment of conservative central bankers

Rogoff (1987; 1989) has suggested that the inflationary bias can be alleviated through the appointment of a conservative central banker, that is, somebody who strongly dislikes inflation and is less willing to accept more inflation in exchange for less unemployment. When the economy is at the natural level, a conservative central banker would be less tempted to embark on a monetary expansion. Central bankers need to appear and sound conservative, whatever views they may hold. This explains why central bank governors are usually reluctant to admit, at least in public, the existence of even a short-run trade-off between unemployment and inflation (Blanchard, 2006).

Inflation–wage contract

Walsh (1995) has developed the idea of inflation–wage job contract. His idea is steeped in the principal–agent approach. If the government appoints a central banker and influences its incentives by assigning a state-contingent wage contract that is designed correctly, inflationary bias can be eliminated. The implementation of such a contract is difficult and may not be effective. The performance-related remuneration contract may not affect the incentives of a central banker as much as postulated since the opportunity cost of being a central banker is very high in terms of pay elsewhere. Furthermore, according to Svensson (1997), there is a practical complication under this regime. The pay contract is expressed in monetary term, while the loss function is expressed in utility units. There is need for translating monetary costs into utility, hence the incorporation of a central banker's marginal utility of money.

Inflation targeting

Svensson (1997) has proposed a solution to the inflationary bias: inflation targeting. He regards inflation targeting as equivalent to that of Walsh's inflation contract. It is a second-best solution when commitment to a rule is not feasible, which eradicates the inflationary bias without unnecessarily destabilising output. Svensson (1997) considers Rogoff's conservative central banker as the third best, since it creates excessive output variability.

Svensson's approach adopts a principal–agent framework in which the society (principal) delegates monetary policy to an agent (central bank). Society assigns a loss function and the central bank is given independence to minimise this loss function, and remains accountable for minimising it. The central bank is given operational but not goal independence. An explicit inflation target is assigned to the central bank, which may differ from that of the socially desired rate (zero). An output target is implicit and, under inflation targeting, is not usually assigned to be the natural level on the ground that this may be a politically unpopular level or that there are difficulties in verifying the natural level of output.

Reputation models of monetary policy

The static models deployed by economists to remove an inflationary bias have provided an intellectually stimulating framework for analysing monetary policy. Some economists, however, suggest that the inflationary bias problem is somewhat exaggerated. When there are lags involved in the conduct of monetary policy, the wage contracts may not be binding by the time the manipulation of monetary instruments takes effect on the actual economy. Only those wage contracts, which remain binding, would be affected.

In practice, the monetary authority is unlikely to be as myopic as the static models suggest. With a time span in office greater than one period, the monetary authority would have regular interactions with private agents and any temptation to cheat to have a one-period gain would therefore be tempered by the resultant inflationary bias and credibility problem that are caused in subsequent periods. Two important strands have emerged in the literature that considers monetary policy in a dynamic setting: models, which emphasise the reputation of policy-makers, and models which deploy a timeless perspective.

Barro and Gordon (1983a; 1983b) developed a dynamic reputation model based on their earlier static model in which reputational forces substitute for formal rules. The idea is that the prospect of reputation loss may motivate policy-makers to abide by the rule that is not so binding. Another type of reputational model is developed by Backus and Driffill (1985). This model assumes a world in which there is imperfect information and as a result there are uncertainties about whether the monetary authority is 'wet' (placing greater concern on output) or 'dry' (regarding inflation as particularly important). In the Backus–Driffill model, the wet central bank mimics the dry, otherwise its identity would be revealed and inflationary expectations would remain high as under discretion. The model is developed in an infinitely repeated game fashion, in which only in the last period the type of central bank would be revealed. Prior to the last period, the wet central bank may well choose zero inflation with the aim of gaining credibility and randomising its strategy. For a dry central bank it is beneficial to set a positive inflation target because in the first period, while its credibility is still in doubt, its pursuit of zero inflation may generate undesirable recession. Therefore, it is possible to have a pooling equilibrium where both types announce a positive inflation rate. However, if the public places high probability on the central bank being of the dry type, it may be more worthwhile for the dry to have inflation very close to zero.

In conclusion, the rule versus discretion debate is far from over. Although the emerging consensus is for a rule-based monetary policy, dynamic inconsistency suggests that unless the rule is binding it may not be credible and the inflation bias problem may remain. Further, there are sceptics who see discretion a better approach to conduct monetary policy (Fischer, 1990).

SUPPLY SHOCKS AND MONETARY POLICY

What kind of monetary policy is appropriate for price stability after a supply shock? This issue has become important since the 1970s, especially in developing countries (Shapiro, 1992). There is consensus that monetary accommodation after the first oil-shock during 1973–74 led to high inflation, which was followed by recession. The simultaneous inflation and high unemployment was tagged as stagflation. This contradicted the traditional Phillips curve relationship that suggests an inverse relationship between inflation and unemployment. Since the 1970s monetary authorities in most countries have treated supply shocks as a transitory phenomenon and avoided accommodating such shocks through money creation. Developing countries remain prone to supply shocks. This section therefore examines this issue in detail.

The monetary theory of aggregate demand shows the relationship between output demanded and the price level when the money market is in equilibrium. To derive such a relationship, an aggregate money demand function is specified below.

The Theory of Money Demand

Assume that the demand for money is derived in the same way as the demand for any other durable good. Real money balances are considered a type of real asset, one form of wealth with the additional property of higher liquidity, providing a flow of non-observable services that enter into individuals' utility functions. All individuals are assumed to maximise their utility functions subject to budget constraints. The demand for real money balances, derived by the utility maximisation principle, would then depend on real income and the opportunity cost of holding money instead of other financial and real assets.

Let M^d be the demand for nominal money balances, P the price level, y the real income or output and π^e the expected inflation. Then the demand for money can be expressed in the following semi-logarithmic form:

$$LM^d - LP = \alpha\, Ly - \beta\pi^e \tag{5.51}$$

where α and β are structural parameters and L represents the logarithmic operator. It shows that the demand for money increases with the increase in real income and decreases with the increase in expected inflation.

Money Market Equilibrium

Equilibrium in the money market refers to a situation where the demand for real money equals the supply of real money, so that at equilibrium $LM^d - LP = LM^s - LP$. Any discrepancy between the demand for, and supply of, money indicates that the money market is in disequilibrium. Any excess money supply (or excess money demand) is expected to spill over to the commodity market. In a closed economy it changes the price level and brings equilibrium in the money market. In a completely open economy where there are no non-traded goods, any disequilibrium in the money market adjusts itself through changes in foreign exchange reserves. When an economy is neither completely closed nor completely open, any disequilibrium in the money market adjusts itself through changes in both the price level and foreign exchange reserves.

An Aggregate Demand Function

The money market equilibrium condition yields the following aggregate demand function

$$Ly = \delta_1 (LM^s - LP) + \delta_2 \pi^e \tag{5.52}$$

where $\delta_1 = 1/\alpha$ and $\delta_2 = \beta/\alpha$.

It shows that when M^s and π^e remain constant, the demand for output is inversely related to the price level. The downward-sloping demand curve shifts to the right, with the increase in both the money supply and expected inflation, and shifts to the left with the reduction in both the money supply and expected inflation.

An Aggregate Supply Function

An expectations-augmented aggregate supply function can be specified in the form of a single reduced-form equation:

$$Ly_t = Ly_{nt} + \gamma_1 (LP_t - LP_t^e) \tag{5.53}$$

where y is measured output, y_n is natural output, determined by factors such as capital, labour and technology, P is the price level, and P^e is the price level expected by workers, given the information available at time t, and γ_1 is the elasticity of output with respect to any discrepancy between the current and expected price levels.

The specified supply function is called the Lucas supply function, although Gordon (1982) prefers to refer it as the Friedman supply function. In terms of Friedman's labour supply analysis, the demand for, and supply of, labour depend on the real wage rate. Employers calculate the real wage rate by evaluating the nominal wage rate in terms of the current price level, but workers calculate the real wage rate by evaluating the nominal wage rate in terms of the expected price level. Therefore, employment and output change only if the monetary authority can adopt such a policy which moves the actual price level, but not simultaneously moving the expected price level for workers. According to Milton Friedman, it is possible that in the short run, due to imperfect information on the part of workers, they can be 'fooled' temporarily but not in the long run. If it is assumed that the price expectations are formed rationally in the sense of Muth (1961) as an unbiased estimator of the actual price level, such output fluctuations do not arise. The aggregate supply curve becomes vertical – its position being determined uniquely by the production function and the conditions of equilibrium in the labour market.[35]

Any supply shock that shifts the production curve downward and the marginal productivity of labour curve leftward, would shift the aggregate supply curve leftward. Therefore, the leftward shift of the aggregate supply curve is the combined effect of the downward shift of the production curve and the lower level of employment. This is because of the decline in the marginal productivity of labour (Branson, 1989).

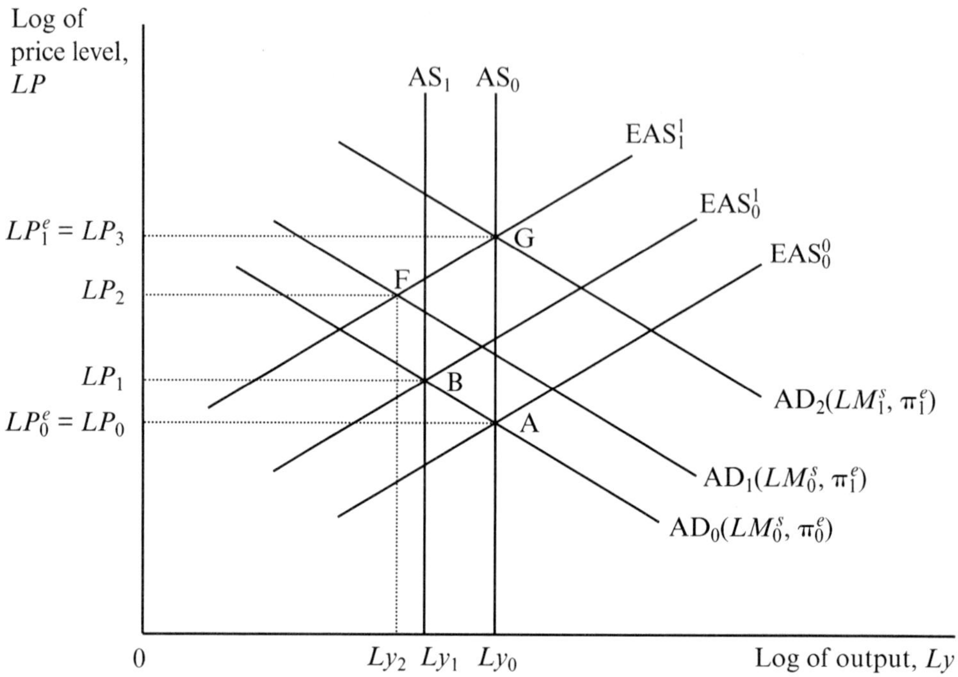

Figure 5.14 The effects on the price level in a closed economy of a hands-off and a hands-on policy by the monetary authority following a supply shock

An Application of the Model in a Closed Economy

In Figure 5.14, the aggregate demand and aggregate supply functions are brought together in order to examine the effects on the price level and output of both a hands-off and a hands-on policy by the monetary authority following a supply shock. The $AD_0(LM_0^s, \pi_0^e)$ line represents aggregate demand with the given money supply M_0^s and expected inflation π_0^e. The AS_0 line represents aggregate supply, which corresponds to a specific production function with equilibrium in the labour market. It actually represents the full capacity output. The EAS_0^0 line represents the expectations-augmented aggregate supply. It cuts the long-run aggregate supply line at the level at which the actual and expected price levels are equal ($LP_0^e = LP_0$). Point A is the initial equilibrium position of the economy with output Ly_0 and the price level LP_0.

Assume that the economy unexpectedly experiences a supply shock and the aggregate supply line AS_0 shifts to the position AS_1, which represents a less than full capacity output. Because the supply shock is unexpected, the expected price level would remain at LP_0^e and the EAS_0^0 line would shift to the position EAS_0^1. The subscript 0 in EAS_0^1 indicates the level of demand represented by $AD_0(LM_0^s, \pi_0^e)$ and the superscript 1 indicates that the aggregate supply line has unexpectedly moved to the position AS_1. After the supply shock, the economy would settle at the temporary equilibrium position B with output Ly_1 and the price level LP_1.

Assume that the supply shock discussed here is a negative agricultural supply shock. Such shocks are random and do not usually persist. Therefore, it is expected that after the one-period supply shock is over, there would be normal production in the next period. It would shift the aggregate supply line AS_1 to the right and settle at the original position AS_0. When that happens, the EAS^1_0 line would move to the original position EAS^0_0 and the price level would fall from LP_1 to LP_0. Thus the impact of any agricultural supply shock on the price level would be temporary if the monetary authority does not intervene and if there is no change in price expectations.

A complex situation may, however, arise if there is a policy intervention by the monetary authority. If the economic agents change their price expectations after the supply shock, any policy intervention by the monetary authority would create a complex and uncertain situation. Consider the case when the expected price level increases from LP^e_0 to LP^e_1. The EAS^0_0 line would then shift to the position EAS^1_1. Since the demand for money depends on expected inflation, an increase in the expected price level would shift the aggregate demand line rightward to the position $AD_1(LM^s_0, \pi^e_1)$. Changes in the expected price level thus shift both the aggregate demand and aggregate supply curves. Given the expected price level LP^e_1, the temporary equilibrium position of the economy is not B, but F, with the price level LP_2 and output Ly_2. But F does not represent a stable equilibrium because the actual and expected price levels are not equal. Whether the economy would remain at the position F, or move towards the position A after the normal production during the next period would depend on how economic agents form their price expectations. Any action by the monetary authority after the supply shock may provide vital information which may influence economic agents in forming their price expectations. Even the monetary authority's behaviour in the past under such circumstances could become the guide to economic agents in forming their price expectations. If the norm is such that the monetary authority adopts a hands-off policy following the supply shock, then it is possible that the one-shot increase in the price level would fall from the peak level after the normal production during the next period. When the expected price level falls, wealth-holders would substitute money for goods which would shift the aggregate demand curve to the left. The expectations-augmented supply curve is also likely to shift to the right after the normal production. The economy may then return to the original position A. In contrast, if the monetary authority increases the money supply after the supply shock, the aggregate demand curve would shift to a further right position, say, $AD_2(LM^s_1, \pi^e_1)$, which would increase the price level to LP_3. If the expected price level remains at LP^e_1, G may be a stable equilibrium because at this point $LP_3 = LP^e_1$. However, if the monetary expansion becomes a source of price expectations, the aggregate supply curve may shift to the left and cause a further increase in the price level.

An Application of the Model in an Open Economy

The model discussed above can be extended to the case of an open economy under both fixed and flexible exchange rate systems. For simplicity, ignore the international trade in financial assets and capital flows so that the capital account in the balance of payments disappears.

The balance of payments and the monetary sector

In an open economy, the national income identity can be written as:

$$GNP = C + I + G + EX - IM \tag{5.54}$$

where GNP is gross national product, C is consumption spending, I is investment spending, G is government spending, EX is exports and IM is imports. All variables are at constant prices.

Total spending, or absorption (A), by domestic residents can be expressed as:

$$A = C + I + G \tag{5.55}$$

Equations (5.54) and (5.55) give

$$A = GNP - EX + IM \tag{5.56}$$

Following the monetary approach to the balance of payments theory, the absorption function can be specified as:

$$A = GNP + \varepsilon(M^s/P - M^d/P) \tag{5.57}$$

where ε is the adjustment coefficient of monetary disequilibrium ($M^s/P - M^d/P$), whose value lies between zero and unity. Equations (5.56) and (5.57) yield:

$$IM - EX = \varepsilon(M^s/P - M^d/P) \tag{5.58}$$

Taking the exponent of both sides in equation (5.51) yields:

$$M^d/P = \exp(\alpha Ly - \beta\pi^e) \tag{5.59}$$

where exp denotes the exponential operator.

Substitution of equation (5.59) into equation (5.58) yields:

$$IM - EX = \varepsilon[M^s/P - \exp(\alpha Ly - \beta\pi^e)] \tag{5.60}$$

This equation demonstrates that the trade balance deteriorates with the increase in both the money supply and expected inflation, and that it improves with the increase in real income.

Supply shock and inflation under the fixed exchange rate system

In an open economy, the effect of supply shock on the price level can be examined by taking into account the possibility that any change in each of fiscal and trade deficits due to a supply shock would change the money supply. However, whether the net effect of a supply shock on the money supply would be positive or negative would depend on the possibility of any increase in the money supply, from increased fiscal deficits, exceeding any decline in the money supply, from the reduction in foreign exchange reserves, due to increased trade deficits.

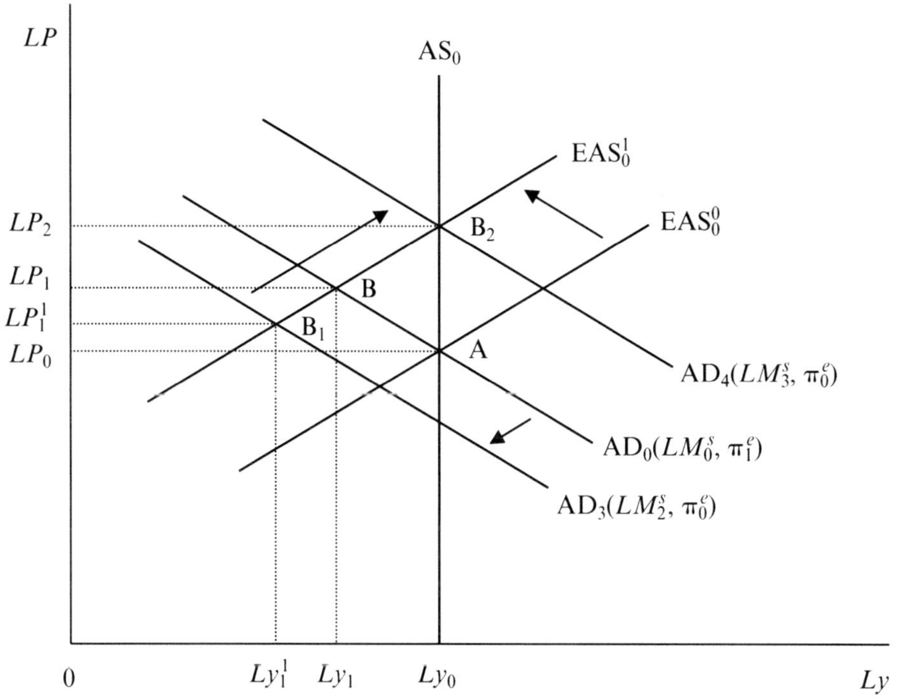

Figure 5.15 The effects on the price level in an open economy of a hands-off and a hands-on policy by the monetary authority following a supply shock

Consider the case when there is a decline in the money supply because of the reduction in foreign exchange reserves at a given level of central bank credit. In Figure 5.15, the decline in the money supply shifts the aggregate demand curve to $AD_3(LM_2^s, \pi_0^e)$. The temporary equilibrium is at B_1 with the price level LP_1^1, rather than LP_1, and the income level Ly_1^1, rather than Ly_1. It shows that in an open economy the decline in output is larger than that in a closed economy.

Given that the government revenue is dependent on income, the supply shock which reduces income may reduce the government revenue and increase the size of the fiscal deficit at a given level of government expenditure. When the government finances fiscal deficits by borrowing from the banking system, it increases the level of the central bank credit component of the money base at a given level of foreign exchange reserves. Assume that such an increase in the money base (or money supply) shifts the aggregate demand curve to the position $AD_4(LM_3^s, \pi_0^e)$ (Figure 5.15).

As indicated earlier, the net effect of supply shocks on the money supply is determined by the combined effect of the reduction in foreign exchange reserves and any increase in the central bank credit because of monetisation of fiscal deficits. Therefore the aggregate demand curve is likely to lie somewhere between $AD_3(LM_2^s, \pi_0^e)$ and $AD_4(LM_3^s, \pi_0^e)$. It shows that even if the government does not increase the money supply, the supply shock has a net effect on the money supply – the direction of which cannot be predicted a priori. The movement of the price level would depend on the movement of the money supply. When such an uncertainty is associated with changes in price expectations, the monetary authority may create complex forces by adopting an active monetary policy, and the effect of which on the price level cannot be predicted a priori.

Supply shock and inflation under the flexible exchange rate system

Consider the following aggregate demand function:

$$y = \tau[b_0 + b_1\, TB(rer) - b_2\, r] \tag{5.61}$$

where y is real output, b_0 is autonomous expenditure, TB is trade balance, rer is the real effective exchange rate, defined as: $rer = NER \bullet P^f/P_d$ (where NER is the nominal exchange rate of the domestic currency), P^f is the foreign price level, P_d is the domestic price level, and r is the real interest rate.

Given the real interest rate, the equation shows that the demand for domestic output is dependent on the real effective exchange rate. A depreciation of the real exchange rate[36] makes the domestic exportable goods competitive in the world market, and induces a switch of domestic demand of residents from imports, thereby increasing the demand for domestic goods. In contrast, an appreciation of the real exchange rate makes domestic exportable goods less competitive in the world market, and induces a switch of domestic demand of residents from domestic to foreign goods, lowering the demand for domestic goods. In the lower part of Figure 5.16, the relationship between the real exchange rate and output is shown as an upward sloping curve.

Assume that the negative supply shock shifts the supply curve EAS_0^0 to EAS_0^1. It increases the price level from P_0 to P_1 and the real exchange rate appreciates from rer_0 to rer_1. The appreciation of the real exchange rate is the result of the increase in the price level due to the supply shock,[37] which has not been associated with an instantaneous depreciation of the currency. However, at the price level P_1 the real wage rate ($W/P = w$) has declined because the nominal wage rate has remained unchanged (W_0); for example, because of short-term wage contracts. The fall in the real wage rate from w_0 ($w_0 = W_0/P_0$) to w_1 ($w_1 = W_0/P_1$) would increase employment and output, moving the economy from E_1 to E_0, which is associated with a depreciation of the real exchange rate as the price level declines.

The adjustment process discussed above rules out any active government intervention in the form of monetary policy. An alternative to automatic adjustment is using expansionary monetary policy to expedite the adjustment process so that the adverse costs of supply shocks are minimised. However, any expansion of the money supply would shift the demand curve rightward and ignite inflation. This is because of the expectations-induced leftward shift of the supply curve and the rightward shift of the demand curve. Therefore, if inflation is a concern to policy-makers, any accommodating monetary policy after the supply shock would be undesirable.

To conclude, the question of whether the monetary authority should adopt a hands-on or a hands-off policy has been analysed by applying a model. It is found that the conduct of active monetary policy after a negative supply shock has the danger of igniting inflation. Therefore, when the danger of inflation is high after a negative supply shock, the monetary authority may even think of adopting a contractionary monetary policy to dampen inflationary expectations (Barro, 1981; Rivera-Batiz and Rivera-Batiz, 1985; Sargent, 1992; Turnovsky, 1987).

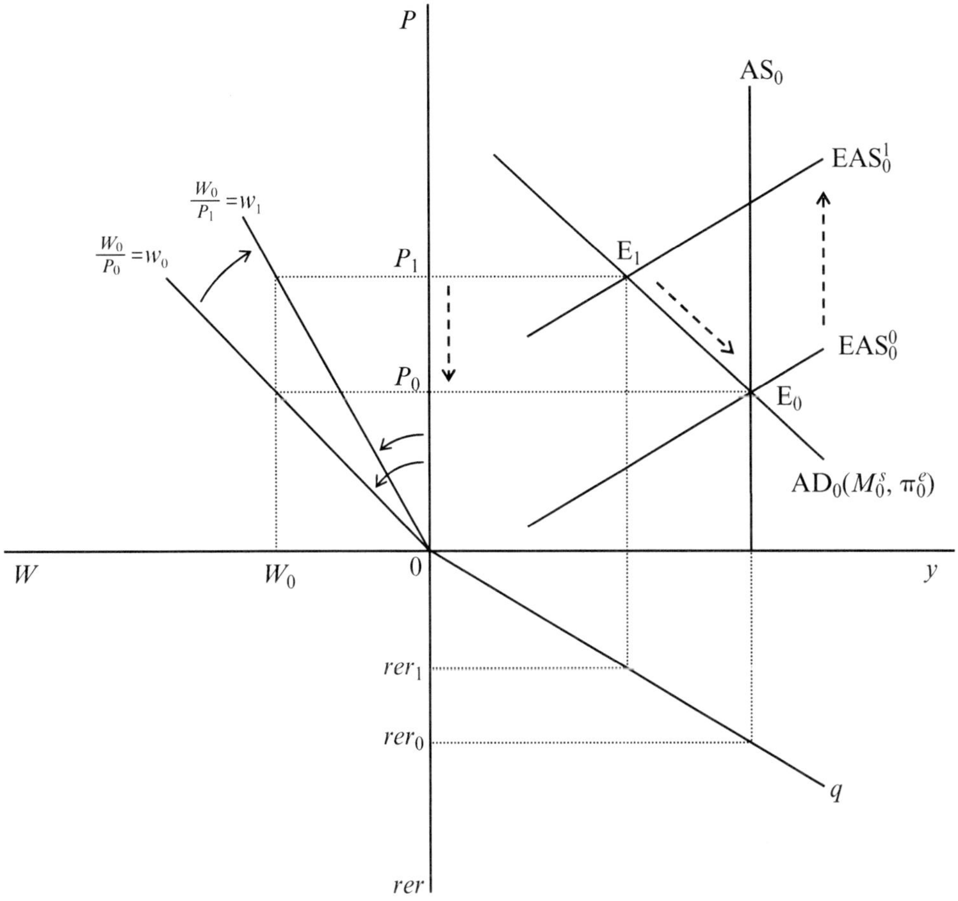

Figure 5.16 The adjustment of an open economy following an adverse supply shock under a floating exchange rate system

SUMMARY AND CONCLUSION

This chapter has reviewed some of the theories, models and approaches to inflation and monetary policy. No attempt has, however, been made to synthesise divergent theories of inflation and monetary policy. The theories and models that have monetary policy implications have been presented topic by topic, albeit at the risk of some commonality between some theories and digression by discussing other theories.

The inflation literature begins with the classical view on inflation, which suggests that inflation in the long run is determined by the growth rate of the money supply. Non-monetary factors affect inflation, but only in the short run. Non-monetary factors, originating from both the demand side and the supply side, cannot lead to a self-sustaining inflation without monetary accommodation. Therefore, control of long-term inflation is equivalent to a control of the growth rate of the money supply (Friedman, 1994).

Determining the sources of high inflation in developing countries requires an understanding of the factors behind the rapid growth of the money supply. One strand of the money growth-inflation literature suggests that in most developing countries budget deficits and money growth are closely related. Therefore inflation can be considered primarily a fiscal phenomenon. Although it is plausible that budget deficits are a source of inflation, the fiscal-monetary part of an inflation model is usually not stable. Any linkage between budget deficits and money growth depends on institutional arrangements which change over time. Furthermore, an understanding of the feedback relationship between budget deficits and inflation in high inflationary economies is essential to comprehend the impact of monetary policy.

Having reviewed the classical model of inflation, this chapter has provided an overview of the conditions that may trigger high inflation or hyperinflation in developing countries. Hyperinflation is a twentieth-century phenomenon, but can still rear its ugly head in developing countries. The episodes of hyperinflation across continents since the 1920s have common elements, albeit overlaid occasionally with unique national characteristics. Still, it is difficult to postulate a general theory of hyperinflation. For an understanding of the high inflationary process in developing countries, this chapter has described some of the common elements and characteristics of hyperinflation. Stabilisation measures for ending hyperinflation and major problems with stabilisation are also discussed.

Building on the review of inflation literature, this chapter has provided an overview of the major theories of money and finance in economic development. The core question in monetary growth theory is whether money has any effect on real variables in a growing economy, either in the steady state or in the transition towards the steady state. In the literature such questions have been examined within the context of neutrality and super-neutrality of money. The review of the literature on neutrality of money reveals that both the Keynesians and the monetarists accept that money is non-neutral in the short run. The short run non-neutrality of money originates from workers' expectational errors or imperfect information. Closely related to the neutrality of money is the concept of super-neutrality of money. The core question with respect to the super-neutrality of money is whether any change in the growth rate of nominal money has an effect on the growth paths of real economic variables, with the exception of real balances. The review of the literature on super-neutrality of money reveals that the super-neutrality condition does not hold in a strict sense, but it can be considered as a reasonable approximation.

While the neutrality and super-neutrality of money has been the focus of growth analysis in developed countries in the context of a fully employed economy, an important branch of the money-economic growth literature has been concerned with the role of inflationary finance in economic growth in developing countries. The review of the literature on inflationary finance and growth reveals that while money creation to finance public investment may have some influence on economic growth, it is unlikely to be a major source of growth. Experience of Latin American countries suggests that inflationary finance is, in fact, a hazardous means of economic growth.

The earlier discussions of financial factors in developing countries were primarily concerned with their role in mobilising savings. This predominantly Keynesian school believes that investment is the constraining factor for growth and prescribes financial repression, characterised by low nominal interest rate and high inflation. While a low interest rate is expected to encourage investment, inflation is used to create forced savings.

On the other hand, the followers of the classical school hold the view that prior savings and financial development are key elements in economic development. According to this view, financial reform enhances the aggregate saving rate, induces financial deepening and improves investment efficiency. These salutary effects in turn contribute to rapid economic growth.

The empirical foundation of the financial liberalisation paradigm has, however, not been so robust. The lack of robustness has been compounded by burgeoning arguments that directly challenge the doctrine of financial liberalisation. A stronger critique of the financial liberalisation hypothesis maintains that a repressed financial system would facilitate rapid economic growth. It is also argued that earlier studies of the adverse affects of financial repression were influenced by large repressions. The large repressions themselves may be symptoms of government failures, making it difficult to conclude whether the adverse growth effect is due to repression per se or to government mismanagement.

It is now increasingly realised that financial markets do much more than mobilising savings – whether 'forced' or 'voluntary'. Financial markets not only deal with intertemporal decisions but also with risk and information. As Stiglitz (1994: 23) observes, 'how well they perform these functions may affect not only the extent to which they can mobilise savings but, more broadly, the overall efficiency and rate of growth of the economy'. Because of the endemic nature of market failures in the financial sector – caused by information asymmetry, moral hazard, and high transaction costs of monitoring and information transfer – a consensus now seems to be emerging that a small degree of repression is possibly even growth promoting. Even the World Bank, which vigorously preached the financial liberalisation programme, itself appears to have accepted the emerging view (World Bank, 1993).

Furthermore, after the initial euphoria with financial liberalisation programme, it is now realised that financial liberalisation is not synonymous with a *laissez-faire* approach. Current developments in the literature as well as the experience of a wide range of countries with financial reforms have brought to the fore the issue of prudential regulation of the financial system. In fact, the choice is not between a *laissez-faire* approach versus dirigiste system, but for a competitive sector within the institutional context of prudential regulation. The global financial crisis that originated in the USA in 2008 is a reminder that the financial sector operates better in a deregulatory environment when it remains under well-designed, prudential regulation and supervision. Australia has largely escaped this crisis which, according to many financial commentators, appears to have struck this balance better than other Organisation for Economic Co-operation and Development (OECD) countries.

The final section of this chapter has reviewed contemporary theoretical developments in the design and conduct of monetary policy. The review has covered the rules versus discretion debate and the importance of transparency in monetary policy to ensure its effectiveness. The rapidly growing literature on time-inconsistency in monetary policy, and various remedial measures that have been suggested by economists to minimise the inflationary bias in discretionary monetary policy, have also been reviewed. The concluding section has provided a detailed analysis of the issue of what kind of monetary policy is appropriate for price stability after a supply shock. In particular, the question of whether the monetary authority should adopt a hands-on or a hands-off policy has been analysed by applying a model. It is found that the conduct of active monetary policy after a negative supply shock has the danger of igniting inflation. Therefore, when the danger of inflation is high after a negative supply shock, the monetary authority may even think of adopting a contractionary monetary policy in the face of declining output to dampen inflationary expectations.

APPENDIX 5A1 MONEY GROWTH AND INFLATION UNDER A FLEXIBLE EXCHANGE RATE SYSTEM

The argument that the main objective of monetary policy should be price stability, rather than the lowering of unemployment and/or promoting economic growth is based on the assumption that there is a one-to-one relationship between money supply growth and inflation in the long run. Although under a fixed exchange rate system the relationship between money supply growth and inflation is not well defined, this is not the case under a flexible exchange rate system. Under a flexible exchange rate system there is an unambiguous relationship between money supply growth and inflation.

A model is developed below to show that inflation in the long run converges with the money supply growth rate.

Assume that the money demand function takes the following form:

$$m^d = y^{\eta_y} e^{-\eta_i i} \tag{5A1.1}$$

where m^d is the demand for real money balances, y is real income, i is the nominal interest rate, η_y is the income elasticity of demand for money, and η_i is the semi-interest elasticity of demand for money.

Assume that the government runs budget deficits and finances them by creating money, such that

$$\hat{M} = P(DEF) \tag{5A1.2}$$

where P is the price level, DEF is the real budget deficit, M is the stock of money supply, and $\hat{M}$ is dM/dt (that is, change in money supply over time).

Following Krugman (1979), assume that the government adjusts its expenditures so as to keep the budget deficit a constant fraction of the money supply, such that:

$$\hat{M} = P(DEF) = \lambda_0 M \tag{5A1.3}$$

Equilibrium in the money market requires that the demand for, and supply of, real money are equal:

$$m^d = m^s = M/P \tag{5A1.4}$$

where m^s is the real money supply.

The flow equilibrium in the money market requires that a change in the demand for real money is associated with an equal change in the supply of real money, such that:

$$dm^d/dt = dm^s/dt = dm/dt \tag{5A1.5}$$

By using the notation $\hat{M}$ equal to dM/dt and $(dP/dt)(1/P)$ equal to π, dm/dt can be written as

$$dm/dt = \hat{M}/P - mx \tag{5A1.6}$$

Since $\hat{M}/P = \lambda_0 m$, equation (5A1.6) can thus be written as:

$$dm/dt = (\lambda_0 - \pi)m \tag{5A1.7}$$

This shows that the growth rate of real money balances $(dm/dt)(1/m)$ is inversely linked with the rate of inflation and that in the steady state (when dm/dt equals 0), λ_0 is equal to π.

Adjustment to Disequilibrium in the Money Market

There can be disequilibrium in the money market as a result of any policy induced (or exogenous) shocks that affect the demand for or supply of real money. Monetarists assume that monetary disequilibrium often originates from the supply side of money. Assume that the money market is in equilibrium but the monetary authority decides to raise the money growth rate from λ_0 to λ_1.

Although neither the money nor the goods market adjusts instantaneously, the adjustment of the money market is quicker than that of the goods market (Dornbusch, 1976). For analytical simplicity, assume that any disequilibrium in the money market adjusts through the partial adjustment mechanism, such that:

$$(dm/dt)(1/m) = \gamma(Lm^d - Lm) \tag{5A1.8}$$

where Lm^d is the log of real money demand and Lm is log of real money supply and γ is the coefficient of adjustment which takes a value between zero and unity.

Since $(dm/dt)(1/m)$ is equal to $\lambda - \pi$, equation (5A1.8) can be written as:

$$\pi = \lambda - \gamma(Lm^d - Lm) \tag{5A1.9}$$

It describes the dynamic behaviour of inflation when there is disequilibrium in the money market. It shows that π would exceed λ if there is excess supply of money (or excess demand for goods and services). From an equilibrium situation, when the growth rate of the money supply is increased from λ_0 to λ_1, then this would create an excess money supply or an excess demand for goods, and thereby accelerate inflation.

Intertemporal Equilibrium Inflation in Developing Economies

Most developing economies are prone to inflation. As the aim of monetary policy is essentially to maintain price stability, the question is whether monetary targeting can stabilise inflation. As shown below, a fixed money supply growth rule can ensure an intertemporal stability in inflation. However, it presupposes that the country follows a flexible exchange rate system and there exists a stable money demand function.

For analytical simplicity, the demand for money is specified here as a function of expected inflation alone. (This is the case of a highly inflationary economy where real income can be considered constant.) Expected inflation in such an economy acts as a better proxy for the opportunity cost of holding money, because the interest rates are not market determined. As indicated in the text, credit markets also cease to exist at very high rates of inflation.

Assuming that actual inflation approximates expected inflation, the money demand function is specified as

$$Lm^d = \varepsilon\,\pi \tag{5A1.10}$$

Substitute equation (5A1.10) in the money market adjustment function (5A1.8) and write it in the following form:

$$\pi = \lambda - \gamma\varepsilon\pi - \gamma\,Lm \tag{5A1.11}$$

Take the time derivative of equation (5A1.11) and, after simplification, this would take the following form (it is assumed that $d\lambda/dt = 0$):

$$d\pi/dt + z\,\pi = z\lambda \tag{5A1.12}$$

where $z = (\gamma/1 - \gamma\varepsilon)$. This is a non-homogeneous linear differential equation. The solution of this equation is given by:

$$\pi(t) = [\pi(0) - \lambda]e^{-zt} + \lambda \tag{5A1.13}$$

This gives a dynamically stable inflation, provided that z is positive. Given that γ and ε are positive, z will be positive if $\gamma\varepsilon < 1$. That is, the e^{-zt} term in the complementary function of the solution tends to zero as t tends to infinity. It implies that when the inflation rate deviates from the equilibrium inflation (given by λ), the actual rate of inflation moves towards the equilibrium rate as time passes. This is shown in the phase diagram in Figure 5A1.1.

Given that the differential equation (5A1.12) is of the form $dy/dt = f(y)$, it is possible to plot $d\pi/dt$ against π. The slope of the phase line is given by 'z' which implies that the phase line slopes downward. That is, $\pi(t)$ converges to equilibrium because, starting from a non-equilibrium position, the convergence of $\pi(t)$ hinges on the prospect that e^{-zt} tends to zero as t tends to infinity. This is clearly the case. Therefore it is possible to say that inflation in the long run would converge to the rate of money supply growth. However, if z is negative (that is, $\gamma\varepsilon > 1$), inflation would diverge from equilibrium. Such a situation arises when the demand for real money balances falls proportionately more than the rise in the rate of inflation.

APPENDIX 5A2 INFLATION AS A SOURCE OF REVENUE

This appendix, adapted from Gordon (1993), explains why developing countries may be tempted to use inflation as a source of revenue.

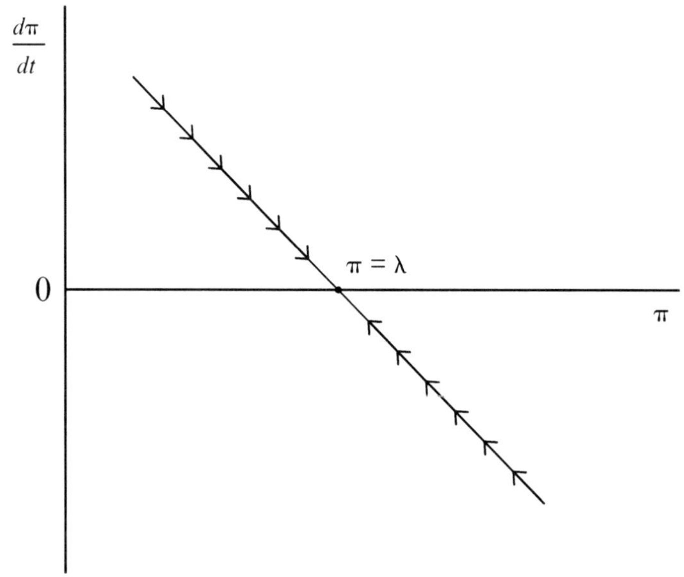

Figure 5A1.1 A phase diagram of inflation

The government's budget constraint can be written in a simplified form as follows:

$$G - T + (i \cdot B/P) = \Delta B/P + \Delta MB/P \quad (5A2.1)$$

where $G - T$ is the basic budget (that is, the deficit excluding interest payments on outstanding bonds), G is government real expenditure, T is real revenues, B is government bonds, i is the nominal interest rate, MB is the money base (or high-powered money) and P is the price level. Since the basic budget deficit $G - T$ is in real terms, the financing terms on the right side are expressed in real terms.

The right side of equation (5A2.1) shows the two methods available for financing the government's budget deficit: (1) the issuance of government bonds, represented by ΔB, and (2) the issuance of additional high-powered money, represented by ΔMB. Assuming that the money multiplier is constant, equation (5A2.1) suggests that when there is a rise in MB, then money supply will increase proportionately.

There is no hard and fast rule for financing budget deficits. Budget deficits may be financed by both monetary and non-monetary means. If financing through issuing bonds is not feasible, money financing could be an alternative. When there is concern about inflation, the government may undertake bond financing. In general, money financing is considered more expansionary than bond financing because the crowding-out effect is avoided in the short run. Therefore, if budget deficits are generated as a policy instrument to stimulate an economy, there could be some preference for money creation compared with bond financing. A higher MB raises the money supply and eliminates the crowding out effect caused by a rise in the interest rate. Deficits financed by MB are stimulative to the economy. The government may therefore finance budget deficits through issuing more MB when the economy is weak, and by issuing more B when the economy is strong.

Developed countries have sophisticated capital markets, so governments can raise funds through issuing bonds. Conversely, developing countries often monetise budget deficits which raise the growth rate of the money supply and cause inflation.

Effects of Inflation

Inflation aggravates the government's problem of financing its basic deficit because, according to the Fisher effect, inflation raises the interest rate that appears on the left side of equation (5A2.1). Rearrange equation (5A2.1) by multiplying the first term on the right side by (B/B) and the second term by (MB/MB). This converts equation (5A2.1) into:

$$G - T + (i \cdot B/P) = \Delta B/P \cdot B/B + \Delta MB/P \cdot MB/MB \qquad (5A2.2)$$

Equivalently, this can be expressed as:

$$G - T + (i \cdot B/P) = \Delta B/B \cdot B/P + \Delta MB/MB \cdot MB/P \qquad (5A2.3)$$

where $\Delta B/B \cdot B/P$ is the percentage change in bonds ($\Delta B/B = \alpha$) times the amount of real bonds outstanding (B/P) and $\Delta MB/MB \cdot MB/P$ is the percentage change in high-powered money ($\Delta MB/MB = \beta$) times the amount of real high-powered money MB/P outstanding.

Equation (5A2.3) suggests that if B/P and MB/P are to remain stable, then the percentage growth rate of B (α) and the growth rate of MB (β) must equal the inflation rate (π), such that

$$\alpha = \beta = \pi \qquad (5A2.4)$$

Substituting from (5A2.4) into (5A2.3) and moving the amount of government interest payments over to the right side, the government's budget constraint with stable (B/P) and MB/P can be expressed as:

$$G - T = \pi \cdot MB/P - (i - \pi) \cdot B/P \qquad (5A2.5)$$

where $\pi \cdot MB/P$ is the inflation tax (seigniorage).

Equation (5A2.5) shows that inflation does not eliminate the government's obligation to pay interest on its outstanding bonds held by households and firms. However, the term $(i - \pi) \cdot B/P$ suggests that the government needs to worry about paying the real interest expense of servicing the outstanding bonds. While the government pays bondholders the nominal interest rate i, bondholders give part of the nominal interest rate back to the government to purchase sufficient additional bonds to keep their real bondings B/P constant.

Thus the government benefits from two ways. First, it obtains seigniorage or the inflation tax. Second, it gains when inflation raises the nominal interest rate less than one for one. A sudden burst of inflation (say during shocks) may raise the nominal interest rate less than one for one. This lowers the real interest rate; this matters for government finance. In developing countries the nominal interest rates are often institutionally determined. The banks also operate under various controls and regulations that make the nominal interest rates relatively inflexible. This explains why financial repression and/or controls over interest rates are attractive to the governments in developing countries due to public finance. Even in developed financial markets, the interest rate may not rise one for one with expected inflation. Mundell (1963) showed that the nominal interest rate does not rise one for one with the rate of inflation, and therefore, the real interest rate tends to fall with the rise in inflation. This is the famous Mundell effect that explains why inflation may affect output.

APPENDIX 5A3 THE PHILLIPS CURVE RELATIONSHIP

Phillips (1958) demonstrated that there was a strong and relatively stable negative relationship between the rate of unemployment and the rate of wage inflation in the UK during 1861–1957. Samuelson and Solow (1960) replicated Phillips's exercise for the USA. They also found a negative relation between CPI-inflation and the rate of unemployment. They labelled this relation the Phillips curve, which later became the cornerstone of macroeconomic policy in developed countries. The theoretical basis of the Phillips curve relationship was later developed by invoking the 'wage-price spiral' thesis. It showed the linkage between nominal wages and prices, given that wage-inflation is linked to the output-gap (Blanchard, 2006).

The Phillips curve relationship gives policy-makers a choice between inflation and unemployment. For example, they can choose a low rate of inflation, provided that they are willing to accept a high rate of unemployment. Similarly, they can choose a low rate of unemployment if they are willing to tolerate a high rate of inflation. Another implication is that policy-makers may be able to keep the unemployment rate at a very low level relative to the 'natural rate of unemployment', as defined below, provided that they are willing to accept an accelerating inflation (Friedman, 1991; Layard, 1992; Phelps, 1992).

The popularity of the Phillips curve relationship was at its peak during the 1960s. The main attack on it came on theoretical grounds during the late 1960s. This came in the form of what was termed the natural rate of unemployment hypothesis (Pesaran, 1992). Friedman (1968a: 8) defined the natural rate of unemployment as follows:

> The natural rate of unemployment . . . is the level that would be ground out by the Walrasian system of general equilibrium equations, provided there is embedded in them the actual structural characteristics of the labor and commodity markets, including market imperfections, stochastic variability in demands and supplies, the cost of gathering information about job vacancies and labor availabilities, the costs of mobility, and so on.

He then argued that a nominal variable, such as money supply growth or inflation, cannot keep the rate of unemployment below the natural rate, except temporarily. In the long-run, there is no trade-off between inflation and unemployment because the unemployment rate in the long run converges to the natural level in response to real forces in the labour market that determine the natural rate. This implies that the long-run Phillips curve is vertical, which represents the classical idea of monetary neutrality.

According to Friedman, the short-run trade-off between inflation and unemployment could be the result of workers' expectational errors. Workers at the beginning of an inflationary period underestimate the price level that would prevail over the period of their work contracts. It overestimates real wages, which induce a greater supply of labour at the prevailing nominal wages than would be the case if their price expectations were correct. The result is employment in excess of the equilibrium level, which creates a trade-off between unemployment and inflation. Expectational errors do not persist long. Therefore, the unemployment level returns to its natural level once expectations errors are corrected. Furthermore, any effort to continually accelerate inflation to exploit a short-run trade off would be defeated by forward-looking adjustment of expectations that take into account the acceleration of inflation.

Formally, Friedman introduced the expectations-augmented Phillips curve relationship. It can be represented as follows:

$$\pi_t = \beta\pi_t^e - \gamma(u_t - u_n) \qquad (5A3.1)$$

where π is the rate of inflation, π^e is the rate of expected inflation, u is the unemployment rate, and u_n is the natural rate of unemployment. Consider the case of a backward-oriented inflationary expectations scheme, in which:

$$\pi^e = \beta\pi_{t-1} \qquad (5A3.2)$$

Such a backward-looking approach to the modelling of expectations was appropriate in the past when there was general price stability and inflation was expected to be adapted in an evolutionary and adaptive process. The use of the adaptive expectations led to the view that an unemployment rate below the natural rate could be maintained by an ever-accelerating rate of inflation (Fischer, 1981).

Substitution of (5A3.2) in Equation (5A3.1) gives:

$$\pi_t = \beta\pi_{t-1} - \gamma\,(u_t - u_n) \qquad (5A3.3)$$

When $\beta = 0$, equation (5A3.3) gives the original Phillips curve relationship:

$$\pi_t = -\,\gamma\,(u_t - u_n) \qquad (5A3.4)$$

When $\beta = 1$, the rate of unemployment affects not the inflation rate, but changes in the rate of inflation, $\pi_t - \pi_{t-1}$:

$$\pi_t - \pi_{t-1} = -\,\gamma\,(u_t - u_n) \qquad (5A3.5)$$

It shows that when actual unemployment is below the natural rate, inflation would accelerate; when unemployment is above the natural rate, inflation would decelerate. In the steady state, inflation is constant and therefore actual unemployment converges to natural unemployment.

The assumption of rational expectations has created a dramatic implication for the Phillips curve relationship. Assume that $\pi^e = E(\pi|I_{t-1})$, where E is the expectational operator and I_{t-1} is the information set at time $t-1$. Under rational expectations, expected inflation on average equals actual inflation. Therefore, the difference between actual and expected inflation $[\pi_t - E(\pi|I_{t-1})]$ is a random error and should be zero on average.

Since expectations are formed rationally, such difference corresponds to the unexpected component of inflation or unexpected money growth. An implication is that monetary policy can influence output or unemployment only by creating inflation surprises. When the government's monetary policy actions are expected by the private sector, there cannot be a surprise with respect to the information set being used by the private sector to form inflationary expectations. Monetary policy would not have any impact on output. Sargent and Wallace (1975) were the first to propose this policy ineffectiveness hypothesis.

The monetary authority can, however, create unexpected inflation by behaving erratically. This could mean sporadically printing lots of money, restricting money at other times. Inflation volatility generated this way can confuse workers, which may produce some real effects of inflation on output (Barro, 2008; Mishkin, 1982).

Lucas (1973) has argued that the extent of the response to an unexpected monetary shock would depend on whether a country's monetary policy has a history of stability or volatility. In an unstable monetary setting, such as in many Latin American countries, households tend to view observed movements in nominal wages and prices as reflections of general inflation. Consequently, monetary expansions do not usually fool workers in these countries into thinking that their real wages have increased. Therefore in a Latin American type environment, monetary shocks would tend to have smaller effects on labour input and real output. In contrast, in a stable monetary setting – such as in the USA and many advanced economies – households may think that the observed movements in nominal wages and prices represent variations in real wages and relative prices. Therefore in stable settings monetary shocks may tend to have significant effects in labour input and real output.

The Lucas hypothesis has received empirical support (Attfield and Duck, 1983; Kormendi and Meguire, 1984; Lucas, 1973). Barro (1981) provides evidence that unanticipated changes in the money supply bring changes in output and unemployment but anticipated changes bring no changes in these areas. He also presents evidence that anticipated changes in the money supply are absorbed completely by inflation, whereas unanticipated changes are partially absorbed by inflation but also bring changes in output and unemployment.

In conclusion, the Phillips curve relationship has generated voluminous literature. The conventional policy trade-off between inflation and unemployment and the successes or failures of deflationary measures to lower inflation without real costs are encapsulated in Figure 5A3.1. The key idea is that when inflation is expected, the economy would stay on the long-run Phillips curve. If there is unexpected inflation, the economy may move along the short-run Phillips curve but would return to the long-run state of the economy once inflationary expectations are adjusted. Available evidence suggests that the short-run Phillips curve relationship is unstable; indeed, it may not even exist. In particular, when the inflation rate is very high, such relationship is unlikely to exist, as inflationary expectations are rapidly adjusted. In another extreme, when there is deflation, or when inflation is close to zero, the Phillips curve type relation simply disappears (Blanchard, 2006).

In cases where the Phillips curve type relation exists, the issue may be how to lower inflation. Deflationary measures may be able to reduce inflation without large costs when such policies are credible and the people have confidence in the authority's ability to maintain lower inflation.

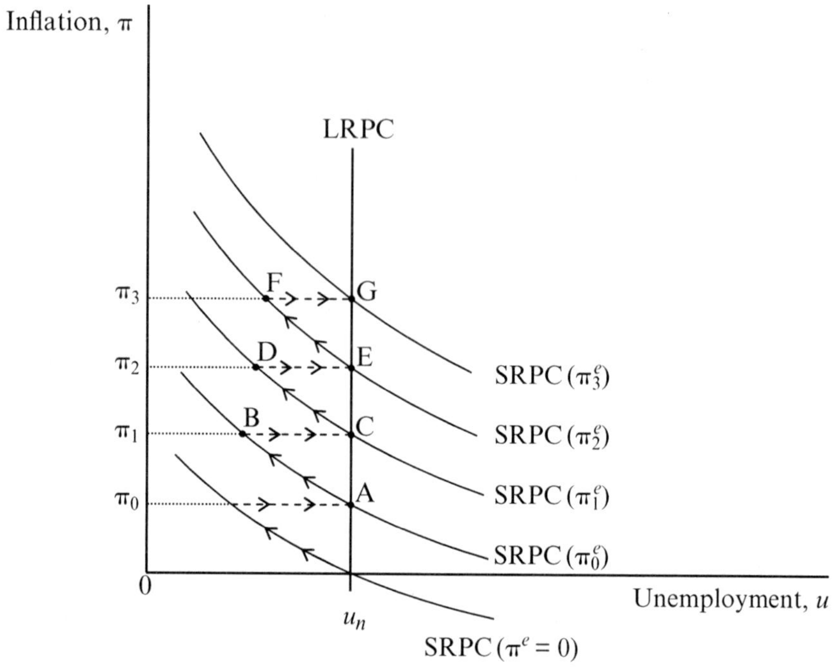

Figure 5A3.1 The Phillips curve relationship

APPENDIX 5A4 INFLATIONARY FINANCE AND ECONOMIC GROWTH

Inflationary finance in developing countries sometimes starts with the objective of achieving higher economic growth. If such policy persists, the developing economy may end up with hyperinflation that may retard economic growth and destroy the fabric of a society. This is the essence of 'macroeconomic populism' that was practised in some countries of Latin America beginning from the 1950s to the 1980s (Dornbusch, 1993; Dornbusch and Edwards, 1990). This is also the essence of the Mundell model of inflationary growth (Mundell, 1965).

In this model, Mundell combined the growth analysis with the quantity theory of money, deriving the following relationship between inflationary finance and economic growth:

$$\pi = [(v/\varphi\rho) - 1]\, g_y \qquad (5A4.1)$$

where π is inflation, g_y is economic growth, v is the velocity of circulation of money, φ is the fractional reserve ratio (in the relation between bank reserves and the nominal money) and ρ is the output–capital ratio.

Substitution of the plausible parameter values of v, φ and ρ ($v = 3$, $\varphi = 0.3$, and $\rho = 0.5$) in equation (5A4.1) yields:

Table 5A4.1 *CPI-inflation and the velocity of money in selected countries of the Asia-Pacific, 1950–2007 (annual average over period; percentage)*

Country	1950–54	1955–59	1960–64	1965–69	1970–74	1975–79	1980–84	1985–89	1990–94	1995–99	2000-2004	2005	2006	2007
Australia														
Inflation	11.2	2.7	1.7	3.2	7.6	11.6	9.0	7.8	3.0	2.0	3.4	2.7	3.5	2.3
Velocity of money (narrow)	2.8	3.6	4.9	5.9	6.8	8.2	9.1	9.3	7.2	5.4	4.0	3.5	3.4	3.2
Velocity of money (broad)	1.6	1.9	2.1	2.1	2.2	2.4	2.6	2.3	1.8	1.6	1.4	1.3	1.2	1.0
Bangladesh														
Inflation	−0.3	7.3	1.4	5.6	30.6	17.5	12.1	10.2	4.5	7.0	4.6	7.1	6.8	9.1
Velocity of money (narrow)	na	na	na	na	12.2	15.9	14.6	13.6	13.8	12.0	11.3	10.4	9.6	9.8
Velocity of money (broad)	na	na	na	na	7.3	9.4	6.8	4.7	4.0	3.6	2.8	2.4	2.3	2.3
China														
Inflation	2.9	0.7	2.7	−1.0	0.0	1.0	2.9	12.0	10.3	5.2	1.1	1.8	1.5	4.5
Velocity of money (narrow)	na	na	na	1.4	1.8	1.5	1.2	1.1	1.2	1.2	6.8	7.9	7.6	7.3
Velocity of money (broad)	na	na	na	2.2	2.7	2.2	1.3	0.8	0.5	0.4	2.6	2.8	2.8	2.7
Fiji														
Inflation	na	na	na	na	12.2	9.1	8.9	6.0	5.1	3.2	2.6	2.4	2.5	4.7
Velocity of money (narrow)	na	na	5.1	5.6	5.5	7.3	9.1	7.9	7.3	6.5	5.6	4.3	4.8	0.0
Velocity of money (broad)	na	na	3.2	3.2	2.9	2.9	2.8	2.4	1.8	2.2	2.4	2.0	1.8	0.0
India														
Inflation	0.3	3.9	4.6	7.7	12.0	3.0	10.5	7.7	10.2	8.9	3.9	4.2	5.8	6.4
Velocity of money (narrow)	5.7	5.3	5.8	6.2	5.9	5.8	6.3	5.9	6.0	6.0	5.4	4.7	4.5	0.0
Velocity of money (broad)	4.7	4.0	4.1	4.3	3.8	3.0	2.5	2.1	2.1	2.0	1.6	1.4	1.3	0.0

Table 5A4.1 (continued)

Country	1950–54	1955–59	1960–64	1965–69	1970–74	1975–79	1980–84	1985–89	1990–94	1995–99	2000-2004	2005	2006	2007
Indonesia														
Inflation	20.8	23.9	107.0	171.3	19.1	14.8	12.4	6.9	8.5	20.5	8.0	10.4	13.1	6.4
Velocity of money (narrow)	na	na	10.4	14.7	11.4	9.6	9.5	9.7	9.3	9.5	9.5	10.2	9.6	8.8
Velocity of money (broad)	na	na	9.4	13.3	7.9	6.1	5.6	3.7	2.4	1.8	2.1	2.3	2.4	2.4
Japan														
Inflation	5.5	0.5	5.5	5.3	10.7	7.5	3.9	1.1	2.0	0.4	−0.5	−0.3	0.3	0.0
Velocity of money (narrow)	3.7	3.8	3.6	3.3	3.0	3.0	3.4	3.5	3.4	2.5	1.5	1.1	1.2	0.0
Velocity of money (broad)	1.7	1.5	1.4	1.3	1.2	1.2	1.1	1.0	0.9	0.9	0.5	0.5	0.5	0.0
Korea, South														
Inflation	141.8	22.9	15.0	11.9	13.8	16.7	12.6	4.2	7.0	4.4	3.2	2.7	2.3	2.5
Velocity of money (narrow)	14.8	12.5	12.0	11.4	9.2	9.8	11.3	11.9	11.4	12.8	11.4	1.7	1.7	1.8
Velocity of money (broad)	13.1	11.0	9.6	5.8	3.3	3.5	3.2	3.0	2.8	2.3	1.4	1.4	1.4	1.5
Malaysia														
Inflation	5.7	−0.3	0.5	1.0	6.9	4.1	5.9	1.4	4.2	3.5	1.5	2.9	3.6	2.0
Velocity of money (narrow)	na	4.2	5.7	6.0	5.5	5.3	5.5	5.1	4.2	3.9	4.1	4.0	4.0	3.6
Velocity of money (broad)	na	3.3	3.8	3.3	2.7	2.2	1.8	1.5	1.3	0.8	0.7	0.8	0.8	0.7
Myanmar														
Inflation	−6.0	0.7	0.5	8.4	11.2	10.5	3.3	16.8	25.5	28.2	23.8	9.4	20.0	35.0
Velocity of money (narrow)	5.0	3.9	4.5	5.9	5.5	4.9	6.7	6.1	7.3	5.0	0.0	0.0	0.0	0.0
Velocity of money (broad)	4.6	3.6	4.2	4.9	4.7	3.5	4.4	4.6	4.7	3.4	0.0	0.0	0.0	0.0

Nepal														
Inflation	na	na	na	5.1	10.6	5.1	10.6	11.1	11.4	7.8	3.2	6.9	7.6	6.1
Velocity of money (narrow)	na	na	13.3	12.0	11.1	9.9	7.8	7.8	7.1	5.4	5.6	5.8	5.6	0.0
Velocity of money (broad)	na	na	12.0	10.5	7.6	5.7	3.7	3.4	3.0	2.4	1.9	1.9	1.8	0.0
New Zealand														
Inflation	6.8	3.2	2.1	4.3	8.6	14.3	12.4	11.6	2.4	1.7	2.5	3.0	3.4	2.4
Velocity of money (narrow)	3.0	3.6	4.1	5.5	6.6	7.4	9.7	9.4	7.7	3.2	6.7	6.9	5.1	5.5
Velocity of money (broad)	2.5	3.2	3.6	4.5	4.4	3.8	3.6	2.4	1.3	1.2	1.1	1.1	1.0	0.9
Pakistan														
Inflation	3.7	1.9	2.1	4.7	12.9	10.4	8.5	6.1	10.5	8.9	4.2	9.1	7.9	7.6
Velocity of money (narrow)	4.6	4.2	4.6	4.6	3.9	4.6	4.5	4.3	4.1	4.5	3.9	2.8	2.8	2.7
Velocity of money (broad)	4.2	3.7	3.8	3.2	2.7	3.1	2.9	2.9	2.9	2.6	2.3	2.0	2.1	2.0
Papua New Guinea														
Inflation	na	na	na	na	12.5	6.8	8.2	4.5	5.3	12.3	12.2	2.0	7.3	10.4
Velocity of money (narrow)	na	na	na	na	na	8.1	9.5	9.0	8.9	7.2	7.2	5.1	0.0	0.0
Velocity of money (broad)	na	na	na	na	na	3.5	3.2	2.8	3.0	2.9	3.3	3.0	0.0	0.0
Philippines														
Inflation	0.0	0.9	5.9	3.4	19.1	10.1	18.4	9.9	11.1	7.9	4.7	7.6	6.2	2.8
Velocity of money (narrow)	6.4	7.9	8.0	8.6	9.5	10.4	11.0	13.9	12.1	10.3	8.8	8.3	8.3	8.6
Velocity of money (broad)	5.0	5.7	5.1	4.4	4.2	4.9	4.3	3.5	3.2	2.2	1.6	1.7	1.8	1.8
Singapore														
Inflation	na	na	1.2	1.2	9.3	2.6	4.9	0.7	2.9	1.0	0.8	0.4	1.1	2.1
Velocity of money (narrow)	na	na	3.2	3.5	3.8	3.7	4.2	4.2	4.4	4.9	4.3	4.2	4.0	3.6
Velocity of money (broad)	na	na	1.8	1.7	1.6	1.6	1.5	1.2	1.1	1.0	0.9	0.9	0.8	0.8

Table 5A4.1 (continued)

Country	1950–54	1955–59	1960–64	1965–69	1970–74	1975–79	1980–84	1985–89	1990–94	1995–99	2000-2004	2005	2006	2007
Sri Lanka														
Inflation	1.4	0.8	1.3	3.1	7.4	6.4	17.1	8.5	13.1	9.5	8.7	11.7	10.0	15.8
Velocity of money (narrow)	5.1	5.3	5.2	5.4	6.9	7.4	8.3	7.8	8.2	10.0	11.2	10.6	11.3	0.0
Velocity of money (broad)	4.6	4.4	3.9	3.7	4.4	4.3	3.2	3.3	3.2	2.6	2.6	2.4	2.4	0.0
Thailand														
Inflation	−1.5	4.0	1.9	2.6	9.0	7.0	8.4	3.2	4.8	5.1	1.7	4.5	4.7	2.3
Velocity of money (narrow)	5.5	5.5	5.9	6.9	7.5	8.8	10.6	10.9	11.2	11.0	8.8	8.2	8.9	8.4
Velocity of money (broad)	5.1	4.7	4.1	3.8	3.1	2.8	2.3	1.6	1.3	1.0	0.9	0.9	1.0	1.0
United States														
Inflation	2.0	1.7	1.2	3.4	6.1	8.0	7.5	3.6	3.6	2.4	2.5	3.4	3.2	2.7
Velocity of money (narrow)	2.7	3.3	3.9	4.5	4.6	5.5	6.3	5.9	5.9	6.4	8.1	8.9	9.6	10.1
Velocity of money (broad)	2.1	2.3	1.6	1.6	1.6	1.6	1.6	1.5	1.6	1.7	1.4	1.3	1.3	1.2

Notes: na = not available, and velocity of money = nominal money income divided by the money stock (narrow or broad), in percentage.

Sources: Author's computations based on IMF, *International Financial Statistics Yearbook* (various years), and IMF, *World Economic Outlook* (various years).

$$\pi = 19g_y \tag{5A4.2}$$

It shows that in order to raise economic growth by 1 per cent, inflation needs to be raised by 19 per cent. However, as the above relation is based on the assumption that the velocity of money is invariant to inflation, Mundell (1971) develops a case in which the velocity of money is an increasing function of inflation, so that

$$v = v_0 + \omega\, \pi \tag{5A4.3}$$

where v_0 is the velocity at zero inflation and ω is the coefficient on inflation. Substitution of equation (5A4.3) into equation (5A4.1) gives the following relation:

$$\pi = [(v_0/\varphi\rho) - 1]\, g_y/[1 - (\omega/\varphi\rho)g_y] \tag{5A4.4}$$

It shows that inflation is not a linear function of economic growth. The ratio of inflation to economic growth rises with economic growth, which means that the greater the growth rate financed by money creation, the larger will be the marginal increment of inflation. A limit will eventually be reached at which inflation will approach infinity, such that

$$g_y = \varphi\rho/\omega \tag{5A4.5}$$

It is the value when the denominator in equation (5A4.5) approximates to zero. For example, when $\omega = 10$ (the case discussed by Mundell), to raise the economic growth by 1 per cent will require an acceleration of inflation by 57 per cent per annum. And the maximum growth rate possible is 1.5 per cent per annum when inflation approaches infinity. The essence of the Mundell model is that short-cut growth strategy that relies heavily on money finance of budget deficits is hazardous and it may lead to high inflation or hyperinflation.

As pointed out at the outset, most Asian developing countries have avoided such a development strategy and therefore have achieved quality economic growth that produced long-term benefits to the society.

NOTES

1. Friedman (1968a) introduced the concept of natural rate of unemployment in the context of the Phillips curve relationship. Appendix 5A3 discusses this concept and related issues.
2. Inflation tax refers to capital losses by moneyholders as a result of inflation. Inflation tax revenue (R^π) is measured as $R^\pi = \pi m$, where π is the inflation rate and m is the stock of real money. Seigniorage (S^μ) is the revenue collected by the government by exercising its monopoly power to print money. It is measured by the purchasing power of the money which is created and put into circulation in a given period, that is, $S^\mu = \lambda \cdot m$, where λ is the growth rate of nominal money. In the steady state, the rate of inflation equals the growth rate of the money stock. Therefore, inflation tax revenue equals the size of seigniorage. These concepts are discussed further in later sections. Sachs and Larrain (1993) have elaborated these concepts.
3. This chapter does not discuss the money supply process, except to note that the money supply may not always remain under the control of the monetary authorities. Under a fixed or pegged exchange rate arrangement, the money supply is endogenous or determined by the money demand factors. Chapter 7 reviews the money supply process and related issues in monetary management.

4. The rise in the general price level is different from the rise in the price(s) of one or more products. Inflation is related to the movement of the general price level, while changes in the prices of individual products are seen as relative price movements. The general price level is determined in the money market when the demand for money equals the supply of money. Relative prices are determined in product markets when the demand for goods equals the supply of goods. A rise in the relative price of food raises the general price level only when the prices of non-food products and services are rigid downward. Such rigidities are assumed in the short run but they are unlikely to remain present in the long run.
5. Monetary policy measures, that are appropriate for avoiding inflation following a supply shock as an originating source of inflation, remain a contentious issue. Part IV of this chapter analyses this issue in the context of developing countries.
6. In developing countries, policy-makers may find it easier to monetise budget deficits than lowering government spending or raising tax revenues. In developed countries, money financing of budget deficits is considered more expansionary than bond financing because the latter may quickly raise the interest rate. The impact of money supply on inflation has a time lag and hence it could be politically attractive as well.
7. The growth rate of the velocity of a broad definition of money can be volatile in the short run but remains generally stable over the long run (Gordon, 1993). The velocity of money remains stable over the long run given that the long-run money demand function is generally stable. Chapter 8 reviews this issue in the context of developing countries.
8. This happens when the central bank, which acts as the government's bank, is required by convention or law to finance the government's budget deficits on a sustained basis.
9. This section draws materials from Sachs and Larrain (1993).
10. This section draws materials from Sachs and Larrain (1993).
11. There are three identifiable time periods when groups of countries succumbed to hyperinflation: the aftermath of the First World War, the aftermath of the Second World War and the debt crisis of the 1980s. In the aftermath of the First World War, five countries in Central Europe and Asia fell into the grips of hyperinflation: Austria, Germany, Hungary, Poland and the Soviet Union. The next round of hyperinflation occurred in the wake of the Second World War when three widely separated countries: China, Greece and Hungary, slid into monetary chaos. The third round of hyperinflation occurred in the 1980s when Argentina, Bolivia, Brazil, Nicaragua, Peru, Poland and Yugoslavia joined in this no longer so exclusive club. In these countries debt repayments represented a large portion of their budgetary expenditures. At the same time, populist policies contributed to the onset of hyperinflation in Latin American countries. The hyperinflation episodes in both Poland and Yugoslavia reflected, in part, the strains of reforming an economy from a planned to a market system (Blanchard, 2006; Dornbusch et al., 2008; Sachs and Larrrain, 1993).
12. The second-order condition of maximisation also holds.
13. Formally, assume that the real budget deficit is $(G - T)$, which is financed by money creation. It follows that $\Delta MB/P = (G - T)$, so that the inflation rate is given by: $\pi = \lambda = \Delta MB/MB = (G - T)/(MB/P) = [(G - T)/Y]/(MB/PY)$. The last term is the ratio of the real deficit to real monetary base (MB/P), and both as fractions of real GDP. In this expression, the denominator is endogenous, which declines with the rise in inflation. All successful stabilisation policies that end hyperinflation periods require that they reduce budget deficits, which are the outcome of policy decisions (Burda and Wyplosz, 2005: 401).
14. Friedman (1983a: 202) acknowledged the possibility of a recession:

    > Unemployment seems to be an unavoidable side effect of curing inflation, just as going to bed is of an operation, and there are many policies that simultaneously add to unemployment and inflation, just as staying in bed may produce illness (though not appendicitis). Why is unemployment a side effect of curing inflation? Because a cure changes the economic environment in ways that were not widely anticipated by the economic actors and that they misinterpret.

15. This model is adapted from Dornbusch (1988a; 1988b).
16. It is also true that an authoritarian government derives its legitimacy from economic well-being that is created on a sustained basis from macroeconomic stability and sound economic policies. This has been the case for some countries in East and Southeast Asia since the 1960s (Quibria, 2000).
17. Per capita real income is used as a measure of economic progress. It is, of course, an imperfect measure of economic welfare. There are other complementary performance criteria, which can be used in developing countries. For a detailed discussion on this issue, see Adelman and Morris (1973), Sen (1988) and Streeten (1981).
18. For example, the Harrod–Domar model shows that the economic growth rate equals the rate of investment multiplied by the reciprocal of the capital–output ratio. When the capital–output ratio is constant, investment becomes the determinant of economic growth (Domar, 1946; 1947; Harrod, 1939). An increase in per capita physical capital may not, however, be enough to raise per capita income because

there is need for both effective utilisation of physical capital (Stiglitz, 1998) and an increase in investment in human capital and intangible productivity-enhancing capital goods (King and Levine, 1993).

19. For a discussion on the major approaches to development finance, see Khatkhate (1972) and Thirlwall (2006).
20. It follows the classical view that since in a fully employed economy the aggregate supply curve is vertical, then any increase in investment demand without lowering consumption demand may generate inflation, but with no real income.
21. Financial repression represents the economic condition in which the government's discretionary policies indiscriminately distort financial prices, discourage saving, lower investment and misallocate financial resources (Fry, 1998).
22. The notion of the quantity theory of money is found in early statements by Hume (1752). For a historical discussion on the quantity theory of money, also see Friedman (1992), Hayek (1933) and Patinkin and Steiger (1989).
23. Individuals suffer from money illusion if they change their economic behaviour after a currency conversion takes place (Patinkin, 1992). Fisher (1926: 4) defined money illusion as a 'failure to perceive that the dollar, or any other unit of money, expands or shrinks in value'.
24. Patinkin (1949) criticises the notion of money illusion as implied by the homogeneity postulate on the grounds that it does not take into account the real balance effect. He defines the absence of money illusion as a condition in which the demand functions of goods are homogeneous of degree zero in money prices and in the initial quantity of financial assets, including money (Patinkin, 1992). Howitt (1992) points out that the absence of money illusion in Patinkin's sense is operationally equivalent to the assumption of rational behaviour of utility maximising economic agents. The inclusion of the real balance effect in the Walrasian monetary model ensures that Say's identity does not hold, for a change in the absolute price level affects the excess demands for all goods. Money is, however, neutral in the sense that a change in the money supply does not change any of the real variables in the general equilibrium system of the economy (Harris, 1985; Patinkin, 1992).
25. Early quantity theorists, such as Hume (1752), also emphasised that prices do not immediately rise proportionately to the increase in the quantity of money, and that in the intervening period it may stimulate production.
26. This presupposes that there is no liquidity trap and investment pessimism. In an open economy, it would require that the exchange rate is sensitive to interest rate changes and net export responds to exchange rate changes.
27. Levhari and Patinkin (1968) also argue that the dropping of the assumption of a constant saving ratio rather than the different definition of disposable income yields their qualitatively different results from those of the Tobin model. However, Bandyopadhyay and Ghatak (1990) show that it is neither the dropping of a constant saving ratio nor the different definition of disposable income, but the form of the money demand function that produces different results.
28. In the original neoclassical model, any decline in the quantity of per capita real balances does not affect real output. It implies that the marginal productivity of real balances is zero. Most monetary economists argue that while it is difficult to treat real balances as a productive service in the same way as labour and capital are treated in the production function, it is an oversimplification to ignore the role of real balances in the production function and to assume that per capita output is a function of only the capital–labour ratio. Stein (1970) argues that the marginal effect of inflation on per capita output $[(\delta y/\delta m)(\delta m/\pi)]$ may be substantial in a developing economy where financial institutions are not fully developed.
29. McKinnon (1973) suggests that households and firms maintain a portfolio balance by holding stocks of monetary assets at a certain proportion of current income. Stocks of monetary assets will be higher relative to income when the real return on holding money is high. Starting from a stationary state with zero net saving, a rise in economic growth will affect households' desired ratio of money to income, inducing them to save from their incremental income to raise their asset position and establish the ratio of money to income. The portfolio effect of growth on saving is more pronounced the higher the desired ratio of money to income, and the higher the rate of growth. Because of the portfolio effect of growth on saving, the propensity to save is not constant, but considered a function of the rate of economic growth.
30. This section draws heavily on Chowdhury and Islam (1993: ch. 8), and Hossain and Chowdhury (1996: ch. 2).
31. Stiglitz (1984) has suggested seven types of market failures in financial markets. They are: monitoring as a public good; externalities of monitoring, selection and lending; externalities of financial disruption; missing and incomplete markets; imperfect competition; Pareto inefficiency of competitive markets; and uninformed investors.
32. The term 'constrained' indicates that the costs of information or of establishing markets have been taken into account.
33. When transactions costs and corresponding information asymmetries between borrowers and lenders

are high and pervasive, lenders cannot efficiently monitor borrowers' activities (Mishkin, 2007a; Stiglitz, 1989). A predictable outcome is credit rationing (Stiglitz and Weiss, 1981). It implies that in a freely functioning capital market, firms relying on external finance may find that investment projects, entailing high ex-ante social rates of return, are crowded out as credit is rationed due to monitoring problems arising from asymmetry of information between borrowers and lenders. Under such circumstances, reliance on the internal capital market and reliance on finance generated through retained earnings or out of depreciation charges, can minimise transaction costs.

34. While the government in such circumstances employs relatively simple rules, the market, by contrast, converts the subjective judgements of a large number of participants into an objective standard (Stiglitz, 1984).
35. Note that even if price expectations are formed rationally, the actual price level may vary independently of the expected price level to the extent that there are random (hence unexpected) demand shocks. This implies a non-vertical, positively sloped AS curve, and thus output fluctuations for any given expected price level.
36. A rise in real exchange rate is depreciation, a fall is appreciation.
37. For the real exchange rate to remain unchanged, any increase in the price level must proportionately depreciate the domestic currency. This follows from the definition of the real effective exchange rate. That is, $\Delta rer/rer = \Delta NER/NER + \pi^f - \pi^d$, where rer is the real exchange rate, NER is the nominal exchange rate, and $\pi^f(\pi^d)$ is the foreign (domestic) inflation rate. When $\pi^f = 0$, ΔNER/NER must equal π^d to keep $\Delta rer/rer = 0$.

6. Choice of the strategy of monetary policy for price stability

INTRODUCTION

During the early 1970s, worldwide inflation and the recession thereafter created a paradigm shift from activist monetary policy for economic stabilisation to one of sustained price stability (Clayton et al., 1977). By researching global economic shocks and other events throughout the 1980s and 1990s, economists began to comprehend the workings of economies better with respect to inflation, balance-of-payments crises and economic growth. With the rapid opening up most economies since the 1980s, the role of macroeconomic factors in economic growth and stability has gained greater significance (Dornbusch and Giovannini, 1990; Fischer, 1990; 1993). In particular, the danger of expansionary monetary policy has become much greater in small open economies. Experiences of different countries have therefore led policy-makers in most countries to acknowledge that monetary policy has a comparative advantage in achieving and maintaining price stability, compared with the Keynesian attempt at moderating business cycles (Friedman, 1968a). It follows the proposition that monetary policy cannot achieve real objectives such as raising economic growth or lowering unemployment except in the short run. The use of monetary policy to achieve real objectives also carries the danger of igniting inflation. As happened in many Latin American developing countries since the 1950s, activist monetary policy often leads to economic and political crises (Diz, 1970; Dornbusch, 1993; Dornbusch and Edwards, 1990).

Consequently, the art of central banking has changed remarkably since the 1990s. Most developed countries have changed their strategies of monetary policy with respect to goals and instruments. To make it effective, the conduct of monetary policy has become transparent. Central banks have gained autonomy in monetary policy and become more accountable to the public in achieving the desired monetary policy objective(s) (Lowe, 1997). Central banks in some developing countries have already started adopting international best practices in monetary policy. The collaboration of central banks across countries and regions, coupled with the surveillance on monetary affairs by international organisations such as the IMF, the World Bank and the Bank for International Settlements, have helped member countries adopt international best practices in monetary policy (Balino and Cottarelli, 1994). This process has accelerated, especially since the financial crises of the 1990s, which have exposed the vulnerabilities of smaller open economies to expansionary policies and external shocks. The danger of populist economic policies has been well documented in the literature. Such policies are incompatible with an outward-oriented growth strategy (Dornbusch, 2000; IMF's *World Economic Outlook*, various issues). As the public support for populist economic policies is diminishing as part of information revolution, most politicians have also changed their rhetoric and settled with disciplined macroeconomic management practices.

The conduct of monetary policy can be improved further by drawing lessons from real-world experiences (Clarida et al., 1999; Mishkin, 2007c). The scientific literature on monetary policy is expanding rapidly. Indeed, this has created optimism that monetary policy can be standardised over time to such an extent that it would appear more as science than an art. Still, as Mishkin (2007b: 29–30) remarks, monetary policy would remain a mixture of objective science and intuitive art: 'The science of monetary policy has come a long way over the past fifty years . . . Monetary policy will however never become as boring as dentistry. Monetary policy will always have elements of art as well as science.'

This chapter provides a review of the strategies of monetary policy and discusses the advantages and disadvantages of these strategies in the context of developing countries.

NOMINAL ANCHOR FOR MONETARY POLICY

The central feature of most strategies of monetary policy is the use of a nominal anchor, which is defined as a nominal variable that the monetary authorities target to tie down the general price level, or its growth rate at a desired level. The conceptual framework for the role of a nominal anchor in monetary policy can be explained as follows.

When a country uses a monetary unit of account, a nominal anchor is needed to determine the price level in terms of domestic currency. The role of a nominal anchor is like a public good and the government has the responsibility of providing such anchor. This idea can be illustrated as follows.

Assume that there are N-markets in the economy. The number of equilibrium relative prices in the economy should therefore be $N - 1$. To determine the entire set of nominal prices in the economy, there only needs to be just one nominal price. The issue is how to determine the nominal price level.

It can be done by invoking the money market equilibrium condition. As discussed earlier, the general price level P is determined in the money market under the condition that $(M/P) = m^d(y,i)$, where M is the nominal money stock, y is real income and i is the nominal interest rate. In this model, real income is determined exogenously by the factors of production such as labour, capital and technology, while the equilibrium interest rate is determined by the relationship: $i = h(y_0, M/P)$. In the model, neither M nor P is determined. If M or P is known from outside sources, the other can be determined. For example, under a fixed exchange rate system, P can be expressed as a function of the nominal exchange rate NER, provided that all goods are tradables. It represents the case of a small economy in which the purchasing power parity proposition holds. It suggests that $P = NER \cdot P^f$, where P^f is the international price in foreign currency and NER is the institutionally set exchange rate of domestic currency per unit of foreign currency. It provides a rationale for the use of the exchange rate as a nominal anchor to the price level. Similarly, if M is set exogenously under a floating exchange rate system, P becomes a function of M, provided that the real quantity of money demanded does not change due to monetary expansion; that is, $P = M/m^d(y,i)$. It is the rationale behind the use of a monetary aggregate as a nominal anchor to the price level.[1]

For a small open economy, depending on the exchange rate regime, the nominal exchange rate (NER) or the stock of money (M) is sufficient to determine the nominal price level (P). Therefore the task of determining the nominal prices involves the choice of an exchange rate regime. If the government chooses a fixed exchange rate regime, the nominal exchange rate would act as a nominal anchor to domestic prices and the money stock would be determined endogenously given the demand for it. In contrast, if the country operates under a floating exchange rate system, the money stock (and the price level) would be determined by the monetary authorities and the nominal exchange rate would be determined endogenously by interactions of the demand and supply factors of domestic and foreign currencies. Once the nominal anchor and the general price level are determined, the relative prices, and real quantities, would be determined by the interactions of demand and supply of goods and services, under general equilibrium conditions. Such relative prices play a role in resource allocation and thereby the composition of output in the economy (Edwards, 1993; Ghosh et al., 1995; Sachs and Larrain, 1993).

The analytical framework outlined above follows the classical dichotomy or monetary neutrality (Patinkin, 1992). It suggests that the nominal exchange rate, or the stock of money, does not matter for real variables. Real variables in the long-run are not affected by the nominal anchor or the specific value that is set for the nominal anchor. In the long run, the price level remains proportional to the level of the nominal anchor; that is, the populace do not suffer from 'money illusion' (Boschen, 1992; Howitt, 1992; Hutton, 1992). Real variables are determined by real factors and not by nominal variables. For example, the real exchange rate ($rer = NER \cdot P^f/P$) is the price of foreign goods and services in terms of domestic goods and services. The real exchange rate is an important relative price, which plays a role in the allocation of resources between the tradable and non-tradable sectors and affects both trade and capital flows. However, the real exchange rate is an endogenous variable. In the long run it does not depend on the exchange rate regime, the conduct of nominal exchange rate policy, or the specific value of the nominal exchange rate (Dornbusch and Kuenzler, 1993: Sorensen and Whitta-Jacobsen, 2005). In the long run the exchange rate policy determines the price level in domestic currency ($NER \approx P$) and not relative prices such as the real exchange rate, $rer = NER \cdot P^f/P$.

Similarly, if the monetary authorities set the nominal exchange rate NER, they cannot control the money supply in the long run. The monetary neutrality proposition suggests that just like the real exchange rate, in the long run real money ($m = M/P$) is independent of the nominal anchor. Also the nominal anchors NER and M cannot be chosen independently or simultaneously. The choice of the nominal exchange rate NER determines P which, through m, determines the required level of M. Similarly, the choice of M determines the required level of NER which is consistent with m. This proposition remains valid, regardless of capital mobility (Khan, 2003; Montiel, 2003).

Types of Nominal Anchor[2]

Over the past two centuries at least three types of nominal anchor have been in use. The first was the fixation of the currency price of one or more commodities (for example, the standardised metallic unit of gold), which are known as commodity standards. This type of anchor was called the *fixed nominal anchor* because under this system, the price level had a tendency to return to the fixed normal level over long periods. The price-level histories in the USA and the UK suggest that the price levels under the gold standard had a tendency to return to the fixed level because inflations were followed by equivalently sized deflations (Cooper, 1982; Flood and Garber, 1984).

The second type of nominal anchors are known as *inflation standards* in which the monetary authorities target a moving nominal anchor such as the monetary target, the inflation target or the nominal income target. Under this system, the inflation rate and the growth rates of other nominal variables have a tendency to return to some acceptable levels over the medium or long run. Such nominal anchors place a limit on the longer-term average rate of inflation. This system is known as the *moving nominal anchor*.

The third type of nominal anchors is the derivative of the first two. It involves a group of countries that agree to operate under a fixed exchange rate arrangement where one or more countries target a fixed nominal anchor and the others target the exchange rates. The exchange rate arrangements under the Bretton Woods Agreement were an example.

When a country operates under a nominal anchor system, it forces the monetary authorities to conduct monetary policy in such a way that the nominal anchor, such as the inflation rate or the money supply growth rate, stays within the set range. The role of a nominal anchor is to limit time-inconsistency in monetary policy. The nominal anchor keeps the price level from growing or falling too fast and preserves the relative stability of the value of the currency. Therefore, the adoption of a nominal anchor such as the nominal exchange rate can promote price stability by keeping inflationary expectations low, provided that the authorities remain committed to keep the exchange rate fixed by maintaining discipline in monetary and fiscal policy. Other strategies of monetary policy also impose restrictions on the behaviour of policy-makers such that their actions can be explained in terms of policy rules and objectives to make them effective.

THE GENERALISED FRAMEWORK OF MONETARY POLICY

This section illustrates a generalised framework of the conduct of monetary policy, in which the basic concepts of goals, targets and instruments of monetary policy are defined. As indicated above, there is an increasing recognition that monetary policy in a deregulated financial environment can achieve and maintain price stability. This can be achieved under different monetary policy frameworks.

Historically, the gold standard was a monetary policy rule that aimed to achieve price stability. Although the gold standard was successful in maintaining long-term price stability, there were wide fluctuations of prices in the short run largely because of unsteady supply of gold (Rockoff, 1992; Rolnick and Weber, 1997). Recognising large resource costs and other considerations, most countries have moved away from commodity standards since the early 1920s. The Bretton Woods exchange rate arrangements since the late 1940s mainly brought monetary stability (Bordo, 1992; Bordo and Kydland, 1995; De Cecco, 1992). Most developing countries were, however, unable to maintain price stability as their expansionary fiscal and monetary policies were not compatible with the fixed exchange rate arrangements. Various supply shocks to commodity exporters also affected their price stability (Cline and Weintraub, 1981; Nelson, 2004; 2005).

Under the present deregulatory financial environment, there is no unique framework for the conduct of monetary policy. Different monetary policy frameworks exist for price stability. It is expected that price stability contributes to economic stability. Countries that have experienced high and unstable inflation and/or have hyperinflationary tendencies are encouraged by the IMF, for example, to introduce a foreign currency or to establish a currency union with other countries in the region. Some countries have introduced capital controls to gain independence in monetary policy under a fixed or pegged exchange rate arrangement. Exchange rate targeting is a monetary policy rule. It has been useful to achieve and maintain price stability in high inflationary countries. Since the 1990s the trend is towards a flexible exchange rate system. Under a floating exchange rate system a country gains monetary policy autonomy. However, a flexible exchange rate system is compatible with low inflation or hyperinflation. Therefore, to maintain low inflation, it is useful to have an inflation anchor. It can be achieved through a monetary aggregate as an intermediate target, or through a credible inflation target that may anchor inflationary expectations, acting as a guidepost for nominal contracts (Corden, 1991, 1993; Dornbusch and Giovannini, 1990; Flood and Mussa, 1994; Lowe, 1997).

The remainder of this chapter reviews the major strategies of monetary policy. In order to facilitate this discussion, a generalised framework of monetary policy is reviewed next. It reveals that the conduct of monetary policy is not arbitrary but can be explained within a general framework. Flood and Mussa (1994:74) have pointed this out: 'in the actual conduct of monetary policy, governments and central banks do not generally behave in a manner that can easily be summarized in a mathematical equation. Almost always, a country's monetary authority exercises some degree of judgment. Nevertheless, the conduct of monetary policy is not random and undisciplined'.

Monetary Policy Framework in a General Form

The strategy that a central bank may undertake for conducting monetary policy can be conceptualised through a flow chart, depicted in Figure 6.1. In the process of designing and implementing monetary policy, the central bank focuses on a host of economic variables that can be classified as instruments, targets, indicators and objectives. At one end of the chart, there are instruments; at the other end, there are policy objectives. The operational and intermediate targets and the indicators or information variables are in the middle (Friedman, 1975; McCallum, 1990).

There are at least two reasons why the monetary policy framework takes the form of a sequential set of actions. First, monetary policy instruments have long, variable lags in their impacts on policy objectives. Second, any link between instruments and objectives is not always direct. It is in this fog of uncertainty that a central bank makes use of operational and intermediate targets in conducting monetary policy, as well as indicators or information variables. The main points of discussion below are related to aspects of instruments, targets and objectives of monetary policy.

The following discussion provides an overview of the conceptual distinctions between variables in terms of their roles as instruments, targets (operational and intermediate) and goals in the conduct of monetary policy. An instrument is a variable that can be controlled directly by the monetary authority. As the term indicates, the intermediate targets are related to both instruments and goals. In a two-stage process, policy-makers first choose a time path for a target, such as the narrow money or the interest rate that is expected to

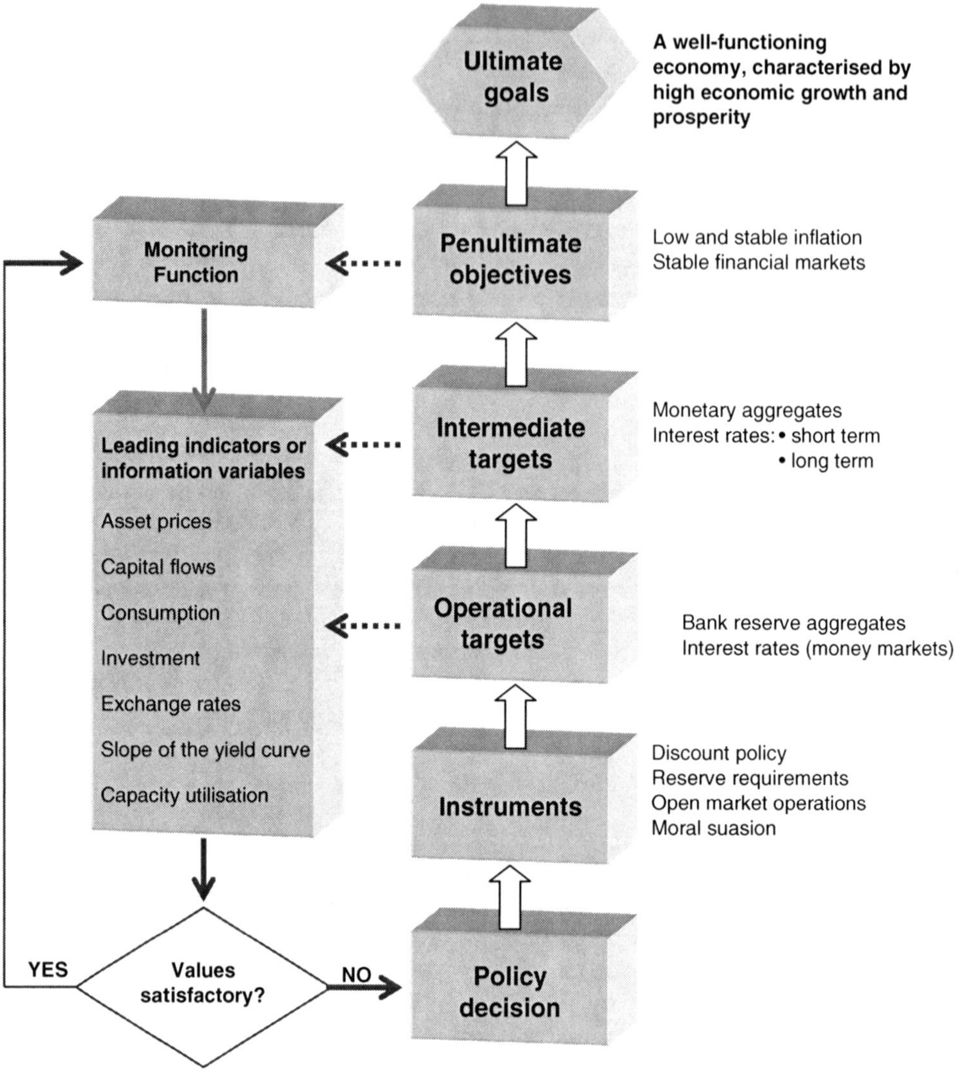

Figure 6.1 Central bank strategy for conducting monetary policy

lead to a desirable outcome for the goal (for example, maintain inflation between 2 and 3 per cent per annum). In the second stage, policy-makers try to attain and maintain the target variable in its defined path by way of manipulating one or more instruments. The goals represent the ultimate objectives of monetary policy, such as price stability with or without an emphasis on economic growth (Mishkin, 2007a).

Conceptually, the operating mechanism of monetary policy is expressed as follows: Instruments → operational targets → intermediate targets → penultimate goals → ultimate goals; or, simply, operating targets → intermediate targets → goals.

Table 6.1 distinguishes variables as instruments, targets and goals.

Table 6.1 Instruments, targets and goals: some examples

Instruments	Operational targets	Intermediate targets	Goals
Direct instruments (e.g., credit controls)	Bank reserve aggregates (reserve money)	Monetary aggregates	Low and stable inflation
Discount rate	Short-term interest rate (money market)	Bank credit aggregates	Financial market stability
Overnight cash rate		Medium- and long-term interest rates	Exchange rate stability
Required reserve ratio			Economic growth and prosperity
Open-market operations, including repo and reverse repo			Improved balance of payments
Moral suasion, etc.			

Instruments, Targets and Goals of Monetary Policy

Intermediate targets are part of the traditional transmission mechanism of monetary policy. An example can make the role of intermediate target clear. Suppose that the aim of monetary policy is to achieve and maintain low inflation. Monetary theory suggests that low inflation can be achieved by keeping the money growth rate low and steady. Having identified the goal of monetary policy, the central bank can announce a target growth rate of the money supply that is consistent with its inflation target.

The practical issue is how to achieve and maintain a low and steady money growth rate. If the money growth rate is high, the central bank does not lower the money growth rate directly. The central bank selects and uses an instrument (or several instruments) to lower the money supply by lowering the growth in reserve money, or by decreasing the value of the money multiplier, or both. Here the intermediate target is not controlled directly but through predetermined operational targets. This indicates that in conducting monetary operations, the monetary authorities may not look at the goal itself; rather, their attention is more on the operational and intermediate targets. In the present case, the intermediate target is the growth rate of the chosen monetary aggregate. Since the central banks use operating targets to affect the intermediate target, the operating targets are part of the monetary policy transmission mechanism. They are placed in between instruments and intermediate targets. The operating targets include the reserve money and short-term interest rates. In the flow chart (Figure 6.1), changes in operational targets are shown to influence the intermediate targets.

STRATEGIES OF MONETARY POLICY

As reviewed in Chapter 5, the current practices of monetary policy are classified under the categories of discretion and rules. The main arguments that compare for and against rules with discretion, are well known. Policy-makers who support discretion believe in the superiority of discretion over rules, on the ground that monetary policy is judgemental and needs to be conducted on the basis of policy-makers' interpretation of economic variables that act as indicators of inflationary trends. Policy-makers favouring rules do still support the adoption of targets, such as monetary targets, pre-announced exchange rate pegs or explicit inflation targets. Their argument is that the attainment of low inflation and later its preservation require policy credibility. Credibility can be gained through consistency, commitment and transparency in policy-making decisions. The monetary authorities' accountability can also be ensured through adoption of explicit targets and procedures, rather than leaving them at the discretion of a few personalities (Fischer, 1990; Kydland, 1992).

Therefore the major decision that a country needs to make is whether the central bank should adopt a discretionary or a rule-based monetary policy in order to achieve and sustain price stability. There are various rule-based strategies of monetary policy. There is, however, no hard and fast rule for making an optimal choice of the strategy of monetary policy. The factors that are important in the decision-making process include the country's inflationary experiences, institutional arrangements and administrative capacity. The emerging consensus on a single objective of monetary policy has certainly made it easier for developed countries to make an informed choice of the strategy of monetary policy. Given their developed money and capital markets, most of them have opted for a rule-based monetary policy. Only a few countries such as the USA and Japan have opted for discretionary monetary policy. The choice of monetary policy strategy has not been simple for developing countries, as it depends on a list of economic factors, including economic structure, financial system, institutional arrangements and economic shocks that the country experiences (IMF's *World Economic Outlook*, various issues).

The growing recognition and acceptance that price stability should be the overriding objective of monetary policy has not precluded countries from adopting varied strategies of monetary policy. What is important is the adoption of a consistent approach to monetary policy that is credible and remains transparent to the public. Some economists suggest that the debate between the discretion versus rule-based monetary policy has been too simplistic. Good practice of monetary policy to achieve price stability involves an integration of the two. For example, the traditionally independent central banks of countries such as Germany, Switzerland and the USA followed discretionary or a rule-based monetary policy and were still successful in sustaining low and steady inflation throughout the 1980s and 1990s. In contrast, some newly independent central banks of Australia, Brazil, Canada, Great Britain, Finland, New Zealand and Spain have adopted inflation targeting. They flirted with monetary targeting during the 1970s and 1980s. These countries have been successful in achieving and sustaining low and steady inflation. Inflation was also relatively low in most developing countries throughout the 1990s (IMF's *World Economic Outlook*, 1996). This was partly due to rapid opening up their economies and the adoption of disciplined macroeconomic policies under the surveillance of the IMF and the World Bank. The recent global upsurge of inflation appears to be driven by supply-side structural factors and both domestic and external shocks. In short, the choice of a strategy of monetary policy remains open for developing countries. Some key features of the strategies of monetary policy need to be considered prior to making any commitment to a particular strategy, or a combination of strategies. Each country's situation is indeed unique and needs to be considered on a case by case basis.

This section reviews the well-known rules-based strategies of monetary policy such as the commodity standards, exchange rate targeting, monetary targeting and inflation targeting. It also reviews specialised monetary arrangements such as currency board, dollarisation and monetary union. The aim of this review is to provide a menu of choice for designing the most appropriate monetary policy strategies in developing countries under different circumstances.

Commodity Standards

The earliest monies were commodity monies. They included both metallic and non-metallic products. Gold and silver, as precious metals, were used as money over centuries. Durability, divisibility and portability made these metals attractive, both as a medium of exchange and a store of value. The commodity monies gave way to commodity standards. The gold standard was the dominant form of monetary system that emerged in the late nineteenth century. The key features of the gold standard were shared by the commodity standards more generally. Although the gold standard was the best known commodity standard, there is no reason why money has to be backed by only gold or silver. Other metals, or even non-metals, can do a similar job (Bordo, 1992; Bordo and Kydland, 1995; Bordo and Schwartz, 1984).

Under a commodity standard, the monetary authority pegs the price of a particular commodity (or a bundle of commodities) by standing ready to purchase and sell the commodity (or the bundle of commodities) in an unlimited quantity at a fixed price, denominated in domestic currency. For example, under a gold standard, the central bank remains ready to purchase and sell standardised gold at a set unit price of, say, $500 per ounce. Such a commitment of the central bank makes the gold standard a binding form of monetary rule.

Gold and other commodity standards are no longer in operation because they are considered rigid. Currently most central banks hold some gold. The market value of gold, however, bears no relation to the liabilities of a central bank. The present fiat monetary system relies on the trust of money-holders that the money in circulation can be exchanged for goods, services and assets.

Under a commodity standard the determination of the price level is straightforward (Barro, 1979). Assume that q denotes the nominal price at which a central bank stands ready to purchase and sell the commodity that backs the currency and that Q_m denotes the stock of commodity that the central bank holds. The stock of money outstanding (M^s) can then be expressed as:

$$M^s = (1/\nu) \cdot q \cdot Q_m \tag{6.1}$$

where ν represents the degree at which the money stock is backed by the commodity and its value lies between zero and one, $0 < \nu \leq 1$. When ν equals one, the currency is fully backed by the commodity.

Assume that the demand for nominal money balances (M^d) depends on the price level P, real income y, the opportunity cost of holding money (for example, expected inflation π^e) and any other factors (z):

$$M^d = Py \cdot f(\pi^e, z) \tag{6.2}$$

At equilibrium, $M^s = M^d$. The general price level is then given by:

$$P = q \cdot Q_m / vf(\pi^e, z)y \tag{6.3}$$

Equation (6.3) shows that the price level is an increasing function of Q_m and π^e and a decreasing function of y. Price stability requires that, *ceteris paribus*, an increase in real income is followed by a proportionate increase in the central bank's holding of the commodity Q_m that backs the currency. It suggests that the price level would fluctuate if Q_m and y do not change proportionately and in the same direction. A rise in π^e is expected to increase the price level by lowering the demand for money.

As a strategy of monetary policy, there is a fundamental distinction between the commodity and fiat money standards for price stability. Under a commodity standard, any rise in the price level due to any shock tends to be reversed, resulting in a stable price level over the medium and long run. Under a fiat monetary standard, there is no such tendency. Instead, sustained inflation could be a part of the fiat monetary system. At the operational level there is also a fundamental difference between the commodity and fiat money standards. Under a commodity standard the monetary authority has no discretionary authority and therefore the commodity standard is considered a rigid rule with regard to monetary management. In contrast, under a fiat money system, the monetary authorities can use various instruments to change the money supply in response to changes in the demand for money.

Those who argue for long-term price stability support a commodity standard, although it may lead to short-term price instability. As indicated earlier, the main objection to a commodity standard is the resource cost of maintaining the commodity base to a level that is compatible with price stability. This cost is weighted against benefits from long-term price stability that the commodity standard may bring. Friedman (1986) suggested that although the resource costs of the commodity system are mentioned, the real resource costs associated with the decline in long-term price stability under a fiat system are rarely mentioned. He cited examples of resource costs associated with a fiat monetary system. They include: real resources that individuals use to insulate against future inflation; resources spent on financial planning and accumulation of precious metals; real resources needed for development of financial instruments, to allow individuals with small asset holdings to benefit from higher interest rates; and real resources that are used to develop new future markets.

Exchange Rate Targeting

As a monetary policy strategy, exchange rate targeting has a long history. Earlier it took the form of fixing the value of domestic currency to a commodity such as gold. This remains the key component of a gold standard. Recently the fixed exchange rate regimes involved fixing the value of domestic currency to that of a large, low-inflation country such as the USA (that is, an anchor country). Another alternative is the adoption of a crawling peg, in which the domestic currency is devalued at a preset rate so that the inflation rate in the pegging country can remain above the level in the anchor country. The ultimate aim of a crawling peg is to avoid an appreciation of the real exchange rate. This is necessary because its inflation may continue to remain at a higher level than that in the anchor country (Quirk 1995; Quirk et al., 1987).

In general, exchange rate targeting induces the tendency of inflation in the pegging country to gravitate to that of the anchor country. This means that under exchange rate targeting, the central bank has instrument, but no goal independence, of monetary policy. The goal is already set by the government, that is, to import low foreign inflation through fixing the exchange rate of domestic currency with the anchor country currency.

Exchange rate targeting is generally recommended to high inflationary countries to bring their inflation rates down (Bruno, 1991; 1993a). The rationale is that the exchange rate peg initially links the domestic price level of the pegged country with internationally traded goods through the purchasing power parity: $P^d = NER \cdot P^f$. If the peg is maintained credibly, it can help the pegging country to gain anti-inflation policy credibility that is enjoyed by the anchor country. By lowering inflationary expectations, the exchange rate peg can bring the inflation rate down with little or no sacrifice in output. This is discussed further below.

The main advantages and disadvantages of exchange rate targeting are reviewed next in a general context.

Advantages

First, the exchange rate as a nominal anchor can keep inflation under control, as it ties the domestic prices of tradables with those of the anchor country. For a small country, the prices of tradables in foreign currency are determined in international markets. The domestic prices of those goods can then be fixed by the exchange rate. When the set exchange rate is credible, in the sense that the monetary authorities commit to keep the exchange rate at the target level, it can anchor inflationary expectations to those in the anchor country. For a relatively large economy, this advantage is limited. The prices of non-tradables are determined within the economy by domestic monetary conditions. Such goods and services generally have a greater weight in the price index. The prices of non-tradables may therefore dominate the movements of the domestic price level.

Second, the exchange rate target provides an implicit rule for the conduct of monetary policy. For example, in order to make the exchange rate target credible, the monetary authorities are required to stick with the principle of tightening or loosening of monetary policy when there is pressure on the domestic currency to depreciate or appreciate. The scope of discretionary, time-inconsistent monetary policy to generate inflationary gains therefore becomes limited. It may not even be an option.

Third, the effectiveness of monetary policy depends on its credibility and simplicity. Exchange rate targeting has the advantage of simplicity. It is understood by the public and can be communicated easily. Also, there is general perception that a hard currency represents a sound economy. Therefore the monetary authorities can make use of such idea as a rallying point for tightening monetary policy for maintaining price stability.

Finally, the public may judge the performance of a central bank and make it accountable by looking at how exchange rate targeting is adhered to without sacrificing output. The political costs of breaking promises with respect to exchange rates could be high for both the government and the central bank. These costs can negate any benefits that the central bank may reap from inflationary surprises. By reducing the central bank's incentives to generate inflation surprises, exchange rate targeting can therefore make monetary policy announcements more credible and effective.

Disadvantages
The exchange rate targeting has some disadvantages. Some of them became evident during the 1990s when many countries across the globe experienced financial crises.

First, under exchange rate targeting with perfect capital mobility, a country cannot pursue an independent monetary policy. This follows the *impossibility theorem*, as reviewed in Chapter 4. It suggests that a country can choose any two of the following three: independent monetary policy, exchange rate stability, and capital market integration, implying perfect capital mobility. By adopting exchange targeting, a country loses its ability to deploy monetary policy as a response to shocks that are independent of those hitting the anchor country.

Second, any shocks to the anchor country can transmit directly to the targeting country because changes in the interest rates in the anchor country lead to corresponding changes in the interest rates in the targeting country. This follows the interest rate parity condition that the domestic interest rate (i^d) equals the interest rate in the anchor country (i^f) plus expected depreciation of the domestic currency (δ). Under a credible fixed exchange rate system, the expected depreciation of domestic currency is zero and therefore, $i^d \cong i^f$.

Third, exchange rate targeting may weaken the accountability of policy-makers, particularly in developing countries. Fixing the exchange rate against a hard currency eliminates useful signals that come from foreign exchange markets. Such signals act as constraints on policy-makers' adoption of a monetary policy stance that is not consistent with declared policy objectives. This problem could be serious for developing countries that do not have bond markets. Bond markets, like the foreign exchange markets, provide early warnings to expansionary, time-inconsistent monetary and fiscal policies.

Fourth, in the absence of external constraints, the central bank can come under political pressure to introduce say expansionary monetary policy. If the central bank gives in, this may take some time to be revealed in macroeconomic indicators. In the meantime, damage could be done to the economy. These problems could be acute in developing countries where the balance sheets of central banks are not transparent. As a result, the policy actions of central banks may not be revealed sooner, especially when they operate under time-bound legislations.

Finally, exchange rate targeting can create an environment for speculative attacks on currencies of targeting countries. These may originate from actual or perceived weaknesses of economic fundamentals. They could also be self-fulfilling prophecies. Even the extreme form of exchange rate targeting, say a currency board, is not immune from speculative attacks. Under this arrangement, the monetary authority's role is restricted to issuing domestic currency against foreign currency at a fixed rate, which is determined by the *law of convertibility*. Therefore the currency board adopting country inherits the interest rate of the anchor country and loses its control over monetary policy. This may not be a problem when the adopting country's sole aim is stabilising the price level and bringing discipline in monetary policy. However, when monetary policy credibility is not achieved and maintained on a sustained basis, the currency board system remains vulnerable to speculative attacks. The case of Argentina is discussed later as a case study to demonstrate how speculative attack on its currency in the late 1990s originated from fiscal problems and Argentinian authorities' inability to use monetary policy to address external shocks (Bennett, 1995).

Exchange rate based stabilisation in developing countries and some problems

Since the 1970s many developing countries have experienced persistently high inflation, large budget deficits, rapid monetary expansion, and crises of confidence among both domestic and foreign investors. In addressing these difficulties, policy-makers adopted exchange rate based stabilisation programmes. The decision to use the exchange rate as the nominal anchor, instead of say a monetary aggregate, was influenced by the alleged instability in the money demand function that made the money growth–inflation relationship unstable. As noted earlier, the adoption of a visible anchor such as the exchange rate enhanced credibility of some stabilisation programmes. This section illustrates the advantages of exchange rate targeting in the context of stabilisation in high-inflationary countries and the problems that it may create.

The domestic inflation converges to foreign inflation

Exchange rate targeting helps to lower inflation quickly, especially when the tradable goods have a large weight (α) in the expenditure basket.[3] This is expressed as follows.

Assume that the inflation rate (π) can be expressed as:

$$\pi = \alpha\,\pi_T + (1 - \alpha)\,\pi_{NT} \tag{6.4}$$

where π_T is the inflation rate for the tradable goods and services, π_{NT} is the inflation rate for the non-tradable goods and services and α is the share of tradables in total expenditure. Under a pegged or fixed exchange rate system, the purchasing power parity condition can be used to express the inflation rate for tradable goods and services as:

$$\pi_T = \Delta NER/NER + \pi^f \tag{6.5}$$

where $\Delta NER/NER$ is the rate of change of the nominal exchange rate, which is approximated to be zero (that is, $\Delta NER/NER = 0$). Equation (6.4) can then be expressed as:

$$\pi = \alpha\,\pi^f + (1 - \alpha)\,\pi_{NT} \tag{6.6}$$

Equation (6.6) shows that if $\alpha = 1$, π converges to π^f.

Greater commitment to inflation and policy credibility

By fixing the exchange rate against a hard currency, the monetary authorities send a strong signal that they are committed to maintain a low and steady inflation. An implicit assumption is that such low inflation can be achieved only through the implementation of restrictive monetary and fiscal policies. As pointed out earlier, fixed exchange rates are not compatible with expansionary monetary and fiscal policies. By fixing the exchange rate, the authorities effectively bind the policy-makers' hands. This does not, of course, preclude the authorities' inconsistent behaviour or temptation to renege the implicit contracts with the public. They could foolishly undertake expansionary policies until all foreign reserves are exhausted. Nevertheless, fixed exchange rates provide the market participants with a device that is easy to observe and understand in comparison to the adoption of monetary targeting. The public can monitor policies and judge whether the monetary and fiscal policies are consistent with the declared policy of exchange rate based price stability. Indeed, the political costs of reneging the implied commitments of the government to maintain policy discipline could be dire.

Reduction of foreign exchange risk

The exchange rate anchor (when credible) can lower foreign exchange risk and facilitate capital inflows that accommodate any increase in money demand. This can avoid high interest rate problems that are associated with money-based stabilisation programmes that freeze or sharply lower the money supply.

Complications: private sector over-borrowing and a boom–bust cycle

There are complications with exchange rate-based stabilisation programmes. Until π converges to the steady state where it equals the foreign inflation rate π^f, the real exchange rate continues to appreciate. This can create current account problems, as explained further.

By definition, $\Delta rer/rer = \Delta NER/NER + (\pi^f - \pi)$. Therefore, since $\Delta NER/NER$ is assumed zero and as long as $\pi > \pi^f$, $\Delta rer/rer$ is negative (indicating appreciation). This implies that the domestic real *ex post* interest rate (r) is lower than its long-run equilibrium rate (r^f) for those who borrow from abroad:

$$r = i - \pi = (i^f + \Delta NER/NER) - \pi$$

$$= (i^f - \pi^f) + (\pi^f - \pi)$$

(given that $\Delta NER/NER = 0$ under a fixed exchange rate system)

$$= r^f + (\pi^f - \pi) \tag{6.7}$$

This shows that if $\pi > \pi^f$, $r < r^f$.

The outcome of this could be increased borrowing from overseas provided that there are no restrictions on capital inflows. The occurrence of a relatively lower real interest rate and capital inflows generally lead to a booming economy with a sharp rise in aggregate demand (absorption). The increased aggregate spending is financed with foreign debt, which is reflected in large and sustained current account deficits. The large capital inflows keep the relative prices of non-tradables rising and the real exchange rate appreciating.

Such booming of the economy cannot continue for long. The boom situation requires reversing at some point in the future. This means cessation of capital inflows or the beginning of capital outflows. The question is how, and when to do it, without jeopardising any reduction in inflation. This requires an exit strategy, which may not be in place. This was the experience of the Southern cone countries during the late 1970s (Edwards and Edwards, 1987). This also happened in Mexico and Argentina after their successful implementation of stabilisation plans during the 1990s.

The issue is why domestic inflation adjusts slowly to the anchor country's inflation. There are at least three reasons. First, there is the existence of backward-looking wage indexation. Indexation introduces sluggishness in domestic inflation and causes a slow convergence of domestic inflation to foreign inflation. Second, capital account liberalisation leads to large-scale capital inflows, which create a boom and raise the relative prices of non-tradables. Third, persistence of inflation may be driven by lack of credibility of the authorities to adhere to the exchange rate rule in the event of adverse shocks. Such credibility problems could be different from those resulting from unsustainability of fiscal policies (IMF's *World Economic Outlook*, various issues).

Despite substantive benefits as an instrument of stabilisation, exchange rate pegging has fallen from favour. The 1990s saw a series of financial crises in countries that followed the exchange rate pegs, starting with the *exchange rate mechanism* crisis in Europe during 1992–93. This was followed by the Mexican crisis in 1994, the Asian crisis in 1997, the Brazilian and Russian crises in 1998, and Turkey's crises in 2000–01. Mishkin (1997; 2000b) suggests that the key reason for the failure of exchange rate pegs is that they do not alleviate the time-inconsistency problem that the monetary authorities confront. Instead of providing a commitment mechanism that allows the governments to resist the temptation to inflate their way out of problems, exchange rate pegs exacerbate the time-consistency problem by making the central bank actions less transparent and less accountable. The reason is that with a pegged exchange rate, the central bank loses useful information on the stance of monetary policy; for example, the daily movements of exchange rates in foreign exchange markets. In the absence of a peg, the fear of sharp depreciation of the currency can prevent a central bank from pursuing a time-inconsistent inflationary monetary policy.

Monetary Targeting

As reviewed in Chapter 5, one of Friedman's most famous propositions is that 'inflation is always and everywhere a monetary phenomenon' (Friedman, 1963: 17). This statement is in the spirit of the classical theory of inflation. This is also a major component of monetarism as a school of thought (Cagan, 1992b; Laidler, 1982; 1990). In short, inflation is interpreted as 'a steady and sustained rise in prices' (Friedman, 1963: 1). Furthermore, Friedman's proposition does not indicate that any shocks that destroy the economy's productive capacity – such as droughts or a capital-destroying earthquake – would not (in the absence of monetary response) lead to an increase in the general price level. Nor does his statement imply that an economy's ongoing inflation rate would be determined solely by the money growth rate. Friedman (1963: 23) acknowledged that the potential output growth and the pace of technical change in the payments industry are relevant in an inflation model. Besides the money supply growth rate, these are the determinants of inflation in the steady state. These factors, however, do not contribute more than a few percentage points of inflation per annum. In a high inflationary economy, these factors can therefore be ignored while suggesting that the money growth rate is the primary (if not the sole) long-term determinant of inflation.

This indicates that it is feasible to bring price stability by keeping the money growth rate low and steady. But, as noted earlier, the present fiat money system does not have an effective constraint on money creation. The government can choose any monetary expansion path, which can be implemented by a subordinate central bank. The result could be high inflation or even hyperinflation. It shows that fixing the money supply growth rate becomes equivalent to fixing the inflation rate. Inflation then becomes a policy variable, a characteristic of independent monetary policy under a floating exchange rate system.

The government's ability to create excessive money through a compliant central bank has prompted economists to argue for a money growth rule, which imposes a limit on the government's capacity of money creation. Monetarists in general propose a money growth rule (such as Friedman's *k*-percent rule) to keep inflation low and steady. Friedman's rule is non-activist in the sense that it eliminates discretion of policy-makers. According to Friedman, the parameter k can be set such that the permanent rate of inflation is zero, although the optimal rate of inflation, on this view, is negative of the real interest rate (Cobham, 1992; Friedman, 1969a, 1969b).

The money growth rule: advantages and disadvantages

As a strategy of monetary policy, monetary targeting has a number of advantages. First, monetary targeting allows the central bank to set an inflation target, which could be different from that in other countries.

Second, monetary targeting provides a signal to the market about the stance of monetary policy in so far as inflation control. It depends on how quickly monetary data are published and whether they are reliable. Provided that the monetary authority's commitment to inflation control is credible, the monetary authority's signals to markets can tie inflationary expectations and this may produce desired inflation outcomes.

Third, monetary targeting may enhance the central bank's accountability in its conduct of monetary policy. When monetary targeting is adhered to, this can lower the monetary authorities' temptation to conduct expansionary, time-inconsistent monetary policy.

Despite its popularity, monetary targeting has a number of disadvantages that have decreased its adoption at a wider scale. First, monetary targeting relies on a stable *causal* relationship between money supply growth and inflation. Underneath this relationship is the assumption of a stable money demand function or velocity of circulation (Cramer, 1992; Hoover, 1991). When this relationship becomes unstable, monetary targeting may fail to achieve its goal. The money demand function has arguably become unstable in most developed countries since they introduced financial deregulation and reforms in the 1980s. Yet there is no conclusive evidence that the money demand function in developing countries has become equally unstable.

Second, to the extent that the money growth–inflation relationship becomes weak, the data for monetary aggregates do not provide signals to markets about the stance of monetary policy. Inflationary expectations cannot then be linked to monetary aggregates. Monetary targets therefore lose their effectiveness as a communication device.

Third, in the absence of a stable link between money growth and inflation, the central bank's accountability cannot be ensured by observing its performance in terms of keeping the monetary aggregate to the target level. Therefore the central bank may become less accountable to the public for its policy actions.

Fourth, monetary targets are unsuited for countries whose inflation record is bad and whose central banks do not have credibility.

Finally, money targets are based on the assumptions that the central banks have full control of the nominal money stock – that is, the money multiplier is stable. In addition, the velocity of money is assumed to be predictable. The stability of the velocity of money underwrites the long run stable relationship between money growth and nominal income growth. In practice, monetary targets are often missed. This could be a reason why the populace question the usefulness of intermediate targets in general and monetary aggregates in particular.

To tie together what is known monetary targeting started as a strategy of monetary policy with a promise in the high inflation environment of the 1970s. It has since been abandoned by most developed countries since the mid-1980s (Friedman, 1996; Grenville, 1997; Judd and Scadding, 1982). In developing countries, with the absence of plausible alternatives, monetary targeting is followed under stabilisation programmes. The future of monetary targeting is uncertain. The question is whether monetary aggregates remain useful to the conduct of monetary policy.

Even the diehard monetarists are not arguing for the return to the Friedmanite *k*-percent growth rule. In general, the main disadvantage of a money growth rule is that it does not appear to have the required flexibility to deal with structural reforms that bring changes in the monetary relationships. The monetarists insist that the long-run money demand relationship remains stable in most countries. This means that the velocity of money can be considered stable. The critics of the money growth rule focus on the changes in the trend of the velocity of money and/or the trend of output growth. Since a money growth rule allegedly does not accommodate such changes, they argue that a strict money growth rule would lead to inflation or deflation. Within a political economy framework, changing the money growth rule may not be straightforward. The problem with permitting frequent amendments to a money growth rule may lose its effectiveness and any adjustment of the parameter *k* could become a hot political issue that may jeopardise the purpose of monetary targeting.

In view of such criticisms, McCallum (1984; 1995b; 1997) has proposed a money growth rule that does not require an amendment. The rule is retrospective and sets the current base money growth equal to a three-year moving average of the difference between the growth rates of real output and of velocity. Thus the rule achieves an automatic adjustment of the base money growth to trend changes in output or velocity. Consequently, it has the desired property of anchoring the price level in the long run.

Hence a money growth rule is not necessarily rigid, as it can be adjusted to capture institutional changes in the economy with economic growth. Still, Fischer (1990) has been highly critical of Friedman's *k*-percent rule in principle. According to Fischer, insulating the central bank from political pressure could be a worthy idea but it does not accord well with the general preference for democratic decision-making. His fundamental criticism is against the idea of policy certainty per se. For example, economic agents want certainty about prices and about output; they have no inherent interest in the behaviour of the stock of money. If a discretionary policy produces an unpredictable path for money but ensures price stability and full employment, then the uncertainty about monetary policy should not be of concern. In short, Fischer argues for discretionary monetary policy that brings price stability and encourages full employment.

Inflation Targeting

Formally, inflation targeting is defined as the public declaration by the government or an independent central bank of a quantitative inflation target for the medium term, and the implementation of a procedure for monitoring the monetary authorities achievement of the target path (Allen, 1999; Bernanke and Mishkin, 1997; Mishkin, 2007a; Mishkin and Posen, 1997). The literature provides a broader definition. For example, according to Mishkin (2007a), inflation targeting encompasses at least five elements:

1. The public announcement of medium-term numerical targets for inflation;
2. An institutional commitment to price stability as the primary goal of monetary policy, to which other goals are subordinated;
3. An information inclusive strategy in which many variables, and not just monetary aggregates or the exchange rate, are used for deciding the setting of policy instruments;
4. Increased transparency of the monetary policy strategy through communication with the public and the markets about the plans, objectives, and decisions of the monetary authorities; and
5. Increased accountability of the central bank for attaining its inflation objectives.

The points enunciated by Mishkin (2007a) suggest that inflation targeting is much more than a public announcement of numerical targets for inflation in years ahead. Since inflation targets are set for the medium term, the conduct of monetary policy is not discretionary over the medium term. In the short term, inflation targeting gives monetary policy-makers some discretion.

A growing number of developed and developing countries have adopted inflation targeting since the early 1990s. They include Australia, Canada, South Korea, New Zealand, the UK and Thailand. Inflation targeting has continued to be successful as a strategy of monetary policy, producing low and stable inflation without lowering output (Bernanke et al., 1999). Notwithstanding, some other developing countries have adopted inflation targeting in recent years with mixed results, for example, Indonesia (Kasa, 2001; Kim and Park, 2006; Leiderman et al., 2006).

Operating mechanism

Currently, monetary authorities in current inflation-targeting countries use a feedback mechanism based on expected, rather than actual, inflation. This method for conducting monetary policy can be illustrated by the following monetary rule:

$$\Delta PI_t = \kappa\,(E_t\pi_{t+j} - \pi_T) \qquad (6.8)$$

where PI_t is the policy instrument, π_T is the inflation target, κ is a positive feedback parameter, j is the number of time periods it takes for policy to have its maximum effect on inflation, and $E_t\pi_{t+j}$ denotes the expected inflation outcome j periods ahead, based on information known through time t.

The transmission mechanism of monetary policy under inflation targeting involves the following four stages:

Stage 1: central bank actions to vary 'very short-term' interest rates (for example, cash rate) in money markets;
Stage 2: very short-term interest rates influence the rest of the term structure and the exchange rate;
Stage 3: interest and exchange rates influence aggregate demand; and
Stage 4: aggregate demand influences inflation.

The interest rate rule

Because inflation is not under the direct control of the central bank, the question arises of how to conduct monetary policy to achieve the target rate of inflation. Taylor (1993) argues that the central bank can use an interest rate rule to change aggregate demand. Following Blanchard (2006: 544–5), the central bank can apply the following Taylor interest rate rule to conduct monetary policy:

$$i_t = i_T + \alpha\,(\pi_t - \pi_T) - \beta\,(u_t - u_n) \tag{6.9}$$

where α and β are positive coefficients, π_t is the actual inflation rate, π_T is the target inflation rate, u_t is the actual unemployment rate and u_n is the natural unemployment rate. The central bank, through open market operations, sets a short-term nominal interest rate. The interest rate rule, as equation (6.9) expresses, can be interpreted as follows.

1. If inflation is equal to the target rate of inflation, $\pi_t = \pi_T$, and the unemployment rate is equal to the natural rate of unemployment, $u_t = u_n$, the central bank should set the nominal interest rate i_t to its target value i_T. A numerical example can be used to set the interest rate path. In the medium run, the real interest rate is equal to the natural real interest rate, r_n, so that the nominal interest rate moves one for one with the inflation rate. If $r_n = 2$ per cent and the targeted inflation rate $\pi_T = 2$ per cent, the target nominal interest rate should be: $i_T = r_n + \pi_T = 2 + 2 = 4$ per cent. If the target inflation rate is 0 per cent, the target interest rate should be: $i_T = 2 + 0 = 2$ per cent.
2. If inflation is higher than the target, $\pi_t > \pi_T$, the central bank should raise the nominal interest rate i_t above i_T. This higher interest rate would increase unemployment, which in turn would lower inflation. The coefficient α should therefore reflect how much the central bank cares about unemployment versus inflation. The higher α the more the central bank would increase the interest rate in response to inflation, the more the economy would slow down, the more unemployment would increase, and the faster inflation would return to the target inflation rate. Taylor pointed out that the value of α should be larger than one. This is because what matters for spending is the real interest rate, not the nominal interest rate. If inflation increases, the central bank, when it intends to decrease spending and output, must increase the real interest rate. In other words, it must increase the nominal interest rate more than one-for-one with inflation.
3. If unemployment is higher than the natural rate of unemployment, $u_t > u_n$, the central bank should decrease the nominal interest rate. The lower nominal interest rate would increase output, leading to a decrease in unemployment. Similar to coefficient α, the coefficient β reflects how much the central bank cares about unemployment relative to inflation. The higher the value β the more the central bank would be willing to deviate from target inflation to keep unemployment close to the natural rate of unemployment.

In stating such a rule, Taylor did not mean that the rule should be followed blindly. Many other events – such as an exchange rate crisis and the need for change in the composition of spending on goods – may justify changing the nominal interest rate. He argued that the rule can provide a useful guideline to be followed under normal circumstances while any deviation from the rule would be acceptable when exceptional circumstances prevail (Sorensen and Whitta-Jacobsen, 2005). Once the central bank has chosen a target rate of inflation, it should try to achieve it by adjusting the nominal interest rate. The rule should take into account not only current inflation but also current unemployment. The inclusion of the output gap (or unemployment gap) in Taylor's rule signifies the importance of the phase of business cycle as a determinant of the present monetary policy stance. The output gap (or unemployment gap) can also be considered a predictor of future inflation (Mishkin, 2007a).

The Taylor rule has generated intense interest, both from researchers and central banks. Researchers, studying the behaviour of both the Fed in the USA and the Bundesbank in Germany, found that although neither of these two central banks thought of itself as following a Taylor rule, such a rule actually described their behaviour. Other researchers explored whether it was possible to improve on this rule, such as whether the nominal interest rate should be allowed to respond not only to current inflation but also to expected inflation. Alternatively, other researchers have discussed whether central banks should adopt and adhere to an explicit interest rate, or whether they should use the rule informally and have freedom to deviate from the rule when appropriate.

While the interest rate has gained importance over the monetary aggregate under inflation targeting, it is possible that monetary aggregates may return to the centre stage in some form. In general, the information on money remains important in the longer term. For developing countries, money remains important irrespective of the strategy of monetary policy. In fact, Taylor (2000: 11–12) suggests that monetary aggregates can be used as an instrument in developing countries under inflation targeting:

> because of the difficulties with the interest rate as an instrument in some emerging market economies, which I mentioned earlier, the monetary base might be a better instrument for achieving the inflation target. In earlier work on policy rule evaluation with an inflation target, such as Taylor (1979), the money supply is the instrument. Inflation targeting is an alternative to fixed or managed exchange rates, not to policies that focus on the monetary aggregates.

On the other hand, *The Economist* (2007: 86) is more optimistic about the return of money to centre stage:

> Money, if not monetarism, is making a comeback in the way central bankers think about and carry out policy. That is a good thing. Monetarism failed the operational test in the early 1980s. But a host of examples stretching back over the centuries bear witness to the long-term link between monetary growth and inflation. Money still matters – as it always has done.

Inflation targeting: advantages and disadvantages

In the early 1990s when inflation targeting was introduced, it was considered a demanding strategy not suitable for all countries. This is because inflation targeting presupposes the following: (1) Central Bank independence (instrument, not goal), (2) no fiscal dominance, (3) no fixation of wages, interest and exchange rates, and (4) developed money and capital markets. Most developing countries do not meet these requirements. Yet in the past decade, inflation targeting has been shown to possess a number of advantages that have made it popular, even in developing countries. Some of the advantages are as follows.

Credibility

Inflation targeting can help to build policy credibility and anchor inflation expectations more rapidly and durably. Inflation targeting emphasises that low inflation is the primary goal of monetary policy. Keeping inflation low and stable involves greater policy transparency to compensate for a greater operational freedom compared with what inflation targeting offers. Inflation targets are also intrinsically clearer, and more easily observable and understandable than other targets, because they do not change over time and are controllable by monetary means. Inflation targeting can help economic agents to better understand and evaluate the performance of a central bank and anchor inflationary expectations faster and permanently compared with other strategies.

Flexibility

Inflation targeting grants flexibility. Since inflation cannot be controlled instantaneously, therefore inflation target is interpreted as a medium-term goal. This implies that central banks pursue the inflation target over a certain horizon, by focusing on keeping inflationary expectations on target. Short-term deviations of inflation from the target are acceptable and do not necessarily translate into losses in credibility. The scope for greater flexibility can reduce output gap variability.

Lower costs of monetary policy failures

Inflation targeting involves lower economic costs in the face of monetary policy failures. The output costs of policy failure under alternative monetary commitments like exchange rate pegs can be large, usually involving massive reserve losses, high inflation, financial and banking crises, and debt defaults. In contrast, the output costs of a failure to meet the inflation target are limited to temporarily higher-than-target inflation and slower growth, as interest rates are raised to bring inflation back to the target level.

Critics of inflation targeting suggest that it has a number of disadvantages. They can be summarised as follows.

First, inflation, especially high inflation, is hard to control. As there can be long lags between monetary policy actions and inflation outcome, inflation targeting does not send immediate and credible signals to the public and markets.

Second, the types of instruments of monetary policy that are used remain at the discretion of central banks. This may weaken the accountability of central banks. The problem becomes serious when inflation is brought down from a relatively high level. Under such circumstances, large forecasting errors and missing targets can lower a central bank's credibility.

Third, for its credibility and success, inflation targeting may need to be rigid for policy-makers. This means that policy-makers may not necessarily respond to shocks. Rigid inflation targeting can lead to excessive output fluctuations. Such concerns have led some economists to propose a variant of inflation targeting (nominal GDP targeting), in which the central banks target the growth in nominal GDP rather than inflation.

Fourth, inflation targeting cannot prevent fiscal dominance, unless there is firm commitment from the government to achieve and maintain price stability. However, exchange rate flexibility, which is a prerequisite for inflation targeting, can cause financial instability, especially in countries that do not have deep foreign exchange markets, are partly dollarised and possessing large foreign-currency denominated debts.

Finally, one of the key requirements of inflation targeting is that the exchange rate should be allowed to move freely. While a freely floating exchange rate system has been found tolerable in developed countries, there is concern about volatility in developing countries. In emerging market economies, exchange rates can overshoot. This results in substantial and sustained shifts of real exchange rates which are not explicable in terms of fundamentals. This may create an exchange rate crisis. Indonesia, for example, entered the crisis in 1997 with its exchange rates only modestly overvalued, yet the currency lost one-fifth of its pre-crisis value. Markets are prone to exhibiting a herd mentality and, once the exchange rate starts to depreciate or a peg is broken, it may be difficult to limit such adjustment to a modest level.

As pointed out above, several developing countries in the Asia-Pacific have adopted inflation targeting. They include Indonesia, South Korea, the Philippines and Thailand. Most South Asian countries, such as Bangladesh, India, Pakistan and Sri Lanka are also considering the possibility of introducing inflation targeting. An increasing body of literature has emerged on issues in inflation targeting for developing countries (Lowe, 1997; Mishkin, 2000a; 2000b; Mishkin and Savastano, 2000).

Discretionary Policy with an Implicit Nominal Anchor

In recent years some developed countries such as the USA and Japan have operated within a monetary framework that has 'no explicit nominal anchor'. As Mishkin (2007c: 50) aptly commented a few years ago: 'I think it is fair to say that the nominal anchor in the United States right now is Alan Greenspan.' The strategy of pre-emptive monetary policy under such a framework involves forward-looking policy strikes against inflation before inflationary pressure appears in the economy. This strategy differs from inflation targeting in that it does not have a nominal anchor and is less transparent in its monetary policy strategy. The proponents of such a strategy argue that this strategy has an advantage that central banks can solve the time-inconsistency problem by engaging in forward-looking behaviour, while retaining some discretion to deal with unforeseen events in the economy. The disadvantage of this strategy is that it lacks transparency and may create financial and economic uncertainty. When they lack transparency, central banks remain relatively unaccountable for their policy actions. As a consequence, central banks remain susceptible to time-inconsistency problem; that is, they may pursue short-term policy objectives at the expense of price stability over the long run. In the absence of a nominal anchor, the people's inflationary expectations also remain susceptible to adverse supply shocks to the economy. Finally, the quality of monetary policy depends on individuals who call the shots. For example, although the USA has had success in keeping inflation low, its monetary policy is not transparent and has the problem of time inconsistency. The success of monetary policy in the recent past depended heavily on a person like Mr Greenspan, who held the position of Chairman, Board of Governors of the Fed. Monetary policy if based on a personality will have inherent weaknesses. This cannot be a substitute for well-defined monetary policy strategy that involves clear nominal anchor for price stability (Cecchetti, 2008; Mayer, 1999; Mishkin, 2007a).

SPECIALISED MONETARY REGIMES

Currency Board

A currency board is a specialised monetary arrangement. It combines at least three key elements: (1) a fixed exchange rate of domestic currency with the anchor currency; (2) automatic convertibility or the right to exchange domestic currency with a foreign currency at the fixed rate whenever desired; and (3) a long-term commitment to the system, which is set out in a central banking law. A currency board becomes credible when the central bank holds enough official foreign exchange reserves to cover its liabilities. A currency board is actually an extreme form of a rule-based monetary system where the domestic currency is backed by foreign reserves, allowing the monetary authorities forgo traditional central bank functions (Walters and Hanke, 1992).

The currency board system dates back to the early nineteenth century, when the British implemented the gold standard regime that discouraged deficit financing. Walters and Hanke (1992) suggest that the principle underpinning the currency board system originated in the provisions of the British Bank Charter Act of 1844, which was known as the Peel's Act. The currency board system was later adopted by the British colonies in Africa, Asia, the Caribbean and the Middle East.

Until the currency board system was introduced in the British colonies, sterling notes and old sovereigns and coins of the imperial power were used as both a medium of exchange and a unit of account. The advantage of this practice was that the sterling notes and coins, having relatively stable value, were accepted in the dispersed colonies. But this practice had two disadvantages for the colonies. First, any loss of currency notes benefited the issuer, for example, the Bank of England. That is, the loss of currency notes was a real loss for the colony. Second, the British earned seigniorage from printing the sterling notes in response to any increase in demand for its currency in the colonies.

The establishment of a currency board system enabled the colonies to avoid losses from accidental destruction of sterling notes. The sterling notes were stored in the board's vaults as reserve assets. On the liability side, the board issued the local currency to the same value. In effect, the local currency was backed 100 per cent by reserve assets. Therefore, any accidental loss of domestic notes did not diminish the net assets of the colony. In addition, the currency board was able to replace the worn out notes from its stock. This avoided the need to have its assets tied-up by sending any battered sterling notes back to London for reissue.

When the British colonies became independent states, most of them abandoned the currency board system and established central banks to manage their currencies. Only a few former colonies adhered to the currency board system. Schwartz (1993) has listed two major reasons why the newly independent countries abandoned the currency board system. First, critics of imperialism alleged that the currency board system was designed to enhance imperial economic objectives. Second, the proponents of central banking argued that the establishment of a central bank in an independent country would allow it to pursue an independent monetary policy. The objectives of monetary policy included macroeconomic stabilisation, economic growth and development. Above all, the establishment of a central bank became the symbol of a sovereign nation.

Schwartz (1993) concludes that the economic fundamentals of colonies favoured the currency board system for at least three main reasons. First, the colonial currencies were linked to the reserve currency, which was based on the gold standard. As the reserve currency was backed by 100 per cent gold reserve, the colonial currencies were effectively backed by 100 per cent gold reserve. Although under the gold standard regime no independent monetary policy was possible, the gold itself became the automatic stabiliser. Second, the major trading partner of most colonies was the 'mother country'. Therefore, it was easy to establish a link of the local currency with the imperial currency. Third, the local banks of most British colonies were often the branches of London-based banks. Therefore, the London offices acted as a lender of last resort under any emergency situation.

Since the 1980s there has been a revival of interest in the currency board system. Hong Kong introduced the currency board system in the early 1980s. Argentina introduced a currency board system in 1991 when it tied the peso to the US dollar at parity. A number of other countries such as Estonia, Bulgaria, Lithuania and Bosnia-Herzegovina also introduced a currency board system since the 1990s. They linked their currencies to the Deutsche mark or Euro. During the height of Asian currency crisis, Indonesia considered the possibility of introducing a currency board system (Enoch and Gulde, 1997, 1998; Goldfajn and Olivares, 2001).

Operation of a currency board system

A currency board system operates much like a commodity standard. Under a currency board system, the stock of money in circulation is backed by foreign reserves. The central bank commits to purchase and sell a foreign currency in an unlimited quantity at a pre-announced exchange rate. Therefore the money supply relationship can be expressed in the following form:

$$M^s = (1/v) \cdot NER \cdot R^\$ \qquad (6.10)$$

where v denotes the degree to which the domestic currency is backed by foreign reserves, *NER* denotes the exchange rate of domestic currency with the foreign currency and $R^\$$ denotes the monetary authority's holding of foreign reserves. Under a pure currency board system, the domestic monetary base is fully backed by foreign reserves so that v equals one. It is, however, common for a currency board to have less than 100 per cent backing of foreign reserves. For example, the Convertibility Law in Argentina that governed its currency board system required only 80 per cent backing of the monetary base by foreign reserves.

Arguments for and against a currency board system

There is a growing body of literature on the currency board system. Despite its occasional popularity, the emerging view is that the case for a currency board remains weak. In countries such as Argentina, Estonia and Latvia, the currency board system worked for a while. However, it was successful because these countries followed macroeconomic policies and structural liberalisation policies that were consistent with a fixed exchange rate system. Recent experiences suggest that currency boards without disciplined macroeconomic policies lead to currency collapse and economic crises. Similarly, when a country introduces disciplined economic policies, it does not need a currency board system for macroeconomic stability. There are specific costs of a currency board system that have also lowered its popularity as a strategy of monetary policy.

First, like other fixed exchange rate systems, a currency board prevents the government or monetary authorities from setting interest rates. The interest rate in a country having currency board follows the interest rate in the pegged currency country. Although it is expected that inflation in the currency board adopting country would converge to the inflation rate in the anchor country, this does not often happen. If the inflation rate in the currency board adopting country remains higher than that in the pegged currency country, its real interest rate could be very low or negative. This can create bubbles in property and share prices. In fact this happened in Hong Kong during the 1990s. If domestic inflation remains at a higher level than that in the anchor country, this can cause exchange rate misalignment and make the economy inefficient and uncompetitive (Latter, 1993).

Second, the government of the currency board adopting country cannot help the economy to adjust to external shocks such as a sharp decline in its export prices or a sharp shift in capital flows. Under a currency board system, the central banks or monetary authorities also cannot act as a lender of last resort. Under such circumstances, external shocks require the downward adjustment of domestic wages and prices. However, wages and prices are sticky downward for most countries, hence their currencies become overvalued. Adjustment of wages and prices is generally slow and painful; therefore, economic damage could be considerable if the exchange rate remains misaligned for a longer time.

Thus, in short, the currency board arrangement is not a good idea for most countries. This may work for small and open economies. In general, price stability and economic flexibility require disciplined and credible economic policies, not a currency board system. Adopting a currency board system can hurt the most when exogenous shocks require a sharp adjustment of the nominal parity to engineer changes in real variables. Of course, there are some benefits of a currency board system as discussed. For example, a country can gain credibility when it introduces a currency board system to escape from hyperinflation. The introduction of a currency board under such an environment may lower the incentive to create, or monetise, budget deficits. The benefits of policy credibility, low inflation and low interest rates that a currency board brings can also be achieved through disciplined monetary and fiscal policies without having a currency board. In general though, currency boards are too restrictive and may cause problems for countries that have a weak financial system and those who remain vulnerable to both economic and political shocks (Balino and Enoch, 1997; Enoch and Gulde, 1998; Ghosh et al., 2000; Zarazaga, 1999).

Case study: currency board in Argentina

Carlos Menem became President of Argentina in 1989 and inherited an economic mess. Inflation was running at more than 30 per cent per month. Output growth was negative. He and his economic minister, Domingo Cavallo, announced the adoption of a currency board system in 1991 to bring the money supply growth rate down and, by implication, bring inflation under control. They pegged the Argentine peso to the US dollar at the symbolic rate of one dollar equals one peso. The central bank then stood ready to exchange pesos for dollars on demand and at an unlimited quantity (Chu and Feltenstein, 1979).

The establishment of the currency board system with a symbolic exchange rate had the objective to convince the financial markets that the government was serious about the exchange rate peg, so much so that it was made difficult for any future governments to give up the exchange rate parity or devalue the peso. By making the fixed exchange rate credible in this way, they lowered the risk of foreign exchange crises.

For a while, the currency board system worked well. Inflation was down to 4 per cent in 1994, as the currency board brought monetary discipline. The sharp decrease in inflation was accompanied by strong output growth, which averaged about 5 per cent per year during 1991–99. Yet in 1999, economic growth in Argentina turned negative. The country entered a long and deep recession. Was this recession caused by the currency board system? The answer is partly yes. Throughout the second half of the 1990s, the dollar appreciated vis-à-vis other world currencies. Since the peso was pegged to the dollar, it appreciated sharply along with the dollar. By the late 1990s it was clear that the peso was grossly overvalued. This lowered Argentinian exports. Output growth fell sharply and trade deficits increased.

The recession was thus the result of an exogenous shock. The currency board system made it harder for Argentina to fight against recession. After all, it did not have an independent monetary policy. The lowering of the interest rate and/or a depreciation of the real exchange rate of the peso could have helped the Argentinean economy to recover. But under the currency board system, this was not an option. An economy-wide cut in wages could have been a policy option. This was also not a politically feasible option (Dornbusch, 2001b; Feldstein, 2002).

In 2001 the recession in Argentina turned into financial and exchange rate crises. Fiscal deficits sharply increased, which led to a rise in public debt. Worried that the government might default on its debt, foreign creditors demanded high interest rates on government debts. This made fiscal deficits even larger and increased the default risk. Therefore, there were expectations that the government would abandon the currency board sooner or later and devalue the currency to fight against recession. These expectations turned out to be true.

In December 2001 the government defaulted on part of its debt. In early 2002, Argentina gave up the currency board system and allowed the peso to float. The peso depreciated sharply, reaching 3.75 pesos for one US dollar by June 2002. The borrowers having, given their early confidence in the peg, borrowing in dollars, found a large increase in the value of their debts in pesos. Although the sharp real depreciation of the peso helped to increase exports, GDP fell by about 11 per cent and unemployment increased to the level of about 20 per cent. It took another two years, until 2003, for output growth to turn to positive.

Was the currency board system the wrong approach for Argentina? Economists have mixed opinions. Some suggest that the currency board was a good idea in principle but Argentina did not go far enough. In fact, it should have simply dollarised: adopting the US dollar as its currency and eliminated the peso altogether. The lesson, they argue, is that even a currency board does not provide a sufficiently hard peg for the exchange rate. Only dollarisation can eliminate the exchange rate risk.

Others argue that the currency board system may have been a good idea at the start but it should not have been kept for so long. Once inflation was under control, Argentina should have moved from a currency board system to a floating exchange rate regime. The problem was that by keeping the fixed exchange rate with the dollar for too long, the peso became grossly overvalued. This made the exchange rate crisis inevitable. Yet without a commitment of long-term continuity of a currency board system, this would not have been credible to the public and therefore would not bring benefits to the economy in the first place. The Argentinean currency board system reveals the difficult choice that a government faces when it adopts an extreme exchange rate system to bring policy discipline, and continues with it past its effective usefulness (Balino and Enoch, 1997; De La Torre et al., 2003).

Dollarisation

In recent years some economists have articulated the view that developing countries should forgo their currencies and use a foreign currency as a medium of exchange. Full dollarisation means a full replacement of domestic currency by a foreign currency, say with the dollar or euro. Partial dollarisation represents a situation in which both domestic and foreign currencies remain in circulation side by side as both a medium of exchange and a store of value. This phenomenon is common in high inflationary countries (Cuddington, 1989; Ize and Levy-Yeyati, 1998; Levy-Yeyati, 2006; Marquez, 1992; Ortiz, 1993).

Yet full-dollarisation remains a controversial idea. Full-dollarisation has actually become an important issue in developing countries in the face of large-scale capital inflows since the mid-1990s. The idea is that in a world of high capital mobility, exchange rate pegs are in fact an invitation to speculative attacks and that only extreme a choice, a firm peg such as the currency board or a free float, are viable options (Fischer, 2001). Advocates of dollarisation argue against both these alternatives. Free floats are not considered a viable option for most developing countries because free floating may result in excessive exchange rate volatility. Similarly, fixed exchange rates may lead to balance-of-payments crises. As reviewed earlier, even the currency board system is not immune from speculative attacks. This happened to both Argentina and Hong Kong. Therefore, it is suggested that full-dollarisation may be a way of avoiding both currency and balance-of-payments crises. Without a domestic currency, there is no possibility of a depreciation of domestic currency. Dollarisation avoids the possibility of a sudden outflow of capital, which may otherwise be motivated by fear of expected devaluation. Given that a country having a foreign currency does not have the option of inflationary finance, dollarisation may strengthen its financial institutions. The resulting macro stability may boost investment and raise economic growth (Balino and Enoch, 1997; Calvo and Rodriguez, 1992; Calvo and Vegh, 1996; Calvo and Reinhart, 2001).

In the literature, the benefits of dollarisation generally include a closer integration with international markets, an exposure to competition from these markets, and the availability of a complete range of financial assets for domestic investors. In countries where high inflationary experiences destroyed the people's confidence in local currency, dollarisation helps to re-monetise those economies, increase domestic intermediation and reverse capital flights (Ramirez-Rojas, 1985).

There are, however, a number of criticisms of dollarisation. First, currency is a national symbol. Abandonment of a currency may not be politically acceptable to many countries, especially those who have gained independence through long and sometimes bloody struggles. This point was lost by (the late) Rudi Dornbusch of the Massachusetts Institute of Technology in the USA, who was an advocate of hard currency for developing countries, also suggesting replacement of domestic currency by a foreign currency. He emphasised economic benefits from dollarisation, but underrated political difficulties in forgoing a national currency (Dornbusch, 2001a). Second, the loss of seigniorage is considerable for a growing economy. Third, there is loss of lender of last resort function of a central bank.

Various case studies suggest that the group of countries that benefit the most from dollarisation are those which are integrated with the US economy. If the economy of a country is not heavily linked to that of the USA, its trade performance could be affected due to dollarisation. In the event of say external shocks, there remains no role for monetary policy in neutralising any effects on trade or capital flows. As dollarisation makes the banking system fragile, it limits the monetary policy options. This raises the role of central bank as lender of last resort (Clements and Schwartz, 1993).

Partial dollarisation and monetary policy

Full dollarisation is not the only option. A growing body of literature has investigated issues in monetary policy under partial-dollarisation. It is generally argued that partial-dollarisation makes monetary policy complicated and less effective. This follows the early literature on currency substitution. The argument is that dollarisation makes the money demand function unstable because it lowers the cost of switching from domestic to foreign currencies when money-holders switch funds to avoid the inflationary tax. Currency substitution, in fact, makes exchange rates more responsive to expected changes in domestic money supply and other factors that affect the money and other asset markets. Calvo and Vegh (1996) have shown that there is a positive correlation between currency substitution and exchange rate volatility.

Although the early concern of dollarisation originated from currency substitution, a similar argument has been made with respect to dollarisation as asset substitution. As previously discussed, the demand for money as a store of value in a dollarised economy becomes more responsive to monetary expansion or changes in interest and exchange rates. Inflation response of monetary shocks can therefore be stronger in a dollarised economy. Levy-Yeyati (2006) has shown that the elasticity of inflation to monetary expansion indeed increases with the rise in dollarisation.

Therefore, dollarisation has important monetary policy implications and they depend on the monetary strategy being adopted (De Zamaroczy and Sa, 2003). In case of monetary targeting, the issue is whether foreign currency assets should be included in the monetary aggregate targeted. If the criterion to choose a monetary aggregate for targeting is its relationship with the price level through the transaction demand for money, currency substitution could be a rationale for inclusion of foreign-currency denominated monetary assets in the definition of money. When foreign-currency assets represent an accumulation of assets (store of value) rather than a means of payment, foreign-currency denominated assets may not need to be included in the monetary aggregate that central banks use for targeting.

Unlike monetary targeting, inflation targeting does not require a stable relationship between money and inflation. It suggests that dollarisation may not create a problem for monetary policy because of its impact on the demand for money. Dollarised economies have a number of disadvantages that may impinge on monetary policy under inflation targeting. They include the relatively higher exchange rate pass-through on prices and the vulnerability of the economy to balance-sheet effects. The higher pass-through effect decreases the monetary authorities' control over inflation under a floating exchange rate system. The vulnerability of the economy to balance-sheet effects makes exchange rate flexibility, as required under inflation targeting, more disruptive and costly to the economy.

Because dollarisation causes the banking system to be more fragile, the central banks need to adopt special prudential measures. The aim is to make the financial system strong so that it can withstand significant exchange rate volatility and/or larger than normal swings in capital flows. Commercial banks and the central bank therefore need to hold large-scale foreign reserves and have access to external lines of credit. To reduce foreign exchange risk, the central bank also needs to monitor the foreign exposure and off-balance-sheet activities of commercial banks and other financial institutions. Steps are also needed to ensure that banks do not incur undue risks in lending to dollar borrowers who do not have the capacity to repay loans when devaluation occurs.

The theoretical literature does not offer an answer as to how partial-dollarisation affects inflation. Cowan and Do (2003) have developed a model which shows that dollarised liabilities can help to correct a devaluation bias by creating a disciplining effect on the central bank. Empirical results provide no evidence that partial dollarisation reduces inflation. Instead, as pointed out above, partial dollarisation hampers monetary policy because it raises the pass-through of the exchange rate to prices. Partial dollarisation may also cause a large currency mismatch because of the immediate impact of devaluation on foreign-currency denominated liabilities.

Trends in dollarisation in Asia

Some Asian countries are heavily or partly dollarised. Although data for foreign currency loans are not available, data for foreign-currency denominated deposits are available for recent years. Both bank deposits and bank loans in foreign currency are expected to be close because the standard banking regulation requires banks to match their assets and liabilities in foreign currency to avoid exchange rate risk (Levy-Yeyati, 2006).

Table 6.2 shows the ratio of foreign currency denominated deposits to total bank deposits in selected countries of Asia. Cambodia remains the most dollarised economy in Asia. The other countries in the list are China, Korea, Malaysia, Thailand and Vietnam.

Dollarisation in Asia has been a reaction to economic instability and high inflation. This was also true for the highly dollarised economies of Latin America. In some highly dollarised economies such as Argentina, Uruguay and Vietnam, inflation reached over 300 per cent per annum. In Cambodia, inflation exceeded 100 per cent in the beginning of the 1990s. Despite the fact that inflation decelerated in these countries during the late 1990s, it did not lower dollarisation significantly (Dodsworth and Associates, 1996; Hung, 1999; Peiris, 2003).

Vietnam has gone furthest in terms of de-dollarisation. This has been associated with a successful disinflation strategy (IMF, 2002). Goujon (2006) has analysed the monetary

Table 6.2 *Dollarisation in selected countries of Asia vis-à-vis other countries, 1990–2004 (percentage)*

Asia and other countries	1990	1995	1998	1999	2000	2001	2002	2003	2004	Average: 1995–2004
Cambodia	na	92	93	92	93	95	94	95	96	94
China	na	na	8	8	9	8	7	6	5	7
Indonesia	na	20	22	19	21	20	17	16	15	19
Israel	28	19	21	19	19	19	na	na	15	19
Korea, South	1	1	5	3	3	4	na	na	na	3
Lao PDR	18	57	76	90	85	83	71	31	33	66
Malaysia	na	na	2	3	3	4	3	3	3	3
Philippines	21	25	33	32	32	31	30	31	32	31
Thailand	0.1	0.3	1	1	1	1	na	na	na	1
Vietnam	na	35	37	39	40	42	39	30	30	37
Argentina	47	57	58	62	65	74	1	2	4	40
Bolivia	82	78	92	93	92	92	92	93	87	90
Chile	19	5	6	9	9	11	11	12	10	9
Ecuador	13	19	37	54	100	100	100	100	100	76
Peru	46	65	64	66	68	66	73	70	68	68
Russia	na	29	44	41	37	34	35	27	28	34
Uruguay	86	79	79	81	82	85	88	89	88	84

Notes:
Dollarisaton is defined as foreign currency deposits to total deposits (percentage).
na = not available.

Source: Alvarez-Plata and Garcia-Herrero (2007).

and exchange rate policies in Vietnam that led to a sharp reduction in inflation. He has concluded that the Vietnamese authorities took two steps during the 1990s that were decisive. First, the authorities maintained a heavily managed floating exchange rate system that created exchange rate stability and lowered uncertainty in the exchange rate of domestic currency. Second, the introduction of a restrictive monetary policy included foreign currency deposits in the broad definition of money.

One broad lesson that emerges is that macroeconomic stability remains the first priority in dealing with dollarisation. This may not, however, be sufficient to reverse dollarisation. Other measures – such the liberalisation of domestic interest rates, the establishment of a competitive domestic currency payments system, and the development of domestic financial instruments – may be needed to de-dollarise the economy. Direct measures for reversing dollarisation are often problematic. For example, regulatory limits on foreign currency deposits and punitive reserve requirements on dollar deposits may drive dollars offshore. Any forced conversion of foreign currency into domestic currency can undermine confidence and encourage capital flights (Dodsworth and Associates, 1996; Levy-Yeyati, 2006).

Currency Union

The establishment of a currency union is equivalent to giving up a country's own currency and embracing a common currency designed for a group of countries with similar economic characteristics. The idea of a common currency has become popular since the successful introduction of the euro to most members of the European Union. The theoretical basis of a currency union is Mundell's Optimum Currency Areas (OCA) (McKinnon, 1963; Mundell, 1961).

The OCA consists of a group of countries which are integrated in product markets and are affected by common economic shocks. Across these countries, labour and capital move freely. Consequently, if there is wage flexibility, they do not lose much by establishing a common currency. As factor mobility can provide a substitute for exchange rate flexibility in promoting adjustments to say external shocks, relative price changes may not be that necessary.

Member countries in a currency union gain because it eliminates foreign exchange transactions costs. Currency union may also expand regional trade, especially intra-industry trade. As currency union removes exchange rate uncertainties, it helps consumers and producers to make consumption and production decisions based on prices of goods and services in a common currency. Assuming that the product markets in member countries have become integrated, this increases competition and raises efficiency. Because of low or zero exchange rate risk and low or no costs of hedging, investors also participate in financial markets and make them efficient. Finally, the formation of a common currency is associated with the establishment of a regional central bank. The independence status of a regional central bank underwrites regional price stability, encouraging both domestic and foreign investment within the region (Krugman and Obstfeld, 2009).

Currency union: advantages and disadvantages

Why should a country have a national currency and under what circumstances should it give up its currency and introduce a currency of another country or a common currency with other countries? To address this question, it is important to consider what the benefits of having a national currency are. For most newly independent countries, national currency is a symbol of independence. Although economists acknowledge a nation's 'patriotic sentiment', they do not consider it that important. Instead, economists emphasise economic policy objectives that a country can achieve through its own currency. Most of the benefits of national currency are interrelated and can be summarised as follows.

First, by changing the real exchange rate, a country can influence its trade flows and stabilise output in response to economic shocks. In general, changes in the real exchange rate alter the pattern of demand and induce reallocation of productive resources across sectors. Therefore, if a country encounters economic shocks, the exchange rate can be used as an instrument to cushion disruptive impacts of shocks and stabilise the economy.

Second, under a floating exchange rate system where the external value of the currency is determined in foreign exchange markets, the country gains the ability to change domestic interest rates (and the shape and level of the yield curve), which may be used to stabilise the economy. In other words, under a floating exchange rate system, a country acquires in its armour an independent policy instrument (monetary policy). In contrast, a fixed exchange rate means that the country, despite having its own currency, loses its monetary policy independence and thereby accepts the monetary policy stance of the pegged currency country. A currency union implies that a country gives up its independent monetary policy for a regional monetary policy.

Third, an independent monetary policy means that a country can choose its own inflation rate (low or high). Inflation then becomes a policy variable for the monetary authorities and the rate they choose may be based on both economic and non-economic considerations.

Finally, having a national currency means that the monetary authorities have the monopoly power to issue a legal tender (print money). For the government of a developing country, the ability to create money (via the central bank) and spend it (commandeer resources) may be important. The literature argues that the government's ability to create money is seen as an inflation tax on the public. There is, however, a limit to generating such revenue; indeed, the associated risk of causing high inflation could be significant. It should be noted that in extreme situations (economic or political), the ability of the central bank to create money could be useful (for example, during war or other emergencies).

The downside of having a national currency is that it could be a curse for a country if it is not managed properly; that is, the currency does not perform its traditional functions such as the medium of exchange and the store of value. For example, if there is excessive money creation resulting in high inflation, then money becomes a 'hot potato', which may lead to hyperinflation. High inflation or hyperinflation adversely affects economic activity and income distribution, often causing economic disaster that destroys the fabric of the society. It is fear of high inflation in developing countries that leads economists to suggest that to ensure price stability, inflation-prone developing countries should consider using a hard foreign currency, or else join other countries to establish a currency union.

Despite the potential danger of high inflation, only a few small developing countries have given up their currencies. For most countries, the benefits of having a national currency seem to outweigh the disadvantages of having one. This is the case under the globalised economic system in which developing countries do not have choice but to maintain disciplined monetary and fiscal policies. Under a floating exchange rate system, changes in the monetary-fiscal policy stance are quickly reflected in foreign exchange rates. Therefore, policy-makers cannot ignore their consequences.

CONCLUSION

This chapter has reviewed the major strategies of monetary policy and discussed issues in specialised exchange rate arrangements in the context of developing countries. It is found that, historically, exchange rate targeting was the most popular strategy of monetary policy for price stability. Since the 1980s there has been a move towards a flexible exchange rate system that requires a nominal anchor for price stability. There is, however, no easy choice of a nominal anchor because countries differ in terms of financial structure and development. They also remain exposed to various shocks and require flexibility in responses to such shocks.

There is general acceptance that price stability should be the overriding objective of monetary policy. What is known is that price stability can be achieved and maintained under varied strategies of monetary policy. It is revealed that price stability requires a consistent approach to monetary policy that over time becomes credible and transparent to the public. It appears that the debate on discretion versus rule-based monetary policy has been simplistic. The good practice of monetary policy to achieve price stability involves the two. The choice of an optimal strategy of monetary policy remains open for developing countries. They need to consider the key features of the strategies of monetary policy prior to making a commitment to a particular strategy. In the end, to achieve price stability, there is also no substitute for disciplined monetary and fiscal policies. Price stability can be achieved on a long-term basis through a policy rule provided that the public find the rule simple and credible. The issue remains whether central banks should exercise their discretion to break policy rules if there are shocks (Sorensen and Whitta-Jacobsen, 2005).

NOTES

1. Monetary neutrality suggests that in the long run real output is independent of the money supply. A one-off change in the money supply also would not change the interest rate in the long run. This can be explained as follows. Assume that the dollar interest rate is i per cent per annum. Giving up one dollar today then buys $\$(1 + i)$ next year. The discount factor $[1/(1 + i)]$ represents the relative price of future dollars in terms of current dollars. This relative price can be interpreted as a measure of the interest rate. This relative price would not change if the real value of a monetary unit is scaled up or down by the same factor on all dates. Consider the money market condition. Assume that the money supply is doubled permanently. The monetary neutrality suggests that this would double the price level so that M/P would remain constant. If y and M/P do not change, i would not change. This means that if \$1 is exchanged for \$1.10 a year from now, a lender would also be willing to lend \$2 today for \$2.20 a year from now. So the interest rate remains at 10 per cent irrespective of scaling up or down of a monetary unit (Krugman and Obstfeld, 2009: 367).
2. This discussion follows Flood and Mussa (1994).
3. This may also happen for a country with a small tradable sector if credibility can be gained by other measures.

7. The money supply process and monetary management

INTRODUCTION

One key principle in monetary theory is that the money supply is determined by the central bank, while the demand for money is determined by money-holders, namely, households and businesses. The stock of money is a nominal variable, and it is exogenously determined under a flexible exchange rate system. The demand for money is the demand for real balances. Real balances in a simplified form depend on real income and the nominal interest rate. Wealth-holders decide on the optimal level of real money holding given wealth and the returns on money vis-à-vis other real and financial assets (Friedman, 1956; 1992).

Central banks implement monetary policy by changing the money supply or the interest rate. Under a deregulated market environment, they cannot change or do not have control simultaneously over both the money supply and the interest rate. In general, the central bank aims to change the money stock or its growth rate to influence the price level and/or economic growth. There are both direct and indirect policy instruments that central banks can use to bring changes in the money supply.

Monetarists generally believe that there exists a stable long-run money demand function. They suggest that changes in the money supply can therefore bring changes in the price level, which re-establishes equilibrium in the real money market. But changes in the money supply can affect output in the short run. Wages and price flexibilities determine the extent to which changes in the money supply affect output and other real variables. Controlling the money supply therefore remains the key task of central banks in developing countries. How much control the central bank may gain over the money supply in the short and long runs still remains a debatable issue, given the exchange rate arrangements.

Until the 1980s most developing countries operated under repressed financial systems. The control of the money supply was therefore direct. Both credit and interest rates were generally controlled and used for monetary control with the goal of maintaining a desired level of foreign exchange reserves (Polak and Argy, 1971). Implementation of monetary policy through direct methods involved the government, the central bank, or both. Commercial banks and other financial institutions were given instructions with respect to credit allocations to the priority sectors, under terms and conditions that included subsidised interest rates. Banks were required to accept deposits to generate funds for lending at zero or very low interest rates. Central banks also remained ready to provide loans to banks and other financial institutions at low discount rates (Aghevli and Khan, 1980; Coates and Khatkhate, 1980).

Since the introduction of financial reforms in the 1980s the implementation of monetary policy has been through indirect methods. These do not generally involve the government or the central bank directly allocating credits to priority sectors and/or selected groups at set interest rates. Commercial banks and other financial institutions are allowed to allocate credits and set interest rates, given the prevailing market conditions. Central banks, however, influence the market conditions that affect credits and interest rates by setting policy interest rates (say the discount rate), or by bringing changes in the money supply through open market operations. The central bank also provides liquidity support to banks and other financial institutions in order to achieve monetary policy objectives such as price stability and economic growth.

The remainder of this chapter reviews the money supply process and analyses key issues in monetary management through various policy instruments in the context of developing countries.

THE MONEY SUPPLY PROCESS

The money supply is considered an exogenous variable set by the central bank. This simplification is for analytical convenience. Determination of the money supply is a complex process. It involves the central bank, commercial banks, government, and both borrowers and depositors. Central banks make the decision about changing the money supply and then deploy instruments at their disposal to bring changes in the high-powered money or monetary base. Commercial banks and financial institutions, including both borrowers and depositors, respond to the central bank's actions. This brings changes in the money supply and/or the interest rates.

By definition, the money stock comprises currency and deposits (demand and fixed). Currency is the most liquid form of asset. The share of currency in the money stock is high in most developing countries. However, currency share in the money stock declines with an increase in income. It indicates that the share of deposits in the money stock increases with an increase in income. Structural changes in the composition of the money supply are considered a major characteristic feature of modern economic growth (Hossain, 1995).

The Money Supply Model

Under a fractional reserve system, the money supply process can be modelled into two parts: the monetary base and the money multiplier. Central banks maintain control over the monetary base or high-powered money. Actual money supply is larger than the monetary base. The money multiplier determines the actual level of the money supply, given the monetary base. The money multiplier is therefore the ratio of the money stock to the monetary base. Its value is greater than one. The monetary base comprises the central bank's currency in circulation and the reserves of commercial banks with the central bank. These reserves back the bank deposits of individuals, businesses and others. Commercial banks hold reserves with the central bank to meet legal requirements. They may also hold excess reserves to meet unexpected withdrawals by depositors, or to meet other emergencies.

The remainder of this section develops a simple money supply model to show the linkages between different components of the monetary base and the money multiplier.

Define the money supply as:

$$M = C + D \tag{7.1}$$

$$MB = C + BR \tag{7.2}$$

where C is currency in circulation, D is deposits, BR is bank reserves with the central bank and MB is the monetary base or high-powered money.

Define the currency–deposit ratio and the reserve–deposit ratio as:

$$cdr = C/D \tag{7.3}$$

$$rdr = BR/D \tag{7.4}$$

Introducing these ratios, equations (7.1) and (7.2) can be rewritten as:

$$M = (cdr + 1)\ D \tag{7.5}$$

$$MB = (cdr + rdr)\ D \tag{7.6}$$

Equations (7.5) and (7.6) can be used to express money stock as a function of its determinants, namely, the currency–deposit ratio (*cdr*), the reserve–deposit ratio (*rdr*) and the monetary base (*MB*). In a simplified form, this gives the money multiplier model as:

$$M = mm \bullet MB \tag{7.7}$$

where *mm* is the money multiplier, which equals $(cdr + 1)/(cdr + rdr)$. The money multiplier value is larger the smaller is the reserve–deposit ratio; it is smaller the higher is the currency–deposit ratio. Since both the *cdr* and *rdr* are relatively high in developing countries, the money multiplier value in relatively low in these countries.

Equation (7.7) shows that changes in the money supply can be attributed to changes in the monetary base and/or changes in the different components of the money multiplier. The above money supply relationship cannot be considered a money supply equation in a behavioural sense. It can, however, be used as an analytical framework for the money supply process by analysing the sources of the monetary base and the factors that determine different components of the money multiplier.

In the money multiplier approach to the money supply, it is assumed that in the long run the money multiplier remains stable. Changes in the money supply depend solely on changes in the reserve money. The money multiplier is stable in the sense that it does not fluctuate much. Its average value is predictable with a certain degree of reliability. However, in the short run the money multiplier may show significant fluctuations around its long-run trend value. This happens because the short-run stability of the money multiplier depends upon the relative movements of its component ratios and upon the extent to which they counterbalance one another. In order to develop a money supply model, the stability of the money multiplier is therefore assumed.

In a more detailed money supply model that distinguishes demand and time deposits, the money multiplier depends on the demand deposits to currency ratio, the total deposits to reserve ratio and the ratio of time to demand deposits. The demand deposits to currency ratio reflects the adoption of banking habits by the people and it is a measure of the people's confidence in the banking system. Interest rates, the level and composition of real income, the income distribution, and the expected rate of inflation are the major determinants of demand deposits to currency ratio. The commercial banks and other financial institutions' portfolio behaviour and policy towards borrowing and lending (together with the statutory reserve requirements) determine the deposits to reserve ratio (Cagan, 1958; Hess, 1971; Hosek, 1970; Hossain, 1995).

Friedman (1971b) has developed a money income model that depends on the money stock. This follows the proposition that given a stable demand for real money balances that leads to a stable velocity of money, an increase in the money stock increases the level of nominal income. Papademos and Modigliani (1990) point out that given the equation of exchange: $m + v = p + y$ where each of the variables is a logarithm of the corresponding uppercase variable, the linkage between m and $p + y$ assumes that $dy/dm = 0$ (money neutrality) and that $dv/dm = 0$, as it is determined by 'institutional and technological factors'. The velocity of money, being the reciprocal of the demand for money, depends on real variables.

There is criticism that there is a reverse relation between income and the money stock. That is, an increase in income increases the money stock. The money multiplier model suggests that income does have some impact on the money stock. This is predominantly through the money multiplier as it affects the deposit–currency ratio, the demand to time deposit ratio and the reserve ratio. An increase in income generally has a positive effect on the deposit–currency ratio, implying that the income elasticity of the demand for currency is smaller than the income elasticity of the demand for demand deposits (Papademos and Modigliani, 1990). Brunner and Meltzer (1990: 392) note that 'the movements of the multipliers induced by the changes in these ratios are too small to explain the observed positive correlation between money and output as the consequence of reverse causation'. They, however, agree that there can be a reverse causation between income and the money stock under a fixed exchange rate system or an interest control policy

The Balance Sheet of a Central Bank and the Monetary Base

Just as commercial banks have a balance sheet which lists assets and liabilities, the central bank maintains a balance sheet. Assets and liabilities in the central bank's balance sheet reveal how changes in the central bank's assets bring about changes in the money supply (liabilities). Given the double-entry bookkeeping principle, assets equal liabilities: the balance sheet always remains in balance.

Assets

The central bank's asset side of the balance sheet includes a number of assets, which are reviewed next.

Securities Central banks hold government securities, which consist primarily of Treasury securities. When the government borrows from the central bank, the Ministry of Finance (or the Treasury) sells securities to the central bank. These securities become part of the central bank's assets. Open market operations (that is, the purchase and sale of Treasury securities) with nominated dealers are the channel through which central banks bring changes in outstanding securities at their disposal. *Ceteris paribus*, changes in outstanding securities on the asset side bring changes on the liability side of the balance sheet (monetary base).

Discount loans Central banks remain ready to provide loans to commercial banks and other financial institutions. By changing the discount rate, central banks attempt to influence commercial banks' borrowing from them. The borrowing of commercial banks from the central bank does depend on credit market conditions and other considerations. Commercial banks also consider the possibility of borrowing from other sources.

Government securities and discount loans are the main interest-bearing assets of the central bank. As the liabilities of the central bank do not generally require interest payment, the central bank makes considerable profits from its holding of interest bearing assets.

Gold and the SDR certificate accounts Central banks hold gold and other precious metals. In the past, gold was the reserve against which the national currency was issued. Under the present fiat monetary system, gold does not back currency, but it still constitutes part of the central bank's assets.

The Special Drawing Rights (SDRs) are issued by the IMF to its member countries. The SDRs help the member countries to settle their debt obligations. They have in fact replaced gold in most international financial transactions.

When the Treasury or the Ministry of Finance receives gold and the SDRs, it issues certificates to the central bank. As these gold and SDRs are considered part of the central bank's assets, the central bank issues deposit balances to the government accounts on the liability side.

Coins The Treasury or the Ministry of Finance mints small-valued coins. Central banks hold these coins and issue deposit balances to the government accounts on the liability side.

Other assets Central banks hold other assets as well. They include deposits and bonds denominated in foreign currencies and physical assets, such as computers, office equipments, buildings and other establishments.

Liabilities

Central bank currency outstanding Central banks issue domestic currency in the form of paper notes, which is usually signed by the governor of the central bank. Central bank currency outstanding is the amount that is in the hands of non-bank public. Currency held by commercial banks is the liability of a central bank but it is considered part of the commercial banks' reserves with the central bank. Currency held by the central bank itself in its vaults is not part of currency outstanding.

Bank reserves All commercial banks and other financial institutions have accounts with the central bank in which they hold deposits. Bank reserves consist of these deposits with the central bank, plus currency that is held by them in their vaults. The latter is called the vault cash because it is literally kept in banks' vaults. Reserves are assets of commercial

Table 7.1 The consolidated balance sheet of a central bank

Assets	Liabilities
Securities	Currency in circulation
Discount loans	Bank deposits (reserves)
Gold and SDR certificate accounts	Foreign and other deposits
Other assets	Other liabilities and capital accounts

banks but they are liabilities of the central bank. Banks can withdraw some deposits with the central bank on demand. Central banks meet their obligation to commercial banks and other financial institutions by making currency notes available on demand to meet excess withdrawals of depositors. When central banks make loans to commercial banks and other financial institutions, their assets increase. Correspondingly, commercial banks' reserves with the central bank increase. It allows the commercial banks to issue liabilities (deposits), which increase the money supply.

Total reserves held by banks can be divided into two categories: required reserves and excess reserves. Central banks by law require commercial banks to hold reserves with them. These reserves are called the required reserves. For example, the central bank may require that for every dollar of deposit at the commercial bank, 5 cents should be held with the central bank as reserve. This fraction is the required reserve ratio, which the central bank can change at any time to bring changes in the money supply. Therefore, the required reserve ratio acts as an instrument of monetary policy. Only since the late 1990s some central banks have started paying interest on bank reserves. Interest rates on reserves are much lower than market interest rates. Some banks keep excess reserves with the central bank to meet emergencies. Excess reserves generally remain sensitive to the market interest rates.

Government deposits The Treasury or the Ministry of Finance holds deposits with the central bank and writes cheques against such deposits. Depending on institutional arrangements, the Treasury or the Ministry of Finance enjoys automatic overdraft facilities with the central bank. It allows the Ministry of Finance to write cheques without facing embarrassment of its cheque being bounced due to shortage of funds.

Foreign and other deposits Foreign governments, foreign central banks, international agencies and other government agencies may hold deposits with a central bank for both economic and non-economic reasons.

Other liabilities and capital accounts This item includes other remaining liabilities of a central bank that are considered part of the balance sheet.

INDIRECT INSTRUMENTS AND THE MONEY SUPPLY PROCESS

This section provides a review of indirect instruments of monetary policy that are used by central banks to change the money supply or the interest rate. The main instruments of monetary policy include the required reserve ratio, the discount rate, open market operations and foreign exchange swaps.

The Required Reserve Ratio

The required reserve ratio is the amount of reserves (as a percentage of deposits) that banks and other financial institutions are required to deposit with the central bank. Such reserves can be held in the form of cash in vaults or as deposits with the central bank. The central bank, by law or convention, decides whether it pays interest on reserves. Changes in the reserve requirements affect the money supply through changes in the value of the money multiplier. An increase in the reserve requirement ratio lowers deposits and hence the money supply given to the monetary base. An increase in the reserve requirement ratio raises the demand for reserves. It may lead to a rise in the interest rate in the money market, such as the inter-bank rate.

In recent years central banks in some developed countries such as Australia, Canada and New Zealand have eliminated the reserve requirements for banks. Most developing countries have also lowered the reserve requirements as part of financial deregulation. The reason is that the provision of required reserves makes commercial banks uncompetitive vis-à-vis non-bank financial institutions. Holding unremunerative reserves with the central bank is a tax on banks. As central banks do not generally pay interest on reserves, the banks lose opportunities to earn interest from reserves with the central bank. In effect, the provision of reserve requirements raises the costs of funds for banks. Non-banking financial intermediaries may not need to hold such reserves, therefore gaining some advantage over banks. Since the deregulation of the financial system in the 1980s, such discrimination between banks and non-bank financial institutions has weakened the health of the banking system across countries. In response, central banks have started lowering the reserve requirements, paying interests on reserves and/or eliminating reserve requirements entirely. These measures have been aimed at making banks competitive and stronger.

As an instrument of monetary management, the required reserve ratio is generally considered blunt. Its advantage is that it affects all banks equally and therefore can cause a powerful impact on the money supply. When a small change in the money supply is required, it cannot however be deployed effectively. Applying the reserve requirement to fine-tune the money supply is analogous to using a jackhammer to cut a diamond. Raising the reserve requirement ratio can also create a liquidity problem for banks with low excess reserves. It may sometimes cause volatility in the inter-bank markets (Mishkin, 2007a).

Discount Rate

The discount rate is the interest rate that central banks charge for loans to commercial banks. In most developing countries, commercial banks and other financial institutions rely heavily on credits from central banks for their lending operations. In countries with developed money and capital markets, banks often can avoid borrowing from central banks. They may borrow instead from other banks in inter-bank markets. In these countries changes in the discount rate may not therefore have immediate impact on the money supply. Changes in the discount rate do however send signals to the financial markets about the intention of central banks with respect to future directions of monetary policy.

The effectiveness of the discount rate as an instrument of monetary policy is not straightforward. It depends on a number of interrelated factors. The discount rate represents the price of borrowing from the central bank. A reduction in the discount rate can therefore encourage banks to increase their borrowings from the central bank. Given the money market rate or the inter-bank rate, a lowering of the discount rate may increase the spread and create opportunities for banks to make profits from increased borrowing from the central bank. Increased borrowing from the central bank increases bank reserves with the central bank. The result is the increase in the money supply. The opposite can happen when there is a rise in the discount rate. It increases the cost of borrowing from the central bank and, given the money market rate, may narrow the interest rate spread. As the opportunity of profitability from borrowing from the central bank diminishes, it may lower the banks' borrowing from the central bank. It reduces banks' reserves with the central bank and therefore may lower the money supply.

Since the deregulation of the financial system in the 1980s, discount lending has played a role in the smooth functioning of the banking sector in most developing countries. In particular, it was useful in preventing financial panics that often resulted from liquidity problems. Through the discount lending window, the central bank performed its role as lender of last resort. Under the present deregulated financial environment, this function of a central bank remains important in both developed and developing countries.

The discount rate as a monetary management tool has some shortcomings. Unless the central bank makes its stance on monetary policy clear, any announcement of changes in the discount rate may create confusion. If the discount rate is changed, this may change the spread between the market rate and the discount rate. It has the potential to create short-term volatility in the money markets (Mishkin, 2007a).

Open Market Operations

Open market operations are the most important monetary policy instrument. They are used widely to bring about changes in interest rates or the monetary base. Open market purchases increase the central bank's outstanding securities and *ceteris paribus*, increase its assets in the balance sheet. On the liabilities side, it increases the monetary base. The increase in the money supply brought out by open market purchases lowers the short-term interest rate. Similarly, open market sales lower the central bank's outstanding securities and raise the interest rate. *Ceteris paribus*, this lowers the central bank's assets in the balance sheet. On the liabilities side, it decreases the monetary base.

There are two types of open market operations – dynamic and defensive. Dynamic open market operations are intended to bring changes in the monetary base, while defensive open market operations are intended to offset movements in the monetary base by such factors as say an increase in the government's deposits with the central bank.

Open market operations have become the most widely used instrument of monetary policy. Central banks initiate open market operations and maintain control over the volume of operations. This contrasts with discount lending. For example, in case of discount operations, the central bank encourages or discourages banks to borrow loans by altering the discount rate. But the central bank does not control the volume of discount loans unless there is excess demand for such loans. On the other hand, open market operations have additional advantages. For example, open market operations are flexible such that they can bring precise change (small or large) in the monetary base through the purchase or sale of securities. Such operations can be reversed quickly if deemed necessary or when mistakes are made in the process of policy-making (Akhtar, 1997; Axilrod and Wallich, 1992; Mishkin, 2007a).

Repo and Reverse Repo

In recent years most central banks have introduced additional open market operations, which are temporary in nature and used only for liquidity management. They are the *repo* and *reverse repo* operations. Under the repo (repurchase operations), the central bank purchases securities from authorised dealers, with an agreement that the latter would repurchase securities from the central bank within a short period, say one to fifteen days from the date of original purchase. Since the effect on the monetary base of a repo is reversed on the day of maturity of the agreement, the repo is a temporary open market purchase. This type of operation is used to conduct a defensive open market purchase with the intention of reversing it shortly. Similarly, when the central bank wants to conduct a temporary open market sale, it can engage in a matched sale-purchase transaction (a reverse repo). In this type of transaction the central bank sells securities and the dealers agree to sell them back to the central bank within a short period. The justification for the repurchase agreement could be that the central bank wants to increase the money base only temporarily. Central bank nominated securities dealers, in general, remain ready to engage the repo and reserve repo operations with the central bank. Such transactions assure risk-free profits for dealers. In contrast, the central bank incurs costs for such transactions but accept them as part of its liquidity management on monetary policy considerations.

Foreign Exchange Swaps

Foreign exchange swaps are financial transactions between two counterparts who exchange specific amounts of two different currencies at the outset and reverse the operations at a future date, according to a set of rules that reflect interest payments and amortisation of principals. Central banks use a simple type of foreign exchange swap transactions where they exchange the principal amounts on the initial and maturity dates at predetermined exchange rates. For example, one party sells foreign dollar spot for domestic dollar and simultaneously buys foreign dollar forward for domestic dollar from the same counterpart. The main objectives of foreign exchange swaps by central banks are liquidity management, foreign exchange reserve management and stimulating domestic financial markets.

When developing countries face shortages of foreign reserves, they sometimes undertake foreign exchange swaps to boost reserves. Such swaps have, however, a number of disadvantages. As swaps raise foreign reserves, any expansionary monetary effect of them requires sterilisation. When a forward market does not exist, a central bank that initiates the swap needs to set a swap rate. When the swap rate does not reflect the market condition, it gives a distorted signal to participants in financial markets. For this reason, central banks keep swap operations confidential. Sometimes these transactions do not always remain confidential and therefore cause problems. When swap operations become a regular phenomenon, developing countries, facing foreign exchange shortages because of structural reasons, are tempted to delay any necessary adjustment to policies. This can damage the economy. When a central bank does not keep its position covered during emergencies such as speculative attacks against the currency, it may be exposed to huge losses.

For these reasons, it is suggested that swap transactions should be temporary and only for short-term technical adjustment of liquidity. It remains a debatable issue whether swap transactions should be rolled over as a strategy of reserve management over a longer period.

FOREIGN EXCHANGE MARKET INTERVENTION AND THE MONEY SUPPLY

The above discussion on monetary management ignored exchange rate arrangements that determine the extent to which the monetary authorities have control over the money supply. Following the discussion in Krugman and Obstfeld (2009), this section provides an overview of monetary management under a managed floating exchange rate system. The managed floating exchange rate regime is a common phenomenon in developing countries. The issue is how central bank's intervention into the foreign exchange markets affects the money supply.

Under a managed floating exchange rate system, monetary authorities intervene into the foreign exchange market to smooth out exchange rate volatility under market conditions. Such an intervention affects the money supply. An intuitive understanding of this linkage requires the use of the central bank's balance sheet. As discussed, changes in the central bank's assets bring changes in the monetary base on the liabilities side. In fact, the central bank has the authority to create money by writing a cheque against itself. For example, when the central bank buys an asset from the public, its payment (whether cash or cheque) increases the monetary base. This is equivalent to suggest that an increase in the central bank's assets is matched by an increase in its liabilities. Similarly, the money supply decreases when the central bank sells an asset to the public. The cash or cheque that the central bank receives in payment goes out of circulation. This reduces the central bank's liabilities to the public.

The Central Bank Balance Sheet Revisited

Recall that the central bank transactions in asset markets (domestic and foreign) can be examined by looking at the central bank's balance sheet. The balance sheet records assets and liabilities of the central bank. Since the central bank's balance sheet is organised according to the principles of double-entry bookkeeping, any acquisition of assets by the central bank results in a positive change on the asset side of the balance sheet. Likewise, an increase in the central bank's liabilities results in a positive change on the balance sheet's asset side. Following this principle, the impact of the central bank's intervention

Table 7.2 The initial balance sheet of a central bank

Assets	
Foreign assets (for example, foreign currency bonds)	$100
Domestic assets (for example, government bonds and loans to banks)	$150
Liabilities	
Bank reserves	$50
Currency in circulation	$200
Net worth	0
Assets − (liabilities plus net worth)	0

Table 7.3 The balance sheet of a central bank after the sale of foreign bonds

Assets	
Foreign assets (for example, foreign currency bonds)	$90
Domestic assets (for example, government bonds and loans to banks)	$150
Liabilities	
Bank reserves	$50
Currency in circulation	$190
Net worth	0
Assets − (liabilities plus net worth)	0

into the foreign exchange market on the money supply can be examined using the hypothetical balance sheet of a central bank.

The balance sheet shows that the central bank's total assets equal its total liabilities plus net worth. For simplicity, net worth is assumed to be zero.

Foreign Exchange Intervention and the Money Supply

To show how foreign exchange intervention affects the money supply, consider the following example. Suppose the central bank sells $10 worth of foreign bonds. The sale reduces the official holdings of foreign assets from $100 to $90. It lowers the asset side of the central bank balance sheet from $250 to $240. The central bank receives payment for those foreign assets and it reduces its liabilities by $10. If the central bank is paid with domestic currency, the currency goes into its own vault and out of circulation. Currency in circulation therefore falls by $10. As a result of the foreign asset sale, the central bank's balance sheet changes, as in Table 7.3.

After the sale, assets equal liabilities. Yet both have declined by $10, equal to the amount of currency that the central bank has taken out of circulation through its intervention in the foreign exchange market. The result would be the same if the central bank is paid with a cheque of $10. This would reduce bank reserves with the central bank by $10, while currency in circulation would remain $200. Liabilities would then equal deposits of banks $40 and currency in circulation $200.

Table 7.4 The balance sheet of a central bank after simultaneous sale of foreign bonds and the purchase of domestic government bonds

Assets	
Foreign assets (for example, foreign currency bonds)	$90
Domestic assets (for example, government bonds and loans to banks)	$160
Liabilities	
Bank reserves	$50
Currency in circulation	$200
Net worth	0
Assets − (liabilities plus net worth)	0

Table 7.5 Summary: effects of central bank's hypothetical foreign exchange interventions on the money supply

Central bank's action	Effect on domestic money supply	Effect on central bank domestic assets	Effect on central bank foreign assets
Non-sterilised foreign exchange purchase	$10	$0	$10
Sterilised foreign exchange purchase	$0	−$10	$10
Non-sterilised foreign exchange sale	−$10	$0	−$10
Sterilised foreign exchange sale	$0	$10	−$10

Sterilisation

Central banks sometimes carry out equal foreign and domestic assets transactions in opposite directions to neutralise the impact of foreign exchange operations on the domestic money supply. This policy is called sterilised foreign exchange intervention (Taylor, 1992).

Suppose that the central bank sells $10 of its foreign assets and receives as payment a $10 cheque from a private bank. This transaction causes the central bank's foreign assets to decline by $10 and therefore there is a decline in the money supply. If the central bank wishes to negate the effect of its foreign asset sale on the money supply, it can buy $10 of domestic assets such as government bonds. This second action would increase the central bank's domestic assets and its liabilities by $10. This action, therefore, offsets the money supply effect of $10 sale of foreign assets. For example, if the central bank purchases the government bonds with a cheque, then the two transactions ($10 sale of foreign assets and a $10 purchase of domestic assets) have the net effect on its balance sheet shown in Table 7.4.

Therefore through sterilisation, the direct link between an external imbalance and the equilibrating change in the money supply is broken. However sterilisation can work only for a short period. Its basic weakness is its dependence on the kind of broad and well-functioning securities market that is not available in developing countries. Fundamentally, sterilisation is limited by the cost of interest payments on the government securities purchased. This cost can escalate rapidly if the central bank sells a large volume of securities to offset large-scale foreign exchange inflows.

KEY ISSUES IN MONEY SUPPLY IN DEVELOPING COUNTRIES

Under financial repression monetary control involves direct control over bank credits. Note that monetary control involves control over both the monetary base and the money multiplier. The key determinants of the reserve money are the central bank's lending to the government and both commercial banks and other financial institutions, commercial banks' lending to the public and net foreign assets of the banking system. The policy issue is whether the reserve money can be considered a policy variable given the exchange rate arrangement.

Monetary Base

Under a fixed or controlled exchange rate system, changes in the money supply are directly related to changes in foreign exchange reserves. Changes in foreign exchange reserves are the net result of export earnings, import payments and the net inflow and outflow of foreign capital. In a macroeconomic framework, export earnings are the product of export prices times the volume of exports. Export prices are determined in the world market, while the quantity of exports is supply determined. Sometimes, export earnings can also be treated as they are demand determined. According to the monetary approach, changes in the money supply – brought about by changes in foreign exchange reserves – reflect changes in the demand for real money balances arising from changes in real income, interest rate and/or expected inflation.

Another important question for developing countries is whether the monetary authorities do sterilise (and are willing to sterilise) the monetary implications of balance of payments, including capital inflows in the form of aid and loans. Bhalla (1981: 76) found that 'reserve changes did have an impact on domestic money supply and that the governments are unwilling or failed to sterilize the reserve flows'. Coates and Khatkhate (1980: 28) suggest that 'with fixed exchange rates a central bank's ability to neutralize foreign sector induced changes in the money supply is limited by its capacity to lose foreign reserves or its willingness to accumulate such reserves'. Such efforts are ultimately futile. Even if the monetary authority changes the domestic component of the money supply (through credit control measures), these changes may be offset by counterbalancing foreign exchange flows through aid and loans. It is also found that a discrete reduction in the rate of monetary expansion frequently precipitates an immediate (though temporary) fall in output in a developing economy, which is clearly undesirable on social and political grounds.

With regard to the fiscal deficit–money supply relationship, an exogenous money supply implies that it is indifferent to fiscal deficits. In other words, monetary institutions are not responsive to fiscal deficits. Such an assumption has been widely criticised, particularly forcefully by Buchanan and Wagner (1977). The main theme of recent literature is that within the existing political and institutional framework, fiscal deficits (whichever way they are financed) ultimately increase the money supply. In developed countries, the government usually finances its deficits by selling bonds and securities; this may put upward pressure on interest rates. In order to reduce adverse effects of rising interest rates on private investment, the monetary authority then increases the money supply to bring the interest rates down. This scenario of fiscal deficit–money supply relationship is based on the assumption that interest rates are the target variables of the monetary authority. In most developing countries, interest rates are institutionally determined at the rates usually below the rates that competitive markets would otherwise have generated. Interest rates are also not very responsive to money market conditions. Furthermore, because of the lack of well-developed financial and capital markets, government borrowing from the private sector is limited. Therefore, it borrows from both the banking system and foreign sources such as aid and loans. In many countries government borrowing from the banking system is relatively easy because the banking system is expected to meet financial needs of the government. For example, according to the Bank of Korea legislation, the bank cannot refuse the government's request for loans.

Interest Rate Control and Credit Rationing

As noted, the interest rate ceiling is another defining characteristic of financial repression. The maintenance of a fixed interest rate or ceiling implies that the monetary authority is following an interest rate target by manipulating monetary aggregates. However, in most cases the authority does not have much control over the money supply. Moreover, the ceiling rate is not an equilibrium rate, as one obtains under the interest rate targeting. The ceiling rate is much below the interest rate that would have prevailed if the demand for money were equal to the supply of money. Thus, when an interest rate ceiling is in place, there would be an excess demand for credit. In such a situation, credit rationing becomes the main feature of monetary policy.

Credit rationing occurs in both direct and indirect manners. Indirect control involves moral suasion and the use of the required reserve ratio. A high reserve requirement for deposits reduces the commercial banks' ability to create credit. High reserve requirements constitute an important instrument of monetary control. Most countries do not pay interest on required reserves. This makes it an attractive instrument from the point of view of inflation tax or seigniorage. If governments are unable to borrow from the non-bank public due to underdevelopment of capital market, they require commercial banks to purchase government securities through liquidity ratios and reserve requirements. This implicitly gives the government an access to low cost bank credits.

The central bank also uses its rediscount facilities, whereby commercial banks borrow from the central bank to restrict credit creation. Direct credit control entails specifying the limit on commercial banks' lending to the private sector. In general, the credit ceiling is derived as a residual after public sector financing requirements are met.

But having both the reserve requirement and direct credit control in the armoury of a central bank does involve a redundancy. Since the two operate on the assets and liabilities sides of the consolidated balance sheet of the banking system, they must always be equal. At any one time, only one of the two instruments will be binding, depending on the institutional framework in which monetary policy is conducted.

Financial Dualism

An important feature of a repressed economy is the dual nature of the financial sector that includes an organised system and an informal sector. Informal financial markets remain largely outside the control of the monetary authority. This raises question about the effectiveness of monetary or credit policy for stabilisation in developing economies where a significant informal sector is often present. Harris (1983), for example, reported increased activities in informal sectors in India when there was credit squeeze in the formal sector. Sundaram and Pandit (1984) argued that highly elastic supplies of funds in the informal sector offset contractionary credit policy. Therefore, restrictive credit policy affects informal money lending only to the extent that it changes the supply of loanable funds. As reviewed in Chapter 5, new structuralists also pointed out a linkage between the formal and informal credit markets.

Controls over Capital Flows

Exchange controls are another feature of financial repression. Control over capital flows enhances the effectiveness of monetary policy. Under a fixed exchange rate system, there is a link between changes in central bank foreign reserves and the monetary base. However, monetary policy cannot change the money supply, rather, only its composition between foreign and domestic components. For example, a restrictive monetary policy through open market selling of government bonds would initially raise the interest rate, which induces foreign capital inflows as foreigners find it more profitable to invest. Foreign capital inflows increase foreign exchange reserves and hence the monetary base. It suggests that a restrictive monetary policy lowers central bank's holding of government securities and an equivalent increase in foreign reserves. The central bank's portfolio is changed but not the money supply. However, restrictions on capital flows can provide the monetary authorities scope to manipulate the money supply in the short run under fixed exchange rate arrangements (Hossain and Chowdhury, 1996).

Open Market Operations

Since the 1980s, an increasing number of developing countries have introduced financial reforms. One key feature of financial liberalisation has been the removal of interest rate ceilings. Most developing countries now rely increasingly on market-based indirect methods of controlling the money supply. Open market operations have emerged as the key instrument of monetary policy, in which government securities and/or central bank securities are being traded. When the central bank sells outstanding government bonds in the open market to the non-bank public, it reduces the money supply as people surrender currency in exchange for these bonds. Increased supply of government bonds lowers the bond price and raises the interest rate. Higher interest rates lower the demand for credits which affects economic activity.

However, open market operations in developing countries are sometimes less effective due to underdeveloped money and capital markets. Some Asian countries – for example, Sri Lanka, Indonesia and the Philippines – have attempted to tackle this problem by issuing central bank's own debt instruments, using private money market securities for open market operations, and taking measures to encourage the development of interbank markets (Tseng and Corker, 1991). Such measures have brought the yields on government securities in line with market interest rates. They have also prevented the central bank from forcing commercial banks to hold government securities to meet prudential regulations.

Reserve Requirements

Liberalisation of interest rates requires that the mandatory reserve requirements be either relaxed or reduced. Otherwise, high interest rates that follow liberalisation would imply a higher burden on the banking system as interest rates are not usually paid on bank reserves with the central bank. It may encourage disintermediation as banks may be reluctant to issue deposits. In recognition of this problem, a number of Asian countries – namely, Indonesia, Korea and Malaysia – have substantially lowered reserve requirements. Nepal and Sri Lanka have also adopted a more flexible system of averaging to meet the reserve requirements and unified reserve ratios for different deposits liabilities. These measures have given banks more flexibility in their portfolio management. The Philippines has adopted a more radical policy of paying interest on bank reserves with the central bank (Tseng and Corker, 1991).

Interest Rate Flexibility and the Money Multiplier

The liberalisation of the interest rate has implications for the control of money supply, as the interest rates affect the money multiplier. In the money multiplier model, the central bank expands or contracts bank credits somewhat mechanically by expanding or contracting the monetary base, assuming that the money multiplier remains constant. One condition for the operation of the money multiplier is that the demand for bank credit is interest elastic. This condition is satisfied when credit is rationed. However, the removal of interest rate ceilings can lower the private sector demand for credits. In such a situation, banks may have excess reserves. It may raise the reserve–deposit ratio and lower the money multiplier. On the other hand, when the opportunity cost of holding excess reserves rises with the rise in the interest rate, banks would economise excess reserves, assuming that the private sector demand for bank credits is relatively inelastic. It may make the money multiplier value larger. Thus the interest rate deregulation potentially can make the money multiplier unstable. Consequently, the linkage between changes in the money base to changes in credits becomes less predictable. The effectiveness of monetary control in a deregulated environment therefore depends on the behaviour of banks with respect to their portfolio choice between excess reserves and loans, given the private sector's demand for bank credits.

Instability in the money multiplier can also arise from the households' portfolio choice between currency and deposits, as hypothesised by McKinnon (1973) and Shaw (1973). When the deposit rate of interest rises, the public substitute bank deposits for currency and other unproductive inflation hedges. It may reduce the currency–deposit ratio and therefore raise the value of the money multiplier. It creates a potential for increased supply of credits. East Asian countries have showed that the interest rate liberalisation increased the money multiplier, with a marked impact on the growth of the money supply (Tseng and Corker, 1991).

Relaxation of Entry Restrictions on Banks and Other Financial Institutions

Another aspect of financial liberalisation is the relaxation of entry restrictions for banks and financial institutions. The increased freedom of entry into the financial market can have significant impact on the financial system. For example, in Indonesia, following deregulation in the 1980s, 47 new private banks and 15 joint ventures with foreign banks were opened, in addition to 600 new branches (Page and Healey, 1993; Zahid, 1995). Furthermore, the competition in the financial sector forced both banks and non-bank financial institutions to be more innovative with their products. These innovations included flexibility in withdrawing from saving deposits, automatic transfer facilities combining current and savings accounts, checkable savings accounts, and automatic teller machines which allow withdrawal from either savings or current accounts. As a result, the distinction between savings and current account (and hence between narrow and broad money) became irrelevant for operational purposes. Time deposits also became more liquid and were increasingly performing the transaction function of money. For example, certificates of deposits have the characteristic of a currency note and they facilitate premature withdrawal and easy borrowing against the security of fixed deposits. It posed a problem for the monetary authority for the use of narrow and broad money as intermediate targets. While narrowly defined monetary aggregates are easier to control, their usefulness may be lost when a broader monetary aggregate such as M2 becomes more liquid. Furthermore, as the deregulated financial sector compete more aggressively with the unregulated sector and other financial institutions for deposits, the distinctions between banks and non-bank financial institutions become blurred. This creates additional problems for the definition of monetary aggregates, and hence their control, because deposits of non-bank financial institutions then become part of broad money. While competing for funds, deregulated institutions accelerate the growth of monetary aggregates which are not necessarily related to changes in economic and financial conditions. If there is no significant correlation between the growth of such monetary aggregates and the growth of output, then the velocity of money would fall. Unpredictable volatility in the velocity of money violates the basic requirement for the successful conduct of monetary policy.

Thus, in short, monetary aggregates cannot be used as reliable intermediate targets, either because they become less controllable or the relationship between their growth and economic activities weakens with financial liberalisation and innovation. This results in a greater use of the interest rate as an instrument of monetary policy. However, the use of interest rate as an intermediate target has limited scope in countries which have removed controls over capital flows. As indicated earlier, the domestic interest rate cannot remain significantly higher from the international rate, as such an interest rate differential may induce large capital inflows. This in turn may add to the inflationary pressure and undermine monetary control. On the other hand, the experience of Southern Cone countries (Argentina, Chile and Uruguay), and the Philippines and Indonesia, have showed that a sharp increase in the domestic interest rate may generate expectations of a large depreciation of domestic currency. It may, in turn, induce capital flights and make domestic currency vulnerable to speculative shocks. If central banks intervene into foreign exchange markets to protect the domestic currency, they then lose control over the money supply.

Foreign Capital Inflows and Monetary Management

As pointed out above, sterilisation was used by East Asian countries prior to the 1997–98 currency crises when they experienced large-scale capital inflows. Through this policy intervention, the capital-receiving countries under a fixed or managed floating exchange rate system tried to prevent monetary expansion associated with rapid accumulation of foreign reserves and/or appreciating their currencies. Their sterilisation efforts were not, however, successful and had negative side effects. Sterilisation through the open market sales of government securities and/or central bank bills prevented the interest rate differential from narrowing. In fact, the open market sales of government securities increased the domestic–international interest rate spread and attracted more short-term capital. Instead of stopping, sterilisation prolonged the capital inflows. In addition, sterilisation had large quasi-fiscal costs that arose from the difference between the yield on foreign exchange acquired by the central banks and the higher interest payments on the government or central bank securities.

Concern with both the costs and ineffectiveness of sterilisation through open market operations induced East Asian countries to increase the reserve requirements. The intention was to lower the value of the money multiplier and the money supply from an increased level of monetary base. Although this technique solved the problem of quasi-fiscal costs, it created a wider spread between the bank loan and deposit rates. Indonesia, Malaysia, Singapore, Taiwan and Thailand sterilised the capital inflows by shifting the public sector or pension funds from commercial banks to the central bank. This reduced banks' reserves with the central bank and therefore their ability to create money. The advantages of this type of sterilisation were threefold. First, it avoided or reduced the central bank quasi-fiscal costs associated with open market operations; second, it did not increase the interest rates as much as the sales of sterilisation bonds; and third, it did not tax bank intermediation as in the case of the increase in reserve requirements.

SUMMARY AND CONCLUSION

This chapter has provided an overview of the money supply process and discussed key issues in monetary management in developing countries under both the repressed and liberalised financial systems. Although the money stock is considered an exogenously determined policy variable, the money supply process remains complex and involves the central bank, commercial banks and both borrowers and lenders. Under a fixed exchange rate system, the money supply is endogenous and determined by the determinants of money demand. This is shown in the form of a linkage between the monetary base and changes in foreign exchange reserves, which are related to the balance of payments. Budget deficits are also linked to the monetary base if the government relies on money financing. Therefore, there are many studies which suggest that the stock of money supply should be considered endogenously determined for a developing country. The money stock remains still under the control of a central bank in a flexible exchange rate system; the central bank can manage the money supply by deploying indirect monetary policy instruments.

For an improved understanding of the money supply process, this chapter has adopted a simple money multiplier approach, in which the sources of the monetary base are identified and the behaviour of the money multiplier components are suggested but not examined. Although the monetary base can be disaggregated into asset or liability components, in the money multiplier model a useful disaggregation of the monetary base is in asset forms. This shows the way the monetary base is created and highlights whether the monetary authority can maintain effective control over reserve money.

Three asset components of the monetary base are: the central bank's net claims with the government, the central bank's net claims with commercial banks, and the net foreign assets of the banking system. In most developing countries, the central bank's net claims with the government are related to the government's budget deficits. The central bank's net claims with commercial banks are linked to the loans of these banks to both the private and public sectors, as commercial banks may depend on borrowings from the central bank for credit creation. Changes in the net foreign assets of the banking system are related to export earnings, import payments, and the net inflow and outflow of foreign capital.

Central banks have a wide range of instruments to control money, under both repressed and deregulated financial systems. Not all of them are effective or necessarily deployed by all central banks. Under financial repression, the money stock was controlled directly by controlling bank credits. Under the present deregulated financial environment, open market operations have become the most widely used technique for liquidity management. Still there is lack of transparency in the way liquidity is managed or how effective is monetary control. As most developing countries operate under a managed floating exchange rate system, central banks in developing countries commonly intervene in foreign exchange markets to maintain exchange rate stability. It affects the monetary base and the money supply. In recent decades, large-scale foreign capital flows into developing countries have also created problems for monetary management. Sterilisation has been the widely used technique but it is found ineffective or costly to central banks.

8. Transmission mechanisms of monetary policy and the demand for money

INTRODUCTION

Monetary policy affects output in the short run but only the price level in the long run. Yet the impact of monetary policy on the economy remains uncertain because of long and variable lags. The emerging consensus is that monetary policy has a comparative advantage in maintaining long-term price stability. Therefore, monetary authorities should use monetary policy for maintaining price stability, rather than attempting to fine-tune the economy (Cagan, 1992b; Friedman, 1961; 1968a).

Transmission mechanisms of monetary policy suggest the plausible channels through which monetary policy actions affect the economy in the short run (Purvis, 1992). As monetary policy is seen as a demand management policy, monetary policy actions are expected to influence aggregate demand directly via its various components. The actions can be indirect depending on instruments being used (Mishkin, 1995; 2007a). As reviewed in Chapter 4, the issue remains whether the monetary authorities should pursue an activist monetary policy to achieve the objective of price stability in the medium and long runs, in conjunction with maintaining steady economic growth and/or stabilising the economy (Fischer, 1990). Identifying the transmission mechanisms of monetary policy is therefore essential for deployment of monetary policy instruments that may influence aggregate demand (and probably aggregate supply), leading to stabilising the price level over the medium term or the business cycle.

When central banks undertake monetary policy, they set in motion a series of economic adjustments that work through both the goods and assets markets. As noted, monetary policy actions affect spending, output and employment in the short run but end up with changes in the price level in the medium and long runs. The early monetary policy literature encompassed both the classical and Keynesian transmission mechanisms. This work suggested interest rate and wealth channels through which monetary policy actions affect the economy. Modern literature reveals other channels through which monetary policy affects the economy in an open economy context (Bernanke and Blinder, 1988a; 1988b; Dornbusch and Giovannini, 1990; Mishkin, 2007a).

What types of monetary policy actions a central bank undertakes in practice depends on the monetary policy framework, the state of the economy and the nature of the financial system. Until recently, the financial systems in most developing countries were repressed and the transmission mechanisms of monetary policy were direct. For example, under a repressed financial system, the central bank maintains controls over bank credits, interest rates and exchange rates and may direct credits to the priority sectors for promoting investment and economic growth (Agenor and Montiel, 1996; Aghevli and Khan, 1980). Relaxation of controls over credits and interest and exchange rates brings structural change in the economy. Monetary policy actions impact the economy through multiple channels in a deregulated environment. The dynamic adjustment of the economy in the short and long runs can then be traced, depending on whether the shocks are nominal or real and whether they are one-off or permanent.

Under a deregulated financial system, monetary policy actions are intended to affect various components of aggregate demand through the price mechanisms. Domestic investment and net exports are the key components of aggregate demand that are often targeted. For example, in countries where the money and capital markets are developed, changes in short-term interest rates are swiftly reflected in the whole interest rate structure (yield curve) and the exchange rates. If there are short-term price and wage rigidities, any changes in the nominal interest rates represent changes in the real interest rates. Therefore, in the short run, changes in the nominal interest rates have a predictable impact on aggregate demand and output via investment and net exports (Lewis and Mizen, 2000). Such monetary policy actions to bring changes in the real economy may not, however, work in high inflationary developing countries. Monetary policy actions may lead to a chain of reactions that can create policy uncertainties and high inflationary expectations such that they raise inflation quickly without a significant gain in output, even in the short run. Therefore, monetary policy actions, instead of achieving output or employment goals, may raise inflation and destabilise the economy (Dornbusch, 1993; Lucas and Sargent, 1981). Lewis and Mizen (2000) point out structural change in the transmission mechanism of monetary policy in a highly inflationary environment.

THE CLASSICAL VERSUS THE KEYNESIAN TRANSMISSION MECHANISMS

In classical economics, the relationship between money and output is direct and derived from the *Quantity Theory of Money*. Consider the following *Equation of Exchange*:

$$MV = Py \tag{8.1}$$

where M is the stock of money, V is the velocity of money, P is the price level and y is real income. This identity can be expressed as a theory of nominal income in which Py depends on the level of money stock, such that

$$M = \theta\, Py \; (\theta = 1/V) \tag{8.2}$$

where θ is the reciprocal of the velocity of money, which is assumed to be predictable but not necessarily constant. The monetary neutrality proposition holds in the long run. Therefore an increase in the exogenously set money supply increases nominal income $Y (= Py)$. In the short run, a monetary expansion increases spending and output but in the long run it increases only the price level. Schematically, the transmission mechanisms of monetary policy are as follows:

$$\Delta M/M \rightarrow \Delta AE/AE \rightarrow \Delta Y/Y \approx \Delta P/P + \Delta y/y \approx \Delta y/y \text{ (that is, } \Delta P/P \approx 0 \text{ in the short run)} \tag{8.3}$$

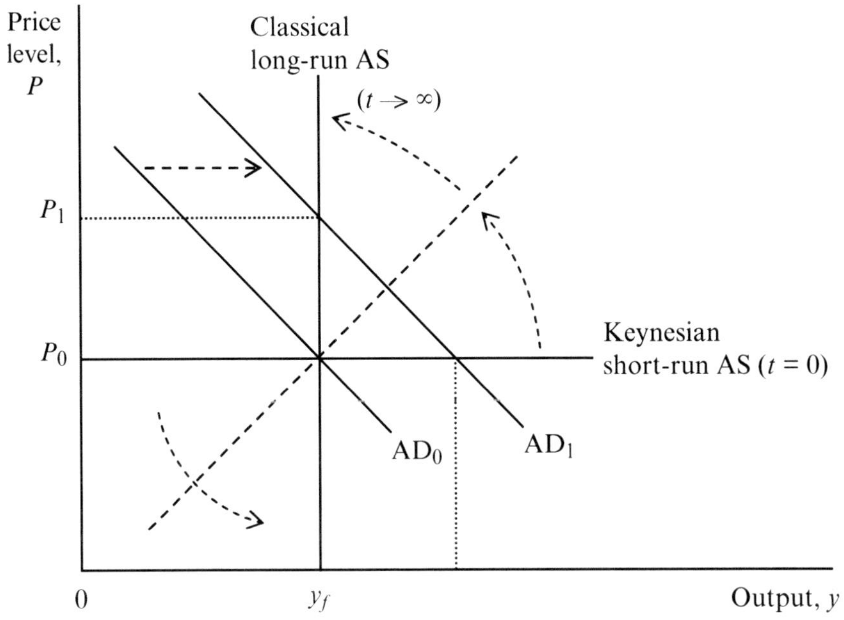

Note: The aggregate demand schedule (AD_0) shifts to the right (AD_1) due to an expansion of the money supply.

Figure 8.1 *Money supply, output and prices*

$$\Delta M/M \rightarrow \Delta AE/AE \rightarrow \Delta Y/Y \approx \Delta P/P + \Delta y/y \approx \Delta P/P \text{ (that is, } \Delta y/y \approx 0 \text{ in the long run)} \quad (8.4)$$

where $\Delta M/M$ is the growth rate of the nominal money supply, $\Delta AE/AE$ is the growth rate of nominal spending, $\Delta Y/Y$ is the growth rate of nominal income, $\Delta P/P$ is the growth rate of the price level, and $\Delta y/y$ is the growth rate of real income.

Underlying the above transmission channels is the idea that since in the short run prices are sticky (implying a horizontal aggregate supply schedule, SRAS), an increase in the money supply shifts the aggregate demand schedule rightward from AD_0 to AD_1 (Figure 8.1). This increases output but no prices. In the long run, output is fixed at the full employment level (y^f). This is represented by the vertical aggregate supply schedule (LRAS). An increase in the money supply therefore translates into a proportionate change in the price level in the long run, leaving output unchanged.

In the above classical model of income determination, the critical assumption is that the velocity of money is constant or predictable. When an increase in the money supply brings an opposite and equal movement in the velocity of money, it would not be transmitted into the price level or output. Any monetary expansion would then be absorbed completely by a change in the velocity of money, with no change in output or the price level. Therefore the direction and extent of the movement of velocity have profound implications for the reliability and effectiveness of monetary policy in bringing changes in output or the price level or both. When the velocity of money is constant, the stock of money would be proportional to the level of nominal output. The implication is that monetary policy can be used to target nominal income, irrespective of the slope of the aggregate supply schedule (Friedman, 1971b; Papademos and Modigliani, 1990). The importance of money demand in the transmission mechanisms comes from the fact that the constancy of the velocity of money requires that the demand for real balances depends primarily and stably on real income which are not highly sensitive to the nominal interest rate. This is a long run condition in which real income and the interest rate are independent of the money supply (Friedman, 1956; 1966; Krugman and Obstfeld, 2009). A stable money demand function leads to a stable velocity of money function. That is, the velocity of money is a constant function, not a number and therefore velocity can vary systematically and predictably in response to variables within the function (Lewis and Mizen, 2000: 159). An implication of it is that the growth rate of the money supply becomes the key determinant of inflation in the long run. To the extent that central banks have control over the money supply, inflation then becomes a policy variable and central banks remain responsible for it. Goodfriend (1997: 9) has articulated this classical theme as follows:

> The theory of money demand implies that control of the money supply is necessary and sufficient to control the trend rate of inflation . . . money demand may be thought of as the fulcrum by which a central bank controls inflation, and the money supply may be thought of as the lever by which it does so.

The Keynesian Transmission Mechanism

The idea that money is an alternative to holding bonds constitutes the essence of the Keynesian monetary theory. According to Keynes, money is demanded for both transactions and speculative purposes. The speculative demand for money is highly sensitive to the expected increase or decrease in bond prices. For example, when the bond prices are low (that is, interest rates are high), then people hold more bonds and less money. Conversely, when bond prices are high (that is, interest rates are low), then people hold less bonds and more money. Monetary policy affects the economy via the interest rate channel. For example, when the money supply increases, then people want to get rid of excess money by purchasing the alternative asset, namely, bonds. By increasing the demand for bonds, it increases bond prices, assuming that the supply of bonds remains unchanged. The resulting decline in the interest rate increases investment and output. Schematically, the Keynesian transmission mechanism is as follows:

$$\Delta M/M \rightarrow \Delta r \rightarrow \Delta I \rightarrow \Delta Y/Y \approx \Delta P/P + \Delta y/y \approx \Delta y/y \text{ (given } \Delta P/P \approx 0) \qquad (8.5)$$

where r is the real interest rate and I is investment.

Thus, in the Keynesian model, money supply affects output via its impact on the interest rate. However, the impact of monetary policy on output is not certain. The impact of monetary policy on output depends on the effect of excess money supply on the interest rate, the responsiveness of investment to the interest rate and the expenditure multiplier. If the interest rate is very low and the demand for money is such that the people hold the entire excess money supply as cash balances for speculative purposes (that is, bond prices are very high and expected to fall), there could be no impact of the increased money supply on the interest rate. This extreme condition is known as the liquidity trap. In the standard IS-LM model the liquidity trap is represented as a horizontal LM curve. Given a downward sloping IS schedule, any expansion of the money supply does not shift the horizontal LM curve downward and therefore the interest rate does not decline further. Hence, monetary policy is ineffective in raising output or employment (Dornbusch et al., 2008). Under normal circumstances the demand for money could be somewhat sensitive to the interest rate, but it does not nullify the role of monetary policy in changing output or prices or both in the short run. Friedman (1969a: 155) makes this point:

> It is important that we try to determine as accurately as possible the characteristics of the demand for money, including the elasticity of demand with respect to interest rates. But in my opinion no 'fundamental issues' in either monetary theory and monetary policy hinge on whether the estimated elasticity can for most purposes be approximated by zero or is better approximated by -0.1 or -0.5 or -2.0, provided it is seldom capable of being approximated by $-\infty$.

How relevant is the Keynesian transmission mechanism of monetary policy to developing economies? Until recently financial markets in developing countries were repressed. Crucially, in a financially repressed economy bond markets are absent and the interest rates are heavily controlled. The Keynesian transmission mechanism through the interest rate channel therefore does not have much relevance (Khan, 1980).

Early studies on money demand in developing countries consistently suggested that the interest elasticity of demand for money was very low, or not significantly different from zero (Adekunle, 1968; Aghevli, 1977). More recent studies (Sriram, 1999; 2000) suggest that the interest elasticity of demand for money remains very low in most developing countries. Therefore it is suggested that the transmission mechanism of monetary policy in developing countries remains close more to the classical description, in the sense that changes in the money supply affect expenditure directly. In most financially repressed developing economies, households remain liquidity constrained. Any expansion of the money supply also creates a large real balance effect, with excess cash balances translating into consumption expenditure.

The idea that excess real money supply affects real expenditure is a major feature of the monetary approach to inflation and the balance of payments theory (Aghevli and Sassanpour, 1982; Hossain, 1995; Khan and Zahler, 1983; Prais, 1961; Swoboda, 1976). According to this theory, the adjustment process to monetary disequilibrium relies on an aggregate private expenditure function which depends not only on disposable income but also on a variable which measures disequilibrium in the money market. Economic agents spend more or less than their disposable income, depending on whether they are running down or accumulating money balances. Therefore, excess money supply positively affects private expenditure and excess demand for money balances results in reduced private expenditure.

A stable money demand function is therefore a necessary condition for changes in the money supply to have predictable effects on inflation, output and balance of payments. The sufficient condition involves the way excess money balances impact aggregate demand via the interest rate effect on investment and the real balance effect on expenditure. This in turn depends on the financial structure, especially the maturity and depth of financial markets and the flexibility of interest rates. In a financially repressed economy where the interest rates are administratively fixed and credit rationing is the principal element of monetary policy, the availability of credit has a direct and immediate impact on expenditure and output. The next section elaborates the transmission mechanisms of monetary policy in financially repressed economies. This provides a historical background of the evolution of monetary policy and its working mechanisms in developing countries.

FINANCIAL REPRESSION AND MONETARY POLICY

As discussed in Chapter 7, in a repressed financial system, the nature of monetary control is direct. Simply, monetary authorities expand the money supply to promote economic growth. The resulting pressure on the price level and balance of payments are mitigated by direct methods, which include credit controls, high reserve requirements, and administrative controls over the interest and exchange rates. Such controls are not always effective because of inconsistency between fiscal and monetary/exchange rate policies and their objectives.

To begin with, the money supply process becomes endogenous under a fixed exchange rate system. The endogeneity originates from the direct link between the monetary base, government budget deficits and balance-of-payments developments. The link between money supply and balance-of-payments developments is the outcome of a fixed or pegged exchange rate policy. In the absence of well-developed money and capital markets, the government also finances budget deficits by borrowing from the central bank. This links fiscal policy with monetary policy (Aghevli and Khan, 1980; Frenkel and Johnson, 1976; 1978).

Ceilings on the interest rate are another defining characteristic of financial repression. The maintenance of a fixed interest rate, or a ceiling on the interest rate, indicates that the monetary authorities follow an interest rate target policy that makes the monetary aggregate endogenous, as it is determined by money demand. When the interest rate ceiling is in place, the demand for loanable funds is not generally matched by the supply of loanable funds. Credit rationing then becomes a feature of monetary policy. Credit rationing occurs both directly and indirectly. Indirect credit controls involve moral suasion and the raising of required reserve ratios. A high reserve requirement for deposits lowers the banks' ability to create credits. Central banks can also use rediscount facilities to limit credit creation. Direct credit controls entail specifying limits on the banks' lending to the private sector. In general, credits to the private sector are determined as a residual once the public sector financing requirements are met (Bell, 1988; 1992; Jaffee, 1992).

On top of credit controls, another feature of financial repression is exchange control. Controls over capital flows enhance monetary policy effectiveness under a fixed exchange rate system. The immediate aim of such controls is, however, to lower pressure on limited foreign reserves (Agenor and Montiel, 1996; Hossain and Chowdhury, 1996; Johnson, 1984; Montiel, 1991).

Transmission Mechanisms of Monetary Policy in a Repressed Economy

Montiel (1991) developed an elaborate model to examine the impact of monetary policy on aggregate demand in a financially repressed economy. Specifically, he examined the impact of four monetary policy instruments: the level of administered bank interest rates, the required reserve ratio, the amount of credit extended by the central bank to

Table 8.1 Effect of monetary policy on aggregate demand in a financially repressed economy

Monetary policy instrument	Interest rate effect	Wealth effect	Fiscal effect	Total effect
Bank credit	Positive	Positive	Positive	Positive
Required reserve ratio	Negative	Negative	Positive	Indeterminate
Administered interest rate	Indeterminate	Positive	Positive	Indeterminate

Source: Author's compilation based on Montiel (1991).

the commercial banks, and the intervention of the monetary authorities in the parallel foreign exchange markets. He showed that any change in each of the above monetary instruments has three effects: the interest rate effect, the household wealth effect and the government fiscal effect. The wealth effect originates from the fact that financial repression entails an implicit system of taxes and subsidies on households as creditors and debtors of the banking system. The present value of these taxes and subsidies changes when changes in the monetary policy instruments affect the effective degree of financial repression, both by changing the rate at which financial repression taxes household portfolios of a given composition and by altering the composition of portfolios in ways that affect the base to which the financial repression tax applies. For example, when the interest rate is not allowed to adjust with inflation, the money-holders lose purchasing power just as when they pay taxes. At the same time, if households hold more nominal money in order to maintain the real value of their money-holdings, then it represents an increase in the tax base. Therefore, an increase in the administered interest rate reduces the degree of repression and increases the net wealth of households.

The fiscal effect arises from the fact that the central bank's profit is a source of revenue for the government. Changes in monetary policy instruments affect the net profit of the central bank. For example, if the administered interest rate is raised, the central bank's profit and hence the government's seigniorage income rise as the central bank generally does not pay interest on reserves of commercial banks.

Table 8.1 presents a summary of the effects on aggregate demand of changes in the four monetary policy instruments. The role of bank credit as a demand management instrument is obvious and unambiguous. Within the Montiel model, an increase in bank credit lowers the demand for loans in the curb market (informal financial market). It lowers the curb market rate. As the interest rate in the curb market falls, the degree of financial repression decreases and increases the level of private wealth. A rise in the level of bank credit may then increase aggregate demand for at least three reasons. First, the fall in the interest rate increases investment spending. Second, the wealth effect increases consumption spending. Third, the supply of bank credit to commercial banks increases the profit level of the central bank, which is transferred to the government for spending on domestic goods and services. However, although the net effect of bank credit on aggregate demand is unambiguous, such an increase in demand would be inflationary if bank credits do not have a supply effect. But there are a number of reasons to believe that an increase in bank credit is likely to raise output in developing countries (Hossain, 1995). To begin with, developing countries suffer from the problem of underutilisation of their capital stocks. An increase in demand would likely just raise their capacity utilisation. Second, as there are many worthwhile projects, an increase in credit is likely to increase investment and hence the productive capacity of the economy. Third, as pointed out by Fry (1998), in financially repressed economies, the supply-constrained volume of real bank credit limits real working capital funds and hence output. Thus, increased credit availability would raise working capital and smooth the production process, at least in the short run.

The effect on aggregate demand and output of any rise in the administered interest rate is ambiguous. Adherents of the McKinnon–Shaw hypothesis maintain that raising interest rates on deposits is likely to increase output in the short run. It happens because the rise in the interest rate may induce an increase in savings, which in turn increases the supply of loanable funds and facilitate private investment. For example, pursuing an anti-inflationary monetary policy in a financially repressed economy brings this observation from Kapur (1976: 778–9):

> the monetary authorities should initially raise the average nominal deposit rate paid on money holdings, thereby reducing the excess supply of money by raising the demand for real balances. Concomitant with this increase in real money balances there will . . . occur an immediate increase in the flow of real bank credit and hence in real output.

On the other hand, the neo-structuralists cite the importance of informal credit markets in providing firms with working capital to purchase their variable inputs (labour, intermediate imports, and so on). Thus the cost of credit forms an important element of the variable cost of production; changes in the interest rate can cause a shift in aggregate supply for real output. Neo-structuralists also emphasise the possibility that increases in bank interest rates would draw funds from the informal market causing the marginal cost of funds to rise, which in turn would have a contractionary effect on both demand and output. Wijnbergen (1982; 1985) cited evidence from South Korea to substantiate this claim. Based on the evidence from the Philippines, Burkner (1982) also argued that, with all asset-holdings unchanged, changes in the informal financial sector and commercial bank deposit holdings must exactly offset each other. The neo-structuralists further claim that such a phenomenon would reduce the overall supply of credit. This is because banks are required to keep reserves, while the informal sector is not, so that the amount of new bank credit created is going to be less than the decline in informal credit. This, however, presupposes that the demand for credit is relatively interest-inelastic. Kapur (1992), on the other hand, argues that the total productive credit may not necessarily decline. He derives his results by considering the motive of the government which receives a 'windfall' seigniorage gain as the monetary base increases, with the rise in reserves as a result of higher deposit takings. The government can channel this newly created monetary base to development banks or to commercial banks themselves.

The impact of an increase in the required reserve ratio on aggregate demand is also ambiguous. The direct interest rate effect is negative. Since an increase in the required reserve ratio raises the degree of financial repression, it lowers the level of aggregate demand through the wealth effect. On the other hand, an increase in the required reserve ratio may raise the government revenue from the increased profits of the central bank.

In sum, although the availability of credit is likely to have a direct impact on aggregate demand, there is considerable ambiguity and lack of consensus about the impact of other monetary policy instruments in a repressed economy.

GENERALISED TRANSMISSION MECHANISMS OF MONETARY POLICY

With the growing importance of monetary policy, economists have investigated a wide range of channels through which monetary policy may affect the economy. There are two conceptual frameworks within which the transmission mechanisms of monetary policy are analysed: the money and credit views on transmission of monetary policy. These are complementary and remain the focus of current research.

The money view is the traditional approach to the transmission mechanism of monetary policy. The assumption is that financial markets are homogenous and perfect. Monetary disturbances have real effects only when there are nominal rigidities in wages and prices. Once financial market imperfections are accounted for, the monetary transmission mechanisms become complex. For instance, financial market imperfections lead to the credit view of monetary policy. Although both the monetary and credit views on the transmission mechanisms of monetary policy share the interest rate as one of the transmission variables, the credit view emphasises bank lending and the firms' financial structure in transmitting monetary policy actions. Market imperfections and asymmetric information in financial markets add other channels through which monetary policy works, for example, exchange rates, asset prices and price expectations. The relative strength of each of these channels varies from one economy to another, and from one regime to another, depending on institutional arrangements and the structure of financial markets (Warjiyo and Agung, 2002).

Since the late 1980s economists have investigated the transmission mechanisms of monetary policy from the asset side of banks' balance sheets, namely, bank credits to the private sector. The credit view of the transmission process is based on the proposition that bank credits are not a perfect substitute for other forms of borrowing. At least for a large group of borrowers, financing by means other than bank credits is not possible. Financing in other forms can be arranged at a higher cost than bank credits. It is suggested that the banks' role in a monetary economy is not limited to intermediation between savers and investors. Banks are well placed to deal efficiently with asymmetric information with respect to borrowers and lenders (Mishkin, 2007a).

The Money View of Transmission Mechanisms

The monetary view of the transmission mechanism of monetary policy focuses on the monetary aggregate, where the short-term interest rate is determined by the supply and demand for money. Changes in the short-term interest rates affect the longer-term interest rates via the term-structure, which in turn affects spending and output. Within this framework, monetary policy actions involve changing bank deposits by changing bank reserves with the central bank. Monetary policy thus focuses on the liability side of both the central and commercial banks' balance sheets. An important assumption behind the money view of the transmission mechanism is that money does not have perfect substitutes. Therefore, economic agents cannot offset completely the impact of monetary policy actions by substituting alternative financial assets. When money substitutes are available, the impact of monetary policy actions on the short-term interest rates is expected to be dampened in proportion to the degree of substitutability.

Interest rate channel

As indicated above, the interest rate is the traditional channel of the monetary policy transmission mechanism. Central banks change the 'very' short-term interest rate through open market operations. Changes in the short-term interest rates are then transmitted into the medium- and long-term interest rates. As discussed in earlier chapters, central banks change the very short-term nominal (but not real) interest rate. Assuming that in the short-run wages and prices are sticky, changes in the nominal interest rates bring changes in the real interest rates. Changes in the real interest rates affect all components of aggregate demand.

The significance of the interest rate impact on aggregate demand remains a contentious issue. Note that the interest rate channel of monetary policy works primarily on the assumption of short-term price stickiness and the fixity of inflationary expectations so that changes in the nominal short-term interest rates are transmitted into the term-structure of the interest rates. Because investment involves a long-term decision-making process, it is questionable whether any long-term investment decisions are based on short-term changes in real interest rates which are brought about by price rigidities. Under the rational expectations hypothesis, inflationary expectations are forward-looking and based on available information on present and future developments, in both real and monetary sectors of the economy. When inflationary expectations are adjusted quickly in a high inflationary economy, changes in the nominal interest rates cannot bring changes in the real interest rates, except temporarily.

Recent monetary literature suggests that financial markets are efficient. Most participants in financial markets acquire and use information from multiple sources. Consequently, inflationary expectations are equal to actual inflation on average. Therefore the issue is what kind of investment remains sensitive to temporary changes in real interest rates such that they could be brought about by unanticipated monetary policy actions. Long-term investment cannot be changed much via changes in the nominal interest rates. Household spending on durables is also unlikely to be sensitive to changes in short-term interest rates. When the interest rates are market determined and remain flexible, households are unlikely to make decisions on purchasing durables with loans of a longer maturity. It follows that changes in short-term real interest rates brought by monetary policy actions may not last over the period of loan repayment for durables.

In short, the monetary policy transmission process through the interest rate channel is not straightforward. Its effectiveness remains uncertain and could be limited. Investment and consumption are long-term decisions, based on factors such as profitability, wealth and risk. Changes in the real interest rates influence inter-temporal decisions on consumption and labour supply and therefore change the wealth positions of borrowers and lenders. Monetary policy actions can bring changes in the real interest rates, but only in the short run when prices are sticky and also when inflationary expectations do not adjust rapidly due to limited information or misperceptions of households and investors. Under the present deregulated and efficient financial markets, it is difficult to see how households and investors remain ignorant of the consequences of monetary policy actions, so much so that they make long-term investment and consumption decisions based on monetary policy actions that have only short-term real effects. What matters are the real interest rates: they cannot be kept different from their equilibrium levels for long (Boschen, 1992).

Exchange rate channel

The exchange rate is an important transmission channel in monetary policy. In the 1960s Mundell (1962) outlined how monetary policy actions influence the exchange rate, which subsequently affects output and inflation. He showed that under perfect capital mobility a simple relationship exists between the short-term interest and exchange rates. Consider the following interest rate parity condition:

$$i^d = i^f + \Delta NER/NER \tag{8.6}$$

where i^d is the domestic interest rate, i^f is the foreign interest rate and $\Delta NER/NER$ is the expected rate of depreciation of domestic currency against the foreign currency.

Equation (8.6) describes the equilibrium condition in the foreign exchange market, which establishes a link between the domestic interest rate, the foreign interest rate and the expected change in the nominal exchange rate. Any change in each of these variables affects equilibrium in the foreign exchange market. For example, if there is an increase in the foreign interest rate, it makes investment abroad more attractive than domestic investment. It may trigger capital outflows and depreciate the domestic currency. An increase in the domestic interest rate may have the opposite effect on the exchange rate if such action triggers capital inflows.

The linkage between money supply growth and the exchange rate can be derived according to what is known as the monetary approach to exchange rate determination.

Consider the purchasing power parity (PPP) relationship:

$$P = NER \bullet P^f \tag{8.7}$$

This can be written as:

$$NER = P/P^f \tag{8.8}$$

Equation (8.8) expresses the relationship between the exchange rate and the domestic price level. It suggests that the higher the domestic price level relative to foreign prices, the higher should be the exchange rate of domestic currency against the foreign currency so that the parity between the domestic and foreign monies can be maintained.

The domestic and foreign money market conditions can then be used to link the domestic and foreign prices to their money demands and supplies. Consider the following money market conditions at home and abroad:

$$M/P = L(y, i) \tag{8.9}$$

$$M^f/P^f = L^f(y^f, i^f) \tag{8.10}$$

Equations (8.9) and (8.10) suggest that

$$P = M/L(y,i) \tag{8.11}$$

$$P^f = M^f/L^f(y^f, i^f) \tag{8.12}$$

Equation (8.8) can now be rewritten as:

$$NER = (M/M^f) \bullet L^f(\ldots)/L(\ldots) \tag{8.13}$$

Equation (8.13) suggests that, *ceteris paribus*, an increase in domestic money supply leads to a depreciation of the exchange rate. However, recall that the real exchange rate (*rer*) is defined as follows:

$$rer = NER \bullet P^f/P \tag{8.14}$$

The real exchange rate influences trade and capital flows, which in turn affect real output. Therefore, just like the interest rate channel, the key issue is how the real exchange rate can be changed by changing the nominal exchange rate. This again is based on the idea of price rigidity that transforms the nominal depreciation of domestic currency to a real depreciation. While it is plausible that changes in the nominal exchange rate may bring change in the real exchange rate temporarily, it is unlikely that such depreciation can be sustained for long because domestic prices are likely to change following monetary expansion that leads to a depreciation of the nominal exchange rate.

Trade and capital flows respond to movements of real exchange rates, only often after a lag. However, temporary changes in real exchange rates are unlikely to make a big difference to trade and capital flows. Real exchange rates are determined by a set of real factors and changes in the nominal exchange rate through monetary policy actions are unlikely to affect the real exchange rate (Edwards, 1989a; 1989b; Hutton, 1992; Neary, 1988). Therefore, although monetary policy actions may affect the nominal exchange rate, its impact on trade and capital flows, and thereby output, is unlikely to be substantial over the medium or long run.

Asset prices in monetary transmission

Since the late 1980s asset price movements have received importance in terms of evaluating the state of economic activity since the late 1980s. Monetary policy actions have wealth and yield effects because of their impact on asset prices. Asset prices contain forward-looking properties. They reflect expectations about future income flows and information on expected inflation and/or interest rates.

Tobin's q-theory of investment and the wealth effect on consumption are two important channels of monetary transmission mechanism. According to Tobin's q-theory, monetary policy actions, such as monetary expansion, transmit into the economy through their impact on equity prices. For example, when the value of q is greater than 1, it suggests that the market price of a firm is high relative to the replacement cost of its capital. Under such circumstances firms issue equities to raise their capital stocks. It increases investment spending because firms purchase more capital equipments with smaller issuance of equities. Similarly, investment decreases when the value of q is less than one. Monetary expansion (reduction) thus affects investment and output through its impact on asset prices (Mishkin, 2007a).

Asset price movements also produce wealth effect on consumption. When the central bank adopts a contractionary monetary policy that raises the interest rate, asset prices fall. Similarly, an increase in the money supply lowers the interest rate and raises asset prices. The Ando–Modigliani life-cycle model suggests that consumption spending is determined by consumers' lifetime resources. With the fall in asset prices, both wealth and consumption decrease accordingly. Empirical studies suggest that the sharp decline in asset prices in Japan (for example, share and land prices) had a negative impact on consumption, contributing to recession that lasted throughout the 1990s (IMF's *World Economic Outlook*, various issues).

The Credit View of Transmission Mechanisms

Recent literature on monetary policy suggests that banks play a crucial role in the monetary transmission mechanism. The credit view of monetary policy highlights banks' special importance in both developed and developing economies. Recall that in the money view of monetary policy, banks operate through the liability side. That is, banks play a role in creating money (liquidity) by issuing deposits (liabilities). Bank deposits change as a result of changes in bank reserves with the central bank. The central bank's monetary policy actions bring changes in banks' reserves. A bank's assets are adjusted to balance its liabilities. The central bank can then use its instruments, such as the discount rate and the required reserve ratio, to change the money supply. For example, an increase in the required reserve ratio lowers banks' ability to issue deposits by lowering the value of the multiplier. Assuming that prices are sticky, it lowers real balances and raises the interest rate. Higher interest rates lower both investment and output.

Bernanke (1983; 1993a; 1993b) and his co-authors have shown the importance of credit in the economy. Bernanke and Blinder (1988a; 1988b) have shown the importance of bank lending in the monetary transmission mechanism. Assume that the central bank adopts a contractionary monetary policy by lowering banks' reserves and deposits. If decreased deposits are not offset by other funds that are not subject to reserve requirements or by a decrease in securities, it would lower bank loans. The result could be decreased investment for borrowers who rely on bank loans for investment. Bank loans are the main source of finance for business enterprises in developing countries. Decreased bank loans can therefore lower investment and economic activity. In Indonesia, bank lending has been found important as a transmission mechanism of monetary policy (Agung, 1998; Goeltom, 2008).

There are two conditions that determine the presence of a bank lending channel. First, the central bank has the ability to constrain the supply of bank loans. Second, bank loans and securities are not perfect substitutes, at least for a section of borrowers. Bernanke and Gertler (1995) suggest that the first condition is questionable on empirical grounds. In order to limit the ability of banks to extend loans after a monetary contraction that lower bank deposits, banks need to be constrained to issue other forms of liabilities. In other words, all bank liabilities (except capital) must be subject to reserve requirements. This is considered a restrictive assumption. For example, public limited banks can issue new equity to generate loanable funds. Still, it can be argued that the central bank through regulatory actions (for example, capital adequacy regulations) can influence the bank's ability to extend loans. Capital adequacy regulations have impact on the banks' willingness to lend. The second condition is generally satisfied in most developing countries. Because of asymmetric information in financial markets, many borrowers find it difficult to issue securities. Banks play a role in overcoming information problem in credit markets. Thus borrowers become dependent on banks.

The credit view of monetary policy has two major implications for policy-makers. First, some economists suggest that credits can serve as a superior instrument for monetary policy because they are a leading indicator for economic activity. Bernanke and Blinder (1988a; 1988b) have argued that if one considers the impact of monetary policy on the ability of the banking system to lend, credits succeed as an intermediate variable where monetary aggregates fail. It happens when the demand for money is unstable. In a deregulated financial environment, policy-makers in particular can predict inflation and longer-term economic growth by observing credits rather than monetary aggregates. Second, the credit channel of monetary transmission permits a better understanding of the nature and characteristics of business cycles. Following Bernanke et al. (1999a), a series of studies during the late 1990s have shown that the impact of monetary policy shocks to the economy tends to be stronger and more persistent than the traditional models predict. The credit channel helps to explain this discrepancy and is believed to contain an amplifying mechanism whereby difficulties in the real sector lead to tightness in credit markets. It lowers investment, which in turn exacerbates economic downturn. Furthermore, shocks to bank credits may have a considerable impact on economic activity. Regulatory changes and past financial distress influence banks to adopt a cautious approach to lending, which has an impact on economic activity (Blinder and Stiglitz, 1983; Khan, 2003).

The balance sheet channel

The basic idea behind the balance sheet channel of monetary transmission mechanism is that monetary policy can affect the borrowers' financial strength (or net worth). It influences the costs of external finance, which affects the borrowers' investment decisions. When the central bank initiates a contractionary monetary policy that raises the interest rate, it influences the borrowers' financial position in two ways. First, it decreases asset prices, which lower the collateral value for borrowers and hence their ability to borrow. Second, a rise in the interest rate raises the cost of servicing of outstanding short-term or floating debt, thereby reducing net cash flows. Because of adverse selection and moral hazard problems and bankruptcy laws, borrowers with a lower net worth have a higher default risk or are less creditworthy on the ground that the lenders have to bear higher costs in the event of project failures. In contrast, the higher the borrowers' net worth, the greater is the value of their collateral and hence the lower is monitoring costs for lenders. Therefore, lenders impose varying premiums for external finance that reflect the costs of monitoring and project evaluation. This indicates that information asymmetries make internal finance of a new project cheaper than external finance. Monetary policy actions influence the wedge between the internal and external finance. A monetary contraction (expansion) increases (decreases) the wedge between the internal and external finance. It impacts both investment and output (Mishkin, 2007a).

SOME LESSONS

The review of the major channels of monetary transmission mechanisms reveals that there are uncertainties and disagreements in different aspects of the transmission process. Although the central bank can set the short-term interest rate, the transmission of monetary policy actions to long-term interest rates and asset prices are not adequately understood. The response of long-term interest rates and asset prices to policy-induced changes in short-term interest rates are difficult to predict. Some other aspects of monetary policy are to be considered. For example, there is no clear indicator of the stance of monetary condition. The dilemma for economists is which indicators are to be used to gauge the stance of monetary policy. Should the monetary aggregates or the real interest rate or equity prices be used? All contain information and could be useful. In so far as developing countries are concerned, there is ongoing debate whether monetary policy can be conducted under a fixed exchange rate system with capital mobility. It is argued that as long as the domestic and foreign assets are not perfect substitutes, there is scope for independent monetary policy even if capital flows are not regulated. The scope of monetary policy in a high-inflationary country is, however, very limited. First, when inflation is high and variable, the real interest rate becomes volatile, which diminishes the importance of interest rate channel in the transmission mechanism. Second, in a highly inflationary environment, the maturity of financial instruments shrinks and the demand for long-term, non-indexed financial assets simply disappear (Shapiro, 2006).

Recent monetary policy experiences in many countries have provided a number of lessons (Mishkin, 2007a). They are useful to the design of monetary policy and for understanding of the monetary transmission mechanisms.

Nominal versus the real interest rate

As Friedman (1968a) emphasised, monetary policy stance cannot be gauged from high or low nominal interest rates. High and rising nominal interest rates could be associated with rapid growth in the quantity of money; conversely, low and falling interest rates could be associated with slow growth in the quantity of money. In short, nominal interest rates are a misleading indicator of whether monetary policy is tight or easy. Central banks can change the very short-term nominal interest rates, while the real interest rates affect investment, consumption and capital flows. Real interest rates are determined by real factors and not by money supply growth.

Asset prices

Besides interest rates, other asset prices contain information on the stance of monetary policy. Share prices, exchange rates, and housing and land prices play an equally important role in the monetary transmission mechanisms. These asset prices have implications for monetary policy effectiveness. For example, when short-term interest rates are low or even zero, other asset prices such as share and land prices could be low and the domestic currency value could be high. This is indicative of tight rather than easy monetary policy.

Very low interest rate and monetary policy effectiveness

Monetary policy can be effective in reviving a weak economy, even when the short-term interest rate is very low or even zero. This is the lesson that has been drawn from the recent deflationary experience of Japan. The conventional wisdom is that when the short-term nominal interest rate is near zero, there is nothing that a central bank can do in order to stimulate the economy. This is not true. Note that the money supply can be increased through the purchase of securities. Open market operations for monetary expansion do not need to be solely on short-term government securities. Purchases of foreign currencies, like purchases of government bonds, can lead to a monetary expansion. Increased liquidity can revive a depressed economy by raising the expected price level. When increased money supply reflates other asset prices, it can stimulate aggregate demand and hence output (Krugman and Obstfeld, 2009; Mishkin, 2007a).

Price stability

Central banks have put greater emphasis on price stability in recent years. The aim is to lower uncertainty in expected prices and their impact on investment and productivity. Unanticipated movements in the price level cause unanticipated fluctuations in output. Price deflations in particular can lead to financial crises. The price stability goal therefore implies that negative inflation is at least as undesirable as high inflation. This goes against the spirit of the Friedmanian view on the optimal inflation rate which, he argued, should be negative of the real interest rate (Mishkin, 2007a).

MONEY DEMAND AND MONETARY POLICY TRANSMISSION

A stable money demand function is the essential condition for the reliable transmission of the impact of changes in the money supply on aggregate expenditure. In the theoretical literature three broadly defined groups of money demand models are dominant. They are the single equation demand theory models, the portfolio theory models and the inventory theory models. The Chicago-school-based demand theory models derive the money demand function in the same way as for the demand for other durable goods. Friedman's (1956) re-statement of the quantity theory of money provided the intellectual inspiration for this model. The portfolio theory models are associated with the Yale-school view of the demand for money. The original insight of this theory is attributed to J.M. Keynes and has been further developed by Tobin (1958). In these models the demand for money is viewed in the context of a portfolio choice problem, with emphasis on risk and the expected returns on various financial assets. The inventory theoretic approach to the transactions demand for money was developed by Baumol (1952) and Tobin (1956), and later extended by Feige and Pearce (1977). This approach focuses on the need to hold money in order to smooth the difference between income and expenditure flows, and explicitly specifies a transactions cost function, where the cost function includes the inventory holding costs as well as brokerage costs.

The portfolio approach to money demand is less appropriate for most developing countries because of the absence of a well-developed capital market and the resultant lack of attractive financial assets of domestic and foreign origin. In developing countries the demand for money is believed to originate from the transactions motive. Therefore, it follows that the Baumol–Tobin transactions demand theory should be more appropriate for such economies. However, the inventory theoretic approach is too rigid in its specification and one faces serious practical difficulties in finding data series on brokerage costs and other forms of transactions costs. Moreover, the fact that money is used primarily for transactions purposes does not necessarily imply that a more general theory of the demand for money is inappropriate for developing countries. As Laidler (1993) pointed out, the theories of money demand based on an application of the general theory of demand are not logically incompatible with the notion that the demand for money arises from its usefulness in making transactions. Nor is it incompatible with the proposition that money is an excellent hedge against the risks inherent in holding other assets. In a world of certainty, the two reasons for holding wealth are to smooth the consumption stream and to earn interest. But in a world of uncertainty, which characterises most developing economies, an important motive for holding wealth is the availability of reserves for emergencies (Friedman, 1957). Of the various forms of wealth, money has always been an attractive asset to wealth-holders because of its versatility (Friedman and Schwartz, 1963a). Thus the Chicago-based demand theory models *à la* Friedman are widely used for empirical studies on money demand in both developed and developing countries.

Issues in Empirical Studies on Money Demand

Perhaps no other economic theory has received as much empirical attention as the demand for money. This section reviews some issues in empirical studies on money demand in developing countries.

The definition of money

In the money demand literature the choice of an appropriate definition of money remains an empirical issue. The choice is between the narrow and broad definitions of money. This is useful for examination of the issue whether the estimated coefficients are different for these two money variables and whether one definition of money is superior to the other, with respect to stability of the money demand function. The demand for money is assumed as a demand for real balances. That is, in the absence of money illusion, an increase in the price level induces a proportionate increase in the demand for nominal money, leaving real balances unchanged. The validity of this proposition is not often tested but is accepted as a maintained hypothesis.

The scale variable

Following the tradition of the asset-theoretic demand for money, a measure of real permanent income (as a surrogate of wealth) is used as a scale variable. There are two reasons for it, at least in principle. First, measured income, due to its volatility, is not a good proxy for wealth and therefore the use of it may suggest instability in an otherwise stable money demand function. Real permanent income can better explain the macroeconomic variables, such as money demand and consumption, in a relatively rapidly growing economy. Second, money may not always act as a key shock absorber for the transitory component of income; other items in the wealth-holder's balance sheet, such as durable goods, consumer credit outstanding, personal debt, and securities, may perform this function (Friedman, 1959b). To the extent that the transitory component of income is stored in the form of money, it may have the characteristic of a 'white' noise in a statistical sense.

The opportunity cost variables

The choice of a proxy for the opportunity cost of holding money remains the most difficult one. In developed countries, the market determined nominal interest rate is the appropriate opportunity cost variable. Ball (2001) suggests that although in the short-run money demand function the commercial paper rate or the Treasury bill rate measures the opportunity cost of holding money, the choice of an interest rate is not critical in the long-run money demand as most interest rates follow a similar trend. However, until recently, this variable played a limited role in money demand for developing countries because the interest rates in these countries were institutionally set at levels below the rates that competitive markets would have otherwise determined. In some instances, the interest rates were kept well below the actual or expected inflation, implying negative real interest rates. Furthermore, in the absence of a broad range of financial assets, asset substitution took place between money and real assets (like land, houses, gold, silver, and consumer durables) and not between money and interest-earning financial assets, since if the prices of alternate assets rise with the general price level, their real returns are zero, whereas the real return on money (given that unlike other assets, its nominal value is fixed) would be minus the inflation rate. Physical assets thus represented the major hedge against inflation and acted as alternative assets in the portfolio of the non-bank public. All these factors have made expected inflation a better proxy for the opportunity cost of holding money, especially in high inflationary developing countries. An empirical issue remains whether expected inflation is significant in the money demand function for a developing country.

Currency and asset substitution

When the money demand model is estimated in an open economy context, an augmentation is necessary, especially if the country's capital accounts remain open and there is scope for foreign currency and asset substitution. In the augmented model, the foreign interest rate and the public's expectations about devaluation of domestic currency are included. In fact, these two variables jointly determine the rate of return on foreign financial assets, such as foreign currency denominated bonds or time deposits. To make a choice between the domestic and foreign financial assets, economic agents compare the rates of return on these assets and make decisions on whether to hold domestic assets or foreign assets.

In most developing countries, capital flows are restricted. Wealth-holders may still have some scope for asset diversification, holding assets at home or overseas through various legal or illegal means. At home, money is the key financial asset, in which the interests are paid only on time deposits. An alternative is to hold foreign financial assets, such as foreign currency denominated bonds or time deposits, in overseas banks and other financial institutions. The rate of return on such assets in domestic currency can be approximated as the sum of a representative foreign interest rate and the actual or expected devaluation of domestic currency against a major foreign currency, such as the US dollar. Given the domestic deposit rate of interest, a rise in the foreign interest rate and/or a devaluation of domestic currency against the foreign currency may decrease money demand, as there could be foreign currency and asset substitution. The coefficient on this variable is expected to bear a negative sign and this may be interpreted as a measure of capital mobility. However, when domestic asset holders substitute foreign currency (not interest-bearing foreign financial assets), the rate of devaluation of domestic currency may capture this phenomenon and a negative coefficient of it may be interpreted as currency substitution. In a general portfolio balance model, Cuddington (1983) has suggested to use both the return on foreign assets and the rate of devaluation of domestic currency in the money demand function.

Income and Interest Elasticities of Money Demand in Developing Countries

There is voluminous empirical literature on the demand for money. They cover issues in both developed and developing countries (Boughton, 1991; Goldfeld and Sichel, 1990; McCallum and Goodfriend, 1992). The early studies on money demand were mostly based on the partial adjustment model, which was introduced by Chow (1966). The recent studies have adopted cointegration and error-correction approaches (Sriram, 1999). Most studies suggest that the demand for real balances in developing countries is a stable function of real income and the actual or expected inflation (Adekunle, 1968; Khan, 1980; Laumas and Mehra, 1977). Empirical findings with regard to the nominal interest rate are mixed. In most studies, the coefficient on the interest rate is not significant because of the fixity of interest rates by administrative regulations (Liang-Siang and Leng Rung, 1970; Mammen, 1970; Mangla, 1979). This section reviews some selective studies on money demand in developing Asia.

Fan and Liu (1970) was one of the early studies on money demand in developing countries of Asia. Using annual data from 1953 to 1968, they investigated the money demand behaviour in Japan, Taiwan, South Korea, India, Pakistan, Myanmar, Sri Lanka, the Philippines and Thailand. For Japan, Korea, the Philippines, Thailand and Myanmar the call money rate and for others the government bond yields were used as a proxy for the interest rate. They did not use any measure of permanent income, as they argued that the concept of permanent income loses its meaning in unstable economies. They found the income variable significant in the money demand function with a positive sign. The estimated value of income elasticity was within a range from 0.79 (Thailand) to 2.55 (Myanmar). The interest rate variable, however, produced mixed signs and was not statistically significant.

Aghevli et al. (1979) used quarterly data to estimate a short-run money demand function for Indonesia, Malaysia, the Philippines, Singapore, Sri Lanka and Thailand. As the interest rates in these countries were administratively fixed during the period of study, they used expected inflation as a measure of the opportunity cost of holding money. Rather than using measured income, the study used permanent income as a scale variable. They found that the demand for money (narrow or broad) was a stable function of real income, the rate of inflation and the lagged real balances. Only in the case of Singapore, the income coefficient was insignificant at the 5 per cent level. The effect of inflation on broad money balances was stronger than what was observed in the narrow money equation. Table 8.2 shows that their findings support the hypothesis that the

Table 8.2 Long-run income elasticities of demand for real balances in developing Asia

Country	Period of study	Narrow money	Broad money
Indonesia	1968 II–1976IV	1.63	1.85
Malaysia	1970 I–1978 I	1.23	1.65
Philippines	1957 II–1977 IV	0.85	1.54
Singapore	1966 II–1976 IV	1.34	1.33
Sri Lanka	1957 II–1976 IV	1.08	1.48
Thailand	1957 III–1977 IV	0.68	1.49

Source: Aghevli et al. (1979).

Table 8.3 Long-run relationship between money, income and the interest rate in developing Asia

Country	Income elasticity		Interest rate elasticity	
	Narrow money	Broad money	Narrow money	Broad money
Indonesia	na	na	−0.66	−2.05
Korea, South	0.79	1.00	−0.84	−0.78
Malaysia	1.11	1.63	not significant	na
Myanmar	1.27	1.43	not significant	not significant
Nepal	1.75	2.60	not significant	not significant
Philippines	0.67	1.47	−1.16	not significant
Singapore	0.86	1.37	−1.17	−2.13
Sri Lanka	0.92	1.22	−1.60	0.46
Thailand	0.85	1.72	−1.53	−2.46

Note: na = not available.

Source: Tseng and Corker (1991).

long-run income elasticity of demand for broad money is larger than that of the demand for narrow money. The income elasticity is also larger than one, irrespective of the definition of money (except for the Philippines and Thailand). The greater than unity income elasticity of the demand for money was interpreted as the result of monetisation of economic activities, limited opportunities to economise on cash balances, and the paucity of alternative financial assets.

Khan's (1980) study of 11 countries included seven Latin American and four Asian countries, namely, India, Malaysia, the Philippines and Thailand. He estimated the money demand function for the period 1962:I–1976:IV. His reported findings were similar to those of Aghevli et al. (1979). He found that the long run income elasticity of demand for broad money is larger than unity. He also found that in high inflationary countries, the money-holders responded quickly to expected inflation because of their greater awareness of the costs of holding money.

Tseng and Corker's (1991) study was different from earlier works in some respects. In their study they used the interest rate rather than expected inflation as a proxy for the opportunity cost variable. Second, to capture any sluggish adjustment of money demand towards desired equilibrium holdings, they specified an error correction model which is more general than the partial adjustment model.

Table 8.3 reports Tseng and Corker's main empirical findings. It shows that the estimated long-run income elasticity of demand for narrow money varies significantly across countries. It ranges from as low as 0.67 for the Philippines to as high as 1.75 for Nepal. Except for Singapore and Nepal, the long-run income elasticities for other countries did not reflect financial development in the sense of monetisation of those economies. For example, income elasticity less than one for Singapore was consistent with its advanced financial system. Similarly, a greater than unity income elasticity for Nepal was explained in terms of its underdeveloped financial system.

With the exception of South Korea, the long-run income elasticities of demand for broad money were larger than unity. Tseng and Corker (1991) maintained that the large income elasticities of demand for broad money did not reflect monetisation – a phenomenon associated with narrow money. Rather, it might have been due to the growth of wealth in excess of the growth of real income in some high-saving countries. In fact, there was rapid growth of savings in the form of time deposits following financial liberalisation in some Asian countries. This explanation was, however, at odds with the high income elasticities of demand for broad money in Nepal and Myanmar.

In the narrow money demand function, the deposit rate of interest was found to be significant with a negative coefficient in most countries. On the other hand, the inflation rate did not fair well as a measure of the opportunity cost of holding narrow money. For Indonesia, South Korea, Malaysia, the Philippines and Thailand the broad money demand was negatively related to the opportunity cost variable measured by the difference between the returns on alternative assets and the average interest rate paid on broad money holdings. The demand for broad money was affected by the relative asset returns as opposed to the general level of interest rates.

Table 8.4 reports recent estimates of the income and interest elasticities of demand for money in selected countries of Asia. The main finding is that the interest elasticity of demand for money remains very low or is not significantly different from zero. The income elasticity of the demand for broad money is significantly greater than 1, while the income elasticity of demand for narrow money is about 1.

STABILITY OF MONEY DEMAND

Stability of the demand for money is a recurring issue in the theory and application of macroeconomic policy. A stable demand for money function satisfies a set of necessary conditions for money to exert a predictable influence on the economy. Provided that the money demand function is stable, the central bank's control over the money supply can be an instrument of economic policy. Friedman (1969a: 155) defines a stable money demand function as follows:

> The important consideration for monetary theory and policy is whether the demand for money can be treated as a reasonably stable function of a fairly small number of variables and whether this function can be empirically specified with reasonable accuracy. Whether one important argument of the function is an interest rate or set of interest rates is much less important. [. . .]

Table 8.4 Recent estimates of income and interest-elasticities of demand for money in selected countries of developing Asia

Country	Author	Study period	Method	Definition of money	Real income elasticity	Interest rate semi-elasticity	Inflation semi-elasticity
Bangladesh	Hossain (2006b)	A: 1973–2002	Cointegration (JJ)	ln (M1/GDPD)	1.17	−0.15	
				ln (M2/GDPD)	1.73	0.26	
China	Tseng et al. (1994)	Q: 1983:1–1988:4	Cointegration (EJ)	ln (CC/RPI)	1.90		−1.23
				ln (M1/RPI)	1.53		−1.51
				ln (M2/RPI)	1.81		−2.21
		Q: 1989:1–1993:4	Cointegration (JJ)	ln (M1/RPI)	1.48		−0.94
				ln (M2/RPI)	1.58		−1.54
India	Moosa (1992)	Q: 1972:1–1990:4	Cointegration (EG)	ln (CC/CPI)	0.87	−0.11	
				ln (M1/CPI)	0.79	−0.03	
				ln (M2/CPI)	1.47	−0.17	
			Cointegration (JJ)	ln (CC/CPI)	0.99	−0.26	
				ln (M1/CPI)	0.80	−0.28	
				ln (M2/CPI)	1.57	−0.86	
Indonesia	Hossain (2007)	A: 1970–2005	Partial adjustment	ln (M1/CPI)	0.93	−0.37	−1.29
Indonesia	Hossain (2008)	A: 1971–2007	Cointegration (JJ)	ln (M1/CPI)	1.50	−0.04	
Korea, South	Arize (1994)	1973:1–1990:1	Cointegration (EY)	ln (M1/CPI)	0.50	−0.03	
				ln (M2/CPI)	0.95		−1.22
			Cointegration (JJ)	ln (M1/CPI)	0.57	−0.03	−9.15
				ln (M2/CPI)	1.16		
Malaysia	Sriram (1999)	M: 1973:8–1995:12	Cointegration (JJ)	ln (M2/CPI)	1.13		−4.89
Pakistan	Arize (1994)	Q: 1973:1–1990:1	Cointegration (EY)	ln (M1/CPI)	0.93		−1.13
				ln (M2/CPI)	0.99	0.003	−1.27
			Cointegration (JJ)	ln (M1/CPI)	1.03		−5.48
				ln (M2/CPI)	0.77	0.038	−7.88
Pakistan	Hossain (1994)	A: 1972–1991	Cointegration (JJ)	ln (M1/CPI)	0.86	−0.54	
				ln (M2/CPI)	1.07	−0.05	
Singapore	Arize (1994)	Q: 1973:1–1990:1	Cointegration (JJ)	ln (M1/CPI)	0.72	−0.33	
				ln (M2/CPI)	1.08	−0.03	

Note: EG = Engle–Granger method; EY = Engle–Yeo method; JJ = Johansen–Juselius approach; M1 = narrow money; M2 = broad money; CPI = Consumer Price Index; GDPD = GP deflator; RPI = Retail Price Index; M = monthly; Q = Quarterly; A = Annual.

Sources: Author's compilation based on Sriram (2000) and other references as listed in the bibliography.

> If the interest elasticity is not zero, there will be movements along the function that is easy to interpret as a sign of instability of the function.

In an empirical context, the notion of a stable money demand function involves at least three key elements. First, the demand for money relationship is highly predictable in a statistical sense, as measured by (a) the usual goodness-of-fit statistics (for example, R^2), (b) precision of estimated coefficients (that is, high t-values), and (c) its ability to forecast accurately out of sample. Second, a stable demand function for money has a relatively few determinants. A relationship that requires knowledge about a large number of variables to verify it down is, in effect, not predictable. Finally, the variables that appear as arguments need to represent significant links to spending and economic activity in the real sector. For example, when the interest rate is considered an argument in the money demand function, any change of interest rate is expected to have some effect on spending or economic activity. In sum, a stable demand function for money means that the quantity of money is predictably related to a small set of key variables linking money to the real sector of the economy (Judd and Scadding, 1982).

The importance of a stable money demand function for monetary policy is illustrated with the standard IS-LM model, in which the interest rate and output are endogenous variables. Within this model, a stable demand for money function translates into a well-defined relationship between money, interest rates and output that allows the slope and position of the LM curve to be determined, given knowledge about the quantity of money. It follows that changes in money exert a predictable effect on output (given knowledge of the IS curve), which in turn implies that control of the money supply gives some measure of output.

Recent debate on the stability of money demand centres on the choice of the strategy of monetary policy. As indicated earlier, monetary targeting is dependent on stability of the money demand function. The abandonment of monetary targeting in developed countries since the mid-1980s in favour of inflation targeting in some countries has been in response to the alleged instability of the money demand function (Boughton, 1981; Goldfeld, 1973; 1976). The debate continues and no consensus has emerged. Harberger (1999: 2) has captured the essence of the debate in the present context:

> You can try fitting as many demand functions for money as you like, and you're not going to find one that has exhibited during recent decades the degree of stability that Friedman was counting on. But at the same time I just don't believe that the demand function for money is not a real and live and important relationship. So we have to deal with a very essential function, central to monetary theory and policy, but with the unfortunate attribute of shifting over time.

Financial Liberalisation and Money Demand

Interest in the stability of the demand for money was rekindled in the 1980s, following financial liberalisation and financial innovations in developing countries. Financial reforms can affect the stability of the money demand function in a number of ways. First, with liberalisation, the interest rate is likely to become a significant variable in the demand for money function. Second, any reform measure that promotes financial market development may create financial assets with attractive yields, which may lead to portfolio shifts away from monetary assets. It would cause a shift in the intercept term of the money demand function. Third, the observed relationships among money, income, prices, and the interest rates may alter following the relaxation of direct controls over bank credits, interest rates and exchange rates and the shift from direct to indirect monetary policy instruments (Jonson and Rankin, 1986; Tseng and Corker, 1991). Any promotion of competition among financial institutions may also lower financial transactions costs, thereby causing money demand to respond differently to interest rate changes than before. Furthermore, financial deregulation may lead to unpredictability of money demand by changing the speed of adjustment at which actual money balances move towards the desired level. In short, financial deregulation may cause a one-time or a gradual shift in the level of money holdings, altering the sensitivity of money demand to changes in income and interest rates.

High inflation and money demand stability

As discussed earlier, there is significant currency substitution in high inflationary developing countries. From the monetary policy viewpoint, the main concern is that currency substitution may make the money demand function unstable (McKinnon, 1981; 1982). Edwards (1993) raised this concern with respect to macroeconomic management in general.

Furthermore, when wealth-holders respond to changes in the relative opportunity costs of holding foreign money balances, foreign monetary disturbances have the potential to destabilise the domestic economy through changes in the demand for domestic money. In other words, currency substitution makes the insulation property of the flexible exchange rates system weaker. To illustrate, if the monetary authority of country A increases its domestic money supply, the inflation rate in A would rise and money-holders would expect A's currency to depreciate. With a flexible exchange rates system, A's monetary authority does not intervene in the foreign exchange market. The expected depreciation of A's currency would then increase the opportunity cost of holding domestic money relative to country B's currency. This would result in a decline in the demand for A's currency and an increase in the demand for B's currency in both countries. If B follows the policy of maintaining a targeted monetary growth, it would mean a higher interest rate in B compared with the case without currency substitution. On the other hand, if B follows the policy of pegging the domestic interest rate, it would have to increase the money supply. Thus, if there is currency substitution, the policy action taken by country A leads to a similar action by country B, even in a world of flexible exchange rates. In other words, with currency substitution the monetary authority cannot have an independent monetary policy which the flexible exchange rate system is supposed to provide (Hossain and Chowdhury, 1996).

Empirical Evidence on Stability of Money Demand

How stable is the demand for money in developing countries? Most empirical studies on money demand in developing countries suggest that the money demand function remains stable, irrespective of financial reforms. It is true for the long-run money demand relationship. There is, however, some instability in the short-run money demand function, which is estimated using high-frequency data. Monetarists suggest that what matters for monetary policy is a long-run stable money demand relationship that underwrites the linkage between money supply growth and inflation (Laidler, 1993).

There are four major money demand studies for Asian countries: Aghevli et al. (1979), Arize (1994), Khan (1980) and Tseng and Corker (1991). The similarity of the estimates of long-run income elasticities in Aghevli et al.'s (1979) study compared with Tseng and Corker's (1991) work suggests that there is a stable long-run money demand function in Asian countries. Indeed, these estimates were not much different from those reported by Fan and Liu (1970). The recent estimates of income and interest elasticities of demand for several developing countries of Asia suggest that the interest elasticity is very low and that the income elasticity is about one for narrow money but greater than one for broad money (Arize, 1994; Hossain, 1993; 1994; 2003; 2005; 2006b; 2007; 2009).

Tseng and Corker (1991) conducted tests for stability of the money demand function for selected Asian countries. They used a two-stage estimation procedure to investigate stability of the money demand function. At the first stage, they applied the co-integration method to test for co-integral relationship between money, income and the interest rate. The significance of co-integration is that two or more non-stationary variables may combine to form a stationary variable and the existence of a co-integral relationship between a group of economic variables can be tested. A rejection of co-integration in the money demand function implies that money, income and interest rate do not exhibit a stable relationship.

Their co-integration tests suggested that at least one monetary aggregate in most sample countries has a stable long-run relationship with income and the interest rate. For example, in the cases of Indonesia, Nepal, Malaysia and Singapore, the long-run relationship for the narrow money demand function remained stable during the sample period. However, the test results for Nepal were not conclusive. And, despite unsatisfactory statistical tests, they argued that there might have been a shift in the long-run narrow money demand function in Indonesia following financial liberalisation in 1983. Similarly, the introduction of financial reforms in the Philippines in the early 1980s and the demonetisation of currency in Myanmar in 1987 caused an intercept term shift in the long-run demand for the narrow money function.

Although the introduction of financial reforms in the late 1970s and early 1980s appears to have shifted the long run demand relationship for narrow money, a weak support for a co-integral relationship was found for broad money for South Korea and Sri Lanka. The estimated long-run relationship for broad money was also found stable for Indonesia and the Philippines. However, it was not so for Singapore, Nepal, and Thailand.

Tseng and Corker (1991) also estimated an error correction model of money demand for sample countries and tested for its stability across different sub-periods. The error correction model was found stable only for four countries – Indonesia, Malaysia (for both narrow and broad money), Korea and Sri Lanka (only for broad money). It implied that financial liberalisation in most of these countries caused instability in the short-run money demand function.

Hossain (1993, 1994) has applied the methods of co-integration and error correction for examining the stability of the money demand function in Bangladesh and Pakistan. His results indicate that the long-run money demand function in these countries has remained stable following financial reforms. He has also investigated money demand behaviour in Bangladesh and Indonesia with recent data and found that the money demand function remains stable in these countries (Hossain, 2006b, 2007, 2009).

Income velocity of money

In general, the income elasticity of the demand for narrow money is one, and that for broad money is greater than one. The finding that the long-run income elasticity of the demand for money is unity establishes the proportionate linkage between the money stock (M) and nominal income (Y). That is, $Y = kM$, where k is the income velocity of money, defined as $k = y/m^d(y)$. In this specification, the demand for real balances is an increasing function of real income (y). If the income elasticity of the demand for money is 1, the implied income velocity of money remains stable with an increase in income. A stable money demand function then suggests a steady income velocity of money. Otherwise, the income velocity of money may show a downward trend given that the income elasticity of the demand for money generally exceeds one in developing countries.

Interest Elasticity of Demand for Money and Effectiveness of Monetary Policy

One issue that has become prominent in the literature on money demand is the structural change in the interest elasticity of demand for money following financial deregulation and financial innovation. In fact, the idea that the proliferation of financial assets and near-monies may affect the relationship between money demand and the interest rate has been the cornerstone of the much debated theory of Gurley and Shaw (1955; 1960). The argument is that the proliferation of the interest-bearing money substitutes would increase the interest elasticity of demand for money and by implication, lower the effectiveness of monetary policy (Johnson, 1962). The Gurley–Shaw thesis has attracted criticism since it was proposed. Marty (1961) argues that the introduction of money substitutes, instead of raising the interest elasticity of the demand for money, would make the money demand schedule less elastic, at least for some range of interest rates. A body of literature has grown on the empirical validity of the Gurley–Shaw thesis. Yet empirical findings are inconclusive. Hossain (2007) shows that the deposit interest elasticity of demand for narrow money has become insignificant in Indonesia since the introduction of financial deregulation and reforms. The demand for narrow money has also become less sensitive to the return on foreign financial assets. This indicates that the money demand function and the velocity of money can be considered relatively stable. Financial liberalisation, instead of increasing, can actually lower the interest sensitivity of money demand. Recall that the velocity of money is a function of expected long-run average income and expected returns on money and other financial and real assets. Since in a competitive financial system, the expected returns on bonds and equity relative to money remain fairly constant with the rise in the interest rate, Friedman (1956) argued that the demand for money and hence velocity should practically be insensitive to the interest rate (Mishkin, 2007a).

Historically, the LM schedule in developing countries was more or less vertical, given that the interest elasticity of demand for money did not greatly differ from zero. The issue is whether financial reforms have caused the slope of the LM curve to change. *Ceteris paribus*, the LM curve probably became a bit flatter in a country like Indonesia during the early phase of financial reforms when the interest elasticity of demand for money became significant. However, the LM curve appears to have become steeper over the past decade or so with a decline in the interest elasticity of demand for money. For Indonesia, this reinforces the potency of monetary policy vis-à-vis fiscal policy for economic stabilisation (given both a floating exchange rate system and open capital accounts). In the debate on the appropriate role of monetary policy, the emerging consensus is that price stability, not economic stabilisation, should be the key (if not the sole) objective of monetary policy. The monetary policy regime (inflation targeting) in some developing countries in Asia has been based on the idea that the money demand function has become unstable. While this may have some truth, it is not necessarily valid for all countries. Any structural change in the money demand function could be a one-off affair. Therefore, the money growth rate can provide information on expected inflation with the potential to become an instrument of monetary policy, until the interest rates become the major channel of the transformation mechanism of monetary policy.

SUMMARY AND CONCLUSION

This chapter has reviewed issues in the transmission mechanisms of monetary policy in the context of developing countries. By reviewing the classical versus Keynesian transmission mechanisms, it is suggested that the classical transmission mechanisms of monetary policy are more appropriate for developing countries. It is also suggested that in a financially repressed economy where the interest rates are administratively fixed and credit rationing is the principal component of monetary policy, the availability of credit has direct and immediate impact on expenditure and output. The chapter then discussed the transmission mechanisms in financially repressed economies, providing a historical background of the evolution of monetary policy and its working mechanisms in developing countries. The money versus credit views provide an important framework in which to design appropriate framework for further analysis of the transmission mechanisms of monetary policy.

In view of the importance of money demand and its stability in the design and conduct of monetary policy, the second part of this chapter has provided a review of relevant issues. It has been found that the income elasticity of the demand for narrow money in most developing countries is around 1. In cases where it exceeds unity, this usually reflects a lower degree of monetisation of the economy and a lack of alternative financial assets. It also implies that the demand for money does not necessarily arise from transaction needs. In most developing countries with high inflation, the rate of inflation has been found to represent a better proxy for the opportunity cost of holding money than the interest rate.

In financially repressed economies, the absence of a well-developed capital market makes open market operations, which normally are an important tool of discretionary monetary policy, somewhat ineffective. In such economies, the transmission mechanism through which changes in the money supply work is close to the classical description rather than the Keynesian. This implies that changes in the money supply are likely to have a direct and immediate impact on aggregate spending and, hence, the price level. However, there is a considerable debate about the net effect of variations in the administered interest rate on aggregate demand in a financially repressed economy.

The long-run demand for money in developing countries has been found mostly stable, even after financial liberalisation. It is the short-run money demand function that does display some instability after financial liberalisation. It was especially so in countries where opening the capital account in the balance of payments increased currency substitution. The instability in the short-run money demand function implies that it would be difficult to use discretionary monetary policy reliably for short-run macroeconomic management. On the other hand, the existence of a stable long-run demand for money function, coupled with the fact that in the long run money supply affects the price level and not real output, suggests that monetary policy should have a long-run target of controlling inflation.

Chapter 9 is devoted to an overview of the conduct of monetary policy in selected countries of the Asia-Pacific.

9. Inflation and monetary policy in selected countries of the Asia-Pacific

One key theme of this book is that monetary policy has played a major role in macroeconomic stability in the Asia-Pacific region. Macroeconomic stability, in turn, has created an environment for rapid economic growth in an increasingly globalised economy. Sustained economic growth has been the main reason behind steady amelioration of poverty in developing Asia (Bhagwati, 2005; Dollar and Kraay, 2002; 2004; Tsai and Huang, 2007). Both monetary and fiscal policies have played a role in maintaining macroeconomic stability in developing Asia. Since the East Asian currency crises of the late 1990s monetary policy in particular has gained increased importance for price stability in this region.

Monetary policy independence and its contribution to price stability, however, depend on exchange rate arrangements and capital flows. Since the 1990s most Asian developing countries have made exchange rates flexible and started removing capital controls. Although some of these countries have given autonomy to central banks, monetary and fiscal policies have not yet been adequately institutionalised. Provided that financial reforms and global economic integration continue in this region, most central banks in developing Asia should steadily gain credibility. This would make monetary policy more effective in achieving price stability (IMF's *World Economic Outlook*, July 2008; Jongwanich and Park, 2008; Mohanty and Klau, 2001).

This chapter provides an overview of inflation and monetary policy in selected countries of the Asia-Pacific. (Some brief comments are also made on monetary policy in the UK.) This is an abridged version of a longer background draft. The discussion covers only key issues in monetary policy.[1] The discussion is organised in an alphabetical order, irrespective of the level of development of a particular country. The coverage of issues is also selective; it varies from country to country. The penultimate section provides a brief overview of the global financial crisis and its implication on monetary and fiscal policies in the Asia-Pacific.

AUSTRALIA

Chapter 3 introduced the RBA and reviewed its key responsibilities. The RBA remains responsible for formulating and implementing monetary policy, which has increasingly gained greater importance. The objectives of monetary policy in Australia, as laid out in the RBA Act of 1959, Section 10(2), have remained broad and unchanged. They are '(a) the stability of the currency of Australia; (b) the maintenance of full employment in Australia; and (c) the economic prosperity and welfare of the people of Australia' (RBA, *Monetary Policy*, http://www.rba.gov.au).

According to Macfarlane (1997a; 1997b; 1998), the post-Second World War monetary policy in Australia has evolved in phases: (1) the fixed exchange rate regime that started in the 1950s and lasted until the early 1970s; (2) monetary targeting between 1976 and 1985; (3) a transitional era since the abandonment of monetary targeting until 1992/93; and (4) inflation targeting since 1993. This section provides a brief overview of monetary policy in Australia under inflation targeting.

Inflation Targeting: 1993 to Present

In 1993 Australia adopted inflation targeting as a strategy of monetary policy. New Zealand was the first country to introduce inflation targeting in December 1989. It was formalised with the passage of the RBNZ Act. Canada adopted this strategy of monetary policy in February 1991. Unlike New Zealand and Canada, inflation targeting in Australia was introduced as a low-key affair. The idea of inflation targeting came to prominence when Mr Fraser, then Governor of the RBA, talked about holding inflation to a rate of 2–3 per cent per annum 'over the course of the cycle'. At that time, the RBA did not want to give any signal of abrupt policy regime shift. In the beginning there was no formal agreement between the government and the RBA on the inflation target. In August 1996 inflation targeting was recognised formally as the strategy of monetary policy (Edey, 2006).

Within the framework of inflation targeting, the RBA sets the CPI-inflation target of 2–3 per cent per annum. Although the headline inflation is the CPI-inflation, the RBA remains concerned about the underlying inflation over the course of business cycle. Subject to achieving the medium-term inflation objective, monetary policy encourages sustainable economic growth. The RBA's view is that inflation control preserves the value of the currency, while low inflation forms the sound basis for long-term economic growth.

The Reserve Bank Board makes decision on the direction of monetary policy. The Board's decision on any variation of the policy interest rate is communicated promptly to the public. The policy interest rate is the cash rate, which is the rate charged on overnight loans between financial intermediaries. While reviewing the monetary policy settings, the RBA considers a number of information indicators. They include the official interest rate, other interest rates for borrowers, the exchange rates, the unemployment levels and trends, economic productivity and capacity, trends in asset values, credit market conditions, and international monetary and economic developments. Although the RBA does not follow any monetary policy rule, such as the Taylor rule, in setting the cash rate, it makes clear that it would use monetary policy tools to vary the cash rate to the extent that the inflation target is achieved over the course of the business cycle (Reserve Bank of Australia, 2009a).

Figure 9.1 exhibits a flowchart of the monetary policy transmission mechanisms in Australia. The transmission mechanisms are based on the assumption of short-term price rigidities, such that changes in nominal interest rates bring changes in real interest rates. The transmission mechanisms of monetary policy in Australia are commonly understood. The movements in the cash rate pass through the whole structure of deposit and lending rates, within short lags. Changes in interest rates affect exchange rates and, through them, import prices. Exchange rate movements in particular affect inflationary expectations, which influence most economic decisions.

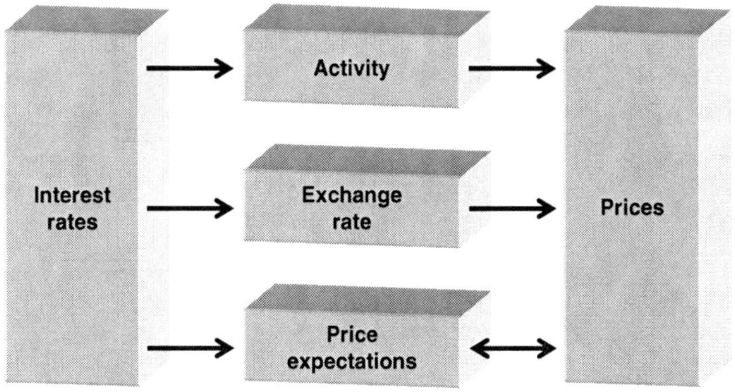

Source: Reserve Bank of Australia website, http://www.rba.gov.au.

Figure 9.1 Transmission mechanisms of monetary policy in Australia

BANGLADESH

The Bangladesh Bank Order No. 1972 is the basis of the conduct of monetary policy in Bangladesh. It provides the Bangladesh Bank with the responsibility of achieving both monetary stability (meaning price stability and exchange rate stability) and economic growth (Hossain, 2003). These objectives are considered complementary (Hossain, 2000).

From the early 1980s to the mid-1990s Bangladesh was under IMF and World Bank supported structural adjustment programmes. Under these programmes, monetary policy, in conjunction with fiscal and exchange rate policies, was aimed at achieving and sustaining macroeconomic stability. Macroeconomic stability indicators included low and steady inflation and a sustainable current account in the balance of payments. Inflation remained relatively high throughout the 1980s but came down sharply in the early 1990s. Inflation started to rise again in 1997. Given the pegged or managed floating exchange rate system throughout the 1980s and 1990s, inflation also remained unstable (Hossain, 2000; 2003).

The pegged exchange rate system, which was introduced in the late 1970s, was replaced by a managed floating exchange rate system on 31 May 2003. The managed floating exchange rate system has given the Bank some scope for conducting an independent monetary policy. Accordingly, in late 2005 the Bangladesh Bank formalised a monetary base targeting framework for the conduct of monetary policy to achieve 'price stability with the highest sustainable output growth' (Bangladesh Bank, 2005).

Under the monetary base-targeting framework, monetary policy is expected to be more credible and effective in maintaining price and exchange rate stability. The conduct of monetary policy has, however, become difficult because of frequent supply shocks and inadequate institutional checks and balances on fiscal policy. The authorities frequently intervene in foreign exchange markets to stabilise the exchange rates which anchor prices.

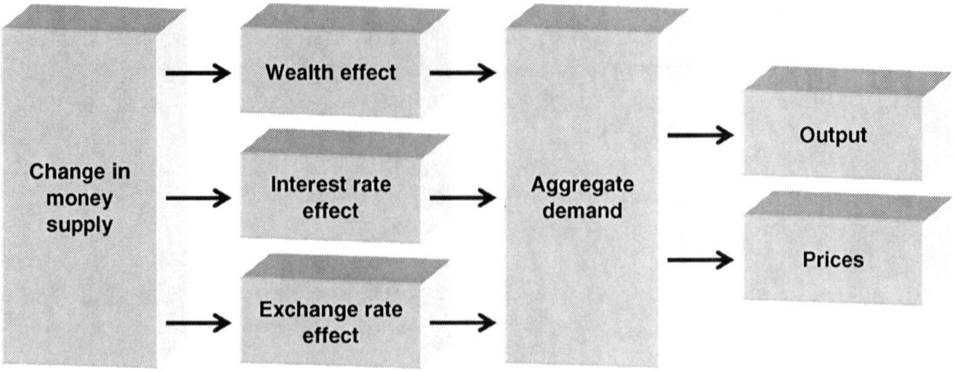

Source: Adapted from Mankiw (1998).

Figure 9.2 Transmission mechanisms of monetary policy in Bangladesh

Transmission Mechanisms of Monetary Policy

Figure 9.2 exhibits a flowchart of the monetary policy transmission mechanisms in Bangladesh. The monetary policy transmission mechanisms include the real balance, interest rate and exchange rate channels. It is assumed that in the short-run prices adjust slowly to money supply changes. The nominal monetary expansion can then have Pigou's wealth effect, Keynes's real interest rate effect and Mundell-Fleming's real exchange rate effect. For example, an increase in money supply represents an increase in real balances. It increases financial wealth, which raises consumption spending. An increase in real balances also lowers the real interest rate, which stimulates investment spending. A decrease in the real interest rate induces an outflow of capital, which depreciates the real exchange rate. This makes domestic goods cheaper relative to foreign goods, which increases net exports and in turn, output. In Bangladesh, the interest rate effect appears limited. Both the wealth and real exchange rate effects are, however, significant. The wealth effect in particular has become significant with financial reforms since the late 1980s (Bangladesh Bank, 2006a).

CHINA

The People's Bank of China (PBC) formulates and implements China's monetary policy. The goal of monetary policy is to maintain stability of the value of currency, which is expected to promote economic growth. The monetary policy department of the PBC remains responsible for research, design and implementation of monetary policy.

China's monetary policy has changed structurally since its extensive economic reforms from 1979. Prior to 1979 monetary policy was passive and the PBC had only limited control over the money stock (Cheng, 1988). Structural changes in China's monetary and financial system since 1979 have been part of the process of economic reforms. Changes in the economy as a whole have created increased demand for financial services and brought changes in the financial system. In particular, financial liberalisation has increased the demand for money at a rapid rate. Some analysts initially interpreted the rapid monetisation in China as a manifestation of 'forced savings' (Feltenstein and Farhadian, 1987; Portes and Santorum, 1987). There was concern that rapid monetisation, in the sense of forced saving, would lead to high inflation. The reality was different: monetisation has sustained over a long period without causing much inflation (Naughton, 1992).

The PBC was designated a central bank in 1983. Since then the PBC has been given more authority that allowed it to use various monetary policy instruments to conduct monetary policy. The role of monetary policy has also increased in recent years, given the spectacular growth of the Chinese economy in a globalised environment.

China had a dual exchange rate regime in the early 1990s. In 1994 the exchange rate regime was unified. Since 1995 the renminbi has maintained a fixed parity relative to the US dollar. Although China retains controls over capital flows, capital accounts have become more open over the past few years. The large size of net errors and omissions in the balance of payments captures this phenomenon. This indicates that the de facto increasing openness of capital accounts has made China's monetary policy less independent, which is limited under a pegged exchange rate regime. Given that the Chinese economy is large and has a significant non-tradable goods sector, there is strong argument that the Chinese authorities should make exchange rates flexible to retain some independence of monetary policy.

Conduct of Monetary Policy

The approach to monetary policy in China has been to use the monetary base as the operational target and the money supply as the intermediate target (Xie, 2004). More recently, the PBC has started using the growth rates of both money and bank lending as explicit intermediate targets. Although the relationship between monetary aggregates and economic activity has not remained stable over time, the growth targets of these two aggregates (because of their observability) have become a device for the PBC to signal its monetary policy intentions and its assessment of economic growth and inflationary prospects. Those primary instruments of monetary policy that the PBC uses include open market operations, the rediscount rate and the reserve requirements. These are complemented by instructive credit plans, credit policy and window guidance.

Given that the Chinese economy has become more market oriented and continues its rapid integration into the global economy, there is increasing need for independent monetary policy to maintain price stability. Provided that China's money demand function remains stable, monetary targeting could be used more effectively under a flexible exchange rate system. Some authors, however, suggest that a money growth targeting is not a good stand-alone nominal anchor for prices in China (Gang, 2008; Goodfriend and Prasad, 2006).

HONG KONG, CHINA

Hong Kong has generally followed a rule-based, non-interventionist exchange rate based monetary policy to maintain price stability. For example, one of its successful policy initiatives has been the well-known currency board system, which has provided price stability and promoted economic growth since the early 1980s.

From 1845 to 1935 Hong Kong's monetary system was under the international silver standard. An Exchange Fund was set up under the Exchange Fund Ordinance of 1935. All note-issuing banks were required to deposit their silver holdings to the Exchange Fund in exchange for the Certificates of Indebtedness which served as legal backing for banknotes. The Sterling Exchange Standard lasted until June 1972. In July 1972, following the UK's decision to float the pound sterling, the Hong Kong government pegged the Hong Kong dollar to the US dollar at the rate of US$ = HK$5.65 (Jao, 1992). In November 1974 the US dollar came under speculative attacks. The Hong Kong government could not maintain its parity with the US dollar, and decided to float the Hong Kong dollar. The Hong Kong dollar by this time was a strong currency. Its flotation in effect led to some revaluation. Although the first two years of the floating regime worked well for Hong Kong dollar, it came under pressure after mid-1977. In the absence of a formal central bank and/or for lack of appropriate monetary policy instruments, Hong Kong lost control over its money stock. This led to a sharp depreciation of the exchange rate of Hong Kong dollar and raised inflation to a double-digit level over the period 1979–83.

Depreciation of the Hong Kong dollar took a serious turn during 1982–83 when China announced its intention to regain sovereignty over Hong Kong from the British. Faced with an imminent collapse of the financial system, the Hong Kong government adopted a two-point currency stabilisation plan. The first measure was the reimposition of a foreign exchange constraint. This required the note-issuing banks to pay in US dollars to the Exchange Fund to obtain the Certificate of Indebtedness (CIs) as cover for their banknotes issued at the fixed rate of US$1 = HK$7.8. The second was the abolition of 10 per cent withholding tax on interest receipts from Hong Kong dollar denominated deposits with financial institutions. These two measures stabilised the Hong Kong dollar and laid the foundation of a US dollar based linked exchange rate system (Hsu, 1985; Jao, 1992; Moreno, 1988). Under the linked exchange rate system, the US dollar has since then become the external nominal anchor to prices in Hong Kong. The money stock has become endogenous, as it is linked to the balance-of-payment developments (Dodsworth and Mihaljek, 1997).

INDIA

The main objectives of monetary policy in India are price stability and the provision of adequate credits to productive sectors of the economy. These twin objectives have governed India's monetary policy since the 1950s. India maintains a monetarist view on inflation and keeps control over money growth by applying both direct and indirect policy instruments. Indian policy-makers are generally conservative and try to keep inflation low. The monetary policy framework in India was not, however, formalised until the 1980s. From the mid-1980s to 1997–98, India's monetary policy framework was characterised as 'monetary targeting with a feedback'. It was established in 1985 on the lines as recommended by the Chakravarty Committee. The Chakravarty Committee did not suggest a rigid monetary growth target rule. Its recommendation was that the targeted money growth rate should be modified on the basis of available information on expected output growth and a tolerable rate of inflation.

Since April 1998, India has adopted what is known as the multiple indicator approach to monetary policy. Concerns about stability of the money demand function caused the shift from monetary targeting with a feedback to the multiple indicator approach. India did not go for inflation targeting because inflation has generally been low. There was also no desire of politicians to go for inflation targeting. This would have required a major change in the framework of monetary policy, including a public declaration of the numerical value of inflation target, making price stability the sole objective of monetary policy, withdrawal of controls over wages and prices, and stopping interventions into foreign exchange markets. Further, given that the RBI does not enjoy full autonomy, there is concern that inflation targeting would lower RBI's credibility further if the targeted inflation is not achieved on a sustained basis. There is the additional fear that supply shocks and/or fiscal profligacy may also compromise the RBI's stance on inflation (Bhattacharya, 2005).

Under the multiple indicator approach, the RBI uses short-term interest rates for demand management. Money and capital markets in India remain underdeveloped and hence the transmission mechanisms of monetary policy are not well known. The RBI claims that the interest rate channel has become important in recent years for demand management over other channels, especially credit and exchange rate channels. The exchange rate channel in particular is not strong because the Indian economy is only modestly open (Reddy, 1999; 2002).

Over the past few years large inflows of foreign capital have created problems for monetary and exchange rate management in India. With the swell of capital inflows, tensions in the monetary policy framework have emerged between exchange rate stability, monetary independence and financial openness. Increased exchange rate flexibility, strengthened monetary operations and effective communication with markets are expected to strengthen monetary policy effectiveness in a more financially open environment.

INDONESIA

Indonesia's monetary policy since 1970 has evolved in line with changes in its exchange rate regimes. Table 9.1 summarises exchange rate regimes and monetary policy in Indonesia.

Exchange Rate Pegging

During the period 1970 to July 1997 Bank Indonesia conducted a limited form of monetary policy under exchange rate pegging. The aim of monetary policy actions was to keep the rupiah exchange rate stable at a certain level or within a fixed range. Monetary policy actions took the form of interventions into foreign exchange markets.

During 1970 to October 1978 the government pegged the Rupiah to the US dollar. To maintain exchange rate stability, Bank Indonesia intervened into foreign exchange markets. The rupiah was not a tradable asset and there was no large speculation on the currency. In addition, the government maintained restrictions over foreign borrowing, foreign

Table 9.1 Exchange rate regimes and monetary policy in Indonesia, 1970–2007

Legal basis	Period	Exchange rate system	Restrictions on capital flows	Strategy of monetary policy	Monetary policy independence
UU 13/1968	1970 to October 1978	Fixed	Semi-controlled (PP No. 64/1970)	Exchange rate targeting	None/limited
	November 1978 to September 1986	Managed floating-I	Semi-controlled	Exchange rate targeting	None/limited
	October 1986 to August 1992	Managed floating-II	Free (PP No. 1/1982)	Exchange rate targeting	None
	September 1992 to July 1997	Managed floating-III (crawling band)	Free	Exchange rate targeting	None
	August 1997 to December 1999	Free floating (since December 1999)	Free	Base money targeting	yes
UU 23/1999	January 2000 to June 2005	Free floating	Free (UU No. 24/1999)	Inflation targeting lite	yes
UU 3/2004	Since July 2005	Free floating	Free	Inflation targeting	yes

Sources: Author's adaptation based on Bank Indonesia (2005) and other Bank Indonesia publications on its website.

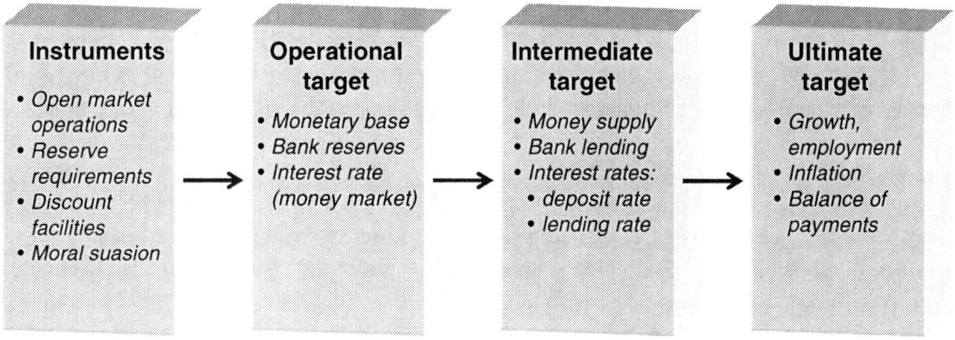

Source: Iljas (1998).

Figure 9.3 Pre-crisis general monetary policy framework in Indonesia

investment and portfolio investment. It gave Indonesia some autonomy in conducting monetary policy under the pegged exchange rate system (Sundararajan and Molho, 1988).

During November 1978 to July 1997 Indonesia allowed the exchange rate to float against a basket of currencies, representing Indonesia's major trading partners and/or competitors. This exchange rate management system was in place over the period 1978–86. During this period the nominal exchange rates remained unchanged, except for occasional adjustments. As capital flows were then small in an underdeveloped financial system, Bank Indonesia did not have difficulties in maintaining stability of the exchange rate as it had desired.

During 1987–97 exchange rate management was designed to create flexibility in the system. It was in response to increasing openness of the Indonesian economy. Large-scale inflows of foreign capital then started to put pressure on the exchange rate. It was therefore realised that excessive interventions into foreign exchange markets in response to capital flows and other capital market developments would create exchange rate misalignments and hence adversely affect the trade balance. From July 1997 the rupiah remained constantly around the lower limit of the intervention band. In mid-July 1997 the rupiah came under pressure, driving it down against the US dollar. The pressure on the rupiah intensified following speculative attacks on Thai baht, which then spread quickly to other countries in the region.

Figure 9.3 shows the pre-crisis framework of monetary policy in Indonesia. Bank Indonesia used a number of instruments, including open market operations, to bring changes in the monetary base and the short-term interest rates. Changes in monetary aggregates and bank credits influenced aggregate demand and aggregate supply conditions, which brought some changes in output, inflation and the balance of payments.

Currency Crisis and the Base Money Targeting

There is no general agreement on factors that triggered the currency crisis in Indonesia. Although Indonesia did not peg the rupiah exchange rate to the US dollar, it maintained, through managed floating, a quasi-fixed exchange rate with the dollar. As a result, the borrowers ignored the exchange rate risk and left their foreign loans unhedged (Hill, 1999). In 1996 the inflation differentials between Southeast Asian countries (including Indonesia) and the USA widened, requiring a depreciation of the rupiah to maintain export competitiveness. This situation was exacerbated when the Japanese yen began to depreciate vis-à-vis the US dollar, which appreciated the real effective exchange rate of the rupiah (Komine, 1998).

An environment was thus created for speculative attacks on the rupiah. The Indonesian authorities ignored other early warning signals because they did not have adequate information on capital inflows, especially the inflows of short-term capital. In the absence of well-regulated capital markets, it was also difficult to keep track of capital movements under open capital accounts. Still, as Bank Indonesia imposed some restrictions on external borrowings, some well-connected conglomerates were able to hide their actual borrowings (Radelet, 1995). Above all, the monetary authorities were complacent because the euphoric condition in the booming economy literally brought prosperity for many local investors.

The 'forced flotation' of the exchange rate of rupiah in July 1997 and the enactment of the Central Banking Law in May 1999 gave Bank Indonesia autonomy in formulating and implementing monetary policy. Unlike the pre-crisis Law, which prescribed the multiple objectives of monetary policy, the 1999 Law stated that the sole objective of monetary policy should be to pursue and maintain price and exchange rate stability, implying 'price stability in an operational sense' (Alamsyah et al., 2001). The Law did not, however, specify any particular monetary policy strategy that Bank Indonesia should introduce. As the exchange rate targeting was untenable and discarded, the plausible rule-based alternative was monetary or inflation targeting.

During 1997–2003 Indonesia was under an IMF stabilisation programme. Bank Indonesia then conducted monetary policy through monetary base targeting. Within this framework, Bank Indonesia set an inflation target and estimated the base money growth rate that was appropriate for this target. This approach was based on the *Quantity Theory of Money*. Apparently, the Quantity Theory was used without examining the underlying monetary relationships, such as the causal relationship between money supply growth and inflation. The existence of a stable money demand function, especially after the crisis, was assumed but not examined.

Strict Inflation Targeting

Despite a 'soft-form' of monetary targeting, inflation was brought to a single digit level during 2000–2003. Bank Indonesia admits that the practice of monetary policy under a 'soft monetary targeting' until 2004 was intended to be pragmatic. It adopted an eclectic approach, in which it used several nominal anchors to keep inflation under control. Given that Bank Indonesia was unable to gain credibility under an eclectic approach to monetary policy, it switched to full-fledged inflation targeting in July 2005 to anchor inflationary expectations.

Bank Indonesia's rationale for the adoption of full-fledged inflation targeting is as follows. First, it would strengthen Bank Indonesia's commitment to keep inflation low and steady. Second, through its commitment to control inflation, Bank Indonesia would gain credibility as an inflation-fighter. Third, inflation targeting would eliminate currency mismatches, which are a cause of exchange rate crisis in developing countries, including Indonesia. Fourth, inflation targeting would allow Bank Indonesia to formulate a forward-looking monetary policy, which is crucial as monetary policy actions have a long and variable effect on inflation. Finally, inflation targeting would improve macroeconomic performance.

The financial crisis of 1997 brought a significant change in the Indonesian economy, which is reflected in monetary policy transmission mechanisms. Before the crisis the Indonesian economy was experiencing an economic boom because of large-scale foreign capital inflows. Empirical findings showed that the interest rates did not affect bank lending prior to the crisis. The exchange rate channel was also not as relevant before the crisis because the economy had operated under a managed floating system. Since the crisis, exchange rates have become an important channel of monetary policy transmission (Agung, 1998; Goeltom, 2008).

JAPAN

Monetary policy in Japan has changed significantly since the mid-1970s. Along with the relaxation of a formal exchange rate objective, the conduct of monetary policy has been affected by a gradual liberalisation of the Japanese financial system. It included decontrol of interest rates, the development of financial instruments and financial markets, and the relaxation of constraints on asset and liability choices of investors, borrowers and financial institutions.

Economists generally attributed the stability of the Japanese economy and low inflation in Japan since the mid-1970s to the adoption by the Bank of Japan of a monetarist policy framework that saw the introduction of a stable long-run money growth to control inflation (Cargill and Hutchison, 1988; Friedman, 1983b). Although the BOJ remained committed to keep inflation low through monetary targeting, financial innovations and deregulation in Japan reduced the usefulness of the monetary aggregate (M2 + CDs) as an indicator of monetary policy. The BOJ then started to use monetary policy to stabilise the exchange rate. The Japanese economy experienced asset bubbles during the late 1980s, caused by excessive money growth. To contain speculation on land and stock prices, the BOJ introduced a tighter monetary policy in 1989 when it sharply lowered the money growth rate. This led to a sharp decline in land and stock prices, with the bubble economy collapsing. The economy experienced a decade long deflation that lasted until 2002 (Ito, 1989; 2004; 2006).

In 1998 the BOJ enacted a new Law. The 1998 Law has given the BOJ the mandate of price stability (Article 2). Unlike most other central banks, the BOJ Law does not mention employment as an objective of monetary policy. Further, the BOJ has been given legal institutional independence in the sense that the governor and monetary policy board members cannot be dismissed by the government, unless they are physically or mentally incapacitated. Their terms of appointment are five years and the government officials can attend the Board meetings only as non-voting members (Cargill et al., 1997; 2001).

For the conduct of monetary policy, the BOJ does not, however, have a nominal anchor of price expectations. The BOJ defines price stability as a rate of inflation that does not distort economic decision-making. It therefore does not have a numerical target to guide monetary policy. The BOJ uses a short-term interest rate for operational purposes.

Since March 2001, the BOJ targeted a specific level of the uncollateralised overnight call rate with open market operations. The aim was to increase the provision of funds when the overnight rate was above the target and to decrease the provision of funds when the overnight call rate was below the target. The funds, whose provision the bank modified in its day-to-day open market operations, were current account balances that private financial institutions held with the BOJ. Under this quantitative easing policy, the BOJ aimed at raising CPI-inflation at a positive level. However, as there was growing concern over potentially excessive equipment investment by corporations, the BOJ ended its formal policy of quantitative easing in March 2006 and its zero interest rate policy in July 2006.

Since the termination of quantitative easing in 2006, the BOJ has not set a monetary or inflation target to guide monetary policy. There is a suggestion that Japan should adopt inflation targeting as a strategy of monetary policy (Speigel, 2000). The BOJ, however, remains sceptical of formal inflation targeting as a solution to deflation. It doubts its ability to influence inflationary expectations and fears that its credibility would suffer enormously if an inflation target is set but not achieved.

SOUTH KOREA

South Korea remained under the fixed/pegged exchange rate system from the 1950s until the financial crisis of the late 1990s. It maintained strict capital controls and hence was able to conduct autonomous monetary policy. Since the 1960s, monetary policy in South Korea was accommodating with respect to the implementation of developmental strategies, such as the export-led growth strategy, the grain-support programme and the promotion of heavy and chemical industries (Amsden, 1989; Cho, 1989). After the second oil price shock in 1979, South Korea switched its monetary policy objective to price stability. The BOK was able to control monetary growth during the first half of the 1980s by using indirect monetary policy instruments. The BOK's control over the money supply, however, weakened with the rapid growth of the external sector and the liberalisation of the economy. During the later half the 1980s, the BOK introduced various direct measures such as the reduction of preferential discounting for export industries, raising reserve requirements and rediscount rates, the reintroduction of marginal reserve requirements, and direct credit controls to supplement open market operations (Amsden and Euh, 1993; Bank of Korea, 2000).

Two-Pillar System of Monetary Policy

South Korea suffered during the 1997–98 financial crises, which led to a flotation of the exchange rate. The financial crises also required South Korea to adopt the IMF rescue financing with a package of policy conditionality (Dooley et al., 2001). For monetary policy, the BOK adopted a broad measure of money (M3) as a reference value, together with a corresponding supply limit for the monetary base. At the same time, the BOK Law was revised in late 1997. This led to the adoption of inflation targeting as the main strategy of monetary policy. The BOK announced a system of monetary policy operations in which a target rate of inflation was made public and the growth rate of M3 was used as the operational target. It was similar to the two-pillar system of monetary policy that the European Central Bank has introduced. The BOK maintained the two-pillar system by setting the target growth rate of M3 because it was concerned about the possible confusion in financial markets that any sudden drop of M3 might cause. During 2001–03 the M3 growth rate target was not set but only monitored. In 2003 the monitoring of the M3 growth rate was discontinued, which ended the transition from the two-pillar to a full-fledged inflation targeting system.

Design of Inflation Targeting Framework

During 1998–99 the BOK used CPI-inflation as the benchmark indicator because it was familiar to the public. The IMF policy conditionality also required the adoption of CPI-inflation as a monetary policy goal. Since 2000 a measure of core CPI-inflation has been chosen as the benchmark inflation indicator. This definition of CPI excludes the prices of petroleum and agricultural products, with the exception of cereals.

The BOK determines inflation target annually in consideration of expected changes in domestic and international economic and financial conditions. The target range of plus or minus 1 per cent is allowed for to take into account economic uncertainties. The call market rate of interest is used as the operational instrument. In setting the call rate target every month, the Monetary Policy Committee follows the 'look-at-everything' approach. The key variables it monitors include production, prices, real estate prices, and output-gap.

South Korea's inflation targeting strategy is considered flexible, in the sense that in addition to price stability, other objectives of monetary policy are considered. Such objectives include economic growth, balance of payments, and financial market stability. This makes inflation targeting eclectic, not focused exclusively on inflation. Nevertheless, monetary policy operations have become transparent since the adoption of inflation targeting (Kim and Park, 2006).

MALAYSIA

The Bank Negara Malaysia has two main objectives for monetary policy: low inflation and a stable exchange rate. It stresses the contributions of low inflation and stable exchange rates to economic growth and development. Since the financial crisis of the late 1990s the BNM has added financial stability as another goal of monetary policy. Unlike other central banks, the BNM considers its multiple goals of monetary policy as a natural outcome for a central bank in a developing country. It takes the view that while in developed countries central banks may focus exclusively on wealth preservation by maintaining price stability, for developing countries wealth creation should be one of the main policy goals. The BNM, therefore, emphasises price stability as the major objective of monetary policy, while supporting the finance of productive investment to raise the country's productive capacity. This explains why monetary policy in Malaysia has been used to promote economic growth in an environment of price stability.

Until the mid-1990s monetary targeting was the monetary policy strategy in Malaysia. It was, however, an internal strategy which was not formally announced to the public. Over the period 1982–92 the BNM influenced the day-to-day volume of liquidity in the money market, which was consistent with the monetary growth target. The idea was to ensure that money supply met the demand, bringing the money supply in line with the BNM's monetary policy objective of price stability. In the early 1990s the money demand relationship became unstable because of financial deregulation; hence the relationship between money growth and inflation broke down. Facing large capital inflows during 1992–93, and the reversal of capital in the following year, also made it difficult for the BNM to maintain control over the monetary aggregate as an intermediate target (Hossain and Chowdhury, 1996).

The BNM shifted its focus from monetary targeting to interest rate targeting in the mid-1990s. However, it continued monitoring monetary aggregates, credit growth and other economic and monetary indicators, including asset prices, consumption and investment. Such a change in the monetary policy strategy was due to a number of factors. First, as part of financial sector deregulation, interest rates were liberalised in 1978, allowing market forces to determine the interest rate. Second, financial deregulation and liberalisation measures enhanced the role of interest rates in the monetary policy transmission mechanisms. Third, there was a shift in the investment financing pattern since the mid-1980s from interest-inelastic markets (that is, government securities markets) to interest-sensitive markets (that is, bank credits and capital markets). Fourth, the BNM adopted the policy of maintaining a positive real interest rate on bank deposits. Finally, the BNM holds the view that interest rate stability is important for financial development and stability, which, in turn, is necessary for the effective transmission mechanisms of monetary policy. The role of financial stability has become apparent since the rapid integration of Malaysia's financial markets with the global money and capital markets in the early 1990s. For all these reasons, the interest-rate oriented monetary policy framework was considered suitable for Malaysia. Malaysia remains a low inflationary economy and hence had minimal need for inflation targeting.

NEW ZEALAND

New Zealand operated under a fixed/pegged exchange rate arrangement and maintained stringent capital controls until the mid-1980s. This provided New Zealand some monetary policy autonomy, although its role was to support fiscal policy. In fact, decisions on monetary policy were the responsibility of New Zealand Treasury, which was headed by the Minister of Finance. Therefore the Reserve Bank of New Zealand did not have much control over the conduct of monetary policy. Further, similar to Australia's experience, the New Zealand government argued that high inflation in this country was due to wage push, coming from trade union militancy. The government maintained such cost-push view on inflation throughout the 1970s and early 1980s. To control inflation, the government introduced direct controls on wages and prices, which were accompanied by rapid monetary expansion.

During 1984–85 New Zealand introduced measures for financial deregulation. They included the introduction of indirect methods to replace the direct controls of money and credit aggregates. The role of monetary policy was changed in favour of price stability. The thinking on monetary policy was, in fact, influenced by the monetarist approach, which reflected international thinking about monetary policy. The monetarist approach highlighted the control of a monetary aggregate for achieving low inflation.

Since the passage of the RBNZ Act in 1989, New Zealand has become the first country to formally embark upon inflation targeting. This Act confers on the RBNZ autonomy in the conduct of monetary policy and recognises that the best contribution monetary policy can make is to keep inflation low and stable. For institutionalisation of monetary policy, the government and the governor have entered into a policy target agreement. The agreement is specified in the form of a CPI-inflation target within the range of 1–3 per cent on average over the medium term. The governor of RBNZ has no obligation to consult with the Minister of Finance, the Treasury or with the Board of the RBNZ for implementation of monetary policy.

Under inflation targeting, transparency has emerged as the key feature of monetary policy strategy in New Zealand. For ensuring a high degree of transparency in an institutional sense, the RBNZ Act requires that the Bank publish a monetary policy statement at least every six months. In addition, there is a review by a select Committee of the Parliament, both explicit, of the Bank's Monetary Policy Statements and implicitly the Bank's handling of monetary policy. The Act also establishes the governor's sole accountability for decisions on the implementation of monetary policy. Interestingly, the assignment of authority and responsibility to an individual rather than a Committee is uncommon amongst inflation targeting central banks. In practice, the governor of the RBNZ has an advisory committee which provides advice to the governor prior to his/her making monetary policy decisions.

Transmission Mechanisms of Monetary Policy

Figure 9.4 shows a flow chart of monetary policy transmission mechanisms in New Zealand. For implementation of monetary policy, the RBNZ controls the cost of liquidity by setting the official cash rate. The official cash rate affects the short-term interest rates as well as the exchange rate. Changes in real interest rates affect the inter-temporal prices of borrowing and spending, while changes in real exchange rates affect the prices of foreign goods in terms of domestic goods. Changes in real interest rates and real exchange rates affect aggregate demand within a lag of about one year. Changes in aggregate demand are expected to affect inflation with a further lag.

PAKISTAN

The main objective of the government's economic policies in Pakistan during the 1950s and 1960s was to promote economic growth without inflation on the understanding that price stability is essential for orderly economic growth. Under a fixed exchange rate arrangement with capital controls, monetary policy had some autonomy. It was, however, conducted to support fiscal policy. Pakistan suffered from high inflation during the 1970s and 1980s (Choudhri and Khan, 2002). Various financial reforms were introduced under IMF-supported structural adjustment programmes. As part of such programmes,

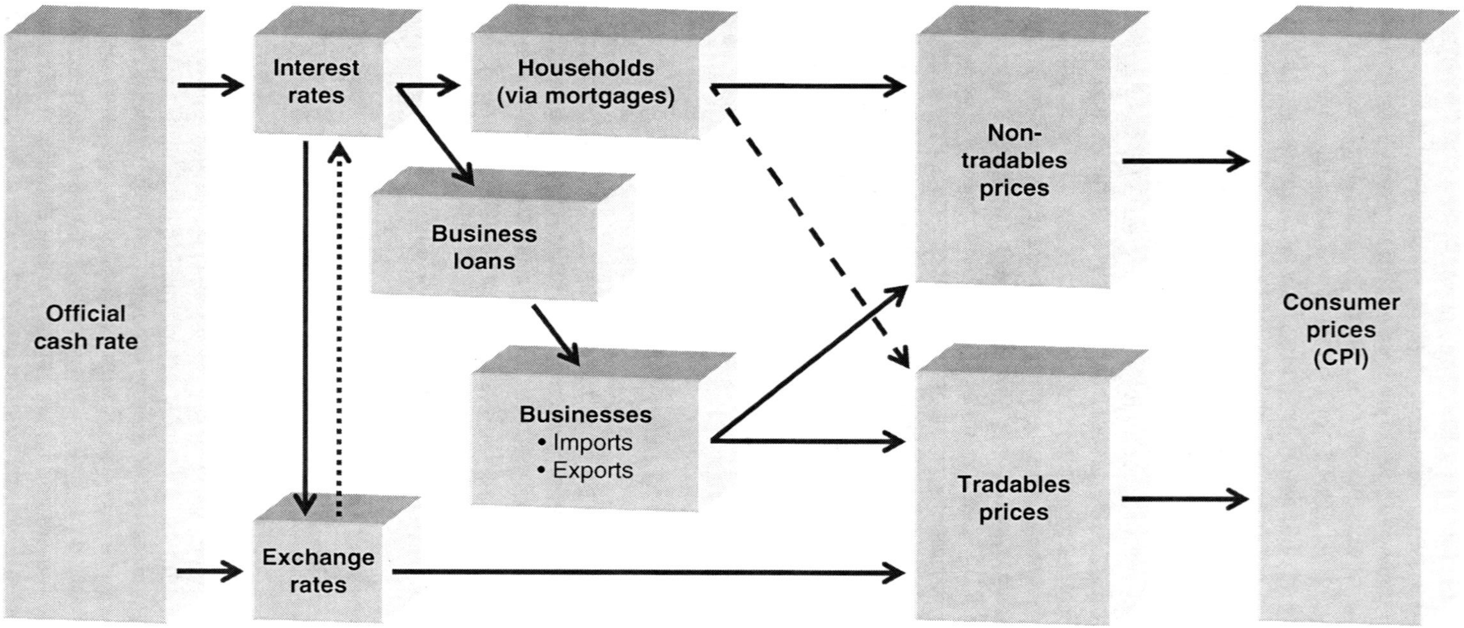

Source: Adapted from Bollard and Karagedikli (2006).

Figure 9.4 Transmission mechanisms of monetary policy in New Zealand financial sector reforms were introduced that raised the importance of monetary policy in macroeconomic stability in general, and price stability in particular. Since the late 1980s Pakistan has adopted a flexible exchange rate management system that aims at avoiding an appreciation of the real effective exchange rate. There is, however, no formal nominal monetary anchor to prices, except that the State Bank of Pakistan uses a broad monetary target for operational purposes or as a guide.

Transmission Mechanisms of Monetary Policy

Figure 9.5 depicts the transmission mechanism of monetary policy in Pakistan. Agha et al. (2005) have found that in addition to the traditional interest rate and bank lending channels, there is an active price channel in Pakistan. The exchange rate channel is less significant by comparison. Private sector credit is considered a superior intermediary aggregate in terms of monetary policy implementation framework. In Pakistan, bank lending remains prominent because of the absence of non-bank sources of finance. The Bank's role has been enhanced in recent years because of financial reforms, market-based credit allocation and crowding-in of private sector credit given diminishing fiscal dominance. Other channels, especially the interest and exchange rate channels, are yet to get prominence. For improvement of monetary policy, the IMF has, therefore, suggested for greater flexibility in interest and exchange rates (IMF, various years).

THE PHILIPPINES

From having a lacklustre performance over the 1980s and mid 1990s, the Philippines has emerged as a dynamic market economy over the past two decades. One feature underlying the recent transformation in the Philippines has been the development of monetary policy institutions and decision-making. In the early 1980s monetary policy in the Philippines was subservient to fiscal policy and lacked coherent focus. The result was the loss of monetary control, spiralling inflation and a balance of payments crisis.

The improvement in monetary policy implementation started after the establishment of a new central bank, the Bangko Sentral ng Pilipinas, in 1993. The old central bank of the Phillipines became insolvent, largely because of its bailing out of domestic banks that ran into financial difficulties. The Bangko Sentral ng Pilipinas was established with a fresh balance sheet. It was recapitalised by the government. Under the revised Central Bank Act of 1993 (Republic Act No. 7653) the mandate of the BSP is to pursue price stability as the key objective of monetary policy. The BSP is the sole formulator and executor of monetary policy. The revised Act has also imposed limits on the amount and maturity of BSP credits to the government. The aim is to diminish fiscal dominance over monetary policy.

During 1993–2002 the BSP conducted monetary policy within the IMF financial programming framework. In fact the IMF programming has been used since 1984 when the then Central Bank of the Philippines adopted a floating exchange rate system. The monetary policy framework revolved around the monetary base programming. The Philippines switched to inflation targeting in 2002 under a flexible exchange rate system; the reason was that the income velocity of money became unstable. Since then the Philippines has liberalised its capital accounts.

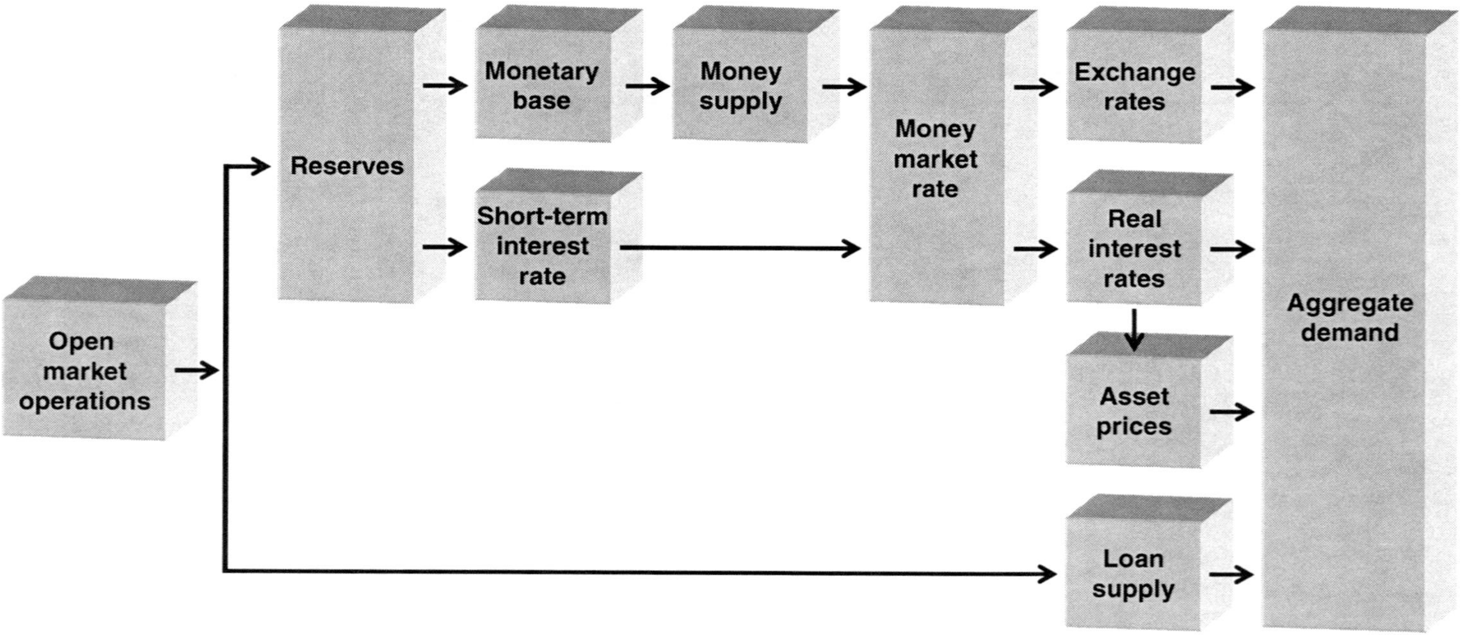

Source: Adapted from Agha et al. (2005).

Figure 9.5 Transmission mechanisms of monetary policy in Pakistan

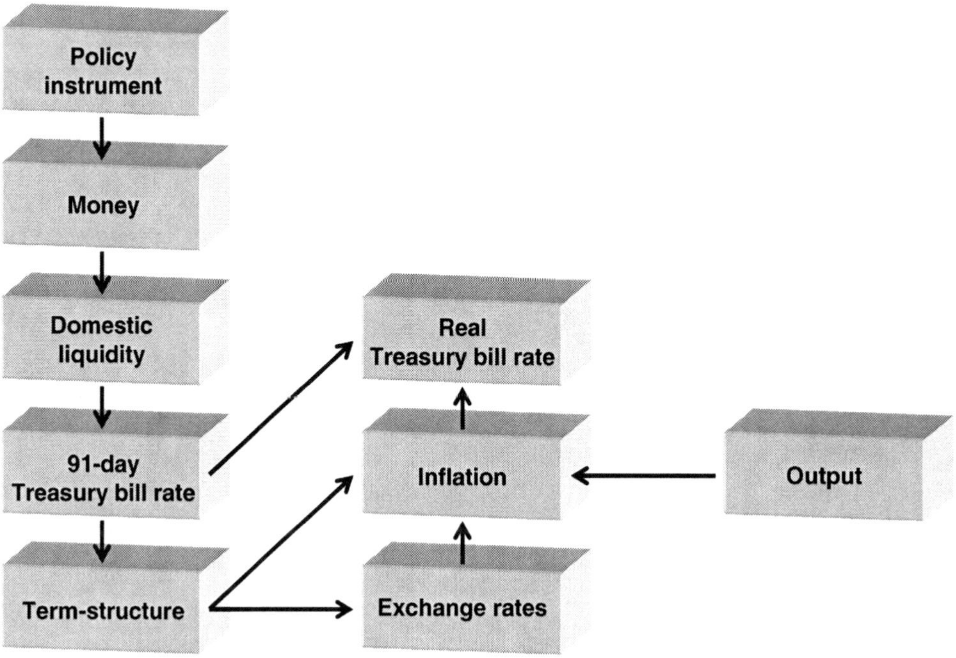

Source: Adapted from Guinigundo (2008: 413).

Figure 9.6 Transmission mechanisms of monetary policy in the Philippines

Transmission Mechanisms of Monetary Policy

Figure 9.6 shows a flow chart of the monetary policy transmission mechanisms in the Philippines. The policy instrument at the disposal of the BSP is the change in the reserve money, which then determines the level of domestic liquidity. Domestic liquidity affects interest rates, in turn influencing the exchange rate and inflation. Domestic liquidity in particular affects the 91-day Treasury bill rate, which in turn alters the term structure of the interest rates. Through the interest rate parity condition, changes in the 91-day Treasury bill rate bring changes in the exchange rate. The exchange rate in turn affects domestic prices. Inflation has a feedback on the exchange rate through the purchasing power parity relationship.

SINGAPORE

Since attaining independence in 1965, Singapore has maintained rapid growth, low inflation and a healthy balance of payments. Singapore's sustained rapid economic growth has been attributed to macroeconomic stability, openness to trade and capital flows, and flexible labour markets. Singapore is therefore seen as an economic success story.

When the Monetary Authority of Singapore was first established in 1971, Singapore operated under a currency board system. The collapse of the Bretton Woods exchange rate arrangement in the early 1970s, coupled with the resulting exchange rate volatilities of major currencies, required Singapore to develop an exchange rate-cum-monetary policy framework (Koh, 1992; Moreno, 1988). Since 1981 Singapore has adopted an exchange rate centred monetary policy framework. As the Singapore economy remains highly open and is exposed to recurrent external shocks, the primary role of monetary policy has been to stabilise inflation and output, caused by external shocks. Singapore, being a small, open economy, does not have the ability to conduct an independent monetary policy, as it intends to maintain exchange rate stability and allow for free capital mobility. The MAS emphasises the price stability objective of exchange rate policy, which is considered the basis of sustained economic growth (Parrado, 2004).

The exchange rate is considered the most effective instrument of monetary policy for price stability. The underlying theory is that the Purchasing Power Parity proposition links domestic prices with external prices via the nominal exchange rate. To ensure price stability, Singapore keeps its dollar strong vis-à-vis its trading partners. Another consideration behind strong Singapore dollar has been to maintain the people's confidence in domestic currency. Liberalised capital flows and a stable currency are considered the key requirements for Singapore's role as an international financial centre.

As a working principle, the MAS intervenes into foreign exchange markets to bring an appreciation or depreciation of the trade-weighted exchange rate of Singapore dollar, depending on whether inflation pressure is strong or weak. Such foreign exchange interventions are supplemented by money market operations to ensure that there is an appropriate level of liquidity in the banking system. The money market tools used for this purpose include foreign exchange swaps, direct lending or borrowing from banks, and transactions involving government securities.

Transmission Mechanisms of Monetary Policy

Figure 9.7 shows a flow chart of the transmission mechanisms of monetary policy in Singapore. Interventions into foreign exchange markets change the trade-weighted nominal exchange rate, which affects prices in both the goods and assets markets. Exchange rate movements directly impact import prices. Exchange rate movements also affect the prices of domestic products that compete with imports or use imported inputs. Depending on the degree of pass-through, the exchange rate movements, therefore, affect consumer prices. The second channel of the impact of exchange rate movements on domestic prices is through their effects on aggregate demand or net trade flows that affect domestic economic activity. The MAS accepts the view that monetary policy has only a short-term effect on the economy and cannot be used for long-term economic growth (MAS, 1999).

SRI LANKA

The Central Bank of Sri Lanka (CBSL) has the responsibility for the design and conduct of monetary policy to attain price stability. Monetary policy operates primarily by influencing the cost and availability of credits. Until June 2001 Sri Lanka operated under a

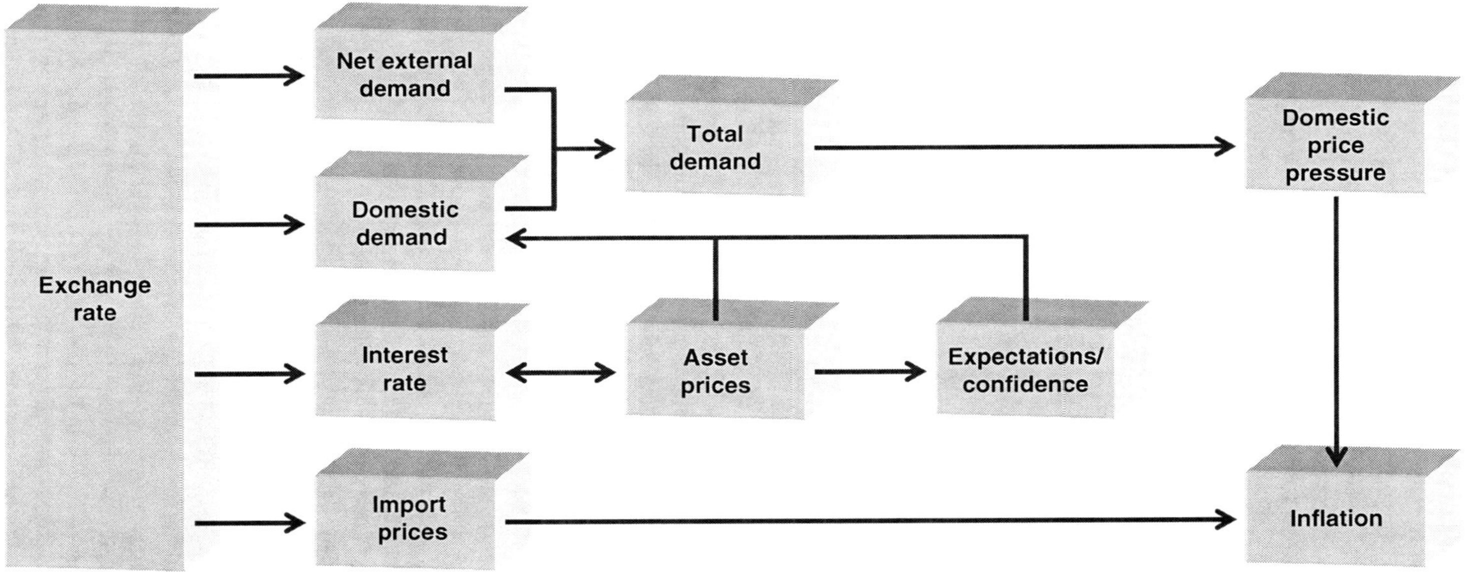

Source: Adapted from Chow (2007: 449).

Figure 9.7 Transmission mechanisms of monetary policy in Singapore fixed/pegged exchange rate system. Since then it has adopted a floating exchange rate system, where the exchange rate system is determined by market forces, reflecting macroeconomic fundamentals. Central bank interventions into foreign exchange markets are conducted to prevent excessive volatility in exchange rates and to maintain a comfortable level of foreign exchange reserves.

The main monetary policy tool that the CBSL uses is the overnight interest rates, called the repurchase (repo) rate (that is, the borrowing rate) and the reverse repurchase rate (the lending rate). Changes in the repo and reverse repo rates have immediate impacts on the interest rates in the inter-bank call money markets. Changes in the call money-market rates lead within a very short period to changes in other short-term rates, such as the yields on Treasury bills and the lending rates of commercial banks to their prime customers. Changes of these interest rates affect the lending rates of commercial banks with a time lag. Changes in market interest rates affect aggregate demand and hence prices and output.

TAIWAN

In accordance with the Central Bank Act, the Central Bank of China (CBC) has the responsibility of maintaining price and exchange rate stability to promote economic growth. To achieve these objectives, the CBC uses monetary targeting as the basic framework of monetary policy. Since 1992, the broad monetary aggregate (M2) has been used as the intermediate target of monetary policy. At the end of each year, the CBC announces the target zone of the M2 growth rate for the next year. The target zone is fixed on the basis of expected economic growth, inflation and interest rates. Using a zone, rather than a fixed number for the M2 growth rate, the CBC allows flexibility in interest and exchange rates. However, note that although Taiwan has moved from the fixed exchange rate system to a floating exchange rate system in 1978, the CBC intervenes into foreign exchange markets to maintain exchange rate stability. Taiwan's exchange rate system is, therefore, considered a de facto managed floating exchange rate system.

For operational purposes, the CBC uses reserve money as the operating target. It uses a variety of instruments to achieve the desired level of reserve money. These include required reserves, discount rates, open market operations, re-deposits from financial institutions, selective credit management, and moral suasion. Re-deposits from financial institutions are indeed an effective instrument for managing reserve money. The CBC is entitled to receive or return re-deposits from the postal savings system, three specialised agricultural banks, and other approved banks. To increase (decrease) reserve money, the CBC can simply return (receive) re-deposits to (from) financial institutions (Yang and Shea, 2005). The CBC has, however, only limited autonomy in conducting monetary policy. Monetary control is, in fact, the joint responsibility of the government and the CBC.

Taiwan has maintained large trade surpluses since the 1980s. It has, therefore, pursued an active monetary policy to sterilise the effects of large balance-of-payments surpluses on the money supply and to counteract monetary disruptions generated domestically (Fry, 1998). Taiwan was able to control the money supply, despite operating under a pegged exchange rate system, through control over capital flows. At times the rapid build-up of foreign reserves has, however, weakened the CBC's control over monetary aggregates. To cope with such situations, Taiwan revalued its exchange rates and raised reserve requirements. In recent years the CBC has intervened in foreign exchange markets to stabilise the exchange rate, as pressure built up on the exchange rate to appreciate from large trade surpluses. It has accumulated large foreign reserves. To maintain control over the growth of reserve money (and hence the growth of M2), the CBC has sterilised foreign market interventions through issuing certificates of deposits and receiving re-deposits from financial institutions.

THAILAND

Monetary and exchange rate policy has played a major role in Thailand's macroeconomic management since the early 1950s. Since then Thailand revealed conservatism in its conduct of monetary policy. This is reflected in low rates of money supply growth, even when the economy was growing rapidly that increased the demand for money because of rapid monetisation of an agricultural economy. Thailand operated under a fixed/pegged exchange rate system from the early 1950s until 1997. The monetary authorities took this exchange rate arrangement seriously. It was only in 2 July 1997 that the authorities abandoned the pegged exchange rate system when the baht came under unexpected speculative attacks. The outcome was a sharp depreciation of both the nominal and real effective exchange rate of the baht. It was the beginning of the Asian currency crisis that lasted until the early 2000.

The Thai economy has since recovered and the authorities have introduced a wide range of financial reforms and deregulatory measures. With the flotation of the baht, Thailand gained monetary policy independence and started conducting monetary policy to maintain price stability through monetary targeting. This was part of the IMF financial programme and it continued until 1999. Since 2000 the authorities have formalised the conduct of monetary policy by adopting inflation targeting. In hindsight, this was a correct decision because Thailand did not lose price stability during the crisis. Later, it introduced institutional reforms to meet the requirements of inflation targeting.

Monetary Policy Transmission Mechanisms in Thailand

Figure 9.8 shows the flow chart of monetary policy transmission mechanisms in Thailand. The BOT uses a very short-term interest rate as a policy instrument. The short-term policy interest rate affects the medium- and long-term interest rates, asset prices and exchange rates. Changes in these prices affect both domestic and external demand for domestic goods and services. Exchange rate movements directly affect the prices of tradable goods, while changes in aggregate demand, through interest and exchange rates, affect the inflationary pressure and hence economic activity.

THE UK

As discussed in Chapter 4, there has been a significant change in the way monetary policy is conducted in the UK. The Bank of England remains a leader in devising

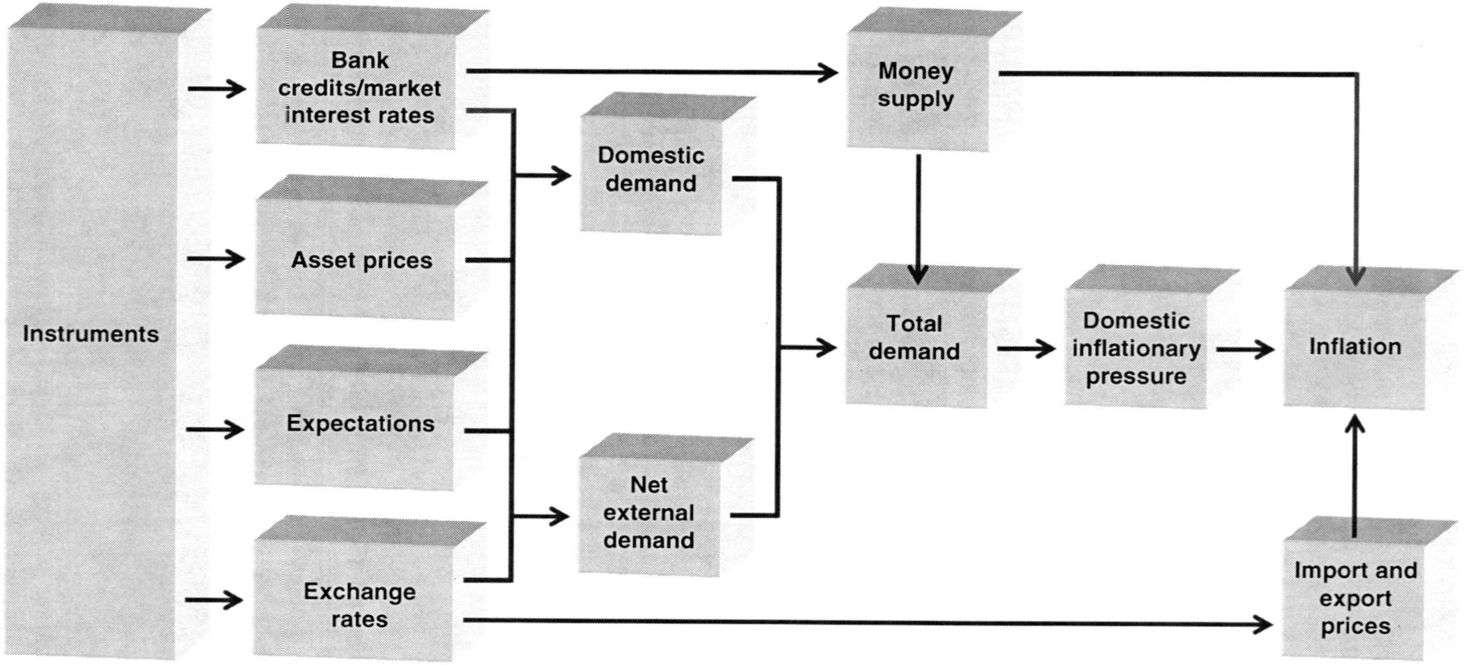

Source: Adapted from Bank of Thailand (2008).

Figure 9.8 Transmission mechanisms of monetary policy in Thailand strategies for the conduct of monetary policy. Many central banks in the Asia-Pacific have institutional set up similar to that at the Bank of England. The relationship between the central bank and the government in some countries of the Asia-Pacific has also evolved, following the British traditions. Some information on recent conduct of monetary policy in the UK is therefore relevant to some developing countries of the Asia-Pacific.

Historically, the Bank of England conducted monetary policy to support fiscal policy. The Chancellor of the Exchequer was the person responsible for the direction of monetary policy. Accordingly, most monetary policy decisions were made by the Bank of England on the basis of directions of the Ministry of Finance. The central banks of Australia, Canada and New Zealand were founded on these traditions.

In late 1973 the UK announced a broad money supply target (M3) in response to high inflationary pressures. Monetary targets were not, however, pursued aggressively. In response to accelerating inflation in the late 1970s, the Thatcher government formally introduced a strategy in 1980 for a gradual deceleration of M3 growth. The Bank of England, however, had difficulties in achieving the M3 growth target because of financial innovations. Beginning in 1983, the BOE shifted its emphasis toward targeting the growth of the monetary base, with an eye toward a gradual reduction in the growth rate of the broad money supply (M3). By this time the money demand function apparently became unstable (Artis and Lewis, 1984).

The UK left the European Monetary System after the speculative attacks on the pound sterling in September 1992 and decided to turn to inflation targeting to replace the exchange rate as the nominal anchor to prices. The BOE at that time did not have the statutory authority over monetary policy and made only recommendations. Therefore the Chancellor of the Exchequer announced the introduction of inflation targeting as a strategy of monetary policy on 8 October 1992. The Governor of the BOE accepted the task of achieving the inflation target. To formalise the institutional set up, the BOE was given autonomy in setting the policy interest rate as the primary instrument of monetary policy in May 1997. To ensure some accountability and transparency, the Governor was required to make a quarterly report on inflation.

The UK's inflation targeting regime is broadly similar in flexibility to the Australian and Canadian frameworks. It stresses a gradual approach to achieving a long-run inflation goal and the focus is on the underlying trend of inflation, rather than on the headline CPI-inflation. To ensure that there is no deflation, there is a commitment to prevent inflation falling below the target. The transparency and accountability of the BOE in all aspects of inflation targeting have improved and standardised since the late 1990s. In fact the BOE's quarterly *Inflation Report* has become a trendsetter in terms of its style and contents. Many inflation targeting central banks now publish such reports at least six-monthly, if not quarterly.

Figure 9.9 illustrates the transmission mechanisms of monetary policy in the UK. The BOE changes the very short-term official interest rate, which then affects asset prices, medium-term and long-term interest rates, exchange rates and inflationary expectations. Changes in asset prices affect aggregate demand and hence consumer prices. Exchange rate movements, in particular, affect import prices and inflation directly.

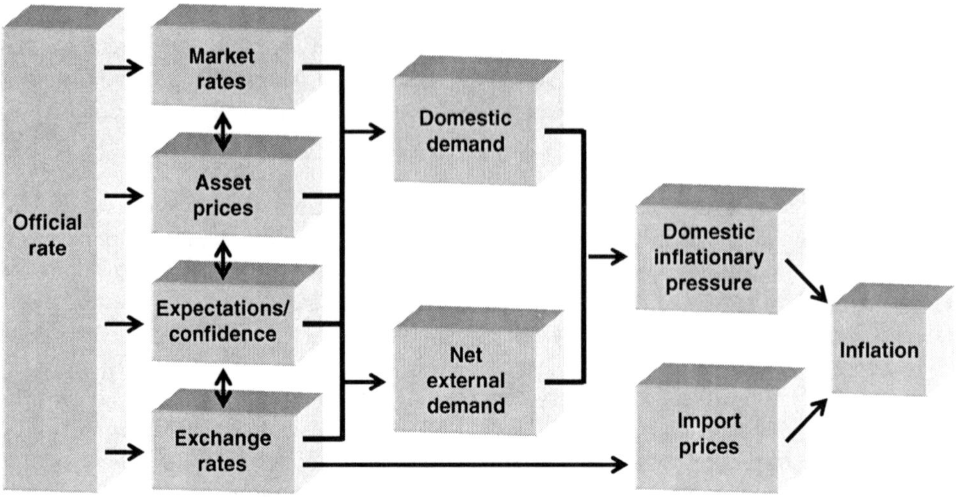

Source: Adapted from Bank of England (1999).

Figure 9.9 Transmission mechanisms of monetary policy in the UK

THE USA

Monetary policy remains a potent instrument for demand management in the USA. The main objectives of monetary policy are to promote high employment and maintain stable prices (Mishkin, 2007a). The relative priority of these twin goals, however, varies depending on economic conditions. The strategy of monetary policy in the USA has changed many times since the 1950s.

In the early 1950s the Federal Reserve System (Fed) took the view that monetary policy should be conducted by taking into account the condition of money market, which is reflected in the nominal interest rate. It formally abandoned the policy of interest rate targeting, which existed during the Second World War, under the Federal Reserve-Treasury Accord in March 1951. According to the provision of the Accord, the Fed was able to conduct an independent monetary policy. It intended to bring control over the money supply. The Fed used free reserves as an operating target, which required the Fed to sell securities when free reserves rose and purchase securities when free reserves fell. This strategy of monetary policy, however, reduced the Fed's control over the money supply. There was widespread criticism of the Fed's pro-cyclical monetary policy. Whether the Fed used interest rate targeting or free reserve targeting, the end result was the same.

In 1970, Arthur Burns became Chairman of the Board of Governors of the Fed. This appointment was welcomed by monetarist economists who strongly criticised the Fed's pro-cyclical monetary policy during the 1950s and 1960s. Burns suggested that the Fed should use monetary aggregates as an intermediate target. The Fed's monetary policy during Burns's tenure in the 1970s, however, remained pro-cyclical because the Fed's commitment to monetary targeting was not strong. It is reflected in the Fed's operating procedure, which was faulty because it effectively continued with the Federal funds rate as an operating target. The use of the Federal funds rate as an operating target made the money supply pro-cyclical. The rationale behind using the Federal funds rate as an operating target was that the Fed remained concerned with achieving interest rate stability (Mishkin, 2007a).

In July 1979 President Carter appointed Mr Volcker as Chairman of the Board of Governors of the Federal Reserve System. He was committed to crushing inflation and chose the monetary aggregates as an intermediate target. He discarded the Federal funds rate as an operating target, but in its place used non-borrowed reserves. This strategy created volatility in the Federal funds rate and also made the money growth rate unstable (Mishkin, 2007a).

In October 1982, the Fed began to pay more attention to the Federal funds rate. It de-emphasised monetary aggregates as a guide for conducting monetary policy. Since then the Fed has conducted monetary policy in a discretionary manner without having the benefit of an explicit nominal anchor to prices. Macroeconomic performance under the Fed's former Chairman Greenspan was highly satisfactory, as inflation in the USA remained low and stable. Real GDP also grew on an average of about 3 per cent per annum since the early 1980s. While Greenspan gained an iconic status in the process, a vigorous debate emerged in the early 2000s about the Fed's monetary policy objectives and how those objectives should be achieved without having any declared nominal anchor to prices. Many US economists argued for 'inflation targeting', so that it can anchor inflationary expectations (Bernanke, 2004; Bernanke and Mishkin, 1997).

The debate on inflation targeting in the USA has heated up since 2003. The debate has become interesting since Mr Bernanke became the Fed's Chairman in 2006. Since becoming the Fed's Chairman, Bernanke has made it clear that any movement towards inflation targeting must result from a consensus within the Federal Reserve. Therefore, it appears that while some movement towards greater transparency is a possibility, how far the Fed would move towards inflation targeting remains uncertain (Mishkin, 2007a). Inflation targeting in the end is a commitment to keep inflation low and stable. This is essentially a rule, which goes against the discretionary form of monetary policy that is conducted in the USA. Some prominent economists also consider inflationary targeting essentially a form of monetary targeting, which does not allow much discretion in the conduct of monetary policy. In this context, Lucas (2007: 2) remarks:

> To me, inflation targeting at its best is an application of Milton Friedman's maxim that 'inflation is always and everywhere a monetary phenomenon', and its corollary that monetary policy should concentrate on the one thing it can do well – control inflation. It can be hard to keep this in mind in financially chaotic times [for example, subprime mortgage crisis], but I think it is worth a try.

VIETNAM

The State Bank of Vietnam (SBV) is governed by the Law on the SBV of December 1997. According to this Law, the SBV is a body of the Vietnamese government (Article 1) and the governor of the SBV is a member of the government (Article 11). The SBV Law makes a distinction between the functions of the SBV and any functions that are related

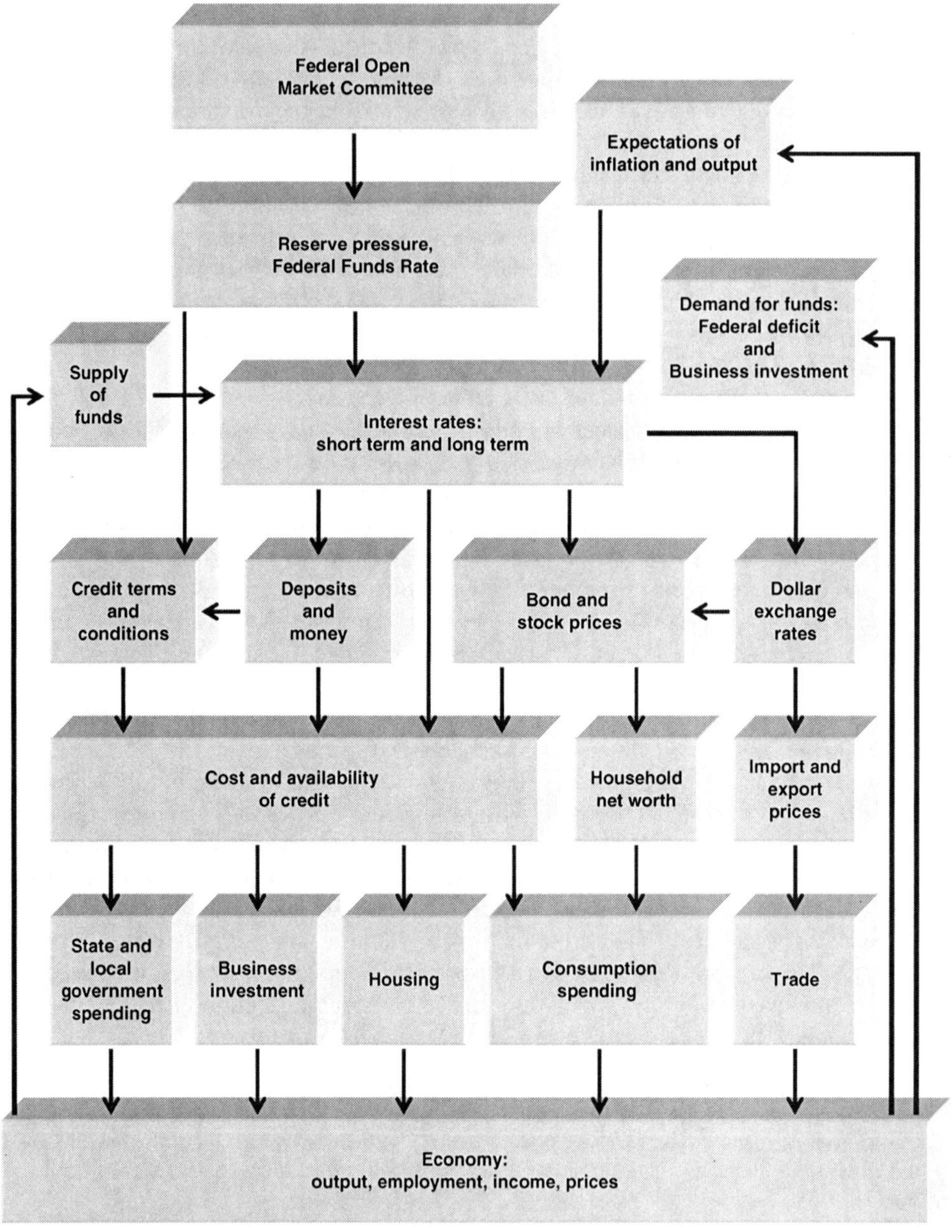

Source: Adapted from Akhtar (1997).

Figure 9.10 Transmission mechanisms of monetary policy in the USA to national monetary policy. Monetary policy, however, is not a whole but 'a component of economic-financial policies of the State' (Article 2). The National Assembly and the government jointly set the objectives of monetary policy, its stance and supervision on the implementation of monetary policy.

While the above institutional arrangement reflects the government's control over monetary policy, the underlying reason behind the National Assembly's control over monetary policy can be explained by Vietnam's experiences with hyperinflation during the 1980s and early 1990s. The government does not want a repetition of high inflation or hyperinflation. Its strong involvement in the implementation of monetary policy indicates that the SBV does not have goal or instrument independence (Camin, 2008; Camin and Genberg, 2005).

Given that monetary policy is a component of economic-financial policies of the State, there are multiple goals of monetary policy. They include stability of the currency value, inflation control, improvement in the people's standards of living, and national defence and security (Article 2). Because of such multiple goals of monetary policy, the primary goal of monetary policy remains unidentified. Having no established hierarchical priority, the multiplicity of goals has the risk of conflict of interest in achieving policy objectives.

The conduct of monetary policy in Vietnam appears to have structuralist elements and is non-transparent. It cannot be discussed in terms of standard instruments, targets and goals. The SBV introduced indirect monetary policy tools in the mid-1990s, as part of financial reforms. Currently the indirect instruments include reserve requirements, refinancing and discount lending facilities, open market operations, and foreign exchange interventions. In addition, the SBV uses its reference rates to influence the interest rates, while the government uses administrative instruments to control some prices.

Vietnam maintains a managed floating exchange rate regime, although the dong remains de facto pegged to the US dollar. Vietnam unified the official exchange rates in March 1989 within a range of 10–20 per cent of the parallel market rates. Since then the authorities have introduced markets for foreign exchange transactions, which include the inter-bank foreign exchange transactions. Vietnam, however, remains a partially dollarised economy. This has been a characteristic feature of the Vietnamese economy since the early 1970s. The increasing use of foreign currency in the Vietnamese economy occurred against a background of large economic and financial imbalances, chronic shortages of basic goods, high and variable inflation, and poor and arbitrary policy implementations.

Vietnam has experienced sustained, impressive economic growth over the past two decades. The Vietnam economy has also opened up significantly and remains exposed to external shocks. With respect to monetary policy, the following principal reform steps have been suggested by the IMF and other international organisations. First, the SBV should be given the responsibility of monetary policy. Second, there should be a hierarchy of monetary policy objectives, with price stability as its primary objective. Third, the monetary policy strategy should be clearly defined and there should be an increase in flexibility of interest and exchange rates. Vietnam can move to monetary or inflation targeting. The choice should depend on stability of the underlying monetary relations, monetary transmission mechanisms, financial structure, and the sources of inflation. These are empirical issues that should be investigated with high priority (Dodsworth and Associates, 1996).

THE GLOBAL FINANCIAL CRISIS AND MONETARY POLICY IN THE ASIA-PACIFIC

It was pointed out at the outset that this book is not about the present global financial crisis and its implications on the conduct of monetary policy. This issue, however, cannot be completely ignored. This section provides an overview of the sources of this crisis and discusses the implications of this crisis on monetary and fiscal policies in developing countries of the Asia-Pacific.

Origins of the Subprime Crisis and Policy Responses

There is no doubt that the global financial crisis that started in the US housing sector in 2007 has spread to most countries and created a global recession. The debate is on the cause of this crisis and about factors that might have contributed to its rapid spread across countries. There are at least two views on the origin of this crisis. The first is that loose monetary policy in the USA during 2002–04 caused the housing bubble, which when busted in 2007 led to mortgage delinquencies and foreclosures in the USA. Subsequently, there was credit squeeze and loss of consumer and business confidence that adversely affected economic activity across countries. As happened in the case of East Asian crisis, financial and trade linkages of most countries with the USA contributed to the spread of the crisis across the globe. Taylor (2008a: 1–2) has provided some empirical evidence to support the 'monetary excess' hypothesis:

> The classic explanation of financial crises, going back to hundreds of years, is that they are caused by excesses – frequently monetary excesses – which lead to a boom and an inevitable bust. In the recent crisis we had a housing boom and bust which in turn led to financial turmoil in the United States and other countries. I begin by showing that monetary excesses were the main cause of that boom and the resulting bust . . . Figure 1 [not reported] shows that the actual interest rate decisions fell well below what historical experience would suggest policy should be. It thus provides an empirical measure that monetary policy was too easy during this period [2002–04], or too 'loose fitting' as *The Economist* puts it. This was an unusually big deviation from the Taylor rule. There was no greater or more persistent deviation of actual Fed policy since the turbulent days of the 1970s. So there is clearly evidence that there were monetary excesses during the period leading up to the housing boom.

The alternative view is that the low interest rates in the USA during 2002–04 were caused by global factors, which were beyond the control of the monetary authorities of the USA. The alternative explanation in particular focuses on the rate of global saving. The argument is that there was excess world saving – a global saving glut – which pushed the interest rates down in the USA and other countries. Taylor (2008a) has discounted this argument on the ground that there was no evidence for a global saving glut. He has based his argument on IMF's *World Development Outlook* (September 2005) data that showed a very low rate of global saving rate (world saving as a fraction of world GDP) during 2002–04.

The question is why did the Fed adopt an ultra-expansionary monetary policy during 2002–04? As many economists pointed out, there was problem with the US strategy of monetary policy. The Fed under Mr Greenspan conducted discretionary monetary policy to achieve multiple objectives. During his era as Chairman of the Fed, in addition to price stability, economic growth got prominence as an object of monetary policy. Moreover, there was political objective of raising the proportion of house ownership, which, many consider was a worthwhile goal but overdone in retrospect (Taylor, 2008a), induced the Fed to maintain a loose monetary policy when the US economy was doing well under a relatively low inflationary environment. Most financial institutions also ignored risks associated with subprime loans during the boom. Mishkin (2008: 2) has highlighted the problems with securitization of mortgages that were ignored by all concerned:

> The subprime crisis exposed problems with the securitization of mortgages. In particular, it became clear how poor the underwriting and credit-risk analysis were for a wide range of products. Some appraisers, brokers, and investment banks were motivated by transaction fees and had little stake in the ultimate performance of the loans they helped to arrange. Many securitized products were complex, and the ownership structure of the underlying assets was opaque. Investors relied heavily on credit ratings instead of conducting due diligence themselves, and credit rating agencies failed to fulfil their raison d'etre. The result has been rising defaults, particularly in the subprime mortgage markets, with losses to both investors and financial institutions.

Some economists have shown the similarities between the 1997 Asian financial crisis and the US subprime mortgage crisis. In both crises there were initially large inflows of foreign capital. In the case of East Asian crisis, large inflows of foreign capital led to a sharp rise in bank lending and corporate borrowings. Foreign investors invested in high-yielding Asian securities or US dollar denominated debt instruments assuming that Asian economies would grow rapidly and currency pegs would hold indefinitely. The boom busted once there was investor panic in the face of uncertainty over the security and valuation of assets (Ee and Xiong, 2008). Consequently, large outflows of capital resulted in a sharp depreciation of domestic currencies. Similarly, in the case of the USA, large inflows of foreign capital financed large current account deficits, which increased from about 1.5 per cent to 5.8 per cent of GDP during 1996–2004. The current account deficits reflected a sharp rise in consumer spending using borrowed funds, which also financed the purchases of houses and financial assets. Financial institutions which invested foreign funds in mortgage-based securities became insolvent once housing boom ended due to the rise in both interest rates and oil prices. Ee and Xiong (2008: 2–4) explained how abundant foreign funds led to imprudent credit expansion that created the housing bubble in the first place:

> In the Asian financial crisis, credit imprudence came in the form of connected lending to large corporate entities or to megaprojects and property developments that were of dubious commercial viability. In the subprime crisis, that search led to the proliferation of mortgage loans in the subprime category, the so-called ninja (no income, no job, and no assets) loans . . . the credit imprudence shown by lenders in both crises reflected the classic principal–agent problem. During the Asian financial crisis, shareholders' interests were ignored by bank managers, who lent indiscriminately to certain companies and projects, either at the behest of governments or because these projects were related to influential shareholders. In the subprime crisis, CDO and MBS investors expected mortgage lenders to maintain credit standard. But with the 'originate and distribute' model, lenders had little incentive to worry about credit standards because they did not retain loans.

The responses of the governments to the subprime crisis were significantly different from those introduced during the Asian crisis. As Ee and Xiong (2008: 4) have pointed this out:

> In the subprime crisis, major central banks have intervened aggressively to provide liquidity to contain disruptions and contagion in financial markets. At the same time, the U.S. Federal Reserve has cut interest rates substantially to ease monetary conditions, and the U.S. Congress has approved a fiscal stimulus package. In the Asian crisis, monetary and fiscal policies were initially tightened to support exchange rates because of massive capital outflows and a run on foreign reserves, which contributed to a downward spiral in the real economy. Only after exchange rates had stabilized at a lower level did governments adopt more expansionary fiscal policies to support the real economies.

Policy Implications

Most countries now face the grim task of avoiding a deep recession. The international financial institutions, including the IMF, have allegedly discarded the idea fiscal prudence and suggested developed countries to use expansionary fiscal policy to avoid a deep recession. Accordingly, some countries, including Australia, China, India, Japan, Singapore and the USA, have introduced large fiscal stimulus measures. These fiscal measures have been in conjunction with expansionary monetary policy although there has been a revival of the view that monetary policy could be ineffective anyway during recession.

Although there is broad support for expansionary policy measures to avoid a deep recession, there is concern that expansionary fiscal policy measures introduced or in the process of adoption are too excessive and that such measures are unlikely to create a rapid recovery of the economy. Taylor (2008b: 8) in particular has been pessimistic about the role of discretionary fiscal policy in bringing sustained economic recovery:

> There is little evidence that short government impulses will jump start an economy adversely affected by other forces. In the current recession, the economy has been pulled down by the housing slump, the financial crisis, and the lagged effects of high energy prices. Expectations of future income and employment growth are low because the effects of the financial crisis are expected to last for years into the future. Unless these effects are addressed, a short-term fiscal stimulus has little chance of causing a sustained recovery. The theory that a short-run stimulus will jump start the economy is based on older 'Keynesian' theories which do not adequately include, in my view, the complex dynamic or general equilibrium effects of a modern international economy.

While the governments across the globe have been enthusiastic about fiscal stimulus as a remedial measure to prevent a recession, they have in the process of justifying large fiscal stimulus package created panic among the public. Even if one does not invoke the Ricardian equivalence proposition, which suggests no major impact of government extra spending on aggregate demand when the public takes into consideration of its impact on future of taxation or money creation, the very fact that there is panic among the public any extra transfer payments to the public or an increase in household disposable income due to tax cuts may simply be saved. This may neutralise the impact of fiscal measures on aggregate demand even in the short run.

For developing countries, the major concern is that expansionary policy measures would create future problems for them, as they only recently brought some fiscal discipline under IMF–World Bank stabilisation and adjustment programmes. The actual or perceived IMF licence for breaking policy discipline (fiscal-monetary) could be a recipe for macroeconomic problems in the future. This is the reason why the IMF has lately cautioned that fiscal stimulus may not be appropriate for low income developing and emerging market countries. The response to the financial crisis should be based on individual country circumstances (IMF's *Survey*, various issues). The problem is that policy-makers in most developing countries can come up with many reasons for expansionary monetary and fiscal policies.

Although there is no certainty about the future course of the global economy, the global crisis has given an impetus to the ongoing debate on the relative importance of monetary and fiscal policy in stabilising the economy. It is unlikely that as a consequence of the present global crisis, there will be a major change in the role of monetary policy in price stability. However, the task of central bankers is likely to be difficult in maintaining price stability in an environment where fiscal policy is given prominence in stabilisation. The danger is that an upgrade of the role of fiscal policy in stabilisation may gradually reinstate the paradigm where there is fiscal dominance over monetary policy. This was a common feature of financial repression during the 1950s to the 1980s.

Asian developing countries have so far not been affected heavily. There is a view that financial reforms that have been undertaken by Asian countries since the 1990s have helped these countries to face the crisis on a stronger footing. Kuroda (2009: 1) has made this point:

> Given the degree of financial integration and global economic interdependence, Asia was bound to be at least somewhat impacted by the crisis. . . . [however] the corrective measures undertaken in the wake of the Asian Financial Crisis have helped the Asian economies to face the latest turmoil with greater confidence and on a much stronger footing. As a result of these reforms, most of the Asian economies have robust economic fundamentals, sound banking supervision and prudential guidelines. As well, commercial banks exposure to toxic foreign assets has been rather limited, resulting in stronger balance sheets. Relative to exports, external debt is far more manageable and exchange rates more flexible. Had Asia not undertaken some of these reform measures, it would have been more susceptible to the contagion effects of the present crisis.

Economists, such as Taylor (2008a), are of the view that to avoid such a crisis, there is need for the return to disciplined monetary policy under policy rules. In the USA, the Federal Reserve in particular should return to the set of principles for setting interest rates that worked well during the 'Great Moderation'. Monetary policy rules remain more important for developing countries. They should maintain monetary discipline and continue developing financial markets and institutions. Central banks in particular should continue improving management of large-scale foreign capital flows, exchange rate risks, credit booms and asset bubbles. Above all, developing countries of the Asia-Pacific should not discard the lessons learnt from the Asian financial crisis and create policy-induced macroeconomic imbalances, even if there are temptations to generate inflation surprises for short-term output or employment gains. Ee and Xiong (2008: 10) have indeed given a timely reminder to policy-makers in developing Asia:

> Asia's healthy long-term growth prospects should mean that the region is poised to ride, or even lead, the next economic boom. The challenge is to ensure that its development does not get derailed by financial land mines along the way. The region should exploit its firmer footing to build on the lessons of the 1997 and current crises.

SUMMARY AND CONCLUSION

This chapter has provided an overview of inflation and monetary policy in selected countries of the Asia-Pacific and the UK. The discussion has covered only key issues in monetary policy and any institutional and organisational developments with monetary policy implications. Due to space constraint, no effort has been made to critically assess country-specific underlying economic relations and issues in the design and implementation of monetary policy.

Since the 1980s most countries of the Asia-Pacific have recognised that the primary role of monetary policy is to achieve and maintain price stability. The strategy of monetary policy has, however, varied across countries. This is reflected in different exchange rate arrangements, restrictions on capital flows, and the coordination between monetary and fiscal policy in these countries. Following the lead of developed countries, the central banks of most Asian developing countries have gained some autonomy under newly enacted central banking laws. This has not, however, improved monetary policy significantly because the governments have managed to retain administrative and financial control over central banking operations and functions. Nevertheless, several central banks in developing Asia, such as Indonesia, the Philippines and Thailand, have shown enthusiasm for developing and protecting their autonomy and building policy credibility through institutional reforms.

Since the currency crises of the late 1990s, monetary authorities in most Asian countries, as part of improving macroeconomic management, have given more importance on monetary and exchange rate policies for price stability. The goal is to sustain high economic growth without creating unsustainable macroeconomic imbalances. Despite the early fear that the 1990s currency crises might have induced East Asian countries becoming protectionist, there has actually been an increase in economic openness in these countries. Although the crises of the 1990s showed the increased importance of macroeconomic stability for sustained economic growth, the ongoing financial crisis that started in the USA in 2007 has exposed the vulnerability of globally interconnected financial institutions. The financial crisis has resulted in global recession. The human cost is the sufferings of the millions of people, especially in developing countries. To avoid such crisis, developing countries of the Asia-Pacific have been correctly advised to maintain macroeconomic stability in general and monetary stability in particular.

NOTE

1. Due to the binding space constraint, no effort is made here to examine the conduct of monetary policy in selected countries in a historical context. In fact this chapter should be seen as a preview of a companion volume on case studies of monetary policy in selected countries of the Asia-Pacific.

10. Summary and conclusion

The main objective of this book has been to provide an overview of central banking and monetary policy issues in developing countries of the Asia-Pacific. The discussion of the book has revolved around the theme that the phenomenal economic progress in East and Southeast Asian countries over the past four decades has taken place within the framework of the East Asian development paradigm that emphasised macroeconomic stability in general and price stability in particular. Accordingly, disciplined monetary and fiscal policies have been credited for the low inflationary economic environment in developing Asia.

The East Asian financial crises of the late 1990s and the 2008–09 global financial crises have, however, exposed the vulnerabilities of most Asian countries to external shocks and developments. Still, for sustained economic growth and poverty reduction, globalisation remains the best option for developing countries. To cope with external shocks, most developing countries of Asia have undertaken economic reforms and improved their financial systems. Some of these countries have also introduced political reforms to develop sound economic policies.

Given the increasing importance of monetary policy in macroeconomic stability, this book has provided an overview of the key concepts and principles of central banking and monetary policy and has reviewed contemporary monetary, fiscal and exchange rate policy issues. At the risk of some repetition, the remainder of this chapter summarises the key ideas, concepts and principles in central banking and monetary policy that have been covered in this book.

CENTRAL BANKING

The book has reviewed the evolution and functions of a modern central bank. The origins of central banking were in the latter half of the seventeenth century in Europe. Central banks were founded primarily for financial advantages that the governments obtained from these institutions, unification of 'chaotic' currency issue systems, centralised management and protection of silver and gold reserves, and the improvement of inter-bank payments systems. Contemporary central banks have evolved as an outcome of institutional adaptation of countries to reduce confidence costs in the fiat monetary system, as well as acting as a conduit for resource transfer from the people to the government for developmental activities. In recent decades central banks have transformed, emerging as national institutions with the explicit role as guardians of monetary and financial stability.

Most central banks in developing Asia have been assigned the responsibility of maintaining price stability through monetary policy for sustained economic growth. Central banks have also been assigned the responsibility of supervising and regulating the financial systems. Without resolving any conflicts between them, the twin objectives of price stability and economic stability have remained in the statute books of central banks in most countries as a reminder that economic stability cannot be ignored, although price stability can be considered as the overriding objective of monetary policy.

INFLATION AND MONETARY POLICY

While reviewing the fundamental concepts and principles of monetary policy, the book has emphasised that there is a close relationship between monetary and fiscal policy in developing countries. Monetary policy cannot be conducted independently of fiscal policy unless there is close coordination between them. The book has also highlighted the policy trilemma in an open economy that needs resolving before monetary policy can be conducted independently. Under a fixed exchange rate system, monetary policy loses its independence unless there are controls over capital flows. In a floating exchange rate system with free capital mobility, the central bank loses control over the exchange rate but gains control over monetary policy. Therefore, central banks are expected to design monetary policy strategies to achieve and maintain price stability. This can be done in the form of a policy rule. The ongoing debate, however, remains whether monetary policy should aim at controlling inflation with or without stabilising the business cycles.

The book has examined this debate in the context of developing countries. Although the literature suggests that there are possibilities of demand disturbances in developing economies originating from both domestic and foreign sources, they are unlikely to be rampant and persistent. The parameter values of the consumption, investment and money demand functions suggest that developing economies are not highly sensitive to demand shocks. Moreover, as real wages and real interest and exchange rates in developing countries are generally flexible, the demand shocks to developing economies are adjusted mostly through price mechanisms. Hence there is less need for stabilisation of the economy in the form of policy interventions. Although demand shocks are not prevalent in developing countries, these countries frequently experience supply shocks originating from the agricultural sector. Agricultural supply shocks, however, are random and do not persist. Monetary policy is usually not effective in stabilising an economy following supply shocks. Therefore, there is consensus that the primary goal of monetary policy should be maintaining low and steady inflation, which is necessary for sustained economic growth and poverty reduction.

Money Growth and Inflation

For an understanding of the inflationary process in developing countries, the book has reviewed some of the theories, models and approaches to inflation and monetary policy. The theme of the literature is that inflation in the long run is determined by the growth rate of the money supply. Non-monetary factors affect inflation, but only in the short run. Non-monetary factors, originating from both the demand side and the supply side, cannot lead to a self-sustaining inflation without monetary accommodation.

One strand of the money growth-inflation literature, however, suggests that budget deficits and money growth are closely related in developing countries. Therefore inflation can be considered primarily a fiscal phenomenon. Although it is plausible that budget deficits are a source of inflation, the fiscal-monetary part of an inflation model is usually not stable, except in hyperinflationary situation. Therefore, control of long-term inflation in general can be considered equivalent to a control of the growth rate of the money supply.

Having reviewed the classical model of inflation, this book has provided an overview of the conditions that may trigger high inflation or hyperinflation in developing countries. The book has described some of the common elements and characteristics of hyperinflation. Stabilisation measures for ending hyperinflation and major problems with stabilisation have also been discussed.

MONEY AND FINANCE IN ECONOMIC GROWTH

An important branch of the money-economic growth literature has been concerned with the role of inflationary finance in economic growth in developing countries. The review of the literature on inflationary finance and growth reveals that while money creation to finance public investment may have some influence on economic growth, it is unlikely to be a major source of growth. The experience of Latin American countries suggests that inflationary finance is, in fact, a hazardous means of economic growth. The phenomenal economic progress in East and Southeast Asia has indeed been in a relatively non-inflationary environment.

In the context of presently deregulated financial systems, the book has emphasised that financial deregulation is not synonymous with a *laissez-faire* approach. Current developments in the literature as well as the experiences of a wide range of countries with financial reforms have brought to the fore the issue of prudential regulation of the financial systems. In fact, the choice is not between a *laissez-faire* approach versus dirigiste system, but for a competitive sector within the institutional context of prudential regulation. The global financial crisis that originated in the USA in 2007–08 is a reminder that the financial sector operates better in a deregulatory environment when it remains under well-designed, prudential regulation and supervision.

STRATEGIES OF MONETARY POLICY

The major decision that a country needs to make is whether the central bank should adopt a discretionary or a rule-based monetary policy in order to achieve and sustain price stability. There are various rule-based strategies of monetary policy. There is, however, no hard and fast rule for making an optimal choice of the strategy of monetary policy. The factors that are important in the decision-making process include the country's inflationary experiences, institutional arrangements and administrative capacity. This book has reviewed the well-known rules-based strategies of monetary policy such as the commodity standards, exchange rate targeting, monetary targeting and inflation targeting. It also reviewed specialised monetary arrangements such as currency board, dollarisation and monetary union. The aim of this review has been to provide a menu of choice for designing the most appropriate monetary policy strategies in developing countries under different circumstances. The rapidly growing literature on time-inconsistency in monetary policy, and various remedial measures that have been suggested by economists to minimise the inflationary bias in discretionary monetary policy, have also been reviewed. The issue of supply shock and monetary policy has gained importance in some countries. The book has provided a detailed analysis of the issue of what kind of monetary policy is appropriate for price stability after a supply shock.

In general, there is an emerging consensus that price stability can be achieved on a long-term context through a policy rule provided that the public find the rule simple and credible. The issue remains whether central banks should exercise their discretion to break policy rules if there are shocks. The global financial crisis has revealed that policy-makers remain keen to break policy rules when there are policy-induced or exogenous shocks. The latest global financial crises suggest that monetary excesses may result even in a highly developed country like the USA when its central bank operates outside the constraint of a policy rule and/or strives for achieving multiple goals through monetary policy.

THE MONEY SUPPLY PROCESS AND MONETARY MANAGEMENT

The book has provided a general overview of the money supply process and discussed issues in monetary management in developing countries. Although the money stock is considered an exogenously determined policy variable, the money supply process remains complex and involves the central bank, commercial banks and both borrowers and lenders. Under a fixed exchange rate system, the money supply is endogenous and determined by the determinants of money demand. This is shown in the form of a linkage between the monetary base and changes in foreign exchange reserves, which are related to the balance of payments. Budget deficits are also linked to the monetary base if the government relies on money financing. The monetary base remains under the control of a central bank in a flexible exchange rate system; the central bank can manage the monetary base by deploying monetary policy instruments.

Although central banks have a wide range of instruments to control money, not all of them are effective or necessarily deployed by central banks. Under financial repression, the money stock was controlled directly by controlling bank credits. Under the present deregulated financial environment, open market operations have become the most widely used technique for liquidity management. Still there is lack of transparency in the way liquidity is managed or how effective is monetary control.

MONETARY POLICY TRANSMISSION MECHANISM

The book has reviewed issues in the transmission mechanisms of monetary policy in the context of developing countries. The classical versus Keynesian transmission mechanisms of monetary policy have been reviewed. The classical transmission mechanisms of monetary policy are, however, found more appropriate for developing countries. It is also suggested that in a financially repressed economy where the interest rates are administratively fixed and credit rationing is the principal component of monetary policy, the availability of credit has direct and immediate impact on expenditure and output. The money versus credit views provides an important framework in which to design an appropriate framework for further analysis of the transmission mechanisms of monetary policy.

In view of the importance of money demand and its stability in the design and conduct of monetary policy, the book has provided a review of relevant issues. The long-run demand for money in developing countries has been found mostly stable, even after financial liberalisation. The existence of a stable long-run demand for money function, coupled with the fact that in the long-run money supply affects the price level and not real output, suggests that monetary policy should have a long-run target of controlling inflation. For many developing countries in Asia this may take the form of controlling monetary aggregates under inflation targeting.

MONETARY POLICY IN THE ASIA-PACIFIC

The penultimate chapter of the book has provided an overview of inflation and monetary policy in selected countries of the Asia-Pacific. The discussion has covered key issues in monetary policy and any institutional and organisational developments with monetary policy implications. The challenge for developing countries of the Asia-Pacific is to maintain low inflation and sustainable current account balances in order to maintain steady economic growth. Improvement in macroeconomic management has, therefore, become the focus of international financial institutions. The strategies that have been put in place by different countries suggest that macroeconomic stability has been taken seriously by most policy-makers in the region. This is despite the fact that most developing countries of the Asia-Pacific are yet to institutionalise the conduct of monetary and fiscal policies, reflective of the way it has happened in developed countries. Therefore, in order to bring transparency in monetary policy in rapidly growing developing Asia, there is a pressing need for institutional development to improve the conduct of monetary policy. This would require the adaptation of basic principles of monetary policy to the conditions of developing economies of Asia. Sustained research on monetary relations and principles therefore remains critical for policy formulation and implementation. Consistent data for macroeconomic variables of most countries of the Asia-Pacific dating from the 1960s are available. Such data can be deployed to econometrically investigate macroeconomic and monetary policy issues. This is an important area of further research and the subject matter of a future companion volume to this book.

Bibliography

Abel, A.B. (1990), 'Consumption and investment', in B.M. Friedman and F.H. Hahn (eds), *Handbook of Monetary Economics,* Amsterdam: Elsevier Science.

Adekunle, J. (1968), 'The demand for money: evidence from developed and less developed economies', *IMF Staff Papers*, **15** (2), 220–66.

Adelman, I. and C.T. Morris (1973), *Economic Growth and Social Equity in Developing Countries*, Stanford, CA: Stanford University Press.

Agenor, P.R. and P.J. Montiel (1996), *Development Macroeconomics*, Princeton, NJ: Princeton University Press.

Agha, A.I., N. Ahmed, Y.A. Mubarik and H. Shah (2005), 'Transmission mechanism of monetary policy in Pakistan', *State Bank of Pakistan-Research Bulletin,* **1** (1), 1–22.

Aghevli, B.B. (1977), 'Inflationary finance and growth', *Journal of Political Economy*, **85**, 1295–307.

Aghevli, B.B. and M.S. Khan (1978), 'Government budget deficits and inflationary process in developing countries', *IMF Staff Papers*, **25**, 383–416.

Aghevli, B.B. and M.S. Khan (1980), 'Credit policy and the balance of payments in developing countries', in W. Coates and D. Khatkhate (eds), *Money and Monetary Policy in Less Developed Countries: A Survey of Issues and Evidence*, Oxford: Pergamon Press.

Aghevli, B.B. and C. Sassanpour (1982), 'Prices, output and the trade balance in Iran', *World Development*, **10**, 791–800.

Aghevli, B.B., M.S. Khan and P. Montiel (1991), 'Exchange rate policy in developing countries: some analytical issues', *Occasional Paper No.78*, Washington, DC: IMF.

Aghevli, B.B., M.S. Khan, P. Narvekar and B. Short (1979), 'Monetary policy in selected Asian countries', *IMF Staff Papers*, **26** (2), 775–824.

Agung, J. (1998), 'Financial deregulation and bank lending channel of monetary policy in developing countries: the case of Indonesia', *Asian Economic Journal,* **12** (3), 273–94.

Ahmad, Z. (1984), 'Concepts and models of Islamic banking: an assessment', paper presented at the seminar on Islamisation of Banking, Karachi, 27–29 November.

Ahmed, A.K.N. (1987), 'Role of central bank in economic development – financing of public and private sectors', *Commerce*, **154** (10 January), 14–23.

Ahmed, I. (1981), 'Wage determination in Bangladesh agriculture', *Oxford Economic Papers*, **33** (2), 298–322.

Ahsan, A., M. Scully and J. Wickramanayake (2007), 'Central bank independence and governance (CBIG) and inflation in Asia-Pacific', draft, Department of Accounting and Finance, Monash University, Clayton, Melbourne.

Akerlof, G.A., W. Dickens and G. Perry (1996), 'The macroeconomics of low inflation', *Brookings Papers on Economic Activity*, **1**, 1–59.

Akhtar, M.A. (1997), *Understanding Open Market Operations*, New York: Public Information Department, Federal Reserve Bank of New York.

Al-Mashat, R. (2004), 'Vietnam's experiences with rapid money growth and low inflation', *Vietnam: Selected Issues*, Washington, DC: IMF.

Alamsyah, H., C. Joseph, J. Agung and D. Zulverdy (2001), 'Towards implementation of inflation targeting in Indonesia, *Bulletin of Indonesian Economic Studies*, **37** (3), 309–24.

Alesina, A. and L.H. Summers (1993), 'Central bank independence and macroeconomic performance: some comparative evidence', *Journal of Money, Credit and Banking*, **25** (2), 151–62.

Alesina, A. and G. Tabellini (1987), 'Rules and discretion with noncoordinated monetary and fiscal policies', *Economic Inquiry*, **25**, 619–30.

Allen, W.A. (1999), 'Inflation targeting: the British experience', *Handbooks in Central Banking Lecture Series No. 1*, Centre for Central Banking Studies, London: Bank of England.

Allen, W.A. (2004), 'Implementing monetary policy', *Handbooks in Central Banking Lecture Series No. 4*, Centre for Central Banking Studies, London: Bank of England.

Alvarez-Plata, P. and A. Garcia-Herrero (2007), 'To dollarize or de-dollarize', *BIS Research Paper*, September.

Amin, A.T.M.N. (1981), 'Marginalisation and dynamism: a study of the informal sector in Dhaka city', *Bangladesh Development Studies*, **9** (4), 77–112.

Amsden, A. (1989), *Asia's Next Giant: South Korea and Late Industrialization,* New York: Oxford University Press.

Amsden, A. and Y. Euh (1993), 'South Korea's 1980s financial reforms: good-bye financial repression (maybe), hello institutional restraints', *World Development*, **21** (3), 379–90.

Ando, A. and F. Modigliani (1963), 'The life-cycle hypothesis of saving: aggregate implications and tests', *American Economic Review*, **53** (March), 55–84.

Argy, V. (1992), *Australian Macroeconomic Policy in a Changing World Environment*, Sydney: Allen and Unwin.

Arize, A. C. (1994), 'A re-examination of the demand for money in small developing economies', *Applied Economics*, **26** (March), 217–28.

Artis, M.J. and M.K. Lewis (1984), 'How unstable is the demand for money in the United Kingdom?', *Economica*, **51**, 473–76.

Asian Development Bank (ADB) (various years), *Asian Development Outlook*, Manila: ADB.

Asian Development Bank (ADB) (various years), *Key Indicators of Developing Asian and Pacific Countries*, Manila: ADB.

Athukorala, P.-C. (2001), *Crisis and Recovery in Malaysia*, Cheltenham, UK and Northampton, MA, USA: Edward Elgar.

Attfield, C. and N. Duck (1983), 'The influence of unanticipated money growth on real output: some cross-country estimates', *Journal of Money, Credit, and Banking*, **15** (November), 442–54.

Auerbach, R. (1985), 'Politics and the Federal Reserve', *Contemporary Policy Issues*, **3** (5), 43–59.

Axilrod, S.H. and H.C. Wallich (1992), 'Open-market operations', in P. Newman, M. Milgate and J. Eatwell (eds), *The New Palgrave Dictionary of Money and Finance*, vol 3, London: Macmillan Press.

Aziz, J., S.V. Dunaway and E. Prasad (eds) (2006), *China and India: Learning from Each Other*, Washington, DC: IMF.

Backus, D. and J. Driffill (1985), 'Inflation and reputation', *American Economic Review*, **75**, 530–38.

Baer, W. and I. Kertenetzky (eds) (1964), *Inflation and Growth in Latin America*, Homewood, IL: Irwin.

Bagehot, W. (1873), *Lombard Street*, London: Henry S. King.

Bailey, M.J. (1956), 'The welfare cost of inflationary finance', *Journal of Political Economy*, **64**, 93–110.

Balino, T.J.T. and C. Cottarelli (eds) (1994), *Frameworks for Monetary Stability*, Washington, DC: IMF.

Balino, T.J.T. and C. Enoch (1997), 'Currency board arrangements: issues and experiences', *Occasional Paper 151*, Washington, DC: IMF.

Ball, L. (1992), 'Why does high inflation raise inflation uncertainty?', *Journal of Monetary Economics*, **29** (3), 371–88.

Ball, L. (2001), 'Another look at long-run money demand', *Journal of Monetary Economics*, **47**, 31–44.

Ball, L. (2006), 'Has globalization changed inflation?', *NBER Working Paper 12678*, New York: NBER.

Ball, L. and N.G. Mankiw (1995), 'Relative price changes as aggregate supply shocks', *Quarterly Journal of Economics* (February), 161–94.

Ball, L. and D. Romer (1990), 'Real rigidities and the non-neutrality of money', *Review of Economic Studies*, **57** (April), 183–203.

Banaian, K., L.O. Laney and T.D. Willett (1983), 'Central bank independence: an international comparison', *Federal Reserve Bank of Dallas Economic Review* (March), 1–13.

Bandyopadhyay, T. and S. Ghatak (1990), 'Monetary growth models: the role of money demand functions', in T. Bandyopadhyay and S. Ghatak (eds), *Current Issues in Monetary Economics*, New York: Harvester Wheatsheaf.

Bangladesh Bank, http://www.bangladeshbank.gov.bd.

Bangladesh Bank (various issues), *Economic Trends*, Dhaka: Bangladesh Bank.

Bangladesh Bank (2005), 'Notes on the monetary policy strategy of the Bangladesh Bank', *Policy Notes Series: PN0602*, Dhaka: Bangladesh Bank.

Bangladesh Bank (2006a), *Monetary Policy Review*, Dhaka: Bangladesh Bank.

Bangladesh Bank (2006b), 'Monetary policy statement: January 2006', Dhaka: Bangladesh Bank.

Bangladesh Bureau of Statistics (BBS) (various years), *Statistical Yearbook of Bangladesh*, Dhaka: BBS.

Bangladesh Bureau of Statistics (2003), *Twenty Years of National Accounting*, Dhaka: BBS.

Bank Indonesia, http://www.bi.gov.in.

Bank Indonesia (2005), 'Inflation targeting framework', Directorate of Economic Research and Monetary Policy (October), Jakarta: Bank of Indonesia.

Bank for International Settlements (BIS) (2003), *Statutes of the Bank for International Settlements*, http:www.bis.org/about/statutes.htm.

Bank of Canada (2000), *Price Stability and the Long-Run Target for Monetary Policy*, Ottawa: Bank of Canada.

Bank of England (1984), *The Development and Operation of Monetary Policy, 1960–1983*, Oxford: Clarendon Press.

Bank of England (1992), 'The case for price stability', Governor's speech, *Bank of England Quarterly Bulletin*, November.

Bank of England (1999), *The Transmission Mechanism of Monetary Policy*, London: Bank of England.

Bank of Japan, http://www.boj.jp.

Bank of Korea (2000), *The Bank of Korea: A History of Fifty Years*, Seoul: Bank of Korea.

Bank of Papua New Guinea, http://www.bankpng.gov.pg.

Bank of Thailand (2008), 'Changes in the monetary transmission mechanism in Thailand', in *Transmission Mechanisms for Monetary Policy in Emerging Market Economies*, BIS Papers No. 35.

Bardhan, K. (1977), 'Rural employment, wages and labour markets in India: a survey of research, part I, part II, and part III', *Economic and Political Weekly*, **12** (26), A34–48, **12** (27), 1062–74, **12** (28), 1108–18.

Bardhan, P. (1979a), 'Labor supply functions in a poor agrarian economy', *American Economic Review*, **69**, 73–83.

Bardhan, P. (1979b), 'Wages and unemployment in a poor agrarian economy: a theoretical and empirical analysis', *Journal of Political Economy*, **87** (3), 479–500.

Barro, R.J. (1972), 'Inflationary finance and the welfare cost of inflation', *Journal of Political Economy*, **80**, 978–1001.

Barro, R.J. (1976), 'Rational expectations and the role of monetary policy', *Journal of Monetary Economics*, **2** (1), 1–32.

Barro, R.J. (1977), 'Unanticipated money growth and unemployment in the United States', *American Economic Review*, **67** (2), 101–15.

Barro, R.J. (1979), 'Money and the price level under the gold standard', *Economic Journal*, **89** (March), 13–33.

Barro, R.J. (1981), 'Rational expectations and the role of monetary policy', in R. Lucas Jr and T. Sargent (eds), *Rational Expectations and Econometric Practice*, London: Allen and Unwin.

Barro, R.J. (1993), *Macroeconomics*, New York: John Wiley and Sons.

Barro, R.J. (1995), 'Inflation and economic growth', *Bank of England Quarterly Bulletin*, May.

Barro, R.J. (2008), *Macroeconomics: A Modern Approach*, Mason, OH: Thomson-South Western.

Barro, R.J. and S. Fischer (1976), 'Recent developments in monetary theory', *Journal of Monetary Economics*, **2**, 133–67.

Barro, R.J. and D.B. Gordon (1983a), 'A positive theory of monetary policy in a natural rate model', *Journal of Political Economy*, **91** (August), 589–610.

Barro, R.J. and D.B. Gordon (1983b), 'Rules, discretion and reputation in a model of monetary policy', *Journal of Monetary Economics*, **12** (1), 101–21.

Baumol, W. (1952), 'The transactions demand for cash: an inventory theoretic approach', *Quarterly Journal of Economics*, **66**, 545–56.

Bell, C. (1988), 'Credit markets and interlinked transactions', in H.B. Chenery and T.N. Srinivasan (eds), *Handbook of Development Economics*, Amsterdam: North-Holland.

Bell, C. (1992), 'Credit markets in developing countries', in P. Newman, M. Milgate and J. Eatwell (eds), *The New Palgrave Dictionary of Money and Finance*, vol. 1, London: Macmillan Press.

Bennett, A.G. (1995), 'Currency boards: issues and experiences', *Finance and Development* (September), 39–42.

Bercuson, K. (ed.) (1995), 'Singapore: a case study in rapid development', *Occasional Paper 119*, Washington, DC: IMF.

Berg, A. and E. Borensztein (2000), 'The choice of exchange rate regime and monetary target in highly dollarized economies', *Journal of Applied Economics*, **3** (2), 285–324.

Berger, H., J. De Haan and S.C.W. Eijffinger (2000), 'Central bank independence: an update of theory and evidence', *Discussion Paper Series No.2353*, London: Centre for Economic Policy Research.

Bernanke, B.S. (1983), 'Nonmonetary effects of the financial collapse in the propagation of the Great Depression', *American Economic Review*, **73**, 257–76.

Bernanke, B.S. (1993a), 'Credit in the macroeconomy', *Federal Reserve Bank of New York Quarterly Review* (Spring), 50–70.

Bernanke, B.S. (1993b), 'How important is the credit channel in the transmission of monetary policy? A comment', *Carnegie-Rochester Series on Public Policy* (December), 47–52.

Bernanke, B.S. (2004), 'Inflation targeting', *Federal Reserve Bank of St. Louis Review*, **86** (4), 165–8.

Bernanke, B. and A.S. Blinder (1988a), 'Credit, money and aggregate demand', *American Economic Review* (June), 257–76.

Bernanke, B.S. and A.S. Blinder (1988b), 'Is it money or credit, or both, or neither? Credit, money, and aggregate demand', *American Economic Review*, **78** (May), 435–39.

Bernanke, B.S. and M. Gertler (1995), 'Inside the black box: credit channel of monetary transmission mechanism', *Journal of Economic Perspective* (Fall), 27–48.

Bernanke, B.S. and F.S. Mishkin (1997), 'Inflation targeting: a new framework for monetary policy?', *Journal of Economic Perspectives*, **11** (2), 97–116.

Bernanke, B.S., M. Gertler and S. Gilchrist (1999a), 'The financial accelerator in a quantitative business cycle framework', in J.B. Taylor and M. Woodford (eds), *Handbook of Macroeconomics*, vol. 1, Amsterdam: Elsevier Science.

Bernanke, B.S., T. Laubach, F. Mishkin and A.S. Posen (1999b), *Inflation Targeting, Lessons from the International Experience*, Princeton, NJ: Princeton University Press.

Bhagwati, J.N. (1984), 'Development economics: what have we learned?', *Asian Development Review*, **2** (1), 23–38.

Bhagwati, J.N. (1991), *Political Economy and International Economics*, ed. by D.A. Irwin, Cambridge, MA: MIT Press.

Bhagwati, J.N. (1992), *India's Economy: The Shackled Giant*, Oxford: Clarendon Press.

Bhagwati, J.N. (1993), *India in Transition: Freeing the Economy*, Oxford: Clarendon Press.

Bhagwati, J.N. (1996), 'The miracle that did happen: understanding East Asia in comparative perspective', keynote speech delivered on 3 May at Cornell University on the occasion of the conference on Government and Market.

Bhagwati, J.N. (1998), 'The capital myth', *Foreign Affairs*, **77** (May–June), 7–12.

Bhagwati, J.N. (2005), 'In defense of globalization: it has a human face', the 2005 Angelo Costa Lecture, Rome.

Bhalla, S. (1981), 'The transmission of inflation into developing countries', in W. Cline and S. Weintraub (eds), *World Inflation and Developing Countries*, Washington, DC: Brookings Institution.

Bhatt, V.V. (1974), 'Some aspects of financial policies and central banking in developing countries', *World Development*, **2** (10–12), 59–67.

Bhattacharya, K. (2005), 'Monetary policy approaches in India', in *BIS Papers 31: Monetary Policy in Asia: Approaches and Implementation*, Basel: BIS.

Bhattacharya, A. and M. Pangestu (1993), *The Lessons of East Asia: Development Transformation and Public Policy*, Washington, DC: World Bank.

Blackburn, K. and M. Christensen (1989), 'Monetary theory and policy credibility', *Journal of Economic Literature*, **27** (1), 1–45.

Blanchard, O.J. (1990), 'Why does money affect output? A survey', in B.M. Friedman and F.H. Hahn (eds), *Handbook of Monetary Economics*, vol. 2, Amsterdam: Elsevier Science.

Blanchard, O.J. (2006), *Macroeconomics*, New York: Pearson-Prentice Hall.

Blanchard, O.J. and S. Fischer (1989), *Lectures on Macroeconomics*, Cambridge, MA: MIT Press.

Blanchard, O.J. and J. Sheen (2007), *Macroeconomics*, Sydney: Pearson-Education Australia.

Blejer, M. and M.S. Khan (1984), 'Government policy and private investment in developing countries', *IMF Staff Papers*, **31**, 379–403.

Blejer, M. and N. Liviatan (1987), 'Fighting hyperinflation: stabilization strategies in Argentina and Israel', *IMF Staff Papers*, **34**, 409–38.

Blejer, M.I., A. Ize and A.M. Leone (eds) (2000), *Inflation Targeting in Practice: Strategic and Operational Issues and Applications to Emerging Market Economies*, Washington, DC: IMF.

Blinder, A.S. (1998), *Central Banking in Theory and Practice*, Cambridge, MA: MIT Press.

Blinder, A.S. (1999), 'Central bank credibility: why do we care? How do we build it?', *NBER Working Paper No. W7161*, New York: NBER.

Blinder, A.S. and J. E. Stiglitz (1983), 'Money, credit constraints, and economic activity', *American Economic Review*, **73** (May), 297–302.

Bodart, V. (1990), 'Central bank independence and the effectiveness of monetary policy: a comparative analysis', draft, Washington, DC: IMF.

Bollard, A. and O. Karagedikli (2006), 'Inflation targeting: the New Zealand experience and some lessons', paper presented at Inflation Targeting: Performance and Challenges Conference at the Central Bank of the Republic of Turkey, Istanbul, 19–20 January.

Bomhoff, E. (1983), *Monetary Uncertainty*, Amsterdam: North-Holland.

Bomberger, W.A. and G.E. Makinen (1983), 'The Hungarian hyperinflation and stabilization of 1945–46', *Journal of Political Economy*, **91** (October), 801–24.

Bordo, M.D. (1989), 'The lender of last resort: some historical insights', *NBER Working Paper Series 3011*, New York: NBER.

Bordo, M.D. (1992), 'Gold standard: theory', in P. Newman, M. Milgate and J. Eatwell (eds), *The New Palgrave Dictionary of Money and Finance*, vol. 2, London: Macmillan Press.

Bordo, M.D. (2007), 'The history of monetary policy', draft, Rutgers University, New Brunswick, NJ.

Bordo, M. and F.E. Kydland (1995), 'The gold standard as a rule: an essay in exploration', *Explorations in Economic History*, **32**, 423–64.

Bordo, M. and A. Redish (1987), 'Why did the Bank of Canada emerge in 1935?', *Journal of Economic History,* **47**, 405–17.

Bordo, M.D. and A.J. Schwartz (eds) (1984), *A Retrospective on the Classical Gold Standard, 1821–1931*, Chicago, IL: Chicago University Press.

Boschen, J.F. (1992), 'Real interest rates', in P. Newman, M. Milgate and J. Eatwell (eds), *The New Palgrave Dictionary of Money and Finance*, vol. 3, London: Macmillan Press.

Bottomley, A. (1965), 'Keynesian monetary theory and the developing countries', *Indian Economic Journal*, **12**, 1–32.

Boughton, J.M. (1981), 'Recent instability of the demand for money: an international perspective', *Southern Economic Journal*, **47** (3), 579–97.

Boughton, J.M. (1991), 'Long-run money demand in large industrial countries', *IMF Staff Papers*, **38**, 1–32.

Branson, W.H. (1989), *Macroeconomic Theory and Policy*, New York: Harper and Row.

Bresciani-Turroni, C. (1937), *The Economics of Inflation*, London: Allen and Unwin.

Brown, A.J. (1955), *The Great Inflation: 1939–1951*, London: Oxford University Press.

Brown, A.J. (1985), *World Inflation Since 1950*, Cambridge: Cambridge University Press.

Brunner, K. (1992), 'Money supply', in P. Newman, M. Milgate and J. Eatwell (eds), *The New Palgrave Dictionary of Money and Finance*, vol. 2, London: Macmillan Press.

Brunner, K. and A. Meltzer (1963), 'Predicting velocity: implications for theory and policy', *Journal of Finance*, **18**, 319–54.

Brunner, K. and A. Meltzer (1968), 'Liquidity traps for money, bank credit and interest rates', *Journal of Political Economy*, **76** (1), 1–37.

Brunner, K. and A. Meltzer (1990), 'Money supply', in B.M. Friedman and F.H. Hahn (eds), *Handbook of Monetary Economics*, vol. 1, Amsterdam: Elsevier Science.

Bruno, M. (1979), 'Stabilization and stagflation in a semi-industrialised economy', in R. Dornbusch and J.A. Frenkel (eds), *International Economic Policy: Theory and Evidence*, Baltimore, MD: Johns Hopkins University Press.

Bruno, M. (1991), 'High inflation and the nominal anchors of an open economy', *Princeton Essays in International Finance No. 183*, Department of Economics, Princeton, NJ: Princeton University.

Bruno, M. (1993a), 'Monetary policy rules in a small open economy', in R. Dornbusch (ed), *Policymaking in the Open Economy: Concepts and Case Studies in Economic Performance*, New York: Oxford University Press.

Bruno, M. (1993b), *Crisis, Stabilization and Economic Reform*, New York: Oxford University Press.

Bruno, M. and W. Easterly (1998), 'Inflation crises and long-run growth', *Journal of Monetary Economics*, **41** (February), 3–26.

Bruno, M. and J. Sachs (1985), *Economics of Worldwide Stagflation*, Oxford: Blackwell.

Bryant, R., P. Hooper and C. Mann (eds) (2003), *Evaluating Policy Regimes: New Research in Empirical Macroeconomics*, Washington, DC: Brookings Institution.

Buchanan, J. and R. Wagner (1977), *Democracy in Deficit*, New York: Academic Press.

Buchanan, J., C. Rowley and R. Tollison (1987), *Deficits*, Oxford: Basil Blackwell.

Burda, M. and C. Wyplosz (2005), *Macroeconomics: A European Text*, New York: Oxford University Press.

Burkner, H.P. (1982), 'The portfolio behaviour of individual investors in developing countries: an analysis of the Philippines case', *Oxford Bulletin of Economics and Statistics*, **44**, 127–44.

Burton, D. and A. Zanello (2007), 'Asia ten years after', *Finance and Development*, **44** (2), 1–9.

Cagan, P. (1956), 'The monetary dynamics of hyperinflation', in M. Friedman (ed), *Studies in the Quantity Theory of Money*, Chicago, IL: University of Chicago Press.

Cagan, P. (1958), 'Demand for currency relative to the total money supply', *Journal of Political Economy*, **66**, 303–28.

Cagan, P. (1992a), 'Hyperinflation: theory', in P. Newman, M. Milgate and J. Eatwell (eds), *The New Palgrave Dictionary of Money and Finance*, vol. 2, London: Macmillan Press.

Cagan, P. (1992b), 'Monetarism', in P. Newman, M. Milgate and J. Eatwell (eds), *The New Palgrave Dictionary of Money and Finance*, vol. 2, London: Macmillan Press.

Calomiris, C.W. and C.P. Himmelberg (1994), 'Directed credit programs for agriculture and industry: arguments from theory and fact', proceedings of the World Bank Annual Conference on Development Economics 1993, 113–54.

Calvo, G.A. (1978a), 'On the consistency of optimal policy in the monetary economy', *Econometrica*, **46** (November), 1411–28.

Calvo, G.A. (1978b), 'Optimal seigniorage from money creation', *Journal of Monetary Economics*, **4**, 503–17.

Calvo, G.A. (ed.) (1996), *Money, Exchange Rates and Output*, Cambridge, MA: MIT Press.

Calvo, G.A. and P.E. Guidotti (1992), 'Speculative attacks', in P. Newman, M. Milgate and J. Eatwell (eds), *The New Palgrave Dictionary of Money and Finance*, vol. 3, London: Macmillan Press.

Calvo, G.A. and F.S. Mishkin (2003), 'The mirage of exchange rate regimes for emerging market countries', *Journal of Economic Perspectives*, **17**, 99–118.

Calvo, G.A. and C.M. Reinhart (2001), 'Reflections on dollarization', in A. Alesina and R.J. Barro (eds), *Currency Unions*, Stanford, CA: Hoover Institute Press.

Calvo, G.A. and C.A. Rodriguez (1992), 'Currency substitution in developing countries: an introduction', *Rivista de Analysis Economico*, **7** (1), 3–28.

Calvo, G.A. and C. Vegh (1996), 'From currency substitution to dollarization: analysis and policy issues', in G.A. Calvo (ed.), *Money, Exchange Rates and Output*, Cambridge, MA: MIT Press.

Camin, U. (2008), 'Monetary policy in Vietnam: the case of a transition country', *BIS Papers*, **31**, 232–52.

Camin, U. and G. Genberg (2005), 'An inflation targeting regime for Vietnam', VERCON First Annual Research Conference, Hanoi.

Campbell, J.Y. and N.G. Mankiw (1987), 'Are output fluctuations transitory?', *Quarterly Journal of Economics*, **102**, 857–80.

Campbell, J.Y. and N.G. Mankiw (1991), 'The response of consumption to income – a cross-country investigation', *European Economic Review*, **35**, 723–67.

Campos, R. (1969), *Reflections on Latin American Development*, Austin, TX: Texas University Press.

Canavese, A. (1982), 'The structuralist explanation in theory of inflation', *World Development*, **10**, 523–30.

Capie, F. (1986), 'Conditions in which very rapid inflation has appeared', *Carnegie-Rochester Conference Series on Public Policy*, **24**, 115–68.

Capie, F. (1997), 'The evolution of central banking', in *Reforming the Financial System: Some Lessons from History*, Cambridge: Cambridge University Press.

Capie, F., C. Goodhart, S. Fischer and N. Schnadt (1994), *The Future of Central Banking: The Tercentenary Symposium of the Bank of England*, Cambridge: Cambridge University Press.

Cardoso, E. (1981), 'Food supply and inflation', *Journal of Development Economics*, **9** (2), 269–84.

Cardoso, E.A and R. Dornbusch (1989), 'Foreign private capital flows', in H.B. Chenery and T.N. Srinivasan (eds), *Handbook of Development Economics*, vol. 2, Amsterdam: Elsevier Science Publishers.

Cargill, T.F. and M.M. Hutchison (1988), 'The response of the Bank of Japan to macro-economic and financial change', in H.S. Cheng (ed.), *Monetary Policy in Pacific Basin Countries*, Boston: Kluwer Academic.

Cargill, T. and M. Hutchison (1990), 'Monetary policy and political economy: the Federal Reserve and the Bank of Japan', in T. Mayer (ed.), *The Political Economy of American Monetary Policy*, New York: Cambridge University Press.

Cargill, T.F., M.M. Hutchison and T. Ito (1997), *The Political Economy of Japanese Monetary Policy*, Cambridge, MA: MIT Press.

Cargill, T.F., M.M. Hutchison and T. Ito (2001), *Financial Policy and Central Banking in Japan*, Cambridge, MA: MIT Press.

Cavallo, D. (1977), 'Stagflationary effects of monetarist stabilization policies', unpublished PhD dissertation, Harvard University, Boston, MA.

Cecchetti, S.G. (2008), *Money, Banking and Financial Markets*, New York: McGraw-Hill.

Chandavarkar, A.G. (1992), 'Of finance and development', *World Development*, **20**, 133–42.

Chapra, M.U. (1982), 'Monetary and fiscal economics of Islam', in M. Ariff (ed.), *Monetary and Fiscal Economics of Islam*, Jeddah: International Centre for Research in Islamic Economics, King Abdulaziz University.

Cheng, H.S. (ed.) (1988), *Monetary Policy in Pacific Basin Countries*, Boston, MA: Kluwer Academic.

Cho, T.J. (1989), 'Finance and development: the Korean approach', *Oxford Review of Economic Policy*, **5** (4), 88–102.

Cho, Y.J. (1990), 'McKinnon-Shaw versus the neostructuralists on financial liberalization: a conceptual note', *World Development*, **18** (3), 477–80.

Cho, Y.J. and D. Khatkhate (1989), 'Lessons of financial liberalization in Asia: a comparative study', *Discussion Paper No. 50*, Washington, DC: World Bank.

Choudhri, E. and M. Khan (2002), 'The exchange rate and consumer prices in Pakistan: is rupee devaluation inflationary?', *Pakistan Development Review*, **41** (2), 107–20.

Chow, G.C. (1966), 'On the long-run and short-run demand for money', *Journal of Political Economy*, **74** (2), 111–31.

Chow, H.K. (2007), 'Singapore's exchange rate policy: some implementation issues', *Singapore Economic Review*, **52** (3), 445–58
Chowdhury, A. and I. Islam (1993), *The Newly Industrialising Economies of East Asia*, New York: Routledge.
Chu, K. and A. Feltenstein (1979), 'Extraordinary inflation: the Argentine experience', *Finance and Development*, **16** (2), 32–5.
Claassen, E.M. (1985), 'The lender-of-last-resort function in the context of national and international financial crises', *Weltwirtschaftliches Archiv*, **121** (2), 217–37.
Clarida, R., J. Gali and M. Gertler (1999), 'The science of monetary policy: a new Keynesian perspective', *Journal of Economic Literature*, **37** (December), 1661–707.
Clayton, G., J. Gilbert and R. Sedgwick (eds) (1977), *Monetary Theory and Monetary Policy in the 1970s*, Oxford: Oxford University Press.
Clements, B. and G. Schwartz (1993), 'Currency substitution: the recent experience of Bolivia', *World Development*, **21** (11), 1883–93.
Cline, W. and S. Weintraub (eds) (1981), *World Inflation and Developing Countries*, Washington, DC: Brookings Institution.
Clower, R.W. (ed.) (1969), *Monetary Theory*, Harmondsworth: Penguin.
Coates, W.L. and D.R. Khatkhate (1980), *Money and Monetary Policy in Less Developed Countries: A Survey of Issues and Evidence*, New York: Pergamon Press.
Cobham, D. (1992), 'Monetary targeting', in P. Newman, M. Milgate and J. Eatwell (eds), *The New Palgrave Dictionary of Money and Finance*, vol. 2, London: Macmillan Press.
Cogley, T. (1997), 'What is the optimal rate of inflation?', *FRBSF Economic Letter*, No. 97-27, 19 September.
Cohen, D. (1985), 'Inflation, wealth, and interest rates in an intertemporal optimizing model', *Journal of Monetary Economics*, **16**, 73–85.
Cole, D. and H. Patrick (1986), 'Financial development in the Pacific Basin market economies', in A. Tan and B.K. Kapur (eds), *Pacific Growth and Financial Independence*, Sydney: Allen and Unwin.
Collier, P. and J.W. Gunning (1999), 'Explaining African economic performance', *Journal of Economic Literature*, **37** (March), 69–111.
Collins, M. (1992a), 'Bank of England', in P. Newman, M. Milgate and J. Eatwell (eds), *The New Palgrave Dictionary of Money and Finance,* vol. 1, London: Macmillan Press.
Collins, M. (ed.) (1992b), *Central Banking in History*, London: Edward Elgar.
Collyns, C. (1983), 'Alternatives to the central bank in the developing world', *Occasional Paper No. 20*, Washington, DC: IMF.
Cooper, R.N. (1982), 'The gold standard: historical facts and future prospects', *Brookings Papers on Economic Activity*, **1**, 1–45.
Corbo, V.L. (1974), *Inflation in Developing Countries: An Econometric Study of Chilean Inflation*, Amsterdam: North-Holland.
Corbo, V.L. (1988), 'Problems, development theory, and strategies of Latin America', in G. Ranis and T.P. Schultz (eds), *The State of Development Economics*, New York: Basil Blackwell.
Corden, W.M. (1991), 'Exchange rate policy in developing countries', in J. de Melo and A. Sapir (eds), *Trade Theory and Economic Reform: North, South, and East*, Oxford: Basil Blackwell.

Corden, W.M. (1993), 'Exchange rate policies for developing countries', *Economic Journal*, **103** (January), 198–207.

Cornwall, J. (1992), 'Stagflation', in P. Newman, M. Milgate and J. Eatwell (eds), *The New Palgrave Dictionary of Money and Finance*, vol. 3, London: Macmillan Press.

Cowan, K. and Q.T. Do (2003), 'Financial dollarization and central bank credibility', *Policy Research Working Paper 3082*, Washington, DC: World Bank.

Coyne, J.E. (1961), 'Remarks to the Annual Conference of the Business Paper Editors Association', Ottawa, 18 January.

Cramer, J.S. (1992), 'Velocity of circulation', in P. Newman, M. Milgate and J. Eatwell (eds), *The New Palgrave Dictionary of Money and Finance*, vol. 3, London: Macmillan Press.

Crockett, A. (2001), 'Monetary policy and financial stability', *Distinguished Lecture No. 4*, Hong Kong: Hong Kong Monetary Authority.

Crockett, A. and S. Nsouli (1977), 'Exchange rate policies for developing countries', *Journal of Development Studies*, **13**, 125–43.

Croushore, D. (1992), 'What are the costs of disinflation?', *Federal Reserve Bank of Philadelphia Business Review*, May–June.

Crow, J. (1988), 'The work of Canadian monetary policy', *Bank of Canada Review* (February), 3–17.

Cuddington, J.T. (1983), 'Currency substitution, capital mobility and money demand', *Journal of International Money and Finance*, **2**, 111–33.

Cuddington, J.T. (1989), 'Review of *Currency Substitutability: Theory and Evidence for Latin America* by V.A. Canto and G. Nickelsberg (Boston: Kluwer)', *Journal of Money, Credit and Banking*, **21** (1), 267–71.

Cukierman, A. (1986), 'Central bank behavior and credibility – some recent developments', *Federal Reserve Bank of St. Louis Review*, **68**, 5–17.

Cukierman, A. (1992), *Central Bank Strategy, Credibility and Independence: Theory and Independence*, Cambridge, MA: MIT Press.

Cukierman, A. and A.H. Meltzer (1986), 'A theory of ambiguity, credibility, and inflation under discretion and asymmetric information', *Econometrica*, **54**, 1099–128.

Cukierman, A., P. Kalaitzidakis, L. Summers and S. Webb (1993), 'Central bank independence, growth, investment and real rates', *Carnegie-Rochester Conference Series on Public Policy*, **39** (December), 95–140.

Cukierman, A., G.P. Miller and B. Neyapti (2002), 'Central bank reform, liberalization and inflation in transition economies – an international perspective', *Journal of Monetary Economics*, **49**, 237–64.

Cuckierman, A., S.B. Webb and B. Neyapti (1992), 'Measuring the independence of central banks and its effects on policy outcomes', *World Bank Economic Review*, **6** (1), 353–98.

Cypher, J.H. and J.L. Dietz (1997), *The Process of Economic Development*, London: Routledge.

Danthine, J.P. (1992), 'Superneutrality', in P. Newman, M. Milgate and J. Eatwell (eds), *The New Pelgrave Dictionary of Money and Finance*, vol. 3, London: Macmillan Press.

Davies, S.G. (1960), *Central Banking in South and East Asia*, Hong Kong: Hong Kong University Press.

De Cecco, M. (1992), 'Gold standard', in P. Newman, M. Milgate and J. Eatwell (eds), *The New Palgrave Dictionary of Money and Finance*, vol. 2, London: Macmillan Press.

De la Torre, A., E. Levy-Yeyati and S.L. Schmukler (2003), 'Living and dying with hard pegs: the rise and fall of Argentina's currency board', *Economia*, Spring, 43–107.

De Long, J.B. (2000), 'The triumph of monetarism?', *Journal of Economic Perspectives*, **14** (1), 83–94.

De Zamaroczy, M. and S. Sa (2003), 'Economic policy in a highly dollarized economy: the case of Cambodia', *Occasional Paper No. 219*, Washington, DC: IMF.

Debelle, G. (1997), 'Inflation targeting in practice', *IMF Working Paper 97/35*, Washington, DC: IMF.

Diaz-Alejandro, C. (1985), 'Good-bye financial repression, hello financial crash', *Journal of Development Economics*, **19**, 1–24.

Dillard, D. (1954), 'The theory of a monetary economy', in K.K. Kurihara (ed), *Post-Keynesian Economics*, London: Allen and Unwin.

Diz, A. (1970), 'Money and prices in Argentina, 1935–62', in D. Meiselman (ed.), *Varieties of Monetary Experience*, Chicago, IL: Chicago University Press.

Dodsworth, J. and Associates (1996), 'Vietnam: transition to a market economy', *IMF Occasional Paper 135*, Washington, DC: IMF.

Dodsworth, J. and D. Mihaljek (1997), 'Hong Kong, China: growth, structural change, and economic stability during the transition', *Occasional Paper 152*, Washington, DC: IMF.

Dollar, D. and A. Kraay (2002), 'Growth is good for the poor'. *Journal of Economic Growth*, **7** (3), 195–225.

Dollar, D. and A. Kraay (2004), 'Trade, growth, and poverty', *Economic Journal*, **114** (493), F22–F49.

Domar, E. (1946), 'Capital expansion, rate of growth, and employment', *Econometrica*, **14** (April), 137–47.

Domar, E. (1947), 'Expansion and employment', *American Economic Review*, **37**, 34–55.

Dooley, M.R., R. Dornbusch and Y.C. Park (2001), 'A framework for exchange rate policy in Korea', paper presented at KIEP/IMF Conference 'Korea Crisis and Recovery', Seoul, 17–19 May.

Dornbusch, R. (1976), 'Expectations and exchange rate dynamics', *Journal of Political Economy*, **84**, 1161–76.

Dornbusch, R. (1988a), 'Lessons from the German inflation experience of the 1920s', in R. Dornbusch, *Exchange Rates and Inflation*, Cambridge, MA: MIT Press.

Dornbusch, R. (1988b), *Exchange Rates and Inflation*, Cambridge, MA: MIT Press.

Dornbusch, R. (1989), 'Stabilization, credibility and unemployment: the experience of Ireland', *Economic Policy*, **7**, 174–209.

Dornbusch, R. (1992a), 'The case for trade liberalization in developing countries', *Journal of Development Perspectives*, **6**, 69–86.

Dornbusch, R. (1992b), 'Purchasing power parity', in P. Newman, M. Milgate and J. Eatwell (eds), *The New Palgrave Dictionary of Money and Finance*, vol. 3, London: Macmillan Press.

Dornbusch, R. (1993), *Stabilization, Debt, and Reform: Policy Analysis for Developing Countries*, New York: Harvester Wheatsheaf.

Dornbusch, R. (2000), *Keys to Prosperity*, Cambridge, MA: MIT Press.

Dornbusch, R (2001a), 'Fewer monies, better monies', *NBER Working Paper No. 8324*, Cambridge, MA: NBER.

Dornbusch, R. (2001b), 'Argentina at the end of the rope', draft, Department of Economics website, MIT, Cambridge, MA.

Dornbusch, R. and S. Edwards (1990), 'The macroeconomics of populism in Latin America', *Journal of Development Economics*, **32**, 247–77.

Dornbusch, R. and S. Edwards (1991), *The Macroeconomics of Populism in Latin America*, Chicago, IL: Chicago University Press.

Dornbusch, R. and S. Fischer (1981), 'Budget deficits and inflation', in J. Flanders and A. Razin (eds), *Development in an Inflationary World*, New York: Academic Press.

Dornbusch, R. and S. Fischer (1986), 'Stopping hyperinflation, past and present', *Weltwirtschaftlichers Archiv*, **1**, 1–47.

Dornbusch, R. and J.A. Frenkel (1973), 'Inflation and growth: alternative approaches', *Journal of Money, Credit and Banking*, **5**, 141–56.

Dornbusch, R. and J.A. Frenkel (1973), 'Inflation and growth: alternative approaches', *Journal of Money, Credit and Banking*, **5**, 141–56.

Dornbusch, D. and A. Giovannini (1990), 'Monetary policy in the open economy', in B.M. Friedman and F.H. Hahn (eds.), *Handbook of Monetary Economics*, vol. 2, Amsterdam: Elsevier Science.

Dornbusch, R. and L.T. Kuenzler (1993), 'Exchange rate policy: options and issues', in R. Dornbusch (ed.), *Policymaking in the Open Economy*, New York: Oxford University Press.

Dornbusch, R. and A. Reynoso (1989), 'Financial factors in economic development', *American Economic Review*, **79** (2), 204–09.

Dornbusch, R., S. Fischer and R. Startz (2008), *Macroeconomics*, New York: McGraw-Hill.

Dornbusch, R., F. Sturzenegger and H. Wolf (1990), 'Extreme inflation: dynamics and stabilization', *Brookings Papers on Economic Activity*, **2**, 1–84.

Dorrance, G.S. (1966), 'Inflation and growth: the statistical evidence', *IMF Staff Papers*, **13**, 82–102.

Dorrance, G.S. (1969), 'The role of central banks in less developed countries', *Finance and Development*, **6** (4), 22–6.

Downes, P. and R. Vaez-Zadeh (eds) (1991), *The Evolving Role of Central Banks*, Washington, DC: IMF.

Driffill, J., G. Mizon and A. Ulph (1990), 'The costs of inflation', in F.H. Hahn and B.M. Friedman (eds), *Handbook of Monetary Economics*, Amsterdam: North-Holland.

Driscoll, M.J. and A.K. Lahiri (1983), 'Income velocity of money in agricultural developing economies', *Review of Economics and Statistics*, **65**, 393–401.

Easterly, W. and K. Schmidt-Hebbel (1993), 'Fiscal deficits and macroeconomic performance in developing countries', *World Bank Research Observer*, **8** (2), 211–39.

Easterly, W. and S. Fischer (1994), 'What can we learn from the Soviet collapse?', *Finance and Development* (December), 2–5.

Easterly, W. and S. Fischer (2001), 'Inflation and the poor', *Journal of Money, Credit and Banking*, **33** (2), 160–78.

Easterly, W., C.A. Rodriguez and K. Schmidt-Hebbel (eds) (1994), *Public Sector Deficits and Macroeconomic Performance*, New York: Oxford University Press.

Economic Report of the President 1962, Washington, DC: US Government Printing Office.

Edel, M. (1969), *Food Supply and Inflation in Latin America*, New York: Praeger.

Edey, M. (2006), 'An Australian perspective on inflation targeting, communication and transparency', *BIS Papers No. 31: Monetary Policy in Asia: Approaches and Implementation*, Basel: Bank for International Settlements.

Edwards, S. (1983), 'The short-run relationship between growth and inflation in Latin America: comment', *American Economic Review*, **73** (3), 477–82

Edwards, S. (1989a), *Real Exchange Rates, Devaluation and Adjustment: Exchange Rate Policies in Developing Countries*, Cambridge, MA: MIT Press.

Edwards, S. (1989b), *Exchange Rate Misalignment in Developing Countries*, Baltimore, MD: Johns Hopkins University Press.

Edwards, S. (1993), 'Exchange rates as nominal anchors', *Review of World Economics*, **129** (1), 1–32.

Edwards, S. (1994), 'The political economy of inflation and stabilization in developing countries', *Economic Development and Cultural Change*, **42** (2), 235–66.

Edwards, S. (1998), 'Capital flows, real exchange rates and capital controls: some Latin American experience', *NBER Working Paper 6800*, Cambridge, MA: NBER.

Edwards, S. and A.C. Edwards (1987), *Monetarism and Liberalization: The Chilean Experiment*, Cambridge, MA: Ballinger.

Edwards, S. and G. Tabellini (1991), 'Explaining fiscal policies and inflation in developing countries', *Journal of International Money and Finance*, **10**, 16–48.

Ee, K.H. and K.R. Xiong (2008), 'Asia: perspective on the subprime crisis', *Finance and Development*, **45** (2), 1–10, http://www.imf.org/external/pubs/ft/fandd/2008/06/khor.htm.

Eiteman, D.K., A.I. Stonehill and M. H. Moffett (2001), *Multinational Business Finance*, New York: Pearson-Addison Wesley.

Enoch, C. and A.-M. Gulde (1997), 'Making a currency board operational', *IMF Paper on Policy Analysis and Assessment, 97/10*, Washington, DC: IMF.

Enoch, C. and A.-M. Gulde (1998), 'Are currency boards a cure for all monetary problems?', *Finance and Development*, **35** (4), 40–43.

Evans, M. (1991), 'Discovering the link between inflation rates and inflation uncertainty', *Journal of Money, Credit, and Banking*, **23**, 169–84.

Fair, D. (1979), 'The independence of central banks', *The Banker*, October.

Fair, R.C. (1987), 'International evidence on the demand for money', *Review of Economics and Statistics*, **69**, 473–80.

Fan, L.S. and Z.R. Liu (1970), 'Demand for money in Asian countries: empirical evidence', *Indian Economic Journal*, **18** (4–5), 475–81.

Fazio, A. (1991), 'Role and independence of central banks', in P. Downes and R. Vaez-Zadeh (eds), *The Evolving Role of Central Banks*, Washington, DC: IMF.

Feder, G. (1982), 'On exports and economic growth', *Journal of Development Economics*, **12** (1–2), 59–74.

Feige, E. and D. Pearce (1977), 'The substitutability of money and near monies: a survey of the time series evidence', *Journal of Economic Literature*, **15** (2), 439–69.

Feldstein, M. (2002), 'Argentina's fall: lessons from the latest financial crisis', *Foreign Affairs*, **81** (2), 7–14.

Feltenstein, A. and Z. Farhadian (1987), 'Fiscal policy, monetary targets, and the price level in a centrally planned economy: an application to China', *Journal of Money, Credit, and Banking*, **19** (2), 137–56.

Fender, J. (1990), *Inflation*, Ann Arbor, MI: University of Michigan Press.

Fischer, S. (1974), 'Money and the production function', *Economic Inquiry*, **12** (4), 517–33.

Fischer, S. (1977), 'Long-term contracts, rational expectations, and the optimal money supply rule', *Journal of Political Economy*, **85** (February), 191–206.

Fischer, S. (1979a), 'Anticipations and the nonneutrality of money', *Journal of Political Economy*, **87** (2), 225–52.

Fischer, S. (1979b), 'Capital accumulation on the transition path in a monetary optimizing model', *Econometrica*, **47**, 1433–9.

Fischer, S. (1980), 'On activist monetary policy with rational expectations', in S. Fischer (ed.), *Rational Expectations and Economic Policy*, Chicago, IL: Chicago University Press.

Fischer, S. (1981), 'Towards an understanding of the costs of inflation: II', *Carnegie-Rochester Conference Series on Public Policy*, **15**, 5–41.

Fischer, S. (1984), 'The benefits of price stability', in *Price Stability and Public Policy*, proceedings of a symposium sponsored by the Federal Reserve Bank of Kansas City, Jackson Hole, WY, 2–3 August.

Fischer, S. (1990), 'Rules versus discretion in monetary policy', in B.M. Friedman and F. Hahn (eds), *Handbook of Monetary Economics*, vol. 2, Amsterdam: Elsevier Science.

Fischer, S. (1992), 'New classical macroeconomics', in P. Newman, M. Milgate and J. Eatwell (eds), *The New Palgrave Dictionary of Money and Finance*, vol. 2, London: Macmillan Press.

Fischer, S. (1993), 'Role of macroeconomic factors in growth', *Journal of Monetary Economics*, **32** (December), 485–512.

Fischer, S. (1994), 'Modern central banking', in F. Capie, C. Goodhart, S. Fischer and N. Schnadt (eds), *The Future of Central Banking*, Cambridge: Cambridge University Press.

Fischer, S. (1995a), 'Central bank independence revisited', *American Economic Review*, **85** (2), 201–06.

Fischer, S. (1995b), 'Central bank independence in the transition economies', revised version of a (1995) lecture delivered at the Seventieth Anniversary Conference of the National Bank of Hungary, Budapest, November 2004.

Fischer, S. (1995c), 'Financial liberalization and central banking in industrializing economies', paper presented at the Bank of Korea's 45th Anniversary Symposium, Seoul, 19 June.

Fischer, S. (1996a), 'Maintaining price stability', *Finance and Development*, December, 34–7.

Fischer, S. (1996b), 'Why are central banks pursuing long-run price stability?, in *Achieving Price Stability*, proceedings of a symposium sponsored by the Federal Reserve Bank of Kansas City, Jackson Hole, WY, 29–31 August.

Fischer, S. (2001), 'Exchange rate regimes: is the bipolar view correct?', *Journal of Economic Perspectives*, **15** (Spring), 3–24.
Fischer, S. (2003), 'Globalization and its challenges', *American Economic Review*, **93** (May), 1–30.
Fischer, S. and W. Easterly (1990), 'The economics of the government budget constraint', *World Bank Research Observer*, **5** (July), 127–42.
Fischer, S., R. Sahay and C.A. Vegh (2002), 'Modern hyper- and high inflations', *Journal of Economic Literature*, **40** (3), 837–80.
Fisher, I. (1911), *The Purchasing Power of Money*, New York: Macmillan.
Fisher, I. (1923), 'The business cycle – largely a dance of the dollar', *Journal of the American Statistical Association*, **18**, 1024–8.
Fisher, I. (1926), *The Money Illusion*, New York: Adelphi.
Fisher, I. (1930), *The Theory of Interest*, New York: Macmillan.
Flavin, M. (1981), 'The adjustment of consumption to changing expectations about future income', *Journal of Political Economy*, **89** (5), 974–1009.
Flood, R.P. and P.M. Garber (1984), 'Gold monetization and gold discipline', *Journal of Political Economy*, **92** (February), 90–107.
Flood, R.P. and M. Mussa (1994), 'Issues concerning nominal anchors for monetary policy', in T.J.T. Balino and C. Cottarelli (eds), *Frameworks for Monetary Stability*, Washington, DC: IMF.
Forder, J. (2000), 'Central bank independence and credibility: is there a shred of evidence?, *International Finance*, **3** (1), 167–85.
Frank, A.G. (1967), *Capitalism and Development in Latin America: Historical Studies of Chile and Brazil*, New York: Monthly Review Press.
Frank, A.G. (1996), 'The development of underdevelopment', in K.P. Jameson and C.K. Wilber (eds), *The Political Economy of Development and Underdevelopment*, New York: McGraw-Hill.
Franzese, R.J.J. (1999), 'Partially independent central banks, politically responsive governments, and inflation', *American Journal of Political Science*, **43** (3), 681–706.
Fraser, B. (1989), 'Reserve bank independence and all that', *Reserve Bank of Australia Bulletin* (December), 8–13.
Fraser, B. (1992), 'Two perspectives on monetary policy', *Reserve Bank of Australia Bulletin*, September, 1–8.
Fraser, B. (1993), 'Some aspects of monetary policy', *Reserve Bank of Australia Bulletin*, April, 1–7.
Freedman, C. (1992), 'Bank of Canada', in P. Newman, M. Milgate and J. Eatwell (eds), *The New Palgrave Dictionary of Money and Finance*, vol. 1, London: Macmillan Press.
Frenkel, J.A. (1991), 'The cost of capital in Japan: a survey', *Pacific-Basin Working Paper*, San Francisco, CA: Federal Reserve Bank of San Francisco.
Frenkel, J.A. and H. Johnson (eds) (1976), *The Monetary Approach to the Balance of Payments*, Toronto: University of Toronto Press.
Frenkel, J.A. and H. Johnson (eds) (1978), *The Economics of Exchange Rates*, London: Addison-Wesley.
Frey, B. and F. Schneider (1981), 'Central bank behavior: a positive empirical analysis', *Journal of Monetary Economics*, **7** (3), 291–315.

Friedman, B.M. (1996), 'The rise and fall of money growth targets as guidelines for U.S. monetary policy', *NBER Working Paper No. 5465*, Cambridge, MA: NBER.

Friedman, B.M. (1999), 'The future of monetary policy: the central bank as an army with only a signal corps?', *International Finance*, **2** (3), 321–38.

Friedman, B.M. and F.H. Hahn (eds) (1990), *Handbook of Monetary Economics*, vols 1 and 2, Amsterdam: Elsevier Science.

Friedman, M. (1948), 'A monetary and fiscal framework for economic stability', *American Economic Review*, **38** (3), 245–64.

Friedman, M. (1956), 'The quantity theory of money: a restatement', in M. Friedman (ed.), *Studies in the Quantity Theory of Money*, Chicago, IL: Chicago University Press.

Friedman, M. (1957), *A Theory of Consumption Function*, New York: National Bureau of Economic Research.

Friedman, M. (1959a), *A Program for Monetary Stability*, New York: Fordham University.

Friedman, M. (1959b), 'The demand for money – some theoretical and empirical results', *Journal of Political Economy*, **67**, 327–51.

Friedman, M. (1961), 'The lag in the effect of monetary policy', *Journal of Political Economy*, **69** (October), 447–66.

Friedman, M. (1962), 'Should there be an independent monetary authority?', in L.B. Yeager (ed), *In Search of a Monetary Constitution*, Cambridge, MA: Harvard University Press.

Friedman, M. (1963), *Inflation: Causes and Consequences*, Bombay: Asia Publishing House.

Friedman, M. (1966), 'Interest rates and the demand for money', *Journal of Law and Economics*, **9**, 71–85.

Friedman, M. (1968a), 'The role of monetary policy', *American Economic Review*, **58** (1), 1–17.

Friedman, M. (1968b), 'Inflation: causes and consequences', in M. Friedman, *Dollars and Deficits*, Englewood Cliffs, NJ: Prentice-Hall.

Friedman, M. (1969a), 'The optimum quantity of money', in M. Friedman (ed.), *The Optimum Quantity of Money and Other Essays*, Chicago, IL: Alpine.

Friedman, M. (ed.) (1969b), *The Optimum Quantity of Money and Other Essays*, Chicago, IL: Alpine.

Friedman, M. (1971a), 'Government revenue from inflation', *Journal of Political Economy*, **79**, 846–56.

Friedman, M. (1971b), 'A monetary theory of nominal income', *Journal of Political Economy*, **79**, 323–37.

Friedman, M. (1973), *Money and Economic Development*, Toronto: Lexington Books.

Friedman, M. (1975), 'Unemployment versus inflation: an evaluation of the Phillips curve', *IEA Occasional Paper No. 44*, London: Institute for Economic Affairs.

Friedman, M. (1977), 'Nobel lecture: inflation and unemployment', *Journal of Political Economy*, **85** (3), 451-72.

Friedman, M. (1983a), *Bright Promises, Dismal Performance: An Economist's Protest*, New York: Harcourt Brace Jovanovich.

Friedman, M. (1983b), 'Monetary variability: United States and Japan', *Journal of Money, Credit and Banking*, **15** (August), 339–43.

Friedman, M. (1984), *Politics and Tyranny*, San Francisco, CA: California Pacific Institute for Public Policy Research.
Friedman, M. (1985), 'The case of overhauling the Federal Reserve', *The Challenge*, **28** (3), 4–12.
Friedman, M. (1986), 'The resource cost of irredeemable paper money', *Journal of Political Economy*, **94** (June), 642–7.
Friedman, M. (1991), *Monetarist Economics*, Oxford: Basil Blackwell.
Friedman, M. (1992), 'Quantity theory of money', in P. Newman, M. Milgate and J. Eatwell (eds), *The New Palgrave Dictionary of Money and Finance*, vol. 3, London: Macmillan Press.
Friedman, M. (1994), *Money Mischief – Episodes in Monetary History*, New York: Harcourt Brace.
Friedman, M. and A.J. Schwartz (1963a), *A Monetary History of the United States, 1867–1960*, Princeton, NJ: Princeton University Press.
Friedman, M. and A.J. Schwartz (1963b), 'Money and business cycles', *Review of Economics and Statistics*, **45** (February), 32–64.
Fry, M. (1991), 'Domestic resource mobilization in developing Asia: four policy issues', *Asian Development Review*, **19** (1), 14–39.
Fry, M. (1992), 'Central banking in developing countries', in P. Newman, M. Milgate and J. Eatwell (eds), *The New Palgrave Dictionary of Money and Finance*, vol. 1, London: Macmillan Press.
Fry, M. (1998), *Money, Interest, and Banking in Economic Development*, Baltimore, MD: Johns Hopkins University Press.
Fry, M., C. Goodhart and A. Almeida (1996), *Central Banking in Developing Countries: Objectives, Activities and Independence*, London: Routledge.
Gang, Y. (2008), 'The monetary policy transmission mechanism in China', *BIS Papers, No. 35*, 179–81.
Gersovitz, M. (1988), 'Saving and development', in H. Chenery and T.N. Srinivasan (eds), *Handbook of Development Economics*, vol. 1, Amsterdam: Elsevier Science.
Ghatak, S. (1983), *Monetary Economics in Developing Countries*, London: Macmillan.
Ghosh, A. and S. Phillips (1998), 'Warning: inflation may be harmful to your health', *IMF Staff Papers*, **45** (December), 672–713.
Ghosh, A.R., A.M. Gulde and H.C. Wolf (2000), 'Currency boards: more than a quick fix?', *Economic Policy*, **31** (October), 269–335.
Ghosh, A.R., A.M. Gulde, J. Ostry and H.C. Wolf (1995), 'Does the nominal exchange rate regime matter?', *IMF Working Paper 95/121*, Washington, DC: IMF.
Giannini, C. (1995), 'Money, trust, and central banking', *Journal of Economics and Business*, **47**, 217–37.
Gillis, M., D. Perkins, M. Roemer and D. Snodgrass (1992), *Economics of Development*, New York: Norton.
Goeltom, M.S. (2008), 'The transmission mechanisms of monetary policy in Indonesia', in *BIS Papers, No. 35*, 309–32.
Goldfajn, I. and G. Olivares (2001), 'On full dollarization: the case of Panama', *Economia*, **1** (2), 101–40.
Goldsbrough and Associates (1996), 'Reinvigorating growth in developing countries:

lesson from adjustment policies in eight economies', *Occasional Paper 139*, Washington, DC: IMF.

Goldfeld, S.M. (1973), 'The demand for money revisited', *Brookings Papers on Economic Activity*, **3**, 577–638.

Goldfeld, S. (1976), 'The case of the missing money', *Brookings Papers on Economic Activity*, **6**, 683–730.

Goldfeld, S.M. and L.V. Chandler (1986), *The Economics of Money and Banking*, New York: Harper and Row.

Goldfeld, S.M. and D.E. Sichel (1990), 'The demand for money', in B.M. Friedman and F.H. Hahn (eds), *Handbook of Monetary Economics*, Amsterdam: Elsevier Science.

Goodfriend, M. (1997), 'Monetary policy comes of age: a 20th century odyssey', *Federal Reserve Bank of Richmond Economic Survey*, **83** (1), 1–22.

Goodfriend, M. and E. Prasad (2006), 'A framework for independent monetary policy in China', *IMF Working Paper WP/06/111*, Washington, DC: IMF.

Goodhart, CA.E. (1988), *The Evolution of Central Banks*, Cambridge, MA: MIT Press.

Goodhart, C.A.E. (1992), 'Central banking', in P. Newman, M. Milgate and J. Eatwell (eds), *The New Palgrave Dictionary of Money and Finance*, vol. 1, London: Macmillan Press.

Goodhart, C.A.E. (1999a), 'Central bankers and uncertainty', *Bank of England Quarterly Bulletin*, **39** (1), 102–14.

Goodhart, C.A.E. (1999b), 'Myths about the lender of last resort', *International Finance*, **2** (3), 339–60.

Gordon, R.J. (1982), 'Price inertia and policy ineffectiveness in the United States, 1890–1980', *Journal of Political Economy*, **90**, 1087–117.

Gordon, R.J. (1993), *Macroeconomics*, New York: HarperCollins College.

Gorton, G. and L. Huang (2001), 'Panics, bank coalitions, and the origin of central banking', draft, The Wharton School, University of Pennsylvania.

Goujon, M.I. (2006), 'Fighting inflation in a dollarized economy: the case of Vietnam', *Journal of Comparative Economics*, **34**, 564–81.

Government of Bangladesh (GOB) (various years), *Bangladesh Economic Review*, Dhaka: Ministry of Finance.

Greene, J. and D. Villanueva (1991), 'Private investment in developing countries: an empirical analysis', *IMF Staff Papers*, **38** (1), 33–58.

Greenwald, B.C. and J.E. Stiglitz (1988), 'Examining alternative macroeconomic theories', *Brookings Papers on Economic Activity*, **1**, 207–70.

Grenville, S.A. (1997), 'The evolution of monetary policy: from money targets to inflation targets', in P.W, Lowe (ed.), *Monetary Policy and Inflation Targeting*, Sydney: Reserve Bank of Australia.

Grilli, V., D. Masciandaro and G. Tabellini (1991), 'Political and monetary institutions and public financial policies in the industrial countries', *Economic Policy*, **13**, 341–92.

Guinigundo, D.C. (2008), 'Transmission mechanisms of monetary policy in the Philippines', *Bank for International Settlements (BIS) Papers*, No. 35, 413–26.

Guitián, M. (1998), 'Capital account convertibility and the financial sector', *Journal of Applied Economics*, **1** (1), 209–29.

Gurley, J.G. and E.S. Shaw (1955), 'Financial aspects of economic development', *American Economic Review*, **45** (4), 515–38.

Gurley, J.G. and E.S. Shaw (1960), *Money in a Theory of Finance*, Washington, DC: Brookings Institution.
Gylfason, T. (1999), *Principles of Economic Growth*, New York: Oxford University Press.
Haberler, G. (1941), *Prosperity and Depression*, Geneva: League of Nations.
Haliassos, M. and J. Tobin (1990), 'The macroeconomics of government finance', in B.M. Friedman and F.H. Hahn (eds), *Handbook of Monetary Economics*, vol. 2, Amsterdam: Elsevier Science.
Hall, R.E. (ed.) (1982), *Inflation: Causes and Effects*, Chicago, IL: University of Chicago Press.
Hall, R.E. and F.S. Mishkin (1982), 'The sensitivity of consumption to transitory income: estimates from panel data on households', *Econometrica*, **50** (2), 461–81.
Hamada, K. and F. Hayashi (1985), 'Monetary policy in postwar Japan', in A. Ando, H. Eguchi, R. Farmer and Y. Suzuki (eds), *Monetary Policy in Our Times*, Cambridge, MA: MIT Press.
Hamann, A.J. and S. Prati (2003), 'Beating inflation: the importance of luck, timing, and political institutions, *Finance and Development* (June), 12–15.
Hansen, B. (1969), 'Employment and wages in rural egypt', *American Economic Review*, **59** (3), 298–313.
Harberger, A.C. (1978), 'A primer on inflation', *Journal of Money, Credit and Banking*, **10**, 505–21.
Harberger, A.C. (1984), 'Economic growth and economic policy', in A.C. Harberger (ed.), *World Economic Growth*, San Francisco, CA: Institute for Contemporary Studies.
Harberger, A.C. (1999). 'Interview with Arnold Harberger', Federal Reserve Bank of Minneapolis, http://woodrow.mpls.frb.fed.pubs/region/99-03/harberger.cfm.
Harris, B. (1983), 'Money and commodities: their interaction in a rural Indian setting', EDI Series in Economic Development, Washington, DC: World Bank.
Harris, L. (1985), *Monetary Theory*, New York: McGraw-Hill.
Harris, R.I.D. (1995), *Using Cointegration Analysis in Econometric Modelling*, Hemel Hempstead: Harvester Wheatsheaf.
Harrod, R. (1939), 'An essay in economic theory', *Economic Journal*, **49**, 14–33.
Hauskrecht, A. and N. Le (2005), 'Capital account liberalization for a small open economy – the case of Vietnam', draft, Kerry School of Business, Indiana University.
Hawtrey, R.G. (1932), *The Art of Central Banking*, London: Longmans, Green.
Hayek, F.A. (1933), *Monetary Theory and Trade Cycle*, London: Jonathan Cape.
Hayek, F.A. (1976), 'Choice in currency: a way to stop inflation', *Occasional Paper 48*, London: Institute of Economic Affairs.
Hayek, F.A. (1978), *Denationalisation of Money – the Argument Refined*, London: Institute of Economic Affairs.
Healy, J. and S. Page (1993), 'The use of monetary policy', in S. Page (ed.), *Monetary Policy in Developing Countries*, London: Routledge.
Hess, A.C. (1971), 'An explanation of short-run fluctuations in the ratio of currency to demand deposits', *Journal of Money, Credit and Banking*, **3**, 666–79.
Hetzel, R.L. (1990), 'Central banks' independence in historical perspective: a review essay', *Journal of Monetary Economics*, **25** (1), 165–76.
Hill, H. (1999), 'An overview of the issues', in H.W. Arndt and H. Hill (eds), *Southeast*

Asia's Economic Crisis: Origins, Lessons and the Way Forward, Singapore: Institute of Southeast Asian Studies.

Hirschman, A.O. (1981), *Essays in Trespassing: Economics to Politics and Beyond*, Cambridge: Cambridge University Press.

Hong Kong Monetary Authority, http://www.hkma.gog.hk.

Honohan, P. (1992), 'Financial repression', in P. Newman, M. Milgate and J. Eatwell (eds), *The New Palgrave Dictionary of Money and Finance*, vol. 2, London: Macmillan Press.

Hoover, K. (1988), *The New Classical Macroeconomics: A Sceptical Inquiry*, Oxford: Blackwell.

Hoover, K. (1991), 'The causal direction between money and prices', *Journal of Monetary Economics*, **27**, 381–423.

Hosek, W.R. (1970), 'Determinants of the money multiplier', *Quarterly Review of Economics and Business*, Summer, 37–46.

Hossain, A. (1989), 'Inflation, economic growth and the balance of payments: a macro-econometric study 1974–85', PhD Thesis, La Trobe University, Australia.

Hossain, A. (1990), 'Real wage determination in Bangladesh agriculture', *Applied Economics*, **22**, 1549–65.

Hossain, A. (1993), 'Financial liberalisation, stability of the money demand function and monetary policy in Bangladesh, *Indian Economic Review*, **28** (1), 85–100.

Hossain, A. (1994), 'The search for a stable money demand function for Pakistan: an application of the method of cointegration', *Pakistan Development Review*, **33** (Winter), 969–81.

Hossain, A. (1995), *Inflation, Economic Growth and the Balance of Payments in Bangladesh: A Macroeconomic Study*, Delhi: Oxford University Press.

Hossain, A. (2000), *Exchange Rates, Capital Flows, and International Trade: The Case of Bangladesh*, Dhaka: University Press.

Hossain, A. (2003), 'An examination of some key issues in the conduct of monetary policy in Bangladesh', in A. Ali, R. Kuddus and S.S. Andaleeb (eds), *Development Issues of Bangladesh-II*, Dhaka: University Press.

Hossain, A. (2005), 'The money demand behavior in Bangladesh', *Bangladesh Journal of Political Economy*, **22** (1 and 2), 365–89.

Hossain, A. (2006a), 'Macroeconomic developments, policies and issues in Indonesia, 1950–2005: a review', *Malaysian Journal of Economic Studies*, **43** (1and 2), 19–67.

Hossain, A. (2006b), 'The money demand behaviour in Bangladesh, 1973–2003: an application of the cointegration and error-correction methods', *Indian Economic Review*, **41** (1), 55–80.

Hossain, A. (2007), 'The narrow money demand behaviour in Indonesia, 1970–2005', *ASEAN Economic Bulletin*, **24** (3), 320–38.

Hossain, A. (2008), 'Rural labour market developments, agricultural productivity, and real wages in Bangladesh, 1950–2006', *Pakistan Development Review*, **47** (1): 89–114.

Hossain, A. (2009), 'In search of a stable money demand function in Indonesia, 1970–2006', forthcoming in *Singapore Economic Review*.

Hossain, A. and A. Chowdhury (1994), 'Monetary policy', in H. Zafarullah, M. Taslim and A. Chowdhury (eds), *Policy Issues in Bangladesh*, New Delhi: South Asian.

Hossain, A. and Chowdhury, A. (1996), *Monetary and Financial Policies in Developing Countries: Growth and Stabilisation*, London: Routledge.

Hossain, A. and A. Chowdhury (1998), *Open-Economy Macroeconomics for Developing Countries*, Cheltenham, UK and Northampton, MA, USA: Edward Elgar.

Hossain, A. and S. Rashid (1996), *In Quest of Development: The Political Economy of South Asia*, Dhaka: University Press.

Howitt, P. (1992), 'Money illusion', in P. Newman, M. Milgate and J. Eatwell (eds), *The New Palgrave Dictionary of Money and Finance*, vol. 3, London: Macmillan Press.

Hsu, J.C. (1985), 'Exchange rate management without a central bank: the Hong Kong experience', *Hong Kong Economic Papers*, 16.

Hughes, H. (1994), 'Development policies and development performance', in E. Grilli and D. Salvatore (eds), *Economic Development*, London: Greenwood Press.

Hughes, H. (1995), 'The myth of Asia's miracle: comment on Krugman', *Policy* (Autumn), 11–12.

Hume, D. (1752), '"Of Money", "Of Interest", and "Of the Balance of Trade"', in E. Rotwein (ed.) (1970), *Writings on Economics*, Madison, WI: University of Wisconsin Press.

Hung, N.T. (1999), 'The inflation of Vietnam in transition', *CAS Discussion Paper, No. 22*.

Hutchison, M. (1986), 'Japan's "money focused" monetary policy', *Federal Reserve Bank of San Francisco Economic Review*, **3** (Summer), 33–47.

Hutton, J.P. (1992), 'Real exchange rates', in P. Newman, M. Milgate and J. Eatwell (eds), *The New Palgrave Dictionary of Money and Finance*, vol. 3, London: Macmillan Press.

Ichimura, S. (1993), *The Role of Japan in Asia,* San Francisco, CA: ICS Press.

Iljas, A. (1998), 'The transmission mechanism of monetary policy in Indonesia', in BIS (ed.), *Transmission Mechanism of Monetary Policy in Emerging Market Economies*, Policy Papers No. 3, 105–26.

International Monetary Fund (IMF) (various issues), *Survey*, Washington, DC: IMF.

International Monetary Fund (IMF) (various issues), *World Economic Outlook*, Washington, DC: IMF.

International Monetary Fund (IMF) (various years), *Exchange Rate Arrangements and Exchange Restrictions*, Washington, DC: IMF.

International Monetary Fund (IMF) (various years), *International Financial Statistics Yearbook*, Washington, DC: IMF.

International Monetary Fund (IMF) (various years), 'Pakistan: Country Reports', http://www.imf.org/publications/country/PAK/htm.

International Monetary Fund (1988), 'Japan's liquidity trap' (Box 4.1), *World Economic Outlook*, Washington, DC: IMF.

International Monetary Fund (1995), *International Capital Markets: Developments, Prospects, and Policy Issues* (August), Washington, DC: IMF.

International Monetary Fund (IMF) (1996), 'The rise and fall of inflation – lessons from the postwar experience', *World Economic Outlook*, chapter VI (October), 100–31.

International Monetary Fund (IMF) (2001), 'The decline of inflation in emerging markets: can it be maintained?', *World Economic Outlook*, chapter IV (May), 116–49.

International Monetary Fund (2002), *Vietnam: Selected Issues and Statistical Appendix*, IMF Country Report No. 02/5, January.

International Monetary Fund (2006), 'How has globalization affected inflation?', *World Economic Outlook* (April), Washington, DC: IMF.

Iqbal, Z. and A. Mirakhor (1987), 'Islamic banking', *Occasional Paper No. 49*, Washington, DC: IMF.

Ito, T. (1989), 'Is the Bank of Japan a closet monetarism? Monetary targeting in Japan, 1978–1988', *NBER Working Paper 2874*, New York: NBER.

Ito, T. (1997), 'How can developing countries learn from East Asia's economic growth?', *Annual World Bank Conference on Development Economics 1997*, 183–200.

Ito, T. (2004), 'Inflation targeting and Japan: why has the Bank of Japan not adopted inflation targeting?', in C. Kent and S. Guttman (eds), *The Future of Inflation Targeting*, Sydney: Reserve Bank of Australia.

Ito, T. (2006), 'Japanese monetary policy: 1998–2005 and beyond', in *Monetary Policy in Asia: Approaches and Implementation, BIS Papers No. 31*, 15–132.

Iyoha, M. (1973), 'Inflation and "openness" in less developed economies: a cross-country analysis', *Economic Development and Cultural Change*, **22** (1), 31–7.

Ize, A. and E. Levy-Yeyati (1998), 'Dollarization of financial intermediation', *IMF Working Paper 98/28*, Washington, DC: IMF.

Jaffee, D.M. (1992), 'Credit rationing', in P. Newman, M. Milgate and J. Eatwell (eds), *The New Palgrave Dictionary of Money and Finance*, vol. 1, London: Macmillan Press.

Jacobs, R. (1977), 'Hyperinflation and the supply of money', *Journal of Money, Credit and Banking*, **9**, 287–303.

James, W.E. and S.M. Stephenson (1993), 'Indonesia's experience with economic policy reform: reversing the conventional wisdom about sequencing', draft, Jakarta.

James, W.E., S. Naya and G.M. Meier (1987), *Asian Development: Economic Success and Policy Lessons*, Madison, WI: University of Wisconsin Press.

Jao, Y.C. (1992), 'Hong Kong monetary and financial system', in P. Newman, M. Milgate and J. Eatwell (eds), *The New Palgrave Dictionary of Money and Finance*, vol. 2, London: Macmillan Press.

Jayaraman, T.K. (1997), 'Fiscal imbalances and real exchange rate movements in Fiji: an empirical study', *Asia-Pacific Development Journal*, **4** (1), 83–104.

Johnson, H.G. (1962), 'Monetary theory and policy', *American Economic Review*, **52**, 335–84.

Johnson, H.G. (1967), *Essays in Monetary Economics*, London: Allen and Unwin.

Johnson, H. (1972), *Macroeconomics and Monetary Theory*, New York: Aldine.

Johnson, H.G. (1978), *Selected Essays in Monetary Economics*, London: Allen and Unwin.

Johnson, O. (1984), 'On growth and inflation in developing countries', *IMF Staff Papers*, **31**, 636–60.

Jongwanich, J. and D. Park (2008), 'Inflation in developing Asia: demand-pull or cost-push?', *ERD Working Paper No. 121*, Manila: Asian Development Bank.

Jonson, P. and R. Rankin (1986), 'On some recent developments in monetary economics', *Economic Record*, **62**, 257–67.

Joshi, V. and I. Little (1994), *India: Macroeconomics and Political Economy*, Washington, DC: World Bank.

Judd, J.P. and J.L. Scadding (1982), 'The search for a stable money demand function: a survey of the post-1973 literature', *Journal of Economic Literature*, **20**, 993–1023.

Kaminsky, G.L., C.M. Reinhart and C.A. Vegh (2003), 'The unholy trinity of financial contagion', *Journal of Economic Perspectives*, **17** (4), 51–74.

Kandil, M. (1991), 'Structural differences between developing and developed countries: some evidence and implications', *Economic Notes*, **20** (2), 254–78.
Kapur, B. (1976), 'Alternative stabilization policies for less developed economies', *Journal of Political Economy*, **84** (4, part I), 777–95.
Kapur, B. (1992), 'Formal and informal financial markets, and the neo-structuralist critique of the financial liberalization strategy in less developed countries', *World Development*, **38** (1), 63–77.
Kasa, K. (2001), 'Will inflation targeting work in developing countries?', *FRBSF Economic Letter*, no. 2001-01.
Keynes, J.M. (1923), *A Tract on Monetary Reform*, London: Macmillan.
Keynes, J.M. (1930), *Treatise on Money*, London: Macmillan.
Keynes, J.M. (1936), *The General Theory of Employment, Interest and Money*, London: Macmillan.
Khan, M.S. (1980), 'Monetary shocks and the dynamics of inflation', *IMF Staff Papers*, **27**, 250–84.
Khan, M.S. (1986), 'Islamic interest-free banking: a theoretical analysis', *IMF Staff Papers*, **33** (March), 1–27.
Khan, M.S. (2003), 'Current issues in the design and conduct of monetary policy', *IMF Working Paper WP/03/56*, Washington, DC: IMF.
Khan, M.S. and A. Mirakhor (1990), 'Islamic banking experiences in the Islamic Republic of Iran and Pakistan', *Economic Development and Cultural Change*, January, 353–75.
Khan, M.S. and A. Mirakhor (1992), 'Islamic banking', in P. Newman, M. Milgate and J. Eatwell (eds), *The New Palgrave Dictionary of Money and Finance*, vol. 2, London: Macmillan Press.
Khan, M.S. and A. Mirakhor (1993), 'Islam and economic system', *Review of Islamic Economics*, **2** (1), 1–29.
Khan, M.S. and A. Mirakhor (1994), 'Monetary management in an Islamic economy', *Journal of King Abdul Aziz University: Islamic Economics*, **6**, 3–21.
Khan, M.S. and C.M. Reinhart (1990), 'Private investment and economic growth in developing countries', *World Development*, **18**, 19–27.
Khan, M.S. and A.S. Senhadji (2001), 'Threshold effects in the relationship between inflation and growth', *IMF Staff Papers*, **48** (1), 1–21.
Khan, M.S. and R. Zahler (1983), 'The macroeconomic effects of changes in barriers to trade and capital flows: a simulation analysis', *IMF Staff Papers*, **30**, 223–82.
Khan, M.S., A.S. Senhadji and B.D. Smith (2006), 'Inflation and financial depth', *Macroeconomic Dynamics*, **10** (2), 165–82.
Khatkhate, D.R. (1972), 'Analytic basis of the working of monetary policy in less developed countries', *IMF Staff Papers*, **19** (3), 533–58.
Kim, J. and L.J. Lau (1994), 'The sources of economic growth of the East Asian newly industrialized countries', *Journal of the Japanese and International Economics*, **8** (3), 235–71.
Kim, S. and Y.C. Park (2006), 'Inflation targeting in Korea: a model of success', in *Monetary Policy in Asia: Approaches and Implementation, BIS Papers No. 31*, Basel: Bank for International Settlements.
Kimbrough, K. (1992), 'Inflation tax', in P. Newman, M. Milgate and J. Eatwell (eds), *The New Palgrave Dictionary of Money and Finance*, vol. 2, London: Macmillan Press.

King, M. (1997), 'Changes in UK monetary policy: rules and discretion in practice', *Journal of Monetary Economics*, **39** (1), 81–97.

King, R.G. and R. Levine (1993), 'Financial intermediation and economic development', in C. Mayer and X. Vives (eds), *Capital Markets and Financial Intermediation*, Cambridge: Cambridge University Press.

Kirkpatrick, C. and F. Nixson (1989), 'Inflation and stabilisation policy in LDCs', in N. Gemmel (ed.) *Survey in Development Economics,* Oxford: Basil Blackwell.

Kisch, C.H. and W.A. Elkin (1928), *Central Banks*, London: Macmillan.

Kochhar, K. and Associates (1996), 'Thailand: the road to sustained research', *Occasional Paper 146*, Washington, DC: IMF.

Koh, A.T. (1992), 'Singapore: monetary and financial system', in P. Newman, M. Milgate and J. Eatwell (eds), *The New Palgrave Dictionary of Money and Finance*, vol. 3, London: Macmillan Press.

Komine, T. (1998), 'Currency crisis and financial turmoil in Asia and the potential for future growth', paper presented at the International Symposium on Foreign Direct Investment in East Asia, Tokyo.

Kormendi, R.C. and P.G. Meguire (1984), 'Cross-regime evidence of macroeconomic rationality', *Journal of Political Economy*, **92** (October), 875–908.

Krueger, A.O. (1993), *The Political Economy of Policy Reform in Developing Countries*, Cambridge, MA: MIT Press.

Krugman, P.R. (1979), 'A model of balance of payments crises', *Journal of Money, Credit and Banking*, **3**, 311–25.

Krugman, P.R. (2000), 'Thinking about the liquidity trap', *Journal of the Japanese and International Economics*, **14** (4), 221–37.

Krugman, P.R. and M. Obstfeld (2009), *International Economics: Theory and Policy*, New York: Pearson-Addison Wesley.

Kuroda, H. (2009), Keynote address at 'High level Conference on Financial Crisis, Global Economic Governance, and Development', Asian Development Bank, 9 February, New Delhi, India.

Kydland, F.E. (1992), 'Rules versus discretion', in P. Newman, M. Milgate and J. Eatwell (eds), *The New Palgrave Dictionary of Money and Finance*, vol. 3, London: Macmillan Press.

Kydland, F.E. and E.C. Prescott (1977), 'Rules rather than discretion: the inconsistency of optimal plans', *Journal of Political Economy*, **85**, 473–91.

Kydland, F.E. and E.C. Prescott (1982), 'Time to build and aggregate fluctuations', *Econometrica*, **51** (November): 1345–70.

Kydland, F.E. and E.C. Prescott (1990), 'Business cycles: real facts and a monetary myth', *Federal Reserve Bank of Minneapolis Quarterly Review* (Spring), 3–18.

Laidler, D. (1982), *Monetarist Perspectives*, Oxford: Phillip Allan.

Laidler, D. (1990), *Taking Money Seriously*, New York: Philip Allan.

Laidler, D. (1993), *The Demand for Money-Theories, Evidence and Problems*, New York: Harper and Row.

Laidler, D. (2004), 'Central banks as lender of last resort – trendy or passe?', *Working Paper 2004–8*, Department of Economics, University of Western Ontario, Canada.

Laidler, D. (2005), 'Free banking and the Bank of Canada', paper presented at the 2005 Annual Meeting of the Canadian Economic Association at McMaster University, May.

Laidler, D. and M. Parkin (1975), 'Inflation: a survey', *Economic Journal*, **85**, 741–809.
Lal, D. (1984), 'Trends in real wages in rural India 1880–1980', *World Bank Research Paper*, Washington, DC: World Bank.
Lal, D. (1985), *The Poverty of Development Economics*, Cambridge, MA: Harvard University Press.
Lane, P.R. (1997), 'Inflation in open economies', *Journal of International Economics*, **42**, 327–47.
Lane, T. and Associates (1999), 'IMF-Supported programs in Indonesia, Korea, and Thailand', *Occasional Paper 178*, Washington, DC: IMF.
Latter, A. (1993), 'The currency board approach to monetary policy', in *Monetary Management in Hong Kong*, proceedings of a seminar on monetary management, sponsered by the Hong Kong Monetary Authority, Hong Kong, 18–19 October.
Laumas, G.S. and Y.P. Mehra (1977), 'The stability of the demand for money function', *Journal of Finance*, **23** (3), 911–16.
Layard, R. (1992), 'Non-accelerating inflation rate of unemployment', in P. Newman, M. Milgate and J. Eatwell (eds), *The New Palgrave Dictionary of Money and Finance*, vol. 3, London: Macmillan Press.
Lee, C.H. (1992), 'The government financial system, and large private enterprises in the economic development of South Korea', *World Development*, **20** (2), 187–97.
Leiderman, L., R. Maino and E. Parrado (2006), 'Inflation targeting in dollarized economies', *IMF Working Paper No. 06/157*, Washington, DC: IMF.
Leijonhufvud, A. (1968), *On Keynesian Economics and the Economics of Keynes*, New York: Oxford University Press.
Leontief, W. (1936), 'The fundamental assumption of Mr Keynes' monetary theory of unemployment', *Quarterly Journal of Economics*, **51**, 192–7.
Levhari, D. and D. Patinkin (1968), 'The role of money in a simple growth model', *American Economic Review*, **58**, 713–53.
Levy-Yeyati, E. (2006), 'Financial dollarization', *Economic Policy*, (January), 61–118.
Lewis, M.K. and P.D. Mizen (2000), *Monetary Economics*, Oxford: Oxford University Press.
Liang-Siang, F. and L. Leng Rung (1970), 'Demand for money in Asian countries: empirical evidence', *Indian Economic Journal*, **18** (4–5), 475–81.
Little, I., R. Cooper, W.M. Corden, M. and S. Rajapatirana (1993), *Booms, Crisis and Adjustment: The Macroeconomic Experience of Developing Countries*, New York: Oxford University Press.
Little, I.M.D. (1982), *Economic Development: Theory, Policy and International Relations*, New York: Basic Books.
Lohmann, S. (1992), 'Optimal commitment in monetary policy: credibility versus flexibility', *American Economic Review*, **82** (March), 273–86.
Long, M. and D. Vittas (1991), 'Financial regulation: changing the rules of the game', *Policy Research Working Papers WPS803*, Washington, DC: World Bank.
Loungani, P. and P. Swagel (2001), 'Sources of inflation in developing countries', *IMF Working Paper WP 01/198*, Washington, DC: IMF.
Lovell, M. (1957), 'The role of the Bank of England as lender of last resort in the crises of the eighteenth century', *Explorations in Entrepreneurial History*, **10**, 8–21.

Lowe, P. (ed.) (1997), *Monetary Policy and Inflation Targeting*, Sydney: Reserve Bank of Australia.

Lucas, R. and T. Sargent (eds) (1981), *Rational Expectations and Econometric Practice*, London: George Allen and Unwin.

Lucas, R.E. Jr (1972), 'Expectations and the neutrality of money', *Journal of Economic Theory*, **4**, 103–24.

Lucas, R.E. Jr (1973), 'Some international evidence on output-inflation trade-offs', *American Economic Review*, **63** (June), 326–34.

Lucas, R. E. Jr (1975), 'An equilibrium model of the business cycle', *Journal of Political Economy*, **83**, 1113–44.

Lucas, R.E. Jr. (1977), 'Understanding business cycles', *Carnegie-Rochester Conference on Public Policy*, **5**, 7–29.

Lucas, R.E. Jr (1981), *Studies in Business-Cycle Theory*, Cambridge, MA: MIT Press.

Lucas, R.E. Jr (1986), 'Principles of fiscal and monetary policy', *Journal of Monetary Economics*, **17**, 117–34.

Lucas, R.E. Jr (1988), 'On the mechanics of economic development', *Journal of Monetary Economics*, **22**, 3–42.

Lucas, R.E. Jr (1996), 'Nobel lecture: monetary neutrality', *Journal of Political Economy*, **104** (August), 661–82.

Lucas, R.E. Jr (2000), 'Inflation and welfare', *Econometrica*, **68** (2), 247–74.

Lucas, R.E. Jr (2007), 'Mortgages and monetary policy', *The Wall Street Journal*, September, http://www-news.uchicago.edu/citations/07/070919.lucas-wsj.html.

Macfarlane, I.J. (1997a), 'The economics of nostalgia', *Reserve Bank of Australia Bulletin*, March, 1–7.

Macfarlane, I.J. (1997b), 'Monetary policy regimes: past and future', *Reserve Bank of Australia Bulletin*, October.

Macfarlane, I.J. (1998), 'Australian monetary policy in the last quarter of the twentieth century', *Reserve Bank of Australia Bulletin*, October, 6–19.

Mahadeva, L. and P. Sinclair (2002), *Monetary Transmission in Diverse Economies*, Cambridge: Cambridge University Press.

Mahadeva, L. and P. Sinclair (2005), *How Monetary Policy Works*, London: Routledge.

Mahadeva, L. and G. Sterne (2000), *Monetary Policy Frameworks in a Global Context*, London: Routledge.

Makinen, G.E. (1992), 'Hyperinflation: experience', in P. Newman, M. Milgate and J. Eatwell (eds), *The New Palgrave Dictionary of Money and Finance*, vol. 2, London: Macmillan Press.

Makinen, G.E. and T. Woodward (1989), 'The Taiwanese hyperinflation and stabilization of 1948–52', *Journal of Money, Credit and Banking*, **21** (February), 90–105.

Mammen, T. (1970), 'A test of Friedman's theory of demand for money with Indian data', *Indian Economic Review*, **17** (4–5), 494–9.

Mangla, I. (1979), 'An annual money demand function for Pakistan: some further results', *Pakistan Development Review*, **18** (1), 21–33.

Mankiw, N.G. (1998), *Principles of Macroeconomics*, New York: Dryden Press.

Marquez, J. (1992), 'Currency substitution', in P. Newman, M. Milgate and J. Eatwell (eds), *The New Palgrave Dictionary of Money and Finance*, vol. 1, London: Macmillan Press.

Marty, A.L. (1961), 'Gurly and Shaw on money in a theory of finance', *Journal of Political Economy*, **69** (1), 56–62.

Marty, A.L. (1967), 'Growth and the welfare cost of inflationary finance', *Journal of Political Economy*, **75**, 71–76

Marty, A.L. (1968), 'The optimal rate of growth of money', *Journal of Political Economy*, **76**, 860–73.

Marty, A.L. (1973), 'Growth, satiety, and the tax revenue from money creation', *Journal of Political Economy*, **81**, 1136–52.

Masciandaro, D. and G. Tabellini (1988), 'Monetary regimes and fiscal deficits: a comparative analysis', in H.S. Cheng (ed.), *Monetary Policy in Pacific Basin Countries*, Boston, MA and London: Kluwer Academic.

Masson, P.R., M.A. Savastano and S. Sharma (1997), 'The scope for inflation targeting in developing countries', *IMF Working Paper 97/143*, Washington, DC: IMF.

Mayer, T. (1999), *Monetary Policy and the Great Inflation in the United States*, Cheltenham, UK and Northampton, MA, USA: Edward Elgar.

McCallum, B.T. (1979), 'The current state of the policy ineffectiveness debate', *American Economic Review*, **69** (May), 240–45.

McCallum, B.T. (1984), 'Monetarist rules in the light of recent experience', *American Economic Review*, **74**, 388–91.

McCallum, B.T. (1990), 'Inflation: theory and evidence', in B.M. Friedman and F.H. Hahn (eds), *Handbook of Monetary Economics*, vol. 2, Amsterdam: North-Holland.

McCallum, B.T. (1995a), 'Two fallacies concerning central bank-independence', *American Economic Review*, **85** (2) (May), 207–11.

McCallum, B.T. (1995b), 'On consequences and criticisms of monetary targeting', *Journal of Money, Credit and Banking*, **17**, 570–97.

McCallum, B.T (1997), 'Issues in the design of monetary policy rules', *NBER Working Paper No. 6016*, Cambridge, MA: NBER.

McCallum, B.T. (2000), 'The present and future monetary policy rules', *International Finance*, **3** (2), 273–86.

McCallum, B.T. and M.S. Goodfriend (1992), 'Demand for money: theoretical studies', in P. Newman, M. Milgate and J. Eatwell (eds), *The Palgrave Dictionary of Money and Finance*, vol. 1, 611–17.

McKinnon, R.I. (1963), 'Optimum currency areas', *American Economic Review*, **53**, 717–25.

McKinnon, R.I. (1973), *Money and Capital in Economic Development*, Washington, DC: Brookings Institution.

McKinnon, R.I. (1974), 'Money, growth, and the propensity to save', in G. Horwich and P.A. Samuelson (eds), *Trade, Stability, and Macroeconomics: Essays in Honor of Lloyd Metzler*, New York: Academic Press.

McKinnon, R.I. (1981), 'Financial repression and the liberalization problem within less developed countries', in E. Grassman and E. Lundberg (eds), *The Past and Prospects for the World Economic Order*, London: Macmillan.

McKinnon, R.I. (1982), 'The order of economic liberalization: lessons from Chile and Argentina', *Carnegie-Rochester Conference Series on Public Policy*, **17**, 159–86.

Meier, G.M. (1985), *Leading Issues in Development Economics*, New York: Oxford University Press.

Meltzer, A.H. (1981), 'Keynes's general theory: a different perspective', *Journal of Economic Literature*, **19** (1), 34–64.

Meltzer, A.H. (1988), *Keynes's Monetary Theory*, Cambridge: Cambridge University Press.

Meltzer, A.H. (2002), 'Japanese monetary and economic policy', *World Economics*, **3** (3), 85–103.

Meltzer, A.H. (2003), *A History of the Federal Reserve*, Chicago, IL: University of Chicago Press.

Metzler, L.A. (1951), 'Wealth, saving, and the rate of interest', *Journal of Political Economy*, **59**, 93–116.

Mikesell, R. (1969), 'Inflation in Latin America', in C. Nisbet (ed.) *Latin America: Problems in Economic Development*, New York: Free Press.

Mill, J.S. (1848), *Principles of Political Economy*, 2 vols, London: John W. Parker.

Mirakhor, A. and I. Zaidi (1991), 'Stabilization and growth in an open Islamic economy', *Review of Islamic Economics*, **1** (2), 1–120.

Mishkin, F.S. (1982), 'Does anticipated monetary policy matter? An econometric investigation', *Journal of Political Economy*, **90**, 22–51.

Mishkin, F.S. (1995), 'Symposium on the monetary transmission mechanism', *Journal of Economic Perspectives*, **9** (4), 3–10.

Mishkin, F.S. (1997), 'Strategies for controlling inflation', in P. Lowe (ed.), *Monetary Policy and Inflation Targeting*, Sydney: Reserve Bank of Australia.

Mishkin, F.S. (2000a), 'Inflation targeting in emerging market economies', *American Economic Review*, **90** (2), 105–09.

Mishkin, F.S. (2000b), 'International experiences with different monetary policy regimes', *NBER Working Paper No. 7044*, Cambridge, MA: NBER.

Mishkin, F.S. (2007a), *The Economics of Money, Banking, and Financial Markets*, New York: Pearson-Addison Wesley.

Mishkin, F.S. (2007b), 'Will monetary policy become more of a science?, draft, Finance and Economics Discussion Series, Divisions of Research and Statistics and Monetary Affairs, Federal Reserve Board, Washington, D.C.

Mishkin, F.S. (2007c), *Monetary Policy Strategy*, Cambridge, MA: MIT Press.

Mishkin, F.S. (2008), 'Global financial turmoil and the world economy', speech given at the Israel Democracy Institute, Eliat, Israel, 2 July, http://www.federalreserve.gov/newsevents/speech/mishkin20080702a.htm.

Mishkin, F.S. and S.G. Eakins (2006), *Financial Markets and Institutions*, New York: Pearson-Addison Wesley.

Mishkin, F.S. and A.S. Posen (1997), 'Inflation targeting: lessons from four countries', *Economic Policy Review*, **3** (3), 9–110.

Mishkin, F.S. and M.A. Savastano (2000), 'Monetary policy strategies for Latin America', *NBER Working Paper No. 7617*, Cambridge, MA: NBER.

Mittra, S. (1977), *Central Bank versus Treasury: An International Study*, Lanham, MD: University Press of America.

Mizen, P. (ed.) (2003), *Central Banking, Monetary Theory and Practice: Essays in Honour of Charles Goodhart*, vol. 1, Cheltemham, UK and Northampton, MA, USA: Edward Elgar.

Modigliani, F. (1944), 'Liquidity preference and the theory of interest and money', *Econometrica*, **12**, 45–88.

Modigliani, F. (1971), 'Monetary policy and consumption', in *Consumer Spending and Monetary Policy: The Linkages*, Conference Series No. 5, proceedings of a monetary conference, Nantucket Island, MA, June, sponsored by the Federal Reserve Bank of Boston, pp. 9–84.

Modigliani, F. (1977), 'The monetarist controversy, or should we forsake stabilization policies?', *American Economic Review*, **67**, 1–19.

Modigliani, F. and R. Brumberg (1954), 'Utility analysis and the consumption function: an interpretation of cross-section data', in K. Kurihara (ed.), *Post-Keynesian Economics*, New Brunswick, NJ: Rutgers University Press.

Mohanty, M.S. and M. Klau (2001), 'What determines inflation in emerging market economies?', *BIS Papers No. 8*, http://www.bis.org/publ/bispap08a.pdf.

Monetary Authority of Singapore (MAS) (1999), 'Monetary policy and the economy', *Economics Explorer 2*, Singapore: MAS.

Monetary Authority of Singapore (MAS) (2001), 'Singapore's exchange rate policy', Singapore: MAS.

Montiel, P.J. (1991), 'The transmission mechanism for monetary policy in developing countries', *IMF Staff Papers*, **38** (1), 83–108.

Montiel, P.J. (2003), *Macroeconomics in Emerging Markets*, Cambridge: Cambridge University Press.

Moosa, I.A. (1992), 'The demand for money in India: a cointegration approach', *Indian Economic Journal*, **40** (July–September), 101–15.

Moosa, I.A. (2004), *International Finance*, Sydney: McGraw-Hill.

Morales, J.A. (1988), 'Inflation stabilization in Bolivia', in M. Bruno, D. Tella, R. Dornbusch and S. Fischer (eds), *Inflation Stabilization*, Cambridge, MA: MIT Press.

Morales, J.A. (1991), 'The transition from stabilization to sustained growth in Bolivia', in M. Bruno, D. Tella, R. Dornbusch and S. Fischer (eds), *Lessons of Economic Stabilization and Its Aftermath*, Cambridge, MA: MIT Press.

Morduch, J. (1995), 'Income and consumption smoothing', *Journal of Economic Perspectives*, **9** (3), 103–14.

Moreno, R. (1988), 'Exchange rates and monetary policy in Singapore and Hong Kong', in H.S. Cheng (ed.), *Monetary Policy in Pacific Basin Countries*, Boston, MA: Kluwer Academic.

Mundell, R.A. (1961), 'A theory of optimum currency areas', *American Economic Review*, **51** (4), 657–65.

Mundell, R.A. (1962), 'The appropriate use of monetary and fiscal policy for internal and external stability', *IMF Staff Papers*, **9** (March), 70–79.

Mundell, R.A. (1963), 'Inflation and real interest', *Journal of Political Economy*, **71**, 280–83.

Mundell, R.A. (1965), 'Growth, stability and inflationary finance', *Journal of Political Economy*, **73**, 97–109.

Mundell, R.A. (1968), *International Economics*, New York: Macmillan.

Mundell, R.A. (1971), *Monetary Theory: Inflation, Interest, and Growth in the World Economy*, Pacific Palisades, CA: Goodyear Publishing Company.

Muth, J.F. (1961), 'Rational expectations and the theory of price movement', *Econometrica*, **29** (2), 315–35.

Myrdal, G. (1971), *Asian Drama: An Inquiry into the Poverty of Nations*, New York: Pantheon Books.

Nam, S.W. (1995), 'Korea's financial markets and policies', in S.N. Zahid (ed.), *Financial Sector Development in Asia: Country Studies*, Manila: Asian Development Bank.

Naughton, B. (1992), 'China: monetary and financial system', in P. Newman, M. Milgate and J. Eatwell (eds), *The New Palgrave Dictionary of Money and Finance*, vol. 1, London: Macmillan Press.

Neary, P. (1988), 'Determinants of the equilibrium real exchange rate', *American Economic Review*, **78** (1), 210–15.

Nelson, E. (2004), 'The great inflation of the seventies: what really happened?', *Federal Reserve Bank of St. Louis Working Paper*, 2004–001.

Nelson, E. (2005), 'Monetary policy neglect and the great inflation in Canada, Australia, and New Zealand', *International Journal of Central Banking* (May), 133–79

Nichols, D.A. (1973), 'Some problems of inflationary finance', *Journal of Political Economy*, **83** (2), 423–30.

Olivera, J. (1967), 'Money, prices and fiscal lags: a note on the dynamics of inflation', *Banca Nazionale del Lavoro Quarterly Review*, **20**, 258–67.

Orphanides, O. and R.M. Solow (1990), 'Money, inflation and growth', in B.M. Friedman and F.H. Hahn (eds), *Handbook of Monetary Economics*, vol. 1, Amsterdam: North Holland.

Ortiz, G. (1993), 'Currency substitution in Mexico: the dollarization problem', *Journal of Money, Credit, and Banking*, **15**, 174–85.

Padoa-Schioppa, T. (2004), 'East Asian monetary arrangements: a European perspective', *International Finance*, **7** (2), 311–23.

Page, S. (ed) (1993), *Monetary Policy in Developing Countries*, London: Routledge.

Page, S. and J. Healy (1993), 'The financial sector', in S. Page (ed.), *Monetary Policy in Developing Countries*, London: Routledge.

Papademos, L. and F. Modigliani (1990), 'The supply of money and the control of nominal income', in B.M. Friedman and F.H. Hahn (eds), *Handbook of Monetary Economics*, vol. 1, Amsterdam: Elsevier Science.

Park, Y.C. (1973), 'The role of money in stabilization policy in developing countries', *IMF Staff Papers*, **20**, 379–418.

Park, Y.C. (1991), 'Financial repression and liberalization', in L. Krause and K. Kihwan (eds), *Liberalization in the Process of Economic Development*, Berkeley, CA: University of California Press.

Parkin, M. (1992), 'Inflation', in P. Newman, M. Milgate and J. Eatwell (eds), *The New Palgrave Dictionary of Money and Finance*, vol. 2, London: Macmillan Press.

Parrado, E. (2004), 'Singapore's unique monetary policy: how does it work?', *IMF Working Paper WP/04/10*, Washington, DC: IMF.

Patinkin, D. (1949), 'The indeterminancy of absolute prices in classical economic theory', *Econometrica*, **17** (1), 1–27.

Patinkin, D. (1956), *Money, Interest and Prices*, New York: Harper and Row.

Patinkin, D. (1972), 'On the short run non-neutrality of money in the quantity theory', *Banca Nazionale del Lavoro Quarterly Review*, No. 100 (March), 3–22.

Patinkin, D. (1992), 'Neutrality of money', in P. Newman, M. Milgate and J. Eatwell (eds), *The New Palgrave Dictionary of Money and Finance*, vol. 3, London: Macmillan Press.

Patinkin, D. (1993), 'Israel's stabilization program of 1985, or some simple truths of monetary theory', *Journal of Economic Perspectives*, **7** (2), 103–28.

Patinkin, D. and O. Steiger (1989), 'In search of the veil of money and the neutrality of money: a note on the origin of terms', *Scandinavian Journal of Economics*, **91** (1), 131–46.

Pazos, F. (1972), *Chronic Inflation in Latin America*, New York: Praeger.

Peiris, S.J. (2003), 'Inflationary dynamics in Vietnam', *Vietnam: Selected Issues*, Washington, DC: IMF.

People's Bank of China, http://www.pbc.gov.cn.

Persson, T. and G. Tabellini (1990), *Macroeconomic Policy, Credibility and Politics*, London: Harwood Academic Publishers.

Persson, T. and G. Tabellini (2000), *Political Economics: Explaining Economic Policy*, Cambridge, MA: MIT Press.

Pesaran, M.H. (1987), *The Limits to Rational Expectations*, Oxford: Basil Blackwell.

Pesaran, M. H. (1992), 'Natural rate hypothesis', in P. Newman, M. Milgate and J. Eatwell (eds), *The New Palgrave Dictionary of Money and Finance*, vol. 3, London: Macmillan Press.

Petrie, P. (1993), 'Common foundations of East Asian success', in *Lessons from East Asia Series*, Washington, DC: World Bank.

Pfefferman, G. (1985), 'Overvalued exchange rates and development', *Finance and Development* (March), 17–19.

Phelps, E.S. (1967), 'Phillips curves, expectations of inflation and optimal unemployment over time', *Economica*, **34** (3), 254–81.

Phelps, E.S. (1968), 'Money-wage dynamics and labor-market equilibrium', *Journal of Political Economy*, Part 2 (August), 678–711.

Phelps, E.S. (1970), 'Introduction: the new microeconomics in employment and inflation theory', in E.S. Phelps (ed.), *Microeconomic Foundations of Employment and Inflation Theory*, New York: Norton.

Phelps, E.S. (1973), 'Inflation in the theory of public finance', *Swedish Journal of Economics*, **75**, 67–82.

Phelps, E.S. (1992), 'Phillips curve', in P. Newman, M. Milgate and J. Eatwell (eds), *The New Palgrave Dictionary of Money and Finance*, vol. 3, London: Macmillan Press.

Phillips, A.W. (1958), 'The relation between unemployment and the rate of change of money wage rates in the United Kingdom, 1861–1957', *Economica*, **25** (November), 283–99.

Polak, J. and V. Argy (1971), 'Credit policy and the balance of payments', *IMF Staff Papers* **16**, 1–24.

Poole, W. (1970), 'Optimal choice of monetary policy instruments in a simple stochastic macro model', *Quarterly Journal of Economics*, **84** (2), 197–216.

Poole, W. (1999), 'Is inflation too low?', *Federal Reserve Bank of St. Louis Review*, July–August.

Porter, R. (1961), 'The dangers of monetary policy in agrarian economies', *Pakistan Development Review*, **1**, 59–72.

Portes, R. and A. Santorum (1987), 'Money and the consumption goods market in China', *Journal of Comparative Economics*, **11** (3), 354–71.

Prais, S. (1961), 'Some mathematical notes on the quantity theory of money in an open economy', *IMF Staff Papers*, **8**, 210–26.

Purvis, D.D. (1992), 'Monetary transmission mechanisms', in P. Newman, M. Milgate and J. Eatwell (eds), *The New Palgrave Dictionary of Money and Finance*, vol. 2, London: Macmillan Press.

Quibria, M.G. (2000), 'Growth and poverty: lessons from the East Asian miracle revisited', *ADB Institute Research Paper Series No. 33*, Tokyo: ADB Institute.

Quirk, P.J. (1995), 'Exchange rate regimes as inflation anchors', *Finance and Development* (March), 42–5.

Quirk, P.J., B.V. Christensen, K.M. Huh and T. Sasaki (1987), 'Floating exchange rates in developing countries', *IMF Occasional Paper 53*, Washington, DC: IMF.

Radelet, S. (1995), 'Indonesian foreign debt: headed for a crisis or financing sustainable growth?, *Bulletin of Indonesian Economic Studies*, **31** (3), 39–72.

Ramirez-Rojas, C.L. (1985), 'Currency substitution in Argentina, Mexico and Uruguay', *IMF Staff Papers*, **32**, 627–67.

Ranis, G. (1987), 'Can the East Asia model of development be generalized? A comment', *World Development*, **13** (4), 543–45.

Rao, V.K.R.V. (1952), 'Investment, income and the multiplier in an underdeveloped economy', *Indian Economic Review*, **1** (1), 55–67.

Reddy, Y.V. (1999), 'Monetary policy in India', *BIS Review 621/1999.*

Reddy, Y.V. (2002), *Parameters of Monetary Policy in India, BIS Review 3.*

Reinhart, C.M. and M.A. Savastano (2003), 'The realities of modern hyperinflation', *Finance and Development* (June), 20–3.

Reisen, H. (1996), 'Managing volatile capital inflows: the experience of the 1990s', *Asian Development Review*, **14** (1), 72–96.

Reserve Bank of Australia, http://www.rba.gov.au.

Reserve Bank of Australia, *History of the RBA*, http://www.rba.gov.au.

Reserve Bank of Australia (1994), 'Measuring underlying inflation', *RBA Bulletin* (August), 1–6.

Reserve Bank of Australia (1996), 'Statement on the conduct of monetary policy by the Treasurer and the Governor (designate) of the Reserve Bank', issued 14 August, http://www.rba.gov.au/about/ab_scmp.html.

Reserve Bank of Australia (2009a), 'About monetary policy', http://www.rba.gov.au/MonetaryPolicy/about_monetary_policy.html.

Reserve Bank of Australia (2009b), 'Governance and accountability of the RBA', http://www.rba.gov.au/AboutTheRBA/governance_and_accountability_of_the_rba.html, accessed 25 April 2009.

Reserve Bank of India, http://www.rbi.org.in.

Reserve Bank of India (2001), *Handbook of Statistics on Indian Economy*, Mumbai: RBI.

Reserve Bank of New Zealand, http://www.rbnz.gov.nz.

Reserve Bank of New Zealand (1991), *Reserve Bank Model of the New Zealand Economy, Model XII*, Auckland.

Ricardo, D. (1817), *Principles of Political Economy and Taxation*, London: Murray.

Ricardo, D. (1824), *Plan for the Establishment of a National Bank*, London: Murray.

Ritter, L.S., W.I. Silber and G.F. Udell (2004), *Principles of Money, Banking and Financial Markets*, New York: Pearson-Addison Wesley.

Rivera-Batiz, F. and L. Rivera-Batiz (1985), *International Finance and Open Economy Macroeconomics*, New York: Macmillan.

Rockoff, H. (1992) 'Gold supply', in P. Newman, M. Milgate and J. Eatwell (eds), *The New Palgrave Dictionary of Money and Finance*, vol. 2, London: Macmillan Press.

Rodrik, D. (1998), 'Who needs capital-market convertibility?', *Should the IMF Pursue Capital-Account Convertibility?* Princeton Essays in International Finance 207 (May), Department of Economics, Princeton University, NJ.

Rodrik, D., A. Subramanium and F. Trebbi (2002), 'Institutions rule: the primacy of institutions over geography and integration in economic development', *Working Paper 9305*, Cambridge, MA: NBER.

Rogoff, K. (1987), 'Reputational constraints on monetary policy', *Carnegie-Rochester Conference on Public Policy*, **26**, 141–82.

Rogoff, K.S. (1989), 'Reputation, coordination, and monetary policy', in R.J. Barro (ed.), *Modern Business Cycle Theory*, Cambridge, MA: Harvard University Press.

Rolnick, A. and W.E. Weber (1997), 'Money, inflation and output under fiat and commodity standards', *Journal of Political Economy*, **105** (December), 1308–21.

Romer, C.D. and D. Romer (1998), 'Monetary policy and the well-being of the poor', *NBER Working Paper No. 6793*, Cambridge, MA: NBER.

Romer, D. (1993), 'Openness and inflation: theory and evidence', *Quarterly Journal of Economics*, **108** (November), 869–903.

Romer, D. (1996), *Advanced Macroeconomics*, New York: McGraw-Hill.

Rosenzweig, M. (1988), 'Labor markets in low-income countries', in H. Chenery and T.N. Srinivasan (eds), *Handbook of Development Economics*, vol. 1, Amsterdam: Elsevier Science.

Roubini, N. (1991), 'Economic and political determinants of budget deficits in developing countries', *Journal of International Money and Finance*, **10** (March), S49–72.

Sachs, J. (1987), 'The Bolivian hyperinflation and stabilization', *American Economic Review*, **77** (2, May), 279–83.

Sachs, J. and F. Larrain (1993), *Macroeconomics in the Global Economy*, New York: Harvester Wheatsheaf.

Saini, K.G. (1982), 'The monetarist explanation of inflation: the experience of six Asian countries', *World Development*, **10** (10), 871–84.

Samuelson, P.A. (1994), 'Panel discussion', in J.C. Fuhrer (ed.), *Goals, Guidelines and Constraints Facing Monetary Policymakers*, Boston, MA: Federal Reserve Bank of Boston Conference Series No. 38.

Samuelson, P.A. and R. Solow (1960), 'Analytic aspects of anti-inflation policy', *American Economic Review*, **50** (May), 177–94.

Santoni, G.J. (1984), 'A private central bank: some old English lessons', *Federal Reserve Bank of St. Louis Review*, (April), 12–22.

Sargent, T.J. (1982), 'The end of four big inflations', in R. Hall (ed.), *Inflation*, Chicago, IL: University of Chicago Press.

Sargent, T.J. (1986), *Rational Expectations and Inflation*, New York: Harper and Row.

Sargent, T.J. (1992), 'Rational expectations', in P. Newman, M. Milgate and J. Eatwell (eds), *The New Palgrave Dictionary of Money and Finance*, vol. 3, London: Macmillan Press.

Sargent, T.J. and N. Wallace (1973), 'Rational expectations and the dynamics of hyperinflation', *International Economic Review*, **14** (April), 169–83.

Sargent, T.J. and N. Wallace (1975), 'Rational expectations, the optimal monetary instrument, and the optimal money supply rule', *Journal of Political Economy*, **83** (2), 241–54.

Sargent, T.J. and N. Wallace (1981), 'Some unpleasant monetarist arithmetic', *Federal Reserve Bank of Minneapolis Quarterly Review*, **5**, 1–17.

Saxena, S. (2008), 'Capital flows, exchange rate regime and monetary policy', *BIS Papers, No. 35*, Basel: Bank for International Settlements.

Sayers, R.S. (1957), *Central Banking After Bagehot*, Oxford: Clarendon Press.

Schwartz, A.J. (1993), 'Currency boards: their past, present and possible future role', *Carnegie-Rochester Conference Series on Public Policy*, **39**, 147–93.

Selgin, G.A. (1988), *The Theory of Free Banking*, Totowa, NJ: Rowman and Littlefield.

Selgin, G.A. and L.H. White (1987), 'The evolution of a free banking system', *Economic Inquiry*, **25** (July), 439–57.

Sen, A.K. (1983), 'Development: which way now?', *Economic Journal*, **93** (December), 745–62.

Sen, A.K. (1988), 'The concept of development', in H. Chenery and T.N. Srinivasan (eds), *Handbook of Development Economics*, vol. 1, Amsterdam: North Holland.

Shambaugh, J.C. (2004), 'The effects of fixed exchange rates on monetary policy', *Quarterly Journal of Economics*, **119** (1), 300–352.

Shapiro, A.C. (2006), *Multinational Financial Management*, New York: John Wiley and Sons.

Shapiro, M.D. (1992), 'Supply shocks in macroeconomics', in P. Newman, M. Milgate and J. Eatwell (eds), *The New Palgrave Dictionary of Money and Finance*, vol. 3, London: Macmillan Press.

Shaw, E. (1973), *Financial Deepening in Economic Development*, New York: Oxford University Press.

Siddiqi, M.N. (1983), *Banking Without Interest*, Leicester: The Islamic Foundation.

Sidgwick, E. (1996), 'The demand for money in Bangladesh: 1973.Q1–1994.Q4', draft, Washington, DC: IMF.

Sidrauski, M. (1967a), 'Inflation and economic growth', *Journal of Political Economy*, **75**, 796–810.

Sidrauski, M. (1967b), 'Rational choice and patterns of growth in a monetary economy', *American Economic Review*, **57** (2), 534–44.

Siklos, P.L. (ed.) (1995), *Great Inflations of the 20th Century*, Aldershot, UK and Brookfield, VT, USA: Edward Elgar.

Siklos, P.L. (2002), *The Changing Face of Central Banking: Evolutionary Trends Since World War II*, Cambridge: Cambridge University Press.

Simons, H.C. (1948), *Economic Policy for a Free Society*, Chicago, IL: University of Chicago Press.

Smith, V.C. (1936), *The Rationale of Central Banking*, London: P.S. King and Son.

Solow, R.M. (1956), 'A contribution to the theory of economic growth', *Quarterly Journal of Economics*, **70**, 65–94.

Solow, R.M. (1957), 'Technical change and the aggregate production function', *Review of Economics and Statistics*, **39**, 312–20.

Sorensen, P. and H.J. Whitta-Jacobsen (2005), *Introduction to Advanced Macroeconomics: Growth and Business Cycles*, New York: McGraw-Hill.

Speigel, M.M. (2000), 'Inflation targeting for the Bank of Japan', *FRBSF, Economic Letter*, no. 2000–11.

Squire, L. (1981), *Employment Policy in Developing Countries: A Survey of Issues and Evidence*, New York: Oxford University Press.

Sriram, S.S. (1999), 'Demand for M2 in an emerging-market economy: an error-correction model for Malaysia', *IMF Working Paper 99/173*, Washington, DC: IMF.

Sriram, S. S. (2000), 'A survey of recent empirical money demand studies', *IMF Staff Papers*, **47** (3), 334–65.

Stein, J.L. (1970), 'Monetary growth theory in perspective', *American Economic Review*, **60**, 85–106.

Stein, J.L. (1971), *Money and Capacity Growth*, New York: Columbia University Press.

Stiglitz, J.E. (1984), 'Price rigidities and market structure', *American Economic Review*, **74**, 350–55.

Stiglitz, J.E. (1989), 'Financial markets and development', *Oxford Review of Economic Policy*, **5** (4), 55–68.

Stiglitz, J.E. (1990), *Economic Role of State*, London: Allen and Unwin.

Stiglitz, J.E. (1994), 'The role of the state in financial markets', proceedings of the World Bank Annual Conference on Development Economics 1993: supplement to *World Bank Economic Review and World Bank Research Observer*, **1**, 19–62.

Stiglitz, J. (1998), 'Sound finance and sustainable development in Asia', http://www.worldbank.org/html/extdr/extme/jssp031298.htm.

Stiglitz, J.E. (2003), *Globalization and Its Discontents*, New York: W.W. Norton.

Stiglitz, J.E. and A. Weiss (1981), 'Credit rationing in markets with imperfect information', *American Economic Review*, **71** (3), 393–410.

Streeten, P. (1981), *Development Perspectives*, London: Macmillan.

Streeten, P. (1993), 'Markets and states: against minimalism', *World Development*, **21** (8), 1281–98.

Summers, L.H. (1991), 'How should long-term monetary policy be determined?', *Journal of Money, Credit and Banking*, **23** (August, part 2), 625–31.

Summers, L. and V. Thomas (1993), 'Recent lessons of development', *World Bank Research Observer*, **8** (2), 235–57.

Sundaram, K. and V. Pandit (1984), 'Informal credit markets, black money and monetary policy: some analytical and empirical issues', *Economic and Political Weekly*, **19** (16), 21 April, 675–82.

Sundararajan, V. and L. Molho (1988), 'Financial reform and monetary control in Indonesia', in H.S. Cheng (ed.), *Monetary Policy in Pacific Basin Countries*, Boston, MA: Kluwer Academic.

Sundararajan, V. and S. Thakur (1980), 'Public investment, crowding out, and growth: a dynamic model applied to India and Korea', *IMF Staff Papers*, **27**, 814–55.

Sunkel, O. (1960), 'Inflation in Chile: an unorthodox approach', *International Economic Papers*, **10**, 107–31.

Sutton, G.D. and J. Tosovsky (2005), 'Financial stability and monetary policy: two sides of the same coin?', paper presented at the Bank Indonesia-IMF International Seminar, Denpasar-Bali, Indonesia, 1–3 December.

Suzuki, Y. (1992), 'Bank of Japan', in P. Newman, M. Milgate and J. Eatwell (eds), *The New Palgrave Dictionary of Money and Finance*, vol. 1, London: Macmillan Press.

Svensson, L.E.O. (1997), 'Inflation forecasting: implementing and monitoring inflation targets', *European Economic Review*, **41** (6), 1111–46.

Svensson, L.E.O. (1999), 'Inflation targeting as a monetary policy rule', *Journal of Monetary Economics*, **43**, 607–54.

Swagel, P. and P. Loungani (1995), 'Supply-side sources of inflation: evidence from OECD countries', *International Finance Discussion Paper No. 515*, Washington, DC: Board of Governors of the Federal Reserve System.

Swan, T.W. (1956), 'Economic growth and capital accumulation', *Economic Record*, **32**, 334–61.

Swinburne, M. and M. Castello-Branco (1991), 'Central bank independence: issues and experience', *Working Paper WP/91/58*, Washington, DC: IMF.

Swoboda, A. (1976), 'Monetary approaches to balance of payments theory', in E. Classen and P. Salin (eds), *Recent Issues in International Monetary Economics*, Amsterdam: North-Holland.

Tabellini, G. and A. Alesina (1990), 'Voting on the budget deficit', *American Economic Review*, **80**, 37–49.

Tanzi, V. (1982), 'Fiscal disequilibrium in developing countries', *World Development*, **10**, 1069–82.

Taylor, J.B. (1993), 'Discretion versus policy rules in practice', *Carnegie-Rochester Conference Series on Public Policy*, **39** (1), 195–214.

Taylor, J.B. (1999), *Monetary Policy Rules*, Chicago, IL: Chicago University Press.

Taylor, J.B. (2000). 'Using monetary policy rules in emerging market economies', paper presented at the 75th Anniversary Conference Stabilization and Monetary Policy: The International Experience, Bank of Mexico, 14–15 November.

Taylor, J.B. (2008a), 'The financial crisis and the policy responses: the empirical analysis of what went wrong', http://www.stanford.edu/~johntayl/FCPR.pdf.

Taylor, J.B. (2008b), 'The lack of empirical rationale for a revival of discretionary fiscal policy', http://www.stanford.edu/~johntayl/AEA_Paper_on_Fiscal_Policy_2009_JBT.pdf.

Taylor, L. (1979), *Macro-Models for Developing Countries*, New York: McGraw-Hill.

Taylor, L. (1983), *Structuralist Macroeconomics*, New York: Basic Books.

Taylor, L. (1988), *Varieties of Stabilisation Experience: Towards Sensible Macroeconomics in the Third World*, Oxford: Clarendon Press.

Taylor, M.P. (1992), 'Sterilized intervention', in P. Newman, M. Milgate and J. Eatwell (eds), *The New Palgrave Dictionary of Money and Finance*, vol. 3, London: Macmillan Press.

Taylor, M.P. (1999), 'Real interest rates and macroeconomic activity', *Oxford Review of Economic Policy*, **15** (2), 95–113.

Terra, C. (1999), 'Openness and inflation: a new assessment', *Quarterly Journal of Economics*, **113**, 641–80.

The Economist (2007), 9–15 June, London.

Thiessen, G.G. (2000), 'Can a bank change? The evolution of monetary policy at the Bank of Canada 1935–2000', public lecture delivered at the Faculty of Social Science, University of Western Ontario, Ontario, 17 October.

Thirlwall, A. (2006), *Growth and Development: With Special Reference to Developing Economies*, London: Palgrave Macmillan.
Thornton, H. (1802), *An Enquiry into the Nature and Effects of the Paper Credit of Great Britain*, London: J. Hatchard.
Timberlake, R.H. Jr (1978), *The Origins of Central Banking in the United States*, Cambridge, MA: Harvard University Press.
Timberlake, R.H. Jr (1984), 'The central banking role of clearinghouse associations', *Journal of Money, Credit and Banking*, **16** (1), 1–15.
Timberlake, R.H. (1992), 'Central banking institutions in the United Kingdom and the United States', in P. Newman, M. Milgate and J. Eatwell (eds), *The Palgrave Dictionary of Money and Finance*, vol. 1, London: Macmillan Press.
Tinbergen, J. (1952), *On the Theory of Economic Policy*, Amsterdam: North-Holland.
Tobin, J. (1956), 'The inter elasticity of transactions demand for cash', *Review of Economics and Statistics*, **38** (3), 241–7.
Tobin, J. (1958), 'Liquidity preference as behaviour towards risk', *Review of Economic Studies*, **25**, 65–86.
Tobin, J. (1965), 'Money and economic growth', *Econometrica*, **33**, 671–84.
Tobin, J. (1968), 'Notes on optimal monetary growth', *Journal of Political Economy*, **76**, 833–59.
Tobin, J. (1972), 'Inflation and unemployment', *American Economic Review*, **62** (March), 1–18.
Tobin, J. (1992), 'Money', in P. Newman, M. Milgate and J. Eatwell (eds), *The New Palgrave Dictionary of Money and Finance*, vol. 2, London: Macmillan Press.
Townsend, R.M. (1995), 'Consumption insurance: an evaluation of risk-bearing systems in low-income economies', *Journal of Economic Perspectives*, **9** (3), 83–102.
Treadgold, M.L. (1990), 'Macroeconomic management in Asia-Pacific developing countries', *Asian-Pacific Economic Literature*, **4** (1), 3–40.
Tsai, P.L. and C.H. Huang (2007), 'Openness, growth and poverty: the case of Taiwan', *World Development*, **35** (11), 1858–71.
Tseng, W. and R. Corker (1991), 'Financial liberalization, money demand, and monetary policy in Asian countries', *Occasional Paper 84*, Washington, DC: IMF.
Tseng, W., H.E. Khor, K. Kochhar, D. Mihaljek and D. Burton (1994), 'Economic reforms in China: a new phase', *Occasional Paper No. 114*, Washington, DC. IMF.
Tun Wai, U. (1959), 'The relation between inflation and economic development: a statistical inductive study', *IMF Staff Papers*, **7**, 302–17.
Tun Wai, U. and C. Wong (1982), 'Determinants of private investment in developing countries', *Journal of Development Studies*, **19**, 19–36.
Turnovsky, S.J. (1987), 'Supply shocks and optimal monetary policy', *Oxford Economic Papers*, **39**, 20–37.
Varian, H.R. (2006), *Intermediate Microeconomics: A Modern Approach*, New York: W.W. Norton.
Vegh, C. (1995), 'Stopping high inflation', in P. Siklos (ed.), *Great Inflations of the 20th Century*, Cheltenham, UK and Brookfield, VT, USA: Edward Elgar.
Veiga, F.J. (1999), 'What causes the failure of inflation stabilization plans?', *Journal of International Money and Finance*, **18** (April), 169–94.
Vines, D. (1992), 'Stabilization policy', in P. Newman, M. Milgate and J. Eatwell (eds),

The New Palgrave Dictionary of Money and Finance, vol. 3, London: Macmillan Press.
Vogel, R. (1974), 'The dynamics of inflation in Latin America', *American Economic Review*, **64**, 102–14.
Wachter, S. (1983), *Latin American Inflation*, Toronto: Heath.
Wade, R. (1988), 'The role of government in overcoming market failure: Taiwan, Republic of Korea and Japan', in H. Hughes (ed.), *Achieving Industrialisation in Asia*, Cambridge: Cambridge University Press.
Wade, R. (1990), *Governing the Market: Economic Theory and the Role of Government in East Asian Industrialization*, Priceton, NJ: Princeton University Press.
Wagner, H. (1997), 'Central banking in transition economies', *IMF Working Paper No. 98/126*, Washington, DC: IMF.
Walsh, C.E. (1995), 'Optimal contracts for central bankers', *American Economic Review*, **85** (1), 150–67.
Walsh, C.E. (1998), *Monetary Theory and Policy*, Cambridge, MA: MIT Press.
Walshe, T.O. (1991), 'Managing a central bank: goals, strategies, and the techniques', in P. Downes and R. Vaez-Zadeh (eds), *The Evolving Role of Central Banks*, Washington, DC: IMF.
Walters, A. and S.H. Hanke (1992), 'Currency boards', in P. Newman, M. Milgate and J. Eatwell (eds), *The New Palgrave Dictionary of Money and Finance*, vol. 1, London: Macmillan Press.
Warjiyo, P. and J. Agung (2002), *Transmission Mechanisms of Monetary Policy in Indonesia*, Directorate of Economic Research and Monetary Policy, Jakarta: Bank Indonesia.
Wijnbergen, S. (1982), 'Stagflationary effects of monetary stabilization policies', *Journal of Development Economics*, **10** (2), 133–69.
Wijnbergen, S. (1985), 'Macroeconomic effects of changes in bank interest rates: simulation results from South Korea', *Journal of Development Economics*, **18**, 541–54.
Willett, T. (ed.) (1988), *Political Business Cycles: The Political Economy of Money, Inflation and Unemployment*, Durham, NC: Duke University Press.
Woodford, M. (1990), 'The optimum quantity of money', in B.M. Friedman and F.H. Hahn (eds), *Handbook of Monetary Economics*, vol. 2, Amsterdam: Elsevier Science.
Woodford, M. (2000), 'Monetary policy in a world without money', *International Finance*, **3** (July), 229–60.
Woodford, M. (2003), *Interest and Prices: Foundations of a Theory of Monetary Policy*, Princeton, NJ: Princeton University Press.
World Bank (various years), *World Development Report*, Washington, DC: World Bank.
World Bank (1993), *The East Asian Miracle: Economic Growth and Public Policy*, New York: Oxford University Press.
Xie, D. (2004), 'Macroeconomic policy coordination under managed floating exchange rate regime – China's case', paper presented at the Bank for International Settlement Workshop on Exchange Rates and Monetary Policy, 28–29 October, Basel.
Yang, Y.H. and J.D. Shea (2005), 'Deflation and monetary policy in Taiwan', *NBER Working Paper 11244*, Cambridge, MA: NBER.
Zahid, S.N. (eds) (1995), *Financial Sector Development in Asia: Country Studies*, Hong Kong: Oxford University Press.

Zahler, R. (1993), 'Financial sector reforms and liberalization: welcome address', in S. Faruqi (ed.), *Financial Sector Reforms in Asian and Latin American Countries: Lessons from Comparative Experience*, Washington, DC: World Bank.
Zarazaga, C. (1999), 'Building a case for currency boards', *Pacific Economic Review*, **4** (June), 139–63.
Zysman, J. (1983), *Government, Markets and Growth: Financial Systems and the Politics of Industrial Change*, Ithaca, NY: Cornell University Press.

Index